The Ultimate PMP® Exam Prep Guide

Wes Balakian, PMP
Timothy S. Bergmann, PMP

Foreword

Welcome to the *Ultimate PMP® Exam Prep Guide*. We are honored and pleased that you have chosen the Ultimate PMP® Exam Prep Guide as your roadmap for achieving your PMP® credential.

In 1996, Hillary Clinton wrote the book *It Takes a Village...* This book validates that concept. It certainly took a "village" of TSI contributors to complete this Exam Prep Guide. This has been a team effort to complete the book and validate the concepts contained within. We have every confidence that this product will serve you well in preparing to pass the PMP® Exam.

This is the first book published in 2009 in a series of books and products that are part of TSI's *Ultimate Project Management Series™*. Please look for other titles and other products at your local bookstore, on Amazon.com and through our Web site: www.truesolutions.com.

As authors, we would like to thank our list of contributors who helped bring this book into being and who made individual contributions to the book.

Our thanks go to participants past and present:

- Lorie Gibbons, PMP
- Laura Johnson
- Sharron Frohner, PMP
- Paul Holland
- Cynthia Hodgkins, PMP
- Pamela Thornton
- Mary Ann Crow, PMP
- Gary W. Griffith
- Ron Darnell, PMP
- Natalie Nix (Introduction photos in chapters 5, 8, 29, 38 and 49)
- Daron Miller

We wish each of you good reading and good luck on your PMP Exam.

Cheers,

Wes Balakian, PMP
CEO, True Solutions Inc.

Timothy S. Bergmann, PMP
CLO, True Solutions, Inc.

Ultimate PMP® Exam Prep Course (5-Day Instructor-Led) First Pass Guarantee

Less than .01 percent of the students who completed our 5-day Instructor-Led Ultimate PMP® Exam Prep Course have taken us up on this guarantee. Our goal is to obviously ensure that you pass the PMP® Exam on your FIRST attempt, and we are extremely effective at helping you accomplish this. But if you successfully completed the entire TSI class, passed our final exam with a 75 or above, and you take the PMP® Exam **no sooner than 7 days and** within 2 months (60 days) of completing our Ultimate PMP® Exam Prep Course and do not pass, TSI will provide you with the following support:

• FREE evaluation of your exam results to uncover subject matter weaknesses

• FREE one-on-one guidance from a senior TSI instructor

• FREE re-registration in a scheduled TSI Ultimate PMP® Exam Prep course

• TSI will pay the exam re-take fee for your second attempt to pass the PMP Exam

Students must notify TSI in writing within 30 days of failing the exam, or the guarantee outlined above will not be honored.

If you fail the exam and choose to retake our Ultimate PMP® Exam Prep course, the course you retake must be based on the same edition of the PMBOK® Guide as your original course.

The First Pass Guarantee only applies to Instructor-Led classes.

Contents

Lesson 1
Your ULTIMATE PMP Exam Prep Guide

Objectives
At the end of this lesson, you will be able to:
- Understand how this book is organized
- Understand how the *Ultimate PMP Exam Prep Guide* gets you ready to pass the PMP® Exam

Roadmap to the PMBOK Guide

	Initiating	Planning	Executing	M & C	Closing
Integration					
Scope					
Time					
Cost	Contains General Management Information Applicable to All Areas of PMBOK® Guide Fourth Edition and Project Management in General				
Quality					
Human Resources					
Communications					
Risk					
Procurement					

In this chapter you will begin learning how to use the *Ultimate PMP Exam Prep Guide* to prepare for your PMP Exam.

Congratulations on your initiative to begin the Project Management Professional (PMP) certification process!

We are honored that you have chosen the *Ultimate PMP Exam Prep Guide* as your road map for achieving your PMP credential. We think that this product will serve you well in preparing you to pass the PMP Exam.

In this lesson, we will work to familiarize you with this Guide. You will begin learning how to use the Guide to prepare for your PMP Exam. The *Ultimate PMP Exam Prep Guide* incorporates lots of exercises to involve all of your learning senses. These exercises are carefully designed to ensure full synthesis of your learning abilities without having to spend hours with tedious memorization or endless flash card drills. We suggest that you simply progress through this Guide and follow the instructions as they are presented. When you have completely worked your way through this Guide, you will have a much better grasp of the materials required to pass your PMP Exam.

Throughout the *Ultimate PMP Exam Prep Guide* there will be direction to read excerpts from the *PMBOK® Guide Fourth Edition*. These readings are essential to your understanding and knowledge transfer prior to attempting the PMP Exam.

How the Ultimate PMP Exam Prep Guide Gets You Ready to Pass

The *Ultimate PMP Exam Prep Guide* prepares you to pass the PMP Exam by developing all the knowledge competencies you need to fully understand exam questions and recognize preferred answers. In addition to mastering the project management learning material, in Lesson 53 you will learn about multiple-choice questions and the science behind answering these questions.

Please follow your Guide faithfully from start to finish and you will be assured of mastering all of the knowledge-based material needed to pass the PMP Exam. Your *Ultimate PMP Exam Prep Guide* employs adult learning techniques to ensure that you learn and understand the material.

- Information is presented in smaller, bite-sized portions. You will not be forced to labor with large blocks of complicated material.

- Effective repetition is used throughout the Guide. Embrace this as it will help in your learning.

- Personal reflection exercises are incorporated to help you understand how the information is applied in real-world project environments.

- Writing exercises are incorporated. Writing the material provides an extended dimension to your learning.

- To help you develop an effective mindset for the exam, much of the material is presented as if you are already a certified PMP project manager.

- To help you better understand how the information is applied in real-world project environments, exercises and lessons-learned narratives are included in the materials.

- Many training organizations present the PMP Exam materials in the same order as the *PMBOK Guide*. In order to facilitate your understanding of the material, we present the processes in a logical sequence like you would use these processes on a typical project. This helps your understanding of process flows throughout the project life cycle.

- Strong visual imagery helps ensure effective recall of information on exam day. Graphics are included in every chapter of this Guide. Additionally, visual review exercises are incorporated to enhance your learning.

- Sample questions are incorporated at the end of each lesson. This helps reinforce understanding of the material. Detailed answers are provided for each question.

- Comprehensive information about the PMP Exam is presented at the beginning of each process group throughout the Guide.

- Exam Tips are provided in Chapter 53 along with an exam-day checklist.

ULTIMATE PMP EXAM PREP GUIDE FORMAT

The *Ultimate PMP Exam Prep Guide* presents the needed information in a series of short lessons to facilitate your learning experience. No lesson in this guide is intended to take more than one hour to read, do the recommended reading, work the exercises, perform the knowledge check, and finish that lesson. This allows the reader to proceed at his or her own pace and study as they have time.

At the beginning of every lesson there is a graphic advising the reader of the lesson number, the name of the lesson — and what parts of the *PMBOK Guide* the lesson refers to. A graphical grid shows what knowledge area and process group the lesson will be referring to.

An example of a lesson introduction is shown below.

Lesson 6
Develop Project Charter

	Initiating	Planning	Executing	M & C	Closing
Integration	■				
Scope					
Time					
Cost					
Quality					
Human Resources					
Communications					
Risk					
Procurement					

Most lessons follow the introduction with a narrative describing the process or process group. After the reader has read the narrative describing the knowledge elements associated with that lesson, then a description of the process inputs, tools and techniques, and outputs will be shown. The process elements are exposed in a narrative and a graphic format.

An example of a process graphic is shown below.

Develop Project Charter
This process formally sanctions a new project or authorizes a project to continue into the next phase

Inputs	Tools and Techniques	Outputs
• Contract • Project Statement of Work (SOW) • Enterprise Environmental Factors • Organizational Process Assets • Business Case	• Expert Judgment	• Project Charter

TSI Study Aid
This chart is part of the study aid poster series available at www.truesolutions.com.

Most processes have specifically defined outputs. These outputs are almost always a document of some sort. After we have discussed the process elements, we will look toward the practical application of the process by exposing the types of documents that would be expected and by showing a sample of a document template for that process.

Again, a sample is shown below (in highly reduced format).

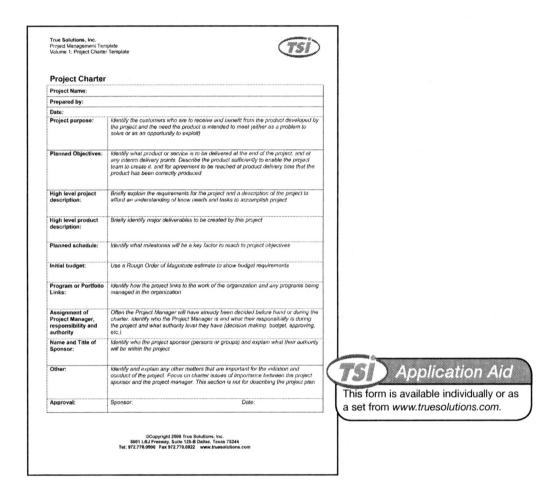

Following the exposition of process documents, most chapters will then discuss typical tasks associated with performing the process.

A Process Application exercise will follow the task discussion. Process Application exercises come in several versions. You may find a Think About It exercise that asks you to compare your practical application of this process in your organization to the way it is depicted in the Guide. There are also Check It Off exercises and Lessons Learned discussions for your knowledge and enjoyment.

Every lesson contains a section of Must Know Concepts. This is a list of elements from the lesson that are essential knowledge for your PMP Exam study.

Every lesson ends with a quiz. This usually consists of three to ten multiple-choice questions. Explanations are found in the back of the *Ultimate PMP Exam Prep Guide* in Appendix A.

BEFORE YOU BEGIN
· ·
Create Your Own PMP Exam Prep War Room

Preparing to pass your PMP Exam is a project in itself. Consider setting up your own project war room to create a dedicated space for working through your preparation activities. A quiet space where you can work undisturbed is best. You will need comfortable seating, desk space, and wall space to display key information. An online computer will be helpful to access the Project Management Institute website, Prometric website, or other websites for applying, scheduling, and gathering information.

Many experts suggest low volume classical music to enhance your learning ability. You may wish to include this as a feature in your PMP Exam Prep war room.

ADDITIONAL READING
· ·
• Read chapter contents on how to use this book

End of Lesson 1

Lesson 2
Applying for the PMP Exam

Objectives

At the end of this lesson, you will be able to:

• Understand how to apply for your PMP Exam
• Understand experience requirements for the PMP application
• Understand the importance of accuracy on your PMP application

Roadmap to the PMBOK Guide

	Initiating	Planning	Executing	M & C	Closing
Integration					
Scope					
Time					
Cost	Contains General Management Information Applicable to All Areas of PMBOK® Guide Fourth Edition and Project Management in General				
Quality					
Human Resources					
Communications					
Risk					
Procurement					

The number of certified project managers continues to grow worldwide; you will be joining an elite group of highly recognized project managers as you obtain your PMP® certification.

The PMP certification is not a certification to be taken lightly. Although the passing score to obtain the PMP certification is not as great as some other certification exams, the PMP certification is a highly regarded professional certification and the exam can be difficult if you do not study the material and have the required project management experience. The PMP certification *exam* is challenging and you must be prepared in order to achieve success.

In this section we will begin discussing some foundation information about project management that you will need to know for the PMP Exam. In this chapter we will discuss the PMP application and examination content information.

The PMP Exam will thoroughly challenge your ability to demonstrate a broad understanding of project management processes, concepts, tools, and techniques. To pass the PMP Exam, you must have a thorough familiarity of the project management knowledge areas as defined in the *PMBOK® Guide Fourth Edition*.

Project Integration Management	Project Human Resource Management
Project Scope Management	Project Communications Management
Project Time Management	Project Risk Management
Project Cost Management	Project Procurement Management
Project Quality Management	

Additionally, you must have a practical understanding of the project life cycle concept, especially with respect to how individual project management processes are applied across the project life cycle. You must have a good understanding of professional and social responsibility and general management competencies.

The PMP Exam is well-crafted. It is not a test of your memorization capability. The PMP Exam tests your ability to recognize particular project management situations and concepts and then draw from your experience and your knowledge of the project management framework defined in the *PMBOK Guide* to select the best response.

The PMP Exam is a straightforward multiple-choice question (MCQ) exam consisting of 200 questions. In North America and Western Europe the PMP Exam is administered via computer at Prometric Testing Centers. Paper versions are available for remote areas.

PMP Value

Project Management Institute (PMI®) was founded in 1969 in order to further the knowledge of project management and to establish a formal career path for project managers. As PMI grew the PMP® credential was developed. The first PMP credentials were granted in 1984 to a small number of project managers.

The number of project managers attaining the PMP credential grew slowly for many years. By the end of 2002 there were approximately 51,000 project managers in the world. An explosion of interest in the PMP credential has caused that number to more than quadruple since the end of 2002. As of this writing it is estimated that there are over 270,000 PMP certified project managers.

If you are a project manager in the corporate world in a typical corporate environment, then the PMP credential provides you with a certification that validates your commitment to the profession, your commitment to your career and professionalism, and validates your project management knowledge base. If you happen to be looking for new opportunities now or in the future, the PMP credential is a key certification to have.

PMP Qualifications

PMI has established a comprehensive set of requirements in order to qualify to take the PMP exam. The applicant must have a specified level of education, must have a minimum level of project management training, and must have a minimum level of experience in project management measured in project management hours and months of experience.

The requirements are broken into two categories: Category One applicants must have an educational background that includes attainment of a bachelor's degree (as a minimum). Category Two applicants must have received a high school diploma.

In Category One the applicant for the PMP credential must have:

• Minimum educational documentation of a bachelor's degree.

• A minimum of thirty-five contact training hours in specific project management training (i.e. general business training for an MBA would *not* count).

• A minimum of 4,500 hours of project management experience that can be documented and verified.

• A minimum of thirty-six calendar months of project management experience that can be documented and verified. The months of experience can go back no more than seven years from the date of application.

In Category Two the applicant for the PMP credential must have:

• Minimum educational documentation of a high school diploma.

• A minimum of thirty-five contact training hours in specific project management training (i.e. general business training for an MBA would *not* count).

- A minimum of 7,500 hours of project management experience that can be documented and verified.

- A minimum of sixty calendar months of project management experience that can be documented and verified. The documented months of experience can go back up to eight years.

The intent of PMI appears to be that the project manager who does not have other educational experience as evidenced by the bachelor's degree, must be a "heads-down" full-time project manager in order to qualify for the PMP credential.

Specific up to date information on PMP application requirements can be obtained at www.pmi.org. PMI periodically updates the requirements on their website. PMI also provides a "PMP Credential Handbook" that can be downloaded from the website by potential applicants.

We recommend that anyone who is contemplating his or her PMP get up-to-the-minute information about applying for the PMP credential from the PMI website.

PMP APPLICATION EXAM COST

PMI bases the cost of the application and exam on whether or not you are a member of PMI.

Cost (as of this writing) of the exam for PMI members: $405

Cost (as of this writing) of the exam for nonmembers: $555

Cost of retaking the exam for a PMI member: $275

Cost of retaking the exam for a nonmember: $375

If you apply to take the exam and are rejected, PMI will retain a $200 application fee regardless of membership status.

PMI Code of Ethics and Professional Conduct

When you visit the Project Management Institute website, please make sure that you obtain and review a copy of the "PMI Code of Ethics and Professional Conduct." This specifies that a member of PMI or a Project Management Professional has responsibilities to several groups. The PMP is generally responsible **to the profession of project management, to customers, and to the public.**

To summarize at a high level, PMI expects Project Management Professionals to act in the most professional manner possible. As part of responsibilities to the profession, the PMP should continue to obtain personal education, should try to promote the profession of project management, and should refrain from actions which might cause harm to the profession. These negative behaviors include mismanagement, fraud, conflicts of interest, or compromising the contents of the PMP exam.

The PMP code of conduct defines specific behaviors that are appropriate and inappropriate toward customers and the public. Misleading potential customers about your qualifications, fraud, conflicts of interest, or not having experience claimed, are all things which violate the code.

In summary, it is our assertion that as long as you follow your common sense — what you know is the right thing to do — you will generally meet the requirements of the code of conduct.

When applying for the PMP Exam, you are agreeing to adhere to and promote the "PMI Code of Ethics and Professional Conduct."

The PMP Application

PMI requires that you provide information to validate your project management experience during the application process. We will not go into specifics in this book about their requirements. PMI changes the application forms periodically. For the most up-to-date information, please visit the PMI website www.pmi.org and download the "PMP Credential Handbook." The application form is contained in the handbook. However, in general you will need to provide many pieces of information.

• Identification information for yourself

• Personal address information

• Company (employment) information

• Industry you are working in

• Education information

• PMI status: whether or not you are a member (be a member!)

• PM training information

• Project specific hours of experience and calendar months of experience

When you apply to PMI you agree to abide by their application process. You should be aware that PMI alone has the ability to approve your application or deny it. Should you disagree with their decision, you may initiate communication with them to discuss and/or appeal their decision. But, keep in mind that PMI has the sole authority to determine whether to allow you to take the PMP exam — or not.

PROJECT VERIFICATION FORM

For each project that you are claiming for experience you must fill out an individual form stating the number of hours of experience you are claiming as well as the months covered. In the verification form you will be asked to provide several items of verifiable information.

- Your job title at the time

- The name of the organization you worked for

- The address for the organization

- An organization contact with a phone number

- Project start and finish dates

- Specific hours for specific activities that you performed

    - The specific hours are broken down by the five process groups

    - The hours must fit into categories defined by PMI in the application for work that the project manager would do during a typical project

FREQUENTLY ASKED QUESTIONS ABOUT THE PROJECT VERIFICATION FORM

Question: Do you have to fill out a Project Verification form for each project that you worked on that you are claiming for experience?

Answer: Yes, sort of. I believe that you can apply some common sense here. If you are claiming experience for a medium size project or larger — that type of project will certainly need an individual experience verification form to be filled out. How do we determine the size of a project? Any project that is two to three months or longer and in excess of $50,000.00 should be considered a medium-sized project. If you work in a predominantly functional or matrix organization where you have many small projects that you manage, historical data suggests that PMI will accept several projects lumped together under certain conditions. The condition appears to be commonality. If you manage the same type of projects over a period of time, projects that do the same thing, have a similar scope, and are executed for a common organization (employer), then you may be able to lump them together as "xx projects for XYZ employer during the period from January 1 to December 31, 201x".

Question: What if I was not officially designated as the "project manager" on the project?

Answer: You do not have to be officially designated as the project manager — but you must have been able to manage some portion of the project work. Business analysts, programmer analysts, and individual contributors perform project management work on portions of large projects. The hours spent performing project management activities should be eligible as part of your project management experience. Work time spent on a deliverable — not on project management related work — is not counted toward project management hours.

Question: What if I do not have a person who can verify my experience? The company I did the work for is no longer in existence.

Answer: It is a necessity to provide a contact person who can verify the experience claimed. If there is a question, it would be the best plan to inform the person who might provide experience verification so that they know you are using them as a reference. Ideally, the person who verifies your experience would be the project sponsor, a manager or director, the project client or a major stakeholder. Since stakeholders include a wide range of project participants, you may be able to find a stakeholder — perhaps a peer — that you are still in contact with to provide verification. In order to prevent the appearance of any conflict of interest, try to avoid using a subordinate as the experience verifier.

HOW TO APPLY

You can apply for your PMP application in a paper format or via an online format. It is my belief that the online format is far superior to the paper format.

If you choose to use the paper format you are going to have to download the forms, duplicate them and fill out many elements of duplicate information. Using paper forms *you* are the quality control element and you have to ensure that you fill in everything correctly, provide all of the information, sign all of the forms, make sure it all adds up, and send in a payment. Forms are part of the "PMP Credential Handbook" that you can download from www.pmi.org.

If you choose to apply online — the website has process checks that ensure that you provide all of the required information before it will allow you to complete the form and submit the final application form to PMI. If you choose to apply online there is an order of events that should happen to make this a pleasant experience.

1. Join PMI. This is a separate process that we recommend you undertake before you begin your PMP Exam application. PMI charges you a higher fee to take the exam if you are not a PMI member. PMI charges you a higher fee for retake if you fail the exam and PMI charges a higher fee for renewals if you are not a member. So, we encourage you to join PMI first, before you do anything else. The cost of joining plus the cost of the exam at the PMI rate is marginally lower than if you take the exam as a nonmember.

2. After you join PMI and get your PMI ID and personal identification number (PIN) you are then ready to begin your application. The online application is available at the PMI website. You will use your PMI ID to login. You will be required to fill in general identifying information about yourself (which has to be done once rather than multiple times on a paper form). You can fill in the experience verification forms on the website. The online application adds up the months and hours to provide totals. There is a check for appropriate numbers — the program will not allow you to complete the application if you are deficient in hours or months of experience.

3. Retain your PMI ID and PIN. This will be used again and again for access to valuable information from PMI. In three years you will be required to recertify your PMP information. This PMI ID and PIN will be used for the recertification application process.

It is our recommendation that all potential PMP's join PMI before they apply. PMI provides valuable information about the profession, current events, and educational opportunities in project management. PMI has local chapters around the country where you can participate in local events, learn about local projects, participate in educational opportunities, and network in your community.

Recertification Overview

PMI has a handbook (available online at www.pmi.org) that defines the requirements, provides the application and the experience verification forms that must be filled out in order to recertify as a PMP. Briefly — in order to recertify you must have 60 Professional Development Units (PDUs) over the three year period. You can accumulate PDUs through various activities:

• 5 PDUs per year for performing as a project manager

• 15 PDU maximum for self-chosen, self-directed learning activities

• PDU value is assigned to each PMI-related activity you attend

- Formal academic education: 1 hour of degree credit at a college or university in a 15 week semester earns 15 PDUs.

- PMI Registered Education Providers will provide a PDU value

- Other education providers: 1 hour of contact learning gives 1 PDU

- 30 PDUs for being the author of a PM article in a refereed journal

- 15 PDUs for being the author of a PM article in a nonrefereed journal

- 10 PDUs for being the speaker on PM at a conference, symposium workshop, or formal course

- 5 PDUs for speaking at a PMI component meeting

- 5 PDUs for being a moderator or panel member at a workshop, conference, or formal course

- 40 PDUs for authoring a PM textbook

- 10 PDUs for developing a seminar or structured learning program

- 10 PDUs for serving as an officer in a PM organization for a year

- 5 PDUs for serving as a committee member in a PM organization for a year

- 5 PDUs for providing PM services to a community or charity group as a volunteer

PMP Exam Preparation Checklist

☐ Determine that you want to become a certified Project Management Professional

☐ Determine if you have a minimum 36 months verifiable project management experience

☐ Determine if you have a minimum 4,500 (or 7,500) hours verifiable project management experience

☐ Go to www.pmi.org to download the "PMP Credential Handbook" to get up-to-date information

☐ Determine if you have the required contact training hours to apply for your PMP Exam

☐ If you need contact training, or want to thoroughly prepare yourself for the PMP Exam, determine what form of training will suit you best and schedule a training class, online training course, or self-study course

☐ Obtain a current copy of the *PMBOK® Guide Fourth Edition* for study purposes

☐ Complete your training course

☐ Compile your experience information and complete your PMP Exam application

☐ Receive notification from PMI approving your application

☐ Schedule your PMP Exam (normally through a Prometric location)

☐ Take your PMP Exam on the scheduled date

☐ Receive official notification from PMI with your exam results

☐ Update your resume to reflect your new certification

☐ Celebrate!

ADDITIONAL READING

- PMP Credential Handbook – available at www.pmi.org

End of Lesson 2

Lesson 3
Project Management Fundamentals

Objectives

At the end of this lesson, you will be able to:

- Understand the definition of a project
- Understand the definition of project management
- Understand the role of the project manager
- Understand how constraints and external factors influence projects

Roadmap to the PMBOK Guide

	Initiating	Planning	Executing	M & C	Closing
Integration					
Scope					
Time					
Cost		Contains General Management Information Applicable to All Areas of PMBOK® Guide Fourth Edition and Project Management in General			
Quality					
Human Resources					
Communications					
Risk					
Procurement					

There is no single way to manage every project. This lesson discusses generally accepted project management concepts that you need to know in order to manage projects effectively.

In this chapter we are going to explore some basic information about project management. Here we will expose basic definitions of projects and project management, discuss organizations and cultural effects on projects and their chances for success.

This chapter will discuss a basic diagram of project management as a whole to educate the student on the minimum required to manage a project.

How the PMBOK Guide Applies Processes

The *PMBOK® Guide* defines material and processes that are "generally recognized as good practices" for project management. In the *PMBOK® Guide Fourth Edition* there are forty-two processes that have been defined.

But will the project manager use each and every one of these processes on every project? The answer to this question is a resounding "maybe."

In the PMBOK Guide, it stresses that there is no specific fixed way that a project must be managed. The project manager must choose the processes, and in what order the processes are performed, based on the needs of the specific project.

Many company project life cycles define specific subsets of processes that should be performed based on the size and complexity of the project. PMI specifies that the project manager must choose what processes are appropriate for the project.

We encourage the project manager to look at the forty-two processes as a checklist. As we delve further into this information, we will discuss the concept that each of the five process groups must be performed in each phase of the project. Since we are using all of the process groups, it provides some logic that each of the forty-two processes might be addressed in each phase of the project as well. While the project manager and project team may not fully perform and address each process in each phase, if the project manager uses the processes as a checklist, then there is a lesser chance that items will be missed on the project.

What Defines a Project?

The definition of a project has three parts. **A project is temporary, it is unique, and it is progressive**.

Temporary

The project always has a beginning and an end. It is a temporary endeavor undertaken to perform a specific set of objectives. The project is usually undertaken to create something.

A project is not an on-going operation. While the project may fulfill the strategic plan of the organization and, via the temporary endeavor, sustain the organizational entity, a project is not an operation.

Even though a project is a temporary experience, there is no specific time frame associated with projects. Whether the project is two days long or two years long, if it is a temporary endeavor and has a defined scope, then it is a project.

Unique

The project is undertaken to perform a specific set of objectives. A project is usually performed to create something, usually a specific unique product or service. Sometimes a project is a temporary endeavor executed for a specific purpose; i.e. Sarbanes-Oxley projects that many companies recently performed. *Projects focus on creating deliverables.*

Progressive

The project is progressive — or more accurately stated, it is progressively elaborated. What do we mean by progressively elaborated? The definition or scope of the project is progressive. At the beginning of the project the project manager and stakeholders will have a high level idea of the scope of the project (work to be performed) and the scope of the product (configuration or requirements definition). As the project progresses the definition is progressively detailed. In the planning portion of the project, the project manager and stakeholders learn more about the project and product and record the details into a scope and requirements document. During executing and monitoring and controlling, the stakeholders learn more and modify the project and the product description in order to ensure that the end product meets needs.

This progressive elaboration can be closely compared to the "Plan-Do-Check-Act cycle" defined by Deming as a quality process. In the Plan portion — you obviously plan and document your intent. Details are documented as they are available and finalized. In the "Do" portion — you do the planned work, create the planned product. In the "Check-Act" portion of the project you make sure you are creating what you defined — and take corrective action if you are not on the right path. Combined with interpersonal skills that project managers must have and use in order to be successful, progressive elaboration is a powerful tool that facilitates project successes.

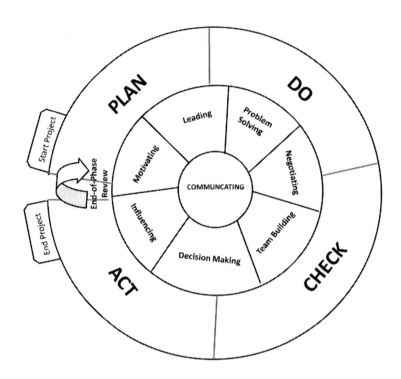

Figure 3.1 Plan-Do-Check-Act

The Definition of Project Management

Project management is "the application of knowledge, skills, tools, and techniques to project activities in order to meet project requirements."

This is the best definition of project management. This is how PMI defines project management in the *PMBOK Guide* on page 8.

There are a few other definitions of project management that can also be considered. One simple definition of project management is **"the management of competing project demands."** Competing demands are most often defined as the project constraints that make up the "triple constraint." In addition, there are several other project elements that fall into this category; the triple constraint is most often defined as:

- Scope

- Schedule (Time)

- Budget (Cost)

Other project constraints or demands include:

- Risk

- Quality

- Resources

The "triple-triple constraint" is depicted in the illustration below.

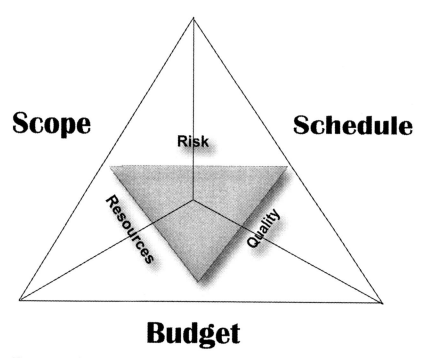

Figure 3.2 Constraints

In addition to the concept of managing constraints, a new vision of project success is emerging. This concept of success includes all of the constraint factors and adds a couple of additional considerations: team satisfaction and value.

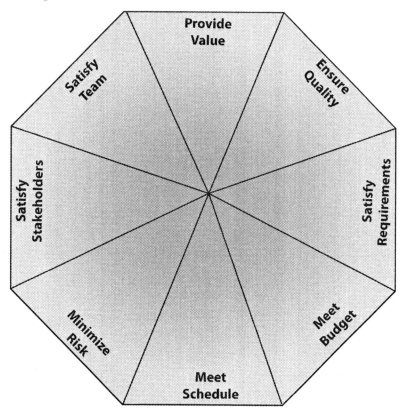

Figure 3.3 Success Factors

Knowledge Required To Be a Successful Project Manager

The **main role of the project manager is to integrate** all of the pieces and parts and elements associated with the project scope and product scope to successfully meet the business need. As the project integrator, the project manager has to have a wide knowledge base in order to be effective. The project manager has to have some areas of specific knowledge and capabilities:

- Knowledge of project management and general management

- Ability to perform

- Personal skills to be able to communicate and interact with stakeholders

Required Project Management Knowledge

The project manager must have project management knowledge and experience to draw on. This experience base will contribute largely to the ability to make decisions based on project management situations.

In addition to general and experience-based project management knowledge, the project manager who is taking the PMP Exam needs to acquire specific knowledge contained in the *PMBOK Guide*. The *PMBOK Guide* specifies nine knowledge areas and forty-two specific project processes contained in five Project Process Groups to be used to manage the project. Each process has inputs, tools and techniques, and outputs to be used for project management. The successful project manager needs to be fully knowledgeable in this area and fully knowledgeable in using these processes.

PMBOK Guide specific project management knowledge and general project management knowledge will be discussed in detail in the portions of the workbook dealing with specific knowledge areas.

General Management Knowledge

The project manager must be able to manage the business environment and the people involved in the project in order to manage the project itself. Projects are a portion of the overall work portfolio of the organization and are executed in order to meet organizational objectives. General management includes knowledge elements like finance and budgeting, human resource processes, regulations and procedures, conflict management and resolution, and other general business knowledge areas.

Knowledge of general management is also required to ensure that the project meets the business needs of the organization. There are multiple areas of general management knowledge that are required.

Finance

The project manager needs to have some basic knowledge of business finance and budgeting in order to be successful. There are several processes defined as part of the forty-two processes that address the project budget. On most projects, the project manager will probably be charged with managing an operating budget. Operating budgets can be defined in several different ways:

- A *Cost Center budget* is used to project and account for the expenses (costs) of an operating unit over a period of time. This type of budget is the most likely budget type that a project manager will use.

- A *Revenue Center budget* projects profits produced by the business unit. Unlike the Cost Center budget, the revenue approach does not take costs into account.

- A *Profit Center budget* projects revenues versus costs to project a profit for the business unit.

In addition to the above budget types, there are some other financial accounting types that the project manager may need.

- Cash budgets are used to show cash flow for the business unit (or project).

- Capital Expenditure budgets are used to track capital investments. Many types of expenses are being capitalized today. The project manager needs to know how to identify capital items and where to account for them.

- Material budgets are used to track specific material expenses.

Strategic Planning

Project managers need to know about operational, long-term, and strategic plans that are part of the enterprise they are working in. Why would the project manager need to understand the plans of the enterprise? Because the project manager wants to make sure that the project being executed fits somewhere in the enterprise plans.

The lowest level of planning for the organization is the *operational plan*. The operational plan focuses on what is needed "now." It is the shortest of the planning variants. Most project plans fall into the operational category since most projects are one year or less in length. Characteristics of operational planning are:

- Operational planning generally covers one year or less; normally the fiscal year is covered by an operational plan.

- Operational planning is usually done by managers and directors and rolled up to higher management levels of the company.

- Operational planning deals with products to be produced, market forecasts, and resource requirements for these products.

- A specific detailed budget is associated with the operational plan.

The next level of planning for the organization is the *long-term plan*. The long-term plan focuses on what is needed in the one to three year term. Most projects look to this category to validate requirements and to determine follow-on projects and activities. Characteristics of long-term planning are:

- Long-term planning generally covers the period from one to three years in the future. Multiple fiscal years are covered by the long-term plan.

- Long-term planning is usually done by directors and senior managers and rolled up to the highest management levels of the company.

- Long-term planning deals with products to be produced, market forecasts, financial returns desired, and organization needs to fulfill these requirements.

- A long-term financial goals-and-objectives statement is associated with the long-term plan.

The highest level of planning for the organization is the *strategic plan*. The operational plan and long-term plan focus on more immediate needs. The strategic plan states the ultimate goals and direction of the company. Most projects look to this category to validate that the project fits in the overall objectives of the company. Characteristics of strategic planning are:

- A statement of the direction and long-term goals of the company. The strategic plan states what business the company is in.

- Strategic planning is usually done by at the highest management levels of the company. The C-level officers, board of directors, and specialized management consultants participate in crafting a statement for the company.

- The structure for strategic planning is unique to the company. Strengths, weaknesses, and opportunities for the enterprise are evaluated.

- General financial goals and objectives are stated in the strategic plan.

Organizing

The project manager must be knowledgeable in organization theory. Organizing the project requires that you establish a framework for managing human and physical elements of the project. In order to organize effectively you have to be aware of several elements.

Unity of Purpose: In order to organize any group or team you have to establish a unity of purpose. Unity of purpose simply means that the people who are working together are working toward the same objectives. Unity of purpose will be achieved when you and your team have the same goals and objectives. This can be also termed "buy-in" for the project. Without establishing unity, without having buy-in for your project, your chances of success are lessened.

Project Staff: In order to have an organization or team, there has to be a staff or a group of persons or physical resources to organize.

Division of Labor: You should have a division of labor. The project manager does one type of work and the subject matter experts do another type of work.

Please note: we are discussing a theoretical "pure" project management environment. In many organizations the division of labor may be clouded.

Organization Framework: There needs to be some method for organizing your team. *Most project organizations fall under a form of matrix organization*, but there are other organization forms that could be chosen:

• Functional organization

• Process oriented organization

• Organization by product

• Organization by market

• Organization by geography

Human Resource Administration

In order to effectively manage the project, the project manager needs to be aware of processes and procedures associated with Human Resource Administration. Human Resource Administration involves regulations and processes which affect hiring and firing, labor relations, career path management, and how to work with people.

The project manager should learn what specific requirements the organization has for:

• Recruiting

• Interviewing

• Selection processes

• Hiring processes

• Separation processes: resignations, terminations, and layoffs

- Labor relations processes: contract terms, grievance procedures

- Compensation available

- Career paths and training available in the organization

- Regulatory requirements for your state and area

Human Resource Administration requires the project manager to know how to manage and work with the assigned staff. The project manager must understand formal and informal groups and potential types of conflict that can exist in the organization. Later in this book we will discuss some processes for project-specific management of human resources.

Interpersonal Skills Used by the Project Manager

Interpersonal skills enable the project manager to perform. Project managers will spend as much as 90% of their time communicating with stakeholders by one means or another during the life a project. With this in mind, we list "Communication" as our first interpersonal skill because it enables all other skills. Having an understanding of these skills will enhance your ability to manage projects.

Communication

Communication is the most important skill a project manager can have. In my opinion, it is not overstated to say that, if you are a good communicator, you have the potential to be a good project manager. Conversely, if you are a poor communicator and the skill does not "flow" from you, you will then need to work on this skill to foster success. A poor communicator will usually be a poor project manager.

Communicating is the exchange of information. Communication is a two-way street. Listening is as important as speaking. Communicating is required to lead, to motivate, to resolve problems and conflicts, to negotiate, and to influence other people.

Common sense would dictate that some subjects are very sensitive and should be minimized or eliminated from the project environment. Politics, personal relationships, religions, sexual conversations, or poorly framed jokes are to be avoided.

Leadership

It may come as a surprise to some that the project management position is considered to be a leadership position. The project manager is expected to do more than just "manage" within the environment. The project manager is expected to lead the project team to fulfill the needs of the enterprise.

Leading includes establishing direction, aligning people in the organization to achieve goals, and motivating the people to reach these goals. When leading the project or performing in a leadership role within the organization, the project manager must keep in mind the characteristics the leader must possess.

The leader must have a vision of what he or she seeks to achieve. Leaders must take the goals and objectives of the enterprise as their own. The leader must have the desire and stamina to lead. Leaders have to show empathy for the situation.

Leaders must be open with their staff, have credibility (knowledge of the specialized application is part of this), must be decisive when required and accountable for their decisions. Leaders must be tenacious, working toward the goal until it is certain whether success or failure will result. Giving up before you are certain is not an option.

One very important additional characteristic for a leader to possess is dependability.

Motivation

In order to achieve better levels of performance from the team, the leader must motivate them. Motivation requires encouragement, gaining buy-in for the goals and objectives, and energizing the team to meet those goals. The leader should probably use several "hands-on" skills in order to motivate the team.

A hands-on skill many overlook but one that is quite effective is the skill of "MBWA: Management By Walking Around." Motivators cannot adequately address the team needs if they "hide" in their office all day. Get out of your office, take a walk, and see what is going on.

While you are out, take a "public opinion bath." Ask people what they think. In leading and motivating, you need to decide which issues are important and which can be deferred. In other words, decide which war(s) to wage. Some deficiencies in output or outcome are clearly worth "fighting over." Some are not. Choose wisely.

Part of motivating the team is to clearly communicate the "why" of what you are doing and accomplishing on an ongoing basis. What value does the project bring to the organization? Always work to remind everyone about basic goals, objectives, and principles that the team will use to reach those goals.

Motivating the team requires the leader to act in a highly professional manner at all times. Try not to let your actions betray your words. Don't let yourself be caught making behavioral exceptions for yourself when you hold the team (or a certain member of the team) to a higher standard. And absolutely, positively never talk about the team or individual team members behind their back. If you as the leader destroy someone's reputation in the company with gossip (real or perceived information), your own reputation as a leader will undoubtedly suffer as a result.

One more motivating factor for the team is to be a good coach. Tell your team when they collectively or individually do well. Advise them when improvements are needed. Forgive and forget mistakes. No one wants to work for a leader who never awards compliments and always remembers mistakes.

Negotiation

The main definition for negotiating is to reach an agreement. *The goal of negotiating is to reach a fair and reasonable decision and to establish a positive relationship with the other parties while negotiating.*

A negotiator tries to reach a fair and reasonable resolution to whatever situation exists. The project manager should establish rules for conflict management up front when initiating and planning the project. If no rules exist, then open conflict can punctuate an otherwise successful project and ruin chances for success.

In order to resolve situations, the leader must determine causes and symptoms of problems, analyze the situation to negotiate a solution, and determine a way to implement that solution.

The strongest method for problem solving is **confronting** the situation directly. But this method takes time. If you have the time then confronting the situation and negotiating a "win-win" solution is the most effective method of problem solving. *Collaborating* is another method to work closely to achieve a "win-win" scenario. Collaborating infers active cooperation and a predetermination that an issue to be negotiated exists.

If you don't have the time, there are a couple of other methods of problem solving that might be used. *Smoothing* can be employed in situations where the problem is not significant to the outcome or deliverable.

Forcing is where the person with the most power makes the decision. Forcing is most often used when time is of the essence and you have to have an immediate decision to resolve the problem.

There are a couple of less effective means of problem solving that might be experienced. *Compromising* can be done between corporate peers. Since compromising often is considered a "lose-lose" situation, it has negative connotations.

Withdrawing can be used effectively as a "cooling off" technique. Sometimes the project manager/leader/staff would find it highly negative if the situation was immediately confronted, but the problem will probably not go away without some intervention.

Remember, your goal as a project manager is to get the project completed. Try to do whatever it takes to accomplish your goal within the prescribed constraints of your project.

Influencing

Influencing is a skill whereby the project manager sometimes shares power and uses interpersonal skills to get others to cooperate.

Influencing enhances your ability to get things done. If you can convince others your project has value and requires support, then your chances of success are enhanced. Influencing requires that the project manager plan to collaborate with others on a long-term basis.

Team Building

Team building is the process of helping the individuals and groups in the organization to work together to accomplish important goals for the organization. Team building skills are discussed and applied using the process of "Develop Project Team."

Team building is essential to project success. Team building is most effective when the highest levels of management support this process. The outcomes from team building such as increased trust, buy-in, and increases in interpersonal communication can enhance the entire organization.

Decision Making

Decision making is essential to the health of the organization and the project. It is essential to have a manager that is empowered to make decisions for a project. Decisions styles generally fall into one of four categories:

- Command (highest-ranking manager makes decision)
- Consult (discuss with group or subject matter experts)
- Consensus (achieve majority agreement)
- Coin-flip or Chance (use some random method to decide).

The project manager must understand the six-step process for decision making:

- Define the problem.
- Define a solution for the problem.
- Define action alternatives.
- Plan the specific action solution.
- Define how decision outcomes will be measured.
- Evaluate the outcome.

Political and Cultural Awareness

Internal and external factors that affect the project make up the project environment. The cultural, economic, societal, religious, and other factors that form the project environment influence the outcome of the project.

The project manager must understand the social and cultural environment they work in. In addition, the project manager should understand what effects the outcome of the project will have on society and the culture that the project is being executed in. In order to understand cultural and social implications, the project manager may need knowledge of religious, ethnic, economic, demographic, education, and other aspects of the people/culture/environment that the project is being executed in.

Part of the project environment is considering the implications of internationalism regarding the project. Are you managing a team of people spread across the world in multiple countries and time zones? If you are, how must you compensate for this team diversity? Holidays, time zones, and local customs all affect the ability of the team to work effectively together—and affect the ability of the project manager to get the job done.

The project environment also includes the organization in which you are working and the organization's view of project management. Many organizations have a loose view of project management and project management processes. Some organizations have highly developed and specified project life cycles with restrictive procedures, tools, and reporting intended to influence successful outcomes. Organization culture also affects the outcome of the project.

Projects, Programs, and Portfolios

Projects, programs, and portfolios interact to manage the overall resource use and work outputs of the organization. In order to understand these three related, yet very different entities, we first need to understand their definitions at a high level. (We have already covered the definition of a project.)

Programs

Programs are simply a group of projects that are managed together in a unified way. An example of a program could be the development of a new subdivision. The development company may have individual projects for installing the infrastructure (streets, drainage, sewer), surveying and subdividing the property, developing home plans, setting up a sales process, creating park spaces, and perhaps designing and building a community center. These are multiple projects that all roll into one program: the "XYZ Subdivision."

Program Management

When projects are rolled together to create a program, a higher form of management takes place. Program management involves managing the multiple projects in order to achieve the objectives and planned benefits of the overall program. While the individual project objectives contribute to this overall benefit, the individual project outcomes are lessened in focus, with the overall focus remaining on the overall or program benefit.

Portfolio Management

A portfolio is a collection of projects or programs or other work within the enterprise. Portfolio management is intended to maximize the benefits from these projects and programs to the enterprise.

Project Portfolio Management is a process that is used in conjunction with other project management techniques. Project Portfolio Management is a method for selecting which projects should be undertaken and which should be shelved

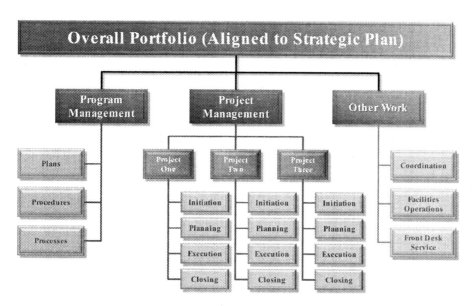

Figure 3.4 Portfolio Management

or discarded. The selection process is usually based on need, profitability, and affordability of the proposed project. It can be simply a method of matching business need to available resources to determine project approval.

Projects, programs, and portfolios interact on a constant basis within the enterprise. There are many interactions that occur between the project and the program. Our graphic below illustrates that information flows both ways between the project and program.

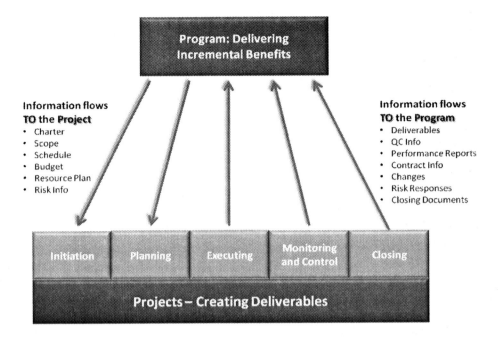

Figure 3.5 Information Flow

In addition to interactions between projects and programs, we need to also consider the role of the portfolio. The portfolio reacts to the strategic plan and objectives of the organization and uses programs and projects (as well as other work) to attempt to achieve those objectives.

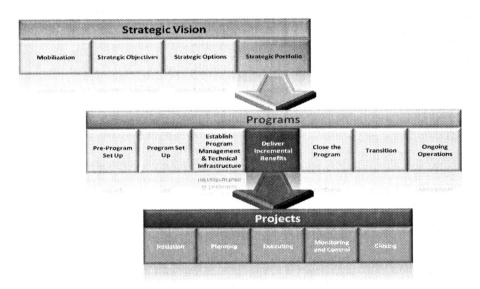

Figure 3.6 Portfolios, Programs, Project Interaction

The Project Life Cycle

The project life cycle (PLC) is created by the performing organization. The project life cycle meets the needs for project management for the organization and meets specific requirements dictated by the specialized application areas in which the organization works.

In general, a project life cycle defines several elements for the project management team. The PLC defines what phases are to be used in executing projects. The PLC defines what type of work is to be done in each phase. The PLC defines what types of roles and organizations are expected in each phase of the project.

If there is a Project Management Office (PMO) within the performing organization, the PMO may be responsible for creating the project life cycle.

A highly detailed project life cycle is often referred to as the project methodology. Project life cycles can be highly detailed or broadly framed depending on the needs of the performing organization. Many life cycles will define levels of detail required based on the size, complexity, cost, and length of the project to be performed.

Product Life Cycle

The product life cycle is not the same as the project life cycle. A product may be envisioned, created, sustained, modified, sustained in its new form, discontinued, remade, and sustained as an ongoing operation for some extended period of time. The product life cycle is usually longer and many times occurs over an open-ended period of time in comparison to a project life cycle.

More importantly, the product life cycle may contain within it several projects.

Project Phases

A phase is part of the defined project life cycle. **Each phase creates one or more deliverables and ends with a review**.

Phases are generally named for the type of work to be performed within the phase. That is, a Discovery phase might be at the beginning of a project, intended to discover all the pertinent facts and define the project. A Design phase might follow the Discovery phase. The Design phase intends to complete all of the planning and definitions for the product of the project. A Development phase could follow, where work would be performed to create the product. And finally, a Deployment phase might be the final phase in the life cycle to implement the product and turn it over to an operational group.

A deliverable is defined as a tangible, verifiable work product.

The end of phase review is a review of the deliverable and a measured decision point at which the decision is made to proceed on the project or to cancel the project.

The end of phase review usually measures project performance to date. This review can also be called a *phase exit*, a *stage gate*, or a *kill point*. The end of a phase creates a logical point to stop the project if it is not proceeding as planned.

The *PMBOK Guide* does not specify what your phase has to contain, what naming convention to use, or how many phases a project life cycle has to have. This will be defined by the performing organization based on the specialized application area where the project is being executed.

Phases can be sequential or overlapping. Your specialized application need will determine which method is best for project management in your organization.

Sequential Phases

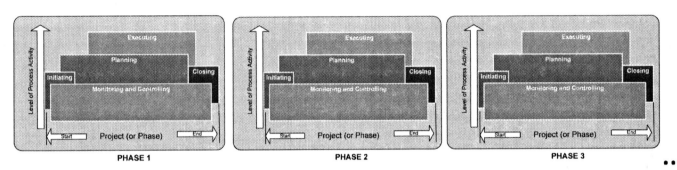

Overlapping Phases

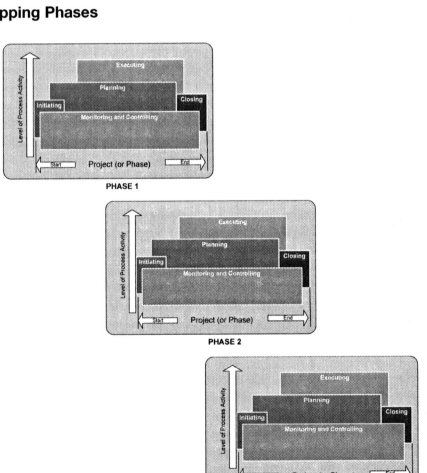

Figure 3.7 Phases

Stakeholders

Stakeholders are the individuals and organizations that are participating in the project, or whose interests are being affected by the project.

Simply stated, stakeholders are those who have a viable interest in the project.

In an ideal world, all of the stakeholders for your project should be identified, considered, consulted, involved, and apprised of project activities. In reality, many times your stakeholders will have individuals or groups who are working on their behalf. If you had to bring all of your stakeholders to each and every project meeting it would probably cause a long and arduous project. Using designated representatives will often provide adequate communication for defining and implementing the project.

You need to consider stakeholders that are apparent and some who might not be. Stakeholders who are close to the project and readily apparent include the project manager, project team members, sponsor, customer, and end user.

Stakeholders that might be a little further removed from the project include individuals and groups such as the executives in the organization, the board, other senior managers (think "synergy"), other departments and groups who might be able to use the product, vendors and suppliers and, sometimes, the general public.

Your job as project manager is to communicate with your stakeholders about the project. Your job includes resolving any communication issues that may be occurring so that there is a common understanding about the project, its definition and intent, performance, and outcome. Several specific processes will be discussed later in this book that are intended to identify and work with stakeholders on the project.

MUST KNOW CONCEPTS

1. A project is a temporary endeavor undertaken to create a unique product, service, or result. A project has a beginning and an end.

2. Project management is the application of knowledge, skills, tools, and techniques to project activities in order to meet project requirements.

3. A project manager must have several areas of skill and knowledge in order to manage projects successfully. These skills and knowledge are grouped into three categories: project management knowledge, the ability to perform, and personal skills.

4 Portfolios are collections of projects, programs, and other work in the organization.

5 Programs are made up of related projects that are managed in a unified manner to achieve planned benefits for the organization.

6 Projects should be organized in terms of phases or stages to form an overall project life cycle.

7 A stakeholder is anyone or any group that is actively involved in the project or whose interests may be affected (positively or negatively) by the project activities or outcome.

8 Initiation and planning are the most important phases of the project. Projects fail at the beginning, not at the end. Stakeholder influence is greatest at the very beginning of the project and then it diminishes as the project progresses.

ADDITIONAL READING
. . . .
- PMBOK Guide – Chapter 1 Introduction
- PMBOK Guide – Chapter 2 Project Life Cycle and Organization

LESSON QUIZ
. . . .

Instructions   Here are some questions to help reinforce your learning. Complete this quiz from memory to the best of your ability. For each question, circle or check your selected answer on this page or a separate piece of paper. When complete, check your results by comparing your answers to the preferred answers provided in Appendix A.

Please note that Knowledge Check questions are not actual PMP Exam questions. These questions are intended to reinforce key terms, concepts and themes. While these Knowledge Check questions are typical of what you can expect on your PMP Exam, many actual PMP Exam questions are more in-depth, designed to challenge your judgment (not rote memory) in applying concepts, processes and methodologies.

1.   Which of these elements is not part of the definition of a project?
    A. Progressively planned
    B. Ongoing operation
    C. Temporary time period
    D. Produces a product or service

2. What is the best definition of project management?
   A. The application of knowledge and skills to project goals in order to complete the project
   B. The application of skills, tools, and techniques, using feelings and intuition to complete the processes and procedures involved with a specific project
   C. The application of knowledge, skills, tools, and techniques to project activities in order to meet project requirements
   D. The application of knowledge, wisdom, art, and science to project activities in order to meet project requirements

3. What is the main role of the project manager on the project?
   A. Manager
   B. Project leader
   C. Integrator
   D. Communicator

4. Which of these elements is not considered part of the "triple constraint" that affects projects and their outcomes?
   A. Schedule
   B. Customer Satisfaction
   C. Budget
   D. Work to be performed

5. Of the interpersonal skills that a project manager must have, which skill is the most important to enable project success?
   A. Leadership
   B. Influencing other people
   C. Political awareness
   D. Communicating

6. What is the primary role of stakeholders on the project?
   A. To provide input to the project manager
   B. To communicate with the project manager and other stakeholders
   C. To communicate among themselves in order to define requirements
   D. To communicate with the project manager when something goes wrong

End of Lesson 3

Lesson 4
Mastering the PMBOK® Guide

Objectives
At the end of this lesson, you will be able to:
- Understand the purpose of the *PMBOK® Guide*
- Understand the content structure of the *PMBOK Guide*
- Understand the application intent of project management processes and process groups

Roadmap to the PMBOK Guide

	Initiating	Planning	Executing	M & C	Closing
Integration					
Scope					
Time					
Cost		Contains General Management Information Applicable to All Areas of PMBOK® Guide Fourth Edition and Project Management in General			
Quality					
Human Resources					
Communications					
Risk					
Procurement					

The *PMBOK Guide* provides a common vocabulary and knowledge base for project management practitioners. The *PMBOK Guide* is the de-facto standard for project management worldwide.

The *PMBOK Guide (A Guide to the Project Management Body of Knowledge)* published by the Project Management Institute is the de-facto global standard for managing projects. In September 1999, the *PMBOK Guide* was formally adopted as an ANSI standard. The *PMBOK Guide* has been updated twice since being adopted; the current version is the *PMBOK® Guide Fourth Edition*, ANSI/PMI 99-001-2008.

As a PMP candidate and eventually as a PMP, it is essential that you understand the intent, content, and context of the *PMBOK Guide*. Many exam questions are designed specifically to test your content knowledge of the *PMBOK Guide*. However, the *PMBOK Guide* is a reference standard, not a learning text. Therefore, the *PMBOK Guide* can be difficult to quickly master.

In this lesson, we will begin to master the *PMBOK Guide* by developing a high-level understanding of its intent, content, and presentation structure. If you have purchased TSI's companion Project Management Process Poster Set, you can see the many processes, process groups, and process flows illustrated in a full-color graphics format.

Study Tips

To purchase TSI's exclusive companion Project Management Process Poster Set, please go to: www.truesolutions.com or call 866-770-0903

Since you have purchased this book, you are eligible to use coupon code "PMGuide" to receive a 25% discount on your poster set.

PMBOK Guide Purpose and Content Structure

The *PMBOK® Guide* defines material and processes that are generally recognized as good practices for project management, those that are applicable to most projects, most of the time.

It is important to understand that these generally accepted practices are not expected to be uniformly applied to all projects, all of the time. It should always be up to the project manager and project team to determine what is most appropriate for any given project. Generally, the level of project management effort should be sensibly proportional to the size and complexity of the project.

The *PMBOK Guide* also provides a common vocabulary and understanding base for project management practitioners around the world.

The PMBOK Guide Fourth Edition
Approximately 459 pages total

Section I – The Project Management Framework

This section provides fundamental information. Basic definitions like the Project Life Cycle, stakeholders, enterprise environmental influences, etc. are covered in this section.

Section II – The Standard for Project Management of a Project

Section II defines project management processes, process groups, and illustrates process interactions.

Section III – The Project Management Knowledge Areas

Section III defines the nine project management knowledge areas and exposes individual project management processes in detail.

Section IV – Appendices

Section IV contains seven appendices. These appendices cover contributor information, changes to the current version of the *PMBOK Guide*, and a section on interpersonal skills.

Section V – Glossary and Index

Section V presents key acronyms, definitions, and references.

Figure 4.1 PMBOK Structure

Project Management Processes

Project management processes usually interact to affect the outcome of the project. Failure to take action in one area of the project will usually directly affect another area of the project. Project management involves managing competing demands. The project management processes defined by PMI in the *PMBOK Guide* address a wide spectrum of project elements and serve as a framework for managing project demands.

A process is defined as "a series of actions bringing about a predefined result." Processes fall into two categories:

Project management processes describe, organize, and complete the work required to complete the project scope.

Product processes specify and create the product of the project. Product processes are generally defined as part of the project life cycle by the performing organization, in order to meet specialized application needs.

Project management processes ensure that the project is managed in a logical and effective manner. Project management processes create a flow of actions and information through the project life cycle.

Product processes deal with the specification and creation of the product of the project. The unique product (project outcome) that is created will dictate the type of product-oriented processes that are to be used. When performing project management, the project manager should have specialized application knowledge and skills appropriate to the industry and product that is being created.

The *Ultimate PMP Exam Prep Guide* and the *PMBOK Guide Fourth Edition* both focus on project management related processes, almost exclusively for product-oriented processes. Two processes make reference to product definitions in Define Scope and configuration management in Integrated Change Control.

The PMP Exam will focus on project management related processes and actions.

Project Management Process Groups

Project process groups are literally collections of processes that are grouped together. The processes have some similarities to their outcomes. Process groups have clear dependencies and interactions. Process groups have a high degree of overlap and all process groups are performed in each phase of the project.

Usually the Inputs, Tools & Techniques, and Outputs in a process group are complimentary and interactive with each other. There are five project management process groups.

Study Tips

Know the Process Groups:

- Initiating
- Planning
- Executing
- Monitoring and Controlling
- Closing

The process groups categorize their processes in relation to the naming convention for the process group.

Initiating processes are used at the beginning of a project or a phase of a project.

Planning processes are used to plan the project at the beginning of a project and are used to validate plans and replan portions of the project in subsequent phases. Planning processes are also reused when a change is being made on the project to redefine whatever element requires change, to ensure project success.

Executing processes are generally used to create deliverables for the project. Executing processes are used in each phase of the project. When using executing processes, the project manager and stakeholders will recognize change requirements; these recognized changes are fed into the next process group and its associated individual processes to manage change.

Monitoring and Controlling processes are used to ensure that changes are recognized as they occur and that changes that are needed to ensure project success are incorporated into the project definition through an approval process. Monitoring and Controlling processes check on progress and are intended to ensure that the project performs as planned and executes the planned work.

Closing processes are used to perform orderly closeout of a project or a phase of a project.

How the Project Life Cycle, Project Process Groups, and Processes Interface

If you view the overall project life cycle in an outline form you can clearly determine how the project management process groups and processes as defined in the *PMBOK Guide* will fit into your project life cycle.

The performing organization will define the project life cycle based on unique needs. This includes the overall definition, the phases, and the activities that take place in the project environment for the organization.

PMI has defined process groups, processes, and unique Inputs, Tools & Techniques, and Outputs for each process.

The project in outline form looks like this:

Project Life Cycle (defined by the user organization)

- *Phases* (defined by the user organization; examples: Discover, Design, Develop, Deploy)

  - *Process Groups* (part of the PMI standard: Initiating, Planning, Executing, Monitoring and Controlling, Closing)

    - *Processes* (part of the PMI standard: forty-two unique processes)

      - *Inputs* (unique to a process)

      - *Tools* (unique to a process)

      - *Outputs* (unique to a process)

        - *Activities* (unique to the specialized application area that the project is being performed in)

It is absolutely critical that the reader understands how the PMI standard fits into the project life cycle of the performing organization. The PMI standard does not try to overpower the need of the organization; the PMI standard does not specify specific elements that have to occur to fulfill the project or activities that have to be performed.

Rather, the PMI standard specifies a framework of process groups and processes along with recommendations for specific inputs, tools, and outputs that can be used to guide the project to success.

A standard is defined as "a recommendation from a recognized body ... defining guidelines and best practices ... with which compliance is not necessary." This is a guideline, a recommendation on the best way to manage a project. You as the reader must know this body of information in order to pass the PMP exam.

In addition to the insertion of process groups and processes into the project life cycle, the reader needs to be aware of how the process groups themselves overlap and interact. The diagram below depicts that interaction.

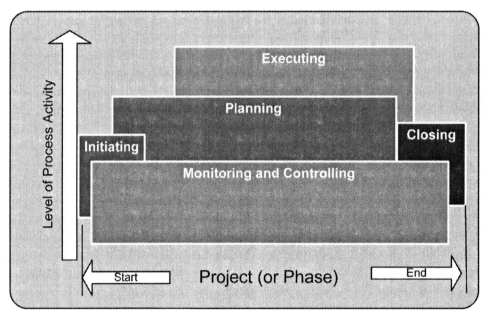

Figure 4.2 Process Group Interaction

To summarize the diagram (and perhaps to oversimplify the description), your project begins with the initiating processes that are resident in the initiating process group. At the beginning of each project or phase of a project, initiating processes are used.

Skipping ahead to the end of the diagram, at the end of a project or phase the project manager will use the closing processes.

In each of the above process groups there are two nice, neat processes that are used at the beginning and at the end.

After Initiating processes are used, the project manager would use the planning processes that are part of the Planning process group. There are twenty processes that are part of the Planning process group. These processes are designed to define the project and how the project will be managed.

There are eight processes that are part of the Executing process group. These processes are intended to produce or create deliverables for the project and to manage the associated project work.

There are ten processes that are part of the Monitoring and Controlling process group. These processes are designed to identify and accommodate change to the definition of the project. These processes also manage understanding of project information and monitor performance on the project.

To clarify the diagram further, remember our timeline? In the beginning of a project or phase the project manager has two nice, neat little processes to initiate the project or phase.

At the end of the project the project manager also has two nice, neat processes to close out the project or phase.

In the middle of the project — all of the project process groups overlap. This essentially means that in the middle of the project or phase, the project manager has the potential to be actively, concurrently using thirty-eight of the forty-two processes at one time.

Initiating processes interact with the Planning, Executing, and Monitoring and Controlling processes — essentially to activate the project or phase. Closing processes similarly interact with the three middle process groups to validate that the plans were fulfilled, deliverables were created, and controls were met before the project or phase of the project is closed.

In the middle, the Planning process group interacts with Executing and Monitoring and Controlling. The Executing process group interacts with the other two and the Monitoring and Controlling process group also interacts with Planning and Executing process groups. This is done to ensure that definitions are completed, deliverables are obtained, and changes are controlled for the project.

A very important interaction is the interaction between the Monitoring and Controlling process group and the Planning process group. This provides a "feedback loop" to Planning so that when changes are required for the project, the planning processes can be reactivated to incorporate the new requirements into the definition of the project.

I encourage the reader to keep an open mind and keep studying. As we go through all of the processes, these interactions and flows will become clear.

KNOWLEDGE AREAS

Project Management Knowledge Areas consist of processes that are grouped together by their knowledge requirements. These processes usually interact with each other and have related Inputs, Tools & Techniques, and Outputs. There are nine Knowledge Areas.

Study Tips

Know the Project Management Knowledge Areas:

- Project Integration Management
- Project Scope Management
- Project Time Management
- Project Cost Management
- Project Quality Management
- Project Human Resource Management
- Project Communications Management
- Project Risk Management
- Project Procurement Management

Project management processes are simultaneously categorized into two categories in the *PMBOK Guide*. Any given process is part of one of the five process groups. Any given process is also part of a specific project management knowledge area. The table on the next page, which is derived from page 43 of the *PMBOK® Guide Fourth Edition*, illustrates this dual relationship for individual processes.

	Initiating Process Group	Planning Process Group	Executing Process Group	Monitoring and Controlling Process Group	Closing Process Group
Project Integration Management	• Develop Project Charter	• Develop Project Management Plan	• Direct & Manage Project Execution	• Monitor and Control Project Work • Perform Integrated Change Control	• Close Project or Phase
Project Scope Management		• Collect Requirements • Define Scope • Create Work Breakdown Structure		• Verify Scope • Control Scope	
Project Time Management		• Define Activities • Sequence Activities • Estimate Activity Resources • Estimate Activity Duration • Develop Schedule		• Control Schedule	
Project Cost Management		• Estimate Costs • Determine Budget		• Control Costs	
Project Quality Management		• Plan Quality	• Perform Quality Assurance	• Perform Quality Control	
Project Human Resource Management		• Develop Human Resource Plan	• Acquire Project Team • Develop Project Team • Manage Project Team		
Project Communications Management	• Identify Stakeholders	• Plan Communications	• Distribute Information • Manage Stakeholder Expectations	• Report Performance	
Project Risk Management		• Plan Risk Management • Identify Risks • Perform Qualitative Risk Analysis • Perform Quantitative Risk Analysis • Plan Risk Responses		• Monitor and Control Risks	
Project Procurement Management		• Plan Procurements	• Conduct Procurements	• Administer Procurements	• Close Procurements

Figure 4.2 Process Matrix

MUST KNOW CONCEPTS

1 The *PMBOK Guide* identifies and describes generally recognized best practices that are applicable to most projects most of the time.

2 The level of project management effort should be sensibly proportional to the size and complexity of the project.

3 The *PMBOK Guide* organizes much of its content as an interrelated set of forty-two well-defined processes, further grouped into five progress groups.

4 The Process groups are: Initiating, Planning, Executing, Monitoring and Controlling, and Closing.

5 The *PMBOK Guide* organizes detailed discussions of the forty-two processes in a set of nine Knowledge Areas: Project Integration Management, Project Scope Management, Project Time Management, Project Cost Management, Project Quality Management, Project Human Resource Management, Project Communications Management, Project Risk Management, and Project Procurement Management.

6 Each of the forty-two *PMBOK Guide* processes is presented as a set of well-defined Inputs, Tools & Techniques, and Outputs.

7 The *PMBOK Guide* is the de-facto global standard for managing projects. The *PMBOK Guide* is an ANSI standard, ANSI/PMI 99-001-2208.

8 Projects should be organized in terms of phases or stages to form an overall project life cycle.

9 The relationship of project processes to specific project management knowledge areas and process groups is an important element to learn for the PMP Exam.

ADDITIONAL READING

• PMBOK Guide – Chapter 3.0 Project Management Processes for a Project

LESSON QUIZ

Instructions   Here are some questions to help reinforce your learning. Complete this quiz from memory to the best of your ability. For each question, circle or check your selected answer on this page or a separate piece of paper.

When complete, check your results by comparing your answers to the preferred answers provided in Appendix A.

Please note that Knowledge Check questions are not actual PMP Exam questions. These questions are intended to reinforce key terms, concepts, and themes. While these Knowledge Check questions are typical of what you can expect on your PMP Exam, many actual PMP Exam questions are more in-depth, designed to challenge your judgment (not rote memory) in applying concepts, processes, and methodologies.

1. How many processes are defined in the *PMBOK® Guide Fourth Edition*?
   A. 40
   B. 42
   C. 44
   D. 39

2. When will you use process groups during phases?
   A. In each phase of the project you will use all process groups.
   B. In each phase of the project you will use process groups only as needed.
   C. You will use the initiating process group only once in each project.
   D. You use initiating processes at the beginning of each phase, but only use the closing processes once, at the end of the project.

3. What portion of the project is most critical for project success?
   A. The phase when the project is initiated and the initial vision is defined
   B. The phase when the project is defining requirements
   C. The phase when the project work is being performed
   D. The phase when the project is being closed

4. Which statement is most true about project management process groups?
   A. Process groups are performed at a specific time on the project.
   B. Process groups are generally performed sequentially.
   C. Process groups have a high level of interaction.
   D. Process groups are selectively performed throughout the life of the project.

Exclusive Book Buyer Content

In many technical or exam preparation books, you might find a CD with an interactive test simulator or other additional information inserted into the book.

TSI has chosen not to provide a CD with this book. We think CDs are so "yesterday," so 1990s. Instead, we want to provide you with some materials that are easier to use and easy to access. We think this is a more environmentally friendly approach to learning and disseminating information.

To register your book so that you can access our test simulator and downloadable audio files, go to: www.truesolutions.com/bookregistration.

End of Lesson 4

Lesson 5
Initiating Process Group

Objectives
At the end of this lesson, you will be able to:
- Understand what processes are used in the Initiating process group
- Understand the purpose for using Initiating processes for the project or project phase

Roadmap to the PMBOK Guide

	Initiating	Planning	Executing	M & C	Closing
Integration	■				
Scope					
Time					
Cost					
Quality					
Human Resources					
Communications	■				
Risk					
Procurement					

It is generally accepted that projects fail at the beginning, due to poor initiating or planning activities, not at the end. Ensuring use of proper initiating processes can start your project towards success.

The Initiating process group consists of two processes that are intended to begin a project or project phase. The primary reason that these Initiating processes are performed is to authorize the project (or phase) and to identify the stakeholders who will be involved and interested in the project as it progresses. Initiating processes occur in the Integration Management knowledge area and the Communications Management knowledge area of the *PMBOK® Guide Fourth Edition*.

An important part of the Initiating process group is the assignment of the project manager to the project. This usually occurs during the authorization process of Develop Project Charter.

If there were a "key-word" that would characterize the Initiating process group, it might be "high-level." When a project is started, the sponsor, project manager, and stakeholders have a high-level view of the project; a vision of what is about to happen. There are usually not specific details available to define the complete project.

At the beginning of subsequent project phases, Initiating processes are used to confirm that the vision for the project is sound and that identified stakeholders still have a role on the project. In subsequent project phases, the Initiating processes will work in conjunction with the Closing processes as part of the Project Life Cycle review, stage, gate, or kill-point decision. The Closing processes are used to review what happened in the phase that is ending; the Initiating processes will confirm that the project vision is sound, the business case is viable, and the project manager who has been assigned can perform effectively on the subsequent phase.

In some cases, the Initiating processes may be performed by external organizational entities such as the portfolio manager or program manager. The *PMBOK Guide* is very clear that the project begins when the Project Charter is issued. Prior to this issuance, there may be feasibility studies, business case development, project selection, and preliminary resource assignments that take place.

When the project manager is assigned, his or her authority level should be defined. This information may be included as part of the Project Charter.

INITIATING TASKS

On your PMP Exam, you will encounter approximately twenty-two questions that will test your understanding of Initiating processes. These twenty-two questions will generally focus on the following Initiating tasks:

- As a PMP or project manager initiating a project (or project phase), you may be required to apply project selection methods to verify that the project being authorized meets customer expectations and a strategic need for the organization.

- As a PMP or project manager initiating a project (or phase), you may be required to define the scope of the project at a high level based on business need.

- As a PMP or project manager initiating a project (or phase), you may be required to identify key stakeholders for the project and interview them to obtain critical information required to start the project.

- As a PMP or project manager initiating a project (or phase), you may be required to identify and document high-level risks, assumptions, and constraints for the project. Project managers typically use previous experience, expert judgment, and historical data (from Organizational Process Assets) to identify these elements.

- As a PMP or project manager initiating a project (or phase), you may be required to develop the project charter through review with key stakeholders to confirm their vision of project scope, risks, issues, assumptions, constraints, and objectives.

- As a PMP or project manager initiating a project (or phase), you may be required to obtain formal approval for the project charter from the sponsor and/or customer to formalize authority, gain commitment and acceptance.

KNOWLEDGE REQUIREMENTS

As a PMP applying Initiating processes in real-world projects, you will be required to possess in-depth knowledge in several project-specific areas, as well as a broad knowledge of project management in general. The PMP Exam will test your understanding of these knowledge specifics.

By developing a familiarity with these knowledge specifics, you will better understand the context of many PMP Exam questions. As you progress through the *Ultimate PMP Exam Prep Guide*, you will see each of these areas mentioned. Please give some thought to each item as it relates to your own project management experiences with past and current projects.

Remember, the PMP or project manager is always required to have a very broad base of knowledge to work from. The project manager has to work across the entire organization spectrum in many cases to effectively perform project management.

As a PMP or project manager applying Initiating processes, you may be expected to have knowledge of:

- Customer needs and expectations

- How to identify stakeholders

- Experience with similar projects or work areas

- Project objectives

- Organizational goals

- Organizational structure, policies, and procedures

- Organization culture

- Business environment

- Presentation techniques

- Information gathering techniques (brainstorming, interviewing, workshops)

- Presentation techniques

- Project Charter development techniques

- Approval procedures

- Organizational templates

- How to identify stakeholder expectations

- Scope definition

- Historical information

- Risks, assumptions, and constraints

- Customer organizational structure

- Risk identification techniques

- Estimation tools and techniques

- Existing skills available in the organization

PERFORMANCE COMPETENCIES

As a PMP applying Initiating processes in real-world projects, there are many specific project management performance competencies (skills) that you may be expected to exercise.

By developing a familiarity with these skills, you will better understand the context of many PMP Exam questions. As you progress through the *Ultimate PMP Exam Prep Guide,* you will see each of these skills mentioned. As you read, please give thought to how use of these skills, related to your past and current project experiences.

As a PMP or project manager applying Initiating process, you may be required to exercise skill in:

- Active listening to identify stakeholders and subject matter experts and to identify requirements and expectations

- Preparing presentations targeted to the audience

- Effective communications skills for working, interviewing, and gathering information from stakeholders

- Analysis and decision-making abilities

- Ability to present and communicate the project vision

- Collecting historical information and lessons learned

- Identifying risk

- Creating estimates for budgets, resource requirements, project durations, and project benefits

- Identifying assumptions and constraints

- Writing skills to create meaningful documents

- Aligning project objectives with organizational objectives

- Aligning project objectives and stakeholder requirements

- Stakeholder analysis techniques

- Brainstorming and interviewing techniques

- Facilitating skills

- Capturing and synthesizing preliminary information into requirements

READ THE PMBOK® GUIDE
FOURTH EDITION

. . . .

> ## Study Tip
>
> The information exposed in our *Ultimate PMP Exam Prep Guide* is often sufficient for you to pass your PMP Exam on the first try … without any other aids or tools.
>
> However, since we are all interested in your success on the PMP Exam, we feel like it is imperative to remind you to read the *PMBOK® Guide Fourth Edition*. Throughout the *Ultimate PMP Exam Prep Guide* you will find references to the *PMBOK*.
>
> In one of our classes, I was asked by a student: "If I just read one thing, would it be the *PMBOK Guide* or the *Ultimate PMP Exam Prep Guide*?" I think the answer is not so simple. As stated above, we think that the *Ultimate PMP Exam Prep Guide* provides you with what you need — but why sell yourself short — or take unnecessary shortcuts. This is an important certification and an important step in your career. We recommend that you thoroughly read *both* documents.

ADDITIONAL READING
. . . .

• PMBOK Guide – Section 3.3

End of Lesson 5

6

Lesson 6
Develop Project Charter

Objectives

At the end of this lesson, you will be able to:

- Describe the purpose of the Develop Project Charter process
- Describe the Inputs, Tools & Techniques, and Outputs of the Develop Project Charter process
- List the key items that should be included in a Project Charter

Roadmap to the PMBOK Guide

	Initiating	Planning	Executing	M & C	Closing
Integration					
Scope					
Time					
Cost					
Quality					
Human Resources					
Communications					
Risk					
Procurement					

Choosing to undertake projects that are not carefully justified can lead to inefficient use of time and resources and perhaps even complete project failure.

In today's increasingly competitive world, we must ensure that projects undertaken have value, provide efficiencies, and meet the organization's strategic objectives. This requires solid planning, execution, and control across the entire project life cycle.

But, even before we begin planning our projects, we must pay close attention to the very projects we choose to undertake. Good project management begins with good project selection.

If corporate management chooses to undertake a project that is not aligned with the organization's strategic goals, or fails to thoroughly consider alternatives up front, then the ability to create real value from the project will be significantly handicapped. Choosing to undertake projects that are not mindfully justified up front can lead to inefficient use of time and resources, and perhaps even project failure.

The Develop Project Charter process is intended to ensure that any project chartered and authorized by management is well thought-through and justified. With a solid beginning, any project has a greater probability of ultimate success.

Applying the Develop Project Charter process encourages management to thoroughly consider all high-level aspects of a proposed project, and then to make an informed selection decision. The process suggests that management employs expert judgment to make good decisions. While not specifically specified as tools in the Develop Project Charter process, informed selection methods usually include Benefit Measurement tools or using some form of Mathematical Models (or application programs) to determine whether or not a project would be valuable to the organization.

When using the Develop Project Charter process, the PMI process model assumes the completion of any feasibility study or analysis, to determine whether or not the project should be performed. In practical application, a feasibility study or preanalysis would be a separate process (or a separate project) that is completed prior to the authorization of the product-creation project, using Develop Project Charter.

When a project is selected, then the Develop Project Charter process suggests that management prepare and issue a formal Project Charter that:

• records the preliminary characteristics of the project or a phase,

• authorizes the project,

• identifies/authorizes the project manager.

A project sponsor or initiator authorizes the project by approving the Project Charter. This person should be at a level that is appropriate for funding the project.

The project initiator may be the Project Management Office (PMO) or the Portfolio Steering Committee.

PROCESS ELEMENTS

The Develop Project Charter process has the following Inputs:

- **Project Statement of Work (SOW)**   Narrative description of the products/services to be delivered by the project

- **Business Case**   Describes the reason the project is worth investing in, from the business standpoint

- **Contract**   Used as an input if the project is undertaken for an external customer/client

- **Enterprise Environmental Factors**   Consideration factors such as culture, systems, procedures, industry standards

- **Organizational Process Assets**   Consideration factors such as processes, procedures, and corporate knowledge base

The Develop Project Charter process uses the following Tools & Techniques:

- **Expert Judgment**   Expert technical and/or managerial judgment (from any qualified source)

The Develop Project Charter process has the following Output:

- **Project Charter**   High-level document that documents business needs, authorizes the project and assigns/authorizes the project manager

Develop Project Charter (4.1)		
This process formally sanctions a new project or authorizes a project to continue into the next phase		
Inputs	**Tools and Techniques**	**Outputs**
• Project Statement of Work (SOW) • Business Case • Contract • Enterprise Environmental Factors • Organizational Process Assets	• Expert Judgment	• Project Charter

TSI *Study Aid*
This chart is part of the study aid poster series available at *www.truesolutions.com.*

PROCESS DOCUMENTS

The Project Charter documents the preliminary project information. As previously discussed, the Project Charter has one main outcome: authorizing the project to start. This authorization allows the project manager to begin the project and begin to use organizational resources. The Project Charter records the initial vision of the project sponsor. This document can be very concise. Many Project Charter documents can be completed in one page.

Some of the elements that might be included in the Project Charter are:

• Project name

• Project purpose

• Business Case and justification for chartering the project

• Planned project objectives

• High-level description of the project overall

• High-level description of the product or service to be created by the project

• A list of potential project risks — identified at a very high level

• Planned schedule

• Initial budget amount

• Results of a feasibility study or project-selection analysis

• Description of how the project links to the organization's work portfolio

• Assignment of a project manager

• Project manager's roles, responsibilities and authority level

• Name and title of person(s) authorizing the project

For specific PMP Exam guidance on the Project Charter document and its contents, please refer directly to the *PMBOK® Guide Fourth Edition*, section 4.1.

The following form reflects a template that can be used to record all of the preliminary project information and define a Project Charter.

True Solutions, Inc.
Project Management Template
Volume 1: Project Charter Template

Project Charter

Project Name:	
Prepared by:	
Date:	
Project purpose:	*Identify the customers who are to receive and benefit from the product developed by the project and the need the product is intended to meet (either as a problem to solve or as an opportunity to exploit)*
Planned Objectives:	*Identify what product or service is to be delivered at the end of the project, and at any interim delivery points. Describe the product sufficiently to enable the project team to create it, and for agreement to be reached at product delivery time that the product has been correctly produced*
High level project description:	*Briefly explain the requirements for the project and a description of the project to afford an understanding of known needs and tasks to accomplish project*
High level product description:	*Briefly identify major deliverables to be created by this project*
Planned schedule:	*Identify what milestones will be a key factor to reach to project objectives*
Initial budget:	*Use a Rough Order of Magnitude estimate to show budget requirements*
Program or Portfolio Links:	*Identify how the project links to the work of the organization and any programs being managed in the organization*
Assignment of Project Manager, responsibility and authority	*Often the Project Manager will have already been decided before hand or during the charter. Identify who the Project Manager is and what their responsibility is during the project and what authority level they have (decision making, budget, approving, etc.)*
Name and Title of Sponsor:	*Identify who the project sponsor (persons or groups) and explain what their authority will be within the project*
Other:	*Identify and explain any other matters that are important for the initiation and conduct of the project. Focus on charter issues of importance between the project sponsor and the project manager. This section is not for describing the project plan*
Approval:	Sponsor: Date:

Application Aid
This form is available individually or as a set from *www.truesolutions.com.*

Study Tip

The Project Charter is one of the three essential documents that each project will require. The other documents are: the Project Scope Statement and Project Management Plan.

PROCESS TASKS

The following is a list of the common tasks associated with the Develop Project Charter process:

1. Identify and document project needs by developing project-related product/service descriptions

- Determine your project's product/service characteristics using expert judgment

- Identify/document your project's constraints and assumptions

- Develop a needs requirement for your project

2. Validate project feasibility study and analysis

- Utilize project selection methods/decision models, including Benefit Measurement methods and mathematical models

- Evaluate historical information from a project involving similar products and services

- Perform a high-level assessment of the organizational resources for your project

- Perform a high-level assessment of the technical and nontechnical requirements of your project

- Document feasibility findings

3. Prepare the Project Charter

- Develop a Project Charter to formally document and link your project to the ongoing work of your organization

- Define your responsibilities as project manager, and those of other organizational managers

- Define the project phases of the project life cycle to be used on the project

- Define the primary components of your Project Charter

- Identify your initial project stakeholders

- Establish your project's purpose, description, assumptions, and constraints

- Define your project's business benefits and benefit measurements

- Define your project's critical success factors

- Validate Business Case for your project

4. Conduct preliminary planning activities

- Identify your customer's expectations with regard to timing of delivery, major milestones, and any schedule and delivery constraints

- Identify internal and external schedule constraints and influences

- Identify your key project milestones

- Develop your initial milestone plan

5. Help prepare a high-level (preliminary) project budget

- Develop your cost-benefit analysis

- Identify your budget constraints

- Determine project quality requirements

6. Determine quality objectives, standards, and levels with input from your stakeholders and the guidance of your higher project authorities to establish the basis for quality outcomes

- Determine your organization's quality policy

- Develop your project quality policies and quality requirements documentation

7. Define the preliminary project organization

- Identify specific organizational role and responsibility assignment processes

8. Determine preliminary project communication needs

- Identify your project/organization communication policies

9. Identify preliminary project risks

- Identify and review your organization's risk management policies and procedures

- Identify risk tolerances of your stakeholders

- Identify preliminary risks

- Develop a high-level preliminary project risk assessment matrix

10. Conduct preliminary procurement planning

- Identify and review your organization's procurement policies and procedures

- Document a preliminary project procurement plan

THINK ABOUT IT

. . . .

Instructions Use this exercise to compare how you practice project management to what is specified in the *PMBOK® Guide Fourth Edition.*

Best Practices suggest that the following items are used during the Develop Project Charter Process.

Which of these items do you use when practicing project management?

- ☐ 1–5 page document
- ☐ High-level overview of project
- ☐ High-level list of deliverables
- ☐ Business Case
- ☐ Planned schedule
- ☐ Initial budget
- ☐ Project manager assignment
- ☐ Authority level for project manager specified
- ☐ Signature of sponsor

How would you change your use of this process in your organization to resolve any gaps in application?

_____

_____

_____

_____

_____

_____

_____

_____

_____

MUST KNOW CONCEPTS

Items 11–17 are general concepts that will be repeated throughout the course

1 The Develop Project Charter process is intended to formally authorize a new project, or authorize an ongoing project to continue into its next phase.

2 Projects must be aligned with the organization's strategic plan (strategic objectives).

3 The primary deliverable (Output) of the Develop Project Charter process is the Project Charter.

4 The Project Charter is a high-level document that communicates preliminary project characteristics, authorizes the project, and identifies and authorizes the project manager.

5 The Project Charter is typically issued by a project initiator or sponsor, external to the immediate project organization, at a funds-providing management level.

6 The project's business need should be clearly defined and documented in the Project Charter.

7 The project's product or service description should be clearly defined during Develop Project Charter and documented in the Project Charter.

8 Chartering a project links the project to the ongoing work of the performing organization.

9 The project manager should be assigned as early as possible, prior to project planning, preferably during Project Charter development.

10 The Project Charter should be relatively brief (broad, not deep), perhaps 1–5 pages in length.

11 Decisions made early in the project life cycle (in Initiating or Planning) tend to have the greatest overall influence on the project outcome.

12 Historical information (from previous projects of similar nature) is considered critical input to many processes, including Develop Project Charter.

13 Constraints are factors that limit the project team's options.

14 Assumptions are factors that are deemed to be certain. Assumptions are best used to define a portion of the project when there are unknown project conditions.

15 Project selection methods fall into two broad categories: Benefit Measurement methods and Mathematical Models.

16 Enterprise Environmental Factors are internal or external factors that influence the project.

17 Organizational Process Assets are assets that may be used to influence project success, such as templates, procedures, historical data, and published guidelines.

ADDITIONAL READING
. . . .
- PMBOK Guide – Section 4.0 Introdution, Project Integration Management
- PMBOK Guide – Section 4.1 Develop Project Charter

LESSON QUIZ
. . . .
Instructions   Here are some questions to help reinforce your learning. Complete this quiz from memory to the best of your ability. For each question, circle or check your selected answer on this page or a separate piece of paper. When complete, check your results by comparing your answers to the preferred answers provided in Appendix A.

Please note that Knowledge Check questions are not actual PMP Exam questions. These questions are intended to reinforce key terms, concepts, and themes. While these Knowledge Check questions are typical of what you can expect on your PMP Exam, many actual PMP Exam questions are more in-depth, designed to challenge your judgment (not rote memory) in applying concepts, processes, and methodologies.

1. The precise description of a physical item, procedure, or service is called a _____.
    A. work breakdown structure (WBS) element
    B. product description
    C. baseline
    D. work package

2. Develop Project Charter inputs include all of the following except _____.
    A. Organizational Process Assets
    B. Enterprise Environmental Factors
    C. contract
    D. Expert Judgment

3. Which of the following statements is most true?
    A. The Project Charter identifies the names of project management team members.
    B. The Project Charter tracks a project's history.
    C. The Project Charter names and authorizes the project manager.
    D. The Project Charter describes the details of what needs to be done to satisfy quality improvement objectives.

4. Your project is characterized by frequent changes to the Project Charter. Authorizing Project Charter changes should typically be the responsibility of _____.
   A. senior management
   B. the project manager
   C. the project management team
   D. project stakeholders

5. Which of the following is most true?
   A. The Project Charter is developed during closing.
   B. The Project Charter is developed during initiating.
   C. The Project Charter is developed during executing.
   D. The Project Charter is developed during planning.

6. In which project life cycle phase would you expect to have the greatest influence on project cost?
   A. Design
   B. Concept
   C. Build
   D. Launch

7. You have served on many of your organization's project teams and, because of your solid performance, have been assigned as project manager on a new company project. You have never managed an entire project. Which of the following is most important to you to help ensure project success?
   A. The project work breakdown structure (WBS)
   B. Your project management training
   C. Organizational process assets
   D. Your common sense and natural organizational skills

8. You can generally say each of the following is true except:
   A. The Project Charter identifies major task interdependencies.
   B. The Project Charter includes the initial product description.
   C. The Project Charter defines the business need(s) that the project was undertaken to address.
   D. The Project Charter is issued by a senior manager external to the project.

End of Lesson 6

Lesson 7
Identify Stakeholders

Objectives

At the end of this lesson, you will be able to:

- Describe the purpose of the Identify Stakeholders process
- Describe the Inputs, Tools & Techniques, and Outputs of the Identify Stakeholders process
- Identify who Key Stakeholders would be for a typical project

Roadmap to the PMBOK Guide

	Initiating	Planning	Executing	M & C	Closing
Integration					
Scope					
Time					
Cost					
Quality					
Human Resources					
Communications	██				
Risk					
Procurement					

A project manager must be sure to identify and list all potential stakeholders for a project in order to facilitate project success.

Very early in the life of a project, it is critical to identify all of the organizations and people who may have an impact on the project, and all those who may be impacted by the project.

A "stakeholder" is any person or organization that is actively involved in a project, or whose interests may be affected positively or negatively by execution of a project. Stakeholders can be internal to the organization or external. In many projects the public at large will become a stakeholder to be considered during the project. The challenge for the project manager when the public is a stakeholder will be to act while considering public needs. Often there is no direct representative of the public to be consulted during project planning and execution.

A project manager must be sure to identify and list all potential stakeholders for a project. Potential stakeholders include but are not limited to:

Competitors	National communities
Employees	Professional associations
Government	Prospective customers
Government regulatory agencies	Prospective employees
Industry trade groups	Public at large (Global community)
Investors	Shareholders
Labor unions	Suppliers
Local communities	

The project manager must document relevant information for all identified stakeholders. This information may include the stakeholder's interests, involvement, expectations, importance, influence, and impact on the project's execution as well as any specific communications requirements. It is important to note that although some identified stakeholders may not actually require any communications, those stakeholders should be identified.

When identifying stakeholders and rating their level of interest and involvement in the project, it will become important to use some sort of a tool — a rating scale, an influence diagram, or a chart form to identify the level of power, influence, interest, or impact that the stakeholder may have on the project. There is a sample of a stakeholder needs and expectations form in the forms section of this lesson.

PROCESS ELEMENTS

The Identify Stakeholders process has the following Inputs:

- **Project Charter**   High-level document that authorizes the project and assigns/authorizes the project manager

- **Procurement Documents**   Identifies procurement contract stakeholders

- **Enterprise Environmental Factors**   Consideration factors such as culture, systems, procedures, industry standards

- **Organizational Process Assets**   Consideration factors such as templates, lessons learned, stakeholder registers from former projects

The Identify Stakeholders process uses the following Tools & Techniques:

- **Stakeholder Analysis**   Gathering and assessing information to determine whose interests should be taken into account for a project

- **Expert Judgment**   Expert technical and/or managerial judgment (from any qualified source)

The Identify Stakeholders process has the following Outputs:

- **Stakeholder Register**   A document identifying all project stakeholder information, requirements, and classification

- **Stakeholder Management Strategy**   Defines the approach to increase stakeholder support and reduce negative impacts represented in a stakeholder analysis matrix

Identify Stakeholders (10.1)
This process identifies all persons/organizations affected by a project and documents their interests, involvement, and impact on the project

Inputs	Tools and Techniques	Outputs
• Project Charter • Procurement Documents • Enterprise Environmental Factors • Organizational Process Assets	• Stakeholder Analysis • Expert Judgment	• Stakeholder Register • Stakeholder Management Strategy

TSI *Study Aid*

This chart is part of the study aid poster series available at *www.truesolutions. com.*

PROCESS DOCUMENTS

During the Identify Stakeholders process two important documents are created. In order to rate each stakeholder's importance and impact on the project you need some form of stakeholder analysis. Stakeholder analysis focuses on the stakeholder's importance to the project, and to the organization, the influence exerted by the stakeholder, plus stakeholder participation and expectations.

A Stakeholder Expectations Questionnaire may be used to analyze specific stakeholder influences and needs. An example of a stakeholder expectations questionnaire is shown below.

True Solutions, Inc.
Project Management Template
Volume 1: Stakeholders Needs & Expectations
Questionnaire Template

(TSI)

PROJECT STAKEHOLDERS NEEDS & EXPECTATIONS QUESTIONNAIRE	Project Management Strategy
Project ID:	Project Name:
Project Sponsor:	Project Manager:

A stakeholder is anyone who will impact, or be impacted by the event.
Please provide the stakeholder with the Project Charter document as an introduction to the project.

Project		Date
Stakeholder	Ext.	Department

A. Objective – What results would you require, expect, or desire from the project? Categories of objectives include; function, cost, time, surprises, flexibility, effectiveness.

Item	Expectation
1	
2	
3	
4	

B. Measures – What measures could we use to validate that we met these objectives?

1	
2	
3	
4	

C. Impact – What changes do you expect your area may make to adjust to this change?

1	
2	
3	
4	

D. Involvement – What do you see as your/your area's role?

E. Your Deliverables and Roles – What items or changes do you think you/your area should provide for the project to be effective? Who would be responsible for these deliverables?

Deliverable	Responsible
1	
2	
3	
4	

©Copyright 2009 True Solutions, Inc.
5001 LBJ Freeway, Suite 125-B Dallas, Texas 75244
Tel: 972.770.0900   Fax 972.770.0922   www.truesolutions.com

(TSI) Application Aid
This form is available individually or as a set from *www.truesolutions.com.*

A Stakeholder Register may be used to record a general overview of each stakeholder and their planned/forecasted role on the project. An example of a potential form for use as a stakeholder register is depicted below.

True Solutions, Inc.
Project Management Template
Volume 1: Stakeholder Register Template

TSI

Stakeholder Register

Project Name:				
Prepared by:				
Date:				

Project Stakeholder Name	Specific Information Needs	Project Interests	Impact on Project	Role
	Types & Frequency of Communication	Specific Areas of Interest and Participation	Positive, Negative, Influencer, Supporter, Roadblock	Decision Maker, Collaborator, Participant, Consultant, Information Recipient

TSI Application Aid
This form is available individually or as a set from *www.truesolutions.com*.

For specific PMP Exam guidance on the Project Charter document and its contents, please refer directly to the *PMBOK® Guide Fourth Edition*, section 4.1.

PROCESS TASKS

The following is a list of some of the common tasks associated with the Identify Stakeholders process:

1. Identify and document a list of all project stakeholders

- Determine who internal stakeholders may be

- Identify/document external stakeholders

- Prioritize the stakeholder list by anticipated participation or importance

2. Validate the Stakeholder Register (list)

- Network with stakeholders to determine specific project interests and needs

- Evaluate stakeholder organization influence to determine stakeholder positioning on the project

3. Create a high-level approach for communicating with all stakeholders

- Prepare a document describing what the overall approach will be toward stakeholder management for the project

- Develop a preliminary communication plan intended to address general stakeholder needs

4. Define your responsibilities as project manager, and those of other stakeholders

- Define which stakeholders will be participating and will have an interest by project phases of the project life cycle to be used on the project

- Communicate the approach to key project stakeholders in order to obtain buy-in

THINK ABOUT IT

When applying the Identify Stakeholders process it is important to note that while this particular process is a new process to the *PMBOK® Guide Fourth Edition*, it is not a new process to project management. It is also a process that is often overlooked—with sometimes disastrous results.

While working as project manager for a major automotive manufacturer during Y2K, I was leading a project to change the way automotive replacement parts were sold and distributed. We already had identified a rather large, overwhelming project team intended to work together to create and deploy the systems and new business processes. But we failed to clearly identify all of the stakeholders and their interests.

When we started the implementation planning it was quickly determined that the end user needs and technical specifications of systems that were in use had not been properly identified. The goals and objectives that the end users had were mostly different from the plan, as documented in the scope statement and the Project Statement of Work. Additionally, political factions within the project began to have internal wars over stated objectives and how to achieve the objectives from a technical standpoint. Major portions of the overall organization considered themselves to be stakeholders, yet were not identified on any list as a project stakeholder.

The immediate program manager, project manager, and team clearly understood what was planned and what the stated goals and objectives were for the program and the project. But, the program and project managers failed to clearly identify who else needed to have input and knowledge of the program.

Using the Identify Stakeholders process effectively could have saved many hours of misdirection and resource misallocation (and lots of money). Ultimately, our project was only moderately successful with a small group of end users that were deployed during that fiscal year. But we could have been highly successful if we had identified all of our stakeholders and their needs before committing to a course of action.

Contributed by Tim Bergmann, PMP

MUST KNOW CONCEPTS

1. A "stakeholder" is any person or organization that is actively involved in a project, or whose interests may be affected positively or negatively by execution of a project.

2. The Identify Stakeholders process is used to identify all people or organizations that may be impacted by or have an impact on a project.

3. A key Output of the Identify Stakeholders process is the Stakeholder Register, which lists the project's stakeholders and relevant information for each stakeholder or stakeholder group.

4. Stakeholder Analysis is a technique used to determine each stakeholder's interest, influence, participation, and expectations for a project.

ADDITIONAL READING

- PMBOK Guide – Section 10.0 Introduction Project Communication Management
- PMBOK Guide – Section 10.1 Identify Stakeholders

LESSON QUIZ

Instructions   Here are some questions to help reinforce your learning. Complete this quiz from memory to the best of your ability. For each question, circle or check your selected answer on this page or a separate piece of paper. When complete, check your results by comparing your answers to the preferred answers provided in Appendix A.

Please note that Knowledge Check questions are not actual PMP Exam questions. These questions are intended to reinforce key terms, concepts, and themes. While these Knowledge Check questions are typical of what you can expect on your PMP Exam, many actual PMP Exam questions are more in-depth, designed to challenge your judgment (not rote memory) in applying concepts, processes, and methodologies.

1.   Which of the following best describes the Identify Stakeholders process?
    A. The Identify Stakeholders process is used to identify all people or organizations that may be impacted by or have an impact on a project.
    B. The Identify Stakeholders process is used to determine the communication needs of project stakeholders.
    C. The Identify Stakeholders process is used to make project information available to project stakeholders.
    D. The Identify Stakeholders process is used to ensure that communications with project stakeholders is productive and meets the needs and desires of those stakeholders.

2.   You have just been appointed as the project manager to an organization that you are not familiar with. One of your first tasks is to identify stakeholders for your project. What are the three steps you would perform to analyze stakeholders?
    A. Identify internal stakeholders, identify external stakeholders, and ask them how they would like to be communicated with
    B. Identify all potential stakeholders, identify the potential impact or support of each stakeholder, and assess how they might respond to various situations

C. Identify all potential stakeholders, ask how they would like to be communicated with, and build alliances with those who are the most important stakeholders

D. Identify all potential stakeholders, identify the potential impact or support of each stakeholder, and build alliances with those who are the most important stakeholders

3. The key Output for Identify Stakeholders includes:
   A. Communications Management plan
   B. Stakeholder Register
   C. Stakeholder Issues report
   D. Stakeholder Analysis

End of Lesson 7

Lesson 8
Planning Process Group

Objectives

At the end of this lesson, you will be able to:

• Understand what processes are used in the Planning process group
• Understand the purpose for using Planning processes for the project or project phase

Roadmap to the PMBOK Guide

	Initiating	Planning	Executing	M & C	Closing
Integration					
Scope					
Time					
Cost					
Quality					
Human Resources					
Communications					
Risk					
Procurement					

During Planning, the project is fully defined. At the end of Planning, the Project Management Plan will be approved and adopted to provide the baseline for all executing activities.

The Planning process group consists of twenty processes that are intended to plan a project or project phase. The primary reason that these Planning processes are performed is to define the elements and work for a project (or phase). Planning processes cover all nine knowledge areas of the *PMBOK® Guide Fourth Edition*.

During the Planning processes, the project is fully defined. At the end of the Planning processes, the Project Management Plan and all related documentation is completed and accepted by the project stakeholders. Usually, after the Project Management Plan and all defining documents are accepted, then change control processes are employed to manage all subsequent changes to the project baseline.

Of particular importance are the project baselines for project scope, schedule, and budget.

In general, when a change is made to the project baseline while the project is in the executing phases of the project, the project manager returns to the Planning processes in order to update the affected documentation.

PLANNING TASKS

On your PMP Exam, you will encounter approximately forty-six questions that will test your understanding of Planning processes. These forty-six questions will generally focus on the following tasks:

- As a PMP or project manager planning a project (or project phase) you may be required to record detailed customer requirements, constraints, and assumptions with stakeholders in order to establish the project deliverables, using requirement gathering techniques (planning sessions, brainstorming, focus groups) and the Project Charter.

- As a PMP or project manager planning a project (or phase) you may be required to identify key project team members, define roles and responsibilities, and create a project organization chart in order to develop critical project documents like the Human Resource Plan and Communications Plan.

- As a PMP or project manager planning a project (or phase) you may be required to create the work breakdown structure with the team, using appropriate Tools & Techniques in order to develop the cost, schedule, resource, quality, and procurement plans.

- As a PMP or project manager planning a project (or phase) you may be required to develop the change management plan by defining how changes will be handled in order to minimize risk.

- As a PMP or project manager planning a project (or phase) you may be required to identify project risks by defining risk strategies and developing the Risk Management Plan in order to reduce uncertainty throughout the project life cycle.

- As PMP or project manager planning a project (or phase) you may be required to obtain project plan approval from the customer or sponsor in order to formalize the project management approach.

- As a PMP or project manager planning a project (or phase) you may be required to conduct a kickoff meeting with all key stakeholders in order to announce the start of the project and review the overall project plan and gain acceptance for the plan.

KNOWLEDGE REQUIREMENTS

As a PMP applying Planning processes in real-world projects, you will be required to possess in-depth knowledge in several project specific areas, as well as a broad knowledge of project management in general. The PMP Exam will test your understanding of these knowledge specifics.

By developing a familiarity with these knowledge specifics, you will better understand the context of many PMP Exam questions. As you progress through the *Ultimate PMP Exam Prep Guide*, you will see each of these areas mentioned. Please give some thought to each item as it relates to your own project management experiences with past and current projects.

Remember, the PMP or project manager is always required to have a very broad base of knowledge to work from. The project manager has to work across the entire organizational spectrum in many cases to effectively perform project management.

As a PMP or project manager applying Planning processes, you may be expected to have knowledge of:

- Project Charter

- Configuration Management Systems

- Organizational structure, policies, and procedures

- Stakeholder expectations

- Requirement gathering techniques

- Communications plans

- Work breakdown structure

- Project deliverables

- Cost plans

- Estimating tools and techniques

- Budgets

- Schedule plans

- Network diagramming
- Simulation techniques
- Scheduling tools
- Resource planning
- Staffing requirements
- Stakeholder analysis
- Quality planning
- Acceptance criteria
- Quality tools
- Procurement processes

- Service level agreements
- Solicitation processes
- Scope management
- Project requirements definition
- Change management plans
- Historical information
- Lessons learned
- Risk management planning
- Project planning

PERFORMANCE COMPETENCIES

As a PMP applying Planning processes in real-world projects, there are many specific project management performance competencies (skills) that you may be expected to exercise.

By developing a familiarity with these skills, you will better understand the context of many PMP Exam questions. As you progress through the *Ultimate PMP Exam Prep Guide*, you will see each of these skills mentioned. As you read, please give thought to how the use of these skills relates to your past and current project experiences.

As a PMP or project manager applying Planning processes, you may be required to exercise skill in:

- Brainstorming
- Negotiating
- Scheduling
- Estimating
- Role-playing
- Facilitating
- Documenting
- Collating
- Forecasting

- Active listening
- Interviewing
- Building consensus
- Leading
- Prioritizing
- Budgeting
- Presenting
- Influencing
- Motivating

ADDITIONAL READING

• PMBOK Guide – Section 3.4

LESSON QUIZ

Process Matching Exercise

Instructions   Read the recommended reading for this lesson before attempting this exercise. After you have read all of the lesson material and the reading in the *PMBOK Guide*, your goal is to match the appropriate processes to the correct process group and knowledge area. All of the processes are listed on the right.

In this exercise, match the correct *planning* process to their knowledge area.

Knowledge Area	Process Group					Project Processes
	Initiating	Planning	Executing	Monitoring & Controlling	Closing	
Integration						Report Performance
						Control Schedule
						Verify Scope
						Plan Risk Responses
						Estimate Costs
						Develop Project Charter
						Identify Stakeholders
Scope						Develop Project Management Plan
						Close Project or Phase
						Monitor & Control Project Work
						Control Scope
						Monitor & Control Project Risk
Time						Direct & Manage Project Execution
						Acquire Project Team
						Plan Quality
						Perform Integrated Change Control
						Define Scope
						Determine Budget
Cost						Define Activities
						Plan Communications
						Manage Stakeholder Expectations
Quality						Manage Project Team
						Control Costs
						Perform Quality Assurance
Human Resource						Administer Procurements
						Develop Human Resource Plan
						Create WBS
						Sequence Activities
						Perform Quality Control
Communication						Close Procurements
						Develop Project Team
						Plan Risk Management
						Conduct Procurements
						Estimate Activity Resources
Risk						Identify Risks
						Perform Qualitative Risk Analysis
						Plan Procurements
						Estimate Activity Durations
						Perform Quantitative Risk Analysis
Procurement						Distribute Information
						Develop Schedule
						Collect Requirements

End of Lesson 8

Lesson 9
Plan Communications

Objectives

At the end of this lesson, you will be able to:

- Describe the purpose of the Plan Communications process
- Describe the Inputs, Tools & Techniques, and Outputs of the Plan Communications process
- Understand the importance of effective communications to the project
- Understand when to perform Plan Communications
- Understand what elements should be included in a communications plan

Roadmap to the PMBOK Guide

	Initiating	Planning	Executing	M & C	Closing
Integration					
Scope					
Time					
Cost					
Quality					
Human Resources					
Communications		■			
Risk					
Procurement					

Planning project communications is critical to success. Failure to plan usually results in confusion, inefficiency and project failure.

Effective communication in project management is considered a critical success factor. When troubled projects are evaluated, it is typical to find poor communication as a major source of negative conflict and negative outcomes. It is a commonly accepted heuristic (rule of thumb) that good project managers spend up to 90% of their time communicating.

Communication provides the vital connections between people, concepts, and information, throughout the project environment. Good communication management ensures that important information is generated, collected, distributed, and stored in an appropriate and effective manner. Effective communications can facilitate success and enable the project to succeed. The lack of effective communications almost always contributes to project confusion, deficiencies, and failure.

The Plan Communications process is applied to determine the communication needs of project stakeholders. This includes determining:

• What information is needed

• When it is needed

• How it will be delivered.

Communications needs for the project are typically determined by first engaging identified project stakeholders (communication requirements analysis), to determine their detailed information needs, then documenting the details in a Communications Management Plan. The initial identification of stakeholders occurs early in the project during project initiation. During the initial identification of stakeholders, communications requirements are identified at a high level. In the Plan Communications process, the initial requirements are further detailed and recorded. The Plan Communications process will be executed at the beginning of planning processes. The fact that this process is performed so early in the project attests to the overall importance of having an effective communications plan.

COMMUNICATION SKILLS

Project Communications Management does not necessarily involve general communication skills. It is more concerned with information structure. However, understanding basic communication skills is essential to good project management. Communicating is one of the key interpersonal skills that a project manager must use to facilitate project success.

Study Tips

Communication is a two-way activity. Communication is not complete until the sender confirms that the receiver has understood the intended message.

Effective listening can be an important part of good communication. It can develop rapport and respect.

It is important for the project manager to understand several elements associated with communicating. The project manager should understand types of interpersonal communications, elements that may prevent or block communications, and how to measure the number of communications channels.

There are five types of Interpersonal Communications:

- Informal Verbal Communication: "hallway chat" and *ad hoc* discussions

- Formal Verbal Communication: formal presentations, briefings

- Non-Verbal Communication: voice tones, body language (Non-verbal communication is much more powerful and expressive than words)

- Informal Written Communication: E-mail messages, memos, text messaging, notes

- Formal Written Communication: legal documents, plans, project reports, standards, procedures, letters, proposals

COMMUNICATIONS INTERFERENCE

Effective communication can become increasingly difficult if "blockers" interfere. Communication blockers can include:

- Language differences between sender and receiver

- Physical distance between sender and receiver

- Physical background noise

- Negative comments from sender or receiver

- Hostility between sender and receiver

• Cultural differences between sender and receiver

Care should be taken to minimize or eliminate blockers before engaging in meaningful communication.

COMMUNICATION CHANNELS

The number of communication channels increases in an exponential fashion as more stakeholders become engaged in a project.

Study Tips

The number of communication channels in a project is calculated using this equation:

$N(N-1)/2$

Where

N = the number of people or stakeholders

As an example, if a project team has eight members, the number of communication channels would be calculated like this:

$8(8-1)/2 = 8(7)/2 = 56/2 = 28$

PROCESS ELEMENTS

The Plan Communications process has the following Inputs:

- **Stakeholder Register**   A document identifying all project stakeholder information, requirements, and classification

- **Stakeholder Management Strategy**   Defines the approach to increase stakeholder support and reduce negative impacts represented in a stakeholder analysis matrix

- **Enterprise Environmental Factors**   Consideration factors such as culture, systems, procedures, industry standards

- **Organizational Process Assets**   Consideration factors such as lessons learned and historical information

The Plan Communications process uses the following Tools & Techniques:

- **Communications Requirements Analysis**   Determining the total of information needs among project stakeholders

- **Communications Technology**   The methodologies used to transfer information among project stakeholders

- **Communications Models**   A model demonstrating how communications occur between two parties

- **Communications Methods**   Individual/group meetings, video/audio conferences, other communication methods, Interactive, push-and-pull communication

The Plan Communications process has the following Outputs:

- **Communications Management Plan**   Details the management of all project communications

- **Project Document Updates**   Updates to other project documentation (i.e. project schedule, stakeholder register, and stakeholder management strategy)

Plan Communications (10.2) This process determines who needs what information, when, and how they get it		
Inputs	**Tools and Techniques**	**Outputs**
• Stakeholder Register • Stakeholder Management Strategy • Enterprise Environmental Factors • Organizational Process Assets	• Communications Requirements Analysis • Communications Technology • Communications Models • Communications Methods	• Communications Management Plan • Project Document Updates

TSI Study Aid
This chart is part of the study aid poster series available at *www.truesolutions.com*.

PROCESS DOCUMENTS
. . . .

The Communications Management Plan is the key output from the Plan Communications process. The Communications Management Plan documents the overall communications needs of project stakeholders at a detailed level. Many organizations have a predetermined Communications Management Plan that will be executed for each project in the organization.

True Solutions, Inc.
Project Management Template
Volume 1: Communications Plan Template

Communications Plan

Project Name:

Prepared by:

Date:

Key Stakeholders (Distribution Schedule) ▼	Stakeholder Issues	Key Messages to Communicate	Communication Methods to be Used (written, one-on-one, electronic, meetings, etc.)	Description of Specific Communications (content, format, level of detail, etc.)	Timing Issues (see also Bar Chart, Project Schedule)	Other
Client						
Senior Management						
Sponsor						
Project Team Members						
Employees						
Subcontractors						
Suppliers						
Unions						
Government Agencies						
News Media						
Community						
Other						

©Copyright 2009 True Solutions, Inc.
5001 LBJ Freeway, Suite 125-B Dallas, Texas 75244
Tel: 972.770.0900 Fax 972.770.0922 www.truesolutions.com

This form is available individually or as a set from *www.truesolutions.com*.

As with any other project management process, the size and complexity of the Communications Management Plan should be in accordance with the procedures of the organization and appropriate to the size and complexity of the project. As a simple example, a two-week project to move a small department within the corporate headquarters building would have minimal communications requirements. An engineering project to create a new jet fighter using multiple corporations working in multiple global locations would require significant communications management activities.

A simple Communications Management Plan could consist of the following elements:

- Identifying Information for the project and plan

    - Project name

    - Project manager

    - Revision number

    - Revision date

- Report (or Communications Document) Name

- Description of document

    - Elements to be included

    - Level of detail

- Document Recipients

- Document Distribution Schedule

- Document Distribution Method (or methods)

COMMON PROCESS TASKS

The following is a list of the common tasks associated with the Plan Communications process:

- Determine the detailed information requirements of your project stakeholders and your project/organization

- Establish your project information storage system

- Document your stakeholder logistic issues

- Identify your external information needs

- Determine format of your information needs

- Develop feedback routines to ensure two-way communication

- Identify communication frequencies by report or document

- Determine the technologies or methods used to transmit your information

- Review the communications plan with the project stakeholders in order to determine if any communications technology related training will be required

- Identify the methods to transmit nonroutine communications

- Document the Communications Management Plan

- Establish a project status reporting process and cycle

- Determine the requirements for project time reporting

- Select a suitable time-reporting mechanism (if required)

THINK ABOUT IT

Instructions The Plan Communications process focuses on planning all communications that will be conducted for the project. Plan Communications does this by involving the stakeholders and meeting their requirements for document formats, frequencies, and distribution. Plan Communications is done by:

- ☐ Involving stakeholders

- ☐ Documenting communications needs

- ☐ Determining what documents to use

- ☐ Determining formats

- ☐ Determining frequency for document to be distributed

- ☐ Determining who the documents will be distributed to

- ☐ Determining what media will be used for distribution

Which of these elements do you use in your organization to plan for communications management?

_____

_____

_____

_____

Which of these elements are you lacking?

_____

_____

_____

_____

_____

What actions might you take to close the identified gap in your communications management process?

_____

_____

_____

_____

_____

MUST KNOW CONCEPTS

1 Effective communications in project management is a critical success factor.

2 It is an accepted heuristic that good project managers spend up to 90% of their time communicating.

3 The primary deliverable (Output) of the Plan Communications process is the Communications Management Plan.

4 The Plan Communications process is applied to determine the communications needs of project stakeholders. This includes what information is needed, when it is needed and how it will be delivered.

5 Communication requirements analysis is a formal activity performed in communications planning to identify project stakeholders, determine their needs and expectations, then decide how best to manage their needs and expectations.

6 Communication is a two-way activity. Communication is not complete until the sender confirms that the receiver has understood the intended message.

7 There are five categories of interpersonal communication: Informal Verbal, Informal Written, Non-Verbal, Formal Verbal, and Formal Written.

8 The number of communication channels within a project increases exponentially as the number of stakeholders increases. The equation used to calculate the number of communication channels is $N(N-1)/2$, where N is the number of stakeholders.

ADDITIONAL READING
• PMBOK Guide – Section 10.2 Plan Communication

LESSON QUIZ

Instructions   Here are some questions to help reinforce your learning. Complete this quiz from memory to the best of your ability. For each question, circle or check your selected answer on this page or a separate piece of paper. When complete, check your results by comparing your answers to the preferred answers provided in Appendix A.

Please note that Knowledge Check questions are not actual PMP Exam questions. These questions are intended to reinforce key terms, concepts, and themes. While these Knowledge Check questions are typical of what you can expect on your PMP Exam, many actual PMP Exam questions are more in-depth, designed to challenge your judgment (not rote memory) in applying concepts, processes, and methodologies.

1. Which of the following statements best describes the Plan Communications process?
   A. The Plan Communications process is applied to determine the number of communication channels within the project and use that data as justification for keeping the number of stakeholders to a minimum.
   B. The Plan Communications process is applied to determine informal verbal communication needs, formal verbal communication needs, informal written communication needs, formal written communication needs, and non-verbal communication needs.
   C. The Plan Communications process is applied to determine the communications needs of project stakeholders, including what information is needed, when it is needed, and how it will be delivered.
   D. The Plan Communications process is applied to satisfy stakeholder wishes.

2. Which statement is most true?
   A. Active listening (effective listening) is an outdated communications technique. It seldom enhances communication between sender and receiver.
   B. Formal written communication is the preferred method for all project communications. This ensures that everything is formally documented for later review and use in lessons learned.
   C. Non-verbal communication is important.
   D. Stakeholders should be provided with information on a strict need-to-know basis. You and your project team are best served by keeping project information closely held.

3. A small project currently has six stakeholders in the communications loop. If two more stakeholders are added, how many more channels of communication will result?
   A. 2
   B. 13
   C. 15
   D. 28

4. You and your team have completed a communication requirements analysis and find that several project stakeholders expressed a desire to be updated on project performance monthly. Your team suggests that a monthly project performance presentation held in the company's main conference room may facilitate the needs of these particular stakeholders. Upon checking back, you find these stakeholders are in agreement, so you include monthly presentations in your communications management plan. These monthly presentations are an example of:
   A. Formal written communication
   B. Informal written communication
   C. Informal verbal communication
   D. Formal verbal communication

End of Lesson 9

Lesson 10
Collect Requirements

Objectives

At the end of this lesson, you will be able to:

- Describe the purpose of the Collect Requirements process
- Describe the Inputs, Tools & Techniques, and Outputs of the Collect Requirements process
- Describe methods for gathering requirements and making decisions
- Describe key documents which come from this process

Roadmap to the PMBOK Guide

	Initiating	Planning	Executing	M & C	Closing
Integration					
Scope		▓▓▓			
Time					
Cost					
Quality					
Human Resources					
Communications					
Risk					
Procurement					

The Collect Requirements process defines and documents the product and project features that are required to meet the business needs, product requirements and stakeholder expectations.

The Collect Requirements process defines and documents the product and project features that are required to meet the expectations and requirements of the project's stakeholders. These "requirements" are the conditions and capabilities that must be achieved through the project's execution. The requirements must be documented in sufficient detail to allow determination of project completion and for determining whether or not the documented requirements have been met.

The identified expectations and requirements will be used in other processes, such as cost, quality, and schedule planning, to ensure that the project is properly planned and will meet stakeholder expectations.

There are many tools and techniques than can be used to help facilitate the identifying of requirements, including focus groups, workshops, brainstorming, mind mapping, surveys, observation, and others.

A key output of this process is the Requirements Documentation. Requirements Documentation describes how the identified requirements fulfill the business needs of the project. This documentation is normally progressively elaborated as a project progresses. As part of this process, a Requirements Management Plan is also created. The Requirements Management Plan defines how requirements are to be described, monitored, and managed throughout the project. In addition, a Requirement Traceability Matrix links each requirement to the business objectives to ensure that each requirement is adding value to the project and organization.

A project's success is directly influenced through this process by the accuracy and completeness of identifying all of the requirements and expectations.

PROCESS ELEMENTS

The Collect Requirements process has the following Inputs:
- **Project Charter** High-level document that authorizes the project and assigns/authorizes the project manager
- **Stakeholder Register** A document identifying all project stakeholder information

The Collect Requirements process uses the following Tools & Techniques:
- **Interviews** Formal and informal approaches used to determine stakeholder information, requirements, and expectations
- **Focus Groups** Bringing together stakeholders and subject matter experts to determine project and product expectations

- **Facilitated Workshops**   Focused cross-functional sessions to define requirements

- **Group Creativity Techniques**   Activities organized to identify project and product requirements

- **Group Decision Making Techniques**   group assessment of alternatives which produce future actions

- **Questionnaires and Surveys**   Form containing a set of questions distributed to gather information from a large number of participants in a timely manner

- **Observations**   Directly viewing individuals or groups in their environment, capturing actual job/task performance

- **Prototypes**   Developing a product model and soliciting feedback prior to the actual build

The Collect Requirements process has the following Outputs:

- **Requirements Documentation**   Documentation describing how individual requirements fulfill the business needs of the project

- **Requirements Management Plan**   Defines how requirements are to be described, monitored, and managed throughout the project

- **Requirements Traceability Matrix**   A table which associates requirement origin and the relationship between requirement origin and history throughout the project life cycle

---

Collect Requirements (5.1)
This process defines and documents the project and product features and functions needed to fill stakeholders' needs and expectations

Inputs	Tools and Techniques	Outputs
• Project Charter • Stakeholder Register	• Interviews • Focus Groups • Facilitated Workshops • Group Creativity Techniques • Group Decision Making Techniques • Questionnaires and Surveys • Observations • Prototypes	• Requirements Documentation • Requirements Management Plan • Requirements Traceability Matrix

TSI **Study Aid**

This chart is part of the study aid poster series available at *www.truesolutions.com.*

PROCESS DOCUMENTS

During the Collect Requirements process, two or three important documents are created. The project manager needs to create:

• Requirements Management Plan

• Requirements Document(s)

• Requirements Traceability Matrix

The Requirements Management Plan is intended to define how specified requirements will be managed during the project life cycle. Elements that may be included in the Requirements Management Plan could be:

• How requirements will be tracked

• Who will track requirements' status and progress

• Reporting mechanisms and frequencies for tracking requirements' fulfillment

• How changes to the requirements will be identified, managed, and accepted

• Who or what level of authority will be required to propose and approve requirements changes

Requirements Documents will be unique to each application area and each enterprise organization. In general, project requirements and product requirements are identified. Some types of requirements are:

• Business need or strategic goals that are to be addressed

• Specific business objectives tied to project deliverables

• Functional requirements

• Technical specifications to achieve the functional requirements

• Nonfunctional requirements like service levels, performance, security, or supportability

• Quality requirements and specifications

• Impacts on internal and external entities

A Requirements Traceability Matrix should be developed that specifies where and who the requirements originate and how the requirements will be tracked during the project. In the sample form below a Project Requirements document template and Traceability Matrix are combined in one form.

True Solutions, Inc.
Project Management Template
Volume 1: Project Requirements Template

Project Requirements and Traceability Matrix

Project Name:								
Prepared by:								
Date:								

	Information Source						Documented Project Requirements	Information Goes to: (List where this information is used - i.e.: Scope Statement, WBS, Quality Plan, Risk Plan, etc.)
Project Area	Interview	Workshop	Questionnaire	Focus Group	Group Creativity	Sponsor		
Business Requirements								
Project Management Requirements								
Delivery Requirements								
Acceptance Requirements								
Assumptions Used								
Constraints Identified								
Traceability Requirements								
Product Area							**Documented Product Requirements**	**Information Goes to:**
Functional Requirements								
Technical Requirements								
Security Requirements								
Performance Requirements								
Quality Requirements								
Support Requirements								
Training Requirements								

Application Aid
This form is available individually or as a set from *www.truesolutions.com*.

Requirement Management Plan

Project Name:	
Prepared by:	
Date:	
Project Manager:	

Requirements:	
How will it be tracked	Insert tracking info here
How will it be planned	Insert planning info here
How will it be reported	Insert planning info here
How changes will be initiated	Insert initiation process here
Analyze	Insert impact here
How will they be traced, tracked, and reported	Insert tracing, tracking, and reporting here
Who will authorize changes	Insert name(s) here
Requirements prioritization process	Insert prioritization here
Requirement attributes for traceability matrix	Insert requirement attributes here
Additional project documents requiring trace	Insert document names here

Additional Notes:

1.

2.

Application Aid

This form is available individually or as a set from *www.truesolutions.com*.

COMMON PROCESS TASKS

The following is a list of the common tasks associated with the Collect Requirements process:

• Analyze the Project Charter and Stakeholder Register

• Define project requirements and product requirements

- Schedule and conduct requirements-gathering sessions (e.g. interviews, workshops, etc.)

- Document findings from requirements-gathering sessions

- Validate requirements/findings with stakeholders

- Determine the level of detail necessary for Requirements Documentation

- Perform progressive elaboration to further define requirements

- Obtain stakeholder acceptance of Requirements Documentation

THINK ABOUT IT

Instructions Think about how this process is defined, used and documented in your organization. Write a brief description of how you use this process:

_____

_____

_____

_____

_____

What specific Inputs, Tools or Techniques do you use as part of this process in your organization?

_____

_____

_____

_____

_____

Are the outcomes from acquiring a project team different in your organization or experiences?

_____

_____

_____

_____

_____

MUST KNOW CONCEPTS

1 The Collect Requirements process defines and documents the product and project features that are required to meet the expectations and requirements of the project's stakeholders.

2 "Requirements" are the conditions and capabilities that must be achieved through the project's execution.

3 A key output of the Collect Requirements process is the Requirements Documentation.

4 The Requirements Documentation describes how the identified requirements meet the business needs of the project.

5 A Requirement Traceability Matrix links requirements to business objectives to ensure each requirement is adding value to the project and organization.

6 A project's success is directly influenced by the accuracy and completeness of identifying all of the requirements and expectations through this process.

7 The Collect Requirements process defines the Requirements Management Plan which is a component of the overall Project Management Plan.

ADDITIONAL READING

- PMBOK Guide – Section 5.0 Introduction, Project Scope Management
- PMBOK Guide – Section 5.1 Collect Requirements

LESSON QUIZ

Here are some questions to help reinforce your learning. Complete this quiz from memory to the best of your ability. For each question, circle or check your selected answer on this page or a separate piece of paper. When complete, check your results by comparing your answers to the preferred answers provided in Appendix A.

Please note that Knowledge Check questions are not actual PMP Exam questions. These questions are intended to reinforce key terms, concepts, and themes. While these Knowledge Check questions are typical of what you can expect on your PMP Exam, many actual PMP Exam questions are more in-depth, designed to challenge your judgment (not rote memory) in applying concepts, processes, and methodologies.

1. Which of the following is most correct regarding the Collect Requirements process?
   A. The Collect Requirements process defines and manages customer expectations.
   B. The Input for Collect Requirements is the Project Charter.
   C. Project requirements include technical, security, and performance requirements.
   D. Product requirements include project management, business, and delivery requirements.

2. Effective group decision making techniques include all of the following, except?
   A. Dictatorship
   B. Majority
   C. Forcing
   D. Plurality

3. Project Scope Management includes the following processes:
   A. Collect Requirements, Verify Scope, and Perform Quality Control
   B. Verify Scope, Create WBS, and Develop Project Management Plan
   C. Collect Requirements, Control Scope, and Create WBS
   D. Define Scope, Control Costs, and Report Performance

4. You are project manager for a project that has a very aggressive schedule. You have a signed Project Charter and the project sponsor wants to begin actual work right away. Which of these choices is probably not appropriate in this situation?
   A. Refuse to start any work until all project and product requirements are fully defined.
   B. Do an initial project and product requirement definition, then document a plan to use rolling-wave planning to define requirements and work as the project progresses.
   C. Identify small work elements that can be started immediately; those work elements that have little or no interdependencies and less risk of rework.
   D. Define requirements and scope for the project; when enough work elements are clearly identified so that subject matter experts are able to start work, begin work while continuing to develop all requirements and scope in detail.

End of Lesson 10

11

Lesson 11
Define Scope

Objectives

At the end of this lesson, you will be able to:

- Describe the purpose of the Define Scope process
- Describe the Inputs, Tools & Techniques, and Outputs of the Define Scope process
- Understand that the Project Scope Statement is critical to project success by providing a common understanding of the project for stakeholders

Roadmap to the PMBOK Guide

	Initiating	Planning	Executing	M & C	Closing
Integration					
Scope		■			
Time					
Cost					
Quality					
Human Resources					
Communications					
Risk					
Procurement					

A clearly defined scope statement is critical to project success. If the project team does not know precisely what work to do, how can they be expected to be successful?

DEFINE SCOPE

The Define Scope process is applied to create the Project Scope Statement. The Project Scope Statement defines the project's deliverables and the work required to create those deliverables.

During scope definition, you and your team build upon the major deliverables, assumptions, and constraints that were defined during project initiation. Stakeholders' needs and desires, as defined in the Requirements Document, are analyzed and developed into firm work requirements. Assumptions and constraints can be further analyzed and the opinions of domain experts can be solicited.

It is important to understand that your Project Scope Statement will serve to provide a common understanding of the project scope among stakeholders. The process of Define Scope creates a detailed Project Scope Statement. The Project Scope Statement is required to complete detailed project planning. The Work Breakdown Structure, Activity List, and Project Schedule will derive from key information that is documented in this process.

During project execution, the original Project Scope Statement will be used to guide decisions. When changes to the project scope are approved, the Project Scope Statement will be updated.

A detailed and thorough Project Scope Statement is critical to the success of a project. The Project Scope Statement is one of three required documents that must be defined for the project. The other two required documents are the Project Charter and Project Management Plan.

PROCESS ELEMENTS

The Define Scope process has the following Inputs:
- **Project Charter**   High-level document that authorizes the project and assigns/authorizes the project manager

- **Requirements Documentation**   Documentation describing how individual requirements fulfill the business needs of the project

- **Organizational Process Assets**   Consideration factors such as processes, procedures, and corporate knowledge base

The Define Scope process uses the following Tools & Techniques:
- **Expert Judgment**   Expert technical and/or managerial judgment (from any qualified source)

- **Product Analysis**   Generally accepted methods for translating high-level product descriptions into tangible deliverables

- **Alternatives Identification**   Technique used to generate different approaches to accomplish the work of the project
- **Facilitated Workshops**   Focused cross-functional sessions to define requirements

The Define Scope process has the following Outputs:
- **Project Scope Statement**   Detailed description of a project's deliverables and work required to create them
- **Project Document Updates**   Updates to other project documentation

Define Scope (5.2)		
This process creates the Project Scope Statement		
Inputs	**Tools and Techniques**	**Outputs**
• Project Charter • Requirements Documentation • Organizational Process Assets	• Expert Judgment • Product Analysis • Alternatives Identification • Facilitated Workshops	• Project Scope Statement • Project Document Updates

TSI Study Aid
This chart is part of the study aid poster series available at www.truesolutions.com.

PROCESS DOCUMENTS

During the Define Scope process one of the most important documents for the project is created. The Project Scope Statement is a narrative description of the scope (work to be performed) of the project. This document should describe the project scope in sufficient detail to provide a common understanding of the project scope for stakeholders.

While the Project Scope Statement can contain a wide variety of information, it is recommended that as a minimum the following be included in the Project Scope Statement:

- Product Scope Description

- Product Acceptance Criteria

- Project Deliverables

- Project Exclusions

- Project Constraints

- Project Assumptions

Previously discussed in the Collect Requirements process, it is important to link project requirements and products requirements to the work of the project. Therefore, Functional Requirements documentation and Technical Requirements documentation are often included in some form as part of the Project Scope Statement. Many times these other documents are referred to and electronically linked to the Project Scope Statement.

Other elements often included in the Project Scope Statement are:

• Planned Schedule

• Planned Budget

• Resource Requirements

• Executive Summary (usually found at the beginning of the document)

• A summary of identified project risks

• Specific approaches planned toward executing the project

Our simplified example of a Project Scope Statement template is shown below.

True Solutions, Inc.
Project Management Template
Volume 1: Scope Statement Template

Scope Statement

Project Name:	
Prepared by:	
Date:	
Revision:	
Product Description:	A brief summary of the product or service description
Project Acceptance Criteria	A statement that defines the criteria and the processes for completed result
Project Deliverables:	A list of the summary-level sub products whose full and satisfactory delivery marks completion of the project
Deliverable A	
Deliverable B	
Deliverable C	
Deliverable D	
Deliverable E	
Known Exclusions	This is where you define what is 'not' in scope
Project Constraints	This is where you would list any constraint that limit your options (like budget)
Project Assumptions	This is where you would put anything you accept to be true (like you can work on a certain day in the future and it won't rain)

©Copyright 2009 True Solutions, Inc.
5001 LBJ Freeway, Suite 125-B Dallas, Texas 75244
Tel: 972.770.0900 Fax 972.770.0922 www.truesolutions.com

TSI *Application Aid*
This form is available individually or as a set from *www.truesolutions.com*.

COMMON PROCESS TASKS

There are several common tasks that are associated with the Define Scope process:

- Evaluate and further define objectives that were originally defined as part of the Develop Project Charter and Collect Requirements processes

- Determine the appropriate level of detail required (project or subproject level) for the Project Scope Statement

- Develop a Project Scope Statement that will be used as the basis for future project decisions and for evaluating project trade-offs

- Develop the Project Scope Statement that will be used as a record of the agreement between your project team and customers or other stakeholders

- Create the Project Scope Statement focused on key project deliverables and objectives

- Determine and document how and when to properly refine or modify a Project Scope Statement

- Review and document alternatives for achieving project deliverables and objectives

THINK ABOUT IT

I was engaged to "rescue" a website project for a business partner. The project was initiated by a business owner. There was not an established technology partner or a project manager. The business owner was working directly with the outside development firm who also did not have a project manager or a project management methodology. The project was approved as an upgrade to the framework of the website; however the scope was never truly defined and agreed upon by the business or the development firm.

The project, which was initially to be a three-month, $20,000 effort, quickly extended to one year and several hundred thousand dollars. Both the business and the outside development firm continued to expand the parameters of the project. Without clear-cut scope, the sky became the limit.

My first order of business when engaged on the project was to quickly understand and document what the business was trying to accomplish with the new site and then to define the scope for the undertaking. We were then able, as a project team, to prioritize deliverables and develop a release schedule for the new site. Unfortunately, the business had an established deadline which was not flexible. This led to us working feverishly to meet our deadlines. In the end, we launched the site on time; however the cost and resource use was significantly over the original project budget.

Using the Define Scope process effectively could have saved many hours of re-work and miscommunication. Ultimately, the business had to compromise on several key deliverables and the site had to undergo additional upgrades and modifications. A clearly defined scope would have provided the project with the proper foundation and would have allowed for a controlled release schedule which would have better utilized resources (people and money) and would have provided higher quality product in the end.

Contributed by Cynthia Hodgkins, PMP

MUST KNOW CONCEPTS

1 The Define Scope process is intended to create the Project Scope Statement.

2 The Project Scope Statement defines the project's deliverables and the work required to create those deliverables.

3 The Project Scope Statement serves to provide a documented basis for common understanding of project scope among stakeholders.

4 The Project Scope Statement provides a documented basis for making many project decisions.

5 Alternatives Identification that is used during Define Scope can serve as a useful technique for generating different approaches for defining and performing project work.

ADDITIONAL READING

• PMBOK Guide - Section 5.2 Define Scope

LESSON QUIZ

Instructions   Here are some questions to help reinforce your learning. Complete this quiz from memory to the best of your ability. For each question, circle or check your selected answer on this page or a separate piece of paper. When complete, check your results by comparing your answers to the preferred answers provided in Appendix A.

Please note that Knowledge Check questions are not actual PMP Exam questions.

These questions are intended to reinforce key terms, concepts, and themes. While these Knowledge Check questions are typical of what you can expect on your PMP Exam, many actual PMP Exam questions are more in-depth, designed to challenge your judgment (not rote memory) in applying concepts, processes, and methodologies.

1. Define Scope Inputs include all of the following except: _____.
   A. Requirements Documentation
   B. Project Charter
   C. Project Scope Statement
   D. Organizational Process Assets

2. Which of the following statements is true?
   A. The Project Scope Statement may serve to provide a documented basis for making many future project decisions.
   B. The Project Scope Statement may serve to provide a documented basis for common understanding of scope among stakeholders.
   C. The Project Scope Statement may be revised as the project progresses, to reflect approved changes to the project scope.
   D. All of the above.

3. The Define Scope process is intended to _____.
   A. create the Project Scope Management Plan
   B. create the project work breakdown structure (WBS), which provides a comprehensive definition of project scope
   C. create the Project Scope Statement
   D. create the Preliminary Project Scope Statement

4. Which of the following is most true?
   A. The Project Scope Statement should include a description of project deliverables, either at a summary-level or in detail.
   B. The Project Scope Management Plan should include the work breakdown structure.
   C. The Project Scope Management Plan should be as brief as possible.
   D. The Project Scope Statement should include the work breakdown structure.

5. As a project increases in size and complexity, the stability (certainty) of project scope _____.
   A. should remain constant, if the Project Scope Statement is properly refined prior to execution
   B. should decrease
   C. should increase in relative proportion to the increase in size and complexity
   D. should cost more to manage

6. You can generally say each of the following statements is true, except:
   A. In large projects, multiple Project Scope Statements may be developed and used by the project management team, typically one for each subproject.
   B. A Project Charter includes the product description.
   C. A Project Scope Statement and a Project Scope Management Plan essentially serve the same purpose.
   D. The Project Charter and Requirements Documentation serve as inputs to the Define Scope process.

7. Product analysis, alternatives identification, and facilitated workshops are examples of _____.
   A. Tools & Techniques used to support the scope definition process
   B. constrained optimization decision models used to aid in project selection
   C. benefit measurement decision models used to aid in project selection
   D. quality control (QC) chart measurement models used to ensure that a project management process is in control

End of Lesson 11

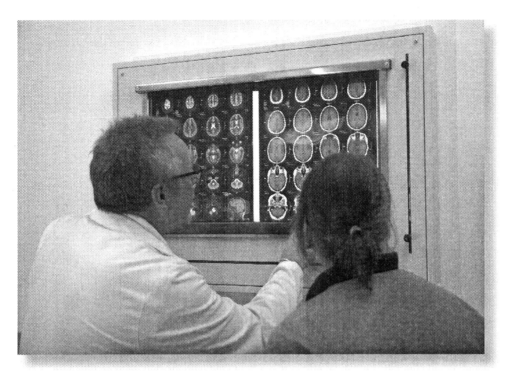

12

Lesson 12
Create WBS

Objectives

At the end of this lesson, you will be able to:

- Describe the purpose of the Create Work Breakdown Structure process
- Describe the Inputs, Tools & Techniques, and Outputs of the Create Work Breakdown Structure process
- Be able to create or interpret a Work Breakdown Structure
- Understand that all of the work on the project should be contained and depicted in the Work Breakdown Structure

Roadmap to the PMBOK Guide

	Initiating	Planning	Executing	M & C	Closing
Integration					
Scope		▓▓▓			
Time					
Cost					
Quality					
Human Resources					
Communications					
Risk					
Procurement					

The Work Breakdown Structure establishes the overall scope baseline for the project. The WBS is always used in project management.

Experienced project managers understand it is simply not possible to visualize and manage an entire project without some sort of tool. Instead of trying to manage the whole project at once, all the time, the project must be broken down into manageable sized pieces, and then the pieces can be easily managed. The Create Work Breakdown Structure process facilitates this goal by decomposing (subdividing) major project deliverables into smaller, more manageable components.

This process is typically the first process applied after the Project Scope Statement has been developed.

The primary deliverable from the Create Work Breakdown Structure process is the Work Breakdown Structure (WBS). The WBS may be the most important tool for management of a project. When properly developed, the WBS illustrates all of the work elements that define the project and serves as the basis for most planning activities from this point forward.

The WBS documents all the work required to successfully complete the project. The WBS must identify *all of the work required, and only the work required*, to successfully complete the project. "Scope Creep" or continual changes in a project's work requirements can be eliminated by carefully defining scope and managing it using the WBS.

Effective application of the Create Work Breakdown Structure process is critical to project success. Work Packages are critical to developing the budget, the schedule and in tracking the project during monitoring and controlling. The completed Project Scope Statement, WBS, and WBS Dictionary form the Scope Baseline for the project.

Study Tips

The following concepts are important in creation of the WBS:

- WBS deliverables should be decomposed (subdivided) to a level where adequate cost and duration estimates are possible

- WBS deliverables should be decomposed to a level where acceptance criteria can be easily defined and the work can be effectively assigned, managed, and measured

- There is no predefined limit to the number of sublevels in a WBS

- The WBS has no time frame — it defines work only

- The lowest level elements of the WBS are termed "Work Packages"

- Work Packages should require no more than eighty hours to complete (the "eighty-hour" thumb-rule/heuristic)

- Detailed Work Package descriptions and information are documented and collected to form a "WBS Dictionary"

The WBS serves as an excellent communication tool, clearly illustrating the total scope of project work to stakeholders and although there is no time associated with a WBS, the first level of decomposition often somewhat defines the project life cycle of the project.

PROCESS ELEMENTS

The Create Work Breakdown Structure process has the following Inputs:

- **Project Scope Statement**   Detailed description of a project's deliverables and work required to create them

- **Requirements Documentation**   Documentation describing how individual requirements meet the business needs of the project

- **Organizational Process Assets**   Consideration factors such as processes, procedures, and corporate knowledge base

The Create Work Breakdown Structure process uses the following Tools & Techniques:

- **Decomposition**   The process of subdividing WBS Work Packages into manageable-sized schedule activities

The Create Work Breakdown Structure process has the following Outputs:

- **Work Breakdown Structure (WBS)**   The deliverables-oriented organization/illustration of all project work (scope)

- **WBS Dictionary**   Companion document to the WBS that details the content of each WBS element

- **Scope Baseline**   Scope Baseline = the approved project scope statement + the WBS + the WBS Dictionary

- **Project Document Updates**   Updates to other project documentation

Create WBS (5.3)		
This process subdivides major deliverables into manageable components		
Inputs	**Tools and Techniques**	**Outputs**
• Project Scope Statement • Requirements Documentation • Organizational Process Assets	• Decomposition	• Work Breakdown Structure (WBS) • WBS Dictionary • Scope Baseline • Project Document Updates

PROCESS DOCUMENTS

During Create WBS we create a Work Breakdown Structure for the project. As previously discussed, the Work Breakdown Structure is where ALL of the work to be performed on the project will be depicted. Work Breakdown Structures can be organized in several ways. Typically a WBS is organized by:

• Phase

• Function to be performed

• Material use

Each WBS will be unique, but the WBS many times is derived from a previous similar WBS which is used as a template to create the new WBS. If your organization has a project management methodology in use, details of how to organize the WBS and what elements must be present will usually be defined as part of the project management methodology.

A sample WBS is depicted below:

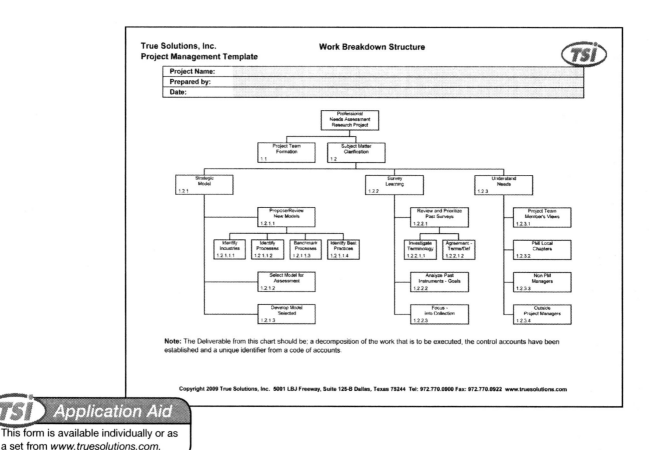

TSI Application Aid
This form is available individually or as a set from *www.truesolutions.com.*

COMMON PROCESS TASKS

The following is a list of the common tasks associated with the Create Work Breakdown Structure process:

- Determine the appropriate level of decomposition detail for your WBS or parts of your WBS

- Develop your WBS, using the proper decomposition techniques

- Communicate the differences between a WBS and other types of breakdown structures

- Determine the utility of a WBS from similar past projects and standardized templates

- Determine the inputs of your project's Create WBS process

- Verify the correctness of your WBS, including your WBS Dictionary

- Identify your specific scope inclusions and exclusions

THINK ABOUT IT

Instructions Use this exercise to compare how you practice project management to what is specified in the *PMBOK® Guide Fourth Edition.*

Think about how this process is defined, used and documented in your organization. Write a brief description of how you use this process:

_____

_____

_____

_____

_____

_____

What specific Inputs, Tools or Techniques do you use as part of this process in your organization?

_____

_____

_____

_____

_____

Are the outcomes from this process different in your organization or experiences?

_____

_____

_____

_____

_____

_____

_____

MUST KNOW CONCEPTS

1. The Create Work Breakdown Structure process is intended to decompose (subdivide) major project deliverables into manageable-sized components.

2. The primary deliverable from the Create Work Breakdown Structure process is the Work Breakdown Structure (WBS).

3. The WBS may be the single most important project management tool.

4. The WBS serves as the basis for most subsequent planning activities.

5. WBS deliverables should be decomposed to a level where adequate cost and duration estimates are possible.

6. The WBS should be subdivided to a level where acceptance criteria can be easily defined and the work can be effectively assigned, managed, and measured.

7. There is no predefined limit to the number of sublevels in a WBS.

8. The WBS has no time-frame.

9. The WBS defines work only.

10. The lowest level elements of the WBS are termed "Work Packages."

11. Work Packages should require no more than eighty hours to complete.

12. Detailed Work Package descriptions are documented and collected to form a WBS Dictionary.

13. The detailed Project Scope Statement, the WBS, and the WBS Dictionary combine to form the Project Scope Baseline.

ADDITIONAL READING

· ·
- PMBOK Guide – Section 5.3 Create WBS

LESSON QUIZ

· ·

Instructions Here are some questions to help reinforce your learning. Complete this quiz from memory to the best of your ability. For each question, circle or check your selected answer on this page or a separate piece of paper. When complete, check your results by comparing your answers to the preferred answers provided in Appendix A.

Please note that Knowledge Check questions are not actual PMP Exam questions. These questions are intended to reinforce key terms, concepts, and themes. While these Knowledge Check questions are typical of what you can expect on your PMP Exam, many actual PMP Exam questions are more in-depth, designed to challenge your judgment (not rote memory) in applying concepts, processes, and methodologies.

1. The decomposed illustration of all project scope (work) is called
    _____.
    A. a project breakdown structure (PBS)
    B. an organizational breakdown structure (OBS)
    C. a Work Breakdown Structure (WBS)
    D. a contractual work breakdown structure (CWBS)

2. The subdivision of major project deliverables, as identified in the Project Scope Statement, into smaller, more manageable components, is performed by applying _____.
    A. configuration management
    B. constrained optimization
    C. the Create WBS process
    D. the eighty-hour rule

3. Create WBS Inputs include all of the following, except?
    A. Requirements Documentation
    B. Scope baseline
    C. WBS templates
    D. Project Scope Statement

4. Which of the following statements is most true?
    A. Creating the WBS results in a compressed project schedule.
    B. Creating the WBS identifies activities on the project's critical path.
    C. Creating the WBS identifies key project risk events.
    D. Creating the WBS can enhance team buy-in.

5. All of the following are false, except:
   A. The Work Breakdown Structure communicates the total project scope (work) to stakeholders.
   B. The Work Breakdown Structure identifies the schedule objectives for defined deliverables.
   C. The Work Breakdown Structure describes the business need for each Work Package.
   D. The Work Breakdown Structure assigns the responsible organization for each major deliverable.

6. The lowest level elements in a Work Breakdown Structure are often termed
   _____.
   A. decompositions
   B. Work Breakdown Structure templates
   C. work authorization packages
   D. Work Packages

7. Detailed descriptions of WBS Work Packages can be documented and collected to form a _____.
   A. Work Breakdown Structure database
   B. scope definition database
   C. Work Breakdown Structure dictionary
   D. work authorization system

8. The methodology used to subdivide major deliverables into smaller, more manageable sized elements is termed what?
   A. Work Package development
   B. Fast-tracking
   C. Resource leveling
   D. Decomposition

9. WBS major deliverables should be subdivided to a level where _____.
   A. components can be adequately estimated for cost, duration, and acceptance criteria
   B. the use of quality control charts can be considered
   C. the component work can be completed by one qualified person (the one-task, one-person rule)
   D. lowest level components will not fall on the critical path

10. Work Breakdown Structure templates and Lessons Learned represent _____.
    A. defined Tools & Techniques to support the Create WBS process
    B. defined Inputs to the Create WBS process
    C. defined Outputs from the Create WBS process
    D. essential project management software tools

End of Lesson 12

13

Lesson 13
Define Activities

Objectives

At the end of this lesson, you will be able to:

- Describe the purpose of the Define Activities process
- Describe the Inputs, Tools & Techniques, and Outputs of the Define Activities process
- Understand how to decompose the Work Breakdown Structure to create the Activity List

Roadmap to the PMBOK Guide

	Initiating	Planning	Executing	M & C	Closing
Integration					
Scope					
Time		■			
Cost					
Quality					
Human Resources					
Communications					
Risk					
Procurement					

The Define Activities process identifies the specific activities necessary to complete the project deliverables; this process is considered an activity-focused extension to the WBS.

The process of Define Activities logically follows the Create WBS process. The WBS identifies the total of all project work in terms of deliverables. The WBS is deliverables-oriented. To adhere to this definition, our WBS should identify work using descriptive nouns, as opposed to action-oriented verbs. We apply the Define Activities process to convert our WBS work packages (lowest level elements) into action-oriented activities.

The Define Activities process identifies the specific activities necessary to complete the project deliverables.

The primary deliverable from the Define Activities process is the project's Activity List; the Activity List becomes an extension of the WBS.

The primary Tool & Technique used to create the Activity List is "decomposition." This is basically the same decomposition method used to create the WBS. The difference is that, in Define Activities, decomposition is used to further subdivide Work Packages into manageable sized activities, and the final Output is described in terms of activities, rather than deliverables. These tasks represent what is needed to complete a Work Package.

Ideally, Define Activities is applied immediately following Create WBS. In real-world practice, however, the two processes are many times applied in parallel. In many projects, Rolling Wave Planning can be an effective tool to support activity definition. In Rolling Wave Planning, only near-term work is planned in detail, leaving future work summarized with less detail. As future work draws nearer, detailed planning is performed.

PROCESS ELEMENTS

The Define Activities process has the following Inputs:
- **Scope Baseline**   The project deliverables, constraints, and assumptions

- **Enterprise Environmental Factors**   Consideration factors such as culture, systems, procedures, industry standards including the Project Management Information System (PMIS)

- **Organizational Process Assets**   Consideration factors such as activity planning related policies, procedures, guidelines, and lessons learned knowledge base

The Define Activities process uses the following Tools & Techniques:
- **Decomposition**   The process of subdividing WBS Work Packages into manageable sized schedule activities

- **Rolling Wave Planning**   A form of progressive elaboration planning where only near-term work is planned in detail

- **Templates** Any existing form (i.e. an activity list from a similar project) that may be used as a template for this process

- **Expert Judgment** Expert technical and/or managerial judgment (from any qualified source)

The Define Activities process has the following Outputs:

- **Activity List** The comprehensive list and description of all schedule activities

- **Activity Attributes** An extension of the activity attributes identified in the Activity List, intended to provide more detail

- **Milestone List** The documented list of both mandatory and optional schedule milestones

Define Activities (6.1)		
This process specifically identifies all schedule activities		
Inputs	**Tools and Techniques**	**Outputs**
• Scope Baseline • Enterprise Environmental Factors • Organizational Process Assets	• Decomposition • Rolling Wave Planning • Templates • Expert Judgment	• Activity List • Activity Attributes • Milestone List

TSI Study Aid
This chart is part of the study aid poster series available at *www.truesolutions.com*.

PROCESS DOCUMENTS

The Activity List documents specific project activities — or tasks — that will be performed on the project. The project management methodology in the organization that you are working in will define the level of granularity or detail that is required in an Activity List. This document can be very high-level or very detailed, based upon project and organization need. Many Activity Lists are developed using Microsoft Project or a similar project management tool.

At a minimum, the Activity List should include:

• Project name

• Project manager

• Date for document

• Project phases

• Project deliverables or milestones

- Project Work Packages

- Project activities (associated with Work Packages)

Typically, additional information such as the duration of the activity, start date, end date, and resources assigned is also shown on an Activity List.

A simple example of an Activity List is shown below.

True Solutions, Inc. Project Management Template	Activity List				TSI
Project Name:					
Prepared by:					
Date:					
Project Phase		Duration	Start Date	End Date	Resource
Deliverable					
Work Package					
Activity					
Development Phase					
Develop Black Box					
Acquire Materials					
Determine specific components					
Order components through Purchasing					
Receive and Inventory components					
Assemble Components					
Attach CPU chip to motherboard					
Attach heat sink and CPU fan					
Attach CPU fan power cable					
Insert RAM chips in motherboard slots					
Install motherboard in CPU case					
Test Assembled Device					
Plug in power supply					
Turn power switch to "on" position					
Check BOIS settings					
Place OS media in media slot					
Boot					

COMMON PROCESS TASKS

The following is a list of the common tasks associated with the Define Activities process:

- Create your Activity List using decomposition of the lowest level of the WBS

- Identify the appropriate level of WBS detail for your Activity List

- Determine the inputs to your Define Activities process

- Validate your WBS by ensuring that performing all activities will complete all deliverables

- Utilize Activity Lists to verify that all activities are within your project scope and that your WBS is correct

- Identify missing deliverables or deliverables requiring clarification, using your WBS as part of the verification process

THINK ABOUT IT

Instructions Think about how this project management process is defined, used, and documented in your organization. Compare your organization's use of this process to the PMI® definition.

Best practices suggest that each of the following items are used during the Define Activities process.

Which of these items do you use when practicing project management?

- ☐ Decompose WBS to create Activity List
- ☐ List individual detailed Activities
- ☐ Document Activity Attributes
- ☐ Document Milestones for the project
- ☐ Use Rolling Wave Planning to detail near term activities

How would you change your use of this process in your organization to resolve any gaps in application?

_____

_____

_____

_____

_____

_____

_____

_____

_____

_____

_____

_____

_____

MUST KNOW CONCEPTS

....

1. The Define Activities process is identifying the specific activities necessary to complete the project deliverables.

2. The Define Activities process is intended to decompose or subdivide WBS Work Packages into manageable sized activities.

3. The primary deliverable (Output) from the Define Activities process is the Activity List.

4. The Activity List may be viewed as an extension of the WBS.

5. Decomposition is the primary methodology (tool/technique) used to create the Activity List.

6. In some projects, Rolling Wave Planning can be an effective tool to support activity definition. In Rolling Wave Planning, only near-term work is planned in detail, leaving future work summarized with less detail. As future work draws nearer, detailed planning is performed.

7. Decomposition in Define Activities differs from decomposition in Create WBS, in that it is used to further subdivide WBS Work Packages into manageable sized activities, and the final Output is described in terms of activities, rather than deliverables.

ADDITIONAL READING

....

- PMBOK Guide – Section 6.0 Introduction, Project Time Management
- PMBOK Guide – Section 6.1 Define Activities

LESSON QUIZ

....

Instructions Here are some questions to help reinforce your learning. Complete this quiz from memory to the best of your ability. For each question, circle or check your selected answer on this page or a separate piece of paper. When complete, check your results by comparing your answers to the preferred answers provided in Appendix A.

Please note that Knowledge Check questions are not actual PMP Exam questions. These questions are intended to reinforce key terms, concepts, and themes. While these Knowledge Check questions are typical of what you can expect on your PMP Exam, many actual PMP Exam questions are more in-depth, designed to challenge your judgment (not rote memory) in applying concepts, processes, and methodologies.

1. The document that identifies all the activities that will be performed on a project is called _____.
   A. the Work Breakdown Structure (WBS)
   B. the Scope Statement
   C. the Activity List
   D. the Work Package List

2. Each of the following is false, except:
   A. The Activity List may be viewed as an extension of the Work Breakdown Structure.
   B. The lowest level elements of the WBS (Work Packages) automatically identify all the project activities necessary to produce identified project deliverables.
   C. The lowest level elements of the WBS (Work Packages) should be documented in terms of action-oriented activities, to help facilitate and expedite the Activity Definition process.
   D. All of the above are false.

3. Define Activities Inputs include all of the following, except _____.
   A. enterprise environmental factors
   B. organizational process assets
   C. scope baseline
   D. milestone list

4. Which of the following statements is true?
   A. Decomposition is the primary methodology (tool/technique) used to further subdivide WBS Work Packages into manageable sized activities.
   B. Decomposition is the primary methodology (tool/technique) used to further subdivide WBS major deliverables into manageable sized Work Packages.
   C. Decomposition is a primary methodology (tool/technique) used in both Create WBS and Define Activities.
   D. All of the above are true.

End of Lesson 13

Lesson 14
Sequence Activities

Objectives

At the end of this lesson, you will be able to:

- Describe the purpose of the Sequence Activities process
- Describe the Inputs, Tools & Techniques, and Outputs of the Sequence Activities process
- Be able to create and interpret a Project Network Diagram

Roadmap to the PMBOK Guide

	Initiating	Planning	Executing	M & C	Closing
Integration					
Scope					
Time		■			
Cost					
Quality					
Human Resources					
Communications					
Risk					
Procurement					

Modern project management tools automate the process of identifying interactivity logical relationships. For the PMP Exam, you need to know how to identify these sequences using manual tools.

Sequence Activities is the process of identifying the interrelationships between individual project activities, then documenting them using, what is generically termed, a Network Logic Diagram. This is an essential step that must be performed accurately prior to the development of a realistic and achievable schedule. Project Network Logic Diagrams are often, though not correctly, referred to as PERT Charts.

Intuitive sense tells us that certain project activities must be completed before others may start. In some cases, certain activities may be performed in parallel. In some cases, certain activities must start before others can finish. There are four possible interactivity relationships:

- Finish-to-Start: One activity must finish before the next activity may start. F-S is the most common type of interdependency

- Finish-to-Finish: One activity must finish before the next activity may finish

- Start-to-Start: One activity must start before the next activity may start

- Start-to-Finish: One activity must start before the next activity may finish. S-F is the least common type of interdependency.

These relationships must be identified and documented in some form of Network Logic Diagram. This is what activity sequencing is all about.

As you might imagine, in a project with hundreds or thousands of identified activities, activity sequencing can be a very complex process. In real-world project planning, most project managers rely on the use of project management software to automate and expedite the process. However, a project manager should have the ability to manually create and analyze simple network diagrams. To accomplish this, the project manager must learn the fundamentals of Network Logic Diagramming, then spend time with hands-on practice.

Because there is a lot of important information in the Sequence Activities process (compared to other processes), expect to devote a little more time learning this process.

PROCESS ELEMENTS

The Sequence Activities process has the following Inputs:

- **Activity List**   The comprehensive list and description of all schedule activities

- **Activity Attributes**   An extension of the Activity List, intended to provide more attribute details

- **Milestone List**   The documented list of both mandatory and optional schedule milestones

- **Project Scope Statement**   Detailed description of a project's deliverables and work required to create them
- **Organizational Process Assets**   Project files from corporate knowledge base used for scheduling methodology

The Sequence Activities process uses the following Tools & Techniques:

- **Precedence Diagramming Method (PDM)**   Activity-on-Node (AON) project network diagramming technique

- **Dependency Determination**   Mandatory dependencies, discretionary dependencies, external dependencies

- **Applying Leads and Lags**   Further defined "overlaps (leads)" and "delays (lags)" in activity dependencies

- **Schedule Network Templates**   Standardized networks used to expedite the creation of Schedule Network Diagrams

The Sequence Activities process has the following Outputs:

- **Project Schedule Network Diagrams**   Schematic displays of the project's activities and their logical relationships

- **Project Document Updates**   Updates to other project documentation (i.e. Activity Lists, Activity Attributes, and Risk Register)

Sequence Activities (6.2)		
This process identifies and documents dependencies among schedule activities		
Inputs	**Tools and Techniques**	**Outputs**
• Activity List • Activity Attributes • Milestone List • Project Scope Statement • Organizational Process Assets	• Precedence Diagramming Method (PDM) • Dependency Determination • Applying Leads and Lags • Schedule Network Templates	• Project Schedule Network Diagrams • Project Document Updates

TSI **Study Aid**
This chart is part of the study aid poster series available at *www.truesolutions.com.*

THE FUNDAMENTALS OF NETWORK LOGIC DIAGRAMS

To master all there is to know about Network Logic Diagramming; we could spend a graduate-level semester dedicated just to this one subject. It can be quite complex with many specific techniques and technique-variations to consider. To prepare for the PMP Exam, however, we need to master only the fundamentals. Here they are.

PRECEDENCE DIAGRAMMING METHOD (PDM)

This is the method used by most modern project management software programs. It constructs the Project Network Diagram using boxes (called *nodes*) to represent project activities, and connects them with arrows which illustrate their interdependencies. Here is a simple network diagram, drawn using PDM:

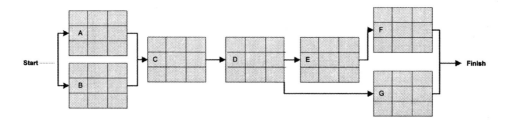

In this simplified example, the project consists of seven activities, A–G. We see that activities A and B have no predecessor constraints and can start right away. We see that A and B must finish before activity C can start. We see that C must finish before D can start. D must finish before E or G can start. E must finish before F can start. Finally, F and G must finish before the project can finish.

• Precedence Diagrams are also called Activity-on-Node (AON) Diagrams (Activity information is identified directly on the node)

• Precedence Diagrams can illustrate four types of interdependencies

• *Finish-to-Start (F-S)*
  Activity A must Finish before Activity B may Start. F-S is the most common type of interdependency.

• *Start-to-Finish (S-F)*
  Activity A must Start before Activity B may Finish. S-F is the least common type of interdependency.

• *Start-to-Start (S-S)*
  Activity A must Start before Activity B may Start. S-S is a less common type of interdependency.

• *Finish-to-Finish (F-F)*
  Activity A must Finish before Activity B may Finish. F-F is a less common type of interdependency.

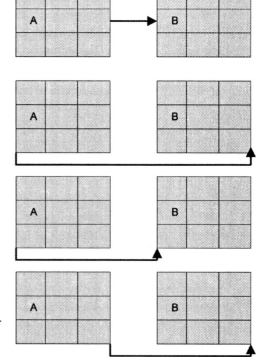

PDM CONVENTIONS

When properly constructed and annotated, Network Diagrams can communicate an enormous amount of essential information. During planning, this helps the project team in creating the project schedule, obtaining resources, and in identifying risks. Here is the way information is typically annotated on PDM Network Diagrams (Activity-on-Node or AON). The numbers indicated in this example are work units. Typically, work units are hours, shifts, days, weeks, etc.

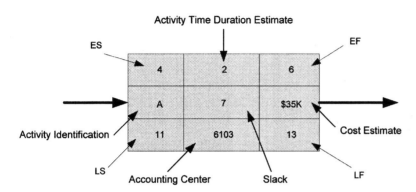

Once the Network is constructed and work units for each activity are estimated, we can then determine the following for each activity:

- **Earliest Start Time (ES) and Earliest Finishing Time (EF).** We can determine ES and EF by making a *forward pass* (left-to-right) through the Network. The earliest starting time (ES) of a successor activity is the latest of the early finish times of its predecessors. The earliest finishing time (EF) is the total of the earliest starting time and the activity duration.

- **Latest Starting Time (LS) and Latest Finish Time (LF).** We can determine LS and LF by making a *backward pass* (right-to-left) through the Network. The latest finishing time (LF) for an activity entering a node is the same as the smallest value latest starting time (LS) of the activities exiting the node. The latest starting time (LS) of an activity is the latest finishing time (LF) minus the activity duration.

- **Slack (also referred to as "float," "reserve," "total float," and "path float").** We can determine Slack in an activity by subtracting its ES from its LS. Many noncritical project activities may have Slack time, allowing greater flexibility in scheduling and resource allocation. Activities on the network's Critical Path typically have zero Slack.

APPLYING LEADS AND LAGS

To accurately define the logical relationship between many project schedule activities, the team will need to apply leads and/or lags. The best time to first apply leads and lags is now, during Sequence Activities.

Leads: Lead time may be viewed as an *overlap* between tasks. For example, in a finish-to-start dependency with a ten-day lead, the successor activity can start ten days before the predecessor has finished. Lead time allows project teams to add realism and flexibility to their schedule.

Lags: Lag time is *waiting time*. For example, if Activity A involves pouring concrete that requires four days to set, then Activity B may have a four-day lag ... meaning Activity B cannot start until four days after Activity A is finished. Lead time is termed "negative lag" in some software programs.

CRITICAL PATH

Network Diagrams illustrate all of the project's activities and their interrelationships/dependencies, from project start to project finish. They also annotate, at minimum, an identification for each activity and the estimated time duration of each activity. Typically a PMP Exam question involving Network Diagramming is very simple and may look something like this:

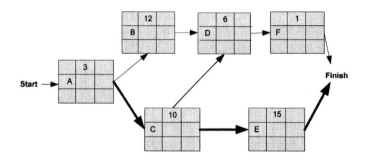

Activity A	3 Days
Activity B	12 Days
Activity C	10 Days
Activity D	6 Days
Activity E	15 Days
Activity F	1 Day

- In this simple example, the project is comprised of six activities, A–F.

- All predecessor/successor relationships are Finish-to-Start (F-S).

- Activity A is estimated to require three days for completion, Activity B twelve days, Activity C ten days, and so on.

- There are three possible paths through this Network from start-to-finish; Path 1, Start-A-B-D-F-Finish; Path 2, Start-A-C-E-Finish; and Path 3, Start-A-C-D-F-Finish.

- Add the associated Activity time estimates to find that Path 1 is 22 days long, Path 2 is 28 days long and Path 3 is 20 days long.

- Path 2 is the longest path through the Network Diagram (28 days), and is therefore identified as the **Critical Path**. *The Critical Path is the longest path through a Network Diagram.* The Critical Path also defines the shortest period of time in which the project may be completed (in this example, 28 days).

- The Critical Path is typically indicated with a heavier arrowed line.

COMMON PROCESS TASKS

The following is a list of the common tasks associated with the Sequence Activities process:

- Determine your interactivity dependencies

- Identify the relationships between your project activities for activity sequencing

- Identify and document the types of interactivity dependencies within your project

- Construct your project Network Diagram

- Identify appropriate diagramming techniques

- Determine Inputs to your sequence activities process

- Complete your Activity List and WBS updates, as well as updates of related supporting documentation

- Define missing activities or activities requiring clarification in your activity list during the development of your project network diagram

THINK ABOUT IT

Instructions Think about how this project management process is defined, used, and documented in your organization.

Use this exercise to compare how you practice project management to what is specified in the *PMBOK® Guide Fourth Edition.*

Think about how this process is defined, used and documented in your organization. Write a brief description of how you use this process:

_____

_____

_____

_____

_____

_____

What specific Inputs, Tools or Techniques do you use as part of this process in your organization?

_____

_____

_____

_____

_____

Are the outcomes from this process different in your organization or experience?

_____

_____

_____

_____

_____

MUST KNOW CONCEPTS
. . . .

1 The Sequence Activities process is intended to identify and document interactivity logical relationships.

2 The primary deliverable (Output) of the Sequence Activities process is the Project Schedule Network Diagram.

3 The Project Schedule Network Diagram becomes the primary input to develop the project schedule.

4 The Project Schedule Network Diagram illustrates all project activities and their predecessor/successor relationships/interdependencies. It also identifies the project's Critical Path and all of the activities on the Critical Path.

5 The Critical Path is the longest path through a Network Diagram. It defines the shortest period of time in which the project may be completed.

6 Network Diagrams are often referred to as PERT Charts (inaccurately). A PERT Chart is a particular type of network diagram widely used in past years.

7 Network Diagrams are typically created and documented using the Precedence Diagramming Method (PDM) technique.

8 PDM is also referred to as Activity-on-Node (AON). In AON diagrams, activities are represented by nodes which are connected by arrowed lines to illustrate their interdependencies.

9 AON diagrams can show four types of interdependencies F-S, S-F, F-F and S-S. Dummies are not needed to illustrate network logic in AON diagrams.

10 A forward pass (left-right through the network) may be performed to determine earliest starting times (ES) and earliest finish times (EF) for each project activity.

11 A backward pass (right-left through the network) may be performed to determine latest starting times (LS) and latest finish times (LF) for each project activity.

12 Slack (also referred to as float, reserve, path float, or total float) for any given activity may be determined by subtracting ES from LS. Activities on the Critical Path typically have zero Slack.

13 Subnet (or fragnet or subnetwork) is a subdivision of a network diagram.

14 Hammock is group of related activities illustrated as a single summary activity.

15 Lead time and Lag time allow project teams to add realism and flexibility to their schedules. Lead time may be viewed as an overlap between tasks. Lag time is waiting time.

ADDITIONAL READING

- PMBOK Guide – Section 6.2 Sequence Activities

LESSON QUIZ

Instructions   Here are some questions to help reinforce your learning. Complete this quiz from memory to the best of your ability. For each question, circle or check your selected answer on this page or a separate piece of paper. When complete, check your results by comparing your answers to the preferred answers provided in Appendix A.

Please note that Knowledge Check questions are not actual PMP Exam questions. These questions are intended to reinforce key terms, concepts, and themes. While these Knowledge Check questions are typical of what you can expect on your PMP Exam, many actual PMP Exam questions are more in-depth, designed to challenge your judgment (not rote memory) in applying concepts, processes, and methodologies.

1. The longest path through a project network diagram is termed, _____.
   A. path float
   B. latest finish time (LF)
   C. latest start time (LS)
   D. critical path

2. Which of the following statements is most true?
   A. A project network diagram may identify more than one critical path.
   B. A project network diagram can illustrate only one critical path. If more than one critical path is identified, a mistake has been made somewhere in construction of the network logic.
   C. A project network diagram should be unique to the project, constructed using the best individual elements of PDM and Conditional Diagramming Methods.
   D. A project network diagram is essentially the same as a project WBS. They are interchangeable.

3. Sequence Activities Inputs include all of the following, except _____.
   A. Activity List
   B. Activity Attributes
   C. Project Schedule Network Diagrams
   D. Milestone List

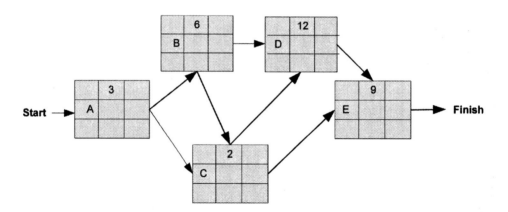

4. In this simplified network diagram (shown above), how many paths exist from project start to project finish?
   A. 6
   B. 1
   C. 5
   D. 3

5. Referring to the project network diagram in question 4, identify the critical path.
   A. Start-A-C-D-Finish
   B. Start-A-C-D-E-Finish
   C. Start-A-B-C-D-E-Finish
   D. Start-A-B-D-E-Finish

6. Referring to the project network diagram in question 4, identify the shortest period of time in which this project may be completed.
   A. 14 days
   B. 20 days
   C. 26 days
   D. 32 days

7. From the given information, determine how many paths exist through this project's network diagram.

Activity	Activity Duration	Predecessors
A	1 week	none
B	7 weeks	none
C	5 weeks	A and B
D	12 weeks	B
E	10 weeks	C and D
F	6 weeks	E
G	3 weeks	F

   A. 1
   B. 2
   C. 3
   D. 4

8. Referring to the information given in question 7, identify the project's critical path.
   A. Start-A-C-E-F-G-Finish
   B. Start-B-D-E-F-G-Finish
   C. Start-B-C-E-F-G-Finish
   D. Start-A-C-E-F-Finish

9. Referring to the information given in question 7, identify the shortest period of time in which this project may be completed.
   A. 25 weeks
   B. 31 weeks
   C. 38 weeks
   D. Insufficient information

10. While reviewing your project network diagram, you note that an activity has an Early Start time of three days and a Late Start time of twelve days. How much float does this activity have?
    A. Zero, because activities on the critical path have zero slack.
    B. +9 days
    C. –9 days
    D. 75%

11. A forward pass _____.
    A. is performed by moving left-to-right through the network diagram to determine the Early Start (ES) and Early Finish (EF) times for each activity
    B. is performed by moving right-to-left through the network diagram to determine the Late Start (LS) and Late Finish (LF) times for each activity
    C. is performed by moving left-to-right through the network diagram to identify the critical path
    D. is performed by moving right-to-left through the network diagram to determine the shortest period of time in which the project may be completed

12. Which of the following is most true?
    A. With the Precedence Diagramming Method (PDM), network diagrams are constructed with activities represented by nodes connected by arrowed lines to complete the network logic.
    B. With the Precedence Diagramming Method Diagramming Method (PDM), network diagrams are constructed with activities represented by arrowed lines connected at nodes to complete the network logic.
    C. Precedence Diagrams normally show only one activity relationship, F-S.
    D. PDM uses dummies and can illustrate all four possible activity relationships, F-S-, S-F, S-S, and F-F.

13. The Sequence Activities process is applied to _____.
    A. identify all of the deliverables-oriented work within the scope of the project
    B. further subdivide Work Packages into clearly defined activities
    C. create the Project Schedule Network Diagram
    D. schedule all of the project's defined activities

End of Lesson 14

Lesson 15
Estimate Activity Resources

Objectives

At the end of this lesson, you will be able to:

- Describe the purpose of the Estimate Activity Resources process
- Describe the Inputs, Tools & Techniques, and Outputs of the Estimate Activity Resources process
- Understand what resources must be estimated

Roadmap to the PMBOK Guide

	Initiating	Planning	Executing	M & C	Closing
Integration					
Scope					
Time		▓			
Cost					
Quality					
Human Resources					
Communications					
Risk					
Procurement					

Resources are the people, equipment, materials or supplies needed to execute the planned project activities.

Estimate Activity Resources is the simple, yet important process of determining the type and quantities of material, people, equipment, or supplies (physical resources) needed. Ideally, resource needs are determined at the lowest level of the WBS (Work Package elements), then rolled-up to higher levels (major deliverables).

The primary deliverable of the Estimate Activity Resources process is a documented description of Activity Resource Requirements. Typically, the resource needs identified here will be obtained by later applying the Acquire Project Team process and Procurement processes.

The Activity Attributes provide the primary data input for Estimate Activity Resources. The Estimate Activity Resources process is closely coordinated with several processes, including Estimate Costs, Acquire Project Team, Estimate Activity Durations, and Plan Procurements process.

PROCESS ELEMENTS

The Estimate Activity Resources process has the following Inputs:

- **Activity List** The comprehensive list and description of all schedule activities

- **Activity Attributes** An extension of the activity list, intended to provide more attribute details

- **Resource Calendars** Information on the availability of resources over the planned activity duration

- **Enterprise Environmental Factors** Consideration factors such as; culture, systems, procedures, industry standards including resource availability and skills

- **Organizational Process Assets** Consideration factors such as policies, procedures, and historical data

The Estimate Activity Resources process uses the following Tools & Techniques:

- **Expert Judgment** Expert technical and/or managerial judgment (from any qualified source)

- **Alternatives Analysis** Used to identify alternatives to account for various resource capabilities, skills, and availability

- **Published Estimating Data** Available published information on production rates and costs for an array of trades, materials, and equipment, and other resources

- **Bottom-Up Estimating**   Deriving project totals by estimating individual activities, then rolling-up the summary
- **Project Management Software**   Any software that may help plan, organize, manage resource estimates and pools

The Estimate Activity Resources process has the following Outputs:
- **Activity Resource Requirements**   Types and quantities of resources needed for each activity
- **Resource Breakdown Structure (RBS)**   Hierarchal structure of identified resources (by category and type)
- **Project Document Updates**   Updates to other project documentation (i.e. Activity List, Activity Attributes, and Resource Calendars)

Estimate Activity Resources (6.3) This process estimates the number of work periods for each schedule activity		
Inputs	**Tools and Techniques**	**Outputs**
• Activity List • Activity Attributes • Resource Calendars • Enterprise Environmental Factors • Organizational Process Assets	• Expert Judgment • Alternatives Analysis • Published Estimating Data • Bottom-up Estimating • Project Management Software	• Activity Resource Requirements • Resource Breakdown Structure (RBS) • Project Document Updates

PROCESS DOCUMENTS

The primary document that comes from this process is the Activity Resource Requirements list. This document contains a list (at an appropriate level of detail) of all resources that are required for the project. This can be also arrayed as a Resource Breakdown Structure (RBS). The RBS can be depicted in list form or in a graphic "organization chart" format.

An example of a Resource Requirements document is shown below.

True Solutions, Inc.
Project Management Template
Volume 1: Resource Requirements Worksheet Template

(TSI)

Resource Requirements Worksheet

Project Name:

Prepared by:

Date:

Work Breakdown Structure Element	Type of Resource Required:	Quantity	Involve Staff Acquisition? (Notes)	Involve Procurement? (Notes)
1.				
2.				
3.				
4.				
5.				
6.				
7.				
8.				

Additional Notes or Comments:

Submitted to:

Name:

Title:

Date:

Name:

Title:

Date:

COMMON PROCESS TASKS

The following is a list of the common tasks associated with the Estimate Activity Resources process:

- Identify physical resources available to your project, including contracted resources

- Evaluate historical resource information related to similar projects

- Comply with organizational policies regarding your resource usage and selection

- Determine and quantify resource needs using your Activity List, Activity Attributes, and resource calendars

- Identify the completeness of your resource requirements document by tracking individual resource requirements to your WBS elements

- Utilize your resource requirements as a basis for acquiring resources and managing other cost activities, including cost estimating

- Evaluate alternative methods to estimate resource requirements

- Develop Activity Resource Requirements

- Develop a Resource Breakdown Structure (RBS)

- Update project documents as required

THINK ABOUT IT

Instructions Think about how this project management process is defined, used, and documented in your organization.

Compare your organization's use of this process to the PMI® definition.

Use this exercise to compare how you practice project management to what is specified in the *PMBOK® Guide Fourth Edition*.

Best Practices suggest that each of the following items are used during the Estimate Activity Resources process:

Which of these items do you use when practicing project management?

- ☐ Define all resources: People, Equipment, Materials, and Supplies

- ☐ List all resources by individual detailed Activities

- ☐ Use a specific resource list

- ☐ Document overall resources in a graphic Resource Breakdown Structure

- ☐ Update all documents when changes to resource plans occur

How would you change your use of this process in your organization to resolve any gaps in application?

_____

_____

_____

_____

_____

_____

MUST KNOW CONCEPTS

. . . .

1. The Estimate Activity Resources process is intended to estimate the type and quantities of material, people, equipment, or supplies required to perform each activity.

2. Physical resources include people, equipment, supplies, and materials.

3. The primary deliverable (Output) from the Estimate Activity Resources process is the documented description of Activity Resource Requirements.

4 Bottom-up estimating generally produces the most confident estimates, but is more costly and time-consuming than its opposite, analogous estimating. Typically, bottom-up estimating is performed by developing detailed estimates for each activity at the Work Package level of the WBS. They are then rolled-up to derive a project total.

5 Identified resource requirements will typically be obtained later by applying the Acquire Project Team process and the Procurement processes.

6 The Estimate Activity Resource process is closely coordinated with the Estimate Cost Process.

ADDITIONAL READING
. . . .
• PMBOK Guide – Section 6.3 Estimate Activity Resources

LESSON QUIZ
. . . .
Instructions   Here are some questions to help reinforce your learning. Complete this quiz from memory to the best of your ability. For each question, circle or check your selected answer on this page or a separate piece of paper. When complete, check your results by comparing your answers to the preferred answers provided in Appendix A.

Please note that Knowledge Check questions are not actual PMP Exam questions. These questions are intended to reinforce key terms, concepts, and themes. While these Knowledge Check questions are typical of what you can expect on your PMP Exam, many actual PMP Exam questions are more in-depth, designed to challenge your judgment (not rote memory) in applying concepts, processes, and methodologies.

1.   The people, equipment, materials, and supplies used to estimate activity resources are termed:
   A. Work Breakdown Structure (WBS) requirements
   B. Physical resources
   C. Work Package requirements
   D. Estimate Activity Resources outputs

2.   The Estimate Activity Resources is applied to:
   A. determine the type of physical resources required to perform each activity
   B. determine the people required to perform each activity
   C. determine the equipment required to perform each activity
   D. determine the materials required to perform each activity

3. Estimate Activity Resources Tools & Techniques include:
   A. Alternatives analysis, expert judgment, and project management software
   B. Resource pool description, expert judgment, and project management software
   C. Organizational policies, expert judgment, and project management software
   D. Resource calendars, expert judgment, and project management software

4. Which of the following statements is most true:
   A. Activity Resource Requirements is the primary Output from Estimate Activity Resources, and describes the physical resources needed to perform/complete project activities.
   B. Activity Resource Requirements is the primary Output from Estimate Activity Resources, and describes the roles and responsibilities of assigned project personnel.
   C. Activity Resource Requirements is the primary Output from Estimate Activity Resources, and describes the resources potentially available to support identified project activities.
   D. Each of the above statements is equally true.

End of Lesson 15

Lesson 16
Estimate Activity Durations

Objectives

At the end of this lesson, you will be able to:

- Describe the purpose of the Estimate Activity Durations process
- Describe the Inputs, Tools & Techniques, and Outputs of the Estimate Activity Durations process
- Understand the available methods for estimating activity durations

Roadmap to the PMBOK Guide

	Initiating	Planning	Executing	M & C	Closing
Integration					
Scope					
Time		▓▓▓			
Cost					
Quality					
Human Resources					
Communications					
Risk					
Procurement					

Activity durations can be estimated using specific estimates or using a range of estimates depending on your project need and organizational processes.

Estimate Activity Durations is the process of estimating time durations for each defined activity resource, which will serve as an essential input for the Develop Schedule process.

In simpler projects, estimates are typically documented as deterministic, single-point values (one number). For example, a single-point estimate may be documented as: 7 days (with no plus/minus flexibility). Single-point estimates are generally less reliable. Using expert judgment or an analogous estimate (also known as top-down estimate) is a simple and quick way of producing a single-point estimate.

In more complex projects, it is common to use sophisticated mathematics to determine probabilistic distributions for each activity, resulting in a time-range estimate instead of a single-time estimate. For example, a probabilistic estimate may be documented as a graphical curve indicating the probability of an activity finishing at any given time on the curve. Probabilistic estimates generally provide for more reliable expectations. Probabilistic estimates usually use a method like three-point estimating to predict a range of outcomes. Duration estimates do not include any lags.

Three-point estimates are sometimes called PERT estimates (Program Evaluation Review Technique).

Three-point estimates use this formula:

$$t_E = \frac{t_O + 4t_M + t_P}{6}$$

This formula is equivalent to the common PERT formula:

E = O + 4ML + P/6

where:

O = optimistic estimate

ML (or M) = most likely estimate

P = pessimistic estimate

Estimates should originate from the person or group of people who have expert familiarity with the activity.

In most of today's project management software, it is common to estimate activity durations in terms of work periods (activity durations). The project team determines how best to define work periods for their particular project, typically days, shifts, hours, or weeks.

PROCESS ELEMENTS

The Estimate Activity Durations process has the following Inputs:

- **Activity List** The comprehensive list and description of all schedule activities

- **Activity Attributes** An extension of the activity list, intended to provide more attribute details

- **Activity Resource Requirements** Types and quantities of resources needed for each activity in a work package

- **Resource Calendars** Information on the availability of resources over the planned activity duration

- **Project Scope Statement** Detailed description of all major deliverables (specifically assumptions and constraints)

- **Enterprise Environmental Factors** Consideration factors such as: culture, systems, procedures, industry standards (i.e. databases, productivity metrics, and published commercial information)

- **Organizational Process Assets** Consideration factors such as historical information, project calendars, scheduling methodology, and lessons learned

The Estimate Activity Durations process uses the following Tools & Techniques:

- **Expert Judgment** Expert technical and/or managerial judgment (from any qualified source)

- **Analogous Estimating** Using actual values from a previous similar project to base current estimates

- **Parametric Estimating** Uses a statistical relationship between historical data and other variables to calculate an estimate for activity parameters (i.e. Total labor hours = 6,000)

- **Three-Point Estimates** Factoring most likely, optimistic, and pessimistic estimates to derive a forecasted estimate

- **Reserve Analysis** Determining the appropriate amount of contingency reserve to compensate for schedule risk

The Estimate Activity Durations process has the following Outputs:

- **Activity Duration Estimates** Quantitative assessments of the time likely needed to complete each activity

- **Project Document Updates** Updates to other project documentation (i.e. Activity Attributes and assumptions)

Estimate Activity Durations (6.4)
This process estimates the number of work periods for each schedule activity

Inputs	Tools and Techniques	Outputs
• Activity List • Activity Attributes • Activity Resource Requirements • Resource Calendars • Project Scope Statement • Enterprise Environmental Factors • Organizational Process Assets	• Expert Judgment • Analogous Estimating • Parametric Estimating • Three-Point Estimates • Reserve Analysis	• Activity Duration Estimates • Project Document Updates

TSI Study Aid
This chart is part of the study aid poster series available at *www.truesolutions.com*.

PROCESS DOCUMENTS

The Activity Duration Estimate can come in many different formats. Shown below is an example of an Activity Duration Estimate given on a separate form dedicated to the duration estimate. Many times the project manager will incorporate the Activity Duration Estimate into an automated project management tool such as Microsoft Project or a similar scheduling tool.

True Solutions, Inc.   **Activity Duration Estimating Sheet (Sample)**   *TSI*
Project Management Template

Project Name:
Prepared by:
Date:

Item #	Work Description	Week Started	Weeks Needed	1	2	3	4	5	6	7	8	9	10	11	12	13	14	15
1	Identify Vendors	1	3															
2	Design Survey	1	4															
3	Email Participants	5	1															
4	Conduct Survey	5	6															
5	Tabulate Results	9	4															
6	Analyze Data	11	3															
7	Write Report	11	4															
8	Publish Report	12	4															

Copyright 2009 True Solutions, Inc. 5001 LBJ Freeway, Suite 125-B Dallas, Texas 75244 Tel: 972.770.0900 Fax: 972.770.0922 www.truesolutions.com

PROCESS TASKS

The following is a list of the common tasks associated with the Estimate Activity Durations process:

• Develop activity duration estimates for your project activities using various tools, such as analogous estimation techniques, parametric analysis, or three-point estimates

• Estimate your number of work periods and possible work duration ranges

• Determine the appropriate time reserves

• Update project documents as required

THINK ABOUT IT

Instructions   Use this exercise to compare with how you practice project management to what is specified in the *PMBOK® Guide Fourth Edition.*

Think about how this process is defined, used and documented in your organization. Write a brief description of how you use this process:

_____

_____

_____

_____

_____

What specific Inputs, Tools, or Techniques do you use as part of this process in your organization?

_____

_____

_____

_____

_____

Are the outcomes from this process different in your organization or experiences?

_____

_____

_____

_____

_____

_____

MUST KNOW CONCEPTS

....

1 The Estimate Activity Durations process is estimating time durations for each defined activity resource. These estimates will ultimately be used to create the project schedule.

2 Care must be taken to differentiate the actual effort time (performance time) required to perform the activity work and the calendar time (elapsed time) required to complete the activity. Some activities may have nonwork waiting time involved.

3 Deterministic (single-point) estimates are typically documented with only one value. Probabilistic (range) estimates typically report estimates in terms of probabilities, instead of hard numbers.

4 Estimating should originate from the person, or group of people, who are most knowledgeable about the activity, ideally by the person or people who will be doing the work.

5 Analogous estimating (also termed top-down estimating) typically involves basing an estimate on a known previous activity performed in the past. Analogous estimates are relatively quick to perform and inexpensive, because no detailed estimating protocols are necessary. All that is involved is recalling history. Analogous estimates are also the least reliable, typically proving to have a significant margin of error after-the-fact.

6 Three-Point Estimates uses the three estimates (pessimistic, most probable, and optimistic) and may be used as a tool to help determine an approximate range for an activity's duration. The three point estimate formula is:

$$t_E = \frac{t_O + 4t_M + t_P}{6}$$

7 Estimators may choose to include reserve time (also termed time buffers) to proportionately compensate for the level of risk associated with the activity.

8 Duration estimates are typically documented in terms of work periods. Work periods are determined by the project team and are typically defined as shifts, hours, days, or weeks.

9 Ideally, estimates should be reported with ranges of possible results such as 8 days ±2 (indicating 6–10 days).

ADDITIONAL READING

- PMBOK Guide – Section 6.4 Estimate Activity Durations

LESSON QUIZ

Instructions   Here are some questions to help reinforce your learning. Complete this quiz from memory to the best of your ability. For each question, circle or check your selected answer on this page or a separate piece of paper. When complete, check your results by comparing your answers to the preferred answers provided in Appendix A.

Please note that Knowledge Check questions are not actual PMP Exam questions. These questions are intended to reinforce key terms, concepts, and themes. While these Knowledge Check questions are typical of what you can expect on your PMP Exam, many actual PMP Exam questions are more in-depth, designed to challenge your judgment (not rote memory) in applying concepts, processes, and methodologies.

1. The estimating technique that typically uses the past actual performance of a similar activity is termed:
   A. Bottom-up estimating
   B. Probabilistic estimating
   C. Analogous estimating (also termed top-down)
   D. Deterministic (single-point) estimating

2. Which of the following is most true?
   A. Work periods should be reported with ranges of possible results such as 10 days +3; or 90% probability of finishing within three weeks.
   B. Work periods should include time reserve (time contingency) to compensate for associated risk.
   C. Work periods are typically defined by the project manager, then communicated to the project team.
   D. Work periods are typically defined in terms of hours, days, shifts, weeks.

3. Estimate Activity Durations outputs include which of the following:
   A. Activity duration estimates, project document updates
   B. Activity duration estimates, three-point estimates
   C. Activity duration estimates, reserve analysis
   D. Activity duration estimates, resource calendars

4. Estimate Activity Durations are best prepared by:
   A. Functional managers, because they are on the front line and close to the work
   B. The project team, to ensure the project manager's expectations will be satisfied
   C. The project manager, to ensure the project schedule can be created to satisfy the sponsor's expectations
   D. The person or people who have the most knowledge about the work

End of Lesson 16

17

Lesson 17
Develop Schedule

Objectives

At the end of this lesson, you will be able to:

- Describe the purpose of the Develop Schedule process
- Describe the Inputs, Tools & Techniques, and Outputs of the Develop Schedule process
- Understand the typical methods that are used to Develop Schedule

Roadmap to the PMBOK Guide

	Initiating	Planning	Executing	M & C	Closing
Integration					
Scope					
Time		■			
Cost					
Quality					
Human Resources					
Communications					
Risk					
Procurement					

A critical part of developing a realistic schedule will be to determine the project calendar. The project calendar will specify what days are worked, work hours and any holidays and non-working days.

Develop Schedule is the process used to create the project schedule based on activity sequences, durations, resource requirements, and schedule constraints. The project schedule is developed as the result of many detailed iterations and progressive elaboration across the entire planning phase.

Scheduling software has become an essential tool to help create the schedule. Most scheduling software today will allow project teams to input raw data, then automate the process of maneuvering it to create the schedule baseline. Once baselined, software can automate changes and tracking throughout the project's remaining phases.

Developing and maintaining a project schedule file can be quite time-consuming and may require expert support. In large projects, it is not unusual to assign one full-time scheduler for every thousand lines in the schedule.

The Develop Schedule process is applied to determine the start/finish dates for project activities.

CREATING A PROJECT SCHEDULE

There are four primary methods used to calculate theoretical early/late start/finish dates for project activities:

- **Critical Path Method (CPM)** CPM determines start/finish dates using one time-duration estimate for each activity by performing forward and backward passes. The Critical Path Method is the "most probable" time-duration estimate.

- **What-if Scenario Analysis** This method computes different scenarios to derive the schedule. Typically, Monte Carlo simulations are performed to support this method.

- **Resource Leveling** Resource leveling is a resource management tool sometimes used to "level" resources across the project schedule, to minimize exaggerated peaks and valleys.

- **Critical Chain Method** This method may be used to modify a project schedule to account for limited resources. Critical chain methodology is characterized by a focus on the use and management of duration buffers.

Completed project schedules are typically illustrated using a bar chart (Gantt chart), milestone chart, or dated network diagram.

COMPRESSING A PROJECT SCHEDULE

There are two primary methods used by project teams to shorten schedules, when feasible:

- **Crashing** The project schedule can sometimes be shortened by "crashing" activities on the critical path. Crashing is the process of adding more resources to the activity. Crashing typically adds cost and potentially increases risk. It is not always a feasible alternative.

- **Fast Tracking** The project schedule can sometimes be shortened by "fast tracking" activities on the critical path. Fast tracking is the process of realigning normally sequential activities to be performed in parallel. Fast tracking typically increases risk and can cause rework. Like crashing, fast tracking is not always a feasible alternative.

PROCESS ELEMENTS

The Develop Schedule process has the following Inputs:

- **Activity List**   The comprehensive list and description of all schedule activities

- **Activity Attributes**   An extension of the Activity List, intended to provide more attribute details

- **Project Schedule Network Diagrams**   Schematic displays of the project's activities and their logical relationships

- **Activity Resource Requirements**   Types and quantities of resources needed for each activity in a Work Package

- **Resource Calendars**   Information on the availability of resources over the planned activity duration

- **Activity Duration Estimates**   Quantitative assessments of the time likely needed to complete each activity

- **Project Scope Statement**   Detailed description deliverables (specifically assumptions and constraints)

- **Enterprise Environmental Factors**   Consideration factors such as; culture, systems, procedures, industry standards (i.e. scheduling tools)

- **Organizational Process Assets**   Consideration factors such as scheduling methodology and project calendar

The Develop Schedule process uses the following Tools & Techniques:

- **Schedule Network Analysis**   Technique that generates the project schedule, employs various analytical methods

- **Critical Path Method**   Calculates schedule dates without regard to resource limitations

- **Critical Chain Method**   Modifies the project schedule to account for limited resources

- **Resource Leveling**   Optimizes the distribution of work among limited resources

- **What-If Scenario Analysis**   Explores various scenarios to bring the schedule into alignment with the plan (i.e. Monte Carlo simulations)

- **Applying Leads and Lags**   Further defined "overlaps (leads)" and "delays (lags)" in activity dependencies to develop a viable schedule

- **Schedule Compression**   Shortens the project schedule without changing scope (fast-tracking and crashing)

- **Scheduling Tool**   Tool used to facilitate creation of the project schedule documentation

The Develop Schedule process has the following Outputs:

- **Project Schedule**   Graphic presentation illustrating planned start and planned finish dates for each activity (i.e. milestone charts, bar charts, Project Schedule Network Diagrams)

- **Schedule Baseline**   Specific version of the project schedule, accepted and approved by the team as the project's schedule baseline

- **Schedule Data**   The schedule milestones, schedule activities, activity attributes, and all documented assumptions and constraints

- **Project Document Updates**   Updates to other project documentation (i.e. Activity Resource Requirements, Activity Attributes, Calendar, Risk Register)

Develop Schedule
This process analyzes activities and constraints to create the project schedule

Inputs	Tools and Techniques	Outputs
• Activity List • Activity Attributes • Project Schedule Network Diagrams • Activity Resource Requirements • Resource Calendars • Activity Duration Estimates • Project Scope Statement • Enterprise Environmental Factors • Organizational Process Assets	• Schedule Network Analysis • Critical Path Method • Critical Chain Method • Resource Leveling • What-if Scenarios Analysis • Applying Leads and Lags • Schedule Compression • Scheduling Tool	• Project Schedule • Schedule Baseline • Schedule Data • Project Document Updates

PROCESS DOCUMENTS

Two important documents are finalized in the Develop Schedule process. The baseline Project Schedule will be developed during this process. Completed project schedules are typically illustrated using a bar chart (Gantt chart), milestone chart, or dated network diagram. An example of the most common form, the bar chart/ Gantt chart, is shown below as well as a Milestone Form template.

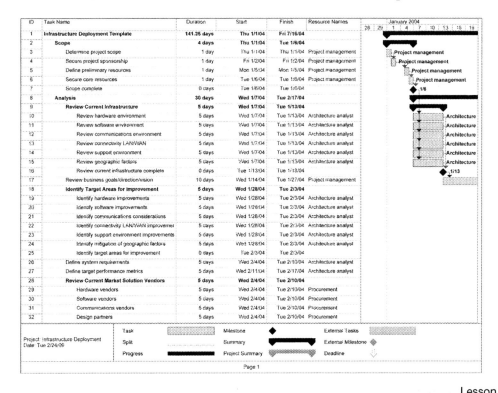

Milestone Chart

Project Name:
Prepared by:
Date:

Current Date
▼

Event	Jan	Feb	March	April	May	June	July	August
Subcontracts Signed	△▼							
Specifications Finalized		△						
Design Reviewed			△					
Subsystem Tested			△					
First Unit Delivered				△				
Production Plan Completed				△				

There are many other acceptable ways to display project information on a milestone chart

Planned	...	△
Actual	...	▼

Note: The arrows above are AutoShapes. Select an arrow from the Key, select Edit->Copy, then select Edit->Paste. Click and drag the new arrow to move to the desired table cell.

TSI Application Aid

This form is available individually or as a set from *www.truesolutions.com*.

In addition to the project schedule baseline that is developed, the project manager must also develop and finalize the Project Schedule Management Plan. The Project Schedule Management Plan documents how the project schedule will be managed and measured during the project. The Project Schedule Management Plan can be as extensive or concise as the project requires. The Project Schedule Management Plan is a subsidiary plan to the Project Management Plan and has several important elements:

• Change Management Procedures

• Precision Level for measuring schedule

• Units of measure used

• Control Thresholds

• Processes to be used for schedule management

Schedule Management Plan

Project Name:		
Prepared by:		
Date:		

Person(s) authorized to request schedule changes (see Schedule Change Request):

Name:	Title:	Location:
Name:	**Title:**	**Location:**
Name:	**Title:**	**Location:**

Person(s) to whom Schedule Change Request forms must be submitted for approval:

Name:	Title:	Location:
Name:	**Title:**	**Location:**
Name:	**Title:**	**Location:**

Acceptable reasons for changes to Project Schedule *(e.g., delays due to material or personnel availability; weather; need to resolve related issue before proceeding; acceleration permitted due to early completion of a phase or process, etc.)*:

Describe how you will calculate and report on the projected impact of any schedule changes *(time, cost, quality, etc.)*:

Describe any other aspects of how changes to the project schedule will be managed:

This form is available individually or as a set from *www.truesolutions.com*.

COMMON PROCESS TASKS

The following is a list of the common tasks associated with the Develop Schedule process:

- Formulate your project and resource calendars

- Modify your activity leads, lags, and constraints

- Determine inputs to your Develop Schedule process

- Select and perform appropriate mathematical analysis, such as critical path method

- Understand the advantages and disadvantages of the different types of project schedule formats

- Determine the completeness of your project schedule

- Develop your Schedule Management Plan, including establishing a schedule baseline, documenting how your schedule variances will be managed, identifying your schedule change control system procedures, and defining appropriate performance measures

- Produce your baseline project schedule

- Update project documents as needed

THINK ABOUT IT

Instructions Think about how this project management process is defined, used, and documented in your organization.

Compare your organization's use of this process to the PMI® definition.

Think about how this process is defined, used and documented in your organization. Write a brief description of how you use this process:

_____

_____

_____

_____

What specific Inputs, Tools, or Techniques do you use as part of this process in your organization?

_____

_____

_____

_____

Are the outcomes from this process different in your organization or experiences?

_____

_____

_____

_____

MUST KNOW CONCEPTS
. . . .

1. The Develop Schedule process is applied to create the project schedule based on activity sequences, durations, resource requirements, and schedule constraints.

2. There are four primary methods used to calculate theoretical early/late start/finish dates for project activities: Critical Path Method (CPM), Critical Chain Method, What-if Scenario Analysis, and Resource Leveling.

3. The primary deliverables (Outputs) of the Develop Schedule process include the project schedule and the schedule baseline.

4. There are two primary methods used to shorten schedules; crashing and fast-tracking.

5. Completed project schedules are typically illustrated using bar charts (also called Gantt charts), milestone charts, or Project Schedule Network Diagrams.

6. Resource leveling is a resource management tool sometimes used to level resources across the project schedule, to minimize exaggerated peaks and valleys.

7. "Heuristic" is an academic term that means thumb-rule. Some modern project management conventions are generally described as heuristics, such as resource leveling heuristics.

ADDITIONAL READING

• PMBOK Guide – Section 6.5 Develop Schedule

LESSON QUIZ

Instructions Here are some questions to help reinforce your learning. Complete this quiz from memory to the best of your ability. For each question, circle or check your selected answer on this page or a separate piece of paper. When complete, check your results by comparing your answers to the preferred answers provided in Appendix A.

Please note that Knowledge Check questions are not actual PMP Exam questions. These questions are intended to reinforce key terms, concepts, and themes. While these Knowledge Check questions are typical of what you can expect on your PMP Exam, many actual PMP Exam questions are more in-depth, designed to challenge your judgment (not rote memory) in applying concepts, processes, and methodologies.

1. The Develop Schedule process is applied to:
    A. Document all duration estimates, using the scheduling software selected by you and your project team
    B. Document how changes to the project schedule will be managed
    C. Add realism and flexibility to the project schedule
    D. Create the project schedule based on activity sequences, durations, resource requirements, and schedule constraints

2. You have been requested to shorten the project schedule by two weeks. You and your project team can:
    A. Explore the feasibility of crashing and/or fast tracking activities on the critical path. But this can result in higher costs and/or greater risk.
    B. Explore the feasibility of resource leveling. But this can result in higher costs and/or greater risk.
    C. Explore the feasibility of employing effective conflict resolution skills to respectfully deny the request. But this can result in hard feelings.
    D. Explore the feasibility of extending lead times and/or shortening lag times. But this can result in unnecessary quality problems.

3. Develop Schedule Outputs include all the following expect:
    A. The schedule baseline
    B. The project schedule
    C. Schedule data
    D. Activity duration estimates

4. Which of the following statements is least true:
   A. Completed project schedules are typically illustrated using bar charts, milestone charts or Network Diagrams.
   B. There are two primary methods used to shorten schedules: crashing and fast-tracking.
   C. Resource leveling heuristics can be used to reduce the number of estimated resources, resulting in lower project costs.
   D. Lead time and lag time allows project teams to add realism and flexibility to their schedule. Lead time may be viewed as an overlap between tasks. Lag time is waiting time.

5. There are four primary methods used to calculate theoretical early/late start/finish dates for project activities. They are:
   A. Critical Path Method (CPM), Resource Leveling, Critical Chain Method, and What if- Scenario Analysis
   B. Critical Path Method (CPM), Program Evaluation and Review Technique (PERT), Graphical Evaluation and Review Technique (GERT), and Crashing
   C. Critical Path Method (CPM), Program Evaluation and Review Technique (PERT), Graphical Evaluation and Review Technique (GERT), and Simulation
   D. Critical Path Method (CPM), Program Evaluation and Review Technique (PERT), Flow-Charting, and Simulation

6. Which of the following is most true?
   A. CPM uses one estimate (the most probable estimate) to determine activity schedule dates.
   B. CPM uses the weighted average of three estimates (pessimistic, most probable, and optimistic) to determine activity schedule dates.
   C. CPM uses Monte Carlo software algorithms to run simulations to determine activity schedule dates.
   D. CPM, PERT, GERT, and Simulation are alternative terms to describe the same method. They all use a broad range of estimates to determine activity schedule dates.

7. Your project team has consulted with several experts to get their opinions on the time duration of a particular project activity that is on the critical path. Their expert opinions varied. The shortest time estimate was six days; the longest estimate was fourteen days; the most probable estimate seemed to be nine days. Based on this information, what is the PERT estimate (three-point estimate)?
   A. 5.67 days
   B. 9.00 days
   C. 9.33 days
   D. 9.67 days

End of Lesson 17

18

Lesson 18
Develop Human Resource Plan

Objectives
At the end of this lesson, you will be able to:
- Describe the purpose of the Develop Human Resource Plan process
- Describe the Inputs, Tools & Techniques, and Outputs of the Develop Human Resource Plan process
- Understand organization types and cultures and their potential effects on the project

Roadmap to the PMBOK Guide

	Initiating	Planning	Executing	M & C	Closing
Integration					
Scope					
Time					
Cost					
Quality					
Human Resources		■			
Communications					
Risk					
Procurement					

Many project processes have a high degree of overlap during project planning. Develop Human Resource Plan is performed as soon as practical in order to facilitate project success.

The Develop Human Resource Plan process is applied to develop, document and assign project roles, responsibilities, and reporting relationships. This typically involves creating a project organization chart, the Human Resource Plan, and defining team policies/procedures.

Logically, human resource planning is one of the earliest processes applied in project planning. Because the organization structure will greatly influence the project's communications requirements, human resource planning is closely linked with communications planning.

Projects can be staffed by people external to the organization, internal to the organization, or by a mix of both. As you may imagine, a project team comprised of staff members who are temporarily borrowed from various groups within an organization will be quite different from a project team comprised of members who are all hired from the outside. To better understand the dynamics of different project organizations, it is helpful to understand the way different organizations tend to staff their projects. Accordingly, this lesson begins with a presentation of some important fundamentals in organizational theory.

ORGANIZATIONAL THEORY

As a project manager, you may be expected to have a practical understanding of different types of organizational structures, especially with relation to project staffing. Generally, we recognize three primary types of organizations:

• Functional Organizations

• Matrix Organizations

• Projectized Organizations

Functional Organizations

In Functional Organizations, little if any cross-functional work is organized/performed as projects. In these organizations, staff members typically work strictly within their functional specialty, such as finance, engineering, marketing, quality, and manufacturing.

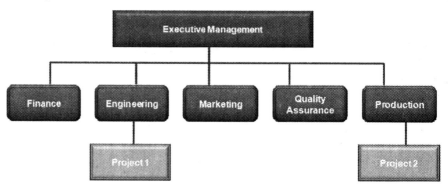

In Functional Organizations, the functional managers usually assume all responsibility and authority. A project manager may be assigned, but only as a project coordinator or project expediter.

Matrix Organizations

In Matrix Organizations, the structure is similar to a functional organization, except some work is organized and performed as projects. Typically, project teams are comprised of people temporarily borrowed from various functional areas within the organization. When their project work is done, they return to their functional area. There are multiple matrix organization variants.

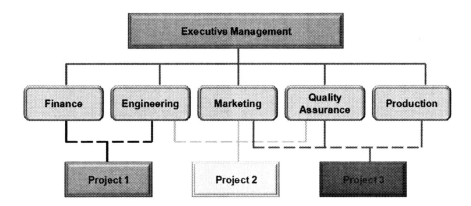

In a balanced matrix organization, the project manager equally shares responsibility and authority with functional managers during the project.

In a strong matrix, the project manager has more authority.

In a weak matrix, the project manager has less authority.

Projectized Organizations

In Projectized Organizations, all work is organized and performed as projects. A building contractor firm could exemplify a Projectized Organization. In these organizations, project teams are usually hired solely to support a project, then let go as soon as their work is done.

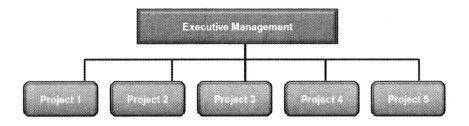

In Projectized Organizations, the project manager usually assumes full profit/loss responsibility and authority.

PROCESS ELEMENTS

The Develop Human Resource Plan process has the following Inputs:

- **Activity Resource Requirements**   Types and quantities of resources needed for each schedule activity

- **Enterprise Environmental Factors**   Consideration factors such as: culture, systems, procedures, industry standards

- **Organizational Process Assets**   Consideration factors such as processes, procedures, and corporate knowledge base

The Develop Human Resource Plan process uses the following Tools & Techniques:

- **Organization Charts and Position Descriptions**   Displays illustrating project reporting relationships and positions

- **Networking**   Informal interaction to better understand political and interpersonal factors in an organization or industry

- **Organizational Theory**   The body of knowledge that describes how people, teams, and organizations behave

The Develop Human Resource Plan process has the following Outputs:

- **Human Resource Plan**   Describes how and when human resources will be applied to the project team

---

Develop Human Resource Plan (9.1)
This process documents project roles, responsibilities, and reporting relationships

Inputs	Tools and Techniques	Outputs
• Activity Resource Requirements • Enterprise Environmental Factors • Organizational Process Assets	• Organizational Charts and Position Descriptions • Networking • Organizational Theory	• Human Resource Plan

---

PROCESS DOCUMENTS

The Human Resource Plan that is the Output from this process is really a collection of documents. The Human Resource Plan combines the Roles and Responsibility Chart (RACI Chart), the Staffing Management Plan (when resources come and go), the Project Organization Chart, and other human resource information into one collection of documents. This is a volume of information that will take multiple pages to define and document.

A simple example of a template for human resource planning is shown below.

True Solutions, Inc.
Project Management Template
Volume 1: Human Resource Management Plan Template

Human Resource Management Plan

Project Name:
Prepared by:
Date:
Project Manager:
Staffing Management Plan Number: (original is #1)
Project Team Roles and Responsibilities:
List Each Team Member and Role: Responsibility, Accountability, Consult, Inform
•
•
Insert Project Organization Chart Here:

Staff Management Plan:

Resource Description	Estimated Number	Projected Timing to Join Project	Projected Completion Date for Release
1.			
2.			
3.			
4.			
5.			
6.			
7.			
8.			
9.			

Projected Approach and Schedule for Updating Staffing Management Plan:

Triggering Event	Expected Timing
•	
•	
•	

Resource Calendar – note differences to standard calendar here:

1.	
2.	

Additional Notes:

TSI *Application Aid*
This form is available individually or as a set from *www.truesolutions.com*.

COMMON PROCESS TASKS

The following is a list of the common tasks associated with the Develop Human Resource Plan process:

- Complete your overall human resource planning process

- Develop your organizational chart for project work

- Describe your project effects on organizational units, technical interfaces, and the presence of different technical disciplines

- Utilize an organizational breakdown structure (OBS) to evaluate unit responsibilities for specific work items on your project

- Develop your project team policies and procedures

THINK ABOUT IT

Instructions Think about how this project management process is defined, used, and documented in your organization.

Compare your organization's use of this process to the PMI® definition.

Best Practices suggest that each of the following items are used during the Develop Human Resource Plan Process.

Which of these items do you use when practicing project management?

☐ Define all Roles and Responsibilities

☐ Create an Organization chart

☐ Use tools like a RACI chart or Responsibility Matrix

☐ Document overall human resources in a histogram form

☐ Document a complete Human Resource Plan to cover the entire project time period

☐ Update all documents when changes to resource plans occur

How would you change your use of this process in your organization to resolve any gaps in application?

_____

_____

_____

_____

_____

_____

_____

MUST KNOW CONCEPTS

1 The Develop Human Resource Plan process is applied to develop, document, and assign project roles, responsibilities, and reporting relationships.

2 The primary output of the Develop Human Resource Plan process is the project's Human Resource Plan.

3 The Human Resource Plan describes how/when human resources will be brought into the project and how/when human resources will leave the project. A Resource Histogram is often used to illustrate some of this information.

4 A Resource Histogram illustrates human resource needs as a function of time.

5 Roles (who does what) and responsibilities (who decides what) are often illustrated using a Responsibility Assignment Matrix (RAM).

6 A Responsibility Assignment Matrix (RAM) illustrates assignments and levels of authority/responsibility, as a function of WBS elements. There is no time associated with a RAM.

7 A RACI Chart (Responsible, Accountable, Consult, Inform) is a type of RAM.

8 Functional Organizations typically do not perform much work as cross-functional projects. When they do, projects are usually the full responsibility of a functional manager. Project managers in Functional Organizations typically have very little authority and are often termed project coordinators or project expediters.

9 In Matrix Organizations, projects are performed using human resources borrowed from functional areas within the organization. In Matrix Organizations, project managers typically share responsibility and authority with functional managers.

10 In Projectized Organizations, most work is performed as projects. In Projectized Organizations, the project manager typically assumes full profit/loss responsibility and authority and staffs the project with dedicated (not borrowed) human resources.

ADDITIONAL READING

- PMBOK Guide – Section 9.0 Introduction, Project Human Resource Management
- PMBOK Guide – Section 9.1 Develop Human Resource Plan

LESSON QUIZ

Instructions Here are some questions to help reinforce your learning. Complete this quiz from memory to the best of your ability. For each question, circle or check your selected answer on this page or a separate piece of paper. When complete, check your results by comparing your answers to the preferred answers provided in Appendix A.

Please note that Knowledge Check questions are not actual PMP Exam questions. These questions are intended to reinforce key terms, concepts, and themes. While these Knowledge Check questions are typical of what you can expect on your PMP Exam, many actual PMP Exam questions are more in-depth, designed to challenge your judgment (not rote memory) in applying concepts, processes, and methodologies.

1. The Develop Human Resource Plan process is applied to _____.
   A. develop, document, and assign the project resource histogram
   B. develop, document, and assign project roles, responsibilities, and reporting relationships
   C. develop the project's Responsibility Assignment Matrix
   D. identify which organizational standards are applicable to the project, then determine how to satisfy them.

2. Which statement is least true?
   A. In Matrix Organizations, project managers typically share responsibility and authority with functional managers.
   B. In strong Matrix Organizations, project managers may have more authority than functional managers.

C. Project managers in Functional Organizations may have little authority and are often termed project coordinators or project expeditors.

D. In Projectized Organizations, the project manager typically assumes no profit/loss responsibility/authority and staffs the project with human resources borrowed from various functional areas within the organization.

3. Develop Human Resource Plan tools and techniques include:

A. staffing management plan, networking, communicating

B. organization charts and position descriptions, networking, organizational theory

C. organization charts and position descriptions, negotiating, organizational theory

D. Project Management Plan, activity/resource requirements, networking

End of Lesson 18

19

Lesson 19
Estimate Costs

Objectives

At the end of this lesson, you will be able to:

- Describe the purpose of the Estimate Costs process
- Describe the Inputs, Tools & Techniques, and Outputs of the Estimate Costs process
- Understand the tools to be used to develop cost estimates
- Understand the different types of cost estimates to be used

Roadmap to the PMBOK Guide

	Initiating	Planning	Executing	M & C	Closing
Integration					
Scope					
Time					
Cost					
Quality					
Human Resources					
Communications					
Risk					
Procurement					

Several progressively more accurate cost estimates will be used to define activity cost estimates for the project. Acceptable ranges for cost estimates will generally be defined by the performing organization, although for the PMP® Exam you should know the specific cost estimate ranges defined here.

Estimate Costs is the process of determining the estimated cost of resources that will be applied to complete all project schedule activities. This includes direct resources such as labor, materials, and equipment plus other indirect costs such as contingency cost reserves, inflation allowances, cost of quality, and overhead. Cost estimates may be documented and reported in detail or in summary form.

It is important to distinguish between cost and price. For example, in a competitive bid scenario, a construction company may estimate its total cost to build an office complex then submit a bid with its price to the client. Typically the price will be higher than the cost. The difference represents the construction company's potential profit. Generally, price is negotiable, whereas cost is not.

The Estimate Costs process is applied not only to produce cost estimates, but to create the Cost Management Plan as well. The Cost Management Plan serves as a subsidiary plan to the overall Project Management Plan and is intended to describe how cost variances will be managed during project execution.

Like activity duration estimates, cost estimates should be prepared and documented with ranges of possible outcomes, instead of inflexible single-point values. For example, $9,300 ± 10\%$.

One tool or technique that is mentioned in this process is the Three-Point Estimate. Three-Point Estimates are estimates derived using three values: most likely estimate, optimistic estimate, and pessimistic estimate. This method of estimating is also known as PERT — Program Evaluation Review Technique. The PMBOK Guide uses a new formula with new designations for the values: most likely value = Cm, optimistic = Co, pessimistic = Cp. Therefore the cost estimate formula looks like: $Ce = Co + 4Cm + Cp / 6$. This is more simply expressed by the old PERT formula of: $O + 4ML + P / 6$.

Many organizations use an established chart of accounts for financial tracking and reporting. It is good practice to code each cost estimate in alignment with the organization's chart of accounts (or with a project-specific chart of accounts, if an existing one is not available). This can facilitate financial tracking and reporting across the project life cycle.

FINANCIAL ACCOUNTING TERMS

Study Tips

As a project manager, you may be expected to work closely at times with financial accounting professionals, primarily to support the cost budgeting, tracking, reporting, and analysis aspects of your project. Therefore, it is very useful to have a general understanding of key accounting terms.

Here are the associated financial accounting terms you are most likely to encounter:

- **Accelerated Depreciation** = Costs amortized over a period of time at some faster rate than straight-line depreciation

- **Benefit Cost Ratio (BCR):** BCR < 1 = costs greater than benefits, BCR > 1 = benefits greater than costs, BCR = 1 means costs equal benefits

- **Direct Costs** = Costs that are directly applied to work on the project

- **Fixed Costs** = Nonrecurring costs that don't change in proportion to the amount of work. One-time setup/teardown costs, special training costs, etc.

- **Indirect Costs** = Overhead items. These are costs typically incurred to cover general administration costs across an organization.

- **Internal Rate of Return (IRR)** = In essence, IRR may be viewed as the interest rate an organization will realize on the money invested in a project.

- **Law of Diminishing Returns** = The more you increasingly put in, the less benefit you increasingly get out. For example: devoting 100 hours of guided study and preparation to pass a certification exam may ensure a passing score of 150. Spending 200 hours may ensure a score of 160. Spending 400 hours may ensure a score of 165. In this example, 100 hours is sufficient to achieve the goal. The first doubling of effort (100 hours to 200 hours) returns only a 5% improvement. The second doubling of effort (200 hours to 400 hours) returns even less, a 2.5% improvement.

- **Net Present Value (NPV)** = The value today of all associated cash flows in the future. It is calculated by adding all of the Present Values (PVs), by accounting period (see Present Value below). For example, if a project is expected to finish two years from now, there may be eight quarterly accounting periods. The NPV equals the sum of the eight quarterly PVs.

- **Opportunity Cost** = The loss associated with deciding to not select a project

- **Payback Period** = The time to recover costs

- **Present Value (PV)** = The value today of cash flows in the future

- **Present Value = FV / (1 + r)n,** where r = interest rate, n = number of time periods, and FV = future value

- **Straight Line Depreciation** = Costs amortized by an equal amount each year

- **Sunk Costs** = Expended costs. Special Note: Accounting standards suggest that sunk costs should not be considered when deciding to continue with a troubled project.

- **Value Analysis** = The systematic use of appropriate techniques to find a less costly way to accomplish the same scope of work

- **Variable Costs** = Costs that change in proportion to the amount of materials, supplies, equipment, and labor applied to the project. More labor, more costs. More supplies, more costs. And so on

- **Working Capital** = The amount of money an organization has available to invest

COST ESTIMATING CONVENTIONS

> ### Study Tips
>
> Estimating cost is a comprehensive professional discipline, with its own rich body of knowledge, processes, and techniques. As a project manager, you may be expected to understand some of the conventions widely accepted in the cost estimating profession.

Here are seven essential cost estimating definitions you may encounter.

- **Order of Magnitude Estimate (or Rough Order of Magnitude [ROM]):** This is one of the three standard project estimating categories. It defines the reliability of an estimate to be ±50%.

- **Budget(ary) Estimate:** This is the second of the three standard project estimating categories. It generally defines the reliability of an estimate to be ±25%.

- **Definitive Estimate:** This is the third of the three standard project estimating categories. It defines the reliability of an estimate to be ±10%.

- **Life Cycle Costing:** Life Cycle Costing is an important concept to factor into project planning. It suggests that post-project operating costs should be carefully considered when planning project strategies. The intent is to avoid strategies that will lower immediate project costs in such a way that they will increase post-project operating costs.

- **Analogous Estimating (top-down):** Analogous Estimating (also termed "top-down estimating") typically involves basing an estimate on a known previous activity performed in the past. Analogous estimates are relatively quick to perform and inexpensive, because no detailed estimating protocols are necessary. All that is involved is recalling history. Analogous estimates are also the least reliable, typically proving to have a significant margin of error after-the-fact.

- **Bottom-up Estimating:** Bottom-up Estimating generally produces the most reliable estimates, but is more costly and time consuming than analogous estimating. Typically, bottom-up estimating is performed by developing detailed estimates for each activity at the Work Package level of the WBS. They are then rolled-up to derive a project total.

- **Chart of Accounts:** Most performing organizations use an established chart of accounts for financial tracking and reporting. It is good practice to code each cost estimate in alignment with the organization's chart of accounts (or with a project-specific chart of accounts, if an existing one is not available). This can help significantly to facilitate financial tracking and reporting across the project life cycle.

PROCESS ELEMENTS

The Estimate Costs process has the following Inputs:

- **Scope Baseline**   Scope Baseline = the approved project scope statement + the WBS + the WBS Dictionary

- **Project Schedule**   Graphic presentation illustrating planned start and planned finish dates for each activity

- **Human Resource Plan**   Describes how and when human resources will be applied to the project team (including personnel rates, staffing attributes, etc.)

- **Risk Register**   List of identified risks and their mitigating costs

- **Enterprise Environmental Factors**   Consideration factors such as culture, systems, procedures, and industry standards (i.e. market conditions and published commercial data)

- **Organizational Process Assets**   Consideration cost factors such as policies, templates, historical information, and Lessons Learned

The Estimate Costs process uses the following Tools & Techniques:

- **Expert Judgment**   Expert technical and/or managerial judgment (from any qualified source)

- **Analogous Estimating**   Using actual results from a previous project to base current estimates

- **Parametric Estimating**   Use of project parameters to calculate predicted costs

- **Bottom-Up Estimating**   Deriving a project total by estimating individual activities, then rolling-up the summary

- **Three-Point Estimates**   Factoring most likely, optimistic, and pessimistic estimates to derive a forecasted estimate

- **Reserve Analysis**   Determining appropriate amount of contingency reserve to compensate for cost risk

- **Cost of Quality**   Total costs incurred to achieve project quality (conformance to requirements)

- **Project Management Estimating Software**   Cost estimating software applications, spreadsheets, simulations, and statistical tools

- **Vendor Bid Analysis**   Analyzing vendor bids (in competitive bid situations) to determine project costs

The Estimate Costs process has the following Outputs:

- **Activity Cost Estimates**   A quantitative assessment of the probable costs required to complete an activity

- **Basis of Estimates**   Documentation that supports the cost estimates by defining how the estimates were derived including assumptions and constraints

- **Project Document Updates**   Updates to other project documentation (i.e. Risk Register)

Estimate Costs (7.1)
This process approximates the costs of resources needed to complete project activities

Inputs	Tools and Techniques	Outputs
• Scope Baseline • Project Schedule • Human Resource Plan • Risk Register • Enterprise Environmental Factors • Organizational Process Assets	• Expert Judgment • Analogous Estimating • Parametric Estimating • Bottom-up Estimating • Three-Point Estimates • Reserve Analysis • Cost of Quality • Project Management Estimating Software • Vendor Bid Analysis	• Activity Cost Estimate • Basis of Estimates • Project Document Updates

TSI Study Aid
This chart is part of the study aid poster series available at www.truesolutions.com.

PROCESS DOCUMENTS

Two important documents come from the Estimate Costs process. First and foremost the project manager will create a Cost Estimate for the project. The Cost Estimate is usually provided in a spreadsheet format using one or more automated tools.

Task Description	Cost	Work Package #	Control Account	Project Cost	Contingency Reserve (Knowns)	Project Baseline	Accuracy Estimate
Develop Prelim Scope	$200						This Budget Estimate is considered the Order of Magnitude estimate with an accuracy of -50%, +100%. Date of Estimate: June 17, 2006
Develop Project Charter	$200	A001			$200		
Develop Project Scope	$400						
Develop Schedule	$300						
Validate Controls	$200						
Finalize Project Plan	$200	A002			$400		
Manage Project Execution	$1,000						
Perform Work	$2,000	B001	8840	$3,500	$500	$4,600	
Perform Change Control	$500						
Measure Performance	$400	B002	8875	$900	$100	$1,000	
Deliver Product	$1,000						
Obtain Formal Acceptance	$200						
Archive Information	$200	B003	8874	$1,400	$400	$1,800	
Totals				$5,800	$1,600	$7,400	

In addition to the Cost Estimate for the project, the project manager will create and document a Cost Management Plan. The Cost Management Plan defines how costs will be managed for the project. Elements that are included in the Cost Management Plan include:

• Precision Level to be used

• Units of Measure

• Control Thresholds

• Change Control Procedures

• Earned Value Rules for performance reporting

• Reporting Formats

• Process Descriptions to be used for Cost Management

Cost Management Plan

Project Name:		
Prepared by:		
Date:		
Person(s) authorized to request cost changes (see Cost Change Request):		

Name:	Title:	Location:
Name:	Title:	Location:
Name:	Title:	Location:

Person(s) to whom Cost Change Request forms must be submitted for approval:

Name:	Title:	Location:
Name:	Title:	Location:
Name:	Title:	Location:

Acceptable reasons for changes in Project Cost *(e.g., approved scope changes, increased raw materials costs, etc.)*:

Describe how you will calculate and report on the projected impact of any cost changes *(time, quality, etc.)*:

Describe any other aspects of how changes to the Project Cost will be managed:

©Copyright 2009 True Solutions, Inc.
5001 LBJ Freeway, Suite 125-B Dallas, Texas 75244
Tel: 972.770.0900 Fax 972.770.0922 www.truesolutions.com

COMMON PROCESS TASKS

The following is a list of the common tasks associated with the Estimate Costs process:

- Develop your project cost estimates at an appropriate level of detail

- Identify and evaluate inputs to your estimating cost process

- Understand the differences between cost estimating and cost pricing

- Identify and document appropriate estimating cost methods

- Evaluate inputs to your cost baseline development process

- Utilize multiple cost baselines to evaluate different aspects of your project cost performance over time

- Verify that your cost estimates are complete and associated with specific resource requirements

- Develop your Cost Change Control Plan

- Identify your performance measurement techniques

THINK ABOUT IT

Instructions Think about how this project management process is defined, used, and documented in your organization.

Compare your organization's use of this process to the PMI® definition.

Think about how this process is defined, used and documented in your organization. Write a brief description of how you use this process:

_____

_____

_____

_____

_____

_____

What specific Inputs, Tools or Techniques do you use as part of this process in your organization?

_____

_____

_____

_____

_____

_____

Are the outcomes from this process different in your organization or experiences?

_____

_____

_____

_____

_____

MUST KNOW CONCEPTS

. . . .

1 The Estimate Costs process is applied to develop cost estimates for each identified project activity. Costs include direct costs for items such as labor, materials, and equipment plus indirect costs for items such as administrative overhead and contingency reserves. These estimates will ultimately be used to create the cost baseline.

2 Estimating should be performed by the person, or group of people, who are most knowledgeable about the activity, ideally by the person or people who will be doing the work.

3 Cost estimates should be prepared and documented with ranges of possible outcomes, instead of inflexible single-point values. For example, $9,300 −10% +25%.

4 An Order of Magnitude (or Rough Order of Magnitude [ROM]) Estimate defines the reliability of an estimate to be ±50%.

5 A Budget(ary) Estimate defines the reliability of an estimate to be ±25%.

6 A Definitive Estimate defines the reliability of an estimate to be ±10%.

7 Analogous Estimating (also termed "top-down estimating") typically involves basing an estimate on a known previous activity performed in the past. Analogous estimates are relatively quick to perform and inexpensive, because no detailed estimating protocols are necessary. All that is involved is recalling history. Analogous estimates are also the least reliable, typically proving to have a significant margin of error after-the-fact.

8 Bottom-up estimating generally produces the most reliable estimates, but is more costly and time-consuming than analogous estimating. Typically, bottom-up estimating is performed by developing detailed estimates for each activity at the Work Package level of the WBS. They are then rolled-up to derive a project total.

9 Life Cycle Costing is an important concept to factor into project planning. It suggests that post-project operating costs should be carefully considered when planning project strategies. The intent is to avoid strategies that will lower immediate project costs in such a way that they will increase post-project operating costs.

10 Cost and price are not the same.

11 In addition to the cost estimates themselves, the Cost Management Plan is defined as a key output of the estimating cost process. The Cost Management Plan is intended to describe how cost will be managed across the project.

12 It is helpful to document cost estimates using a coding structure aligned with some selected chart of accounts, typically the chart of accounts already in use by the performing organization.

ADDITIONAL READING
. . . .
- PMBOK Guide – Section 7.0 Introduction, Project Cost Management
- PMBOK Guide – Section 7.1 Estimate Costs

LESSON QUIZ
. . . .
Instructions   Here are some questions to help reinforce your learning. Complete this quiz from memory to the best of your ability. For each question, circle or check your selected answer on this page or a separate piece of paper. When complete, check your results by comparing your answers to the preferred answers provided in Appendix A.

Please note that Knowledge Check questions are not actual PMP Exam questions. These questions are intended to reinforce key terms, concepts, and themes. While these Knowledge Check questions are typical of what you can expect on your PMP Exam, many actual PMP Exam questions are more in-depth, designed to challenge your judgment (not rote memory) in applying concepts, processes, and methodologies.

1. Life cycle costing:
   A. Is a financial accounting term that will not likely appear on the PMP Exam
   B. Represents an important planning concept that suggests it is not advisable to develop cost-lowering project strategies at the expense of creating higher post-project operating costs
   C. Includes labor, materials, supplies, and equipment plus indirect costs such as general overhead and administration
   D. Is a highly reliable estimating technique that typically involves developing detailed cost estimates at the Work Package level of the WBS, by the person who will be doing the actual work

2. When a project manager prepares cost estimates during the initiation phase, what is the range of a rough order of magnitude (ROM)?
   A. ±75%
   B. ±40%
   C. ±50%
   D. ±25%

3. Estimating costs Tools & Techniques include which of the following:
   A. Analogous estimating, bottom-up estimating, and chart of accounts
   B. Bottom-up estimating, parametric modeling, and activity duration estimating
   C. Analogous estimating, bottom-up estimating, and parametric estimating
   D. Bottom-up estimating, parametric estimating, and estimating publications

4. Which of the following statements is least true?
   A. The estimating cost process is applied to create the cost baseline.
   B. The estimating cost process is applied to develop cost estimates for each schedule activity.
   C. Costs can include labor, materials, equipment, supplies, variable costs, indirect costs, and direct costs.
   D. The project Cost Management Plan is developed as part of estimating costs process.

5. Which of the following statements is most true?
   A. Price and cost are essentially interchangeable.
   B. Price includes all direct project costs, whereas cost includes all indirect project costs.
   C. Price and cost are not the same.
   D. Price should be considered as life cycle costing factor, whereas costs should not.

6. When reporting cost estimates:
   A. It is preferred to report them with ranges of possible outcomes, as opposed to inflexible, single-point values
   B. It is preferred to report them using some form of parametric modeling
   C. It is preferred to report them as definitive estimates
   D. It is preferred to report them as ROM estimates

7. A coding structure for individual project cost categories generally describes what?
   A. Analogous estimating
   B. Chart of accounts
   C. Quantitative cost analysis
   D. Parametric modeling

8. Cost estimates are best developed by:
   A. The project team
   B. The project manager
   C. The project cost engineer
   D. The person, or people, who will be doing the actual work

9. One estimate cost technique involves developing detailed estimates at the Work Package level of the WBS, then rolling them up to derive the project's total cost. This technique also tends to produce estimates with higher reliability. What is this technique commonly called?
   A. Analogous (top-down) estimating
   B. Parametric estimating
   C. Bottom-up estimating
   D. Probabilistic estimating

End of Lesson 19

20

Lesson 20
Determine Budget

Objectives

At the end of this lesson, you will be able to:

- Describe the purpose of the Determine Budget process
- Describe the Inputs, Tools & Techniques, and Outputs of the Determine Budget process
- Understand the tools used to develop the Project Cost Performance Baseline
- Understand how the Project Cost Performance Baseline is documented

Roadmap to the PMBOK Guide

	Initiating	Planning	Executing	M & C	Closing
Integration					
Scope					
Time					
Cost		■			
Quality					
Human Resources					
Communications					
Risk					
Procurement					

The Performance Measurement Baseline (PMB) defined in Determine Budget will be used throughout the project as the guide for monitoring cost performance.

The Determine Budget process is applied to formally aggregate all activity (and/or Work Package) cost estimates into a cohesive project budget and approved cost baseline.

The project budget is sometimes termed the "Cost Performance Baseline" or "Performance Measurement Baseline" (PMB). Formally, the cost performance baseline is the time-phased budget. It is used to monitor and measure project cost performance across remaining project phases. When measuring the project using Earned Value Techniques, the Performance Measurement Baseline is represented by the Budget at Complete (BAC) value. Cost performance baselines are typically illustrated using graphs. Plotted cost baselines usually form an S-curve appearance.

Management and contingency reserves are established in the Determine Budget Process. However, reserves are excluded in the baseline.

PROCESS ELEMENTS

The Determine Budget process has the following Inputs:

- **Activity Cost Estimates**   a quantitative assessment of the probable costs required to complete an activity

- **Basis of Estimates**   Documentation that supports the cost estimates by defining how the estimates were derived

- **Scope Baseline**   Scope Baseline = the approved Project Scope Statement + the WBS + the WBS Dictionary

- **Project Schedule**   Graphic presentation illustrating planned start and planned finish dates for each activity

- **Resource Calendars**   Information on the availability of resources over the planned activity duration

- **Contracts**   Applicable contract information for products and services to be purchased from external sources

- **Organizational Process Assets**   Consideration factors such as cost policies, procedures, guidelines, and cost budgeting tools and reporting methods

The Determine Budget process uses the following Tools & Techniques:

- **Cost Aggregation**   The process of aggregating schedule activity cost estimates by Work Packages

- **Reserve Analysis**   Determining the appropriate amount of contingency and management reserves to compensate for project risk

- **Expert Judgment** Expert technical and/or managerial judgment (from any qualified source)

- **Historical Relationships** Analogous and Parametric Models used for cost estimation

- **Funding Limit Reconciliation** The scheduling of work to avoid large variations in periodic expenditures

The Determine Budget process has the following Outputs:

- **Cost Performance Baseline** The time-phased budget used to measure, monitor, and control project cost performance : also known as Budget at Completion (BAC)

- **Project Funding Requirements** Simply the funding needed and when it will be needed

- **Project Document Updates** Updates to other project documentation (i.e. Risk Register, cost estimates, and project schedule)

Determine Budget (7.2)
This process aggregates individual activity costs to establish the project's Cost Performance Baseline

Inputs	Tools and Techniques	Outputs
• Activity Cost Estimates • Basis of Estimates • Scope Baseline • Project Schedule • Resource Calendars • Contracts • Organizational Process Assets	• Cost Aggregation • Reserve Analysis • Expert Judgment • Historical Relationships • Funding Limit Reconciliation	• Cost Performance Baseline • Project Funding Requirements • Project Document Updates

PROCESS DOCUMENTS

The main document that is created as a result of the Determine Budget process is the Project Budget Baseline — also known as the Cost Performance Baseline or the Budget at Completion (BAC). This Cost Performance Baseline is the best estimate of all costs of resources, reserves, and other costs for the overall project. The Cost Performance Baseline is a progressively elaborated document based on original cost estimates. The Cost Performance Baseline could be depicted as a spreadsheet or as an S-curve graphic.

Task Description	Cost	Work Package Cost	Control Account	Project Cost	Contingency Reserve (Knowns)	Project Baseline	Management Reserve (Unknowns)	Total Project Budget
Develop Prelim Scope	$200							
Develop Project Charter	$200	$400			$200		$100	
Develop Project Scope	$400							
Develop Schedule	$300							
Validate Controls	$200							
Finalize Project Plan	$200	$1,100			$400		$200	
Manage Project Execution	$1,000							
Perform Work	$2,000	$3,000	8840	$3,500	$500	$4,600	$500	$5,400
Perform Change Control	$500							
Measure Performance	$400	$900	8875	$900	$100	$1,000	$-0-	$1,000
Deliver Product	$1,000							
Obtain Formal Acceptance	$200							
Archive Information	$200	$1,400	8874	$1,400	$400	$1,800	$-0-	$1,800
Totals				$5,800	$1,600	$7,400	$800	$8,200

COMMON PROCESS TASKS

The following is a list of the common tasks associated with the Determine Budget process:

- Allocate your overall costs to individual activities

- Utilize a chart of accounts to associate your quantitative cost assessments with related resource requirements

- Determine contingency and management reserves

- Develop your cost baseline to establish cost performance guidelines

THINK ABOUT IT

Instructions Think about how this project management process is defined, used, and documented in your organization.

Compare your organization's use of this process to the PMI® definition.

Use this exercise to compare how you practice project management to what is specified in the *PMBOK® Guide Fourth Edition*.

Think about how this process is defined, used and documented in your organization. Write a brief description of how you use this process:

_____

_____

_____

What specific Inputs, Tools or Techniques do you use as part of this process in your organization?

_____

_____

_____

_____

_____

Are the outcomes from this process different in your organization or experiences?

_____

_____

_____

_____

_____

_____

MUST KNOW CONCEPTS

1. The Determine Budget process is applied to formally aggregate all activity cost estimates into a cohesive project budget, also known as the Cost Performance Baseline.

2. The primary deliverable (Output) of the Determine Budget process is the Cost Performance Baseline (performance measurement baseline or PMB).

3. The Cost Performance Baseline is the project's time-phased budget.

4. The Cost Performance Baseline is used to monitor and measure project cost performance across project phases.

5. Cost Performance Baselines are typically illustrated using graphs. Plotted Cost Performance Baselines usually form an S-curve.

6. Reserves are excluded from the Cost Performance Baseline.

ADDITIONAL READING

• PMBOK Guide – Section 7.2 Determine Budgets

LESSON QUIZ

. . . .

Instructions   Here are some questions to help reinforce your learning. Complete this quiz from memory to the best of your ability. For each question, circle or check your selected answer on this page or a separate piece of paper. When complete, check your results by comparing your answers to the preferred answers provided in Appendix A.

Please note that Knowledge Check questions are not actual PMP Exam questions. These questions are intended to reinforce key terms, concepts, and themes. While these Knowledge Check questions are typical of what you can expect on your PMP Exam, many actual PMP Exam questions are more in-depth, designed to challenge your judgment (not rote memory) in applying concepts, processes, and methodologies.

1. The Determine Budget process is applied to:
    A. Formally estimate the cost of each identified Work Package
    B. Formally organize all activity cost estimates into a cohesive project budget
    C. Formally document the estimated cost of each WBS Work Package
    D. Formally document the estimated cost of each activity identified on the project's Activity List

2. Your project team has just completed development of the Cost Performance Baseline. The Cost Performance Baseline is:
    A. A formal document that describes how Earned Value Management (EVM) will be applied to measure and report project cost performance
    B. A formal document that describes how project cost variances will be managed
    C. A time-phased budget, used to monitor and measure cost performance
    D. A time-phased budget, used as supporting detail to justify activity cost estimates

3. Determine Budget Inputs include all the following except:
    A. Cost Performance Baseline
    B. Activity cost estimates
    C. Resource calendars
    D. Project schedule

4. Which of the following statements is most true?
    A. Cost Performance Baselines are typically illustrated using graphs. Plotted cost baselines usually form an S-curve.
    B. Cost Performance Baselines are typically documented informally, as they are likely to change frequently.
    C. Cost Performance Baselines are typically documented as a subsidiary plan to the overall project plan.
    D. Cost Performance Baselines are typically illustrated using Gantt charts (bar charts) or milestones charts.

End of Lesson 20

Lesson 21
Plan Quality

Objectives

At the end of this lesson, you will be able to:

* Describe the purpose of the Plan Quality process
* Describe the Inputs, Tools & Techniques, and Outputs of the Plan Quality process
* Understand fundamental quality definitions

Roadmap to the PMBOK Guide

	Initiating	Planning	Executing	M & C	Closing
Integration					
Scope					
Time					
Cost					
Quality		▓▓			
Human Resources					
Communications					
Risk					
Procurement					

Quality means conformance to identified requirements and fitness for use as defined by the functional product specification.

The Plan Quality process is applied to identify which quality standards are applicable to the project and then determine how to satisfy them. Quality planning is often applied in parallel with other processes during project planning.

The term "quality" means different things to different people, depending on their specific orientation and application environment. For our purposes in project management, quality means delivering precisely what is promised. When a project team delivers on-time, within budget, and has satisfied all scope requirements, then quality has been achieved.

It is important to understand, quality must be "planned-in" to the project, not "inspected in".

It is also helpful to understand that the terms "quality" and "grade" are not identical. Quality is the totality of characteristics to satisfy requirements. Grade is a measurement of technical characteristics. For instance, a high-grade product would be characterized by having many complex features. A low-grade product would have few features. Both could be of high-quality. When speaking of quality and grade, low-quality is a problem, low-grade is not.

QUALITY TERMS

The following are the key terms and concepts related to Project Quality:

- **Quality Policy** An organization's quality commitment is generally referred to as its "quality policy." The quality policy originates from the highest management levels in the organization. A corporate Quality Management Manual could serve to document the quality policy. In some projects, the organization's quality policy can be adopted directly, to serve the project's quality needs. In other projects, it may be necessary to create a project-specific quality policy. In all projects, the quality policy must be communicated to stakeholders and its requirements must be met.

- **Cost of Quality (COQ)** The cost of quality is defined as a quality tool/ technique. It includes all costs expended to achieve product/service quality objectives. Quality = conformance to requirements. These costs typically include prevention costs (planned-in quality), appraisal costs (quality control) and failure costs (warranty, rework).

- **Design of Experiments (DOE)** Design of experiments is a quality tool/ technique that employs statistical methods to analyze trade-offs. For instance, the project team may wish to evaluate the schedule/cost trade-offs associated with using senior engineers (higher costs, lower risks, possible shorter duration) opposed to using junior engineers (lower costs, higher risks, possible longer duration). Simulations (experiments) may be run to determine the optimum combination of junior engineers and senior engineers.

- **Flowcharting**   Flowcharts (also termed "process maps" or "systems flowcharts") are often used as a quality tool/technique. Flowcharts are graphical illustrations that show how elements of a system relate. A project network diagram is a flowchart.

- **Cause-and-Effect Diagrams (also called "fishbone diagrams" or "Ishikawa diagrams")**   A cause-and-effect diagram is a specific type of flowchart. These types of diagrams are often used to illustrate how different factors are linked to problems and are especially helpful for generating ideas when analyzing quality problems.

- **Benchmarking**   Benchmarking is defined as a quality tool/technique. Benchmarks are established standards and/or practices that may be used for comparison when the project team establishes its standards for measuring project performance. Benchmarks may be internal or external to the performing organization.

- **ISO 9000**   ISO 9000 is an international quality standard used by organizations to ensure adherence to their own quality policies. ISO 9000 is part of The International Organization for Standardization's 9000 series. ISO 9000 is a brief document, not a detailed QA/QC policy. ISO 9000 certified organizations are still responsible for developing their own specific quality policies. ISO 9000 certification simply ensures adherence to those organization-specific quality policies.

- **Just-in-Time (JIT)**   JIT is the manufacturing management concept/ practice of maintaining minimal inventory (ideally zero). JIT implementation typically requires higher quality standards to compensate for lower inventories (high failure rates cannot be tolerated in a JIT environment).

- **Quality Metrics (also called "operational definitions")**   Metrics are the specific parameters for measuring quality performance. These are the project elements selected for measurement and the quality control system that will be used to measure them.

- **Process Improvement**   Project teams should be ever-vigilant in looking for ways to improve project performance (cost reduction, schedule reduction) across the entire life cycle, not just during planning. Such improvements increase overall benefits to project stakeholders. This is process improvement. Process improvement is any action taken to improve efficiency and effectiveness in project performance.

- **Total Quality Management (TQM)**   TQM is a concept/practice intended to help organizations achieve quality improvement objectives.

PROCESS ELEMENTS

The Plan Quality process has the following Inputs:

- **Scope Baseline** Scope Baseline = the approved Project Scope Statement + the WBS + the WBS Dictionary

- **Stakeholder Register** A document identifying all project stakeholder information

- **Cost Performance Baseline** The time-phased budget used to measure, monitor, and control project cost performance

- **Schedule Baseline** Specific version of the project schedule, accepted and approved by the team as the project's schedule baseline

- **Risk Register** List of identified risks

- **Enterprise Environmental Factors** Consideration factors such as: government regulations, rules, standards, guidelines, and conditions of the project/product which may affect quality

- **Organizational Process Assets** Consideration factors such as quality policies, procedures, guidelines, historical databases, and Lessons Learned

The Plan Quality process uses the following Tools & Techniques:

- **Cost-Benefit Analysis** The use of financial measures to assess the desirability of identified alternatives

- **Cost of Quality** Total costs incurred to achieve project quality (cost of conformance and cost of nonconformance)

- **Control Charts** Charts used to determine if processes are stable and performing in a predictable manner

- **Benchmarking** Comparing performance to a selected "standard" primarily to generate ideas for improvement

- **Design of Experiments (DOE)** A statistical method to help identify optimal solutions, factoring-in specific variables

- **Statistical Sampling** Statistical analysis using a small group from an entire population

- **Flowcharting** Diagramming methods that can help analyze how problems in a system occur

- **Proprietary Quality Management Methodologies** Other quality management methodologies (for example, Lean 6 Sigma)

- **Additional Quality Planning Tools** Affinity diagrams, force field analysis, matrix diagrams, and others

The Plan Quality process has the following Outputs:

- **Quality Management Plan** Describes how the team will implement the organization's quality policy

- **Quality Metrics** Operational definitions. Project elements, and how they are to be measured by quality control

- **Quality Checklists** Structured forms used to verify that a set of required steps has been performed in quality control

- **Process Improvement Plan** Describes the steps for analyzing processes to eliminate wasteful activities (i.e. boundaries, configuration, metrics, and targets for improved performance)

- **Project Document Updates** Updates to other project documentation (i.e. Stakeholder Register and RAMs)

Plan Quality (8.1)		
This process identifies project quality standards and defines how they will be satisfied		
Inputs	**Tools and Techniques**	**Outputs**
• Scope Baseline • Stakeholder Register • Cost Performance Baseline • Schedule Baseline • Risk Register • Enterprise Environmental Factors • Organizational Process Assets	• Cost-Benefit Analysis • Cost of Quality • Control Charts • Benchmarking • Design of Experiments • Statistical Sampling • Flowcharting • Proprietary Quality Management Methodologies • Additional Quality Planning Tools	• Quality Management Plan • Quality Metrics • Quality Checklists • Process Improvement Plan • Project Document Updates

TSI Study Aid
This chart is part of the study aid poster series available at www.truesolutions.com.

PROCESS DOCUMENTS

Two documents are critical outputs from the Plan Quality process: the Quality Management Plan and the Process Improvement Plan.

The Quality Management Plan depicts (as a minimum):

• Quality Organization

• Roles and Responsibilities (toward quality actions)

- Resources Required

- Quality Assurance actions planned

- Quality Control actions planned

- Continuous Improvement Plan

The Quality Management Plan serves to describe how the project team will implement its organization's quality policy. The Quality Management Plan may be brief or comprehensive, whichever best suits the size and complexity of the project. The Quality Management Plan will become a subsidiary plan to the overall Project Management Plan. A Quality Management Plan template is shown on the next page.

The Process Improvement Plan depicts (as a minimum):

- Process Boundaries (owner, purpose, process description)

- Process Configuration (flowcharts)

- Process Metrics (control parameters)

- Target for Process Improvement

The Process Improvement Plan details the steps for analyzing processes to identify wasteful activities, thus increasing stakeholder value. The Process Improvement Plan may be brief or comprehensive whichever suits the size and complexity of the project. The Process Improvement Plan will become a subsidiary plan to the overall project Management Plan.

COMMON PROCESS TASKS

The following is a list of the common tasks associated with the Plan Quality process:

- Develop your project quality policies and ensure they are aligned with your organization's quality policy

- Utilize standard project quality Tools & Techniques

- Develop your project quality metrics and performance checklists

- Develop your project Quality Management Plan

- Evaluate your project quality control, assurance, and improvement issues

- Develop your process improvement plan

Quality Management Plan

Project Name:	
Prepared by:	
Date:	
Description of Project Quality System:	

Describe in as much detail as needed specifically what will be required in each of the following areas to manage quality on this project:

ORGANIZATIONAL STRUCTURE

ROLES AND RESPONSIBILITIES

PROCEDURES

PROCESSES

RESOURCES

Describe how each of the following aspects of quality management will be addressed on this project:

QUALITY CONTROL

QUALITY ASSURANCE

QUALITY IMPROVEMENT

TSI Application Aid

This form is available individually or as a set from *www.truesolutions.com.*

THINK ABOUT IT

. . . .

Instructions Think about how this project management process is defined, used, and documented in your organization.

Use this exercise to compare to how you practice project management to what is specified in the *PMBOK® Guide Fourth Edition.*

Think about how this process is defined, used and documented in your organization. Write a brief description of how you use this process:

_____

_____

_____

_____

_____

_____

What specific Inputs, Tools or Techniques do you use as part of this process in your organization?

_____

_____

_____

_____

_____

_____

Are the outcomes from this process different in your organization or experiences?

_____

_____

_____

_____

_____

_____

MUST KNOW CONCEPTS

. . . .

1 The Plan Quality process is applied to identify the quality standards that are applicable to the project then determine how to satisfy them.

2 The primary outputs of the Plan Quality process are the project's Quality Management Plan and the Process Improvement Plan.

3 In project management, quality means delivering precisely what is promised. When a project team delivers on-time, within budget, and has satisfied all scope requirements, then high quality has been achieved.

4 Quality must be planned-in to a project, not inspected-in.

5 Quality and grade are not the same. Low-quality is a problem; low-grade is not.

6 A quality policy is an organization's quality commitment. Many times, a quality policy is documented in the form of an organization's Quality Assurance Manual.

7 Cost of quality includes all costs expended to achieve product/service quality objectives.

8 Design of experiments is a quality tool/technique that employs statistical methods to analyze trade-offs.

9 Flowcharts (also termed process maps or systems flowcharts) are graphical illustrations that show how elements of a system relate.

10 Cause-and-effect diagrams (also termed "fishbone diagrams" or "Ishikawa diagrams") are often used to illustrate how different factors are linked to problems and are especially helpful in generating ideas when analyzing quality problems.

11 Benchmarks are established standards and/or practices that may be used for comparison when the project team establishes its standards for measuring project performance.

12 ISO 9000 is an international quality standard used by organizations to ensure adherence to their own quality policies.

13 Just in Time (JIT) is the manufacturing management concept/practice of maintaining minimal inventory (ideally zero).

14 Quality metrics (also called "operational definitions") are the specific parameters a project team selects for measuring quality performance.

15 Process improvement is any action taken to improve efficiency and effectiveness in project performance, providing increased benefits to project stakeholders.

16 Total Quality Management (TQM) is a concept/practice intended to help organizations achieve quality improvement objectives.

ADDITIONAL READING
· ·
- PMBOK Guide – Section 8.0 Introduction, Project Quality Management
- PMBOK Guide – Section 8.1 Plan Quality

LESSON QUIZ
· ·
Instructions   Here are some questions to help reinforce your learning. Complete this quiz from memory to the best of your ability. When complete, check your results by comparing your answers to the preferred answers provided in Appendix A.

Please note that Knowledge Check questions are not actual PMP Exam questions. These questions are intended to reinforce key terms, concepts, and themes.

1. The Plan Quality process is applied to:
   A. Help ensure high-grade, high-quality project performance
   B. Create quality improvement
   C. Develop the project's cause-and-effect diagram
   D. Identify which quality standards are applicable to the project, then determine how to satisfy them

2. Which statement is most true?
   A. ISO 9000 is a comprehensive quality policy that can be adopted by any organization to serve as their Quality Assurance Manual.
   B. Quality must be planned-in to a project, not inspected-in.
   C. JIT and TQM are two quality standards that offer international certification for quality organizations.
   D. Just in Time (JIT) is an international quality standard that emphasizes low inventory.

3. Plan Quality Tools & Techniques include:
   A. Cost-benefit analysis, benchmarking, and Cost of Quality (COQ)
   B. Quality baseline, benchmarking, and Cost of Quality (COQ)
   C. Cost-benefit analysis, quality checklists, and Cost of Quality (COQ)
   D. Cost-benefit analysis, benchmarking, and quality metrics

4. Which of the following statements is least true?
    A. Flowcharts (also termed "process maps" or "systems flowcharts") are graphical illustrations that show how elements of a system relate.
    B. Cause-and-effect diagrams (also termed "fishbone diagrams" or "Ishikawa diagrams") are often used to illustrate how different factors are linked to problems and are especially helpful in generating ideas when analyzing quality problems.
    C. Cost of Quality (COQ) includes all costs expended to achieve product/ services quality objectives.
    D. Grade is another term for quality in some application areas. The two terms may be used interchangeably.

5. You and your project team have been studying the performance of a recently completed project that was a big success in your organization. That project was very similar in nature to yours. You decide to use several successful milestone achievements from the earlier project to set measurement standards for your own project. This is an example of:
    A. Historical data
    B. Using templates
    C. Benchmarking
    D. Lessons learned

6. You and your project management team completed the project on-time, within budget, and you successfully delivered all that was defined in the scope of work, precisely to specification … but an executive in the organization is not pleased. Based on this scenario, which of the following statements is most true?
    A. You and your project team have achieved quality.
    B. You and your project team must have missed some important project objective. A company executive is displeased.
    C. You and your project team should immediately request a meeting with the project sponsor.
    D. You and your project team should immediately plan a job search.

End of Lesson 21

Lesson 22
Plan Risk Management

Objectives

At the end of this lesson, you will be able to:

- Describe the purpose of the Plan Risk Management process
- Describe the Inputs, Tools & Techniques, and Outputs of the Plan Risk Management process
- Know the definition of risk to be used for project management
- Understand the categories of risk to be considered on the project

Roadmap to the PMBOK Guide

	Initiating	Planning	Executing	M & C	Closing
Integration					
Scope					
Time					
Cost					
Quality					
Human Resources					
Communications					
Risk		▓			
Procurement					

If your organization utilizes a comprehensive risk management methodology, your organizational processes will normally be utilized on your project. The PMP candidate should know the six Risk Management processes thoroughly for the PMP Exam.

Project Risk Management is a knowledge area that has been largely overlooked in past years, but is now recognized as one of the most important areas in all of modern project management.

Risk infiltrates each and every aspect of a project. Even though risk is found everywhere in the project environment, it can be identified, analyzed, and managed to minimize potential negative impacts and maximize potential positive impacts.

There are six closely associated processes in Project Risk Management. The first is Plan Risk Management. In Plan Risk Management, we decide how to approach and plan our risk management activities for a particular project. The Plan Risk Management process is applied to develop the project's Risk Management Plan.

There are several important things to understand concerning risk:

Study Tip

Project risk is any uncertain event or condition that, if it occurs, has a positive or negative effect on a project objective.

Project risks can be positive or negative!

Negative risks are Threats and should be avoided.
Positive risks are Opportunities and should be pursued.

PROCESS ELEMENTS

The Plan Risk Management process has the following Inputs:

- **Project Scope Statement**   Detailed description of a project's deliverables and work required to create them

- **Cost Management Plan**   Defines how risk budgets, contingencies, and management reserves will be managed

- **Communications Management Plan**   Details the management of all project communications

- **Schedule Management Plan**   Defines how schedule contingencies will be reported

- **Enterprise Environmental Factors** Consideration factors such as risk attitudes and tolerances

- **Organizational Process Assets** Consideration factors such as risk categories, risk definitions, formats, templates, roles and responsibilities, Lessons Learned, and Stakeholder Register

The Plan Risk Management process uses the following Tools & Techniques:

- **Planning Meetings and Analysis** Project team meetings held to develop the risk management plan

The Plan Risk Management process has the following Output:

- **Risk Management Plan** Describes how project risk management will be structured and performed across the project

Plan Risk Management (11.1)		
This process documents how to approach and plan risk management activities		
Inputs	**Tools and Techniques**	**Outputs**
• Project Scope Statement • Cost Management Plan • Schedule Management Plan • Communications Management Plan • Enterprise Environmental Factors • Organizational Process Assets	• Planning Meetings and Analysis	• Risk Management Plan

TSI Study Aid

This chart is part of the study aid poster series available at *www.truesolutions.com.*

PROCESS DOCUMENTS

The primary output from the Plan Risk Management process is the Risk Management Plan. The Risk Management Plan serves to document how project risk activities will be approached and planned. The Risk Management Plan can be brief or comprehensive, based on the needs of the project. The Risk Management Plan will become a subsidiary plan to the overall Project Management Plan.

Here is a possible Risk Management Plan template:

True Solutions, Inc.
Project Management Template
Volume 1: Risk Management Plan Template

Risk Management Plan

Project Name:	
Prepared by:	
Date:	
Description of Risk Management Methodology to be Used:	
Approaches	
Tools	
Data Sources	
Roles and Responsibilities:	
Risk Management Action:	
Team Leader	
Team Members	
Support	
[Add sections as needed]	
Budget:	
Timing: (Describe how risk management will relate to the project life cycle, and at what points it will be reviewed during the execution of the project)	
Risk Categories: (you can generalize here or use the Project Risk Categorization Worksheet; similar to RBS[Risk Breakdown Structure])	
Risk Probability and Impact: (you can generalize here or use the Rating Impact for a Risk)	

In conjunction with completing the Risk Management Plan, the project manager may use a worksheet of some sort to categorize potential project risks. A sample form is shown below:

COMMON PROCESS TASKS

The following is a list of the common tasks associated with the Plan Risk Management Process:

- Identify roles, responsibilities, and levels of authority for your risk management decision-making

- Review and expand your preliminary risk assessment matrix

- Develop your Risk Management Plan

- Develop the process by which your risk identification and quantification will be maintained

THINK ABOUT IT

Instructions Think about how this project management process is defined, used, and documented in your organization.

Compare your organization's use of this process to the PMI® definition.

Use this exercise to compare how you practice project management to what is specified in the *PMBOK® Guide Fourth Edition.*

Think about how this process is defined, used and documented in your organization. Write a brief description of how you use this process:

_____

_____

_____

_____

_____

_____

What specific Inputs, Tools or Techniques do you use as part of this process in your organization?

_____

_____

_____

_____

_____

Are the outcomes from this process different in your organization or experiences?

_____

_____

_____

_____

MUST KNOW CONCEPTS

1. Project risk is any uncertain event or condition that, if it occurs, has a positive or negative effect on a project objective.

2. Project risks can be positive or negative.

3. Negative risks are Threats and should be avoided.

4. Positive risks are Opportunities and should be pursued.

5. Project risk management is comprised of six closely associated processes.

6. Plan Risk Management is the first of the five processes and is applied to decide and document how project risk will be approached and planned.

7. The primary deliverable (Output) of the Plan Risk Management process is the Risk Management Plan.

ADDITIONAL READING

- PMBOK Guide – Section 11.0 Introduction, Project Risk Management
- PMBOK Guide – Section 11.1 Plan Risk Management

LESSON QUIZ

Instructions Here are some questions to help reinforce your learning. Complete this quiz from memory to the best of your ability. When complete, check your results by comparing your answers to the preferred answers provided in Appendix A.

Please note that Knowledge Check questions are not actual PMP Exam questions. These questions are intended to reinforce key terms, concepts, and themes.

1. Project risk is properly defined as:
   A. Any negative event or condition that, if it occurs, has an effect on a project objective
   B. Any cause that has a negative consequence to a project objective
   C. Any uncertain event or condition that, if it occurs, has a negative or positive effect on a project objective
   D. Any event or condition that has a negative or positive effect on a project objective

2. Which of the following statements is most incorrect?
   A. A risk has a cause and, if it occurs, a consequence
   B. There are negative risks and positive risks.
   C. Positive risks may be viewed as opportunities and should be pursued.
   D. Negative risks must be eliminated before project plan execution.

3. Plan Risk Management Inputs include all the following, except:
   A. Organizational process assets
   B. The Risk Management Plan
   C. The Project Scope Statement
   D. The communications management plan

4. The six project risk management processes are:
   A. Plan Risk Management, Identify Risk, Perform Qualitative Risk Analysis, Perform Quantitative Risk Analysis, Plan Risk Responses, and Monitor and Control Risks
   B. Plan Risk Management, Identify Risk, Perform Qualitative Risk Analysis, Perform Quantitative Risk Analysis, Perform Risk Response Planning, and Risk Avoidance
   C. Plan Risk Management, Identify Risk, Perform Qualitative Risk Analysis, Perform Probabilistic Risk Analysis, Perform Risk Response Planning, and Perform Risk Mitigation
   D. Plan Risk Management, Identify Risk, Perform Qualitative Risk Analysis, Perform Quantitative Risk Analysis, Perform Risk Mitigation, and Perform Risk Acceptance

End of Lesson 22

23

Lesson 23
Identify Risks

Objectives

At the end of this lesson, you will be able to:

- Describe the purpose of the Identify Risks process
- Describe the Inputs, Tools & Techniques, and Outputs of the Identify Risks process
- Understand methods for identifying project risk

Roadmap to the PMBOK Guide

	Initiating	Planning	Executing	M & C	Closing
Integration					
Scope					
Time					
Cost					
Quality					
Human Resources					
Communications					
Risk		▓▓			
Procurement					

Risk Identification often identifies many risks for the project. Practical considerations usually dictate that all risks cannot be addressed with a specific planned response due to time or budget constraints.

Identify Risks is the second of our five risk processes that occur in the Planning process group. The Identify Risks process is applied to determine which risks may affect the project and to document their characteristics.

The primary objective of this process is to create a list of identified risks, along with the indications that the risk has occurred or is about to occur. These indications are termed "triggers" or "risk symptoms" or "warning signs." Each identified risk will be analyzed during the application of subsequent risk management processes. To help identify as many risks as possible, many knowledgeable people should participate in the process. Several iterations are likely before an exhaustive list of risks is developed.

While most risk identification is done during planning, identifying risks is a process that should be encouraged frequently throughout the project life cycle. In many projects, new risks can surface daily.

IDENTIFY RISKS FUNDAMENTALS

First of all, remember the definition of risk: *Project risk is an uncertain event or condition that, if it occurs, has a positive or negative effect on a project objective. A risk has a cause, and if it occurs, a consequence.*

It is common in project management to encounter documented risks that are not risks at all.

Study Tip

Some project managers experience difficulty identifying actual risks. Here are a few helpful tips:

- Risk is an uncertain event or condition. Uncertainty is key. If an event or condition is certain, then it is not a risk.

- A problem is not a risk. It is a certain negative condition.

- An issue is not a risk. It is a matter to be decided.

There are four generally accepted categories of risk in project environments. These four categories are sometimes expressed as a Risk Breakdown Structure (RBS):

- **Technical, quality, performance risks**   These types of risks may be caused by a reliance on unproven technology and/or unrealistic performance goals

- **Project management risks**   These types of risks may be caused by poor use of project management disciplines

- **Organizational risks**   These types of risks may be caused by resource conflicts, incompatible goals, and/or inadequate funding

- **External risks**   These types of risks are typically caused by regulatory issues and/or natural disasters

Information-gathering techniques are useful in engaging others to help identify project risks. They include:

- **Brainstorming Sessions**   with knowledgeable people

- **Delphi Technique**   This technique solicits and shares information among experts on an anonymous basis, to build consensus without personal bias

- **Interviewing**   Simple one-on-one interviews with key people can be very productive

- **Root Cause Identification**   Investigation to determine essential causes of project risks

- **SWOT Analysis**   This is another technique for analyzing the organization's Strengths, Weaknesses, Opportunities, and Threats—a technique that can bring risks to the surface

Diagramming techniques can be applied to help identify project risks. They include:

- **Cause and Effect Diagrams (also termed "fishbone diagrams" or "Ishikawa diagrams")**   These can help identify the causes of risk

- **Systems Flowcharts (or process maps)**   Analyzing the project network diagram, for example, can bring risks to light

- **Influence Diagrams**   help identify associated causes

PROCESS ELEMENTS

The Identify Risks process has the following Inputs:

- **Risk Management Plan**   Describes how project risk management will be structured and performed across the project

- **Activity Cost Estimates**   a quantitative assessment of the probable costs required to complete an activity

- **Activity Duration Estimates**   Quantitative assessments of the likely time needed to complete each activity

- **Scope Baseline**   Scope Baseline = the approved Project Scope Statement + the WBS + the WBS Dictionary

- **Stakeholder Register** A document identifying all project stakeholder information, requirements, and classification

- **Cost Management Plan** Defines how risk budgets, contingencies, and management reserves will be managed

- **Schedule Management Plan** Defines how changes to the project schedule will be managed

- **Quality Management Plan** Describes how the team will implement the organization's quality policy

- **Project Documents** Additional project documentation that aids in identification of risks (i.e. assumptions log, work performance reports, earned value reports, network diagrams, and baselines)

- **Enterprise Environmental Factors** Consideration factors such as: published information, academic studies, published checklists, benchmarking, industry studies, and risk attitudes

- **Organizational Process Assets** Consideration factors such as project files, organizational and project process controls, risk statement templates, and Lessons Learned

The Identify Risks process uses the following Tools & Techniques:

- **Documentation Reviews** A structured review of all project documentation

- **Information Gathering Techniques** Various techniques used to help in identification of risks (i.e. brainstorming, Delphi technique, interviewing, root cause analysis)

- **Checklist Analysis** Checklists based on historical risks identified for previous similar projects

- **Assumptions Analysis** Analysis of project assumptions to identify possible risks

- **Diagramming Techniques** Risk diagramming techniques (for example, Cause and Effect diagrams, system flowcharts, influence diagrams)

- **SWOT Analysis** Strengths, Weaknesses, Opportunities, and Threats

- **Expert Judgment** Expert technical and/or managerial judgment (from any qualified source)

The Identify Risks process has the following Output:

- **Risk Register** List of identified risks

Identify Risks (11.2)
This process identifies risks associated with the project

Inputs	Tools and Techniques	Outputs
• Risk Management Plan • Activity Cost Estimates • Activity Duration Estimates • Scope Baseline • Stakeholder Register • Cost Management Plan • Schedule Management Plan • Quality Management Plan • Project Documents • Enterprise Environmental Factors • Organizational Process Assets	• Documentation Reviews • Information Gathering Techniques • Checklist Analysis • Assumptions Analysis • Diagramming Techniques • SWOT Analysis • Expert Judgment	• Risk Register

PROCESS DOCUMENTS

As an output from the Identify Risks process, the project manager and stakeholders create the Risk Register. The document created at this stage of the project is not the final Risk Register document. The current document output from Identify Risks is the preliminary list of risks for the project. Subsequent processes will make updates to this Risk Register by providing more detail.

True Solutions, Inc.
Project Management Template — Risk Register/Evaluation Grid — *TSI*

Project Name:
Prepared by:
Date:

Risk ID#	Risk Description	Risk Owner	Rating or Priority of Risk	Symptoms & Warning Signs	Root Cause	Trigger	Impact (P/I Score)	Quantitative Score	Risk Response Action Type	Response Trigger	Response Owner	Response Description	Expected Impact

COMMON PROCESS TASKS

The following is a list of the common tasks associated with the Identify Risks process:

- Identify your potential project risk events

- Identify the sources of your possible internal/external risk events

- Develop flowcharts to determine the causes and effects of risk

- Classify your potential risk events, the ranges of possible outcomes, and risk interactions anticipated during various project phases

- Identify your risk symptoms or triggers

THINK ABOUT IT

During the early days of e-commerce over the Internet, I was assigned to replace the existing project manager on a project to create a website for a paint company. What I found when I took over the project was that there was very little documentation available. Most of the project had been managed very loosely by the previous project manager and from the documentation that was available there were only a short list of project risks that had been developed.

This paint company website was planned to have all of the usual tools for the customer to find information about paint, help with choosing paint, help with applying paint, and search options to locate specific products that they could use to paint their home or business. But one particular feature was a very risky element for the entire project.

The person or persons who had collected the requirements and defined the scope for the project had included a feature to allow customers to go online and match *customized* paint colors over the Internet. Now when I began to ask the technical staff involved with the project about this, they told me this was not a problem, since the customer would be expected to have (or purchase?) a special monitor calibration tool — a special piece of hardware and software that would read the monitor colors and calibrate them so that the matching of paint would come out correctly.

I suspect that you already know the outcome of this particular project. We were not able to economically create this website feature. In the end, the customer felt like the project was a failure since they did not get the "special feature" (paint matching) that they wanted. The performing organization felt like the project was a failure since they did not get to build and maintain the special feature and since the project terminated early as a result (less money for the company). And the technical resource personnel were all disappointed since they did not get to play with the technical feature for days, weeks, and months (years?) to make it work.

Proper risk identification at the beginning of the project would have identified how difficult it would have been to build this special paint-match feature. Proper risk identification would have determined how immature the technology was and how unlikely it would be that a customer who wanted to match paint would have a monitor color calibration tool or would be willing to purchase one. Again, proper use of project management processes, in their appropriate order, would have saved everyone involved from disappointment and misuse of resources.

Contributed by Tim Bergmann, PMP

MUST KNOW CONCEPTS

1. Project risk is an uncertain event or condition that, if it occurs, has a positive or negative effect on a project objective. A risk has a cause and, if it occurs, a consequence.

2. The Identify Risks process is applied to determine which risks may affect the project and to document their characteristics.

3. Identifying risks is a process that should be encouraged frequently throughout the project life cycle. In many projects, new risks can surface daily.

4. There are four generally accepted categories of risk in project environments: technical risks (technical, quality, performance), project management risks, organizational risks, and external risks.

5. Information gathering techniques used to help identify project risks include: brainstorming, Delphi technique, interviewing, and root cause identification.

6. Diagramming techniques can be applied to help identify project risks including: cause and effect diagrams (also termed "fishbone" or "Ishikawa"), systems flowcharts (also termed "process maps"), and influence diagrams.

7. SWOT analysis is another technique for analyzing the organization's Strengths, Weaknesses, Opportunities, and Threats—a technique that can bring risks to the surface.

8. Indications that a risk has occurred, or is about to occur, are termed "triggers" (or "risk symptoms" or "warning signs").

9. The primary output of the Identify Risks process is the Risk Register. The Risk Register is created during risk identification and then used to capture the outputs of all subsequent risk processes. The Risk Register becomes a subsidiary plan to the overall Project Management Plan.

ADDITIONAL READING

- PMBOK Guide – Section 11.2 Identify Risks

LESSON QUIZ

Instructions Here are some questions to help reinforce your learning. Complete this quiz from memory to the best of your ability. When complete, check your results by comparing your answers to the preferred answers provided in Appendix A.

Please note that Knowledge Check questions are not actual PMP Exam questions. These questions are intended to reinforce key terms, concepts, and themes.

1. The Identify Risks process is applied to:
    A. Determine which risks are serious enough to warrant further analysis
    B. Determine which risks may affect the project and to document their characteristics
    C. Determine which risks are low enough to accept
    D. Determine which risks should be mitigated

2. Project risk categories include:
    A. Technical, project management, organizational, and external
    B. Quality, performance, opportunities, and threats
    C. Positive, negative, causal, and consequential
    D. Triggers, symptoms, warning signs, and uncertainties

3. Identify Risks Tools & Techniques include the following:
    A. Information gathering techniques, diagramming techniques, and documentation reviews
    B. Assumptions analysis, checklist analysis, and diagramming techniques
    C. Diagramming techniques, documentation reviews, and assumptions analysis
    D. All the above

4. Which of the following statements is most true?
    A. Identifying risks is a process that must be applied properly during project planning because once execution begins there are no more opportunities to incorporate new risks in the plan.
    B. Identifying risks is a process that is normally contained to members of the project core team.
    C. Identifying risks is a process that should be encouraged frequently throughout the project life cycle. In many projects, new risks can surface daily.
    D. Identifying risks is a process that should be performed by functional managers, because they are closest to the work.

5. Diagramming techniques can be applied to help identify project risks. These techniques may include:
   A. Cause and effect diagrams (also termed "fishbone" or "Ishikawa")
   B. Systems flowcharts (also termed "process maps")
   C. Influence diagrams
   D. All of the above

6. Indications that a risk has occurred, or is about to occur, are termed:
   A. Uncertainties
   B. Triggers (or risk symptoms or warning signs)
   C. Consequences
   D. Threats

7. Project risk is an uncertain event or condition that, if it occurs, has a positive or negative effect on a project objective. A risk has a _____, and if it occurs, a _____. Which set of terms below, when used to fill-in the blanks, best completes this key definition?
   A. reason, problem
   B. negative impact, positive solution
   C. positive impact, positive solution
   D. cause, consequence

End of Lesson 23

24

Lesson 24
Perform Qualitative Risk Analysis

Objectives

At the end of this lesson, you will be able to:

- Describe the purpose of the Perform Qualitative Risk Analysis process
- Describe the Inputs, Tools & Techniques, and Outputs of the Perform Qualitative Risk Analysis process
- Understand how to apply a Risk Matrix in order to score and prioritize risks for the project

Roadmap to the PMBOK Guide

	Initiating	Planning	Executing	M & C	Closing
Integration					
Scope					
Time					
Cost					
Quality					
Human Resources					
Communications					
Risk		▩			
Procurement					

Qualitative Risk Analysis is performed to identify risk scores and rank risks using risk probability and impact ratings.

Perform Qualitative Risk Analysis is the process of assessing the impact and likelihood of identified risks. It is the third of five risk planning processes, and is logically applied as the next step after the Identify Risks process.

Perform Qualitative Risk Analysis is intended to help prioritize identified risks and identify those risks serious enough to warrant further analysis. As you may imagine, some identified risks have very little probability of occurring, and if they occur, would have only a slight impact. As a result of the Perform Qualitative Risk Analysis process, these risks would be appropriately listed low in priority. Other identified risks may have high probabilities of occurring and/or significant impact if they occur. These risks may be listed high in priority.

A probability/impact (P-I) risk rating matrix is used as the primary tool in Qualitative Risk Analysis to determine the impact and likelihood of identified risks.

PROBABILITY/IMPACT (P-I) RISK RATING MATRIX

A probability/impact (P-I) matrix is a tool that combines both risk probability and risk impact into a single score. It is used to help determine qualitative risk rankings.

		Low	Moderate	High	Very High
		1	4	7	10
	.9				
	.8				
	.7				
	.6				
	.5				
	.4				
	.3				
	.2				
	.1				
	Risk Impact	Low--→High			

(Y-axis: Probability of Risk Occurring, Low → High)

Using this P-I matrix type of qualitative assessment, each identified risk may be assigned a score by plotting it appropriately in the matrix. In this simple P-I matrix example, risks that are assessed with scores in the lower left portion of the matrix indicate low-probability with low-impact. Risks scored in the upper right indicate high-probability with high-impact.

Typically, high or very high risks would receive higher priority for either further analysis or for immediate action. Notice that the probability y-axis goes no higher than 0.9 in this example. By definition, the probability of a risk occurring must be less than 100%. If the probability is 100%, then the event or condition is certain to occur and therefore not a risk at all. Risks are *uncertain* events or conditions.

PROCESS ELEMENTS

The Perform Qualitative Risk Analysis process has the following Inputs:

- **Risk Register**   List of identified risks

- **Risk Management Plan**   Describes how project risk management will be structured and performed across the project

- **Project Scope Statement**   Detailed description of a project's deliverables and work required to create them

- **Organizational Process Assets**   Consideration factors such as similar completed projects, studies, risk databases

The Perform Qualitative Risk Analysis process uses the following Tools & Techniques:

- **Risk Probability and Impact Assessment**   Qualitative assessment of individual risk probability/impact

- **Probability/Impact Matrix**   A matrix that rates and prioritizes risks by combining probabilities and impacts

- **Risk Data Quality Assessment**   Technique to determine the level (confidence) to which a risk is useful

- **Risk Categorization**   Technical risks, external risks, project management risks, organizational risks

- **Risk Urgency Assessment**   Identification of risks which may require near-term responses

- **Expert Judgment**   Expert technical and/or managerial judgment (from any qualified source)

The Perform Qualitative Risk Analysis process has the following Output:

- **Risk Register Updates**   updates to the list of identified risks

Perform Qualitative Risk Analysis (11.3)		
This process prioritizes risks by analyzing their combined probability and impact		
Inputs	**Tools and Techniques**	**Outputs**
• Risk Register • Risk Management Plan • Project Scope Statement • Organizational Process Assets	• Risk Probability and Impact Assessment • Probability/Impact Matrix • Risk Data Quality Assessment • Risk Categorization • Risk Urgency Assessment • Expert Judgment	• Risk Register Updates

TSI *Study Aid*
This chart is part of the study aid poster series available at www.truesolutions.com.

PROCESS DOCUMENTS

The Perform Qualitative Risk Analysis process documents results by populating the probability/impact matrix shown previously in this chapter. Risk scores which result from the P-I matrix will be entered into the Risk Register as an update.

COMMON PROCESS TASKS

The following is a list of the common tasks associated with the Perform Qualitative Risk Analysis Process:

- Document the manifestations of your risk events

- Confirm your stakeholder risk tolerances

- Estimate your risk event probabilities, consequences, and frequencies

- Estimate risk event values and related ranges of possible project costs

- Develop your Probability/Impact Risk Rating Matrix

- Develop your list of prioritized risks

- Determine the overall risk ranking for your project

THINK ABOUT IT

Instructions Think about how this project management process is defined, used, and documented in your organization. Compare your organization's use of this process to the PMI® definition. Do you:

☐ Identify risks in a separate process before you rank risks

☐ Rank risks using a probability/impact matrix

☐ Use a cardinal scale (numbers) to score risks

☐ Use an ordinal scale (descriptive words; low, medium, high) to score risks

☐ Identify a single risk score for each risk

☐ Normally have more risks than you can address due to constraints

Are the outcomes from this process different in your organization or experiences?

_____

_____

_____

_____

_____

_____

_____

MUST KNOW CONCEPTS
. . . .

1 The Perform Qualitative Risk Analysis process is applied to assess the impact and likelihood of identified risks. It is intended to help prioritize identified risks and identify those risks serious enough to warrant further analysis.

2 A probability/impact (P-I) risk rating matrix is a tool that combines both risk probability and risk impact into a single score. It is used to help determine qualitative risk rankings.

3 The primary output of the Perform Qualitative Risk Analysis process is new input to the Risk Register, including a list of risks for additional analysis, a list of prioritized risks, a list of risks requiring near-term response, risks grouped by category, and more.

ADDITIONAL READING
. . . .

• PMBOK Guide – Section 11.3 Perform Qualitative Risk Analysis

LESSON QUIZ
. . . .

Instructions   Here are some questions to help reinforce your learning. Complete this quiz from memory to the best of your ability. When complete, check your results by comparing your answers to the preferred answers provided in Appendix A.

Please note that Knowledge Check questions are not actual PMP Exam questions. These questions are intended to reinforce key terms, concepts, and themes.

1. The Perform Qualitative Risk Analysis process is applied to:
   A. Assess the probability/impact of high priority risks. It is intended to mitigate those risks that pose immediate threats or encourage those risks that offer immediate opportunities.
   B. Determine which risks may affect the project and to document their characteristics
   C. Further assess those risks that scored high-high on the probability/impact (P-I) matrix
   D. Assess the impact and likelihood of identified risks. It is intended to help prioritize identified risks and identify those risks serious enough to warrant further analysis.

2. A probability/impact (P-I) risk rating matrix is:
   A. A defined tool/technique of the Perform Qualitative Risk Analysis process
   B. A defined input to the Perform Qualitative Risk Analysis process
   C. A tool that combines both risk probability and risk impact into a single score
   D. Both A and C.

3. Perform Qualitative Risk Analysis Tools & Techniques include all the following except:
   A. Risk data quality assessment
   B. Risk Register
   C. Probability/impact (P-I) matrix
   D. Risk urgency assessment

Probability of Risk Occurring (Low → High)		Low	Moderate	High	Very High
		1	4	7	10
	.9				
	.8				
	.7				
	.6				
	.5				
	.4				
	.3				
	.2				
	.1				
	Risk Impact	Low--→High			

4. Which of the following statements is most true?
   A. Risks that are assessed with scores in the lower left portion of a typical P-I matrix indicate low-probability with low-impact.
   B. Risks that are assessed with scores in the lower left portion of a typical P-I matrix indicate high-probability with high-impact.

C. Risks that are assessed with scores in the upper right portion of a typical P-I matrix indicate low-probability with low-impact.

D. Risks that are assessed with scores in the upper right portion of a typical P-I matrix indicate high-probability with low-impact.

5. Using the P-I matrix shown, you and your team determine that an identified risk has a 0.3 probability of occurring and, if it occurs, an impact potential of 7. What is the overall score for this risk?

A. 0.21

B. 2.10

C. 21.0

D. None of the above

6. Using the P-I matrix shown, what is the highest possible risk score and the lowest possible risk score?

A. 9.0, 0.1

B. 0.9, 0.1

C. 90.0, 1.0

D. 0.9, 0.001

7. Using the P-I matrix shown, you and your project team assess an identified risk with a score of 0.1. Where in the matrix does it appear, and what does it signify?

A. Lower right, signifying low-probability but high-impact

B. Upper right, signifying high-probability but low-impact

C. Lower left, signifying low-probability but low-impact

D. Upper right, signifying high-probability but high-impact

End of Lesson 24

25

Lesson 25
Perform Quantitative Risk Analysis

Objectives

At the end of this lesson, you will be able to:

- Describe the purpose of the Perform Quantitative Risk Analysis process
- Describe the Inputs, Tools & Techniques, and Outputs of the Perform Quantitative Risk Analysis process
- Understand that this process is applied when it is necessary for project success

Roadmap to the PMBOK Guide

	Initiating	Planning	Executing	M & C	Closing
Integration					
Scope					
Time					
Cost					
Quality					
Human Resources					
Communications					
Risk		■			
Procurement					

Quantitative Risk Analysis is performed when required, to create probabilistic forecasts of project outcomes, usually for time or cost parameters.

The Perform Quantitative Risk Analysis process is applied to guide the additional analysis of individual risks, to determine the numerical value of its probability of occurrence and the numerical value of its consequence on project objectives, should it occur. This process is also applied to determine a numerical value for overall project risk. Perform Quantitative Risk Analysis is the fourth of five risk planning processes and is normally applied as the logical next step following Perform Qualitative Risk Analysis.

Today's powerful desktop computers and application software allow project teams to perform sophisticated quantitative risk analyses, which contributes to higher confidence in schedule estimates, cost estimates, and overall quality. Monte Carlo simulation and expected monetary value analysis are commonly used tools to apply perform quantitative risk analysis.

QUANTITATIVE RISK ANALYSIS TOOLS

There are numerous Tools & Techniques available to support quantitative risk analysis. Four Tools & Techniques stand out as generally recognized and practiced in a widespread fashion throughout the project management community. The tools fit into two categories.

Modeling Techniques

Expected Monetary Value Analysis (EMV): EMV is calculated by multiplying the value of each possible outcome by its probability of occurrence, then adding them all together. A common way to show EMV is using *decision tree analysis*. Decision tree diagrams illustrate the decision being considered, along with all of the implications of choosing various alternatives, including costs, risks, and rewards. Solving a decision tree yields the path with greatest expected value.

Sensitivity Analysis: Sensitivity analysis is a simple risk analysis technique that looks at the overall project risk in a somewhat cursory fashion. Here is an example: Assume that Project X has a cost of $100,000, with a projected return on investment (ROI) of 400% and a 60% probability of complete failure. Project XX has the same cost of $100,000, but with a potential ROI of 35% and a 10% probability of complete failure. Using sensitivity analysis, the project selection decision is based on the level of risk our organization is willing to take. An organization that is willing to accept high risk may find Project X appealing, while Project XX may be better suited for a more risk-averse organization.

Simulation: Today's powerful desktop computers allow project teams of any size to perform sophisticated computer simulations. These simulations can provide reliable numerical analyses for cost risk, schedule risk, and other project risks.

Monte Carlo algorithms provide the underlying "engines" of many simulation software packages. Using Monte Carlo, project managers can input specific parameter values into a program, then automatically run hundreds or thousands of simulations. The results are typically reported in graphical form to predict project performance. One such application could be to predict activity time durations. In this application, activity time duration estimates would be input to a simulation program, along with other key information. When the simulation is run and reported, the result is a graph that illustrates the probability of completion on any calendar date on the curve. Some project risk specialists believe that Monte Carlo simulation programs serve as today's best available quantitative analysis tool ... and they predict actual project performance with a high degree of accuracy

Data Gathering and Representation Techniques

Interviewing: Interviews with stakeholders and subject matter experts (SMEs) can be an effective approach in quantifying risks. For instance; you, as interviewer, could ask an expert stakeholder to estimate the cost for a particular activity; a high estimate, a low estimate, and a most-probable estimate. With these estimate ranges, you and your project risk team can perform a sophisticated quantitative analysis that should provide a complete and confident range of numerical cost probabilities for that activity.

PROCESS ELEMENTS

The **Perform Quantitative Risk Analysis** process has the following Inputs:

- **Risk Register**   List of identified risks

- **Risk Management Plan**   Describes how project risk management will be structured and performed across the project

- **Cost Management Plan**   Defines how risk budgets, contingencies, and management reserves will be managed

- **Schedule Management Plan**   Defines how changes to the project schedule will be managed

- **Organizational Process Assets**   Consideration factors such as similar completed projects, studies, risk databases

The **Perform Quantitative Risk Analysis** process uses the following Tools & Techniques:

- **Data Gathering and Representation Techniques**   Interviewing and probability distributions

- **Quantitative Risk Analysis and Modeling Techniques**   Sensitivity analysis, EMV, decision tree, simulation

- **Expert Judgment**   Expert technical and/or managerial judgment (from any qualified source)

The Perform Quantitative Risk Analysis process has the following Output:
- **Risk Register Updates**   Updates to the list of identified risks

Perform Quantitative Risk Analysis (11.4)		
This process numerically analyzes the effect of risks on overall project objectives		
Inputs	**Tools and Techniques**	**Outputs**
• Risk Register • Risk Management Plan • Cost Management Plan • Schedule Management Plan • Organizational Process Assets	• Data Gathering and Representation Techniques • Quantitative Risk Analysis and Modeling Techniques • Expert Judgment	• Risk Register Updates

PROCESS DOCUMENTS

Process documents used in this process will vary, depending on the tools employed. Interview records, simulation outcomes, and probability distributions all may be employed and documented as part of this process. The results from using these tools will be documented in the Risk Register as updates.

COMMON PROCESS TASKS

The following is a list of the common tasks associated with the Perform Quantitative Risk Analysis Process:

- Conduct risk interviews with your project stakeholders and subject matter experts to support your quantitative risk analysis

- Conduct sensitivity analysis on your probable risk events

- Utilize simulation to analyze the behavior/performance of your project system

- Develop decision tree analysis to depict your key interactions

- Communicate your limitations of risk quantification in order to avoid false impressions of risk assessment reliability

- Prepare your probabilistic risk analysis for the project

THINK ABOUT IT

Instructions Think about how this project management process is defined, used, and documented in your organization.

Compare your organization's use of this process to the PMI® definition. In the *PMBOK® Guide Fourth Edition*, the following tools are used:

- ☐ Interviewing subject matter experts to determine ranges of probabilities

- ☐ Using probability distributions

- ☐ Using sensitivity analysis

- ☐ Expected Monetary Value analysis forecasts

- ☐ Modeling or simulation of outcomes

- ☐ Decision trees

Which of these do you use in your organization?

_____

_____

_____

_____

Which of these do you find valuable?

_____

_____

_____

_____

MUST KNOW CONCEPTS

1. The Perform Quantitative Risk Analysis process is applied to guide the additional analysis of individual risks, to determine the numerical value of its probability of occurrence and the numerical value of its consequence on project objectives, should it occur. This process is also applied to determine a numerical value for overall project risk.

2 Sensitivity analysis is a simple risk analysis technique used to help make project decisions based on the general risk sensitivity of an organization, person, or group of people.

3 Simulation is a quantitative risk analysis tool that can produce probability-based predictions for many project parameters. Monte Carlo algorithms provide the underlying engines in many of today's simulation software programs. Monte Carlo works by running numerous simulations with project-specific information.

4 Expected Monetary Value (EMV) analysis is a quantitative risk analysis tool. EMV is calculated by multiplying the value of each possible outcome by its probability of occurrence, then adding them all together. $EMV = V \times P$, where V is value in dollars, and P is probability. Decision tree analysis illustrates the decision being considered, along with all the implications of choosing various alternatives. Solving a decision tree yields the path with the greatest expected value.

5 The primary output of the Perform Quantitative Risk Analysis process is new input information to the Risk Register including probabilistic analysis of the project, probability of achieving cost and time objectives, a prioritized list of quantified risks, and more.

ADDITIONAL READING
· ·
- PMBOK Guide – Section 11.4 Perform Quantitative Risk Analysis

LESSON QUIZ
· ·
Instructions   Here are some questions to help reinforce your learning. Complete this quiz from memory to the best of your ability. When complete, check your results by comparing your answers to the preferred answers provided in Appendix A.

Please note that Knowledge Check questions are not actual PMP Exam questions. These questions are intended to reinforce key terms, concepts, and themes.

1. The Perform Quantitative Risk Analysis process is applied to:
   A. Develop the project's risk management plan
   B. Determine which risks may affect the project and to document their characteristics
   C. Assess the impact and likelihood of identified risks
   D. Guide the additional analysis of an individual risk, to determine the numerical value of its probability of occurrence and the numerical value of its consequence on project objectives, should it occur

2. After careful comparison, the decision is made by your project sponsor to choose one particular project strategy over another, because the chosen strategy has less associated risk. This decision is consistent with her risk averse policies. This could be an example of using _____ to base a decision.
   A. subjective analysis
   B. expert power
   C. title power
   D. sensitivity analysis

3. Perform Quantitative Risk Analysis Tools & Techniques include:
   A. Probability/impact matrix, quantitative risk analysis and modeling techniques
   B. Data gathering and representation techniques, probability/impact matrix
   C. Data gathering and representation techniques, quantitative risk analysis, and modeling techniques
   D. Checklist analysis, quantitative risk analysis, and modeling techniques

4. Which of the following statements is least true?
   A. Using Monte Carlo simulations, project managers can input project-specific parameter values into a program, then automatically run hundreds or thousands of simulations.
   B. When an activity duration Monte Carlo simulation is run and reported, the result is normally a graph that illustrates the probability of completion on any calendar date on the curve.
   C. Simulations can provide confident numerical analyses for cost risk.
   D. Monte Carlo simulations can be used effectively to predict stakeholder expectations.

5. To help determine and justify a cost contingency for your project, you decide to further evaluate four identified risks using EMV analysis. Risk 1 has a 10% probability of occurring, and if it occurs, will result in $10,000 added cost to the project. Risk 2 has a 70% probability of occurring, and if it occurs, will result in $8,000 added cost to the project. Risk 3 has a 60% probability of occurring, and if it occurs, will result in $10,000 less cost to the project. Risk 4 has a 20% probability of occurring, and if it occurs, will result in $800 added cost to the project. What is the combined EMV of these four risks?
   A. –$12,760
   B. $760
   C. –$760
   D. Not enough information

End of Lesson 25

Lesson 26
Plan Risk Responses

Objectives

At the end of this lesson, you will be able to:

- Describe the purpose of the Plan Risk Responses process
- Describe the Inputs, Tools & Techniques, and Outputs of the Plan Risk Responses process
- Understand the risk responses for negative risks
- Understand the risk responses for positive risks
- Understand different options for response plans

Roadmap to the PMBOK Guide

	Initiating	Planning	Executing	M & C	Closing
Integration					
Scope					
Time					
Cost					
Quality					
Human Resources					
Communications					
Risk		■			
Procurement					

When identifying risk responses for your project, it is important to consider available time and available funds that might be used for contingency planning purposes.

The Plan Risk Responses process is applied to:

Develop options and determine actions to enhance opportunities (positive risks), and to develop options and determine actions to reduce threats (negative risks).

A primary objective of the Plan Risk Responses process is to create the project's Risk Response Plan as part of the Risk Register.

Once a risk has been identified and analyzed (qualitatively and/or quantitatively), a decision must be made on what to do about the risk. It is the intent of Plan Risk Responses to guide that decision, by planning an appropriate response to the risk.

For instance: Inclement weather is a risk that threatens many outdoor events. A project team managing such an event may choose to respond to this negative risk by planning in advance. That planning may be:

- to change the plan, making it an indoor event (this action avoids the risk).

- to arrange in parallel an alternate indoor venue that may be substituted at the last minute, should the risk occur (this action accepts the risk, with a contingency plan in place).

- to purchase insurance to cover losses, should the risk occur and the event is canceled (this action transfers the risk, shifting the consequence to another party).

- to plan one or more rain dates (this action mitigates the risk by lowering the probability of complete cancellation, should the risk occur).

An example of a positive risk in relation to the above outdoor event might be if the weather is much better than usual for that time of the year and the crowd is much larger than planned. Positive risk response options:

- If the project team determines thirty days or so prior to the event that the long-term weather outlook is positive, they may choose to advertise the event further in advance or advertise the forecasted weather (attempting to enhance the risk).

- If the project team determines immediately prior to event that a highly positive condition exists, they may attempt to notify the public or advertise a special event fee or expanded events (exploiting the risk).

- Accepting this risk might involve a contingency plan (as above — only geared to the positive outcomes). An example of a contingency plan might be to plan for more food consumption at the event or arrange for more contingent parking.

- Sharing the risk might involve bringing other organizations into the event if positive conditions are present.

ALTERNATIVES TO CONSIDER DURING PLAN RISK RESPONSES:

Strategies for Negative Risks or Threats

- **Avoidance:** Avoidance is any action that changes the project plan, or condition within the plan, to eliminate the risk. If feasible, risk avoidance is the best option available to reduce overall negative project risk. If an avoidance strategy can be reasonably implemented for a particular negative risk, then the risk is completely eliminated.

- **Transference:** Risk transfer is the action of shifting the consequence and ownership of a risk to a third party. It is important to understand that this does not eliminate the risk (avoidance eliminates a risk). It transfers the consequence and ownership. For instance: Risk may be transferred by (a) purchasing insurance; (b) obtaining guarantees, warranties, and/or performance bonds; (c) using fixed-price contracts, transferring cost risk to the seller; and (d) transferring liability through a contract.

- **Mitigation:** Mitigation is any action that reduces the probability and/or impact of an adverse risk to an acceptable threshold. Many creative possibilities may exist to develop reasonable mitigation plans.

- **Accept:** This strategy is used when the team decides that no changes to the Project Management Plan will occur for a specific risk, or when no response strategy can be defined for that risk.

Strategies for Positive Risks or Opportunities

- **Exploit:** Seeking ways to make the opportunity happen

- **Share:** Sharing the opportunity with a third party, who may be better able to make it happen

- **Enhance:** Seeking to increase the size and/or probability of the opportunity

- **Accept:** Used when no action is planned for taking advantage of a positive risk

Accepting a risk (with no other actions) is a reasonable response strategy in many instances, especially when the risk probability/impact is low. Risks may be accepted actively or passively.

Active acceptance requires the advance development of an appropriate contingency action to respond to the risk, should it occur. An active acceptance strategy for any particular risk could include (a) developing a contingency action plan, (b) developing a fallback action in advance, or (c) adding a contingency reserve (contingency allowance) to the project schedule and/or budget as appropriate.

Passive acceptance is a reasonable option with very low probability/impact risks. Passive acceptance requires no response action planned in advance. Instead a planned action is developed only if and when the risk occurs (a work-around).

PROCESS ELEMENTS

The **Plan Risk Responses** process has the following **Inputs:**

- **Risk Register**   List of identified risks

- **Risk Management Plan**   Describes how project risk management will be structured and performed across the project

The **Plan Risk Responses** process uses the following **Tools & Techniques:**

- **Strategies for Negative Risks or Threats**   Avoid, transfer, mitigate, or accept

- **Strategies for Positive Risks or Opportunities**   Exploit, share, enhance, or accept

- **Contingent Response Strategy**   Responses planned for implementation if/when certain conditions occur

- **Expert Judgment**   Expert technical and/or managerial judgment (from any qualified source)

The **Plan Risk Responses** process has the following **Outputs:**

- **Risk Register Updates**   Updates to the list of identified risks

- **Risk-Related Contract Decisions**   Insurance, services, and/or other items contracted to address specific risks

- **Project Management Plan Updates**   Updates to the Project Management Plan as a result of this process (i.e. schedule/cost/quality/procurement/human resource management plans, WBS, schedule baseline, cost performance baseline)

- **Project Document Updates**   Updates to other project documentation (i.e. assumptions log updates, technical documentation updates)

Plan Risk Responses (11.5)

This process develops options and actions to reduce threats and enhance opportunities

Inputs	Tools and Techniques	Outputs
• Risk Register • Risk Management Plan	• Strategies for Negative Risks or Threats • Strategies for Positive Risks or Opportunities • Contingent Response Strategies • Expert Judgment	• Risk Register Updates • Risk-Related Contract Decisions • Project Management Plan Updates • Project Document Updates

PROCESS DOCUMENTS

The main output from this process is an update to the Risk Register. As an output from Plan Risk Responses, the Risk Register is now the complete document with all risk information documented.

In addition to the completed Risk Register, there are potential updates to many of the ancillary plans that make up the Project Management Plan. Common management plans that are part of the Project Management Plan like scope, time, and cost may be updated. Other project management elements like quality, procurement, and human resources plans may also get updates.

While not shown in this lesson, each of these Project Management Plan elements is shown in its respective lesson.

COMMON PROCESS TASKS

The following is a list of the common tasks associated with the Plan Risk Responses process:

• Work with stakeholders to develop your risk responses

• Determine procurement feasibility as a risk reduction tool

• Develop your contingency plans, implementation criteria, and alternative strategies

• Determine your insurance coverage needs

• Determine your risk events warranting responses

• Assign risk owners

- Identify other processes affected by your risk planning iterations

- Estimate the price of nonconformance to your identified risks

- Determine and document the appropriateness of your specific risk event strategies

- Describe potential differences in your risk event estimates depending on the project phase

- Determine your contingency reserve amounts needed

- Update your Risk Register, including responses

THINK ABOUT IT

Instructions Think about how this project management process is defined, used, and documented in your organization. Compare your organization's use of this process to the PMI® definition.

Use this exercise to compare how you practice project management to what is specified in the *PMBOK® Guide Fourth Edition.*

Think about how this process is defined, used and documented in your organization. Write a brief description of how you use this process:

_____

_____

_____

_____

_____

What specific Inputs, Tools or Techniques do you use as part of this process in your organization?

_____

_____

_____

_____

_____

_____

Are the outcomes from this process different in your organization or experiences?

_____

_____

_____

_____

_____

MUST KNOW CONCEPTS

1 The Plan Risk Responses process is applied to develop options and determine actions to enhance opportunities (positive risks), and to develop options and determine actions to reduce threats (negative risks).

2 The primary Output of the Plan Risk Responses process is the project's completed Risk Register.

3 Avoidance is one of the strategies for negative risks or threats. Avoidance involves changing the project plan, or condition within the plan, to eliminate the risk.

4 Transference is one of the strategies for negative risks or threats. Risk transfer involves shifting the consequence and ownership of a risk to a third party. Transfer does not eliminate the risk.

5 Mitigation is one of the strategies for negative risks or threats. Mitigation involves reducing the probability and/or impact of a negative risk to an acceptable threshold.

6 Acceptance is a strategy for both threats and opportunities. With active acceptance, a contingency plan is developed in advance to respond to the risk, should it occur. With passive acceptance, a response action is developed only if and when the risk event occurs.

7 Exploit, share, and enhance are strategies for positive risks or opportunities.

8 Secondary risks are those risks that arise from the implementation of risk response actions.

9 Residual risks are those risks that remain after response actions have been implemented. Residual risks also include those risks that have been accepted.

10 Contingency action is any planned response action to a risk, should it occur.

11 Contingency allowance (or contingency reserve) is a cost buffer or time buffer included in the project plan to compensate for risk and to help reduce the probability of overruns.

ADDITIONAL READING

• PMBOK Guide – Section 11.5 Plan Risk Responses

LESSON QUIZ

Instructions   Here are some questions to help reinforce your learning. Complete this quiz from memory to the best of your ability. When complete, check your results by comparing your answers to the preferred answers provided in Appendix A.

Please note that Knowledge Check questions are not actual PMP Exam questions. These questions are intended to reinforce key terms, concepts, and themes.

1. The Plan Risk Responses process is applied to:
    A. Develop options and determine actions to create positive risks and develop options and determine actions to mitigate negative risks
    B. Develop options and determine actions to enhance opportunities (positive risks) and develop options and determine actions to reduce threats (negative risks)
    C. Develop options and determine actions to eliminate (avoid) negative risks and develop options and determine actions to accept positive risks
    D. Develop options and determine actions to create opportunities for positive risks and develop options and determine contingency actions for negative risks

2. After reviewing the detailed analysis of a risk associated with a particular project activity, you and your project team decide to respond to the risk by contracting with a specialist outside of your organization who is willing to guarantee successful completion of the activity, on time, and with a firm fixed price contract. This could be an example of:
    A. Active acceptance
    B. Passive acceptance
    C. Mitigation
    D. Transference

3. Plan Risk Responses Outputs include:
   A. Risk Register updates, risk-related contractual decisions, and project management plan updates
   B. Risk Response Plan updates, list of residual risks, and list of secondary risks
   C. Risk Response Plan updates, secondary risks, and contractual agreements
   D. Risk Response Plan, secondary risks, and list of potential responses

4. Which of the following statements is least true?
   A. Contingency allowance (or contingency reserve) is a cost buffer or time buffer included in the project plan to compensate for risk and to help reduce the probability of overruns.
   B. Residual risks are those risks that remain after response actions have been implemented. Residual risks also include those risks that have been accepted.
   C. Contingency allowance (or contingency reserve) is a defined passive acceptance risks response action strategy.
   D. Secondary risks are those risks that arise from the implementation of risk response actions.

End of Lesson 26

Lesson 27
Plan Procurements

Objectives

At the end of this lesson, you will be able to:

- Describe the purpose of the Plan Procurements process
- Describe the Inputs, Tools & Techniques, and Outputs of the Plan Procurements process
- Understand general criteria for the make-or-buy decision.
- Understand contract types and applications

Roadmap to the PMBOK Guide

	Initiating	Planning	Executing	M & C	Closing
Integration					
Scope					
Time					
Cost					
Quality					
Human Resources					
Communications					
Risk					
Procurement		■			

When making the decision to purchase resources external to the performing organization, the project manager must consider what is best for the project, what is best for the organization and what complies with organization best practices.

The Plan Procurements process is the planning process used to document decisions regarding the purchasing and acquisition of required project resources. In addition, this process identifies potential sellers for required resources.

It is important to understand that the required resources include more than just physical materials or components, but can include services and labor from outside the immediate project organization. For example, some construction projects may require special permits. The Plan Procurements process would be used to specify who and how those permits will be purchased or obtained.

There are three primary activities during the Plan Procurements process:
• Make-or-buy decision making

• Selecting the type of contract(s) to be negotiated with suppliers

• Creating the Procurement Management Plan

This process, as required, identifies how materials and services will be purchased, how sellers will be selected, and the types of contracts to be used, based on project requirements and constraints. Make-or-buy decisions can often be difficult.

Some elements to consider when making the decision to make the product are:
• Cost of using internal resources

• Ability to use readily available experienced subject matter experts

• Having more control of the work

• Maintaining control of the intellectual property

• Possibly considering the presence of proprietary data

When making the decision to buy you may also consider:
• Cost; many times external resources can be more efficient or a pre-manufactured product is available that can be customized

• In-house expertise may not be available

• Whether efficiency outweighs intellectual property considerations

• Whether the needed skills are readily available from vendors

The Plan Procurements process is closely related to the Develop Schedule and Estimate Activity Resources processes. It also must factor in consideration for project risks involved in purchasing decisions. If it is determined during Plan Procurements that there are no products or services that need to be acquired or developed outside of the project team, then the remaining project procurement management processes do not need to be performed.

TYPES OF CONTRACTS

There are three broad categories of contract types. From them, many possible variations (hybrids) may be crafted to suit specific project needs:

- **Fixed Price** (also termed "firm fixed price" or "lump sum") Fixed price contracts require the seller to provide all contracted items for one firm price. When executed well, fixed price contracts provide reliable, stable costs to the project, avoiding cost overruns. As a result, fixed price contracts can reduce cost risk to the buyer. Fixed price contracts are often used in projects, for the express purpose of reducing cost risk.

- **Cost Reimbursable** Cost reimbursable contracts [sometimes structured as Cost-Plus-Fee (CPF), Cost-Plus-Fixed-Fee (CPFF), Cost-Plus-Incentive-Fee (CPIF), or Cost-Plus-Percentage of Cost (CPPC)] require the buyer to reimburse the seller for his/her costs, plus some agreed-upon fee. Total cost to the buyer will vary, depending on the amount and types of items supplied.

- **Time and Materials (T&M)** T&M contracts reimburse the seller at an agreed-upon rate for each item to be provided. Total cost to the buyer will vary, depending on the amount and types of items supplied

At a very high level, there are some general reasons for choosing one contract form over another.

	Fixed Price	Cost Reimbursable	Time & Materials
Contract Forms	FP = Fixed price FPIF = Fixed price incentive fee FPEPA = Fixed Price economic price adjustment	CR = Cost Reimbursable CPFF = Cost plus fixed fee CPPC = Cost Plus percent of cost CPIF = Cost Plus Incentive Fee	T&M T&E = Time and Expense
Advantages	Less work for buyer to manage, less cost risk to buyer. Seller has incentive to control costs. Buyer knows total cost.	Simpler scope of work, sometimes provides lower cost since seller does not need to factor in as much risk.	Quick to create SOW, good choice for staff augmentation.
Best to use when	You know precisely what you need done.	You need help in determining what needs to be done.	Short term staff augmentation. Need someone right away.
Disadvantages	Seller may attempt to add-on with change orders. Needs a detailed SOW – changes have to be controlled closely.	Buyer has to closely control each seller invoice to avoid overpaying. Seller has a moderate incentive to control costs.	Seller has no incentive at all to control costs or to work efficiently. Requires daily management by the buyer.
Scope of work	Detailed – has to define all the work specifically.	Moderate detail – wants seller to help define the work.	Brief SOW – usually specified on a daily basis to resource.

PROCESS ELEMENTS

The Plan Procurements process has the following Inputs:

- **Scope Baseline**   Scope Baseline = the approved Project Scope Statement + the WBS + the WBS Dictionary

- **Requirements Documentation**   Documentation describing how individual requirements fulfill the business needs of the project

- **Teaming Agreements**   Legal contractual agreements between parties to form partnerships or joint ventures

- **Risk Register**   List of identified risks

- **Risk-Related Contract Decisions**   Insurance, services, and/or other items contracted to address specific risks

- **Activity Resource Requirements**   Types and quantities of resources needed for each schedule activity

- **Project Schedule**   Graphic presentation illustrating planned start and planned finish dates for each project activity

- **Activity Cost Estimates**   A quantitative assessment of the probable costs required to complete an activity

- **Cost Performance Baseline**   The time-phased budget used to measure, monitor, and control project cost performance

- **Enterprise Environmental Factors**   Consideration factors such as; culture, systems, procedures, and industry standards

- **Organizational Process Assets**   Consideration factors such as processes, procedures, and corporate knowledge base

The Plan Procurements process uses the following Tools & Techniques:

- **Make-or-Buy Analysis**   General management technique used to determine which resources must be purchased outside of the organization

- **Expert Judgment**   Expert technical and/or managerial judgment (from any qualified source)

- **Contract Types**   Consideration and selection of an appropriate contract types for the intended purchases

The Plan Procurements process has the following Outputs:

- **Procurement Management Plan**   Describes how the procurement process will be managed from documentation through contract closure

- **Procurement Statements of Work**   Detailed description of the "procurement item," for prospective suppliers (sellers)

- **Make-or-Buy Decisions**   The documented decisions of what will be developed in-house and what will be purchased

- **Procurement Documents**   Documents used to solicit proposals from prospective sellers

- **Source Selection Criteria**   Criteria used to help score or rate proposals submitted by prospective project suppliers (sellers)

- **Change Requests**   Request for changes to scope, schedule, costs, or processes, or other project documentation

---

Plan Procurements (12.1)
This process documents purchasing decisions, the procurement approach, and identifies potential sellers

Inputs	Tools and Techniques	Outputs
• Scope Baseline • Requirements Documentation • Teaming Agreements • Risk Register • Risk-Related Contract Decisions • Activity Resource Requirements • Project Schedule • Activity Cost Estimates • Cost Performance Baseline • Enterprise Environmental Factors • Organizational Process Assets	• Make-or-Buy Analysis • Expert Judgment • Contract Types	• Procurement Management Plan • Procurement Statements of Work • Make-or-Buy Decisions • Procurement Documents • Source Selection Criteria • Change Requests

TSI Study Aid

This chart is part of the study aid poster series available at *www.truesolutions.com.*

PROCESS DOCUMENTS

The Plan Procurements process will use some form of documentation to record the outcomes from the process. See below for a simple checklist to be used when planning procurements to ensure that all procurement areas are considered prior to actual purchases.

True Solutions, Inc.
Project Management Template
Volume 1: Procurement Management Planning Checklist
Template

Procurement Management Planning Checklist

Project Name:		
Prepared by:		
Date:		
Identify types of contracts being used		
Independent estimates required?	Yes	No
If Yes, who will prepare?		
By when?		
Actions that Project Management Team can take independent of Procurement Department		
Source of standardized procurement documents, if needed		
How will multiple providers be managed?		
How will you coordinate Procurement with the following aspects of the project?		
Scheduling		
Performance Reporting		
Human Resources		
Other		

Application Aid
This form is available individually or as a set from *www.truesolutions.com*.

©Copyright 2009 True Solutions, Inc.
5001 LBJ Freeway, Suite 125-B Dallas, Texas 75244
Tel: 972.770.0900 Fax 972.770.0922 www.truesolutions.com

COMMON PROCESS TASKS

The following is a list of the common tasks associated with the Plan Procurements process:

- Utilize make-or-buy analysis to identify which of your project needs are best met by procuring products and/or services

- Communicate Inputs to your Plan Procurements process

- Determine the contract types available for your project procurement planning purposes

- Develop rating and scoring evaluation criteria for your project procurement planning purposes

- Determine the different types of procurement documents

- Develop your Procurement Management Plan

THINK ABOUT IT

Instructions Think about how this project management process is defined, used, and documented in your organization. Compare your organization's use of this process to the PMI® definition.

Use this exercise to compare how you practice project management to what is specified in the *PMBOK® Guide Fourth Edition*.

Think about how this process is defined, used and documented in your organization. Write a brief description of how you use this process:

_____

_____

_____

_____

_____

_____

_____

What specific Inputs, Tools or Techniques do you use as part of this process in your organization?

_____

_____

_____

_____

_____

_____

Are the outcomes from this process different in your organization or experiences?

_____

_____

_____

_____

_____

_____

MUST KNOW CONCEPTS
. . . .

1. The Plan Procurements process is the planning process used to document decisions regarding the purchasing and acquisition of required project resources.

2. A primary output of the Plan Procurements process is the Procurement Management Plan, which defines the purchasing decisions for the project.

3. If it is determined during the Plan Procurement process that there are no products or services that need to be acquired or developed outside of the project team, then the remaining Project Procurement Management processes (Conduct Procurements, Administer Procurements, Close Procurements) do not need to be performed.

4. There are three primary activities during the Plan Procurements process: make-or-buy decision making, selecting the type of contract(s) to be negotiated with suppliers, and creating the Procurement Management Plan.

5 There are the three broad categories of contract types: Fixed Price (also termed "firm fixed price" or "lump sum"), Cost Reimbursable [sometimes structured as Cost-Plus-Fee (CPF), Cost-Plus-Fixed-Fee (CPFF), Cost-Plus- Incentive-Fee (CPIF), or Cost-Plus-Percentage of Cost (CPPC), and Time and Materials (T&M).

6 The Plan Procurements process is also applied to develop documents to be used to support the Conduct Procurements process.

7 Statements of work are prepared in sufficient detail to allow prospective sellers to bid on the work.

8 Procurement documents are prepared to inform sellers of the project need. Common procurement document forms include RFP (Request for Proposal), RFQ (Request for Quote), and IFB (Invitation for Bid).

9 Evaluation criteria should be developed during this process to ensure that procurement is handled in a fair and equitable manner.

ADDITIONAL READING

- PMBOK Guide – Section 12.0 Introduction, Project Procurement Management
- PMBOK Guide – Section 12.1 Plan Procurements

LESSON QUIZ

Instructions   Here are some questions to help reinforce your learning. Complete this quiz from memory to the best of your ability. When complete, check your results by comparing your answers to the preferred answers provided in Appendix A.

1. After reviewing the detailed analysis associated with a particular project activity, you and your project team decide to transfer the risk consequence by contracting with a specialist outside of your organization. You then prepare a document for prospective contractors that details the complete scope of expected work, plus other important terms. This document is an example of _____.
    A. A work package
    B. A contractor's project charter
    C. A contract statement of work (SOW)
    D. Risk transference

2. Which of the following is *most* true?
   A. Creating the procurement management plan can also have an influence the project schedule.
   B. Make-or-buy analysis only considers the direct costs associated with the procurement of an item.
   C. The amount of risk shared between the seller and the buyer is determined by teaming agreements.
   D. The Procurement Management Plan includes the selection of the seller for all procured items.

3. Which of the following statements is least true?
   A. Fixed price contracts (also termed "firm fixed price" or "lump sum") require the seller to provide all contracted items for one firm price. Fixed price contracts can reduce cost to the buyer.
   B. Cost reimbursable contracts (sometime termed "cost plus fixed fee") require the buyer to reimburse the seller for his/her costs plus some agreed-upon fee. Total cost to the buyer will vary, depending on the amount and types of items supplied.
   C. Time and material (T&M) contracts reimburse the seller at an agreed-upon rate for each item to be provided. Total cost to the buyer will vary, depending on the amount and types of items supplied.
   D. Fixed price contracts (also termed "firm fixed price" or "lump sum") require the seller to provide all contracted items for one firm price. Fixed price contracts can increase cost risk to the buyer.

4. Plan Procurements process Outputs include:
   A. Procurement Management Plan, make-or-buy decisions, and procurement statements of work
   B. Procurement documents, source selection criteria, and contract types
   C. Requirements documentation, Risk Register, and procurement documents
   D. Procurement Management Plan, source selection criteria, and make-or-buy analysis

5. When preparing bid documents, the project team decides to include a section requiring each prospective seller to demonstrate their (a) financial capacity, (b) technical depth, (c) management depth, and (d) understanding of scope. The team's intent is to provide important nonprice information for them to consider when selecting the supplier. This could be an example of _____.
   A. Standard forms
   B. Expert judgment
   C. Source Selection criteria
   D. Benchmarking

End of Lesson 27

Lesson 28
Develop Project Management Plan

Objectives
At the end of this lesson, you will be able to:
- Describe the purpose of the Develop Project Management Plan process
- Describe the Inputs, Tools & Techniques, and Outputs of the Develop Project Management Plan Process
- Understand what ancillary management plans make up the Project Management Plan
- Understand that the project schedule is part of but is not the Project Management Plan

Roadmap to the PMBOK Guide

	Initiating	Planning	Executing	M & C	Closing
Integration		■			
Scope					
Time					
Cost					
Quality					
Human Resources					
Communications					
Risk					
Procurement					

The Project Management Plan must be approved by all of the stakeholders in order to facilitate future project success. Failure to gain acceptance for the plan will most likely result in impaired results.

The Develop Project Management Plan process represents the final step in project planning. It simply defines, integrates, and coordinates all subsidiary plans and the Outputs from other planning processes into a single, cohesive document; the Project Management Plan.

Once approved and authorized, the Project Management Plan is used to:

- serve as the baseline for monitoring and measuring project performance during execution and control

- facilitate stakeholder communications during execution and control

- guide all aspects of the project through execution, monitoring and control, and closing

- document project planning decisions, strategies, alternatives, and assumptions

The Project Management Plan is progressively elaborated through updates throughout a project's life cycle.

The Project Management Plan and a Project Schedule are not one and the same. In common speech, many persons, including project managers, tend to use "project plan" to mean a schedule such as a Microsoft Project Schedule; however these documents are two separate and distinct things.

PROCESS ELEMENTS

The Develop Project Management Plan process has the following Inputs:
- **Project Charter** High-level document that authorizes the project and assigns/authorizes the project manager

- **Outputs from Planning Processes** Planning documents from the other project planning processes

- **Enterprise Environmental Factors** Consideration factors such as; culture, systems, procedures, and industry standards

- **Organizational Process Assets** Consideration factors such as processes, procedures, and corporate knowledge base

The Develop Project Management Plan process uses the following Tools & Techniques:
- **Expert Judgment** Expert technical and/or managerial judgment (from any qualified source)

The Develop Project Management Plan process has the following Output:

- **Project Management Plan** The consolidated package of the subsidiary management plans and baselines

---

Develop Project Management Plan (4.2)
This process documents all actions required to define, prepare, integrate, and coordinate all subsidiary plans

Inputs	Tools and Techniques	Outputs
• Project Charter • Outputs from Planning Processes • Enterprise Environmental Factors • Organizational Process Assets	• Expert Judgment	• Project Management Plan

TSI Study Aid

This chart is part of the study aid poster series available at *www.truesolutions.com*.

PROCESS DOCUMENTS

The Project Management Plan is a collection of documents that define the baseline and the approach for the project. Since it is a collection of documents, each document has its own format, based on the needs of that particular portion of the project.

The Project Management Plan could consist of:

- Project Charter (not formally defined as part of the plan in the PMBOK)

- Project Requirements Plan and Traceability Matrix

- Project Management Approach*

    - Processes to be used

    - Level of detail required

    - Documentation of specialized considerations for the project

    - Authority levels for the project manager

    - Steering committees or other support elements for the project

    - Work management processes to be used

- Project Scope Baseline

- Schedule Baseline

- Cost Performance Baseline

- Change Management Plan

- Configuration Management Plan

- Scope Management Plan*

- Schedule Management Plan*

- Cost Management Plan*

- Project Quality Management and Quality Improvement Plan

- Communications Management Plan

- Risk Management Plan

- Procurement Management Plan

*This item is created as part of general project direction, not as the direct result of a specific process output.

Study Tip
Know what documents form the project management plan.

PROCESS TASKS

The following is a list of the common tasks associated with the Develop Project Management Plan process:

- Determine your Project Management Plan development methodology

- Identify your interface points with other projects within the organization

- Define and utilize your Project Management Information System (PMIS) to assist in the gathering, integration, interpretation, and dissemination of the Inputs and Outputs of all project processes

- Identify and develop your integrated project plan, including all components and subsidiary plans

- Determine your overall Project Management Plan for use in managing and controlling project execution

- Determine how updates to the Project Management Plan will be identified and implemented during the executing portions of the project.

THINK ABOUT IT

Instructions Think about how this project management process is defined, used, and documented in your organization.

Compare your organization's use of this process to the PMI® definition.

Use this exercise to compare how you practice project management to what is specified in the *PMBOK® Guide Fourth Edition*.

Think about how this process is defined, used and documented in your organization. Write a brief description of how you use this process:

_____

_____

_____

_____

What specific Inputs, Tools or Techniques do you use as part of this process in your organization?

_____

_____

_____

_____

Are the outcomes from this process different in your organization or experiences?

_____

_____

_____

_____

_____

MUST KNOW CONCEPTS

1 The Develop Project Management Plan process represents the final step in project planning.

2 The Develop Project Management Plan process is applied to gather the Outputs from all other planning processes, all subsidiary plans, then assemble them into a single, cohesive document, the Project Management Plan.

3 The primary deliverable (Output) of the Develop Project Management Plan process is the Project Management Plan.

4 The Project Management Plan documents project planning decisions, strategies, alternatives, and assumptions.

5 The Project Management Plan serves as the baseline for monitoring and measuring project performance during execution, monitoring and control, and closing.

6 The Project Management Plan facilitates stakeholder communications during execution, monitoring and control, and closing.

7 The Project Management Plan guides all aspects of the project through execution, monitoring and control, and closing.

ADDITIONAL READING

• PMBOK Guide – Section 4.2 Develop Project Management Plan

LESSON QUIZ

Instructions   Here are some questions to help reinforce your learning. Complete this quiz from memory to the best of your ability. When complete, check your results by comparing your answers to the preferred answers provided in Appendix A.

1. Which of the following best describes the Develop Project Management Plan process?
   A. The Develop Project Management Plan process may use a PMIS to help assemble the integrated project plan.
   B. The Develop Project Management Plan process represents the last step in project planning.
   C. The Develop Project Management Plan process is applied to gather the Outputs from all other planning processes, along with all subsidiary plans, and assemble them into a single, cohesive document, the Project Management Plan.
   D. The Develop Project Management Plan process is ongoing throughout the project planning phase.

2. You and your project team may use your Project Management Plan to
   _____.
   A. document project planning decisions, strategies, alternatives, and assumptions
   B. serve as the baseline for monitoring and measuring project performance during execution and control
   C. guide all aspects of your project through execution, monitoring and control, and closing
   D. all of the above

3. Develop Project Management Plan Inputs include all of the following except:
   A. Project Charter
   B. Past project files
   C. Expert judgment
   D. PMIS

4. Most project planning work is now complete and your project team is preparing to assemble the integrated Project Management Plan. They look to you for guidance. Your best recommendation may be what?
   A. The size and complexity of the Project Management Plan should be in sensible proportion to the size and complexity of the project.
   B. The Project Management Plan must include all planning Outputs, in as much detail as is available.
   C. The Project Management Plan must be as condensed as possible, so as not to overwhelm risk averse stakeholders.
   D. All of the above.

5. The Project Management Plan includes all of the following except:
   A. Communications Management Plan
   B. Quality Management Plan
   C. Scope Verification Plan
   D. Procurement Management Plan

End of Lesson 28

Lesson 29
Executing Process Group

Objectives

At the end of this lesson, you will be able to:

- Understand what processes are used in the Executing Process Group
- Understand the purpose for using Executing processes for the project or project phase

Roadmap to the PMBOK Guide

	Initiating	Planning	Executing	M & C	Closing
Integration			▓		
Scope					
Time					
Cost					
Quality			▓		
Human Resources			▓		
Communications			▓		
Risk					
Procurement			▓		

The Executing Process Group is where the majority of resources are expended for the project. During these processes, work is completed and deliverables are created.

The Executing Process Group consists of eight processes that are intended to manage the work during a project or project phase. The primary reason that these Executing processes are performed is to manage the work so that the intended deliverables of the project or phase are created as planned. Executing processes occur in integration, quality, human resource, communication, and procurement management knowledge areas in the *PMBOK® Guide Fourth Edition*.

If there were a "key word" that would characterize the Executing Process Group, it might be "deliverables." The most important Output of the entire process group is the deliverables created for the project.

The Executing processes have a high degree of interaction with each other. In addition, these Executing processes also work very closely with the processes in the Monitoring and Controlling process group. Executing processes focus on producing deliverables, the Monitoring and Controlling processes concentrate on confirming that the planned deliverables are created and that these Outputs meet the planned specifications and requirements.

EXECUTING TASKS

On your PMP Exam, you will encounter approximately fifty-four questions that will test your understanding of Executing processes. These fifty-four questions will generally focus on the following Executing process tasks:

- As a PMP or project manager executing a project (or project phase), you may be required to execute the tasks as defined in the project plan in order to achieve the project goals.

- As a PMP or project manager executing the project (or project phase), you may be required to ensure a common understanding for setting expectations and resolving issues in accordance with the project plan in order to align the stakeholders and team members.

- As a PMP or project manager executing a project (or project phase), you may be required to implement the procurement of project resources in accordance with the procurement plan.

- As a PMP or project manager executing a project (or project phase), you may be required to manage resource allocation proactively by ensuring that appropriate resources and tools are assigned to the tasks according to the project plan.

- As a PMP or project manager executing a project (or project phase), you may be required to implement the Quality Management Plan to ensure that work is being performed according to documented quality standards.

- As a PMP or project manager executing a project (or project phase), you may be required to implement approved changes according to the Change Control Management Plan in order to ensure the successful completion and integration of all tasks.

- As a PMP or project manager executing a project (or project phase), you may be required to implement the approved actions and workarounds required to mitigate project risk events in order to minimize the impact of the risks on the project.

- As a PMP or project manager executing a project (or project phase), you may be required to improve team performance by building team cohesiveness, leading, mentoring, training, and motivating in order to facilitate cooperation, ensure project efficiency, and boost morale.

KNOWLEDGE REQUIREMENTS

As a PMP applying Executing processes in real-world projects, you will be required to possess in-depth knowledge in several project-specific areas, as well as a broad knowledge of project management in general. The PMP Exam will test your understanding of these knowledge specifics.

By developing a familiarity with these knowledge specifics, you will better understand the context of many PMP Exam questions. As you progress through the *Ultimate PMP Exam Prep Guide*, you will see each of these areas mentioned. Please give some thought to each item as it relates to your own project management experiences with past and current projects.

Remember, the PMP or project manager is always required to have a very broad base of knowledge to work from. In many cases, the project manager has to work with all levels of the organization to effectively perform project management.

As a PMP or project manager applying Executing processes, you may be expected to have knowledge of:

- Project plans

- Statements of Work

- Organizational structure, culture, and procedures

- Existing skills available in the organization

- Configuration management

- Stakeholders, interests, expectations, and limitations

- Procurement processes and plans

- Cost estimating and management techniques

- Contract administration techniques

- How to manage budget and time constraints

- Quality plans and conformance to requirements

- Requirements and specifications

- Change Management Plans

- Risk Management Plans and techniques

- Motivation factors for the team

- Team member skills

- Team member interests

PERFORMANCE COMPETENCIES

As a PMP applying Executing processes in real-world projects, there are many specific project management performance competencies (skills) that you may be expected to exercise.

By developing a familiarity with these skills, you will better understand the context of many PMP Exam questions. As you progress through the *Ultimate PMP Exam Prep Guide*, you will see each of these skills mentioned. As you read, please give thought to how use of these skills relates to your past and current project experiences.

As a PMP or project manager applying Executing processes, you may be required to exercise skill in:

• Leading	• Problem Solving
• Facilitating	• Communicating
• Negotiating	• Influencing
• Presenting	• Documenting
• Analyzing	• Mentoring

Study Tip

Be sure to understand the Process Group Interactions

We have previously exposed and discussed information about process group interactions. During the Executing phases or portions of the project, a high degree of interaction occurs between the Executing *process group* and the Monitoring and Controlling *process group*.

The intent of the Executing process group is to create project deliverables. The intent of the Monitoring and Controlling process group is to make sure they are the right deliverables.

When completing the work of the project, processes from both process groups have to work together very closely and interact frequently in order to manage the project and its outcomes.

As you read the *Ultimate PMP Exam Prep Guide, remember to look for process flows (defined by one Output becoming the Input to another process) that define the interactions that occur during a typical project.*

ADDITIONAL READING
. . . .

• PMBOK Guide – Section 3.5

LESSON QUIZ

. . . .

Process Matching Exercise

Read the recommended reading for this lesson before attempting this exercise. After you have read all of the lesson material and the reading in the *PMBOK Guide*, your goal is to match the appropriate processes to the correct process group and knowledge area. All of the processes are listed on the right.

In this exercise, match the *Executing* processes to their correct knowledge area.

Knowledge Area	Process Group					Project Processes
	Initiating	Planning	Executing	Monitoring & Controlling	Closing	
Integration						Report Performance
						Control Schedule
						Verify Scope
						Plan Risk Responses
						Estimate Costs
						Develop Project Charter
						Identify Stakeholders
Scope						Develop Project Management Plan
						Close Project or Phase
						Monitor & Control Project Work
						Control Scope
						Monitor & Control Project Risk
Time						Direct & Manage Project Execution
						Acquire Project Team
						Plan Quality
						Perform Integrated Change Control
						Define Scope
						Determine Budget
Cost						Define Activities
						Plan Communications
						Manage Stakeholder Expectations
Quality						Manage Project Team
						Control Costs
						Perform Quality Assurance
Human Resource						Administer Procurements
						Develop Human Resource Plan
						Create WBS
						Sequence Activities
						Perform Quality Control
Communication						Close Procurements
						Develop Project Team
						Plan Risk Management
						Conduct Procurements
						Estimate Activity Resources
						Identify Risks
Risk						Perform Qualitative Risk Analysis
						Plan Procurements
						Estimate Activity Durations
						Perform Quantitative Risk Analysis
Procurement						Distribute Information
						Develop Schedule
						Collect Requirements

End of Lesson 29

30

Lesson 30
Direct and Manage Project Execution

Objectives

At the end of this lesson, you will be able to:

- Describe the purpose of the Direct and Manage Project Execution process
- Describe the Inputs, Tools & Techniques, and Outputs of the Direct and Manage Project Execution process
- Describe the key interpersonal skills which are required for effective project management in project environments

Roadmap to the PMBOK Guide

	Initiating	Planning	Executing	M & C	Closing
Integration			■		
Scope					
Time					
Cost					
Quality					
Human Resources					
Communications					
Risk					
Procurement					

The understanding and appropriate use of general management skills is most important during project execution in order to create the required project deliverables.

In carrying out the Project Management Plan, Direct and Manage Project Execution is the process of coordinating and directing all the resources that exist across the project. To successfully execute the Project Management Plan, the project manager and team must constantly monitor and measure performance against baselines, so that timely corrective action can be taken, as appropriate. Also, final cost and schedule forecasts must be updated periodically, as appropriate.

Typically, most project resources are expended during project execution.

The understanding and appropriate use of general management skills is most important during project execution. Accordingly, this chapter begins with primers in three essential people-skills in project environments: conflict management, negotiation, and leadership.

CONFLICT MANAGEMENT PRIMER
Three Truths about Conflict in Project Environments

1. Conflict manifests when there are incompatible goals, thoughts, or emotions within or between individuals or groups.

2. Conflict is inevitable in project environments but it does not have to be destructive.

3. Project staff should be sensitive to both the positive and negative values of conflict and its effect on performance.

The "Seven Sources of Conflict" in Project Environments

From studies conducted by Thamhain and Wilemon (1975) and Posner (1986), there are seven primary sources of conflict in project environments:

1. Schedules

2. Cost/budget

3. Priorities

4. Human resources

5. Technical trade-offs

6. Personality

7. Administrative procedures

Resolving Conflict in Project Environments

Here are six common approaches for resolving conflicts. Project managers should select the approach most appropriate for any particular situation.

- **Confronting** (also termed "problem solving" or "negotiating")   Confronting tackles the disagreement head-on. Successful confronting usually requires mature, competent parties who are genuinely interested in finding an acceptable solution. Confronting takes longer but can provide an ultimate resolution.

- **Collaborating**   This may be a good approach when the situation can't be compromised. It incorporates viewpoints from both parties to help build a consensus resolution. Collaborating can provide a long-term resolution.

- **Compromising** (also termed "bargaining")   Compromising incorporates the use of trade-off exchanges, to bring some satisfaction to both parties. A permanent resolution can be achieved but some aspects of the issue may be compromised. With compromising, both sides lose something and hard feelings can return.

- **Smoothing** (also termed "accommodating")   This can be a good interim approach to temporarily keep the peace. With smoothing, agreements are emphasized, disagreements are avoided. Smoothing typically provides short-term relief, but fails to provide a permanent resolution.

- **Withdrawing** (also termed "avoidance")   May also be considered throwing-in-the-towel, retreat, refusal to deal with the conflict, ignoring it, or denial. This may not be an ideal approach, as withdrawing never resolves a conflict. It can, however, be a sensible temporary approach when "cooling off" will help.

- **Forcing**   This involves the use of dominance. Forcing is typically a technique of last resort reserved for times when there is no common ground, when time is of the essence, or when the parties are uncooperative. Forcing can be fast and decisive but generally leaves hard feelings. Forcing can provide a definitive resolution.

NEGOTIATING IN PROJECT ENVIRONMENTS

Negotiating in project environments typically involves bargaining for resources, bargaining for information, and/or bargaining for actual work.

Negotiation is the process through which parties with differing interests reach agreement.

Negotiable items in the project environment may include:

- Issues
- Scope changes
- Services and supplies
- Schedule changes
- Budget changes
- Resources
- Performance criteria

Negotiating partners you may encounter in the project environment can include:

- Executive managers
- Functional managers
- Subject matter experts
- Other project managers
- Clients
- Procurement specialists

There are three primary steps to successful negotiating:

1. **Separate the problem from the people**
   - Put yourself in the other person's position
   - Separate the substance of negotiation from relationships and personalities
   - Find ways to give credit for the advice and ideas of others
   - Develop options that are fair to all parties
   - Attack the problem, not each other

2. **Focus on common interests**
   - Explore your shared interests instead of opposing views
   - Acknowledge the interests of the other party
   - Be firm in dealing with the problem, but flexible in exploring solutions and ideas

3. **Create options that include shared interests**

   - Before starting negotiation, create possible solutions that reflect shared interests

   - Focus on adjusting the most mutually attractive solution to reach a final agreement

LEADERSHIP PRIMER

Leadership in project environments is the process of:

- creating a vision

- communicating that vision to others

- communicating a realistic plan to achieve the vision

- translating the vision into reality *through* people rather than *over* people

Effective leadership skills are essential to ensure long-term success as a project manager. Successfully managing a project team, motivating stakeholders and creating a high-performance, innovative project environment requires good leadership, influence skills, and political awareness.

There are several types of power found in the leadership role. These types of power include:

- **Reward power**   This type of power is derived from the leader's authority to reward desired behavior ... with salary increases, promotions, vacations, perks, and/or other positive incentives.

- **Punishment power**   This type of power is derived from the leader's authority to punish undesirable behavior ... with termination, pay docking, reprimands, and/or other negative incentives.

- **Referent power**   Referent power is earned power. Leaders who are admired by others as a role model usually get desired behavior from their people through this referent (or earned) power.

- **Expert power**   This is closely related to referent power. It is earned when the leader is viewed as an expert and gains desired behavior because people believe their leader "knows best."

- **Title power**   This is the type of power derived by the actual title or position of the leader, as authorized by senior/executive management.

- **Information power**   This type power is derived by controlling the distribution of key information to people. "Information is power."

- **Charismatic power**   This type of power is derived through the use of extraordinary communication skills. This type of "influence" power can be very useful for project managers who function in environments where they have limited formal authority.

- **Contacts power**   This type of power is derived through alliances and networks with influential people in the organization.

Total power is often derived from a combination of several individual sources.

PROCESS ELEMENTS

The Direct and Manage Project Execution process has the following Inputs:

- **Project Management Plan**   The consolidated package of the subsidiary management plans and baselines

- **Approved Change Requests**   Documented, authorized changes that expand or reduce scope

- **Enterprise Environmental Factors**   Consideration factors such as; culture, systems, procedures, and industry standards

- **Organizational Process Assets**   Consideration factors such as processes, procedures, and corporate knowledge base

The Direct and Manage Project Execution process uses the following Tools & Techniques:

- **Expert Judgment**   Expert technical and/or managerial judgment (from any qualified source)

- **Project Management Information System (PMIS)**   Automated system to help the team execute planned activities

The Direct and Manage Project Execution process has the following Outputs:

- **Deliverables**   Results, products, and/or capabilities (unique, verifiable outcomes) of activities performed

- **Work Performance Information**   Raw data related to deliverable status, schedule progress, and costs incurred

- **Change Requests**   Requests for changes to scope, cost, budget, schedule, or policies and procedures

- **Project Management Plan Updates**   Updates to the Project Management Plan as a result of this process

- **Project Document Updates**   Updates to other project documentation

Direct and Manage Project Execution (4.3)
This process executes the work defined in the Project Management Plan

Inputs	Tools and Techniques	Outputs
• Project Management Plan • Approved Change Requests • Enterprise Environmental Factors • Organizational Process Assets	• Expert Judgment • Project Management Information System	• Deliverables • Work Performance Information • Change Requests • Project Management Plan Updates • Project Document Updates

TSI *Study Aid*

This chart is part of the study aid poster series available at *www.truesolutions.com.*

PROCESS DOCUMENTS

The key result from the Direct and Manage Project Execution process is work results or deliverables. The project manager may manage work through use of a work authorization system. Most work authorization systems employ specific documentation to track work results.

An example of a simple work results document is shown below.

True Solutions, Inc.
Project Management Template
Volume 1: Work Results Guidelines Template

TSI

Work Results Guidelines

Project Name:
Prepared by:
Date:

Deliverable #1

Completed as of Scheduled Date:
Not completed as of Scheduled Date:
Reason, if not completed

Quality Standards:	Met	Not Met
Quality Issues		

Costs Incurred

On Budget	Under Budget by	Over Budget by

Additional Remarks:

Deliverable #2

Completed as of Scheduled Date:
Not completed as of Scheduled Date:
Reason, if not completed

Quality Standards:	Met	Not Met
Quality Issues		

Costs Incurred

On Budget	Under Budget by	Over Budget by

Additional Remarks:

Reported by	Date

Application Aid

This form is available individually or as a set from *www.truesolutions.com*.

©Copyright 2009 True Solutions, Inc.
5001 LBJ Freeway, Suite 125-B Dallas, Texas 75244
Tel: 972.770.0900 Fax 972.770.0922 www.truesolutions.com

COMMON PROCESS TASKS

The following is a list of the common tasks associated with the Direct and Manage Project Execution process:

1. Execute Scope

- Utilize your WBS to manage project deliverables
- Conduct work scope in accordance with your plans
- Establish review and approval processes for your project deliverables
- Apply the Project Schedule

2. Employ mechanisms to measure, record, and report progress of activities in relation to your agreed schedule and plans

- Conduct ongoing analysis of options to identify variances and forecast the impact of changes on your schedule
- Review progress throughout the project life cycle and implement agreed schedule changes to ensure consistency with changing scope, objectives, and constraints related to time and resource availability
- Develop and implement agreed responses to perceived, potential, or actual schedule changes, to maintain your project objectives

3. Execute the Cost Baseline

- Implement agreed financial management procedures and processes to monitor your actual expenditures and to control costs
- Select and utilize cost analysis methods and tools to identify cost variations, evaluate options, and recommend actions to your higher project authority
- Implement, monitor, and modify agreed actions to maintain your financial and overall project objectives throughout the project life cycle

4. Implement Project Time Reporting

- Execute requirements and processes for time reporting to all project stakeholders, including time-reporting data in regular progress reports

5. Execute the Risk Response Plan, including preventive actions as necessary

- Initiate and manage change requests as a response to risk events
- Manage change to your risk response plan as a result of evolving circumstances

6. Manage Human Resources

- Manage changes in your organizational plans

- Monitor results of your team-building activities

- Monitor effectiveness of your programs for enhancing project team performance

- Monitor your rewards and recognition plan

7. Manage and Review Contract Performance

- Review contractor costs, schedules, and technical performance levels

- Implement your contract change control system

8. Other actions

- Identify and execute preventive actions or modifications to the project plan using a structured approach

- Utilize structured communication methods

- Utilize regularly scheduled project status reviews

- Utilize project information systems to provide project information

- Utilize negotiating strategies

- Apply problem solving techniques in managing your project

- Implement methods used to influence behavior and preventive action

- Manage various project related technical and/or organizational interfaces

- Utilize work authorization systems and procedures for approving project work to ensure proper work sequencing

- Know products and services and have the ability to monitor and react to project changes initiated by your sponsor

- Document work results and quality outcomes, including completion of your project deliverables

- Identify change requests during work processes and determine potential project scope changes

THINK ABOUT IT

. . . .

Instructions Think about how this project management process is defined, used, and documented in your organization. Compare your organization's use of this process to the PMI® definition.

Use this exercise to compare how you practice project management to what is specified in the *PMBOK® Guide Fourth Edition.*

Think about how this process is defined, used and documented in your organization. Write a brief description of how you use this process:

_____

_____

_____

_____

_____

_____

What specific inputs, Tools or Techniques do you use as part of this process in your organization?

_____

_____

_____

_____

_____

_____

Are the outcomes from Direct and Manage Project Execution different in your organization or experiences?

_____

_____

_____

_____

_____

_____

MUST KNOW CONCEPTS

1. The Direct and Manage Project Execution process is applied by the project manager and project team to coordinate and direct all the resources that exist across the project, in carrying out the Project Management Plan.

2. To successfully execute the Project Management Plan, the project manager and team must constantly monitor and measure performance against baselines, so that timely corrective action can be taken.

3. The primary Outputs of the Direct and Manage Project Execution process are work results (deliverables).

4. The effective use of people-skills is essential to achieve success during project execution.

5. In most projects, most of the project budget is spent during the project execution phase.

6. Formal work authorization systems are helpful to control project work, especially with respect to minimizing unnecessary scope expansion (so-called "scope creep").

7. Sources of conflict in projects often include (in rank order): schedules, budgets, priorities, human resources, technical trade-offs, personalities, and administrative procedures.

8. The six commonly applied techniques for conflict resolution include: withdrawing, forcing, smoothing, confronting, collaborating, and compromising.

9. Items typically requiring negotiation in projects include: human resources, budgets, schedules, changes, performance criteria, issues, scope, and supplies.

10. Negotiation in projects typically involves people such as: functional managers, executive managers, contractors, other project managers and clients.

11. Sources/types of leadership power in projects includes: reward power, punishment power, referent power, expert power, title power, information power, charismatic power, and contacts power.

ADDITIONAL READING

. . . .

• PMBOK Guide – Section 4.3 Direct and Manage Project Execution

LESSON QUIZ

. . . .

Instructions   Here are some questions to help reinforce your learning. Complete this quiz from memory to the best of your ability. When complete, check your results by comparing your answers to the preferred answers provided in Appendix A.

1.   All of the following regarding change requests are true except:
   A. They can be internally or externally initiated
   B. They may cover corrective or preventative actions
   C. They are legal/contractually mandated
   D. They can impact scope, cost, budget, and schedule

2.   The conflict resolution technique in which both sides lose something is called:
   A. Bargaining
   B. Negotiating
   C. Problem Solving
   D. Accommodating

3.   Which of the following is *least* true?
   A. To successfully execute the project management plan, the project manager and team must constantly monitor and measure performance against baselines, so the timely correction action can be taken.
   B. The effective use of people skills is essential to achieve success during project execution.
   C. In most projects, most of the project budget is spent during the project execution phase.
   D. Formal work authorization systems are used to account for project spending, by category, in accordance with the cost budget chart of accounts.

4.   Direct and Manage Project Execution Outputs include:
   A. Deliverables and project documents
   B. Deliverables and Project Management Plan updates
   C. Deliverables and project schedule
   D. Deliverables and stakeholder register

5. You, as project manager, are in the fortunate position of having a loyal, motivated and respectful project core team. This is largely due to the fact that you have thirty years of hands-on experience, successfully managing projects on time, on budget, and within scope. This position of personal leadership power you possess could be an example of

_____.

   A. expert power
   B. title power
   C. contacts power
   D. charismatic power

6. Project resources include:
   A. Individuals
   B. Meeting rooms
   C. Equipment
   D. All of the above

End of Lesson 30

31

Lesson 31
Acquire Project Team

Objectives

At the end of this lesson, you will be able to:

- Describe the purpose of the Acquire Project Team process
- Describe the Inputs, Tools & Techniques, and Outputs of the Acquire Project Team process
- Describe common methods to acquire the project team
- Describe when the project manager will acquire the project team

Roadmap to the PMBOK Guide

	Initiating	Planning	Executing	M & C	Closing
Integration					
Scope					
Time					
Cost					
Quality					
Human Resources			■		
Communications					
Risk					
Procurement					

Acquiring the Project Team is often done in steps. Early in the project a core team is assigned. As the project planning progresses and clear roles are defined, additional resources are acquired or assigned as needed.

The Acquire Project Team process is applied to get needed human resources assigned and working on the project.

When considering people to support the project, the project team should factor in things such as experience, availability, competencies, personal characteristics, and whether or not the potential resource has an interest in working on the project. Many times, especially in matrix organizations, you as project manager may need to use your best negotiating skills to get the people you want from their functional manager(s).

The Acquire Project Team process is defined as an executing process in the *PMBOK® Guide Fourth Edition*. This does not mean that the project manager has to wait until late in the project to acquire the project team. Best practice guidelines would suggest that a core project team will be acquired early in the project — immediately after the Project Charter is issued. Other human resources will be brought on throughout the project as needed. It will be important that the project manager plan carefully and not acquire resources without first considering the Develop Human Resource Plan process and its outcomes: the Staffing Management Plan and Roles and Responsibilities for the project.

An important consideration for the project manager will be to negotiate for and acquire resources which have the needed levels of competency that are required to execute the project. If the available resources do not have the required competencies and experience, if there are not sufficient resources available to perform project activities, or if resources cannot be acquired in a timely manner, the project manager will return to the planning processes and replan portions of the project that are affected by differences in planned human resources.

The Acquire Project Team process is complete when the project is reliably staffed with appropriate people. Many project teams publish a formal team directory when staffing is complete.

PROCESS ELEMENTS

The Acquire Project Team process has the following Inputs:
- **Project Management Plan** The consolidated package of the subsidiary management plans and baselines

- **Enterprise Environmental Factors** Consideration factors such as culture, systems, procedures, and industry standards

- **Organizational Process Assets** Consideration factors such as processes, procedures, and corporate knowledge base

The Acquire Project Team process uses the following Tools & Techniques:

- **Pre-Assignment**   Predefined project staff assignments. Example: Staff was identified in the Project Charter

- **Negotiation**   Influential discussions (typically with functional managers) to fill project staff assignments

- **Acquisition**   Obtaining project staff from outside sources (if necessary), using project procurement management

- **Virtual Teams**   Teams with shared goals working with little or no face-to-face communications

The Acquire Project Team process has the following Outputs:

- **Project Staff Assignments**   The appropriate people, reliably assigned to staff the project

- **Resource Calendars**   Documents the time periods each team member can work on the project

- **Project Management Plan Updates**   Updates to the Project Management Plan as a result of this process

Acquire Project Team (9.2)		
This process obtains needed project human resources		
Inputs	**Tools and Techniques**	**Outputs**
• Project Management Plan • Enterprise Environmental Factors • Organizational Process Assets	• Pre-Assignment • Negotiation • Acquisition • Virtual Teams	• Project Staff Assignments • Resource Calendars • Project Management Plan Updates

TSI *Study Aid*

This chart is part of the study aid poster series available at *www.truesolutions.com.*

PROCESS TASKS

The following is a list of the common tasks associated with the Acquire Project Team process:

- Determine your human resource requirements for individual tasks with input from stakeholders and guidance from higher project authorities, to provide a basis for determining project staffing levels and competencies

- Establish your project organizational structure and directory to align individual and group competencies with project tasks

PROCESS TASKS, Continued

· ·

- Negotiate with appropriate internal functional managers to acquire required resources

- Procure resources using procurement processes if acquiring external human resources

- Allocate your project staff to and within the project, or within the organization, as directed by a higher project authority, to meet competency requirements throughout the project life cycle

- Communicate your designated staff responsibilities, authority, and personal performance measurement criteria, to ensure clarity of understanding of the work and to provide a basis for ongoing assessment

THINK ABOUT IT

· ·

Instructions Think About It! Use this exercise to compare how you practice project management to what is specified in the *PMBOK® Guide Fourth Edition*

Think about how Acquire Project Team is defined, used and documented in your organization. Write a brief description of how you use this process:

_____

_____

_____

_____

_____

_____

What specific Inputs, Tools or Techniques do you use as part of this process in your organization?

_____

_____

_____

_____

_____

_____

Are the outcomes from acquiring a project team different in your organization or experiences?

_____

_____

_____

_____

_____

MUST KNOW CONCEPTS

1. The Acquire Project Team process is applied to obtain and assign needed human resources (people) to the project.

2. The project manager will negotiate with functional managers and other sources of possible project team members as necessary to obtain the people a project manager desires.

3. The project manager will use procurement processes to acquire staff if external staff are used for the project.

4. The primary deliverable (Output) of the Acquire Project Team process is project staff assignments.

ADDITIONAL READING

• PMBOK Guide – Section 9.2 Acquire Project Team

LESSON QUIZ

Instructions   Here are some questions to help reinforce your learning. Complete this quiz from memory to the best of your ability. For each question, circle or check your selected answer on this page or a separate piece of paper. When complete, check your results by comparing your answers to the preferred answers provided in Appendix A.

Please note that Knowledge Check questions are not actual PMP Exam questions. These questions are intended to reinforce key terms, concepts, and themes. While these Knowledge Check questions are typical of what you can expect on your PMP Exam, many actual PMP Exam questions are more in-depth, designed to challenge your judgment (not rote memory) in applying concepts, processes, and methodologies.

1. Which of the following best describes the Acquire Project Team process?
   A. The Acquire Project Team process is applied to obtain needed human resources (people) from functional managers.
   B. The Acquire Project Team process is applied to assign needed human resources (people) to the project directory.
   C. The Acquire Project Team process is applied to assign project team roles and responsibilities.
   D. The Acquire Project Team process is applied to obtain and assign needed human resources (people) to the project.

2. Which statement is least true?
   A. In Matrix Organizations, project managers may have to negotiate with functional managers to obtain needed people.
   B. In strong Matrix Organizations, project managers may have more authority than functional managers.
   C. In Functional Organizations, it is the project sponsor's responsibility to assign project staff.
   D. A Responsibility Assignment Matrix (RAM) illustrates assignments and levels of authority/responsibility, as a function of WBS elements. There is no time associated with a RAM.

3. Acquire Project Team Tools & Techniques include:
   A. Pre-assignment and resource calendars
   B. Negotiation and acquisitions
   C. Virtual teams and resource calendars
   D. Project staff assignments and acquisitions

4. You are assigned to manage an important project for your organization. This project is the direct result of your company winning a competitive bid. You are told that your project team is already selected and assigned. What is the likely reason for staff being assigned before the project even begins?
   A. Your project sponsor does not fully trust you to make staff assignment decisions.
   B. Specific staff members were part of your company's winning proposal.
   C. Staff assignment is the responsibility of your company's Human Resources department.
   D. Your company assigns the same personnel to every project.

End of Lesson 31

32

Lesson 32
Develop Project Team

Objectives

At the end of this lesson, you will be able to:

- Describe the purpose of the Develop Project Team process
- Describe the Inputs, Tools & Techniques, and Outputs of the Develop Project Team process
- Understand ways that the project manager can facilitate team building within the project team

Roadmap to the PMBOK Guide

	Initiating	Planning	Executing	M & C	Closing
Integration					
Scope					
Time					
Cost					
Quality					
Human Resources			■		
Communications					
Risk					
Procurement					

The project manager exerts considerable interpersonal skills in order to enable the project team to work together effectively. Develop Project Team is focused on enhancing individual and group competencies.

Develop Project Team is the process of enhancing the ability of individual team members (skills and team cohesiveness) to enhance overall project performance. In practice, team development is a continuous process applied from the time the project team comes together until the team disbands. In concept, stronger individuals will naturally create a stronger team.

Generally, Develop Project Team tools include:

• training

• team-building activities

• reward and recognition systems

• colocation

Some project managers like to establish a project war room where core team members can be colocated to work in close proximity during the project.

In some Matrix Organizations, team development can be extra challenging when team members report to both the project manager and to their functional manager. In most organizations, the resource will be more closely aligned with their functional manager and will minimize input from the project manager on any organizational issues other than those directly related to the project.

Because motivation is a key management skill in team development, we begin this lesson with a motivation primer.

Study Tips

Successful team development requires a practical understanding of the dynamics of human behavior to create a project environment in which team members feel motivated to excel.

• Team members should desire to stay and grow with the project.

• Team members should desire to fulfill their responsibilities and perform assigned tasks.

• Team members should desire to go beyond average performance, to demonstrate creativity and innovation.

MOTIVATION THEORIES

Motivation is internal, triggered by the needs and desires that create drive in people. Motivational theories are broken into two categories.

Content Theories focus on motivating desired behavior by satisfying specific motivation factors, such as money, shelter, security, growth, and achievement.

- Maslow's Hierarchy of Needs: This is probably the best-known content theory. Maslow identifies five levels of needs, in ascending order of priority: Physiological Needs, Safety Needs, Social Needs, Esteem, Self Actualization. According to this theory, a person must satisfy lower level needs before ascending the pyramid. Maslow believes it is "unfulfilled needs" that serve as motivators. The diagram is shown below.

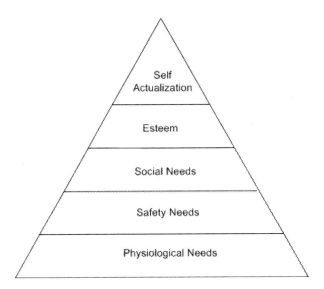

- Alderfer's ERG Needs: Alderfer maintains that people have three sets of equally important fundamental motivators: Existence Needs (food, shelter), Relatedness Needs (relationships), and Growth Needs (development).

- Herzberg's Motivator/Hygiene Theory: Herzberg maintains that hygiene factors (money, environment, relationships) are essential to maintaining harmony, but do not motivate. Herzberg's motivators include advancement, recognition, and responsibility.

Process Theories focus on producing desired behavior by employing specific motivational processes.

- McGregor's Theory X/Theory Y: Probably the best-known process theory, McGregor maintains that Theory X managers assume all people dislike work and try to avoid it. They motivate accordingly, usually with a strict hand. Theory Y managers assume all people can be high achievers when motivated, then motivate accordingly.

- Morse and Lorsch's Contingency Theory: Motivation is driven by the core desire to achieve competence

- Latham and Locke's Goal-setting Theory: Motivation is driven by the desire to achieve goals.

- Vroom's Expectancy Theory: Motivation is driven by the expectation of a reward.

- Skinner's Reinforcement Theory: Motivation is driven by the influence of a previous experience by the person, positive or negative.

- Adams's Equity Theory: Motivation is driven by a core desire to be treated equitably.

PROCESS ELEMENTS

The Develop Project Team process has the following Inputs:

- **Project Staff Assignments**   The appropriate people, reliably assigned to staff the project

- **Project Management Plan**   The consolidated package of the subsidiary management plans and baselines

- **Resource Calendars**   Documents the time periods each team member can work on the project

The Develop Project Team process uses the following Tools & Techniques:

- **Interpersonal Skills**   The broad set of "soft skills" important to team development

- **Training**   Activities designed to enhance the competencies of project team members

- **Team-Building Activities**   Actions designed to enhance interpersonal relationships among team members

- **Ground Rules**   Documented team rules to establish clear expectations with respect to acceptable behavior

- **Colocation**   The placing of team members in the same physical location, to enhance team performance

- **Recognition and Rewards**   Formal management actions that recognize and reward desirable behavior

The Develop Project Team process has the following Outputs:

- **Team Performance Assessments**   Formal and/or informal assessments of the team's effectiveness

- **Enterprise Environmental Factors Updates**   Updates to employee training records and skill assessments

Develop Project Team (9.3)		
This process improves people's competencies in order to enhance performance		
Inputs	**Tools and Techniques**	**Outputs**
• Project Staff Assignments • Project Management Plan • Resource Calendar	• Interpersonal Skills • Training • Team-Building Activities • Ground Rules • Colocation • Recognition and Rewards	• Team Performance Assessment • Enterprise Environmental Factors Updates

TSI Study Aid
This chart is part of the study aid poster series available at *www.truesolutions.com.*

COMMON PROCESS TASKS

The following is a list of the common tasks associated with the Develop Project Team process:

- Utilize your project team policies and procedures

- Perform team-building activities

- Establish a colocated team

- Implement programs that enhance your project team performance, including use of conflict/stress reduction techniques

- Implement rewards and recognition according to your plan

THINK ABOUT IT

. . . .

Instructions Think about how this project management process is defined, used, and documented in your organization.

Compare your organization's use of this process to the PMI® definition.

Use this exercise to compare how you practice project management to what is specified in the *PMBOK® Guide Fourth Edition.*

Best practices suggest that each of the following items are used during the Develop Project Team Process.

Which of these items do you use when practicing project management?

☐ Training

☐ Co-Location of the Team

☐ Ground Rules for Behavior

☐ Team Building Activities

☐ Reward and Recognition Systems

Which of these tools do you use in your application of project management?

_____

_____

_____

_____

_____

What types of Team Building activities do you commonly use?

_____

_____

_____

_____

_____

MUST KNOW CONCEPTS

1. Develop Project Team is the process of enhancing the ability of individual team members (skills and team cohesiveness) to enhance overall project performance.

2. In some Matrix Organizations, team development can be extra challenging when team members report to both the project manager and to their functional manager.

3. The primary deliverable (Output) of the Develop Project Team process are team performance assessments.

4. It may be helpful to colocate team members to a single work location during the project.

5. A war room is sometimes established to serve as a temporary office, to function as a single working headquarters for the project team.

6. Rewards and recognition are management actions intended to encourage desired behavior.

7. Important content theories of motivation include Maslow's Hierarchy of Needs and Herzberg's Motivator/Hygiene Theory.

8. Important process theories of motivation include McGregor's Theory X/Theory Y.

ADDITIONAL READING

• PMBOK Guide – Section 9.3 Develop Project Team

LESSON QUIZ

Instructions   Here are some questions to help reinforce your learning. Complete this quiz from memory to the best of your ability. For each question, circle or check your selected answer on this page or a separate piece of paper. When complete, check your results by comparing your answers to the preferred answers provided in Appendix A.

Please note that Knowledge Check questions are not actual PMP Exam questions. These questions are intended to reinforce key terms, concepts, and themes. While these Knowledge Check questions are typical of what you can expect on your PMP Exam, many actual PMP Exam questions are more in-depth, designed to challenge your judgment (not rote memory) in applying concepts, processes, and methodologies.

1. Develop Project Team Inputs include all of the following except:
   A. Project staff assignments
   B. Resource calendars
   C. Team-building activities
   D. Project Management Plan

2. Which of these statements best describes the Develop Project Team process?
   A. Develop Project Team is the process of creating the project's rewards and recognition procedures.
   B. Develop Project Team is the process of enhancing the ability of individual team members to enhance overall project performance.
   C. Develop Project Team is the process of creating the project team's motivation procedures.
   D. Develop Project Team is the process of colocating team members to a single project war room; which will serve as the team's headquarters facility during the project.

3. The highest level in Maslow's Hierarchy of Needs is:
   A. Safety
   B. Esteem
   C. Self Actualization
   D. Self Preservation

4. Which of the following statement is most true?
   A. Colocation can include moving team members into a more central area when team members already work at the same physical location, but should not include relocating team members from other geographic locations.
   B. Team Development is generally easier in Functional Organizations.
   C. In some organizations, team development can be extra challenging when team members report to both the project manager and to their functional manager.
   D. Team development procedures should be developed during Develop Project Charter.

End of Lesson 32

Lesson 33
Manage Project Team

Objectives

At the end of this lesson, you will be able to:

- Describe the purpose of the Manage Project Team process
- Describe the Inputs, Tools & Techniques, and Outputs of the Manage Project Team process
- Understand the use of an Issues Log in managing resources

Roadmap to the PMBOK Guide

	Initiating	Planning	Executing	M & C	Closing
Integration					
Scope					
Time					
Cost					
Quality					
Human Resources			■		
Communications					
Risk					
Procurement					

The project manager will use interpersonal skills in Manage Project Team to manage the individual behavior of the team members assigned to the project.

We apply the Manage Project Team process to address performance, behavior, issues, and conflicts associated specifically with project team members.

The process involves tracking and appraising team member performance, resolving issues, observing team behavior, managing conflicts and providing feedback. In Matrix Organizations, dual reporting roles of team members typically create complications that must be managed properly by the project manager. Effectively managing these dual reporting situations is often a critical success factor in project environments.

Of course, the intended outcome of the Manage Project Team process is enhanced overall project performance.

PROCESS ELEMENTS

The Manage Project Team process has the following Inputs:

- **Project Staff Assignments**   The appropriate people, reliably assigned to staff the project

- **Project Management Plan**   The consolidated package of the subsidiary management plans and baselines

- **Team Performance Assessments**   Formal and/or informal assessments of the team's effectiveness

- **Performance Reports**   S-curves, bar charts, tables, histograms, etc., that summarize team member performance

- **Organizational Process Assets**   Consideration factors such as processes, procedures, and corporate knowledge base

The Manage Project Team process uses the following Tools & Techniques:

- **Observation and Conversation**   Used to stay in touch with project work and team member attitudes

- **Project Performance Appraisals**   Formal and/or informal appraisals to provide feedback to team members

- **Conflict Management**   Used to enhance productivity and create positive working relationships

- **Issue Log**   Written log identifying specific issues, issue owners, and resolution target dates

- **Interpersonal Skills**   The broad set of "soft skills" important to team development

The **Manage Project Team** process has the following Outputs:

- **Enterprise Environmental Factors Updates**   Updates to employee training records and skill assessments

- **Organizational Process Assets Updates**   Updates to corporate documents, guidelines, procedures, historical information, etc.

- **Change Requests**   Request for changes to scope, schedule, costs, or processes or other project documentation

- **Project Management Plan Updates**   updates to the Project Management Plan as a result of this process

Manage Project Team (9.4)		
This process tracks team member performance to enhance overall project performance		
Inputs	**Tools and Techniques**	**Outputs**
• Project Staff Assignments • Project Management Plan • Team Performance Assessments • Performance Reports • Organizational Process Assets	• Observation and Conversation • Project Performance Appraisals • Conflict Management • Issue Log • Interpersonal Skills	• Enterprise Environmental Factors • Organizational Process Assets Updates • Change Requests • Project Management Plan Updates

TSI Study Aid

This chart is part of the study aid poster series available at *www.truesolutions.com*.

PROCESS DOCUMENTS

One of the most important documents that will be used in this process is the Issues Log. The Issues Log as applied to project management can be a public document concerned directly with all issues that are being addressed on the project. In this case, many times the project manager is addressing and documenting sensitive human resource issues. The issues log as applied here may be a semi-public document that is held by the project manager and discussed only with human resource personnel and project senior managers.

Sometimes this human resources issues log is simply a journal kept by the project manager — unless personnel action is required. The project manager should determine what is appropriate for the project and organizational culture that they are working in.

A generic Issues Log that is suitable for common project issues will be shown later in Manage Stakeholder Expectations.

COMMON PROCESS TASKS

The following is a list of the common tasks associated with the Manage Project Team process:

- Tracking team member performance

- Providing team member feedback and documented appraisals

- Applying conflict resolution skills

- Maintaining an Issue Log

- Coordinating changes to enhance project team member performance

THINK ABOUT IT

We all know there will be conflicts on projects. In many cases, these situations can be resolved quickly. However, there are times when conflicts with team members cannot be resolved. In this situation, I was brought in as the program manager from outside of an organization. Upon my arrival, one of the project managers appeared distant and uncooperative. We met and discussed her concerns. She explained she was previously promised my position and was extremely unhappy regarding my arrival at the project management office. After reviewing her concerns with my sponsor, I discovered her performance was not meeting the sponsor's expectations and he felt she was not ready to take on the additional responsibility. However, the sponsor and her supervisor had not documented their concerns nor communicated them to her during the past year.

The project manager and I sat down and put a plan together to position her to ultimately assume my role, since I had only planned to remain in this position for six months. The first month was great, however, the second month I noticed her behavior reverting back to the original dissatisfactions. We continued to meet and I began to document the negative behavior on an Issue Log, reviewed only by the sponsor and myself. Despite the attempts to correct the problems, the project manager could not get past her resentment and anger over not having the program manager position. Finally, she was released from the company. The Issue Log became a key document used to make the case and show the attempts to resolve the problems.

Fortunately, within two weeks of her departure, the team improved their overall performance and that impacted the entire organization. Unfortunately, her behavior was left unaddressed for a year and that negatively affected the organization. If an Issue Log had been used and her negative behavior addressed in a timely manner, she may have been the appropriate choice when the program manager position became available.

Contributed by Sharron Frohner, PMP

MUST KNOW CONCEPTS

1. The Manage Project Team process is applied to address performance, behavior, issues, and conflicts associated specifically with project team members.

2. Observation and conversation are key methods to stay in touch with the work and attitudes of project team members.

3. Successful conflict management results in greater productivity and positive working relationships.

ADDITIONAL READING

• PMBOK Guide – Section 9.4 Manage Project Team

LESSON QUIZ

Instructions   Here are some questions to help reinforce your learning. Complete this quiz from memory to the best of your ability. For each question, circle or check your selected answer on this page or a separate piece of paper. When complete, check your results by comparing your answers to the preferred answers provided in Appendix A.

Please note that Knowledge Check questions are not actual PMP Exam questions. These questions are intended to reinforce key terms, concepts, and themes. While these Knowledge Check questions are typical of what you can expect on your PMP Exam, many actual PMP Exam questions are more in-depth, designed to challenge your judgment (not rote memory) in applying concepts, processes, and methodologies.

1. Manage Project Team Inputs include:
   A. Team performance assessments, performance reports, organizational process assets, and Issue Log
   B. Team performance assessments, performance reports, organizational process assets, and project staff assignments
   C. Observation and conversation, project staff assignments, Issue Log, and change requests
   D. Project performance appraisals, interpersonal skills, project staff assignments, and performance reports

2. Which of the following is most true?
    A. Staffing changes do not have to be processed through the Perform Integrated Change Control process.
    B. An Issue Log is a written document which provides visibility and tracking of responsible party and resolution due dates for a particular issue.
    C. Issues are also known as risks.
    D. Conflict should be avoided at all costs during a project.

3. The Manage Project Team process is applied to:
    A. Enhance the performance of project team members, to enhance the overall project performance
    B. Coordinate training for project team members and to create the project's reward and recognition system
    C. Address performance, behavior, issues, and conflicts associated specifically with project team members
    D. Develop options and determine actions to create opportunities for project team member advancement

End of Lesson 33

34

Lesson 34
Perform Quality Assurance

Objectives
At the end of this lesson, you will be able to:
- Describe the purpose of the Perform Quality Assurance process
- Describe the Inputs, Tools & Techniques, and Outputs of the Perform Quality Assurance process
- Understand the use of the Quality Audit

Roadmap to the PMBOK Guide

	Initiating	Planning	Executing	M & C	Closing
Integration					
Scope					
Time					
Cost					
Quality			▓▓▓		
Human Resources					
Communications					
Risk					
Procurement					

Quality Assurance is a critical process intended to ensure that the project fulfills the operational metrics and continuous improvement goals defined as part of the Quality Management Plan.

Quality Assurance (QA) is the application of quality activities intended to ensure that the project will employ all processes necessary to satisfy recognized requirements. Quality activities should be applied across the entire project life cycle.

An intended outcome of applying the Perform Quality Assurance process is continuous process improvement. Continuous process improvement includes all actions to reduce waste and nonvalue-added activities, to increase project efficiency and effectiveness. An example of process improvement could be reducing the overall project cost by 2% through more efficient use of resource leveling. Continuous process improvement is sometimes termed "Kaizen," representing the quality philosophy of achieving improvement via small incremental steps. Note that process improvement is focused on improved project performance, not improved functionality of the product of the project.

While many organizations support quality assurance with dedicated departments, it is important to understand that project quality management is the responsibility of the project manager.

PROCESS ELEMENTS

The Perform Quality Assurance process has the following Inputs:
- **Quality Metrics**   Operational definitions and project elements, and how they are to be measured by quality control

- **Project Management Plan**   The consolidated package of the subsidiary management plans and baselines which contains the Quality Management Plan and the Process Improvement Plan

- **Work Performance Information**   Performance results such as performance measures, status deliverables, schedule progress, and incurred costs

- **Quality Control Measurements**   Results of all quality control activities

The Perform Quality Assurance process uses the following Tools & Techniques:
- **Plan Quality and Perform Quality Control Tools and Techniques**   The same Tools & Techniques used for the Plan Quality process and the Perform Quality Control process

- **Quality Audits**   Structured reviews to identify ineffective/inefficient processes/procedures as well as best practices and Lessons Learned

- **Process Analysis**   Implements the process improvement plan, to identify needed improvements

The Perform Quality Assurance process has the following Outputs:

- **Organizational Process Assets Updates**   Updates to quality standards

- **Change Requests**   Requests for changes to take corrective action, preventive actions, and/or perform defect repair

- **Project Management Plan Updates**   Updates to the Project Management Plan as a result of this process, specifically the Quality Management Plan, Schedule Management Plan and the Cost Management Plan

- **Project Document Updates**   Updates to other project documentation (i.e. quality audit reports, training plans, and process documentation)

Perform Quality Assurance (8.2)		
This process ensures that the project employs all processes needed to meet requirements		
Inputs	**Tools and Techniques**	**Outputs**
• Quality Metrics • Project Management Plan • Work Performance Information • Quality Control Measurements	• Plan Quality and Perform Quality Control Tools and Techniques • Quality Audits • Process Analysis	• Organizational Process Assets Updates • Change Requests • Project Management Plan Updates • Project Document Updates

PROCESS DOCUMENTS

The main purpose of the Perform Quality Assurance process is to determine if the project is progressing in the manner in which it was planned. Best practices for project management and creation of the project product (metrics) are measured during the Perform Quality Assurance process.

A template for measuring quality metrics is shown below.

True Solutions, Inc.
Project Management Template
Volume 1: Quality Metrics Template

Quality Metrics

Project Name:		
Prepared by:		
Date:		
Project Manager:		
Project Phase:	**Overall Project Status:**	
Metrics Date:	**Metrics Number:**	**Metrics Leader:**
Metrics Team:		
Goal(s) of This Specific Metrics:		

Metrics of Management of Project:

1. On time performance	**Assessment:**	**Comment:**
2. Budge Control	**Assessment:**	**Comment:**
3. (required project objective #3)	**Assessment:**	**Comment:**
4. (required project objective #4)	**Assessment:**	**Comment:**

Overall Assessment of Management of Project:

Recommended Action(s)/Lessons Learned Regarding Management of the Project:
1.
2.
3.

Metrics of the Product of the Project:

1. Defect frequency	**Assessment:**	**Comment:**
2. Failure rate	**Assessment:**	**Comment:**
3. Reliability	**Assessment:**	**Comment:**
4. Test Coverage	**Assessment:**	**Comment:**
5. (required product characteristic #5)	**Assessment:**	**Comment:**
6. (required product characteristic #6)	**Assessment:**	**Comment:**

Overall Assessment about the Product of the Project:

Recommended Action(s)/Lessons Learned Regarding the Product of the Project:
1.
2.
3.

Additional Metrics Comments:
1.
2.
3.

Have you attached additional material(s)?	yes	no

Name(s) of attachment(s):
1.
2.

Metrics Report Submitted To:	**Date:**

 **Application Aid**

This form is available individually or as a set from *www.truesolutions.com*.

COMMON PROCESS TASKS

The following is a list of the common tasks associated with the Perform Quality Assurance Process:

- Perform project quality control testing and measurement

- Determine the benefits/costs of your project quality efforts

- Document your project quality outcomes in a format suitable for comparison and analysis

- Identify and implement actions needed to increase your project effectiveness and efficiency

- Document Lessons Learned for improved performance

- Implement process improvements using your project change control processes

- Execute project quality control, assurance, and improvement processes

THINK ABOUT IT

Instructions Think about how this project management process is defined, used, and documented in your organization. Compare your organization's use of this process to the PMI® definition.

Use this exercise to compare how you practice project management to what is specified in the *PMBOK® Guide Fourth Edition*.

Think about how this process is defined, used and documented in your organization. Write a brief description of how you use this process:

_____

_____

_____

_____

_____

_____

_____

What specific Inputs, Tools or Techniques do you use as part of this process in your organization?

_____

_____

_____

_____

_____

_____

Are the outcomes from this process different in your organization or experiences?

_____

_____

_____

_____

_____

MUST KNOW CONCEPTS
. . . .

1 Quality Assurance is the application of all quality activities intended to ensure the project will employ all processes necessary to satisfy recognized requirements.

2 Quality activities should be applied across the entire project life cycle.

3 An intended outcome of applying the Perform Quality Assurance process is continuous process improvement.

4 Continuous process improvement (quality improvement) is sometimes termed Kaizen, representing the quality philosophy of achieving improvement via small incremental steps.

5 Continuous process improvement is focused on improved project performance, not improved functionality of the product of the project.

6 Project quality management is the responsibility of the project manager.

ADDITIONAL READING
. . . .

• PMBOK Guide – Section 8.2 Perform Quality Assurance

LESSON QUIZ

Instructions   Here are some questions to help reinforce your learning. Complete this quiz from memory to the best of your ability. When complete, check your results by comparing your answers to the preferred answers provided in Appendix A.

1. Which of the following best describes the Perform Quality Assurance process?
    A. The Perform Quality Assurance process provides confidence that the project will satisfy relevant quality standards.
    B. The Perform Quality Assurance process is applied to measure project performance, using quality assurance control charts.
    C. The Perform Quality Assurance process is applied to measure project performance, using earned value management (EVM).
    D. The Perform Quality Assurance process is applied to improve the functionality of the product of the project.

2. The responsibility for project quality management lies with:
    A. The project manager
    B. The project core team member assigned to manage project quality
    C. The highest ranking QA/QC manager in the performing organization
    D. The organization's QA/QC manager assigned to oversee quality activities for this particular project

3. Perform Quality Assurance Outputs include:
    A. Process analysis
    B. Change requests
    C. Quality audits
    D. Results of quality control measurements

4. Which of the following statements is least true?
    A. Quality Assurance (QA) is the collective total of all activities intended to ensure that the project satisfies recognized quality requirements.
    B. Quality activities should be applied across the entire project life cycle.
    C. Process improvement is sometimes termed Kaizen, representing the quality philosophy of achieving improvement via small incremental steps.
    D. Process improvement is focused on the improving functionality of the product of the project.

End of Lesson 34

35

Lesson 35
Distribute Information

Objectives

At the end of this lesson, you will be able to:

- Describe the purpose of the Distribute Information process
- Describe the Inputs, Tools & Techniques, and Outputs of the Distribute Information process
- Understand that all project documents become part of "organizational process assets"

Roadmap to the PMBOK Guide

	Initiating	Planning	Executing	M & C	Closing
Integration					
Scope					
Time					
Cost					
Quality					
Human Resources					
Communications			▓		
Risk					
Procurement					

One of the many challenges for the project manager is to effectively manage the distribution of communications during the project. Distribute Information is done to fulfill the Communications Management Plan.

Distribute Information is the communications process of making project information available to project stakeholders, as determined and documented in the Communications Management Plan.

It should be noted that information distribution may be facilitated by keeping orderly records. Orderly record keeping can assist in information distribution only when there are effective distribution methods chosen. Information distribution methods should be appropriate to the project, the timeliness required, and the culture of the organization that you are working in.

Distribution of information can be done effectively if there are effective retrieval systems available and put into use. And finally, in order to effectively distribute information, the project manager must possess good general communications skills. Information is often distributed to stakeholders that is clouded with technical terms or acronyms which are not readily understandable by managers or customers.

Effective distribute information techniques include:

• Sender-receiver models: Understanding feedback and barriers to communication

• Choice of media: Written, verbal, or electronic; based on the needs of the project

• Writing styles: Using active vs. passive

• Meeting management: Agendas and effective means for addressing conflict

• Presentation: Body language and presentation aids

• Facilitation: Obtaining consensus and overcoming obstacles

It is important to be mindful that communication is not complete until the sender is confident that the receiver understands the information, as intended. In a later process, Manage Stakeholders Expectations, the project manager will address any issues that arise from the distribution of information. Project success is most likely when all stakeholders have a common understanding of the current condition of the project.

PROCESS ELEMENTS
. . . .

The Distribute Information process has the following Inputs:

• **Project Management Plan**   The consolidated package of the subsidiary management plans and baselines specifically the Communications Management Plan

• **Performance Reports**   S-curves, bar charts, tables, histograms, etc., that summarize work performance measurements

• **Organizational Process Assets**   Consideration factors such as policies, procedures, guidelines, templates, and historical information

The Distribute Information process uses the following Tools & Techniques:

- **Communication Methods**   Individual/group meetings, video/audio conferences, other communication methods

- **Information Distribution Tools**   Hard copy documents, electronic distribution, web-based distribution, etc.

The Distribute Information process has the following Output:

- **Organizational Process Assets Updates**   Updates to stakeholder notifications, project reports, project presentations, project records, feedback from stakeholders, and lessons Learned documentation (all distributed information becomes part of Organizational Process Assets and ultimately part of the project archives at the end of the project).

Distribute Information (10.3)
This process provides needed information to stakeholders in a timely fashion

Inputs	Tools and Techniques	Outputs
• Project Management Plan • Performance Reports • Organizational Process Assets	• Communication Methods • Information Distribution Tools	• Organizational Process Assets Updates

TSI Study Aid

This chart is part of the study aid poster series available at *www.truesolutions.com*.

PROCESS DOCUMENTS

This process is intended to deliver a wide variety of project documents to project stakeholders. The process gets its basis from the planning process: Plan Communications. The Communications Management Plan document might be used in this process as a checklist to ensure that the appropriate documents are distributed to project stakeholders.

COMMON PROCESS TASKS

The following is a list of the common tasks associated with the Distribute Information process:

- Implement your project Communications Management Plan

- Implement your project information retrieval system

- Respond to expected and unexpected information requests

- Maintain your project records

THINK ABOUT IT

While working on a project to implement a new system at a company in another city, I learned the value and the dangers associated with using a document management system for document storage and review.

It has always been my assertion that one of the primary responsibilities of the project manager is to communicate effectively with stakeholders. I have always purported that timely communication is important. As well as being timely, the feedback component is also important. The perception held by the stakeholder is their reality. In order to determine what that perception or understanding of information is, you have to communicate directly with stakeholders to ascertain their views.

On our project we decided to use Microsoft Sharepoint as our status and performance reporting tool for the project. While Sharepoint is a lovely tool for storage and dissemination of information, it does lack a bit as far as feedback or interaction between the project manager and stakeholders. I was assured that it was part of that corporate culture that everyone always used Sharepoint for information storage and that everyone was used to retrieving information from the system.

Since I was a contractor and since I was traveling part of the time, I first learned the value of timely status reporting. The status report was due on Friday before 5:00 p.m. If I did not have the status report in the Sharepoint file at the appropriate time, I got five or six e-mails asking where the status report was. That meant that the process worked, right? Well, as I said, I would get five or six e-mails; but there were over forty stakeholders officially identified for the project. So what about those folks?

Well, I am sure you can guess the answer ... the remainder of the project stakeholders were not concerned about the status report since they never retrieved it and read it. Several of these very same folks would arrive for the biweekly status meeting totally devoid of any knowledge about what was happening on the project.

Distribution of information cannot be complete without some sort of mechanism to ensure that the distributed information is read, acknowledged, or acted upon in some manner.

Contributed by Tim Bergmann, PMP

MUST KNOW CONCEPTS

1 Distribute Information is the communications process of making project information available to project stakeholders, as determined and documented in the Communications Management Plan.

2 Communication is not complete until the sender is confident that the receiver understands the information, as intended.

3 Orderly record keeping, effective distribution methods (meetings, project intranet, presentations, e-mail), effective retrieval systems, and good general communication skills facilitate information distribution.

ADDITIONAL READING

• PMBOK Guide – Section 10.3 Distribute Information

LESSON QUIZ

Instructions   Here are some questions to help reinforce your learning. Complete this quiz from memory to the best of your ability. When complete, check your results by comparing your answers to the preferred answers provided in Appendix A.

1.   Distribute Information _____.
   A. is the communications process of distributing project performance reports to project stakeholders, as determined and documented in the Communications Management Plan
   B. is the communications process of making project information available to project stakeholders, as determined and documented in the Communications Management Plan
   C. is the communications process of distributing earned value reports to project stakeholders, as determined and documented in the Communications Management Plan
   D. is the communications process of preparing and delivering progress presentations to project stakeholders, as determined and documented in the Communications Management Plan

2. You and your project team have just commenced the execution/controlling phases of the project. Today, at the end of week one, your first weekly project performance report was prepared, reviewed/approved by the project core team, and sent to the appropriate distribution list via electronic mail. Based on this information, select the best statement.

   A. Your communication obligation is satisfied. Your weekly performance report, as agreed to in the Communications Management Plan, has been prepared and distributed, on-time, to the appropriate stakeholders. Stakeholders must accept ownership of their obligation to acknowledge receipt, then read, and understand the information.

   B. Your communication obligation is not yet satisfied. Although your weekly performance report, as agreed to in the Communications Management Plan, has been prepared and distributed, on-time, to the appropriate stakeholders, you must verify that the reports were received for communication to be complete. It may be a good idea to use electronic receipt verification to automate this process.

   C. Your communication obligation may not yet be satisfied. Although your weekly performance report, as agreed to in the Communications Management Plan, has been prepared and distributed, on-time, to the appropriate stakeholders, you should verify that the reports were received and that the recipients understood the information, as it was intended. It may be a good idea to interview a few recipients to ensure the reports satisfy their intended purpose, especially after distribution of the very first report.

   D. Your communication obligation is satisfied. Your weekly performance report, as agreed to in the Communications Management Plan, has been prepared and distributed, on-time, to the appropriate stakeholders. You may confidently move to the next activity.

3. Distribute Information Inputs include all the following except:
   A. Project Management Plan
   B. Performance reports
   C. Organizational process assets
   D. Communication methods

End of Lesson 35

Lesson 36
Manage Stakeholder Expectations

Objectives

At the end of this lesson, you will be able to:

- Describe the purpose of the Manage Stakeholder Expectations process
- Describe the Inputs, Tools & Techniques, and Outputs of the Manage Stakeholder Expectations process
- Understand what management skills are necessary to resolve issues with project stakeholders

Roadmap to the PMBOK Guide

	Initiating	Planning	Executing	M & C	Closing
Integration					
Scope					
Time					
Cost					
Quality					
Human Resources					
Communications			■		
Risk					
Procurement					

Issue resolution is a key part of any project. The project manager will work closely with stakeholders to facilitate and enable open communications about project issues in order to achieve common understanding of events, goals and objectives.

The Manage Stakeholder Expectations process is used to ensure that communication with project stakeholders is productive and meets the needs and desires of those stakeholders. This process also deals with resolving issues that arise from communications issues.

There is often a great deal of communication between the project management team and the project stakeholders. For the project to be managed effectively and efficiently the project manager should ensure that the stakeholder communications needs/desires are being met and that stakeholders are not being flooded with excessive and unnecessary communications.

In addition, successfully managing stakeholder expectations helps foster project acceptance and support and helps to reduce overall project risk. This will also limit disruptions during the project.

PROCESS ELEMENTS

The Manage Stakeholder Expectations process has the following Inputs:

- **Stakeholder Register**   A document identifying all project stakeholder information

- **Stakeholder Management Strategy**   Defines the approach to increase stakeholder support and reduce negative impacts

- **Project Management Plan**   The consolidated package of the subsidiary management plans and baselines specifically the Communications Management Plan

- **Issue Log**   Written log identifying specific issues, issue owners, and resolution target dates

- **Change Log**   A log used to track changes that occur during a project

- **Organizational Process Assets**   Consideration factors such as communication requirements, issue management procedures, change control procedures, and historical information

The Manage Stakeholder Expectations process uses the following Tools & Techniques:

- **Communication Methods**   Individual/group meetings, video/audio conferences, other communication methods

- **Interpersonal Skills**   The broad set of "soft skills" important to team development

- **Management Skills**   Presentation, writing, and public speaking skills as well as other general management skills

The Manage Stakeholder Expectations process has the following Outputs:

- **Organizational Process Assets Updates**   Updates to causes of issues, supportive documentation for corrective actions, and Lessons Learned

- **Change Requests**   Request for changes to scope, schedule, costs, or processes or other project documentation

- **Project Management Plan Updates**   Updates to the Communications Management Plan

- **Project Document Updates**   Updates to other project documentation (i.e. stakeholder management strategy, Stakeholder Register, and Issue Log)

Manage Stakeholder Expectations (10.4)		
This process manages communications to satisfy stakeholders' requirements		
Inputs	**Tools and Techniques**	**Outputs**
• Stakeholder Register • Stakeholder Management Strategy • Project Management Plan • Issue Log • Change Log • Organizational Process Assets	• Communication Methods • Interpersonal Skills • Management Skills	• Organizational Process Assets Updates • Change Requests • Project Management Plan Updates • Project Document Updates

This chart is part of the study aid poster series available at www.truesolutions.com.

PROCESS DOCUMENTS

In this process the project manager communicates directly with the project stakeholders to resolve any project issues as they arise. While some issues may be of a sensitive nature and might not appear in a public Issue Log, the majority of project issues will be listed on an Issue Log.

A sample of an Issue Log is shown below.

True Solutions, Inc.
Project Management Template
Volume 1: Project Issues and Questions Tracking Log
Template

PROJECT ISSUES AND QUESTIONS TRACKING LOG
Project Management Strategy

Project ID: Project Name:

Project Sponsor: Project Manager:

No.	From	Sent To	Assigned To	Item	Result	Sent Closed	Dates Due	Status
1								
2								
3								
4								
5								
6								
7								
8								
9								
10								
11								
12								
13								
14								
15								
16								
17								
18								
19								
20								
21								
22								
23								
24								
24								
26								
27								
28								
29								

Application Aid
This form is available individually or as a set from *www.truesolutions.com*.

COMMON PROCESS TASKS

The following is a list of the common tasks associated with the Manage Stakeholder Expectations process:

- Utilize your project communications policies and procedures

- Utilize your project Communications Management Plan

- Apply interpersonal and management skills

- Implement programs that enhance stakeholder communication, including use of issue resolution techniques

THINK ABOUT IT

Instructions Think about how this project management process is defined, used, and documented in your organization.

Use this exercise to compare how you practice project management to what is specified in the *PMBOK® Guide Fourth Edition*.

Think about how this process is defined, used and documented in your organization. Write a brief description of how you use this process:

_____

_____

_____

_____

_____

_____

What specific Inputs, Tools or Techniques do you use as part of this process in your organization?

_____

_____

_____

_____

_____

Are the outcomes from this process different in your organization or experiences?

_____

_____

_____

_____

_____

MUST KNOW CONCEPTS

1. The Manage Stakeholder Expectations process is applied to ensure that communications with project stakeholders is productive and meets the needs and desires of those stakeholders.

2. Actively managing project stakeholders increases the likelihood that the project will not be negatively impacted by unresolved stakeholder issues.

3. An Issue Log (or action-item log) is used to document and monitor the resolution of issues.

ADDITIONAL READING

• PMBOK Guide – Section 10.4 Manage Stakeholder Expectations

LESSON QUIZ

Instructions   Here are some questions to help reinforce your learning. Complete this quiz from memory to the best of your ability. When complete, check your results by comparing your answers to the preferred answers provided in Appendix A.

1. The Manage Stakeholder Expectations process is applied to:
   A. Ensure each stakeholder is familiar with the Project Management Plan, to the extent appropriate for the particular stakeholder
   B. Quantitatively determine the number of communication channels in a project environment
   C. Satisfy the needs of, and resolve issues with, project stakeholders
   D. Enhance the abilities of individual stakeholders to improve all project performance

2.	During project execution, a key stakeholder becomes very upset. She claims that she was not aware of a Project Management Plan element that impacts her division. Your best response would be:
   A.	As soon as possible, arrange a face-to-face meeting with your sponsor to plan a resolution
   B.	As soon as possible, arrange a face-to-face meeting with the stakeholder
   C.	As soon as possible, with your project management team, create a work-around plan
   D.	As soon as possible, document the stakeholder's concern and communicate it to your sponsor/customer

3.	Manage stakeholder Tools & Techniques include:
   A.	Communication methods and communications plan
   B.	Communication methods and Issue Log
   C.	Communication methods and interpersonal skills
   D.	Management skills and Issue Log

End of Lesson 36

37

Lesson 37
Conduct Procurements

Objectives

At the end of this lesson, you will be able to:

- Describe the purpose of the Conduct Procurements process
- Describe the Inputs, Tools & Techniques, and Outputs of the Conduct Procurements process
- Understand the notification, proposal, and seller selection elements within this process

Roadmap to the PMBOK Guide

	Initiating	Planning	Executing	M & C	Closing
Integration					
Scope					
Time					
Cost					
Quality					
Human Resources					
Communications					
Risk					
Procurement			■		

When procuring goods or services from a source external to the performing organization, it is intended that all processes used will be performed in a fair and impartial manner. Performing in such a manner is critical to compliance with the PMI Code of Ethics.

The Conduct Procurements process is used to solicit and obtain the project's external resources. This process includes obtaining seller responses and bids, selection of a seller or sellers, and awarding contracts. During the process of Conduct Procurements, the project manager (or purchasing department) will notify sellers of the potential need by providing appropriate procurement documents to the sellers. In response, the project manager (or purchasing department) will receive proposals from the seller on how the need can be satisfied by the vendor. Statements of work and evaluation criteria developed during Plan Procurements may be used in conjunction with notifying the vendors and evaluating their responses or proposals.

This process is often repeated many times within the life cycle of the project. In its simplest form, this may include searching for parts via the Internet (for example) and placing an order from the cheapest source, or it can be a more complicated process of submitting procurement packages, reviewing seller bids, seller evaluations, negotiations, and contract awards.

Successful procurement is often very critical to project success and can greatly impact the project's expenses.

PROCESS ELEMENTS

The Conduct Procurements process has the following Inputs:

- **Project Management Plan** The consolidated package of the subsidiary management plans and baselines

- **Procurement Documents** Documents used to solicit proposals from prospective sellers

- **Source Selection Criteria** Criteria used to help score or rate proposals submitted by prospective project suppliers (sellers)

- **Qualified Seller List** Final list of prospective suppliers (sellers)

- **Seller Proposals** Supplier (seller) responses that describe ability and willingness to provide requested services

- **Project Documents** Risk Register and Risk Related Contract Decisions

- **Make-or-Buy Decisions** The documented decisions of what will be developed in-house and what will be purchased

- **Teaming Agreements** Legal, contractual agreements between parties to form partnerships or joint ventures

- **Organizational Process Assets** Consideration factors such as processes, procedures, and corporate knowledge base

The Conduct Procurements process uses the following Tools & Techniques:

- **Bidder Conferences**   Q&A-type meetings with prospective project suppliers (sellers) prior to proposal preparation

- **Proposal Evaluation Techniques**   Formal evaluation process defined by procurement policies

- **Independent Estimates**   Prepared estimates used for benchmark on proposed seller responses

- **Expert Judgment**   Expert technical and/or managerial judgment (from any qualified source)

- **Advertising**   Public advertisements used to solicit potential sellers for contracted project goods and/or services

- **Internet Search**   Use of the Internet to research and procure required resources or materials

- **Procurement Negotiations**   Used to clarify structure and requirements for purchases between seller and purchaser

The Conduct Procurements process has the following Outputs:

- **Selected Sellers**   List of sellers selected using the process Tools & Techniques

- **Procurement Contract Award**   The contract package for selected sellers

- **Resource Calendars**   Information on the availability of resources over the planned activity duration

- **Change Requests**   Request for changes to scope, schedule, costs, or processes or other project documentation

- **Project Management Plan Updates**   Updates to the Project Management Plan as a result of this process

- **Project Document Updates**   Updates to other project documentation

PROCESS DOCUMENTS

As previously stated in the introduction to this process, there are multiple documents that can be used during the process of Conduct Procurements. The project manager or purchasing department will use the Inputs from Plan Procurements as a guide for this process. As Outputs the project manager or purchasing department receive proposals (the format for each proposal could be set by the buyer or seller). Ultimately, the project manager or purchasing department will award a contract to the selected seller.

The Contract Award Template lists common elements such as:

- Contract statement of work

- Schedule and performance criteria

- Pricing

- Payment terms

- Penalties

- Incentives

- Other information appropriate to the contract

An example of the Contract Award Template is shown below.

True Solutions, Inc.
Project Management Template
Volume 1: Procurement Contract Award Template

Procurement Contract Award

Project Name:	
Prepared by:	
Date:	
Statement of Work or Project Deliverables:	A statement of work that defines the need or deliverable from buyer that will meet sellers standard
Schedule Baseline	A statement that defines approximately when the buyer will be needed
Performance Reporting	The standard of work that is expected from buyer to meet the seller requirements
Pricing	The fixed price that is agreed upon by buyer and seller
Payment Terms	The method in which the obligation between buyer and seller will be satisfied
Fees and Retainage	The method of how the seller will be paid and what monies will be retained for warranty purposes
Inspection & Acceptance Criteria	The standard of work that is expected is agreed upon and acceptance criteria set
Penalties	If the standard of work is not met, what conditions will be placed upon buyer
Incentives	If the standard of work is met, what conditions will be placed upon seller
Insurance & Performance Bonds	This is protection for the buyer where a seller is required to pay for an insurance on work performed
Change Request Handling	This is the documentation that states how changes of work will be handled
Termination & ADR	This is where it is stated how termination of a seller is handled and how disputes about that are resolved

This form is available individually or as a set from www.truesolutions.com.

COMMON PROCESS TASKS

The following is a list of the common tasks associated with the Conduct Procurements Process:

- Conduct solicitation activities to obtain bids/proposals from your prospective sellers.

- Conduct bidder conferences.

- Collect proposals for evaluation.

- Evaluate proposals utilizing proposal evaluation techniques.

- Conduct contract negotiations.

- Award contract to selected seller/vendor.

THINK ABOUT IT

Instructions Think about how this project management process is defined, used, and documented in your organization. Compare your organization's use of this process to the PMI® definition. Do you use:

☐ Statements of work previously defined and documented

☐ Make-or-buy analysis results

☐ List of prequalified vendors

☐ Vendor evaluation criteria

☐ Teaming agreements

☐ Standard contract forms

☐ Procurement award checklist

How does your process differ?

_____

_____

_____

_____

How would you address any gaps that are apparent between the best practice definition and the way you perform this process today?

_____

_____

_____

_____

MUST KNOW CONCEPTS

1. Conduct Procurements is the process of obtaining bids and proposals from sellers and selecting a seller to provide resources for the project.

2. The primary deliverable from this process is selected sellers.

3. Objective bid evaluations should be performed to determine the successful bidders.

4. When performing a large procurement it may be helpful to narrow the field to a short list, then enter into more detailed negotiations with the remaining bidders.

5. The project manager should play an integral role throughout the contracting process.

6. Contracts are legally binding agreements between buyer and seller. The project team should be aware of the project's contractual legal obligations.

7. Contracts may be simple or complex, proportional to the size and complexity of the procurement.

ADDITIONAL READING

• PMBOK Guide – Section 12.2 Conduct Procurements

LESSON QUIZ

Instructions Here are some questions to help reinforce your learning. Complete this quiz from memory to the best of your ability. When complete, check your results by comparing your answers to the preferred answers provided in Appendix A.

1. Conduct Procurements Tools & Techniques include _____.
   A. bidder conferences
   B. project documents
   C. teaming agreements
   D. source selection criteria

2. Which of the following statements is *most* true?
   A. The Internet is a useful tool for conducting a bid-based procurement effort.
   B. Independent estimates are required in complex procurement efforts.
   C. Bidder conferences are conducted to ensure that all prospective sellers clearly understand the procurement process and that all prospective sellers are treated equally and fairly.
   D. Advertising for prospective bidders is best managed by advertising professionals.

3. The Conduct Procurements process is performed to _____.
   A. develop and document the project's procurement management plan
   B. obtain responses, select a seller, and award a contract
   C. determine the qualified sellers list
   D. advertise to prospective sellers to add to the company's vendor list

End of Lesson 37

Monitoring
and
Controlling

38

Lesson 38
Monitoring & Controlling Process Group

Objectives

At the end of this lesson, you will be able to:

- Understand what processes are used in the Monitoring and Controlling Process Group
- Understand the purpose for using Monitoring and Controlling processes for the project or project phase

Roadmap to the PMBOK Guide

	Initiating	Planning	Executing	M & C	Closing
Integration				■	
Scope				■	
Time				■	
Cost				■	
Quality				■	
Human Resources					
Communications				■	
Risk				■	
Procurement				■	

Monitoring and Controlling processes are part of the "Check and Act" portion of the "Plan-Do-Check-Act" cycle. The project manager checks to ensure that performance is appropriate, if performance is found to be variant, then action is taken to bring performance into compliance with plans.

The Monitoring and Controlling Process Group consists of ten processes that are intended to control the work during a project or project phase. The primary reason that these Controlling processes are performed is to ensure that the work performed is the work planned or is changed to meet the requirements of the project in a controlled manner. Monitoring and Controlling processes occur in all knowledge areas except the Human Resource Management area in the *PMBOK® Guide Fourth Edition*.

A key-word that might characterize the Monitoring and Controlling Process Group could be "check." The most important element of Monitoring and Controlling is to check against the plan and the execution to ensure that the project is on track.

The Monitoring and Controlling processes have a high degree of interaction with each other. In addition, these processes also work very closely with the processes in the Executing Process Group. Executing processes focus on producing deliverables, the Monitoring and Controlling processes concentrate on confirming that the planned deliverables are created and that these outputs meet the planned specifications and requirements.

When a change occurs on the project, the project manager will return to the Planning processes to update affected project documents to ensure that the entire project is constantly and properly documented.

MONITORING AND CONTROLLING TASKS

On your PMP Exam, you will encounter approximately forty-two questions that will test your understanding of Monitoring and Controlling processes. These forty-two questions will generally focus on the following Monitoring and Controlling tasks:

- As a PMP or project manager monitoring and controlling a project (or project phase), you may be required to measure project performance using appropriate tools and techniques in order to monitor the progress of the project, identify and quantify any variances, perform any corrective actions, and communicate with stakeholders.

- As a PMP or project manager monitoring and controlling a project (or project phase), you may be required to manage changes to the project scope, schedule, and budget using appropriate verification techniques in order to keep the project plan accurate, updated, reflective of authorized changes as defined in the change management plan, and to facilitate customer acceptance.

- As a PMP or project manager monitoring and controlling a project (or project phase), you may be required to ensure that project deliverables conform to quality standards established in the project quality plan, using appropriate tools and techniques (e.g., testing, inspection) in order to adhere to customer requirements.

- As a PMP or project manager monitoring and controlling a project (or project phase), you may be required to monitor the status of all identified risks by identifying any new risks, taking corrective actions, and updating the risk response plan in order to minimize the impact of the risks on the project.

KNOWLEDGE REQUIREMENTS

As a PMP applying Monitoring and Controlling processes in real-world projects, you will be required to possess in-depth knowledge in several project specific areas, as well as a broad knowledge of project management in general. The PMP Exam will test your understanding of these knowledge specifics.

By developing a familiarity with these knowledge specifics, you will better understand the context of many PMP Exam questions. As you progress through the *Ultimate PMP Exam Prep Guide*, you will see each of these areas mentioned. Please give some thought to each item as it relates to your own project management experiences with past and current projects.

Remember, the PMP or project manager is always required to have a very broad base of knowledge to work from. In many cases, the project manager has to work across the entire organization to effectively perform project management.

As a PMP or project manager applying Monitoring and Controlling processes, you may be expected to have knowledge of:

- Performance measuring and tracking techniques

- Status reporting and distribution

- Time management

- Conflict resolution

- Cost analysis

- Project control limits

- Prioritization and decision-making techniques

- Project templates and metrics

- Variance and trend analysis

- Quality measurement tools

- Quality standards and conformance criteria

- Industry best practices and standards

- Reporting procedures

- Process analysis

- Change control processes

- Project plan management

- Risk identification and analysis

- Risk response techniques

- Facilitation techniques

PERFORMANCE COMPETENCIES

As a PMP applying Monitoring and Controlling processes in real-world projects, there are many specific project management performance competencies (skills) that you may be expected to exercise.

By developing a familiarity with these skills, you will better understand the context of many PMP Exam questions. As you progress through the *Ultimate PMP Exam Prep Guide*, you will see each of these skills mentioned. As you read, please give thought to how the use of these skills relates to your past and current project experiences.

As a PMP or project manager applying Monitoring and Controlling processes, you may be required to exercise skill in:

- Communicating with stakeholders

- Problem solving

- Analyzing and interpreting performance data

- Implementing corrective actions in a proactive manner

- Developing root cause analysis

- Evaluating the impact of changes to the project

- Negotiating with stakeholders and getting approval for changes and corrective actions

- Identifying and analyzing issues to decide if changes are warranted

- Inspecting and reviewing

- Analyzing and elaborating project reports

- Observing processes to identify deviations

- Active listening

- Motivating and getting commitment

- Problem solving regarding risk responses

- Using experience and expert judgment to identify risks and corrective actions

---

Study Tip

Be sure to understand the Process Group Interactions

We have previously exposed and discussed information about Process Group Interactions. During the Executing phases or portions of the project a high degree of interaction occurs between the Executing *process group* and the Monitoring and Controlling *process group.*

The intent of the Executing process group is to create project deliverables. The intent of the Monitoring and Controlling process group is to make sure they are the right deliverables.

When completing the work of the project, processes from both process groups have to work together very closely and interact frequently in order to manage the project and its outcomes.

As you read the ***Ultimate PMP Exam Prep Guide***, remember to look for process flows (defined by one output becoming the input to another process) that define the interactions that occur on a typical project.

ADDITIONAL READING

- PMBOK Guide – Section 3.6

. . . .

Process Matching Exercise

Read the recommended reading for this lesson before attempting this exercise. After you have read all of the lesson material and the reading in the *PMBOK Guide*, your goal is to match the appropriate processes to the correct process group and knowledge area. All of the processes are listed on the right. In this exercise, match the correct *Monitoring and Controlling* processes to their knowledge area.

Knowledge Area	Process Group					Project Processes
	Initiating	Planning	Executing	Monitoring & Controlling	Closing	Report Performance
Integration						Control Schedule
						Verify Scope
						Plan Risk Responses
						Estimate Costs
						Develop Project Charter
						Identify Stakeholders
Scope						Develop Project Management Plan
						Close Project or Phase
						Monitor & Control Project Work
						Control Scope
						Monitor & Control Project Risk
Time						Direct & Manage Project Execution
						Acquire Project Team
						Plan Quality
						Perform Integrated Change Control
						Define Scope
Cost						Determine Budget
						Define Activities
						Plan Communications
Quality						Manage Stakeholder Expectations
						Manage Project Team
						Control Costs
Human Resource						Perform Quality Assurance
						Administer Procurements
						Develop Human Resource Plan
						Create WBS
Communication						Sequence Activities
						Perform Quality Control
						Close Procurements
						Develop Project Team
						Plan Risk Management
Risk						Conduct Procurements
						Estimate Activity Resources
						Identify Risks
						Perform Qualitative Risk Analysis
						Plan Procurements
						Estimate Activity Durations
Procurement						Perform Quantitative Risk Analysis
						Distribute Information
						Develop Schedule
						Collect Requirements

End of Lesson 38

39

Lesson 39
Control Scope

Objectives

At the end of this lesson, you will be able to:

- Describe the purpose of the Control Scope process
- Describe the Inputs, Tools & Techniques, and Outputs of the Control Scope process
- Understand how the process of Control Scope interacts with the process of Perform Integrated Change Control

Roadmap to the PMBOK Guide

	Initiating	Planning	Executing	M & C	Closing
Integration					
Scope				▓	
Time					
Cost					
Quality					
Human Resources					
Communications					
Risk					
Procurement					

Scope creep is a common occurrence in many projects. Control Scope is performed to monitor scope and make only necessary changes for the project.

Control Scope is the process of effectively managing changes in project scope, then integrating those changes across the entire project through the Perform Integrated Change Control process. In Scope Control, scope changes are identified by utilizing the variance analysis tool. After a scope change has been identified, it becomes an Output from this process (as a change request), which becomes an Input to Integrated Change Control.

It is important to understand that it is the project manager's responsibility to discourage unnecessary scope changes. It is also important to understand that, when changes are warranted, they must be made in strict accordance with the project's scope change control process, and the established scope baseline must remain intact. Rebaselining scope is appropriate only in extreme situations.

Some organizations utilize a change control board (CCB) to evaluate and approve/ disapprove scope change requests.

PROCESS ELEMENTS

The Control Scope process has the following Inputs:

- **Project Management Plan**   The consolidated package of the subsidiary management plans and baselines

- **Work Performance Information**   Raw data related to deliverable status, schedule progress, and costs incurred

- **Requirements Documentation**   Documentation describing how individual requirements fulfill the business needs of the project

- **Requirement Traceability Matrix**   A table which associates requirement origin and the relationship between the requirement's origin and history throughout the project life cycle

- **Organizational Process Assets**   Consideration factors such as processes, procedures, and corporate knowledge base

The Control Scope process uses the following Tools & Techniques:

- **Variance Analysis**   Comparing scope performance objectives to actuals, to assess the magnitude of variation

The Control Scope process has the following Outputs:

- **Work Performance Measurements**   Collection of project status information; technical performance measures, etc.

- **Change Requests**   Request for changes to scope, schedule, costs, or processes or other project documentation

- **Organizational Process Assets Updates**   Updates to corporate documents, guidelines, procedures, historical information, etc.

- **Project Management Plan Updates**   Updates to the Project Management Plan as a result of this process

- **Project Document Updates**   Updates to other project documentation

Control Scope (5.5)		
This process controls changes to project scope		
Inputs	**Tools and Techniques**	**Outputs**
• Project Management Plan • Work Performance Information • Requirements Documentation • Requirements Traceability Matrix • Organizational Process Assets	• Variance Analysis	• Work Performance Measurements • Change Requests • Organizational Process Assets Updates • Project Management Plan Updates • Project Document Updates

TSI *Study Aid*

This chart is part of the study aid poster series available at *www.truesolutions.com*.

PROCESS DOCUMENTS

The main document that may be used in this process would be a Scope Change Request. Sometimes a generic change request will be used instead of the more specific Scope Change Request.

True Solutions, Inc.
Project Management Template
Volume 1: Scope Change Request Template

(TSI)

Scope Change Request

Project Name:	
Prepared by:	
Date:	
Person(s) Requesting Change:	
Change Number:	
Detailed Description of Scope Change Requested:	
Reason for Scope Change Requested:	

Effect on Project Cost:

☐ Projected Cost *Overrun* of approximately   %

☐ Estimated Cost *Reduction* of approximately   %

Effect on Schedule:

☐ Planned Project Completion Date:

☐ New Project Completion Date:

Additional Remarks:

Approval	Project Manager	Date
Approval	(Other)	Date

 **Application Aid**

This form is available individually or as a set from *www.truesolutions.com*.

©Copyright 2009 True Solutions, Inc.
5001 LBJ Freeway, Suite 125-B Dallas, Texas 75244
Tel: 972.770.0900 Fax 972.770.0922 www.truesolutions.com

COMMON PROCESS TASKS

The following is a list of the common tasks associated with the Control Scope process:

- Evaluate the degree to which changes would affect your project scope

- Implement your scope change control system

- Use variance analysis to determine scope condition for the project

- Evaluate alternatives to scope modifications

- Implement approved changes, manage related work tasks, and integrate approved scope changes into other project control processes

THINK ABOUT IT

One might typically consider law firms to be customers who love to document. In this example, that is no exception. The project was a two-phased approach to internal software implementations. During the initiation process of phase one, a change control board was established to consider future changes.

One day, a key stakeholder (one of the attorneys) decided she wanted to make a change to the e-mail software during phase one of the project. I reminded her that we agreed to put all changes through the change control process and present the change to the change control board for consideration. The next day, the change control board met and I noticed this request was missing from the agenda. After the meeting, I asked her why it was not on the agenda. She explained she completed the request and realized the change would affect the time, cost, and scope of the project.

After we both sat down and reviewed the request, it was evident this change would ultimately better satisfy and meet the goals and expectations of other stakeholders but would be more applicable to the second phase of the project.

Using the Control Scope process and having an established change control board prior to starting the project were excellent ways to ensure that the project scope was controlled in phase one. It would have been easy to ignore and move onto the next phase and not consider her changes. However, being open to changes that would meet and satisfy the organization's strategic goals and applying them in the appropriate time is also important.

Contributed by Sharron Frohner, PMP

MUST KNOW CONCEPTS

1 Control Scope is the process of effectively managing changes in project scope, then integrating those changes across the entire project through the Perform Integrated Change Control process.

2 The primary deliverables (Outputs) of the Control Scope process include updates to all associated project plans and documents.

3 It is the project manager's responsibility to discourage unnecessary scope changes.

4 When legitimate scope changes are warranted, they should be made in accordance with the project's scope change control system.

5 For monitoring and performance measurement purposes, the established project scope baseline should remain unchanged.

6 Rebaselining project scope is appropriate only in extreme situations.

7 Some organizations utilize a change control board (CCB) to evaluate and approve/disapprove project scope change requests.

ADDITIONAL READING

- PMBOK Guide – Section 5.5 Control Scope

LESSON QUIZ

Instructions   Here are some questions to help reinforce your learning. Complete this quiz from memory to the best of your ability. When complete, check your results by comparing your answers to the preferred answers provided in Appendix A.

1. Legitimate scope changes may be necessitated/justified by many conditions. Of the following, which does *not* typify a condition that would justify a scope change?
    A. A sponsor's decision to reestimate activity costs
    B. A client's decision to add a feature to the product of the project
    C. A newly available technology that was not an option when project scope was initially documented
    D. A newly enacted government regulation

2. Control Scope Inputs include all of the following *except*:
   A. Requirements documentation
   B. Project Management Plan
   C. Change requests
   D. Work performance information

3. All of the following regarding Control Scope are true *except*:
   A. Control Scope ensures that requested changes go through the Perform Integrated Change Control process.
   B. Scope creep may result from uncontrolled changes in a project.
   C. Control scope is the process of effectively managing changes in project scope, then integrating those changes across the entire project.
   D. Control Scope is applied to guide the project change control board (CCB) in approving or denying Work Breakdown Structure change requests.

4. Scope Control_____.
   A. is applied to guide the project change control board in approving or rejecting WBS change requests
   B. is applied to determine and document how changes in project scope will be managed
   C. is the process of rebaselining scope
   D. is the process of effectively managing changes in project scope, then integrating those changes across the entire project

5. As a project manager, your first priority in relation to scope changes is to_____.
   A. manage each scope change immediately upon becoming aware of the request, in accordance with scope change control procedures
   B. discourage and prevent unnecessary changes
   C. ensure that all scope changes are properly documented
   D. discuss each scope change request with your project sponsor to ensure you have their approval before requesting the change

End of Lesson 39

Lesson 40
Control Schedule

Objectives

At the end of this lesson, you will be able to:

- Describe the purpose of the Control Schedule process
- Describe the Inputs, Tools & Techniques, and Outputs of the Control Schedule process
- Understand how Control Schedule interacts with the process of Perform Integrated Change Control

Roadmap to the PMBOK Guide

	Initiating	Planning	Executing	M & C	Closing
Integration					
Scope					
Time				■	
Cost					
Quality					
Human Resources					
Communications					
Risk					
Procurement					

When monitoring and controlling the project, scope, schedule and cost are critical elements to be constantly monitored. Schedule control is a particular concern since one missed schedule activity can often cause a cascade of schedule changes.

Control Schedule is the process of monitoring the status of the project to update project progress and manage changes to the schedule baseline, then integrating those changes across the entire project through the Perform Integrated Change Control process. In Control Schedule, schedule changes are identified using various tools, including variance analysis. After a schedule change has been identified, it becomes an Output from this process in the form of a change request, which then becomes an Input to Perform Integrated Change Control.

It is important to understand that it is the project manager's responsibility to discourage unnecessary schedule changes. It is also important to understand that, when changes are warranted, they must be made in strict accordance with the project's Schedule Change Control process, defined in the Schedule Management Plan, and that the established schedule baseline must remain intact. Rebaselining the schedule is appropriate only in extreme situations.

Some organizations utilize a change control board (CCB) to evaluate and approve/disapprove schedule change requests.

PROCESS ELEMENTS

The Control Schedule process has the following Inputs:
- **Project Management Plan**   The consolidated package of the subsidiary management plans and baselines which contains the schedule management plan and the schedule baseline

- **Project Schedule**   The most recent version of the project schedule with updates

- **Work Performance Information**   Project progress such as which activities have started, their progress, and which activities have finished

- **Organizational Process Assets**   Consideration factors such as existing formal and informal schedule, control-related policies, procedure, and guidelines, schedule control tools, and monitoring and reporting methods to be used

The Control Schedule process uses the following Tools & Techniques:
- **Performance Reviews**   Reviews to measure, compare, and analyze schedule performance

- **Variance Analysis**   Assessing the magnitude of variation from the original schedule baseline

- **Project Management Software**   Any software that can track planned dates versus actual dates, and forecast the effects of changes to the project schedule

- **Resource Leveling**   Technique applied to create efficient resource limits

- **What-If Scenario Analysis**   Explores various scenarios to bring the schedule into alignment with the plan (i.e. Monte Carlo simulations)

- **Adjusting Leads and Lags**   Used to find ways to bring project activities that are behind into alignment with the plan

- **Schedule Compression**   Used to find ways to bring project activities that are behind into alignment with the plan: (i.e. fast-tracking and crashing)

- **Scheduling Tool**   Tool used to perform schedule network analysis to generate an updated project schedule

The Control Schedule process has the following Outputs:

- **Work Performance Measurements**   Collection of project status information and calculated SV and SPI values

- **Change Requests**   Request for changes to schedule baseline and/or other components of the Project Management Plan

- **Organizational Process Assets Updates**   Updates to causes of variances, corrective action chosen, and the reasons, and other types of Lessons Learned from project schedule control

- **Project Management Plan Updates**   Updates to the Project Management Plan as a result of this process, specifically the schedule baseline, schedule management plan, and cost baseline

- **Project Document Updates**   Updates to other project documentation (i.e. schedule data and project schedule)

Control Schedule (6.6)		
This process controls changes to the project schedule		
Inputs	**Tools and Techniques**	**Outputs**
• Project Management Plan • Project Schedule • Work Performance Information • Organizational Process Assets	• Performance Reviews • Variance Analysis • Project Management Software • Resource Leveling • What-if Scenario Analysis • Adjusting Leads and Lags • Schedule Compression • Schedule Tool	• Work Performance Measurements • Change Requests • Organizational Process Assets Updates • Project Management Plan Updates • Project Document Updates

TSI Study Aid
This chart is part of the study aid poster series available at *www.truesolutions.com*.

PROCESS DOCUMENTS

In the Control Schedule process the primary document that might be used would be the Schedule Change Request. Again, the performing organization may choose to use a generic change request that covers all change areas instead of this more specific document. A sample is shown below.

True Solutions, Inc.
Project Management Template
Volume 1: Schedule Change Request Template

TSI

Schedule Change Request

Project Name:	
Prepared by:	
Date:	
Person(s) Requesting Change:	
Change Number:	
Detailed Description of Schedule Change:	
Reason for Schedule Change Requested:	

Effect on Project Cost:
    ☐ Projected Cost *Overrun* of approximately   %
    ☐ Estimated Cost *Reduction* of approximately   %

Overall Effect on Schedule:
    ☐ Planned Project Completion Date:
    ☐ New Project Completion Date:

Additional Remarks:

Approval	Project Manager	Date
Approval	(Other)	Date

Application Aid
This form is available individually or as a set from *www.truesolutions.com*.

COMMON PROCESS TASKS

The following is a list of the common tasks associated with the Control Schedule Process:

- Define the procedure by which your project schedule may be changed

- Implement your Schedule Change Control system

- Integrate schedule activities with your Integrated Change Control system

- Determine the need for a schedule change

- Determine the magnitude of a schedule change and the need for reestablishing your baseline

- Determine overall plan adjustments resulting from schedule updates

- Determine the need for schedule fast-tracking or crashing

- Initiate corrective actions to ensure that additional schedule changes are minimized

- Integrate approved schedule changes with your other project control processes

THINK ABOUT IT

Instructions Think about how this project management process is defined, used, and documented in your organization.

Compare your organization's use of this process to the PMI® definition.

Use this exercise to compare how you practice project management to what is specified in the *PMBOK® Guide Fourth Edition.*

 Think about how this process is defined, used and documented in your organization. Write a brief description of how you use this process:

_____

_____

_____

_____

_____

_____

_____

What specific Inputs, Tools or Techniques do you use as part of this process in your organization?

_____

_____

_____

_____

_____

Are the outcomes from this process different in your organization or experiences?

_____

_____

_____

_____

_____

MUST KNOW CONCEPTS

1. Control Schedule is the process of effectively monitoring the project progress and managing project schedule baseline changes, then integrating those changes across the entire project through the Perform Integrated Change Control process.

2. The primary deliverables (Outputs) of the Control Schedule process include updates to all associated project plans and documents.

3. Control Schedule uses earned value to calculate SV and SPI values for the project schedule

4. It is the project manager's responsibility to discourage unnecessary schedule changes.

5. When legitimate schedule changes are warranted, they should be made in accordance with the project's Schedule Change Control system.

6. For monitoring and performance measurement purposes, established project schedule baselines should remain unchanged, regardless of project changes.

7. Schedule rebaselining is appropriate only in extreme situations.

8. Some organizations utilize a change control board (CCB) to evaluate and approve/disapprove project schedule change requests.

ADDITIONAL READING

• PMBOK Guide – Section 6.6 Control Schedule

LESSON QUIZ

Instructions   Here are some questions to help reinforce your learning. Complete this quiz from memory to the best of your ability. When complete, check your results by comparing your answers to the preferred answers provided in Appendix A.

1. Which of the following best describes the intended application of the control schedule process:
    A. Control schedule is the process of effectively monitoring the project progress and managing project schedule baseline changes, then integrating those changes across the entire project
    B. Control schedule is the process applied to prevent changes to the schedule baseline
    C. Control schedule is the process applied to guide the project manager when making approval/denial decisions with respect to schedule baseline change requests
    D. Control schedule is the process applied to determine the potential benefit value of schedule change requests

2. The project Schedule Change Control system is intended to do what?
    A. Provide the procedural guidance by which schedule change requests are to be managed
    B. Provide the procedural guidance to integrate schedule change requests with the Project Management Information System (PMIS)
    C. Provide the procedural guidance to initiate corrective action with respect to the project schedule
    D. Provide the procedural guidance for the project manager and project team to ensure they authorize schedule changes in accordance with the performing organization's QA/QC standards

3. Control Schedule Tools & Techniques include all the following expect:
    A. Performance reviews
    B. Variance analysis
    C. Project schedule
    D. Project management software

End of Lesson 40

Lesson 41
Control Costs

Objectives

At the end of this lesson, you will be able to:

- Describe the purpose of the Control Costs process
- Describe the Inputs, Tools & Techniques, and Outputs of the Control Costs process
- Understand how to use earned value measurement to measure the project and report performance

Roadmap to the PMBOK Guide

	Initiating	Planning	Executing	M & C	Closing
Integration					
Scope					
Time					
Cost				■	
Quality					
Human Resources					
Communications					
Risk					
Procurement					

Earned Value Technique is an integral part of controlling the project using the Performance Measurement Baseline developed during Determine Budget. Earned Value results are often depicted in a dashboard format with "Red, Yellow or Green" status.

Control Costs is the process of effectively managing changes to the project budget, then integrating those changes across the entire project through the Perform Integrated Change Control process. It is important to understand that it is the project manager's responsibility to discourage unnecessary budget changes. It is also important to understand that when changes are warranted, that they be made in strict accordance with the project's Cost Change Control process, and that the established cost baseline remains intact. Rebaselining the budget is appropriate only in extreme situations.

In Control Costs, the application of earned value measurement (EVM) is a key tool used to measure project performance. Earned value measurement, aka: earned value management, earned value analysis, earned value technique, integrates cost, scope, and schedule to derive measurement values that accurately assess project progress to date, as well as forecast future performance.

Consider that schedule, scope, or cost values alone can create false impressions. For example, a project can be well under budget at any given time. This may appear favorable. However, if the under-budget performance is the result of being well behind schedule, then the project may not be in a favorable status. Earned value analysis corrects such issues.

As well as managing change to the cost parameter for the project, a key element to the process of Control Costs is the use of earned value measurement to measure project performance. Earned value measurement allows project teams to determine a number of critical project factors:

• Schedule performance: Is the project ahead or behind schedule?

• Time efficiency: How efficiently is the project using time?

• Forecast completion: When is the project likely to be completed?

• Cost performance: Is the project over or under budget?

• Resource efficiency: How efficiently is the project utilizing resources?

• Forecast costs: What will the remaining project work cost? What will be the final project total cost?

Earned value measurement relies on four key data points:

☐ **Planned Value (PV):** (also termed Budgeted Cost of Work Scheduled or BCWS) Planned value is the established baseline that indicates the amount of money planned for spending to date, at any particular point in time (regardless of what actual work has been performed).

☐ **Earned Value (EV):** (also termed Budgeted Cost of Work Performed or BCWP) Earned value is the established baseline that indicates the amount of money planned for spending on the actual work performed to date, at any particular point in time (regardless of other planned objectives).

☐ **Actual Cost (AC):** (also termed Actual Cost of Work Performed or ACWP) Actual cost is the amount of money spent on the actual work performed to date, at any particular point in time (regardless of other planned objectives).

☐ **Budget at Completion (BAC):** Budget at completion is simply the amount of money planned for spending on the entire project.

Based on these data points, EVM Performance Analysis and Forecasting can be accomplished. Once values for PV, EV, AC, and BAC are identified, the project team can factor them into specific equations to determine:

Variances

• Schedule Variance (SV)

• Cost Variance (CV)

• Variance at Completion (VAC)

Indices

• Schedule Performance Index (SPI)

• Cost Performance Index (CPI)

Forecasts

• Estimate at Completion (EAC)

• Estimate to Complete (ETC)

• To-Complete Performance Index (TCPI)

VARIANCE CALCULATIONS

The following describes the calculations to determine variance values:

Schedule Variance (SV)

SV = EV – PV

SV reveals schedule status ... at this time, is the project ahead of schedule or behind schedule? SV > 0 = ahead of schedule. SV < 0 = behind schedule.

Cost Variance (CV)

CV = EV – AC

CV reveals cost status ... at this time, is the project under budget or over budget? CV > 0 = under budget. CV < 0 = over budget.

Variance at Completion (VAC)

VAC = BAC – EAC

VAC forecasts final cost status ... when the project is complete, will it be under budget or over budget? VAC > 0 = under budget. VAC < 0 = over budget.

INDEX CALCULATIONS

The following describes the calculations to determine index values:

Schedule Performance Index (SPI)

SPI = EV / PV

SPI indicates time efficiency ... at present, how efficiently is the project utilizing time? SPI > 1 = ahead of schedule. SPI < 1 = behind schedule.

Cost Performance Index (CPI)

CPI = EV / AC

CPI indicates cost efficiency ... at present, how efficiently is the project utilizing resources? CPI > 1 = under budget. CPI < 1 = over budget.

FORECAST CALCULATIONS

The following describes the calculations to determine forecast values:

Estimate at Completion (EAC)

EAC = AC + ETC when using a bottom-up ETC estimate

EAC = AC + BAC – EV for work at budgeted rate

EAC = BAC/CPI; use when factoring CPI into forecast

EAC = AC + [(BAC – EV) / (CPI × SPI)] to factor in both CPI and SPI performance

EAC forecasts final project costs ... at present, what is the updated estimate for final/total project costs?

To-Complete Performance Index

TCPI = (BAC – EV)/(BAC – AC) or

TCPI = (BAC – EV)/(EAC – AC)

TCPI forecasts how efficient the remainder of the project must be in order to achieve project cost performance goals.

Formula #1 is used when the Budget at Completion is used as the cost performance goal.

Formula #2 is used when the Estimate at Completion is used as the cost performance goal. The EAC based formula is often used when management determines that the original BAC is not achievable and wants to use a more realistic measurement when calculating performance for the remainder of the project.

PROCESS ELEMENTS

The Control Costs process has the following Inputs:
- **Project Management Plan**   The consolidated package of the subsidiary management plans and baselines which contains the cost performance baseline and cost management plan

- **Project Funding Requirements**   Simply the funding needed and when it will be needed

- **Work Performance Information**   Project progress such as which activities have started, their progress, and which activities have finished

- **Organizational Process Assets**   Consideration factors such as existing formal and informal schedule control-related policies, procedures, and guidelines, cost control tools and monitoring and reporting methods to be used

The Control Costs process uses the following Tools & Techniques:
- **Earned Value Measurement (EVM)**   Integrates scope, cost, and schedule measurements to measure project performance and progress

- **Forecasting**   Estimates the project completion (ETC and EAC)

- **To-Complete Performance Index (TCPI)**   Calculated projection of cost performance that must be achieved on the remaining work

- **Performance Reviews**   Reviews to compare cost performance over time, schedule under-runs/over-runs, and future expenditures forecasts

- **Variance Analysis** Assess the magnitude of variation to the original cost baseline

- **Project Management Software** Any software that provides information on the three EVM dimensions (PV, EV, and AC)

The Control Costs process has the following Outputs:

- **Work Performance Measurements** Collection of project status information and calculated CV, SV, CPI, and SPI values

- **Forecasts** Calculated EAC value or bottom up EAC

- **Change Requests** Request for changes to cost baseline and/or other components of the Project Management Plan

- **Organizational Process Assets Updates** Updates causes of variances, corrective action chosen, and the reasons, and other types of Lessons Learned from project cost control

- **Project Management Plan Updates** Updates to the Project Management Plan as a result of this process, specifically the cost baseline, and Cost Management Plan

- **Project Document Updates** Updates to other project documentation (i.e. cost estimates and basis of estimates)

Control Costs (7.3)		
This process controls changes to project costs		
Inputs	**Tools and Techniques**	**Outputs**
• Project Management Plan • Project Funding Requirements • Work Performance Information • Organizational Process Assets	• Earned Value Measurement • Forecasting • To-Complete Performance Index • Performance Reviews • Variance Analysis • Project Management Software	• Work Performance Measurements • Budget Forecasts • Change Requests • Organizational Process Assets Updates • Project Management Plan Updates • Project Document Updates

TSI Study Aid

This chart is part of the study aid poster series available at *www.truesolutions.com*.

PROCESS DOCUMENTS

The Control Costs process uses earned value (EV) to determine cost performance for the project. The results of these EV calculations will be output in some performance report format, a spreadsheet (table format), S-curve format (showing the planned cost curve and the actual cost curve), or a dashboard type of report (usually showing a green-yellow-red status). Performance report documents are discussed in more detail in the next lesson, Report Performance.

A simple tabular format performance report is illustrated below.

Task Description	Task Cost	Planned Budget PV $	Earned Earned Value EV $	Cost Actual Cost AC $	Variance Cost Variance (EV-AC)	Variance Sched Variance (EV-PV)	Indexes CPI (EV/AC)	Indexes SPI (EV/PV)
Develop Prelim Scope	$200							
Develop Project Charter	$200	$400	$400	$500	($100)	$-0-	0.8	1.0
Develop Project Scope	$400							
Develop Schedule	$300							
Validate Controls	$200							
Finalize Project Plan	$200	$1,100	$1,000	$1,100	($100)	($100)	.91	.91
Manage Project Execution	$1,000							
Perform Work	$2,000	$3,000	$2,500	$3,500	($1,000)	($500)	.71	.83
Perform Change Control	$500							
Measure Performance	$400	$900	$900	$800	$100	$-0-	1.13	1.0
Deliver Product	$1,000							
Obtain Formal Acceptance	$200							
Archive Information	$200	$1,400	$100	$100	$-0-	($1,300)	1.0	.07
Totals		$6,800	$4,900	$6,000	($1,100)	($1,900)	.82	.72

COMMON PROCESS TASKS

The following is a list of the common tasks associated with the Control Costs process:

- Implement your cost change control system

- Integrate cost changes within your overall change control system

- Implement cost controls

- Define and evaluate factors that may potentially cause cost changes

- Revise cost estimates and evaluate the degree to which your cost baseline has changed using performance techniques such as earned value analysis

- Integrate approved cost changes with your other project control processes

- Determine modifications needed to estimates for completion

EARNED VALUE APPLICATION EXERCISE

Your project has four tasks. Task A planned value is $1,000. Task B planned value is $5,000. Task C planned value is $500. Task D planned value is $2,000. Based on today's date, you are supposed to be completely done with Task A and 50% done with Task B. However, your Work Performance Information indicates you are completely done with Task A and 75% done with Task B. And, you have spent $5,000 so far on this project. Based on this information, how do you determine the components of your earned value?

Step 1: Draw out the project and document your assumptions:

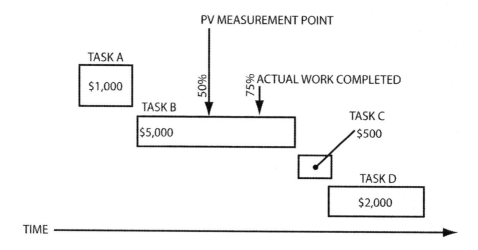

Project ABC

There are four tasks in this project:

Task A is 100% completed, Task B is 75% completed. (EV)

$5,000 has been spent to date on this project. (AC)

Based on today's date, you should have completed 100% of Task A and 50% of Task B. (PV)

Step 2: Define the key data points:

PV (Planned Value)   What is the money value based on where you are supposed to be on this date (based on the authorized budget)? Also known as the performance measurement baseline (PMB)
$1000 (Task A) + $2500 (50% of Task B) = $3,500 PV

EV (Earned Value)	What is the money value based on where you actually are (based on assigned work of the project schedule)?
	$1000 (Task A) + $3750 (75% of Task B) = $4,750 EV
AC (Actual Cost)	What is the actual amount of money spent (incurred) to date? $5,000 = AC
BAC (Budget at Completion)	What is the amount of money planned for spending on the entire project (total planned value)?
	$1000 (Task A) + $5000 (Task B) + $500 (Task C) + $2000 (Task D) = $8,500

Step 3: Determine variances:

$CV = EV - AC$	Cost variance: How far is the project from the cost baseline (planned cost value)?
	$4,750 (EV) – $5,000 (AC) = –$250 (CV)
	Project is OVER budget by $250 (<0)
	OR value of work completed compared to progress made
$SV = EV - PV$	Schedule variance: What is the monetary value of the schedule baseline (behind or ahead of schedule)?
	$4,750 (EV) – $3,500 (PV) = $1,250 (SV)
	Project is AHEAD of schedule by $1,250 (>0)
	OR project achieved compared to project planned

Step 4: Determine indices: (note, same data points but dividing instead of subtracting)

$CPI = EV / AC$	Project's cost performance to date: How efficient is the project budget?
	$4,750 (EV) / $5,000 (AC) = 0.95 (CPI)
	Project is OVER budget (<1)
	OR cost efficiency for the work completed
$SPI = EV / PV$	Project's schedule performance to date: How efficient is the project schedule?
	$4,750 (EV) / $3,500 (PV) = 1.36 (SPI)
	Project is AHEAD of schedule (>1)

TCPI (based on BAC)	(BAC − EV) / (BAC − AC)
	($8,500 − $4,750) / ($8,500 − $5,000) = 1.07
TCPI (based on EAC)	(BAC − EV) / (EAC − AC)
	($8,500 − $4,750) / ($8,947 − $5,000) = 0.95

Step 5: Determine forecasts:

ETC = (BAC − EV) / CPI	Estimate to Complete
	What is the amount of money you expect to spent to complete the project from this point?
	($8,500 − $4,750) / 0.95 = $3,947 (ETC)
	Based on past performance we plan to spend $3,947
EAC = ETC + AC	Estimate at Completion
	What is the expected cost for the entire project?
	$3,947 (ETC) + $5,000 (AC) = $8,947 (EAC)
	You expect to spend $8,947 that includes any current over- or under-runs
VAC = BAC − EAC	Variance at Completion
	Will the project be under or over budget at completion?
	$8,500 (BAC) − $8,947 (EAC) = −$447 (VAC)
	You will be OVER budget by $447 at the end of your project

This is important information for managing the project:

• It shows you how large your gaps are from your cost and schedule baselines based on where you are on your project and where you are supposed to be on your project.

• It shows you how efficient you are on your budget and schedule.

• It helps you to determine how much more money you plan to spend based on your over- and under-runs.

• It helps you to determine how much money you will spend on your entire project based on over- and under-runs.

• It helps you to determine how much you will be over/under at the end of the project.

MUST KNOW CONCEPTS

1. Control Cost is the process of effectively managing changes to the project budget, then integrating those changes across the entire project through the Perform Integrated Change Control process.

2. It is the project manager's responsibility to discourage unnecessary cost changes.

3. When legitimate budget changes are warranted, they should be made in accordance with the project's Cost Change Control system.

4. Earned value measurement (EVM) is a key tool used to measure project performance. Earned value analysis integrates cost, scope, and schedule to derive measurement values that accurately assess project progress to date, as well as forecasted future performance.

5. Planned Value (PV): (also termed Budgeted Cost of Work Scheduled or BCWS) is the established baseline that indicates the amount of money planned for spending to date, at any particular point in time (regardless of what actual work has been performed).

6. Earned Value (EV): (also termed Budgeted Cost of Work Performed or BCWP) is the established baseline that indicates the amount of money planned for spending on the actual work performed to date, at any particular point in time (regardless of other planned objectives).

7. Actual Cost (AC): (also termed Actual Cost of Work Performed or ACWP) is the amount of money spent on the actual work performed to date, at any particular point in time (regardless of other planned objectives).

8. Budget at Completion (BAC) is simply the amount of money planned for spending on the entire project.

9. Schedule Variance (SV): $SV = EV - PV$. $SV > 0$ = ahead of schedule. $SV < 0$ = behind schedule.

10. Cost Variance (CV): $CV = EV - AC$. $CV > 0$ = under budget. $CV < 0$ = over budget.

11. Variance at Completion (VAC): $VAC = BAC - EAC$. $VAC > 0$ = under budget. $VAC < 0$ = over budget.

12. Schedule Performance Index (SPI): $SPI = EV / PV$. $SPI > 1$ = ahead of schedule. $SPI < 1$ = behind schedule.

13. Cost Performance Index (CPI): $CPI = EV/AC$. $CPI > 1$ = under budget. $CPI < 1$ = over budget.

14 Estimate to Complete (ETC): ETC = EAC – AC. ETC forecasts remaining project costs.

15 Cost Estimate at Completion (EAC): EAC = BAC / CPI. EAC forecasts final project cost total.

16 TCPI (based on BAC): TCPI = (BAC – EV) / (BAC – AC). TCPI based on BAC is the forecast of how efficient future project performance must be in order to conform to the planned BAC for the project.

17 TCPI (based on EAC): TCPI = (BAC – EV) / (EAC – AC). TCPI based on EAC is the forecast of how efficient future project performance must be in order to conform to the planned EAC (based on new outcome predictions) for the project.

ADDITIONAL READING

• PMBOK Guide – Section 7.3 Control Costs

LESSON QUIZ

Instructions Here are some questions to help reinforce your learning. Complete this quiz from memory to the best of your ability. When complete, check your results by comparing your answers to the preferred answers provided in Appendix A.

1. Of the following statements, which best describes the intended application of the control cost process?
    A. Control Cost is the process of effectively managing changes to the project cost baseline, then integrating those changes across the entire project.
    B. Control Cost is the process applied to prevent changes to the cost baseline.
    C. Control Cost is the process applied to guide the project manager when making approval/denial decisions with respect to cost baseline change requests.
    D. Control Cost is the process applied to determine the potential benefit value of cost change requests.

2. As budget changes are requested and approved during the execution/control phases of your project, it is most appropriate to:
    A. Integrate the changes as approved, then document/communicate a new project budget each time a change is made
    B. Document and communicate new project budgets, but only after all changes have been made and integrated

C. Ensure your sponsor and key stakeholders are made aware of the changes as soon as possible after each change is made and integrated

D. Integrate budget changes as you are authorized, but maintain the original cost baseline

3. The project Cost Change Control system is intended to do what?
   A. Provide the procedural guidance by which cost change requests are to be managed
   B. Provide the procedural guidance to integrate cost changes with the Project Management Information System (PMIS)
   C. Provide procedural guidance to initiate corrective action with respect to the project budget
   D. Provide procedural guidance for the project manager and project team to ensure they authorize cost changes in accordance with the performing organization's QA/QC standards

4. Control Cost Tools & Techniques include all the following except:
   A. Variance analysis
   B. Performance reviews
   C. Forecasting
   D. Cost Change Control system

5. At the end of month three into a four-month project, you find yourself 50% complete and have spent $600,000. You originally planned to spend $212,500 each month, with your work activities evenly scheduled at 25% each month. The total project budget is $850,000. What is the VAC?
   A. –$425,000
   B. $350,000
   C. $1,200,000
   D. –$350,000

6. While reviewing a progress report you see that the schedule variance is zero, the estimate to complete is $14,500 and the budgeted cost of work performed is $6,000. The earned value is:
   A. $8,500
   B. $20,500
   C. $6,000
   D. Not enough information

7. One way to determine the SPI is to:
   A. Subtract estimate at completion (EAC) from budget at completion (BAC)
   B. Divide budget at completion (BAC) by the cost performance index (CPI)
   C. Subtract actual cost of work performed (ACWP) from budgeted cost of work performed (BCWP)
   D. Divide budget cost of work performed (BCWP) by budgeted cost of work scheduled (BCWS)

8. A project was estimated to cost $1.5 million and scheduled to last six months. After three months, the earned value analysis shows: BCWP = $650,000, BCWS = $750,000, ACWP = $800,000. What are the schedule and cost variances?
   A. SV = +$100,000 / CV = +$150,000
   B. SV = +$150,000 / CV = –$100,000
   C. SV = –$50,000 / CV = +$150,000
   D. SV = –$100,000 / CV = –$150,000

9. At the end of month three into a four-month project, you find yourself 50% complete and have spent $600,000. You originally planned to spend $212,500 each month, with your work activities evenly scheduled at 25% each month. The total project budget is $850,000. What is your ETC?
   A. $212,500
   B. $600,000
   C. $1,062,500
   D. $425,000

End of Lesson 41

Lesson 42
Report Performance

Objectives

At the end of this lesson, you will be able to:

- Describe the purpose of the Report Performance process
- Describe the Inputs, Tools & Techniques, and Outputs of the Report Performance process
- Understand options for reporting project performance

Roadmap to the PMBOK Guide

	Initiating	Planning	Executing	M & C	Closing
Integration					
Scope					
Time					
Cost					
Quality					
Human Resources					
Communications				■	
Risk					
Procurement					

The project manager will create performance reports from the data derived from Earned Value results and work performance information. Reliable status reporting is often a factor that facilitates successful project communication.

Report Performance is the communications process of providing project stakeholders with performance information, through the use of status reporting, progress reporting, and forecasting. Information included in forecasts and reports typically includes scope, cost, schedule, quality, risk, and procurement. The most common form of performance reporting is the periodic project status report.

In project management, the application of earned value analysis (EVA) is a key tool used to measure project performance. Earned value analysis integrates cost, scope, and schedule to derive measurement values that accurately assess project progress to date, as well as forecasted future performance.

The level and detail of reporting should be appropriate to the intended audience. Providing an excessive amount of performance data where it is unneeded or unwanted should be avoided.

In many industries, performance reports rely heavily on earned value analysis, presented in the form of bar charts, S-curves, histograms, and/or spreadsheets.

PROCESS ELEMENTS

The Report Performance process has the following Inputs:
- **Project Management Plan** The consolidated package of the subsidiary management plans and baselines

- **Work Performance Information** Project progress such as deliverables status, schedule, and costs

- **Work Performance Measurements** Collection of project status information (planned vs. actuals); technical performance measures, etc.

- **Organizational Process Assets** Consideration factors such as report templates, policies, procedures, and organizationally defined variance limits

- **Budget Forecasts** Forecasts for the remaining work and estimates for completion of project work

The Report Performance process uses the following Tools & Techniques:
- **Variance Analysis** Comparing planned performance objectives to actual in order to assess the magnitude of variation

- **Forecasting Methods** Predicting future project performance trends based on actual performance to date

- **Communication Methods**   Individual/group meetings, video/audio conferences, other communication methods
- **Reporting Systems**   Typically software related, spreadsheet, graphics, presentation, table reporting

The Report Performance process has the following Outputs:

- **Performance Reports**   S-curves, bar charts, tables, histograms, etc., that summarize project performance

- **Organizational Process Assets Updates**   Updates to report formats and Lessons Learned

- **Change Requests**   Request for changes to scope, schedule, costs, or processes or other project documentation

Report Performance (10.5)		
This process collects and distributes status reports and forecasts		
Inputs	**Tools and Techniques**	**Outputs**
• Project Management Plan • Work Performance Information • Work Performance Measurements • Organizational Process Assets • Budget Forecasts	• Variance Analysis • Forecasting Methods • Communication Methods • Reporting Systems	• Performance Reports • Organizational Process Assets Updates • Change Requests

TSI Study Aid

This chart is part of the study aid poster series available at *www.truesolutions.com.*

PROCESS DOCUMENTS

Performance reports can be produced in a narrative format, as an S-curve diagram, as a histogram, or as a tabular performance report (spreadsheet). The most commonly used report format is the periodic status report. An example of a status report is shown in two pages below.

True Solutions, Inc.
Project Management Template
Volume 1: Project Status Report Template

TSi

Department/Client Name
Status Report

Date of Status:	
Project Name:	
Project Manager:	
Project Sponsor:	
Delivery Manager	
Technical Lead:	
Start Date:	
Estimated End Date:	
Overall Status:	R/Y/G
Schedule Status:	R/Y/G
Resource Status:	R/Y/G
Technical Status:	R/Y/G
Cost Status:	R/Y/G

Project Description	High level description	Status: (R,Y,G)
	Phase 1: Description	
	1. Deliverable 1	
	2. Deliverable 2	
	3. Deliverable 3	
	4. Deliverable 4	
	Phase 2: Description	
	1. Deliverable 1	
	2. Deliverable 2	
	3. Deliverable 3	
	4. Deliverable 4	

(You will need to quantify what each color means for the project during planning.)

TSi Application Aid

This form is available individually or as a set from *www.truesolutions.com*.

Current Period's Accomplishments	• Phase 1 high level status with % complete
	• Key Status Point 1
	• Key Status Point 2
	• Key Status Point 3
	• Etc.

Next Period's Action Items	• Detailed deliverable/action with date/cost estimate where applicable.
	• Detailed deliverable/action with date/cost estimate where applicable.
	• Detailed deliverable/action with date/cost estimate where applicable.
	• Etc.

Milestones Status	Due Date	Revised Date	Status	Comments
Phase # - Milestone Name			R/Y/G	
Phase # - Milestone Name			R/Y/G	
Phase # - Milestone Name			R/Y/G	
Phase # - Milestone Name			R/Y/G	

#	Risks and Issues	Date Added	Assigned To	Status
01	Risk Description			Open/Closed
02	Risk Description			Open/Closed
03	Risk Description			Open/Closed
04	Risk Description			Open/Closed

Application Aid
This form is available individually or as a set from *www.truesolutions.com*.

COMMON PROCESS TASKS

The following is a list of the common tasks associated with the Report Performance process:

• Implement project performance reviews

• Generate and disseminate status, progress and forecast reports to appropriate stakeholders, i.e. variance, trend, earned value, etc.

• Create change requests based on performance reports

• Monitor compliance to ensure that timely and accurate data are available

THINK ABOUT IT

When creating a status report for your project (or for your organization) you need to keep the corporate culture in mind when creating the report. In this book I have previously discussed Lessons Learned in terms of distributing information to project stakeholders. Lessons Learned carries over into the type of performance or status reporting that you choose to use. The tendency on the part of many stakeholders is to not read the information thoroughly. Most stakeholders are working on or participating in multiple projects most of the time — and usually they still have a "day-job" to work as well. Stakeholders are busy. Therefore it is often best to consider their workload when crafting your project status report format.

I suggest that there are five major areas that need to be covered in a weekly status report:

• Red Flag items (issues that may stop the project execution)

• Risks and Issues

• Progress toward Objectives

• Forecast for work to be performed in the next reporting period

• Other (everything else that is happening on the project)

Some of my peers have accused me of being highly negative by putting "Red Flags" and "Risks and Issues" first in this format. I think this is just being realistic. If you think that your stakeholders are pressed for time and not going to have time to read your status report thoroughly, what portions of the report do you want them to read? Do you want them to understand that there are some risks and issues on the project? Or do you want them simply to see the progress section and assume that all is well and the project is going great?

Contributed by Tim Bergmann, PMP

MUST KNOW CONCEPTS

1 Report Performance is the communications process of providing project stakeholders with performance information, through the use of status reporting, progress reporting, and forecasting.

2 Information included in performance reports typically include scope, cost, schedule, quality, risk, and procurement.

③ Normally, performance reports reflect current project status and forecasted future performance.

④ In many industries, performance reports rely heavily on earned value analysis, presented in the form of bar charts, S-curves, histograms, and/or tables.

ADDITIONAL READING

• PMBOK Guide – Section 10.5 Report Performance

LESSON QUIZ

Instructions   Here are some questions to help reinforce your learning. Complete this quiz from memory to the best of your ability. When complete, check your results by comparing your answers to the preferred answers provided in Appendix A.

1. One common way to compute estimate-at-completion (EAC) is to take the project budget-at-completion, then:
   A. Divide it by the schedule performance index
   B. Multiply it by the schedule performance index
   C. Multiply it by the cost performance
   D. Divide it by the cost performance index

2. Your most recent project status report contains the following information: BCWP = 3,000, ACWP = 3,500, and BCWS = 4,000. The schedule variance is:
   A. +1,000
   B. +500
   C. –500
   D. –1,000

3. While reviewing a progress report you see that the earned value is $8,000 and the budget at completion is $24,000. The budgeted cost of work performed is:
   A. $8,000
   B. $16,000
   C. $32,000
   D. Not enough information

4. Upon reviewing the most recent progress report, you see that your project currently has a CPI of 1.13. This means:
   A. Your project is going to cost 87% more than originally planned
   B. Your project is progressing at 113% of the rate originally planned
   C. Your project is progressing at only 87% of the rate originally planned
   D. Your project is getting $1.13 for every $1.00 invested

End of Lesson 42

Lesson 43
Perform Quality Control

Objectives

At the end of this lesson, you will be able to:

- Describe the purpose of the Perform Quality Control process
- Describe the Inputs, Tools & Techniques, and Outputs of the Perform Quality Control process
- Understand that Perform Quality Control is focused mostly on the product of the project
- Understand how various tools can be applied to measure the product of the project

Roadmap to the PMBOK Guide

	Initiating	Planning	Executing	M & C	Closing
Integration					
Scope					
Time					
Cost					
Quality				■	
Human Resources					
Communications					
Risk					
Procurement					

Perform Quality Control leans heavily towards measuring the outputs or project deliverables. Deliverables will be measured against requirements and functional specifications to determine compliance. Making sure that the project attains quality is a key role for the project manager.

Perform Quality Control (QC) is the process of monitoring specific project results to ensure they comply with the project's quality standards. Like quality assurance (QA), quality control should be applied across the entire project life cycle. The quality control process is also intended to identify ways to eliminate quality problems such as causes of weak processes or poor product quality. Process improvement is a natural adjunct of the Perform Quality Control process.

Quality control monitors both product-related deliverables (Work Packages) and project management deliverables (cost/schedule/scope performance). This process focuses on outputs and uses tools that measure these outputs.

To effectively manage the QC aspects of a project, the project manager and project team should have a practical understanding of basic statistical quality control and probability. Accordingly, this lesson begins with a QC primer.

STATISTICAL QUALITY CONTROL
. . . .

Standard deviation (sigma): For QC purposes, standard deviation is a measure indicating the distance from the mean (average). In the control chart illustration (next page), the upper control limit (UCL) and lower control limit (LCL) could be established at 3 sigma from the mean, or perhaps 6 sigma from the mean

Normal Distribution		
1 Sigma	±68.26%	1 Standard Deviation
2 Sigma	±95.46%	2 Standard Deviations
3 Sigma	±99.73%	3 Standard Deviations
6 Sigma	±99.99%	6 Standard Deviations

Statistical Sampling: Statistical sampling is used as a QC technique to test a sample number of items from a larger population of items (opposed to testing every item). Statistical sampling can be effective and it can reduce overall QC costs. Statistical sampling has a body of knowledge all of its own.

OTHER STATISTICAL QUALITY CONTROL TERMS

Prevention = keeping errors out of the process

Inspection = keeping errors out of the hands of the customer

Attribute Sampling = results are determined as compliant or not compliant; go/no-go

Variables Sampling = results are measured on a continuous scale indicating degree of conformity

Special Causes = unusual events

Random Causes = normal process variation

Tolerances = results are acceptable if within tolerance ranges

Control Limits = result is in-control if it is within specified control limits

COMMON QUALITY CONTROL TOOLS

- **Pareto Diagrams:** A Pareto diagram is a histogram, applied as a QC analysis tool to help illustrate the frequency of occurrences by category of causes. Pareto's law (the 80/20 principle) suggests that 80% of problems are caused by 20% of all possible causes. Pareto diagrams typically identify the root causes of quality problems, allowing the project team to focus their corrective actions on the small number of areas causing the largest number of problems.

- **Run Charts:** Line graphs that illustrate the history and pattern of variation (trends)

- **Scatter Diagrams:** Illustrate the pattern of relationship between two variables

- **Cause and Effect Diagrams:** (Ishikawa diagrams, fishbone diagrams) Illustrate how various factors may be linked to potential problems

- **Flowcharts (Process maps):** Illustrate how various elements of a system interrelate

PROCESS CONTROL CHARTS

Control Charts are graphic displays of process results over time. They are used to monitor a process, to verify its continued stability. Control charts are used to monitor the results of any process, including project management processes. A typical control chart may look like this.

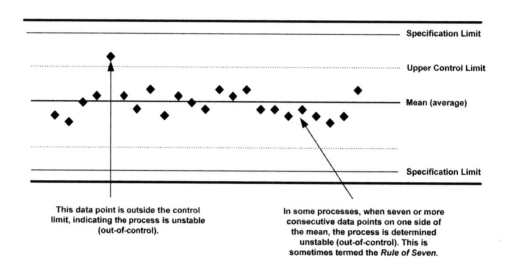

| This data point is outside the control limit, indicating the process is unstable (out-of-control). | In some processes, when seven or more consecutive data points on one side of the mean, the process is determined unstable (out-of-control). This is sometimes termed the *Rule of Seven*. |

PROCESS ELEMENTS

The Perform Quality Control process has the following Inputs:

- **Project Management Plan**   The consolidated package of the subsidiary management plans and baselines

- **Quality Metrics**   Operational definitions. Project elements, and how they are to be measured by quality control

- **Quality Checklists**   Structured forms used to verify that a set of required steps has been performed in quality control

- **Work Performance Measurements**   Collection of project status information (planned vs. actuals); technical performance measures, etc.

- **Approved Change Requests**   Documented, authorized changes (i.e. defect repairs, revised work methods, and revised schedule)

- **Deliverables**   Results, products, and/or capabilities (unique, verifiable outcomes) of activities performed

- **Organizational Process Assets**   Consideration factors such as quality standards and policies, work guidelines, issue and defect reporting procedures, and communication policies

The Perform Quality Control process uses the following Tools & Techniques:

- **Cause and Effect Diagrams** (fishbone diagrams, Ishikawa diagrams). Illustrate how various factors may be linked to a problem or effect

- **Control Charts** Charts used to determine if processes are stable and performing in a predictable manner

- **Flowcharting** Diagramming methods that can help analyze how problems in a system occur

- **Histogram** Bar chart showing distribution of variables. Can help identify cause of problems

- **Pareto Chart** A specific type of histogram that can help identify nonconformities. Pareto's law = 80/20 principle

- **Run Chart** A line graph that illustrates the history and pattern of variation in a process, to determine trends (used to monitor technical, cost, and schedule performances)

- **Scatter Diagram** Illustrates the pattern of relationship between two variables, to study changes in the two variables

- **Statistical Sampling** Statistical analysis using a small group from an entire population

- **Inspection** Measuring, examining, testing (reviews, audits, walkthroughs) to ensure results conform to requirements and to validate defect repairs

- **Approved Change Request Review** A review of all approved change requests to verify implementation

The Perform Quality Control process has the following Outputs:

- **Quality Control Measurements** Results of all quality control activities

- **Validated Changes** Notification of acceptance or rejection of changed or repaired items

- **Validated Deliverables** Completed deliverables checked using the Perform Quality Control process

- **Change Requests** Request for changes to take corrective action, preventive actions, and/or perform defect repair

- **Organizational Process Assets Updates** Updates to corporate docs, guidelines, procedures, historical information, etc.

- **Project Management Plan Updates** Updates to other project documentation (i.e. quality management plan and process improvement plan)

- **Project Document Updates** Updates to completed checklists and Lessons Learned documentation

Perform Quality Control (8.3)

This process monitors project results against relevant quality standards

Inputs	Tools and Techniques	Outputs
• Project Management Plan • Quality Metrics • Quality Checklists • Work Performance Measurements • Approved Change Requests • Deliverables • Organizational Process Assets	• Cause and Effect Diagrams • Control Charts • Flowcharting • Histogram • Pareto Chart • Run Chart • Scatter Diagram • Statistical Sampling • Inspection • Approved Change Request Review	• Quality Control Measurements • Validated Changes • Validated Deliverables • Change Requests • Organizational Process Assets Updates • Project Management Plan Updates • Project Document Updates

TSI Study Aid
This chart is part of the study aid poster series available at www.truesolutions.com.

PROCESS DOCUMENTS

Documents that come from the process of Perform Quality Control can be created in conjunction with other project management processes. In this process you may have the results of one or more tools being applied to project or product measurement and inspection. You may also use a Project Audit template as part of this process.

Quality Control actions, specifically "inspection," are often tied to the Verify Scope process to verify that the work was completed and that it has been completed satisfactorily, meeting requirements and functional specifications. In this case, a formal acceptance form might be used in this process.

All forms, templates, and records that are produced in this process become "organizational process assets updates" and will be included later in the project archives.

COMMON PROCESS TASKS

The following is a list of the common tasks associated with the Perform Quality Control Process:

- Monitor specific project results to ensure compliance with your requirements (relevant quality standards) using appropriate checklists

- Perform inspections, reviews, and walkthroughs to ensure that items are properly documented as accepted, rejected, or identified for rework

- Utilize techniques, including Pareto analysis, cause/effect diagrams, trend analysis, and statistical sampling for your inspections

- Implement process adjustments to ensure quality improvement efforts

- Complete all quality related documentation

THINK ABOUT IT

Instructions Think about how this project management process is defined, used, and documented in your organization. Compare your organization's use of this process to the PMI® definition. Do you use these tools in your quality control processes?

☐ Cause and effect diagrams

☐ Control charts

☐ Flowcharts

☐ Histograms

☐ Pareto charts

☐ Run charts

☐ Scatter diagrams

☐ Statistical sampling

☐ Inspection procedures

If you do not use these tools, are there any of these tools that you see a need for?

_____

_____

_____

_____

How can you close the gap between your current practices and best practices defined in the *PMBOK Guide*?

_____

_____

_____

_____

MUST KNOW CONCEPTS
. . . .

1 Perform Quality Control is the process of monitoring specific project results to ensure they comply with the project's quality standards.

2 The primary deliverable (Output) of the Perform Quality Control process is validated deliverables.

3 Perform Quality Control monitors both product-related deliverables (Work Packages) and project management deliverables (cost/schedule/scope performance).

4 Prevention is defined as keeping errors out of the process. Inspection is keeping errors out of the hands of the customer.

5 Attribute Sampling is determining if results are compliant or not compliant; go/no-go.

6 Variables Sampling is when results are measured on a continuous scale indicating degree of conformity.

7 Special Causes are unusual events.

8 Random Causes mean normal process variations.

9 Tolerances are where results are acceptable if within tolerance ranges.

10 Control Limits define where a result is in-control if it is within specified control limits.

11 Statistical sampling is used as a QC technique to test a sample number of items from a larger population of items (compared to testing every item). Statistical sampling can be effective and it can reduce overall QC costs.

12 A Pareto diagram is a histogram, applied as a QC analysis tool to help illustrate the frequency of occurrences by category of causes. Pareto's law (the 80/20 principle) suggests that 80% of problems are caused by 20% of all possible causes. Pareto diagrams typically identify the root causes of quality problems, allowing the project team to focus their corrective actions on the small number of areas causing the largest number of problems.

13 Standard deviation (sigma) is a measure indicating the distance from the mean (average). 1 sigma = 1 standard deviation = ±68.26%. 2 sigma = 2 standard deviations = ±95.46%. 3 sigma = 3 standard deviations = ±99.73%. 6 sigma = 6 standard deviations = ±99.99%.

14 Control Charts are graphic displays of process results over time. They are used to monitor a process, to verify its continued stability. Control charts are used to monitor the results of any process, including project management processes.

15 Scatter diagrams, run charts, flowcharts, cause and effect diagrams and histograms are commonly used quality control tools.

ADDITIONAL READING
. . . .
• PMBOK Guide – Section 8.3 Perform Quality Control

LESSON QUIZ
. . . .
Instructions   Here are some questions to help reinforce your learning. Complete this quiz from memory to the best of your ability. When complete, check your results by comparing your answers to the preferred answers provided in Appendix A.

1.   Perform Quality Control (QC) is the process of:
   A. Applying statistical testing to detect and analyze quality trends
   B. Monitoring the product of the project to ensure it satisfies product performance specifications
   C. Developing performance tolerance criteria, then documenting actual performance using a control chart
   D. Monitoring specific project results to ensure they comply with the project's quality standards

2.   The upper control limit (UCL) and lower control limit (LCL) on a typical control chart indicates what?
   A. Process specification limits
   B. Product (of the project) performance specification limits
   C. Statistical validation that the product of the project satisfies performance specifications
   D. The acceptable range (upper and lower) of variation in a process

3. Perform Quality Control Tools & Techniques include all the following except:
   A. Statistical sampling
   B. Pareto charts
   C. Control charts
   D. Quality metrics

4. Standard deviation (sigma):
   A. In project quality control is a performance measurement of how close you are to the schedule baseline at any given time in the project
   B. In project quality control is a performance measure of how far you are from a determined mean (average)
   C. In project quality control is a performance measurement of the precision of any statistical sample
   D. In project quality control is a performance measurement of how far out-of-control a process is at any given time

5. In project quality control, out-of-control could be indicated by:
   A. A charted process sample data point that falls outside (above or below) 1 sigma
   B. Any project core team member who has been authorized to declare an-out-of-control condition
   C. A charted process sample data point that falls outside an upper or lower control limit
   D. A charted process sample data point that violates the rule-of-seven

6. Which of the following is most true?
   A. 3 sigma = 3 standard deviations = $\pm99.73\%$
   B. 6 sigma = 6 standard deviations = $\pm99.73\%$
   C. 2 sigma = 2 standard deviations = $\pm68.26\%$
   D. 1 sigma = 1 standard deviation = $\pm95.46\%$

7. Which of the following is least true?
   A. Prevention over inspection is a preferred project quality concept
   B. Pareto diagrams typically identify the 20% of all possible root causes that are responsible for 80% of the problems
   C. Project QC monitors both product-related deliverables (Work Packages) and project management deliverables (cost/schedule/scope performance)
   D. Statistical sampling is a QC technique that requires inspection of only 50%, instead of 100% of the population, thus reducing testing time by half

End of Lesson 43

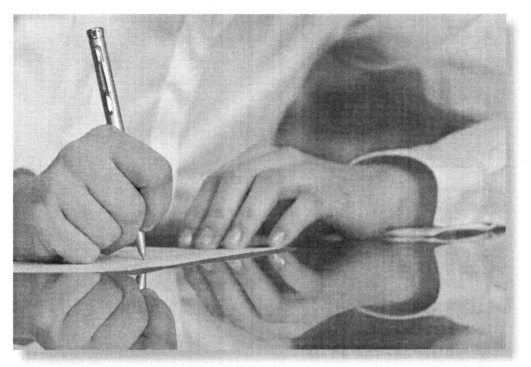

Lesson 44
Verify Scope

Objectives

At the end of this lesson, you will be able to:

- Describe the purpose of the Verify Scope process
- Describe the Inputs, Tools & Techniques, and Outputs of the Verify Scope process
- Understand the relationship between Verify Scope, Perform Quality Control, and Close Project or Phase

Roadmap to the PMBOK Guide

	Initiating	Planning	Executing	M & C	Closing
Integration					
Scope				██	
Time					
Cost					
Quality					
Human Resources					
Communications					
Risk					
Procurement					

Verification of scope, work output or deliverables is a key part of the overall acceptance processes for the project. Scope verification is often done in conjunction with Perform Quality Control.

Verify Scope is the process of obtaining formal acceptance of project deliverables. It must be understood that a project deliverable is not complete until it has been formally accepted, by the individual or group authorized to accept it.

Scope verification differs from quality control. Quality control focuses on the correctness of work. Scope verification focuses on formal acceptance of the work. In practice, both are normally performed in parallel.

Formal acceptance must be documented. Scope verification can occur at any level of the project; it can be done for work, for a specific deliverable, for a milestone, for a phase, or for the project overall. Verify Scope is often a predecessor to the closure of a project phase or when closing the overall project.

PROCESS ELEMENTS

The Verify Scope process has the following Inputs:

- **Project Management Plan** The consolidated package of the subsidiary management plans and baselines

- **Requirements Documentation** Documentation describing how individual requirements fulfill the business needs of the project

- **Requirements Traceability Matrix** A table which associates requirement origin and the relationship between requirement origin and history throughout the project life cycle

- **Validated Deliverables** Completed deliverables checked using the Perform Quality Control process

The Verify Scope process uses the following Tools & Techniques:

- **Inspection** Measuring, examining, and testing (reviews, audits, walkthroughs) to ensure results conform to requirements

The Verify Scope process has the following Outputs:

- **Accepted Deliverables** Documentation of accepted deliverables from the Verify Scope process

- **Change Requests** Request for changes to scope, schedule, costs, or processes or other project documentation

- **Project Document Updates** Updates to other project documentation

Verify Scope (5.4)

This process formalizes acceptance of completed project deliverables

Inputs	Tools and Techniques	Outputs
• Project Management Plan • Requirements Documentation • Requirements Traceability Matrix • Validated Deliverables	• Inspection	• Accepted Deliverables • Change Requests • Project Document Updates

TSI *Study Aid*

This chart is part of the study aid poster series available at *www.truesolutions.com.*

PROCESS DOCUMENTS

Verify Scope focuses on formal acceptance of project work. Verify Scope is often tied directly to the Perform Quality Control process so that the accuracy of the work is inspected during the formal acceptance process.

True Solutions, Inc.
Project Management Template
Volume 1: Formal Acceptance of Product or Phase Template

TSI

Formal Acceptance of Product or Phase

Project Name:	
Prepared by:	
Date:	
Name of Product:	
Name of Phase, if applicable:	
Name of Specific Deliverable, if applicable:	
Name of Client or Sponsor:	

Statement of Formal Acceptance:

The undersigned formally accepts as complete the above-identified product, project phase, or major deliverable and do hereby states that this project, project phase, or major deliverable meets or exceeds agreed-upon performance standards for quality, schedule, and cost, and we state that we have seen documentation that all relevant legal and regulatory requirements have been met or exceeded.

[*In the case of a Phase:*] Acceptance of this Phase of the Project is conditional on the following: (e.g., satisfactory completion of all subsequent phases and meeting overall objectives of entire project)

Accepted by (name of client, sponsor, or other official)	*Date*
Accepted by (name of client, sponsor, or other official)	*Date*
Accepted by (name of client, sponsor, or other official)	*Date*

Signed form distributed to:

Stakeholder name	*Date*
Stakeholder name	*Date*
Stakeholder name	*Date*

Application Aid

This form is available individually or as a set from *www.truesolutions.com*.

COMMON PROCESS TASKS

The following is a list of the common tasks associated with the Verify Scope process:

• Participate in project inspections, reviews, audits, and walkthroughs

• Determine that deliverables are completed correctly

• Document deliverables acceptance by your stakeholders

THINK ABOUT IT

Instructions Think about how this project management process is defined, used, and documented in your organization.

Think about how this process is defined, used and documented in your organization. Write a brief description of how you use this process:

_____

_____

_____

_____

_____

What specific Inputs, Tools or Techniques do you use as part of this process in your organization?

_____

_____

_____

_____

Are the outcomes from this process different in your organization or experiences?

_____

_____

_____

_____

_____

MUST KNOW CONCEPTS

1 Verify Scope is the process of obtaining formal acceptance of project deliverables.

2 The primary deliverable (Output) of the Verify Scope process is accepted deliverables.

3 A project deliverable is not complete until it has been formally accepted, in writing by the individual or group authorized to accept it.

4 Scope verification differs from quality control which focuses on the correctness of work while scope verification focuses on formal acceptance of the work.

ADDITIONAL READING

- PMBOK Guide – Section 5.4 Verify Scope

LESSON QUIZ

Instructions Here are some questions to help reinforce your learning. Complete this quiz from memory to the best of your ability. When complete, check your results by comparing your answers to the preferred answers provided in Appendix A.

1. Which of the following statements best depicts the difference between Verify Scope and Perform Quality Control?
   A. Scope verification is primarily focused on the acceptance of project deliverables; Quality control is primarily focused on the correctness of deliverables.
   B. Quality control is primarily focused on the acceptance of project deliverables; Scope verification is primarily focused on the correctness of deliverables.
   C. Quality control is always performed before Scope verification.
   D. Scope verification is primarily focused on whether deliverables meet the requirements; Quality control is primarily focused on the correctness of deliverables.

2. Verify Scope Inputs include all of the following *except*:
   A. Requirements documentation
   B. Requirements traceability matrix
   C. Validated deliverables
   D. Scope Management Plan

3. Which of the following statements best describes the Verify Scope process?
   A. Verify Scope is applied to guide the parallel performance of quality control and formal acceptance of a project deliverable.
   B. Verify Scope is applied to verify the correctness of project deliverables.
   C. Verify Scope is the process of obtaining formal acceptance of project deliverables.
   D. Verify Scope is the process of verifying the correctness of identified project scope items.

End of Lesson 44

Lesson 45
Monitor and Control Risks

Objectives

At the end of this lesson, you will be able to:

- Describe the purpose of the Monitor and Control Risks process
- Describe the Inputs, Tools & Techniques, and Outputs of the Monitor and Control Risks process
- Understand the use of workaround plans for responding to unanticipated project risk

Roadmap to the PMBOK Guide

	Initiating	Planning	Executing	M & C	Closing
Integration					
Scope					
Time					
Cost					
Quality					
Human Resources					
Communications					
Risk				■	
Procurement					

As the project progresses it is critical that the project manager and project team keep looking for risk symptoms and new risks. Risk should be discussed in all team meetings throughout the project.

The Monitor and Control Risks process is applied to perform several functions for the project:

• monitor identified risks

• identify new risks

• ensure the proper execution of planned risk responses

• evaluate the overall effectiveness of the risk management plan in reducing risk

If a risk event occurs during project execution, there is a likelihood it was identified sometime earlier, it was analyzed, and an appropriate response action was planned to deal with it (captured in the Risk Register). For the most part, Monitor and Control Risks is the process of putting into action all of the risk planning done earlier in the project life cycle.

It is important to understand that risk monitoring is intended to be a daily, ongoing process across the entire project life cycle. Project team members and stakeholders should be encouraged to be vigilant in looking for risk symptoms, as well as for new project risks. It is suggested that project risk always be an agenda item for all team meetings. Newly identified risks and symptoms of previously identified risks should be communicated immediately for evaluation and/or action.

PROCESS ELEMENTS

The Monitor and Control Risks process has the following Inputs:
- **Risk Register**   List of identified risks

- **Project Management Plan**   The consolidated package of the subsidiary management plans and baselines which contains the risk management plan

- **Work Performance Information**   Project performance related to deliverable status, schedule progress, and costs incurred

- **Performance Reports**   S-curves, bar charts, tables, histograms, etc., that summarize project performance

The Monitor and Control Risks process uses the following Tools & Techniques:
- **Risk Assessment**   New risk identification and frequent reassessment of existing risks

- **Risk Audits**   Examination and documentation of the effectiveness of risk responses and risk management processes

- **Variance and Trend Analysis**   Examination of project trends to help determine the impact of threats/opportunities

- **Technical Performance Measurement**   Comparison of planned technical accomplishments to actual achievements
- **Reserve Analysis**   Determining appropriate amount of contingency reserve to compensate for project risk
- **Status Meetings**   Typically, risk management is an agenda item at each project status meeting

The Monitor and Control Risks process has the following Outputs:

- **Risk Register Updates**   Updates to the list of identified risks

- **Organizational Process Assets Updates**   Updates to templates, RBS, Lessons Learned

- **Change Requests**   Recommended corrective actions and recommended preventive actions

- **Project Management Plan Updates**   Updates to the Project Management Plan as a result of this process, specifically the risk management plan

- **Project Document Updates**   Updates to other project documentation (i.e. plan risk responses)

Monitor and Control Risks (11.6)		
This process executes risk response plans and evaluates their effectiveness		
Inputs	**Tools and Techniques**	**Outputs**
• Risk Register • Project Management Plan • Work Performance Information • Performance Reports	• Risk Assessment • Risk Audits • Variance and Trend Analysis • Technical Performance Measurement • Reserve Analysis • Status Meetings	• Risk Register Updates • Organizational Process Assets Updates • Change Requests • Project Management Plan Updates • Project Document Updates

TSi Study Aid

This chart is part of the study aid poster series available at www.truesolutions.com.

PROCESS DOCUMENTS

During Monitor and Control Risks, two functions occur: identified risks are monitored to determine if the risk is occurring and new risks are identified. If identified risks occur, the project manager often has a documented risk response prepared that can be put into action. When an identified risk occurs, two documents will be addressed: the project manager will fill out a Change Request Form to request that the risk response be implemented and the Risk Register will be updated.

If a new risk occurs, it is likely that this risk was not previously identified, so it would not currently appear on the Risk Register. Responding to this previously unidentified risk would be done in the form of a workaround plan. The project manager would update the Risk Register to reflect the newly identified risk, use a Change Request Form to request a risk response be implemented and use a Workaround Planning Worksheet to document the workaround plan.

True Solutions, Inc.
Project Management Template
Volume 1: Workaround Planning Worksheet Template

TSI

Workaround Planning Worksheet

| Project Name: |
| Prepared by: |
| Date: |
| Description of Emerging Risk Identified: |
| Person(s) Responsible: |
| Results from Risk Analysis (if applicable): |
| Description of Plan to Respond (avoidance, transference, mitigation, acceptance): |
| Description of Residual Risk Level: |
| Action Steps: |
| Budget & Time for Response: |
| Contingency/Fallback Plans: |
| Additional Notes: |

TSI *Application Aid*
This form is available individually or as a set from *www.truesolutions.com*.

COMMON PROCESS TASKS

The following is a list of the common tasks associated with the Monitor and Control Risks process:

- Create workarounds for unplanned risk events

- Implement workarounds for unplanned risk events

- Implement contingency plans

- Quantify actual risk events (for comparison and evaluation with your risk plan)

- Complete risk event updates as part of the project control process

- Update Risk Register, including adjustments to risk probabilities and risk values

THINK ABOUT IT

Instructions Think about how this project management process is defined, used, and documented in your organization. Compare your organization's use of this process to the PMI® definition.

Think about how this process is defined, used and documented in your organization. Write a brief description of how you use this process:

_____

_____

_____

_____

_____

_____

What specific Inputs, Tools or Techniques do you use as part of this process in your organization?

_____

_____

_____

_____

_____

_____

Are the outcomes from this process different in your organization or experiences?

_____

_____

_____

_____

_____

MUST KNOW CONCEPTS

1. The Monitor and Control Risks process is applied to monitor identified risks, identify new risks, ensure proper execution of planned risk responses, and evaluate overall effectiveness of the Risk Management Plan in reducing risk.

2. Workarounds (or workaround plans) are responses to unanticipated (surprise) risk events after they occur. Workarounds are for risk events that were not previously identified, and have no planned response action. Workaround plans should be documented and incorporated into the Risk Register as soon as they are developed.

3. Risk monitoring is intended to be a daily, ongoing process across the entire project life cycle, from project start to project finish.

4. Project team members and stakeholders should be vigilant in looking for risk symptoms, as well as for new project risks.

ADDITIONAL READING

• PMBOK Guide – Section 11.6 Monitor and Control Risks

LESSON QUIZ

Instructions Here are some questions to help reinforce your learning. Complete this quiz from memory to the best of your ability. When complete, check your results by comparing your answers to the preferred answers provided in Appendix A.

1. The Monitor and Control Risks process is applied to:
   A. Implement risk avoidance, risk transference, risk mitigation, and risk acceptance (passive and active)
   B. Develop options and determine actions to enhance opportunities (positive risks) and develop options and determine actions to reduce threats (negative risks)
   C. Monitor identified risks, identify new risks, ensure proper execution of planned risk responses, and evaluate overall effectiveness of the Risk Management Plan in reducing risk
   D. Develop options and determine actions to create opportunities for positive risks and develop options and determine contingency actions for negative risks

2. During project execution, an odd risks event occurs, a risk that no one imagined in advance. But now that is has occurred, the project team must act. An appropriate response would be to:
   A. Request guidance from the project sponsor
   B. Create a new risk response plan
   C. Create a workaround plan
   D. Transfer the risk as soon as possible

3. Monitor and control risks Tools & Techniques include:
   A. Risk audits, reserve analysis, and status meetings
   B. Workaround plans, reserve analysis, and status meetings
   C. Risk audits, Risk Register updating, and status meetings
   D. Risk audits, reserve analysis, and recommended preventive actions

4. Which of the following statements is least true?
   A. Unanticipated risks (those not identified in advance) that occur during project execution must be ignored, because no advance plans exist to deal with them. The project must simply accept the consequences (either negative or positive).
   B. Project team members and stakeholders should be vigilant in looking for risk symptoms, as well as for new project risks.
   C. Risk monitoring is intended to be a daily, ongoing process across the entire project life cycle, from project start to project finish.
   D. Workarounds (or workaround plans) are responses to unanticipated (surprise) risk events after they occur.

End of Lesson 45

Lesson 46
Administer Procurements

Objectives

At the end of this lesson, you will be able to:

- Describe the purpose of the Administer Procurements process
- Describe the Inputs, Tools & Techniques, and Outputs of the Administer Procurements process
- Understand the need to integrate the vendor team as part of the overall project team

Roadmap to the PMBOK Guide

	Initiating	Planning	Executing	M & C	Closing
Integration					
Scope					
Time					
Cost					
Quality					
Human Resources					
Communications					
Risk					
Procurement				■	

The vendor is often a critical member of the project team – albeit a member who has a closely defined, limited scope of work. It is important to integrate the vendor team into the project and manage the team to the level defined by the procurement contract.

Monitoring the relationships created by a project's procurement needs, monitoring contract performance, and making procurement changes and corrections are accomplished through the Administer Procurements process. Part of this process includes validating that a seller's performance is meeting requirements and contract obligations.

In many organizations, the role of contract monitoring and control is performed by a specialized contracts department. This is often done because of the legalities associated with contracts. Regardless of who is performing administration of procurements, project team members should be aware of the legal obligations and the impact of their actions in regard to contracts.

During the application of this process, each seller's performance should be recorded and documented. A performance review of sellers can lead to identification of issues to be resolved, and can provide additional data for similar future projects in regards to contracts and purchases with sellers.

When applying this process, the project manager will have a high degree of interaction with several other processes. It is important to integrate the vendor project team into the overall project team and stakeholder organization. Project management elements for managing work, for verifying work and deliverable conformance, for managing change, and for developing the team are important during this process. Some processes that may be closely coordinated with Administer Procurements are:

• Direct and Manage Project Execution

• Monitor and Control Project Work

• Verify Scope

• Perform Quality Control

• Develop Project Team

• Manage Project Team

• Control Scope

• Control Schedule

• Control Cost

• Perform Integrated Change Control

• Close Procurements

• Close Project or Phase

PROCESS ELEMENTS

The Administer Procurements process has the following Inputs:

- **Procurement Documents**   Documents used to solicit proposals from prospective sellers

- **Project Management Plan**   The consolidated package of the subsidiary management plans and baselines which contains the procurement management plan

- **Performance Reports**   S-curves, bar charts, tables, histograms, etc., that summarize project performance

- **Approved Change Requests**   Documented, authorized changes that expand or reduce scope

- **Work Performance Information**   Project performance related to quality standards being satisfied, paid invoices, and costs incurred

- **Contract**   Procurement contract and information

The Administer Procurements process uses the following Tools & Techniques:

- **Contract Change Control System**   A system that defines the process by which a contract may be modified

- **Procurement Performance Reviews**   A procurement performance review of seller's conformance to contract terms

- **Inspections and Audits**   Required by the buyer, supported by the seller, and conducted to verify seller's compliance

- **Performance Reporting**   Management information to assess the contractual performance of project suppliers

- **Payment Systems**   Reviews, approvals, and payments made in accordance with contract terms

- **Claims Administration**   Procedures for resolving disputed/contested changes between buyer and seller

- **Records Management System**   Used by the project manager to manage contract documentation and records

The Administer Procurements process has the following Outputs:

- **Procurement Documentation**   Contract, supporting schedules, requested contract changes, unapproved change requests, and approved change requests

- **Organizational Process Assets Updates**   Updates to correspondence, payment schedules and requests, and seller performance evaluation documentation

- **Change Requests**   Request for changes to scope, schedule, costs, the Procurement Management Plan or other project documentation

- **Project Management Plan Updates**   Updates to the Project Management Plan as a result of this process, specifically the Procurement Management Plan and baseline schedule

---

Administer Procurements (12.3)
This process manages procurement relationships and contract performance

Inputs	Tools and Techniques	Outputs
• Procurement Documents • Project Management Plan • Performance Reports • Approved Change Requests • Work Performance Information • Contract	• Contract Change Control System • Procurement Performance Reviews • Inspections and Audits • Performance Reporting • Payment Systems • Claims Administration • Records Management System	• Procurement Documentation • Organizational Process Assets Updates • Change Requests • Project Management Plan Updates

PROCESS DOCUMENTS

As previously stated in this lesson, Administer Procurements is closely linked to other project management processes in real-world applications. The documents associated with these other processes will be used as part of this process.

Unique to this process is the need to communicate with a vendor company to notify them of status, change, conflict, etc. Formal communication (usually a letter) to the vendor company will become part of Organizational Process Assets Updates and ultimately part of the overall project archive.

COMMON PROCESS TASKS

The following is a list of the common tasks associated with the Administer Procurements process:

- Reviewing contractors' work to determine work completion and acceptability

- Creating payment requests (making payments) to compensate vendors for work performed

- Reviewing contractors' change requests and disseminating contract changes to appropriate parties

- Integrating procurement administration within the broader context of the project management plan, quality control processes, and the overall project performance reporting systems

THINK ABOUT IT

Instructions Think about how this project management process is defined, used, and documented in your organization.

Compare your organization's use of this process to the PMI® definition. When applying the Administer Procurement process do you:

☐ Communicate directly with the vendor to check on work

☐ Perform Quality Control processes to check work accuracy

☐ Create payment requests or make payments to compensate the vendor

☐ Integrate vendor activities with other project management processes

☐ Communicate formally with the vendor on all changes or requests

☐ Formally accept work throughout the project

If you do not practice procurement administration in this manner, what gaps can you identify in your practices?

_____

_____

_____

_____

_____

What actions can you identify that you need to address in order to conform to best practice recommendations within your organization?

_____

_____

_____

_____

_____

MUST KNOW CONCEPTS
. . . .

1 The Administer Procurements process is used to manage procurement relationships, monitor contract performance, and making changes and corrections to procurements.

2 Many organizations utilize a contract administration department or office to administer procurement contracting because of the legal aspects of formal contracting.

3 Seller performance should be formally documented for use in future decisions and in evaluation of sellers.

4 Contract changes can be kept to a minimum by proper and thorough procurement planning but changes can be used to reduce risk, or when such amendments are beneficial for the buyer, the seller, or both.

ADDITIONAL READING
. . . .

• PMBOK Guide – Section 12.3 Administer Procurements

LESSON QUIZ
. . . .

Instructions   Here are some questions to help reinforce your learning. Complete this quiz from memory to the best of your ability. When complete, check your results by comparing your answers to the preferred answers provided in Appendix A.

1. Administer Procurements is:
   A. The procurement process of interfacing with the organization's central contract group
   B. The procurement process of approving and paying sellers involved in a timely fashion
   C. The procurement process of ensuring that the seller's performance satisfies contractual obligations
   D. The procurement process of minimizing the number of contractors' change requests

2. You and your project team have completed evaluations of several proposals and have decided that one in particular appears to present the most attractive offer overall. However, while checking references, you find this seller has a history of bidding low to get the work, then demanding many change requests to increase their revenue. You also found their quality of work is consistently excellent. Which of the following represents the best approach to this situation?
   A. Disqualify this seller's proposal. Their history demonstrates low integrity.
   B. Disqualify this seller's proposal. Your project may suffer schedule delays and cost overruns due to the many contract change requests you will certainly face from the seller.
   C. Do not disqualify this seller's proposal. They present the best offer. But, if you do ultimately select them, assign a core team member to watch them closely. They should not be trusted.
   D. Do not disqualify this seller's proposal. As long as you are confident that scope of work and terms are well-defined, contract changes should be minimal. Select this seller with confidence.

3. Administer Procurements Inputs include all the following except:
   A. Contract
   B. Project Management Plan
   C. Change requests
   D. Work performance information

4. Which of the following statements is least true?
   A. Once negotiated and executed, a buyer/seller contract becomes a legally binding agreement and cannot be changed.
   B. If a contract is well-planned and negotiated, then the need for contract changes should be minimized.
   C. Contract changes that are needed to improve project performance should be facilitated, but in accordance with the project's change control system.
   D. Unnecessary contract changes should be discouraged.

End of Lesson 46

Lesson 47
Monitor and Control Project Work

Objectives

At the end of this lesson, you will be able to:

- Describe the purpose of the Monitor and Control Project Work process
- Describe the Inputs, Tools & Techniques, and Outputs of the Monitor and Control Project Work process
- Understand that this process is where many corrective actions are identified for the project

Roadmap to the PMBOK Guide

	Initiating	Planning	Executing	M & C	Closing
Integration					
Scope					
Time					
Cost					
Quality					
Human Resources					
Communications					
Risk					
Procurement					

This process is intended to identify variance conditions, create forecasts and make corrective action recommendations. This is another critical checking process for overall project management.

The U.S. Apollo space missions to the moon during the 1960s and 1970s were proud successes shared by the entire world. What few people realize is that at any given moment during a space capsule's flight to the moon, the trajectory is considerably off-course. Allowed to continue on its path at any given time, the capsule would miss its target by a significant margin. Technology at that time was not capable of automating the capsule's flight path.

To compensate, ground controllers would continuously monitor the flight path and, using tiny on-board firing jets, make frequent corrective adjustments to bring the capsule back on course. Ultimately, the capsule reached its objective.

This is a good example of the Monitor and Control Project Work process.

As project managers, it is our responsibility to continuously monitor project work, and when we detect some aspect is heading off course, we make controlling adjustments, as necessary, to bring the project back in alignment, to ultimately achieve our defined objectives.

We apply the Monitor and Control Project Work process to:

• monitor all other processes through initiation, planning, executing, and closing

• take/make corrective/preventive actions, as needed

PROCESS ELEMENTS

The Monitor and Control Project Work process has the following Inputs:
- **Project Management Plan**   The consolidated package of the subsidiary management plans and baselines

- **Performance Reports**   S-curves, bar charts, tables, histograms, etc., that summarize team member performance

- **Enterprise Environmental Factors**   Consideration factors such as culture, systems, procedures, and industry standards

- **Organizational Process Assets**   Consideration factors such as processes, procedures, and corporate knowledge base

The Monitor and Control Project Work process uses the following Tools & Techniques:
- **Expert Judgment**   Expert technical and/or managerial judgment (from the project team)

The Monitor and Control Project Work process has the following Outputs:
- **Change Requests**   Request for changes to scope, schedule, costs, or processes or other project documentation

- **Project Management Plan Updates** Updates to the Project Management Plan as a result of this process

- **Project Document Updates** Updates to other project documentation

Monitor and Control Project Work (4.4)		
This process monitors and controls the processes used by the project team		
Inputs	**Tools and Techniques**	**Outputs**
• Project Management Plan • Performance Reports • Enterprise Environmental Factors • Organizational Process Assets	• Expert Judgment	• Change Requests • Project Management Plan Updates • Project Document Updates

PROCESS DOCUMENTS

Information gathered during the Monitor and Control Project Work process will be used in several other processes. Forecasts and performance information updates will be used in Report Performance. Calculations based on the information collected in this process will be used in Control Cost and Control Schedule processes. Issues identified here will be recorded and reviewed in Manage Stakeholder Expectations and other processes. Please review these documents in the chapters cited here.

COMMON PROCESS TASKS

The following is a list of the common tasks associated with the Monitor and Control Project Work process:

- Compare actual project performance with the Project Management Plan and determine the need to take/make corrective/preventive actions

- Analyze, track, and monitor project risks (for comparison and evaluation with your Risk Management Plan)

- Maintain an accurate information base

- Prepare and distribute project cost and project schedule forecasts

- Monitor the implementation of approved changes

THINK ABOUT IT

· ·

Instructions Think about how this project management process is defined, used, and documented in your organization. Compare your organization's use of this process to the PMI® definition.

Use this exercise to compare how you practice project management to what is specified in the *PMBOK® Guide Fourth Edition*.

Think about how this project management process is defined, used and documented in your organization. Write a brief description of how you use this process:

_____

_____

_____

_____

_____

_____

_____

What specific Inputs, Tools or Techniques do you use as part of this process in your organization?

_____

_____

_____

_____

_____

_____

Are the outcomes from this process different in your organization or experiences?

_____

_____

_____

_____

_____

_____

MUST KNOW CONCEPTS

1 The Monitor and Control Project Work process is applied to monitor all other processes through initiation, planning, executing, and closing in order to take/make corrective/preventive actions, as needed.

2 Corrective actions are actions required to bring expected future project performance into conformance with the Project Management Plan.

3 Preventive actions are actions required to reduce the probability of negative consequences associated with project risks.

4 Defect repairs identify a flaw or defect in a project component and recommend to either repair or replace the component.

ADDITIONAL READING

• PMBOK Guide – Section 4.4 Monitor and Control Project Work

LESSON QUIZ

Instructions Here are some questions to help reinforce your learning. Complete this quiz from memory to the best of your ability. When complete, check your results by comparing your answers to the preferred answers provided in Appendix A.

1. The monitor and control project work process is applied to _____.

    A. monitor all executing processes and take/make corrective/preventive actions, as needed
    B. monitor all other processes through initiation, planning, executing, and closing and implement risk response actions, if/when risk events occur
    C. monitor all other processes through initiation, planning, executing, and closing and take/make corrective/preventive actions, as needed
    D. provide guidance for all other monitoring and controlling processes and take/make corrective/preventive actions, as needed

2. During project execution, an opportunity arises to make a change that will significantly reduce the probability of an identified negative risk from occurring. You suggest making the change. This is an example of what?
    A. Expert judgment
    B. A preventive action
    C. A workaround plan
    D. A corrective action

3. Monitor and Control Project Work Outputs include:
   A. Rejected change requests, recommended corrective actions, and requested changes
   B. Forecasts, work performance information, and requested changes
   C. Project management plan updates, project document updates, and change requests
   D. Forecasts, recommended corrective actions, and requested changes

End of Lesson 47

Lesson 48
Perform Integrated Change Control

Objectives

At the end of this lesson, you will be able to:

- Describe the purpose of the Perform Integrated Change Control process
- Describe the Inputs, Tools & Techniques, and Outputs of the Perform Integrated Change Control process
- Understand how Perform Integrated Change Control interacts with other control processes
- Understand how Configuration Management and Change Control work together

Roadmap to the PMBOK Guide

	Initiating	Planning	Executing	M & C	Closing
Integration				▓	
Scope					
Time					
Cost					
Quality					
Human Resources					
Communications					
Risk					
Procurement					

When a change is formally requested, it must be considered using Integrated Change Control processes. Allowing only necessary changes to be approved will lead towards project success.

Perform Integrated Change Control is the process of effectively managing changes and integrating them appropriately across the entire project. It is important to understand that it is the project manager's responsibility to discourage unnecessary changes. It is also important to understand that when changes are warranted, they must be made in strict accordance with the project's change control system, and that established project baselines remain intact. Rebaselining is appropriate only in extreme situations.

Configuration management is applied in conjunction with change control processes to control changes to the project baselines and product specifications. Configuration management is focused on specifications surrounding the deliverables and the specifications for processes that are used on the project. Change control works with configuration control. Change control documents and controls changes to the project baseline (Scope, Schedule and Cost parameters) and product (deliverables) baseline. To oversimplify the description, configuration management applies mostly to the framework or specifications for the product and project processes. Change control deals with the Deliverables planned for the project.

Configuration management activities included in this process include configuration identification (identifying the basis for the product definition), configuration status accounting (identifying and documenting when and how to check on the product configuration), and configuration verification and audit (auditing done to make sure the product configuration meets functional requirements).

Project changes, although often initiated verbally, should always be documented to allow tracking and control. Additionally, all project changes should be formally approved or rejected.

Change Requests that are used as inputs to the Perform Integrated Change Control process come from many sources. This process works closely with Control Scope and Control Schedule to manage change requests for formal approval or rejection. Other processes like Direct and Manage Project Execution, Monitor and Control Project Work, Perform Quality Assurance, Perform Quality Control, and others also provide change requests to this process.

Some organizations utilize a change control board (CCB) to evaluate and approve/disapprove project change requests.

PROCESS ELEMENTS

The Perform Integrated Change Control process has the following Inputs:

- **Change Requests**   Request for changes to scope, schedule, costs, or processes or other project documentation

- **Organizational Process Assets**   Consideration factors such as processes, procedures, and corporate knowledge base

- **Project Management Plan**   The consolidated package of the subsidiary management plans and baselines

- **Work Performance Information**   Raw data related to deliverable status, schedule progress, and costs incurred

- **Enterprise Environmental Factors**   Consideration factors such as; culture, systems, procedures, and industry standards

The Perform Integrated Change Control process uses the following Tools & Techniques:

- **Expert Judgment**   Expert technical and/or managerial judgment (from any qualified source)

- **Change Control Meetings**   Change Control Board meetings to review change requests and approve/reject changes

The Perform Integrated Change Control process has the following Outputs:

- **Change Request Status Updates**   Processed change requests

- **Project Management Plan Updates**   Updates to the Project Management Plan as a result of this process

- **Project Document Updates**   Updates to other project documentation

---

Perform Integrated Change Control (4.5)
This process reviews, approves, and controls changes to project deliverables

Inputs	Tools and Techniques	Outputs
• Change Requests • Organizational Process Assets • Project Management Plan • Work Performance Information • Enterprise Environmental Factors	• Expert Judgment • Change Control Meetings	• Change Request Status Updates • Project Management Plan Updates • Project Document Updates

TSI *Study Aid*

This chart is part of the study aid poster series available at *www.truesolutions.com.*

PROCESS DOCUMENTS

Two primary documents are associated with Perform Integrated Change Control: the Change Request Form and Change Control Log. Examples of each are shown below.

True Solutions, Inc.
Project Management Template
Volume 1: Change Request

TSI

Generic Change Request

| Project Name: |
| Prepared by: |
| Date: |
| Person(s) Requesting Change: |

Change Number:

Type of Change Requested:

| | Project Scope Change | | Project Budget Change | | Project Schedule Change |
| | Project Procurement/Contract Change | | Other (specify) | | |

Detailed Description of Change:

Reason for Change Requested:

Effect on Project Cost:

| ☐ Projected Cost *Overrun* of approximately | % |
| ☐ Estimated Cost *Reduction* of approximately | % |

Effect on Schedule:

| ☐ Planned Project Completion Date: |
| ☐ New Project Completion Date: |

Additional Remarks:

| Approval | Project Manager | Date |
| Approval | (Other) | Date |

Application Aid

This form is available individually or as a set from *www.truesolutions.com*.

True Solutions, Inc.   **Change Management Log Example**

Project Management Template

Change Management Log

Project Name: _____   Project ID#: _____

Project Manager: _____   Customer: _____

ID#	Requester	Title of Change	Status	Priority	Date Required	Approved		Area of Impact		
						Yes	No	Schedule	Scope	Budget
001										
002										
003										
004										
005										
006										
007										
008										
009										
010										
011										
012										
013										
014										
015										
016										
017										
018										
019										
020										
021										
022										
023										
024										
025										
026										
027										
028										
029										
030										

TSI *Application Aid*
This form is available individually or as a set from *www.truesolutions.com*.

COMMON PROCESS TASKS

The following is a list of the common tasks associated with the Perform Integrated Change Control process:

- Verify that a change has occurred

- Determine that a change is needed and that change request documentation has been properly completed

- Adhere to the steps by which your official project documents may be changed

- Determine whether variances from your plan require corrective action, need new or revised cost estimates, should result in a modification of activity sequences, or require the development of additional risk response alternatives

- Utilize the powers and responsibilities of your change control board or other governing body

- Document and implement procedures to process changes that may be accepted without prior review by a change control board or other governing body

- Employ proactive, structured change management procedures to properly influence your project stakeholders

- Utilize your performing organization's change control system

- Complete project plan modifications, including integration with various project baselines

- Utilize configuration management procedures to integrate change across all areas of your project

THINK ABOUT IT

My company was engaged to provide project management of an implementation project for a software company. The actual project was to create a custom website portal for a financial organization so that they could access their financial system and upgrade to the newest version of the financial software package.

The project team consisted of a project manager and developers from the software company and a project manager and developers from a website company (most of the resources were off-shore) who were responsible for design and coding of the website portal. In addition, the customer team had a project manager and multiple functional experts.

The project had been delayed multiple times and was over budget by about $5,000,000. The customer was threatening to sue the software company for not delivering the implementation of the software. The software company had lost all credibility and did not know how to fix the problem so they brought in my company as a third party program manager to be the neutral party and see if the project and the relationship could be recovered.

Our PM came in and within a week, assessed scope, requirements, and project plan. The problem was identified as a lack of cohesive planning across all project teams and entities. Each of the above teams had a different scope document and working from different versions of the requirements. There were no plans or processes in place to synchronize their scope, requirements, and changes.

The solution was getting all three parties to agree to a single scope and requirements document and then implementing stringent integrated change control for all parties. This solution was facilitated by holding requirement review sessions and producing one set of controlled requirements (owned by the functional users), and integrating all of the schedules into one master project schedule. Then we could see the gaps, issues, and take action to put the project back on track. While the project ultimately ended with a severe cost overrun, the end result of the project was an upgraded financial system that was usable and Internet accessible.

Contributed by Lorie Gibbons, PMP

MUST KNOW CONCEPTS

1. Perform Integrated Change Control is the process of effectively managing changes and integrating them appropriately across the entire project.

2. The primary deliverables (Outputs) of the Perform Integrated Change Control process include Project Management Plan Updates and Project Document Updates.

3. Configuration management applies mostly to the framework or specifications for the product and project processes. Configuration management is an especially useful tool when the product of the project is very complex.

4. It is the project manager's responsibility to discourage unnecessary changes.

5. When legitimate changes are warranted, they should be made in accordance with the project's change control system.

6 For monitoring and performance measurement purposes, established project baselines should remain unchanged, regardless of project changes. Rebaselining is appropriate only in extreme situations.

7 Some organizations utilize a change control board (CCB) to evaluate and approve/disapprove project change requests.

ADDITIONAL READING
· ·
• PMBOK Guide – Section 4.5 Perform Integrated Change Control

LESSON QUIZ
· ·
Instructions   Here are some questions to help reinforce your learning. Complete this quiz from memory to the best of your ability. When complete, check your results by comparing your answers to the preferred answers provided in Appendix A.

1. The Perform Integrated Change Control process occurs

    _____.
    A. during Execution only
    B. during Initiation and Executing
    C. throughout the project life cycle
    D. during Executing and Monitoring and Controlling

2. All of the following are Perform Integrated Change Control process Outputs except:
    A. Project document updates
    B. Change request status updates
    C. Project Management Plan updates
    D. Change control meetings

3. Perform Integrated Change Control is _____

    _____.
    A. the process applied to guide the project change control board (CCB) in their decisions to approve or deny project change requests
    B. the process of effectively managing changes and integrating them appropriately across the entire project
    C. the process applied to encourage the project manager to use effective influencing skills to discourage unnecessary changes
    D. the process applied to guide the use of configuration management procedures across the project life cycle

End of Lesson 48

Lesson 49
Closing Process Group

Objectives

At the end of this lesson, you will be able to:

• Understand what processes are used in the Closing Process Group
• Understand the purpose for using Closing processes for the project or project phase

Roadmap to the PMBOK Guide

	Initiating	Planning	Executing	M & C	Closing
Integration					
Scope					
Time					
Cost					
Quality					
Human Resources					
Communications					
Risk					
Procurement					

Closing processes are intended to closeout procurement actions and other actions of the project. These processes are usually done at the end of each phase of the project.

The Closing Process Group consists of two processes that are intended to end or close a project or project phase. The primary reason that these Closing processes are performed is to authorize the project (or phase) to end. End of phase reviews will be held as part of Closing processes. Closing processes occur in the Integration Management knowledge area and the Procurement Management knowledge area of the PMBOK® Guide Fourth Edition.

An important part of the Closing Process Group is the authorization for the vendor to terminate activities and for the overall project (or phase) to terminate.

When a project is closed, the sponsor, project manager, and stakeholders have the final view of the project. Approvals for work, the product that was created, and the project overall are obtained prior to closing the project or phase.

Once the project team and/or vendor team is released from the project, unless there is some form of warranty verbiage in contracts, then the team is done and the project is officially closed.

The *PMBOK Guide* is very clear that the project ends when final approvals for work, for the product, and for the project are obtained.

CLOSING TASKS

On your PMP Exam, you will encounter approximately eighteen questions that will test your understanding of Closing processes. These eighteen questions will generally focus on the following Closing tasks:

• As a PMP or project manager closing a project (or project phase), you may be required to formalize final acceptance for the project from the sponsor by ensuring that the delivered products and services comply with the agreed deliverables list, agreed scope, and any organizational procedures in order to close contractual obligations and document the project's success.

• As a PMP or project manager closing the project (or project phase), you may be required to obtain financial, legal, and administrative closure (final payments, warranties, contract sign-off, etc.) for internal and external vendors and customers using generally accepted accounting principles (GAAP) and Sarbanes-Oxley (SOX) accounting compliance in order to ensure no further expenditures and to communicate formal project closure.

• As a PMP or project manager closing a project (or project phase), you may be required to release all project resources using appropriate organizational policies and procedures (financial and human resources) and to provide performance feedback in order to make the resources available for future project assignments.

- As a PMP or project manager closing a project (or project phase), you may be required to communicate Lessons Learned by means of team discussions, 360-degree surveys, supplier performance evaluations, and workshops in order to create and/or maintain knowledge and experience that could be used in future projects, improve overall project management processes and decision making, and to capitalize on best practices.

- As a PMP or project manager closing a project (or project phase), you may be required to distribute the final project report using all project closure related information in order to highlight project variances, open issues, Lessons Learned, deliverables, and to provide a final project status report to all stakeholders.

- As a PMP or project manager closing a project (or project phase), you may be required to archive project records, historical information and documents (Schedule, Project Management Plan, Lessons Learned, Surveys, Risk Register, and Issue Log, etc.) in order to retain organizational knowledge, comply with statutory requirements, and ensure availability of data for potential use in future projects and internal or external audits.

- As a PMP or project manager closing a project (or project phase), you may be required to measure customer satisfaction at the end of the project by capturing customer feedback using appropriate interview techniques and surveys in order to gain, maintain, and improve long-term customer relationships.

KNOWLEDGE REQUIREMENTS

As a PMP applying Closing processes in real-world projects, you will be required to possess in-depth knowledge in several project-specific areas, as well as a broad knowledge of project management in general. The PMP Exam will test your understanding of these knowledge specifics.

By developing a familiarity with these knowledge specifics, you will better understand the context of many PMP Exam questions. Please give some thought to each item as it relates to your own project management experiences with past and current projects.

Remember, the PMP or project manager is always required to have a very broad base of knowledge to work from. In many cases, the project manager has to work across the entire organization to effectively perform project management.

As a PMP or project manager applying Closing processes, you may be expected to have knowledge of:

- Project Scope and objectives

- Deliverables

- Acceptance criteria

- Organizational structure, policies, and procedures

- Contract and statutory requirements

- Budgeting and expenditure processes

- Conflict resolution

- Skills assessment

- Performance metrics

- Historical information

- Stakeholders

- Project contracts

- Industry best practices

- Archiving processes

- Project documents and records

PERFORMANCE COMPETENCIES

As a PMP applying Closing processes in real-world projects, there are many specific project management performance competencies (skills) that you may be expected to exercise.

By developing a familiarity with these skills, you will better understand the context of many PMP Exam questions. As you progress through the Ultimate PMP Exam Prep Guide, you will see each of these skills mentioned. As you read, please give thought to how the use of these skills relates to your past and current project experiences.

As a PMP or project manager applying Closing process, you may be required to exercise skill in:

- Negotiating

- Presenting

- Interviewing

- Decision making

- Document writing

- Managing conflict

- Communicating

- Managing relationships

- Coordinating

- Motivating

- Appraising

- Objectivity

- Facilitating

- Statistical sampling

READ THE PMBOK® GUIDE FOURTH EDITION

Study Tip

The information exposed in our *Ultimate PMP Exam Prep Guide* is often sufficient for you to pass your PMP Exam on the first try ... without any other aids or tools.

However, since we are all interested in your success on the PMP Exam, we feel that it is imperative to remind you to read the *PMBOK® Guide Fourth Edition*. Throughout the *Ultimate PMP Exam Prep Guide* you will find references to the *PMBOK Guide*.

This is an important certification and an important step in your career. We recommend that you thoroughly read *both* documents.

ADDITIONAL READING

- PMBOK Guide – Section 3.7

End of Lesson 49

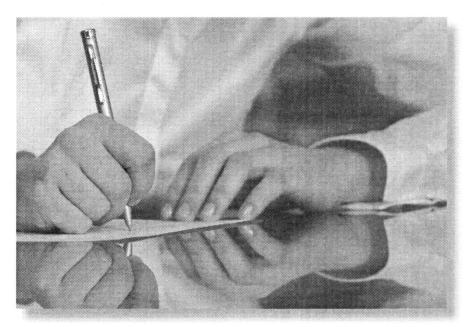

Lesson 50
Close Procurements

Objectives

At the end of this lesson, you will be able to:

- Describe the purpose of the Close Procurements process
- Describe the Inputs, Tools & Techniques, and Outputs of the Close Procurements process
- Understand how Close Procurements interacts with Close Project or Phase and other processes

Roadmap to the PMBOK Guide

	Initiating	Planning	Executing	M & C	Closing
Integration					
Scope					
Time					
Cost					
Quality					
Human Resources					
Communications					
Risk					
Procurement					■

In Close Procurements, the vendor is provided with formal acceptance for the work, for the product produced and for their project overall. The vendor resources are released from the project in this process.

The Close Procurements process is used to formally validate that all of the requirements for each of the project's procurement activities have been met and are acceptable for both seller and buyer.

This process, in conjunction with the Close Project or Phase process, is used to complete a project. This process is also used throughout the project's life cycle to bring a formal termination to a procurement or procurement contract.

This process is usually preceded by the Verify Scope process and Perform Quality Control process in order to verify that work was completed and that the work or deliverables created are acceptable for project use.

The process of Close Procurements is similar to, but slightly different from, the process of Close Project or Phase. First of all, Close Procurements is closing only a portion of the overall project, whereas Close Project or Phase is used to close the overall project or phase. In addition to that difference, there is a difference in activity flow in the process.

During Close Procurements, the majority of formal approval or acceptance flows from the project to the vendor. During Close Project or Phase, the project manager obtains or receives formal acceptance from the sponsor.

Formal Acceptance for:	Close Procurements	Close Project or Phase
Work	Given to Vendor	Received from Sponsor
Product		
Project		
Resource Release		
Documentation	Received from Vendor and archived	Provided to Sponsor and Organization; then archived

When closing any procurement, information, Lessons Learned, and other procurement data should be archived to aid in future projects.

PROCESS ELEMENTS

The Close Procurements process has the following Inputs:

- **Project Management Plan**   The consolidated package of the subsidiary management plans and baselines

- **Procurement Documentation**   Contract, supporting schedules, scope, quality, cost performance, contract change documentation, payment records, and inspection results

The Close Procurements process uses the following Tools & Techniques:

- **Procurement Audits**   Structured lessons learned-type reviews of the project's procurement process

- **Negotiated Settlements**   Final settlement of all outstanding issues, claims, and disputes

- **Records Management System**   Used by the project manager to manage contract documentation and records

The Close Procurements process has the following Outputs:

- **Closed Procurements**   Formal written notice of the closure of the procurement

- **Organizational Process Assets Updates**   Updates to procurement files, deliverable acceptance, and Lessons Learned documentation

Close Procurements (12.4)		
This process formally terminates the project procurements		
Inputs	**Tools and Techniques**	**Outputs**
• Project Management Plan • Procurement Documentation	• Procurement Audits • Negotiated Settlements • Records Management System	• Closed Procurements • Organizational Process Assets Updates

TSI Study Aid
This chart is part of the study aid poster series available at www.truesolutions.com.

PROCESS DOCUMENTS

This process focuses on providing formal acceptance to the vendor for work, for the product of the project, and for the project overall. The project manger will probably use acceptance documents similar to the document shown in the Verify Scope process.

COMMON PROCESS TASKS

The following is a list of the common tasks associated with the Close Procurements process:

- Verify work, performance, quality, and product

- Provide formal acceptance to vendor

- Resolve any open issues

- Document Lessons Learned

- Archive all contract documentation

THINK ABOUT IT

Instructions Think about how this project management process is defined, used, and documented in your organization. Compare your organization's use of this process to the PMI® definition. Does your organization perform these items during Close Procurements?

- ☐ Verify work completion and acceptance

- ☐ Review vendor performance

- ☐ Provide formal acceptance to the vendor

- ☐ Use a process to make final payments

- ☐ Resolve any open issues before formal acceptance is provided

- ☐ Document Lessons Learned

- ☐ Archive all contract documents

What gaps can you identify between the recommended best practice for Close Procurements and the actions you take in your organization?

_____

_____

_____

_____

_____

What actions could you take to close these identified gaps?

_____

_____

_____

_____

_____

MUST KNOW CONCEPTS

1. The Close Procurements process is used to formally validate that all of the requirements for each of the project's procurement activities have been met and are acceptable for both seller and buyer.

2. The deliverables (Outputs) of the Close Procurements process are the closed procurements and updates to the Organizational Process Assets.

ADDITIONAL READING

- PMBOK Guide – Section 12.4 Close Procurements

LESSON QUIZ

Instructions Here are some questions to help reinforce your learning. Complete this quiz from memory to the best of your ability. When complete, check your results by comparing your answers to the preferred answers provided in Appendix A.

1. Close Procurements:
   A. Is the procurement process of verifying that the final seller invoices have been approved and paid
   B. Is the procurement process of formally validating that all the requirements for each of the project's procurement activities have been met and are acceptable
   C. Is the procurement process of documenting that the seller has been formally notified of contract end, regardless of the reason for termination
   D. Is the procurement process of formally transferring the contract to central contracting to ensure the final contract documents (including Lessons Learned) are properly archived

2. Among the following statements, which is least true?
   A. Close Procurements is performed by verifying that contracted work was completed correctly and contract terms and conditions were satisfied.
   B. During Close Procurements, formal acceptance is documented and contract records are archived.
   C. Close Procurements is applied once, at the very end of the final project phase, like all closing processes.
   D. Close Procurements is applied only if services/supplies are contracted/purchased to support the project.

3. Which of the following is a Close Procurements tool/technique?
   A. Procurement audits
   B. Closed procurements
   C. Organizational process assets updates
   D. Procurement documentation

End of Lesson 50

51

Lesson 51
Close Project or Phase

Objectives

At the end of this lesson, you will be able to:

- Describe the purpose of the Close Project or Phase process
- Describe the Inputs, Tools & Techniques, and Outputs of the Close Project or Phase process
- Understand the interaction with other processes that is required to close a project or phase

Roadmap to the PMBOK Guide

	Initiating	Planning	Executing	M & C	Closing
Integration					▉
Scope					
Time					
Cost					
Quality					
Human Resources					
Communications					
Risk					
Procurement					

In Close Project or Phase, the project manager works with the stakeholders and sponsor to obtain formal acceptance for work for the product and for the project overall. After formal acceptance has been obtained, the resources are released and project records are archived for future use.

Close Project or Phase is the process of formally ending either the project or project phase. This process documents project results to formalize the acceptance of the product of the project or project phase. Close Project or Phase is also utilized for projects that are terminated prior to their completion.

Close Project or Phase is performed by collecting project records, analyzing project performance, analyzing Lessons Learned and archiving all project information for future review and use.

This process is intended to deliver two primary Outputs:

• The final product/service/result of the project (formally accepted)

• Organizational process updates

PROCESS ELEMENTS

The Close Project or Phase process has the following Inputs:

- **Project Management Plan**   The consolidated package of the subsidiary management plans and baselines

- **Accepted Deliverables**   Documentation of accepted deliverables from the Verify Scope process

- **Organizational Process Assets**   Consideration factors such as processes, procedures, and corporate knowledge base

The Close Project or Phase process uses the following Tools & Techniques:

- **Expert Judgment**   Expert technical and/or managerial judgment (from any qualified source)

The Close Project or Phase process has the following Outputs:

- **Final Product, Service, or Result Transition**   The progression of the final product, service, or result of the project or project phase

- **Organizational Process Assets Updates**   Updates to corporate documents, guidelines, procedures, historical information, etc.

Close Project or Phase (4.6) This process formally terminates the project or project phase		
Inputs	**Tools and Techniques**	**Outputs**
• Project Management Plan • Accepted Deliverables • Organizational Process Assets	• Expert Judgment	• Final Product, Service or Result Transition • Organizational Process Assets Updates

PROCESS DOCUMENTS

The main focus for this particular process is the formal acceptance of the project or the phase. A formal acceptance document similar to the one shown below will be used.

In addition to obtaining formal acceptance for the project or phase during this process, the project manager will gather (if not already collected) all of the project documentation for inclusion in the project archives. The project archives form the Organizational Process Assets that can be used in the future to assist in planning future projects in the performing organization.

True Solutions, Inc.
Project Management Template
Volume 1: Formal Acceptance and Closure Template

(TSI)

Formal Acceptance and Closure

Project Name:

Prepared by:

Date:

Name of Client or Sponsor:

Review of Scope Verification
☐ Yes ☐ No

Statement of Formal Acceptance:

The undersigned formally accepts as complete the above-identified project, and do hereby state that this project, project phase, or major deliverable meets or exceeds agreed-upon performance standards for scope, quality, schedule, and cost, and states that we have seen documentation that all relevant legal and regulatory requirements have been met or exceeded.

Additional Remarks:

Accepted by (name of client, sponsor, or other official)	*Date*
Accepted by (name of client, sponsor, or other official)	*Date*
Accepted by (name of client, sponsor, or other official)	*Date*

Signed form distributed to:

Stakeholder name	*Date*
Stakeholder name	*Date*
Stakeholder name	*Date*

(TSI) **Application Aid**
This form is available individually or as a set from *www.truesolutions.com*.

COMMON PROCESS TASKS

The following is a list of the common tasks associated with the Close Project or Phase process:

- Define and implement closure at the end of the project by collecting all project records, documenting the degree to which each project phase was properly closed after its completion, and verifying all project results in preparation for formal acceptance

- Document performance measures resulting from performance reviews, as well as variance, trend, and earned value analyses

- Review final specifications and analyze project success and effectiveness

- Document your final project scope

- Document Lessons Learned

- Formalize the acceptance/sign-off of the product by your sponsor, client, or customer

- Perform final appraisal reviews of your team members

- Archive relevant project documentation

Conduct Close Project or Phase with Regard to Risk Management

- Review project outcomes to determine effectiveness of your risk management processes and procedures

- Identify, document, and report risk issues to recommend improvements to your higher project authority for application in future projects

Conduct Close Project or Phase with Regard to Integration

- Document Lessons Learned from project integration, including causes of activities requiring corrective action, types of activities requiring corrective action, reasons for selecting certain corrective actions, and classification of changes for subsequent analysis

Conduct Close Project or Phase with Regard to Scope

- Identify causes of variances in project scope

- Identify the reasoning behind corrective actions chosen through Scope Change Control

- Determine and document Lessons Learned with regard to scope

- Perform a post-project review

Conduct Close Project or Phase with Regard to Time

- Document Lessons Learned, including causes of activities leading to schedule changes, types of schedule changes, reasons for selecting specific corrective actions, and classification of schedule change causes for further analysis

Conduct Close Project or Phase with Regard to Cost

- Document Lessons Learned, including causes of activities leading to cost changes, types of cost changes, reasons for selecting specific corrective actions, and classification of cost changes for further analysis

Conduct Close Project or Phase with Regard to Quality

- Document Lessons Learned, including causes of activities leading to quality changes, types of quality changes, reasons for selecting specific corrective actions, and classification of quality change causes for further analysis

Conduct Close Project or Phase with Regard to Human Resource Management

- Implement transition activities to return resources to parent organization

- Document Lessons Learned, including causes of activities leading to people changes, types of changes, reasons for selecting specific corrective actions, and classification of change causes for further analysis

THINK ABOUT IT
. . . .

Instructions Think about how this project management process is defined, used, and documented in your organization.

Compare your organization's use of this process to the PMI® definition.

Use this exercise to compare how you practice project management to what is specified in the *PMBOK® Guide Fourth Edition.*

 Think about how this process is defined, used and documented in your organization. Write a brief description of how you use this process:

_____

_____

_____

_____

_____

What specific Inputs, Tools or Techniques do you use as part of this process in your organization?

_____

_____

_____

_____

_____

Are the outcomes from this process different in your organization or experiences?

_____

_____

_____

_____

_____

MUST KNOW CONCEPTS
. . . .

1 Close Project or Phase is the process of formally ending either the project or project phase.

2 Close Project or Phase documents project results to formalize the acceptance of the product/service/result of the project (or project phase).

3 The primary deliverables (Outputs) of the Close Project or Phase process include the formally accepted product/service/result transition and Organizational Process Assets updates.

4 Close Project or Phase is performed by collecting project records, analyzing project performance, analyzing Lessons Learned, and archiving all project information for future review and use.

ADDITIONAL READING
. . . .

• PMBOK Guide – Section 4.6 Close Project or Phase

LESSON QUIZ

Instructions Here are some questions to help reinforce your learning. Complete this quiz from memory to the best of your ability. When complete, check your results by comparing your answers to the preferred answers provided in Appendix A.

Remember that these questions are similar to those that could appear on your PMP exam, but they are not exact. Actual PMP Exam questions may be more comprehensive and may describe project scenarios where you will be asked to use your knowledge and experience to choose the best answer.

1. _____ best describes the Close Project or Phase process.
   A. Preparing and distributing the final project performance report
   B. Archiving the performance evaluations of project core team members
   C. Bringing an orderly end to the seller's contractual obligations
   D. Formally ending either the project or project phase

2. Close Project or Phase is intended to be applied _____.
   A. repeatedly, upon the completion of each WBS Work Package.
   B. at the end of each project life cycle phase, including the very last project phase
   C. at the end of the final project life cycle phase, concluding the entire project
   D. each time a significant project document needs to be formally archived

3. Close Project or Phase Inputs include which of the following?
   A. Expert judgment
   B. Final product transition
   C. Accepted deliverables
   D. WBS

4. Which of the following is most true?
   A. You (as project manager) are responsible for performing and documenting Lessons Learned.
   B. Your key project stakeholders are responsible for performing and documenting Lessons Learned.
   C. Your sponsor is responsible for performing and documenting Lessons Learned.
   D. You (working with your project management team) are responsible for performing and documenting Lessons Learned.

End of Lesson 51

52

Lesson 52
Professional and Social Responsibility

Objectives
At the end of this lesson, you will be able to:
- Understand what groups the project manager is responsible to
- Understand professional and social responsibility in a project management context
- Understand how culture plays a role in project success

Roadmap to the PMBOK Guide

	Initiating	Planning	Executing	M & C	Closing
Integration					
Scope					
Time					
Cost		Contains General Management Information Applicable to All Areas of PMBOK® Guide Fourth Edition and Project Management in General			
Quality					
Human Resources					
Communications					
Risk					
Procurement					

In today's diverse global culture, the project manager must be culturally aware and must always choose to do the right thing when managing projects.

Your PMP Exam will include approximately eighteen questions designed to test your knowledge competency and judgment in the area of professional and social responsibility. This represents a significant overall percentage of exam questions and may actually provide a benefit to the exam taker. For many PMP candidates, professional and social responsibility questions are considered easy to answer correctly.

Many professional responsibility questions can be answered simply by using common sense.

Part of your additional reading assignment (listed at the back of the chapter) is to read the "PMI Code of Ethics and Professional Conduct." This code governing the conduct of project managers and PMP's has been developed since the 1980s. The "PMI Code of Ethics and Professional Conduct" responds to changes in the world of project management that have occurred during that time. The new code applies to all members of PMI and certification holders. This code addresses Mandatory Standards which have to be met and Aspirational Standards which are desirable.

In general, this code is intended to instill confidence in the profession of project management by providing a common frame of behavior for project managers. In general, compliance with this code should facilitate each practitioner becoming more proficient as they comply with the code.

PROFESSIONAL RESPONSIBILITY TASKS

- As a PMP or project manager you will be required to ensure personal integrity and professionalism by adhering to legal requirements, ethical standards, and social norms in order to protect the community and all stakeholders and to create a healthy working environment.

- As a PMP or project manager you will be required to contribute to the project management knowledge base by sharing Lessons Learned, best practices, research, etc., within appropriate communities in order to improve the quality of project management services, build the capabilities of colleagues, and advance the profession of project management.

- As a PMP or project manager you will be required to enhance professional competence by increasing and applying knowledge in order to improve project management services.

- As a PMP or project manager you will be required to promote interaction among team members and other stakeholders in a professional and cooperative manner by respecting personal and cultural differences in order to ensure a collaborative project management environment.

- As a PMP or project manager you will be required to uphold the "PMI Code of Ethics and Professional Conduct" by acting in a professional and socially aware manner and by reporting ethics violations to appropriate parties.

KNOWLEDGE REQUIREMENTS

As a PMP applying professional services in real-world projects, you will be required to possess in-depth knowledge in several project-specific areas, as well as a broad knowledge of project management in general. The PMP Exam will test your understanding of these knowledge specifics.

By developing a familiarity with these knowledge specifics, you will better understand the context of many PMP Exam questions. Please give some thought to each item as it relates to your own project management experiences with past and current projects.

Remember, the PMP or project manager is always required to have a very broad base of knowledge to work from. In many cases, the project manager has to work across the entire organization to effectively perform project management.

As a PMP or project manager applying professional services, you may be expected to have knowledge of:

- Legal requirements

- Ethical standards

- Social norms

- Community and stakeholder values

- Communication techniques

- Body of knowledge of project management

- Techniques for knowledge transfer

- Research techniques

- Personal strengths and weaknesses

- Instructional methods and tools

- Appropriate professional competencies

- Training options

- Self-assessment strategies

- Interpersonal skills

- Cultural differences

- Team motivation strategies

PERFORMANCE COMPETENCIES

As a PMP performing professional services in real-world projects, there are many specific project management performance competencies (skills) that you may be expected to exercise.

By developing a familiarity with these skills, you will better understand the context of many PMP Exam questions. As you read, please give thought to how use of these skills relate to your past and current project experiences.

As a PMP or project manager performing professional services, you may be required to demonstrate and exercise skill in:

- Exercising judgment

- Researching local laws, regulations, ethical standards, organization values, and cultural norms

- Gathering, assessing, compiling, and documenting information

- Negotiating effectively

- Resolving conflicts

- Communicating effectively

- Transferring knowledge

- Coaching, mentoring, and training

- Using research techniques

- Planning personal development

- Attaining and applying new project management practices

- Respecting cultural differences

- Motivating teams

PROFESSIONAL RESPONSIBILITY

ADHERING TO THE "PMI CODE OF ETHICS AND PROFESSIONAL CONDUCT"

You should familiarize yourself with the "PMI Code of Ethics and Professional Conduct." If you do not currently have a copy, please go to www.pmi.org to download a copy for yourself. The code is relatively brief; it addresses four major areas of concern for the project management practitioner. The code has aspirational and mandatory elements.

- Responsibility

  - Taking the best actions for a specific situation

  - Taking actions supported by knowledge

  - Fulfilling project and professional requirements

  - Protecting sensitive information

  - Upholding the code

  - Compliance with all applicable laws and regulations (mandatory)

  - Reporting unethical or illegal behavior (mandatory)

- Respect

  - Keeping informed about cultural norms and customs

  - Listening to stakeholders

  - Addressing conflict as required

  - Behaving professionally at all times

- Negotiating in good faith with customers and suppliers (mandatory)

- Refraining from personal enrichment (mandatory)

- Not acting abusively (mandatory)

- Respect for others property rights (mandatory)

- Fairness

  - Making decisions in a transparent manner

  - Acting impartially

  - Providing equal access to information

  - Providing equal opportunity when acquiring resources

  - Avoiding conflicts of interest (mandatory)

  - Acting fairly when hiring — do not base decisions on personal considerations (mandatory)

  - Do not discriminate against individuals based on social prejudices (mandatory)

  - Applying rules impartially (mandatory)

- Honesty

  - Seeking the truth

  - Speaking the truth

  - Making commitments in good faith

  - Do not engage in or condone dishonesty (mandatory)

Business ethics is currently emerging as a dedicated field of interest with its own body of knowledge. New books on the subject are being published at a rapid rate and it is likely that ethics will become a more pronounced discipline associated with project management in the future. Recent social and economic upheavals at a global level continue to increase awareness of ethics, ethical dilemmas, and doing "the right thing" in business and social settings.

CULTURAL COMPETENCE

In today's global society it is important for project managers to be aware of how to manage a culturally diverse project team. Many project managers find themselves managing multicultural project teams, managing teams from different locations around the globe, and managing teams that have highly diverse expectations for work ethics and conditions. As a result, cultural competency is becoming a critical skill for successful project managers. Here are a few areas that a project manager needs to be familiar with, to help develop cultural awareness, sensitivity, and practical competence.

Awareness and Sensitivity of Cultural Differences: Understand that differences exist … between countries, between communities, between people.

Monetary policies	Governments	Social groups	Religions
Education	Body language	Class structure	Perceived time
Genders	Negotiating practices	Managements styles	Risk thresholds
Local laws	Quality standards	Infrastructure	Language
Physical time	Procurement Practices	Trust	Races

Awareness and Sensitivity of Cultural Priorities: Understand that cultural priorities can be quite different.

• Developed, industrialized countries are sometimes characterized by excess. Priorities tend to be driven by a desire for continuous improvement.

• There is no excess in less developed countries. A close balance between needs and resources exists. These cultures tend to be driven by a desire to achieve what fully developed countries have accomplished.

• Cultures in third world countries tend to be driven by the need to meet basic necessities. Most times, needs exceed resources.

Developing Practical Cultural Competence: Fundamental cultural competence may be developed by following a few practical guidelines.

Practice your awareness of cultural differences. Just being yourself will not facilitate cross-cultural competence. Do not assume similarity.

Be realistic with expectations for yourself and others. Do not try to adopt the orientations of the other culture. Adapting is helpful, adopting is not.

Be forgiving. Accept that you will make mistakes. Remain confident. Maintain your sense of humor.

Practice patience. Slow your pace. Take time to establish relationships. Practice integrity.

Maintain your objectivity. Don't evaluate the other culture in terms of good or bad. Don't blame. Do not compare the other culture with your own.

MUST KNOW CONCEPTS

1. Perceptions and behaviors are different between cultures.

2. It is important to maintain a professional sensitivity to cultural differences.

3. It is important to respect cultural differences.

4. As a PMP or a member of PMI you agree to adhere to and support the "PMI Code of Ethics and Professional Conduct."

5. As a PMP or PMI member you agree to maintain a high integrity in all professional activities and commitments.

6. As a PMP or PMI member you agree to respond to ethical challenges by choosing to do the right thing.

ADDITIONAL READING

- PMI Code of Ethics and Professional Conduct
- www.pmi.org

LESSON QUIZ

1. Among the following statements, which is *most* true?
   A. To help minimize communications challenges in projects with team members who speak different languages, project performance reports should be prepared and distributed using visual illustrations with little or no text.
   B. It is generally known that developing countries have unstable economies. Projects in such countries should be financed with short-term money.
   C. In global projects, using the *PMBOK Guide* could provide a common language to help facilitate good communication.
   D. In global projects with several different time zones involved, it is common practice to establish staggered work hours to ensure that the team works simultaneously, regardless of their respective locale.

2. Communications challenges are ever present in many project environments. These challenges become even more pronounced in project environments where several geographic regions around the world are involved. Which of the following is probably not a potential source of communications challenges in global projects?
   A. Mistrust
   B. Inadvertent misinterpretation of the cultural communications matrix
   C. Inadvertent misinterpretation of body language
   D. Language barriers and educational differences

3. You are the project manager assigned to a landfill cleanup project. Environmental monitoring indicates that your activities have inadvertently caused low-toxicity chemicals to leach into the local aquifer. Of the following, what is your most appropriate course of action?

   A. Immediately notify authorities, as appropriate, and be fully accessible to address public concerns in a fully truthful and open fashion.

   B. Do nothing/say nothing unless you are specifically asked by authorities. Addressing public concerns is beyond the scope of expertise for most project managers.

   C. If forced to address public concerns, play down possible problems. Part of your job as project manager is to always present the project in the utmost positive manner.

   D. Immediately investigate the cause and identify the responsible individual(s). Document your findings and communicate them right away to authorities and to the public. It is essential for all involved to know, as soon as possible, who is at fault.

End of Lesson 52

Lesson 53
Mastering the PMP® Exam

Objectives

At the end of this lesson, you will be able to:

- Understand the fundamentals of multiple-choice question (MCQ) exams, including successful test taking techniques
- Understand test anxiety and stress
- Learn the Ultimate PMP Exam Day Test Strategy to help achieve anxiety-free peak performance

Roadmap to the PMBOK Guide

	Initiating	Planning	Executing	M & C	Closing
Integration					
Scope					
Time					
Cost		Contains General Management Information Applicable to All Areas of PMBOK® Guide Fourth Edition and Project Management in General			
Quality					
Human Resources					
Communications					
Risk					
Procurement					

The PMP Exam is a challenging 200 question multiple choice exam that must be completed in four hours. Make sure that you are fully prepared before you take your exam!

To be successful in passing your PMP Exam, just knowing the material may not be enough. You must also develop some practical test taking skills. In this lesson, we will discuss important fundamentals in test taking, then present a proven test taking strategy to help you achieve peak performance on Exam day.

Throughout your academic experience it is likely that you have encountered many types of test question formats, such as oral questions, essay questions, fill-in-the-blank questions, and true or false questions. Your PMP Exam employs a multiple-choice question (MCQ) format.

MCQ exams have been proven to be highly effective for testing complex intellectual knowledge, reasoning ability, and understanding. Good MCQ exams (like the PMP Exam) are both objective and reliable.

To pass, MCQ test takers must study for recall, but more importantly for understanding. Good MCQ exams require you to (1) recognize answers to problems, (2) recognize correct reasons for relationships, (3) establish causal links, and (4) demonstrate an understanding of principles and standards.

Good MCQ exams make liberal use of reasonable appearing distracters. Distracters are incorrect answers that are designed to include common misconceptions or partially correct information. Distracters are intended to discriminate between those who truly know the correct or best answer and those who have only a cursory familiarity on the subject.

The PMP Exam presents all questions with four unique multiple-choice answer options. There are no true/false questions and there are no combination answers where two or more answers form a correct choice. The test taker must choose the best answer from the presented choices. In some cases, one or more answer options may be correct or have some degree of correctness; the test taker must determine the best answer from his or her understanding of the subject matter.

THE SCIENCE OF ANSWERING MCQ EXAM QUESTIONS

. . . .

Step 1: Know How to Read the MCQ

- Approach each MCQ as a mutually exclusive independent event. Read the MCQ carefully, looking to determine precisely what the question is really asking for:

  - Identify the correct answer?

  - Identify the best answer?

- Identify the first best action?

- Identify the least best action?

- Identify the exception?

- Identify the incorrect alternative?

- Many MCQs will be straightforward, but many will include irrelevant information and other distracters. Be thankful for the straightforward questions, but expect distracters.

- Be on the lookout for distinguishing terms. Directly in the wording of many MCQs, you will find some distinguishing term or phrase. For example, *fast tracking* may appear in a question. You should recognize *fast tracking* as a key project management term. It may be the distinguishing term in this particular MCQ. If you focus some attention on the distinguishing term, you may be able to identify the correct answer even before reviewing the answer options.

- If the MCQ is presented as a double-negative (i.e. *All of the following are false, except. . .*) then you may consider converting it to a positive before reviewing the answer options. In the example, *All of the following statements are false, except. . .*, logic tells us that all of the answer options are false except one. The correct answer is the one *true* statement So, instead of identifying the false statements and eliminating them, look to identify the one true statement and selecting it.

- Before looking at the answer options, try to answer the question based on your recall and understanding. Many times, this will help you quickly identify the correct answer.

THE SCIENCE OF ANSWERING MCQ EXAM QUESTIONS

Step 2: Know How to Review the Answer Options and Select the Best One

- Once you feel confident that you understand what the MCQ is asking you to identify (correct, best, least, most, exception), review the answer options.

- Read *all* answer options carefully.

- If the answer doesn't come quickly, look for more clues in the question. For example; if the question indicates the answer is plural, then it may be possible to eliminate answers that are singular. Some MCQs purposely contain awkward grammar, but most are straightforward.

- If the answer is still elusive, begin eliminating options. Use scratch paper to cross off options that you know are wrong.

- If you are still unsure, mark the question for later review. Do not attempt an answer at this time. The general rule of thumb is to labor no more than two minutes over a difficult question. Mark it and save it for later.

- When your first pass through the questions is complete, revisit unanswered questions, as well as any low-confidence questions. It is possible to encounter clues to some correct answers in other questions.

- Changing answers on an MCQ exam is neither good nor bad. If you have a sensible reason to change one or more of your answers, go ahead and make the change.

- Do not leave blanks on your completed Exam. Provide an answer for *all* of the questions. There is no added penalty for answering questions incorrectly on your PMP Exam. Correctly answered questions are tallied as one. Incorrect and unanswered questions are tallied as zero. On impossible questions, a wild guess is better than no answer at all. If you can't eliminate even one of the options, a wild guess will still give you a theoretical 25% probability of being correct.

Formal examination confrontations almost always generate significant test taking anxiety and stress. This creates a special challenge. When under extreme stress, many people do not perform well in mental recall and logical reasoning. Mastering the material does help to reduce test taking anxiety, but specific stress reducing techniques are needed to maintain relative calm during the exam.

MCQ exams tend to create added stress through their extensive use of distracters. These distracters force test takers to read and reread many questions to fully understand what is being said. The level of focus and concentration needed throughout a long MCQ exam can be very draining.

KNOW THE CHALLENGES YOU WILL ENCOUNTER

Expectation 1: Every question on your PMP Exam will be new to you. You have never seen any of them before. No matter how many practice exam questions you have mastered, these new questions will create uncertainty, anxiety and will challenge your confidence. In the extreme, you may even be somewhat shocked.

Expectation 2: Although you are fully prepared with material knowledge, there is no way to prepare for specific Exam questions. Many questions will require you to integrate several facts to derive the correct answer. This will challenge your logical reasoning.

Expectation 3: Many questions will purposely include irrelevant information and distracters. This will be somewhat disorienting.

Expectation 4: Some questions may force you to select correct answers that you fundamentally disagree with. This may generate a bit of resentment.

Expectation 5: Some questions will include alternate terminology to test your deeper understanding of a concept. This will challenge your confidence.

Expectation 6: Many questions present long situational scenarios. These questions take excessive time to read and understand. These questions can disorient your pacing, challenge your focus/concentration, add to anxiety and erode your confidence.

Expectation 7: Some questions will include obscure terms or concepts that you have never seen before. This will challenge your confidence.

Expectation 8: Your Exam may present a consecutive sequence of long difficult questions. This tends to disorient your pacing and challenge your confidence.

Expectation 9: Your Exam screen will feature an ever-present four-hour countdown clock, which does not stop when you take a break. This adds to anxiety.

The ULTIMATE PMP Exam Day Strategy

Use this integrated PMP Exam taking strategy to ensure you achieve peak performance on Exam day, with as little stress as possible.

Pre-Exam Day Rehearsals

1. Prometric allows you to use scratch paper, pencil and a four-function calculator during the PMP exam. They provide these items for you. It is very useful, to do a *memory-dump* before you initiate the Exam. Your memory-dump is done jotting down key equations and reminders on scratch paper as soon as you sit down to your computer station. This is perfectly legal, acceptable, even encouraged. Here is a possible memory dump sheet:

Memory Dump

Standard Deviation
1 Sigma = ± 68.26%
2 Sigma = ± 95.46%
3 Sigma = ± 99.73%
6 Sigma = ± 99.99%

$PERT = (P + 4M + O)/6$

Communication Channels
$N(N - 1)/2$

EV = BCWP
PV = BCWS
AC = ACWP

SPI = EV/PV
CPI = EV/ACBCWS
SV = EV − PV
EAC = BAC/CPI
CV = EV − AC
ETC = BAC − EV
or (BAC − EV)/CP
VAC = BAC − EAC

TCPI = (BAC − EV)/(BAC − AC) or
TCPI = (BAC − EV)/(EAC − AC)

---

2. As you study and prepare, practice your memory-dump immediately prior to tackling a set of practice exam questions. On Exam day, it will be a quick & easy process.

3. A week or so before your PMP Exam, drive to your Prometric testing center to learn the route and traffic patterns. Ask a facility representative to familiarize you with testing protocols.

4. The day before your Exam, take a break. Don't study. Relax. Get a good night's sleep.

On Exam day:

1. Pack a snack and a drink (if allowed) and a sweater.

2. Eat a light, nourishing meal before you go.

3. Leave in time to arrive thirty minutes early.

4. In addition to items in #1, plan on taking only your picture ID and one other ID into the testing center

5. Once processed in and seated at your testing station, perform your memory dump.

6. Take the optional computer tutorial, primarily to acclimate yourself and to relax.

7. Before signaling to your test proctor that you are ready to initiate the Exam, take a minute to relax, get centered. Close your eyes, breathe easily, relax your muscles, and stretch a bit.

8. Begin your exam.

9. Treat each question as an independent event. For each question, follow the two-step protocol for answering MCQ exams.

10. Take periodic breaks in your seat. Sit back, close your eyes, breathe easy, relax your muscles, stretch a bit, and then return to your exam.

11. Maintain your focus and concentration. Don't think about anything except executing your Exam strategy. Pay attention to your exam strategy — your passing score will take care of itself.

12. Take all of the time allotted.

13. When you feel confident that you have answered all of the questions to the best of your ability, the computer will prompt you to end the exam.

14. Your pass/fail notification will be presented in a few seconds. A printout of your result will be waiting for you as you exit the testing room.

15. The PMP Exam is a stressful event, mentally and physically. Give yourself the rest of the day off to celebrate and to recover.

ADDITIONAL READING
. . . .
• PMBOK Guide – Chapters 1–12
• PMBOK Guide – Glossary

End of Lesson 53

Lesson 54
Simulated PMP Exam

200 Questions—Finish in four (4) hours or less
· ·
Multiple Choice

Choose the best answer for the question and circle it.

1. You are a member of the PMO for a large commercial bank and you have just received a request from a new manager in the Adjustments department to initiate a new project to consolidate data reports from several departments into one report with a consistent reporting format. Currently, the manager receives management reports from each department and each report is a different format. It is difficult for the new manager to know which accounts need adjustment. Therefore, a new project has been authorized by the PMO. This would have been a result of which of the following?
   A. Organizational need
   B. Legal requirement
   C. Customer request
   D. Technological advance

2. Given the following information, is the project budget under or over at this measurement point? EV = 105, PV = 95, AC = 1
   A. Over, because the result of the variance measurement is negative
   B. Under, because the result of the variance measurement is positive
   C. Under, because the result of the variance measurement is negative
   D. Over, because the result of the variance measurement is positive

3. You are an adjustor for a third-party insurance administration company. You are the manager of the Major Accounts Division which performs property and casualty claims for the company's key clients. The Major Accounts Division performs negotiation and pay settlement for property and casualty claims that are filed against its clients. This is a large department, with several smaller sections that deal with specific accounts; for example, large retail clients with multiple locations. You have received your first set of management reports and cannot interpret information. Each section appears to use a different methodology to audit their work and record the data for the management report. You request a project manager from the PMO to come down and get started right away on a project to streamline this process and make the data and reports consistent. This project came about as a result of which of the following?
   A. Technological advance
   B. Legal requirement
   C. Business need
   D. Stakeholder request

4. Before a reliable cost baseline and schedule baseline can be developed, the outputs of several critical planning processes must first be available. Which of the following planning outputs is LEAST useful to support budget and schedule development?
   A. Work breakdown structure
   B. Integrated project management plan
   C. Network diagram
   D. Activity list

5. What is the document that formally authorizes a project or a phase and documents initial requirements that satisfy the stakeholders' needs and expectations?
   A. Project charter
   B. Project management plan
   C. Project statement of work
   D. Feasibility plan

6. If the Budget at Completion (BAC) or Estimate at Completion (EAC) are not viable at any point in project monitoring, a cost control tool and technique is performed to determine a calculated projection of cost performance that must be achieved on the remaining work. What tool of the Control Cost process does this describe?
   A. Cost performance index
   B. To-Complete performance index
   C. Schedule performance index
   D. Forecasting

7. You are a project manager working on developing a new learning toy for toddlers. Your company wanted the new toy displayed on the store shelves for the holiday season. To make this schedule come true, you contracted out the entire production of the toy assembly so the deliverable would make the holiday buyer season. Now that all of the work is done, you need to begin the Close Procurements process. You need to gather the technical specifications for the toy from the vendor to archive. Where will this information be filed?
   A. Product documentation
   B. Historical information file
   C. Procurement documentation
   D. Records Management System

8. You are working as a project manager for a firm that designs and constructs certain portions of the buildings for hotel chains. Some of the work can be staffed from your firm, and when it can, you manage those projects and the deliverables. However, the project you are working this time also required that you procure contracted resources. You set the work packages so that the contracted work would be completed before the work that your organization is completing. The key deliverables of the work that was contracted is complete and marks the end of the design phase of the project. There is one project phase remaining. Which of the following Closing processes should be performed, if any?
   A. Close Project or Phase only
   B. Close Procurements and Close Project or Phase
   C. Close Procurements only
   D. No closing process should be performed, since all project work is not completed

9. Which process will be used to determine all people or organizations, either positively or negatively, that may impact project planning?
   A. Stakeholder management
   B. Stakeholder identification
   C. Stakeholder analysis
   D. Team member analysis

10. Which document listed below correctly describes the official written acknowledgement that a project exists and documents initial requirements that satisfy the stakeholders' needs and expectations?
    A. Project Management Plan
    B. Project Integration Plan
    C. Project Charter
    D. Project Statement of Work

11. Performance reports are an important input to the Distribute Information process within Communications Management. Which of the following statements is not true regarding performance reports?
    A. Performance reports are not only used to distribute project information but also status information.
    B. Performance reports will state how well the policies and procedures regarding information distribution are being followed.
    C. Performance reports include forecasts that are updated and reissued based on work performance measurements provided as the project is executed.
    D. Performance reports include forecast information that is generated using earned value methods.

12. What activity is not performed as part of the Direct and Manage Project Execution process?
    A. Staffing, training, and managing the project team
    B. Establishing, documenting, and managing communication channels
    C. Managing and implementing risk response activities
    D. Obtaining and managing resources including materials, tools, and equipment

13. Which statement below is incorrect about the Conduct Procurements process?
    A. This process obtains seller responses, selects a seller, and awards a contract.
    B. This process determines the source selection criteria to rate seller proposals.
    C. This process can request seller responses and evaluate those responses repeatedly on major procurement items.
    D. This process can use a weighting system to select sellers.

14. Management has authorized the development of a new product line for its European markets. Using this authorization, the project team develops a project charter and obtains approval from the key sponsors to begin project planning. Initially the team develops a broad overview of what the project entails, what the desired future state of the new product should be, and the general methods used to achieve management's stated objectives. Then utilizing a series of integrated processes involving research, careful planning, and discovery the project team develops a concise document that details the work involved in, and the expectations of, the project; how the project will be controlled, measured, and managed; and how the project should progress through time. Then the project management team creates a baseline

document that can be updated throughout the project utilizing the project's integrated change control process. Which of the following statements best describes this team activity?

A. The project team is performing the planning process of creating an integrated change control plan for the project.

B. The project team is performing the develop project schedule process.

C. The project team is performing the scope definition process to produce a project execution plan using rolling wave planning.

D. The project team is performing the develop project management plan process to produce a project management plan that is progressively elaborated over the project lifecycle.

15. As the new project manager responsible for a project where activities will be performed in twelve countries on three continents, you should anticipate issues will arise due to _____.

A. scope definition

B. communication management planning

C. organizational planning

D. language, cultural, and time-zone differences

16. You are a project manager for Booster Club Outfitters, Inc. (BCO). The project steering committee has selected a project and requested you as the project manager. The project involves manufacturing team logo bobble-head dolls that will be sold along with the team logo jerseys BCO currently sells. The marketing department has conducted a market analysis study and believes this product combination will increase BCO's market penetration. The project sponsor thinks that this is urgent and wants you to start manufacturing right away. How should you respond?

A. Require a project charter be written and signed by the project steering committee and other stakeholders as appropriate.

B. Agree and begin manufacturing because the sponsor is from management and has a lot of authority and power.

C. Suggest that a project statement of work be written since it will outline the project objectives and assist in the development of the scope statement and project planning processes.

D. Ask for preliminary budget, resource assignments, and notify the manufacturing managers of your plan.

17. You have been assigned a project that is already in progress to build a new jail for your county. When you start your research on the jail project, you find that the numbers of the project are: estimated project cost of $625,000 with a project timeline of forty-eight weeks. Planned value for the project is $518,750. Actual cost is $300,000. The earned value is $312,500 since only 50% of the work has been completed. What is the budget at completion (BAC)?

A. $100,000

B. $168,750

C. $625,000

D. $300,000

18. Which statement is least correct for a reason that early termination of a contract would occur?
    A. As a result of a mutual agreement of both parties
    B. As a result of economic conditions raising project costs in excess of project cost estimates
    C. As a result of the default of one party
    D. For the convenience of the buyer, if provided for in the contract

19. When you are the project manager with deliverables that are outsourced for completion, what will you do first when the project closes down?
    A. Close Procurements process
    B. Release the resources
    C. Close Project or Phase process
    D. None of these

20. As a Project Manager on a large construction project with many stakeholders, you have worked with your team to define a strategy and an approach to manage the stakeholders throughout the project life cycle. After completing your stakeholder management approach, what process would the Project Manager do next?
    A. Plan Communications
    B. Collect Requirements
    C. Distribute Information
    D. Manage Stakeholders Expectations

21. Projects are authorized due to internal business needs or external influences. This usually triggers the creation of a needs analysis, business case or similar documentation. Therefore, the project charter links the project to the strategy and ongoing work of the organization. Who would issue the project charter?
    A. A senior manager within the project management organization
    B. A senior manager external to the project team
    C. A functional manager that will have the most resource assigned to the project
    D. The project manager assigned to the project

22. Which statement about the Distribute Information process outputs is not true?
    A. No output in this process relates to feedback received from stakeholders.
    B. Project records include correspondence, memos, and meeting minutes.
    C. Project reports include formal and informal project reporting on status and lessons learned.
    D. Stakeholder notification information provides stakeholders with resolved issues, approved changes, and general project status.

23. An approved corrective action is:
    A. A response to management about a customer complaint
    B. Production of the quality management plan

C. A course correction to bring the project activities into compliance with the baselined schedule

D. Finding the cause and effect in the quality assurance process

24. A procurement contract award will be given to each selected seller. Which procurement process has the contract award as an output?
    A. Administer Procurements
    B. Close Procurements
    C. Plan Procurements
    D. Conduct Procurements

25. You are a project manager for a growing real estate management company. It owns and leases properties in the southwestern region of the United States and is expanding its holdings and leasing operations to California. Your company is in the process of purchasing commercial properties in order to begin leasing operations. The project team member in charge of IT infrastructure deployment reported some hardware problems at the last project team meeting. You are also working with other project leads who are having problems coordinating and integrating other elements of the project. Which of the following statements is most true?
    A. You and your project team are performing the Direct and Manage Project Execution process.
    B. You and your project team are performing the Monitor and Control Project Work process.
    C. You and your project team are performing the Perform Integrated Change Control process.
    D. Your project team is not communicating project status according the project communication management plan.

26. When planning and/or conducting project meetings, which of the following is the LEAST important consideration?
    A. Keeping the meeting focused on objectives
    B. Ensuring the meeting is attended by appropriate participants
    C. Developing and distributing the meeting agenda, beforehand
    D. Controlling what participants say and don't say during the meeting

27. Which of these elements is not part of the definition of a project?
    A. Progressively planned
    B. Ongoing operation
    C. Temporary time period
    D. Produces a product or service

28. The scope baseline is a key input to the Plan Procurements process. However, it is also the primary output of another project management process. Which project management process is the scope baseline an output of?
    A. Create WBS
    B. Develop Schedule
    C. Collect Requirements
    D. Define Scope

29. You are the project manager working for a television station. Your project is to redesign the news center, since the same on-air set has been there for nearly five years. The estimated project cost is $200,000 with a project timeline of sixteen weeks. It is week twelve of the schedule and the budgeted cost of scheduled is $150,000. Accumulated costs are $138,000. The work is 73% completed, resulting in an earned value of $146,000. The estimate to complete is $62,000. What is the schedule variance?
   A. −$8,000
   B. $62,000
   C. $50,000
   D. −$4,000

30. Which of the following is not a tool and technique of the Close Procurements process?
   A. Closed procurements
   B. Negotiated settlements
   C. Records Management System
   D. Procurement audits

31. You work at a book publisher and are managing projects associated with book publication. The project you just managed, which deployed four new print machines, is now complete and you and your team are in the process of evaluating how the project went. Presently, some of the team is analyzing what went well and what didn't, while others are evaluating the approved change requests that were applied toward the project deliverables. You, as the project manager, are documenting information for the project sponsor and management team. What phase of the project is your team in the process of completing?
   A. Monitoring and Controlling
   B. Executing
   C. Closing
   D. Lessons Learned

32. Once stakeholders are identified, a stakeholder register is to be completed as one of the main outputs of the process. All of the following are details related to the stakeholder register except:
   A. Name, organizational position, location, role in project, and contact information
   B. Stakeholder classification as to being internal or external, supporter, or resistor
   C. Stakeholder classification as to risk categorization and project phase of influence
   D. Assessment information for stakeholder potential influence in the project

33. You are a seasoned project manager at a recreational equipment firm. Your project will be to design safer playground equipment. You have been e-mailed the project charter from the project sponsor and it authorizes you to be the project manager. You discover that the project charter has been signed by three individuals. What is the least correct answer for how this could affect your management of the project?

A. You will coordinate with all who signed as equal sponsors for project deliverables.

B. You will need to determine which sponsor is associated to their appropriate project deliverable.

C. You will need to ensure that each sponsor can propose and approve project changes, within the change control system, only for their deliverables.

D. A project charter should only have a single project sponsor and you need to determine which of the three who signed the charter will perform that role throughout the project life cycle.

34. You are mentoring a new project manager who has just been hired. He is the CEO's son who wants to be an anthropologist, but his dad wants him to try his business skills before he goes onto school for his four-year degree. You worked with him through all planning processes and it was a challenge, as he didn't understand nor support all the need for planning and "just wanted to get working." Now the project is in the executing phase and you attended his project team meeting and observed that the meeting was completely off track. He always ended up off topic, let project team members run longer than needed for status updating, and allowed others to bring up side items and out-of-scope ideas. Which of the following would improve his meetings?

A. Send him to communication training.

B. Mentor him on the communication method of preparing an agenda and, before the meeting, publishing it to all meeting participants.

C. Mentor him on how to manage his project team for effective communication.

D. Write his communication failures in your status report for his father's review.

35. All of the following are activities that are part of executing the project management plan, except:

A. Applying defect repairs to fix flaws and problems identified through quality control

B. Applying corrective actions to bring future project performance into compliance with the project management plan

C. Analyzing project trends and measurements to improve the project

D. Applying preventive actions to avoid negative risks within the project

36. A project manager or procuring organization can use the independent estimate tool and technique to serve as a benchmark on proposed contract responses. What statement is false regarding the benefits of using independent estimates for conducting procurements?

A. Independent estimates should always be used on complex procurements.

B. Independent estimates can identify significant differences in cost estimates.

C. Independent estimates can identify such significant differences that the procurement SOW can be deemed as deficient or ambiguous.

D. Independent estimates can be developed by using an outside professional estimator.

37. You are a project manager for Fantastic Toys and you are currently assigned to a new educational toy project that is scheduled for completion for the next holiday season. You are currently performing reporting tasks and comparing actual project results against the project management plan, analyzing performance data, and determining if corrective or preventive action should be recommended, analyzing project risks, documenting all appropriate product information throughout the life of the project, gathering and recording project information, and monitoring approved change requests. Which process are you performing?
    A. Perform Quality Control
    B. Monitor and Control Project Work
    C. Perform Quality Assurance
    D. Direct and Manage Project Execution

38. A large roadway construction project was successfully completed over a year ago. The prime contractor performed all work under the terms of a fixed-price contract and finished on time and within spec. Now, a year after the fact, a local advocacy group is publicly accusing the contractor of price gouging and demanding to see the contractor's accounting records. The group threatens to seek a court order if the contractor does not voluntarily comply. What is the contractor's obligation in this situation?
    A. There is no obligation. With a firm fixed-price contract, there is no requirement for the contractor to share cost and margin information.
    B. It is unknown. The court will need to decide.
    C. The contractor will need to vigorously oppose the group to keep the matter out of the courts.
    D. The contractor should admit wrongdoing and quickly offer a reasonable rebate.

39. What is the best definition of project management?
    A. The application of knowledge and skills to project goals in order to complete the project
    B. The application of skills, tools and techniques, using feelings and intuition to complete the processes and procedures involved with a specific project
    C. The application of knowledge, skills, tools, and techniques to project activities in order to meet project requirements
    D. The application of knowledge, wisdom, art, and science to project activities in order to meet project requirements

40. Which statement below best describes Teaming Agreements?
    A. Teaming agreements are contractual agreements between two or more entities to form a partnership or joint venture, or some other arrangement as defined by the parties.
    B. Teaming agreements are commitments that the project team makes at the project execution kickoff meeting.
    C. Teaming agreements are agreements from functional managers to staff the project team.

D. Teaming agreements are permanent agreements between two or more organizations.

41. You've decided to use your project management skills for a home improvement project. You are building a new garage with the help of your sons. The work is planned for four weeks. Using your earned value skills from your project management job, determine your performance from these figures: Task A is worth $500 and is 100% completed, and actual costs are $550. Task B is worth $600 and is 95% completed and actual costs are $530. Task C is worth $400 and is 90% complete and actual costs are $420. Your total budget is $3500. What is the cost variance for the tasks listed?
    A. $1,500
    B. -$70
    C. $1,430
    D. Not enough information

42. The major output of the Close Procurements process is closed procurements. The sole remaining output is key updates to the organizational process assets that may include all of the following except:
    A. Procurement file
    B. Procurement terms and conditions updates
    C. Deliverable acceptance
    D. Lessons learned documentation

43. All of the following statements are false regarding project closure except which one?
    A. Close Project or Phase process does not verify the product deliverables in order to consider the project or phase closed.
    B. Close Project or Phase process reviews the accepted deliverables output from the Verify Scope process before considering the project closed.
    C. Close Project or Phase process does not use lessons learned that were developed from previous processes on the project since they are now outdated. New lessons learned will be created before considering the project closed.
    D. Close Project or Phase process uses lesson learned as its sole tool and technique when performing administrative closure activities.

44. Joe Hansen has signed the project charter after evaluating the business needs for the project. He did this because he will pay for the project and own the product when the project deliverables are completed. What is Joe's role in this project?
    A. Senior Management
    B. Project Management Office
    C. Functional Management
    D. Sponsor

45. During what project phase should lessons learned documentation take place?
    A. At the end of the project
    B. At the end of each project phase
    C. Throughout the project life cycle
    D. Whenever an issue turns into a lesson learned

46. Change requests may occur as a result of performing this process:
A. Plan Quality
B. Schedule Development
C. Direct and Manage Project Execution
D. Perform Integrated Change Control

47. When you are performing the executing portion of your project and the project team is involved with negotiating a contract that will result in selection of a vendor to perform work under contract, what process is the team involved in?
A. Plan Procurements
B. Direct and Manage Project Execution
C. Administer Procurements
D. Conduct Procurements

48. You are a project manager for Teleflex Systems. Teleflex writes telecommunications billing and provisioning software for mobile telephone companies. You are assigned to an implementation project that has been progressing as planned for a new client. At a recent meeting the customer requested that you implement a change to the current project schedule. You tell the customer to submit this request in writing and you explain that project change control is concerned with all of the following except:
A. Reviewing, approving or denying all recommended corrective or preventive actions
B. Coordinating changes across the entire project including schedule changes
C. Maintaining an accurate, timely information base concerning the project's product(s) and their associated documentation through project completion
D. Reviewing, analyzing, and approving change requests

49. One estimating technique involves developing an estimate for each WBS work package, then rolling them all up to derive the project total. This technique can be time-consuming and costly, but will likely produce highly realistic estimates. This estimating technique is termed _____.
A. analogous (or top-down)
B. bottom-up
C. expert judgment
D. accepted practice

50. Which of these elements is not considered part of the "triple constraint" that affects projects and their outcomes?
A. Schedule
B. Customer Satisfaction
C. Budget
D. Work to be performed

51. You've decided to use your project management skills for a home improvement project. You are building a new garage with the help of your sons. The work is planned for four weeks. Using your earned value skills from your project management job, determine your performance from these figures: Task A is worth $500 and is 100% completed, and actual costs are $550. Task B is worth $600 and is 95% completed and actual costs are $530. Task C is worth $400 and is 90% complete and actual costs are $420. Your total budget is $3500. Being a project manager, you summarize your research about your garage project. Which statement is the most correct?
    A. You are concerned with the project performance so far, you are over budget by about 5%.
    B. You are happy with the project performance, you are under budget by 5%.
    C. You are happy with the project performance, you are under budget by 5% and ahead of schedule by 10%.
    D. You are concerned with the project performance since you are over budget by 5% and behind schedule by 10%.

52. You work for a company that designs and constructs new playground equipment for elementary schools. A new customer gave you a contract statement of work and all seems fine in the contract terms and conditions and with the mutual agreements for contract type and fees. You are managing the work as outlined in the contract and are in the monitoring and controlling process of contract administration when the customer notifies your firm that the land on which the playground equipment was to be placed has been found to have contaminated dirt and the contract needs to be terminated. What should you do first?
    A. Finish the contract administration work until the contract can be checked for early termination clauses
    B. Perform a procurement audit to determine the compensation owed from the customer for the early termination
    C. Perform the Close Procurements process
    D. Perform Close Project or Phase process due to the early contract termination

53. If a project is terminated prior to completion, which statement is false?
    A. The project still goes through the Close Project or Phase process.
    B. The formal documentation stating the early termination gives procedures for the transfer of the finished deliverables of the canceled project to others.
    C. The formal documentation stating the early termination contains the reason that the project was terminated.
    D. The formal documentation stating the early termination gives procedures for the transfer of the finished and unfinished deliverables of the canceled project to others.

54. There are valid reasons for the requesting organization or customer to write a business case. The business case is contained within the project charter and states whether or not the project is worth the required investment. All of the following are valid business needs that could result in the production of a business case, except:
    A. Market demand
    B. Legal requirements
    C. Marketplace conditions
    D. Ecological impacts

55. Reasons that a project team would complete lessons learned documentation include all of the following except:
    A. So that the causes of issues can be documented
    B. So that the project team can show what they have accomplished
    C. So that the lessons learned will become part of the historical database(s)
    D. So that the reasoning behind the corrective actions that were taken can be documented

56. Work performance information is routinely collected as the project is executed. Work performance information can be related to mainly three performance results, including all but which option?
    A. Cost incurred
    B. Quality assurance metrics
    C. Deliverables
    D. Schedule progress

57. You work as a project manager for the city. You have been assigned a project to install security cameras at key city office locations. You are ready to meet with potential vendors for the security equipment and subsequent installation. The city council, your project sponsor, wants you to invite the vendors to visit the properties and show them the details of the work that they would be involved in, as well as to answer any questions that they may have before their proposals are submitted. The council has a small budget and feels this effort will save money in the long run. What action is the project sponsor asking you to perform?
    A. Bidder conferences
    B. Plan Procurements
    C. Proposal evaluation techniques
    D. Selected seller interviews

58. Armadillo Productions specializes in producing television commercials and you are the project manager for their most recent advertising campaign. The project required extensive filming while on location in Arizona. This phase of the project is complete and the editing phase is scheduled to begin next week. As the project manager you have collected work performance information for the filming phase to include in the project archives. What is the purpose of the work performance information?
    A. The work performance information is used as part of the formal acceptance process to verify contract expenditures.

B. The work performance information is used to determine the status of project activities and make certain the project goals and objectives are met.

C. The work performance information is used as historical information for future projects that are similar in scope to this project.

D. The work performance information is included in the project archive documentation after its accuracy is confirmed.

59. You and your project team are into week four of a dedicated six week planning session for a major business improvement project within your organization. As more information has become available during planning, you and your team have been able to further refine the WBS every few days. Your WBS is much more detailed and reliable now, compared to its initial version in week one. This may be an example of what?

   A. Team development
   B. Learning curve
   C. Progressive elaboration
   D. Expert judgment

60. What portion of the project is most critical for project success?

   A. The phase when the project is initiated and the initial vision is defined
   B. The phase when the project is defining requirements
   C. The phase when the project work is being performed
   D. The phase when the project is being closed

61. As an output of the contract closure process, the buyer needs to approve or reject the deliverable(s). Which statement below is false?

   A. The buyer will usually provide the seller with a formal written notice that the deliverables are accepted or rejected.
   B. The buyer uses the procurement audit results to determine the deliverable acceptance.
   C. Requirements for formal deliverable acceptance and how to address nonconforming deliverables are defined in the contract.
   D. At contract close, the buyer usually works through the authorized procurement administrator for deliverable acceptance/rejection.

62. Collect Requirements is the process of defining and documenting stakeholders' needs to meet the project objectives. Requirements include the quantified and documented needs and expectations of the sponsor, customer, and other stakeholders. These requirements need to be elicited, analyzed, and recorded in enough detail to be measured once project execution begins. Many organizations categorize requirements into two general areas. Which best describes these categories?

   A. High-level requirements and detailed requirements
   B. Business justification and management requirements
   C. Business requirements and project requirements
   D. Product requirements and project requirements

63. One of the project team members suggests employing the use of a formal work authorization system. After discussing all the advantages and disadvantages associated with such a system, the idea is enthusiastically endorsed by the entire team, including yourself. Two team members are subsequently assigned the job of creating a system for the project, complete with procedures, forms, and training (if training is determined necessary). What is the PRIMARY benefit the team expects to realize by instituting their work authorization system?
   A. Improved control of scope
   B. Improved control of human resources assigned to specific tasks
   C. Improved quality of project documents
   D. Improved ability to measure performance against baseline

64. The precise description of a physical item, procedure, or service is called a
   _____.
   A. scope statement
   B. product description
   C. configuration description
   D. work package

65. Which statement is the least correct about negotiated settlements for contract disputes?
   A. Alternate dispute resolutions, including mediation and arbitration, can be explored instead of using negotiation.
   B. Negotiation is the best method to a final and equitable settlement of all claims and disputes.
   C. When a settlement cannot be reached through negotiation, alternate dispute resolution should be explored.
   D. Litigation should always be considered if initial negotiation attempts fail.

66. One of the project manager's primary functions is to accurately document the deliverables and requirements of the project and then manage the project so that they are produced according to the agreed-upon criteria. Deliverables describe the components of the goals and objectives in a quantifiable way. Requirements are the specifications of the deliverables. The project manager should use the project charter as a starting point for identifying and progressively elaborating project deliverables, but it's possible that only some of the deliverables will be documented there. Remember that the charter is often written by a manager external to the project, and it was the first take at defining the project objectives and deliverables. As the project manager, it's your job to make certain all the deliverables are identified and documented in the project scope statement. What is the primary objective of the project scope statement?
   A. The scope statement serves as the agreement among stakeholders regarding what project objectives and deliverables will be produced in order to meet and satisfy the requirements of the project.
   B. The scope statement serves as a detailed contract between the project team and project stakeholders.

C. The scope statement is the document used by the project team to manage project deliverables.

D. The scope statement serves as the project financial baseline.

67. Cost of Quality. Which of the following BEST represents this term?
    A. Cost of ensuring life cycle costing objectives
    B. Cost of performing bottom-up estimates
    C. Cost of performing benefit/cost analyses
    D. Cost of ensuring quality objectives

68. Develop Project Charter inputs include all of the following except _____.
    A. organizational process assets
    B. enterprise environmental factors
    C. contract
    D. expert judgment

69. Your company, National Equine Products, has appointed you project manager for its new signature saddle product line introduction. This is a national product rollout and all the company's affiliated retail stores across the country need to have the first models of new saddles in stock before the advertising campaign begins. The complete product line involves three new models, which will be introduced at different times over a three-year period. The last two models will be progressively defined in more detail closer to the product's release date, while the first two products will be elaborated in great detail now. The scope management plan has just been completed. Which of the following is true? (Choose the best response.)
    A. The WBS encompasses the full scope of work for the project and the technique in the question is called rolling wave planning.
    B. The WBS template from a previous project, a tool and technique of the Create WBS process, was used to create the WBS for this project. The WBS encompasses the major deliverables for the project.
    C. Only the deliverables associated with the work of the project should be listed on the WBS. Since product number three isn't being released until a later date it should not yet be included on the WBS.
    D. The WBS should be created next, and it encompasses the full scope of work for the project. Only the work of the project is listed on the WBS.

70. As a contracted project management consultant to an intact project team, you created a unique project communications plan template for the team. Another organization wishes to contract your services and asks to review samples of your most recent work. You would like to provide a copy of the communications plan template, but have a confidentiality agreement with the first client. How should you approach this situation?
    A. Respectfully refuse to provide work samples
    B. Seek permission from the first client
    C. Arrange for the sample template to be sent by someone other than yourself
    D. Send the sample template, but white-out any information that links to the first client

71. Which of the following best describes the Identify Stakeholder process:
    A. The Identify Stakeholder process is used to identify all people or organizations that may be impacted or have an impact on a project.
    B. The Identify Stakeholder process is used to determine the communication needs of project stakeholders.
    C. The Identify Stakeholder process is used to make project information available to project stakeholders.
    D. The Identify Stakeholder process is used to ensure that communications with project stakeholders is productive and meets the needs and desires of those stakeholders.

72. You are the project manager of a software project for a large consumer electronics manufacturing company. Consumer purchases within the industry are down 10% this year due to poor global economic conditions. As a result, management has implemented a corporate-wide hiring freeze and laid off many company employees including several members of the company's technical staff assigned to your project team. Your project is 80% of the way through the programming and testing work when the staff reductions are announced and you were informed that work on your project will be suspended until the company can resume hiring or until the remaining technical personnel are released from higher priority projects. Which of the following addresses the purpose of the Verify Scope process in this case?
    A. Verify Scope process documents the correctness of the work according to stakeholders' expectations.
    B. Verify Scope process determines if the project results comply with quality standards.
    C. Verify Scope process documents the level and degree of completion.
    D. Verify Scope process determines the correctness and completion of all the work.

73. You are the project manager for a WAN infrastructure project. The project product is the complete deployment of 300 network nodes at company retail locations throughout the United States. As project manager you have been monitoring the success of the project and product scope and managing changes to the scope baseline. You ensure that all requested changes and recommended corrective or preventative actions are processed through the Perform Integrated Change Control process. You are also managing actual changes when they occur to prevent scope creep. Which of the following tools and techniques are you using to determine if a change has occurred?
    A. Process analysis
    B. Inspection
    C. Variance analysis
    D. Statistical sampling

74. You and your team are working on the detailed planning for your project and have completed the scope baseline. The PMO is asking that you schedule a schedule buy-in meeting with your team and other key project stakeholders as a condition for approving funding for project execution. Before you can obtain team buy-in you will need to schedule project work such that project deliverables will be met. What is your first task?
    A. Decompose the WBS work packages into smaller components
    B. Decompose the project scope by performing the Create WBS process
    C. Calculate the theoretical early start and early finish then calculate last start and late finish dates for your project so that you know if you can deliver the project scope as expected by the project stakeholders
    D. Create a roles and responsibilities matrix and RBS so that you can assign project team members to schedule activities as you

75. While analyzing an identified risk, the team determines that the risk has a 30% probability of occurring and, if it occurs, will add $10,000 to project costs. What is the expected monetary value associated with this risk?
    A. –$3,000
    B. $3,333
    C. $10,000
    D. –$10,000

76. You have just been appointed as the project manager to an organization that you are not familiar with. One of your first tasks is to identify stakeholders for your project. What are the three steps you would perform to analyze stakeholders:
    A. Identify internal stakeholders, identify external stakeholders, and ask them how they would like to be communicated with
    B. Identify all potential stakeholders, identify the potential impact or support of each stakeholder, and assess how they might respond to various situations
    C. Identify all potential stakeholders, ask how they would like to be communicated with, and build alliances with those who are the most important stakeholders
    D. Identify all potential stakeholders, identify the potential impact or support of each stakeholder, and build alliances with those who are the most important stakeholders

77. The key output for identify stakeholders includes:
    A. Communication Management Plan
    B. Stakeholder register
    C. Stakeholder issues report
    D. Stakeholder analysis

78. You're going to paint your house but, unfortunately, it's fallen into a little disrepair. The old paint is peeling and chipping and will need to be scraped before a coat of primer can be sprayed on the house. After the primer dries, the painting can commence. In this example, the primer activity depends on the scraping. You should not prime the house before scraping off the old paint. The painting activity depends on the primer activity in the same way. What is the dependency relationship between these activities?
    A. Finish-to-finish (FF)
    B. Finish-to-start (FS)
    C. Start-to-finish (SF)
    D. Start-to-start (SS)

79. All projects, from the smallest to the largest, require resources. The term "resources" in this case does not mean just people; it means all the physical resources required to complete the project. The *PMBOK® Guide Fourth Edition* defines resources as people, equipment, and materials. This includes people, equipment, supplies, materials, software, hardware, and so on, depending on the project. Which process is concerned with determining the types of resources (both human and material) and quantities for each schedule activity within a work package?
    A. Develop Activity Resource Plan
    B. Estimate Activity Resources
    C. Develop Human Resource Plan
    D. Develop Schedule

80. You are the project manager of Happy Builders Construction. You and your project team are performing detailed planning for a large residential and retail building in the central business district of a major city. Your project team has requested activity duration estimates from the SME for each trade that will be working on the project. They were asked to provide the following duration estimates: most likely, best-case, and worst-case. Your team is performing which activity duration estimating technique?
    A. Critical chain estimating
    B. Parametric estimating
    C. What-if scenario
    D. Three-point estimating

81. A dated project network diagram indicates that Activity 4.2.3.2 cannot start until two days after its predecessor, Activity 4.2.3.1, finishes. This two-day period represents _____.
    A. lead time (or overlap)
    B. lag time (or waiting time)
    C. an external dependency
    D. slack

82. The conflict resolution technique of last resort, when others fail, or sometimes necessary when time is of the essence, is _____.
    A. forcing
    B. lose-lose

C. withdrawing

D. smoothing

83. Which statement is most true?

    A. Active listening (effective listening) is an outdated communications technique. It seldom enhances communication between sender and receiver.

    B. Formal written communication is the preferred method for all project communications. This ensures everything is formally documented for later review and use in lessons learned.

    C. Non-verbal communication is important.

    D. Stakeholders should be provided with information on a strict need-to-know basis. You and your project team are best served by keeping project information closely held.

84. A small project currently has six stakeholders in the communications loop. If two more stakeholders are added, how many more channels of communication will result?

    A. 2

    B. 13

    C. 15

    D. 28

85. You are a project manager for Weddings-R-Us. Your company specializes in the production of weddings in exotic locations around the globe. You have been assigned to a wedding that will take place in Fiji next June. You have a sequenced list of the schedule activities required to ensure that the bride, groom, and their families have a wonderful wedding experience. You're developing the project schedule for this undertaking and have determined the critical path. Which of the following statements is true?

    A. You calculated the most likely start date and most likely finish dates, float time, and weighted average estimates.

    B. You calculated the optimistic, pessimistic, and most likely duration times and the float times for all activities.

    C. You calculated the early and late start dates, the early and late finish dates, and float times for all activities.

    D. You calculated the activity dependency and the optimistic and pessimistic activity duration estimates.

86. The schedule analyst from your project team has prepared a report for the next team meeting with the project sponsor. One section of the report contains the schedule baseline completion dates and the actual completion date for work performed and an estimate of completion dates for future work. The schedule analyst has completed a/an _____.

    A. Earned Value analysis

    B. Milestone analysis

    C. What-if Scenario analysis

    D. Variance analysis

87. The Project Manager is creating an estimate for raised flooring in a computer room that is being built. The customer is now creating his budget for the next calendar year and needs this estimate as soon as possible. A Senior Project Manager has managed many projects that required raised floors and is considered an expert. The Project Manager asks the Senior Project Manager to e-mail the cost estimating parameters used for prior projects so that they can be used to estimate the raised floor for the current project. Which of the following estimating techniques is the project manager using?
   A. Parametric estimating
   B. Analogous estimating
   C. Bottom-up estimating
   D. Expert judgment

88. At the very beginning of a new project, you search for any and all past records of similar projects, both from within your organization and from outside sources within your industry. You want to learn as much as possible about past successes and failures so you can incorporate the best practices from those who went before you, as well as avoid the mistakes they made. You are successful in accumulating an enormous amount of material. Upon reviewing an archived project plan, you study a section that features the project's time-phased budget at completion (BAC) that was used for earned value calculations when monitoring and measuring project cost performance. Plotted, it forms an S-curve appearance. What is this?
   A. Cost Baseline
   B. Cost Variance Baseline (CVB)
   C. Performance Measurement Baseline (PMB)
   D. Funding Reconciliation Curve (FRC)

89. You are the new project manager tasked with taking over for a project manager who left six weeks before. Some of the numbers that you find in your initial research are as follows:

   Estimated project cost: $675,000

   Project timeline: 24 weeks

   This is week 16.

   Accumulated costs are $300,000.

   Twenty-five percent of the work has been completed.

   What is the CPI?
   A. 0.25
   B. 0.6750
   C. 0.3731
   D. 0.5625

90. You and your project team have been studying the performance of a recently completed project that was a big success in your organization. That project

was very similar in nature to yours. You decide to use several successful milestone achievements from that project to set measurement standards for your own project. This is an example of _____.

A. benchmarking
B. lessons learned
C. benefit analysis
D. using templates

91. You work for an office furniture manufacturer. Your current project assignment is the design and production of a net executive desk chair. You have finished planning and are in the project execution phase. You have just received the first design verification samples off of the product assembly line and have found a few problems with the product and at the last project review you found that the project is over budget. You have informed your manager, the PMO, and the project sponsor of this situation. You have also requested the authority and resources to perform an examination of the problems the project has experienced and a root cause analysis to identify the underlying causes of these problems and formulate preventative actions. What have you proposed to your manager and the PMO?

A. Lessons learned analysis
B. Quality audit
C. Process analysis
D. Statistical analysis

92. Which of the following is most true?

A. Advertising for prospective bidders is best managed by advertising professionals.
B. Pre-bid conferences should be conducted with one bidder (prospective seller) at a time, so as not to have all bidders in one room at one time.
C. Conduct Procurements is a procurement process applied only if/when resources and/or supplies are purchased to support the project.
D. Care must be taken to ensure that bidders (prospective sellers) are not aware of other companies competing for project work.

93. The product of your project is rich with features. This exemplifies what?

A. A high-grade product
B. A high-quality product
C. A product that can command a higher price in the marketplace
D. A complex project

94. Which of the following is most correct regarding the Collect Requirements process?

A. The Collect Requirements process defines and manages customer expectations.
B. The input for Collect Requirements is the Project Charter.
C. Project requirements include technical, security, and performance requirements.
D. Product requirements include project management, business, and delivery requirements.

95. Which of the following statements is true?
    A. The Project Scope Statement may serve to provide a documented basis for making many future project decisions.
    B. The Project Scope Statement may serve to provide a documented basis for common understanding of scope among stakeholders.
    C. The Project Scope Statement may be revised as the project progresses, to reflect approved changes to the project scope.
    D. All of the above.

96. You are the project controller for a large construction project. The project may have as many as 200 workers on site at a time. Your company has a PMIS that updates the schedule based on the time reports approved by the construction foremen. However, when you prepare earned value reports for the project management team the schedule variance indicates that the project is behind schedule. The construction foremen always disagree and say that they are on schedule and possibly a little ahead of the plan. Your project manager asked you to investigate this because it is important that the schedule reflect the most current information since the project funding is based on schedule completion percentage. You discuss this with the foremen and discover that they are having problems approving the time reports for their direct reports. To present this information to your project manager you prepare a histogram that orders by frequency of occurrence the problems the foremen are experiencing in regards to late time reporting. What type of histogram did you prepare?
    A. Ishikawa chart
    B. Pareto diagram
    C. Scatter chart
    D. Run chart

97. You are a project manager who works for a commercial development company that has won a contract to develop a new city-funded homeless shelter. You have been assigned to the team that will complete the project work. You identify the people responsible for schedule activities within your organization, the designers, engineers, installers, management, and so on. You will interface with functional managers to coordinate employees' availability, financing to arrange procurement of resources needed for project completion, and with senior management to report the status of the project work.

    You will work and communicate with government officials for approval of the design, change requests, and overall schedule of the project. You anticipate that there will be safety issues, design questions, and other concerns that will come up as the project progresses. You will also need to communicate project status and other issues with external stakeholders such as the people who live and work near the new homeless shelter, the greater community at large, and various government officials. These stakeholders will need to be involved in the planning and design of the shelter to ensure it satisfies the community's needs.

Which project management planning document do you need to develop to understand the all of the roles, responsibilities, and other factors involved with the project's numerous stakeholders?

A. Process improvement plan
B. Communications management plan
C. Resource activity plan
D. Human resource plan

98. You are negotiating with functional managers and making project staff assignments. You have a list of several candidates for a position on the project team that requires specific technical qualifications and industry certifications required by the customer and stipulated in the project contract. All of the candidates appear to meet these qualifications. You also consider their personal interests, characteristics, availability, and compensation requirements. Which of the following is true?

A. You are considering the staffing management plan input of the Develop Human Resource Plan process.
B. You are considering the organizational process assets input of the Develop Project Team process.
C. You are considering the roles and responsibilities input of the Acquire Project Team process.
D. You are considering the enterprise environmental factors input of the Acquire Project Team process.

99. You have a team member who is ready to make the move into a team lead role but she does not have any actual experience as a team lead. You and the PMO decide to give her some exposure by assigning her to a limited amount of schedule activities in a lead capacity, provide her with some training if needed, and be available to coach and mentor where needed. What project management process are you performing in this case?

A. Manage Project Team
B. Manage Stakeholder Expectations
C. Develop Project Team
D. Develop Human Resource Plan

100. As a result of recent reductions in revenue and missed market expectations executive management at Zendar Corporation has decided to make significant organizational changes. They have reduced staffing globally by 3,000 people and sold two under-producing divisions to a major competitor. However, one executive director in one of these divisions has demonstrated exceptional management ability by consistently exceeding expectations. Management decided to assign the executive director to a leadership role within one of the remaining divisions within the company.

To accomplish this management decides to split the division into two independent groups. The executive director is now in charge of the product development group. Shortly after assuming the new position the executive director summarily cancels many existing projects, reduces the scope of many of the remaining projects, and announces a staff reduction in all functional areas. Then the executive director inserts her core team from her former division and announces the formation of a new PMO and a new reporting structure for all project teams.

Which of the following best describes the current situation at Zendar Corporation in regards to the executive director's actions?

A. The executive director who is managing the division is leading the organization and influencing the project team utilizing her position power.

B. The executive director is utilizing an autocratic management style and is creating additional risk for the project teams to manage.

C. The executive director who is managing the division is leading the organization and influencing the project team utilizing her confronting/problem solving interpersonal skills.

D. The executive director is managing organizational conflict utilizing a forcing conflict management technique.

101. The method that integrates cost, scope, and schedule to derive measurement values that accurately assess project progress to date, as well as forecasted future performance is termed what?

A. Earned value analysis

B. Variance analysis

C. Integrated change control

D. Estimate at completion (EAC)

102. Each of the following is false, except:

A. The activity list may be viewed as an extension of the work breakdown structure.

B. The lowest level elements of the WBS (work packages) automatically identify all the project activities necessary to produce identified project deliverables.

C. The lowest level elements of the WBS (work packages) should be documented in terms of action-oriented activities, to help facilitate and expedite the Define Activities process.

D. All of the above are false.

103. You are making a presentation to the executive steering committee regarding the status of a project you are managing. The project scope has been approved and your team is in the process of completing detailed planning. During the presentation you noted that you will be purchasing and implementing a new Internet portal for the use of external team members. When you presented this project requirement the VP of information technology (IT) expressed concern that, if the project is implemented as planned, he will have to purchase and hire additional network security resources to support the portal since it will expose the corporate intranet to the public Internet. The cost is substantial and was not taken into consideration in the project budget and the portal exposes the company's information technology infrastructure to external threats.

The VP of IT wants to suspend planning the project until the project can be revised to assess the potential risks and a strategy is developed to mitigate them and until the project budget can be revised to accommodate the additional cost. However, the project sponsor insists that the project must go forward as originally planned or the customer will suffer. Which of the following is true?

A. The conflict should be resolved in favor of the customer.

B. The conflict should be resolved by not implementing the internet portal.

C. The VP of IT is correct and the project team should revise the project plan.

D. The conflict should be resolved in favor of the project sponsor.

104. You are the project manager for the state symphony orchestra. You have been assigned to the summer pops tour for next summer and you have started planning the tour. You have published the project scope and created a scope management plan. You have also created a document that describes project interfaces and who will receive copies of project planning and future project status information, how and when it should be distributed, and who will be responsible for its preparation. What project management document have you created?

A. Information distribution plan

B. Roles and responsibilities plan

C. Communications management plan

D. Project documents update plan

105. Your project team consists of eleven team members colocated in our office building, three team members from a vendor in Australia, eight team members people from your company's European office in Munich, seven team members for you company's Piscataway, New Jersey office, and fifteen technical team members located in Mumbai, India. Your office is in the central time zone but works different hours than all the other offices in the area to accommodate the time differences of its team members. You use tools like web conferencing and e-mail to distribute information to the team. Which of the following best describes your project team and its situation?

A. This scenario describes staff assignments from the Acquire Project Team process and communication methods from the Distribute Information process.

B. The scenario describes virtual teams from the Develop Project Team process and information distribution methods from the Distribute Information process.

C. This scenario describes the staffing management plan from the Manage Project Team process and communication skills from the Distribute Information process.

D. The scenario describes virtual teams from the Acquire Project Team process and information distribution tools from the Distribute Information process.

106. Jim is the project manager for the Global Implementation project and he is collecting information from project team members regarding project progress, project accomplishments, project issues, and reporting it to the stakeholders. Jim is managing these communication needs and resolving issues according to the project communication management plan. Which of the following is most true?

   A. Jim is creating project document updates reports and a stakeholder register, which are both outputs of the Report Performance process.
   B. Jim is using both the Report Performance and Manage Stakeholder Expectations processes, which are both part of the Project Communications Management knowledge area.
   C. Jim is using the Report Performance Reporting process, which involves reporting project progress and accomplishments to the stakeholders.
   D. Jim is using the stakeholder management strategy (an input) and issue logs (a tool and technique) of the Manage Stakeholder Expectations process.

107. You are making a presentation to the executive steering committee regarding the status of a project you are managing. The project scope has been approved, your team has completed detailed planning and project execution is underway. As part of your presentation you present a high-level report that includes an analysis of past performance, the current status of risks and issues, work completed to date, and work to be completed, a summary of approved change requests, and other relevant information that warrants review and discussion. What project management process are you performing?

   A. Quality assurance
   B. Risk management
   C. Report performance
   D. Requirements reporting

108. While carrying out closure activities at the end of the project, you are quite surprised to learn that the customer is unhappy. Your project was completed on schedule, within budget, and met all contractual requirements. The contract between you and your customer is:

   A. Not yet complete, because stakeholder satisfaction has not been achieved
   B. Complete, because you satisfied the terms of the contract
   C. Complete, because you are carrying out closing activities
   D. Not yet complete, because you must have omitted some work

109. A senior project manager in your organization established a project management community of practice (PM-COP) last year and it has been a big success. The PM-COP meets quarterly for the purpose of sharing lessons learned and best practices. This exemplifies what?

   A. Contributing to the project management knowledge base to improve quality and build capabilities
   B. Expert (referent) leadership power
   C. Good stakeholder management
   D. A progressive organization

110. After reviewing the detailed analysis of a risk associated with a particular project activity, you and your project team decide to respond to the risk by purchasing insurance. This could be an example of

_____.

    A. active acceptance
    B. passive acceptance
    C. mitigation
    D. transference

111. The longest path through a project network diagram is termed

_____.

    A. path float
    B. latest finish time (LF)
    C. latest start time (LS)
    D. critical path

112. Which of the following statements is most true?
    A. A project network diagram may identify more than one critical path.
    B. A project network diagram can illustrate only one critical path. If more than one critical path is identified, a mistake has been made somewhere in construction of the network logic.
    C. A project network diagram should be unique to the project, constructed using the best individual elements of PDM and Conditional Diagramming Methods.
    D. A project network diagram is essentially the same as a project WBS. They are interchangeable.

113. Mary is a project manager for a large well-known manufacturing company. She is working on a new project to release a new international product line. This is her company's first project to produce products for international markets and everyone is expecting great success with this new product line. Many of the project stakeholders are apprehensive about the project and they usually proceed cautiously and take a considerable amount of time to examine information before making final project decisions. The project entails producing localized versions of a current product that the company produces for its domestic markets. This is the first time that the company has attempted to create a product that is not only localized in the local language but is also designed for cultural coexistence. History with other companies indicates that subtle miscalculations in this area can offend consumers and result in a loss of market share for all of the company's products. A new vendor is engaged to perform the language translations and test the cultural coexistence of the product. After speaking with one of your stakeholders, Mary discovers that this will be the first project for your organization to work with this new vendor. Which of the following statements is true given the information in this question?
    A. This scenario describes the interviewing tool and technique used during the Risk Identification process.
    B. This scenario describes a risk that requires a response strategy from the positive risk category.

C. This scenario describes risk triggers that are derived using interviewing techniques and recorded in the risk register during the Qualitative Risk Analysis process.

D. The scenario describes risk tolerance levels of the stakeholders, which should be considered as an input to the Plan Risk Management process.

114. You are a new project manager for a company that develops sales and compensation applications for the multilevel marketing industry. Your company recently closed a contract for an application integration project and you have been selected as the principle project manager. The project team plans to conduct several iterations of the Identify Risks process. What information gathering techniques might be used to identify risk for your project?

A. Brainstorming, PERT, interviewing, root cause identification, and SWOT analysis.

B. Brainstorming, Delphi technique, benchmarking, and SWOT analysis.

C. Brainstorming, Delphi technique, sensitivity analysis, root cause identification, and SWOT analysis.

D. Brainstorming, Delphi technique, interviewing, root-cause identification, and root cause analysis.

115. Organizations can improve the project's performance by focusing on high-priority risks. Therefore, the PMO has established a procedure that is repeated on a periodic basis throughout the life cycle of all the organization's projects. The project management team is required to assess the priority of identified risks using their relative probability or likelihood of occurrence, the corresponding impact on project objectives if the risks occur, as well as other factors such as the time for response and the organization's risk tolerance associated with the project constraints of cost, schedule, scope, and quality. Such assessments reflect the attitude of the project team and other stakeholders to risk. Which Project Management process is the PMO requiring the project team to perform periodically throughout the project lifecycle?

A. Perform Risk Sensitivity Analysis

B. Perform Quantitative Risk Analysis

C. Perform Risk Response Analysis

D. Perform Qualitative Risk Analysis

116. Interview techniques draw on experience and historical data to quantify the probability and impact of risk on project objectives. The information needed depends on the type of probability distributions that will be used. Documenting the rationale of the risk ranges and assumptions behind them are important components of the risk interview because they can provide insight on the reliability and credibility of the analysis. You are using the interviewing technique of the Perform Quantitative Risk Analysis process on your current project. You intend to use normal and lognormal distributions. All of the following statements are true regarding this question except which one?

A. Interviewing techniques are used to quantify the probability and impact of the risks on project objectives.

B. Distributions graphically display the impacts of risk to the project objectives.

C. Triangular distributions rely on optimistic, pessimistic, and most likely estimates to quantify risks.

D. Normal and lognormal distributions use mean and standard deviation to quantify risks.

117. The petroleum refinery project manager informed the project team that the site director has determined the risks associated with handling certain chemicals are too high for the project team. The project sponsor agreed to reduce this risk and approved a change request to change the project plan and hire an experienced chemical handling company on a firm fixed-price contract to complete this task. This is an example of which of the following?

A. Avoidance

B. Acceptance

C. Transference

D. Mitigation

118. Monitor and control project risks can involve choosing alternative strategies, executing a contingency or fall-back plan, taking corrective action, and modifying the project management plan. The risk response owner reports periodically to the project manager on the effectiveness of the plan, any unanticipated effects, and any correction needed to handle the risk appropriately. Which of the following best describes the steps for implementing a contingency plan or a work-around when performing the Monitor and Control Risks process?

A. Implement the contingency according to the risk response plan and then prepare a change request and submit it to the Perform Integrated Change Control process.

B. Conduct a risk audit, then implement the workaround or contingency plan.

C. Notify the project sponsor that a risk event has occurred and obtain authorization to implement the contingency or work-around.

D. Prepare a change request based on the risk response plan and submit it to the Perform Integrated Change Control process.

119. All of the following are examples of legitimate causes for scope change, except:

A. A regulatory change that affects the project

B. Incorporating new technology that was not available when the project was planned

C. Omission of a critical feature when the project was planned

D. Upgrading the current version of your scheduling software

120. The two project closing processes are:

A. Close project or phase and close procurements.

B. Scope verification and administrative closure.

C. Close procurements and verify scope.

D. Product verification and formal acceptance.

121. From the given information, determine how many paths exist through this project's network diagram.

Activity	Activity Duration	Predecessors
A	1 week	none
B	7 weeks	none
C	5 weeks	A and B
D	12 weeks	B
E	10 weeks	C and D
F	6 weeks	E
G	3 weeks	F

A. 1
B. 2
C. 3
D. 4

122. Referring to the information given in question 121, identify the project's critical path.
A. Start-A-C-E-F-G-Finish
B. Start-B-D-E-F-G-Finish
C. Start-B-C-E-F-G-Finish
D. Start-A-C-E-F-Finish

123. You are the project manager for a software development project to create a network provisioning system for a telecommunications company that will be network-aware and can be accessed through a VPN connection via the Internet. Based on your research, you have discovered it will cost you $250,000 to write the application utilizing integral resources. Once the code is written, you estimate you'll spend $30,000 per month updating the software with client information, government regulations, and maintenance.

You have found a vendor who can develop the application for your company and charge a recurring fee based on the number of active communication devices using the application every month. The vendor will charge you $5 per month per active device. You will have roughly 12,000 clients using the system each month. However, you'll need an in-house accountant to manage the time and billing of the system, so this will cost you an extra $1,200 per month. How many months can you use the system before it's better to write your own code rather than hire the vendor?
A. 8 months
B. 6 months
C. 10 months
D. 15 months

124. You are working on a national infrastructure project for a large title insurance company. During the resource planning process the team decided to utilize a technology services company for technicians to perform some of the project work. The procurement department has scheduled meetings to ensure that all prospective sellers have a clear and common understanding of the procurement. What are these meetings called?

A. Contract negotiation meeting
B. Advertising conference
C. Bidder conferences
D. Qualified sellers list meeting

125. You are working on a national infrastructure project for a large title insurance company. During the resource planning process the team decided to utilize a technology services company for technicians to perform some of the project work. Your procurement department selected a suitable vendor and the project is 95% complete. The vendor is sending you weekly work performance reports, you have authorized product inspection of their deliverables, and you have authorized weekly payments through the accounts payable system to the technology services company. What project management process have you, the buyer, and the technology services company, the seller, been interacting in?

A. Administer procurements
B. Close Contracts
C. Conduct procurements
D. Contract administration

126. Jack's project to implement an electronic funds management system for a multinational investment bank has just completed. The project was fraught with procurement issues over the entire project life cycle. What would be the most appropriate action to ensure that the procurement problems are resolved for future projects?

A. Document this in a lessons learned meeting so project managers on future projects will be aware of the situation
B. Submit corrective and preventative action documentation to the PMO
C. Perform a procurement audit
D. Correct the problem through the contract change control system

127. The project management plan is used for all of the following, except to:

A. facilitate communication among stakeholders
B. provide a baseline for progress measurement and project control
C. document project planning assumptions and decisions regarding alternatives chosen
D. provide a unique learning reference to improve the project management knowledge and skills of team members

128. When project deliverables completely satisfy the client:

A. Quality is achieved
B. Rework is minimized
C. Project costs are lower
D. Stakeholder satisfaction is achieved

129. You are working with a group of senior executives brainstorming the acquisition and deployment of a new accounting software package that promises to significantly enhance efficiency across your entire organization. They clearly indicated they want to have a high-level project scope statement documented before the brainstorming session ends. Everyone agrees that a particular installation vendor represents a critical success factor, but it will take several days to confirm availability of this vendor. Even though the vendor availability is unknown, to complete the high-level project scope statement by the end of the session, you document that the vendor will perform the work. This could exemplify what?
    A. Sole-source procurement
    B. A high risk threshold
    C. An assumption
    D. A go/no-go decision gate

130. A quality control chart can help the team with all of the following, except:
    A. Determining whether or not project spending is tracking within acceptable variation limits
    B. Determining whether or not project schedule performance is in-control
    C. Determining whether or not the project schedule is tracking within acceptable variation limits
    D. Identifying the 20% of all possible causes likely responsible for 80% of the problems

131. Only three weeks into the execution phase of your six month project schedule, things are going terribly wrong. Every day, new surprises seemingly come out of nowhere, forcing you and the team to stop planned work to address the problem and decide how to go about fixing it. For example, this morning the team was shocked to learn that a new government regulation will become effective in two weeks that will dramatically expand project scope. The team met for a full hour and still doesn't know how it will approach the problem. This one surprise alone could require complete replanning. Based on the current situation, what did this team OVERLOOK during project planning?
    A. Scope management
    B. Stakeholder management
    C. Risk management
    D. Quality management

132. When the number of items to be tested is prohibitively large, which of the following may represent a reasonable alternative?
    A. Statistical sampling
    B. Expanding both upper and lower control limits
    C. Opting not to apply the rule-of-seven
    D. Expanding both upper and lower specification limits

133. Eighty percent of your project's human resources are provided by one functional manager. Well into project execution, with performance tracking smoothly, the functional manager stuns you by saying most of your staff

is no longer available, including several members of your core project management team. You learn that the functional manager reassigned your people to a new pet project. This is extra shocking, because the new pet project seems to be of far less importance to the organization. What is your BEST course of action?

A. Immediately solicit the help of your sponsor to seek senior management attention.

B. With your core project management team, evaluate the impact of this development.

C. Suspend all project activities until new staff can be acquired.

D. Authorize the use of cost contingency reserves to immediately recruit new staff.

134. Referring to the information in the table below, identify the shortest period of time in which this project may be completed.

Activity	Activity Duration	Predecessors
A	1 week	none
B	7 weeks	none
C	5 weeks	A and B
D	12 weeks	B
E	10 weeks	C and D
F	6 weeks	E
G	3 weeks	F

A. 25 weeks
B. 31 weeks
C. 38 weeks
D. Insufficient information

135. You have a reputation within the organization for being somewhat of a "project management evangelist." Admittedly, you take every opportunity available to emphasize the value that good project management offers. Your most popular project management mantra is "Communication, Communication, Communication." You believe so strongly in the importance of good communication in the project environment that every project you are assigned begins with development of the project communication management plan. Every communications management plan you develop includes all of the following, except:

A. A description of what information will be gathered, how it will be gathered, and how often it will be gathered.

B. A description of the methods that will be used for accessing information.

C. A listing of the stakeholders to whom information will flow and how the information will be distributed.

D. A large open section in the back of the plan binder to collect all project documents.

136. The precise description of a physical item, procedure, or service is called a
_____.
    A. work breakdown structure (WBS) element
    B. product description
    C. baseline
    D. work package

137. The Sequence Activities process is applied to _____.
    A. identify all of the deliverables-oriented work within the scope of the project
    B. further subdivide work packages into clearly defined activities
    C. create the project schedule network diagram
    D. schedule all of the project's defined activities

138. The people, equipment, materials, and supplies used to estimate activity resources are termed:
    A. Work breakdown structure (WBS) requirements
    B. Physical resources
    C. Work package requirements
    D. Estimate activity resources outputs

139. You were just called by your project sponsor and asked to come up to the office right away. When you arrive, you find your sponsor and the organization's CFO waiting for you. It appears that during a recent audit of your project's financial performance, it was discovered that most of your material suppliers are routinely invoicing extra fees for rush deliveries and your service contractors are routinely escalating their contract values with numerous contract changes. The CFO sees this as wasteful spending. It is true that your service contractors request escalation changes frequently, but this is necessary because the original contracts accidentally left out much of the intended work. Plus, it is true that materials are often shipped overnight, but this is necessary because the team just keeps forgetting to order materials until inventories are depleted. What is the MOST LIKELY cause of this situation?
    A. The absence of a procurement management plan
    B. Unethical suppliers and contractors
    C. The absence of an organization central contracting group
    D. Lack of direct oversight by the project sponsor

140. Which of the following statements is most incorrect?
    A. A risk has a cause and, if it occurs, a consequence.
    B. There are negative risks and positive risks.
    C. Positive risks may be viewed as opportunities and should be pursued.
    D. Negative risks must be eliminated before project plan execution.

141. A budget change is requested and approved during the execution/control phase of the project. What is your MOST appropriate action following approval?
    A. Integrate the changes as approved, then create a new cost baseline.

B. Create a new cost baseline, but only after all changes have been made.

C. Notify your project sponsor.

D. Integrate budget changes, but maintain the original cost baseline.

142. The Estimate Activity Resources is applied to:
   A. determine the physical type resources required to perform each activity
   B. determine the people required to perform each activity
   C. determine the equipment required to perform each activity
   D. determine the materials required to perform each activity

143. The estimating technique that typically uses the past actual performance of a similar activity is termed
   A. Bottom-up estimating
   B. Probabilistic estimating
   C. Analogous estimating (also termed top-down)
   D. Deterministic (single-point) estimating

144. The Develop Schedule process is applied to:
   A. Document all duration estimates, using the scheduling software selected by you and your project team
   B. Document how changes to the project schedule will be managed
   C. Add realism and flexibility to the project schedule
   D. Create the project schedule based on activity sequences, durations, resource requirements, and schedule constraints

145. You can generally say each of the following is true except:
   A. The project charter identifies major task interdependencies.
   B. The project charter includes the product description.
   C. The project charter defines the business need(s) that the project was undertaken to address.
   D. The project charter is issued by a manager external to the project.

146. Indications that a risk has occurred, or is about to occur, are what?
   A. Uncertainties
   B. Triggers (or risk symptoms or warning signs)
   C. Consequences
   D. Threats

147. Your project team has consulted with several experts to get their opinions on the time duration of a particular project activity that is on the critical path. Their expert opinions varied. The shortest time estimate was six days, the longest estimate was fourteen days, the most probable estimate seemed to be nine days. Based on this information, what is the PERT estimate (three-point estimate)?
   A. 5.67 days
   B. 9.00 days
   C. 9.33 days
   D. 9.67 days

148. The Develop Human Resource Plan process is applied to _____.
   A. develop, document, and assign the project resource histogram
   B. develop, document, and assign project roles, responsibilities, and reporting relationships
   C. develop the project's Responsibility Assignment Matrix
   D. identify which organizational standards are applicable to the project, then determine how to satisfy them

149. Your stakeholder analysis indicates that several project stakeholders want to be updated on project performance biweekly. Your team suggests that a biweekly project performance presentation held in the project office may facilitate the needs of these particular stakeholders. Upon checking back, you find these stakeholders are in agreement, so you include biweekly presentations in your communication management plan. These presentations are an example of what?
   A. Formal written communication
   B. Informal written communication
   C. Informal verbal communication
   D. Formal verbal communication

150. After several years of working as an independent project management consultant, you have had the fortunate opportunity to get a firsthand inside look at the project management systems used in many organizations around the world. One of your observations is that many organizations have a project office, but these project offices differ widely in how they function to support their organization. You have noticed some called Project Management Office, some called Program Management Office, some called Project Office and some just PMO. Which of the following is generally NOT TRUE with respect to a project office?
   A. Some PMOs provide comprehensive support functions to project managers in their organization.
   B. Some PMOs provide templates and learning materials to project managers in their organization.
   C. Some PMOs assume full responsibility for the results of projects in their organization.
   D. Some PMOs assume full responsibility for the marketing and sales of the product of the project for some defined period of time after the project has ended.

151. At the end of year one into a planned three-year roadway expansion project, you are conducting annual performance appraisals for each of your core team members. Three members of your team have consistently demonstrated some minor weaknesses during this first year. You should_____.
   A. replace them, to improve team performance in year two
   B. discuss the weaknesses you have observed and, together, develop an improvement plan, to be monitored occasionally during year two
   C. recruit additional team members to compensate for the observed weaknesses, to improve overall team performance

D. formally document their appraisals, start a file, and continue to document/file every problem they create, just in case you need documented justification to fire them sometime in the future

152. The customer requests a change that will likely decrease your probability of achieving on schedule project performance. What is your most appropriate FIRST action?
   A. Go to your project sponsor for resolution.
   B. Use the decision tree tool to quantify the schedule delay.
   C. Together with your project management team, analyze the impact of the change request.
   D. Respectfully deny the request, unless it was previously identified as a risk.

153. Your project team has just completed development of the cost performance baseline. The cost performance baseline is:
   A. A formal document that describes how earned value management (EVM) will be applied to measure and report project cost performance
   B. A formal document that describes how project cost variances will be managed
   C. A time-phased budget, used to monitor and measure cost performance
   D. A time-phased budget, used as supporting detail to justify activity cost estimates

154. The plan quality process is applied to:
   A. Help ensure high-grade, high-quality project performance
   B. Create quality improvement
   C. Develop the project's cause-and-effect diagram
   D. Identify which quality standards are applicable to the project, then determine how to satisfy them

155. Project risk is properly defined as:
   A. Any negative event or condition that, if it occurs, has an effect on a project objective
   B. Any cause that has a negative consequence to a project objective
   C. Any uncertain event or condition that, if it occurs, has a negative or positive effect on a project objective
   D. Any event or condition that has a negative or positive effect on a project objective

156. The Identify Risks process is applied to:
   A. Determine which risks are serious enough to warrant further analysis
   B. Determine which risks may affect the project and to document their characteristics
   C. Determine which risks are low enough to accept
   D. Determine which risks should be mitigated

157. Which of these statements best describes the develop project team process?
  - **A.** Develop project team is the process of creating the project team performance record
  - **B.** Develop project team is the process of enhancing the ability of individual team members in order to enhance overall project performance
  - **C.** Develop project team is the process of creating the project team building plan
  - **D.** Develop project team is the process of collocating team members to a single project war room, which will serve as the team headquarters

158. Of the following, which BEST represents a way project managers can contribute to their organization's knowledge base?
  - **A.** Practicing and promoting formal project reviews and lessons learned
  - **B.** Enforcing and promoting the protection of company proprietary information
  - **C.** Ensuring all project plans are complete and comprehensive
  - **D.** Practicing and promoting good stakeholder management

159. Network diagram Activity 3095 indicates Early Start (ES) as six days and Late Start (LS) as fifteen days. Based on this information, how much slack does Activity 3095 have?
  - **A.** 60%
  - **B.** –60%
  - **C.** 9 days
  - **D.** –9 days

160. Project risk categories include:
  - **A.** Technical, project management, organizational, and external
  - **B.** Quality, performance, opportunities, and threats
  - **C.** Positive, negative, causal, and consequential
  - **D.** Triggers, symptoms, warning signs, and uncertainties

161. The perform qualitative risk analysis process is applied to:
  - **A.** Assess the probability/impact of high priority risks. It is intended to mitigate those risks that pose immediate threats or encourage those risks that offer immediate opportunities.
  - **B.** Determine which risks may affect the project and to document their characteristics
  - **C.** Further assess those risks that scored high-high on the probability/impact (P-I) matrix
  - **D.** Assess the impact and likelihood of identified risks. It is intended to help prioritize identified risks and identify those risks serious enough to warrant further analysis.

162. Using a typical P-I matrix, you and your project team assess an identified risk with a score of 0.1. Where in the matrix does it appear, and what does it signify?
  - **A.** Lower-right, signifying low-probability but high-impact
  - **B.** Upper-right, signifying high-probability but low-impact

C. Lower-left, signifying low-probability but low-impact
D. Upper-right, signifying high-probability but high-impact

163. After careful comparison, the decision is made by your project sponsor to choose one particular project strategy over another, because the chosen strategy has less associated risk. This decision is consistent with her risk-averse policies. This could be an example of using _____ to base a decision.
   A. Subjective analysis
   B. Expert power
   C. Title power
   D. Sensitivity analysis

164. Given that the pessimistic estimate for a particular activity time duration is six days, the optimistic estimate is two days and the most probable estimate is five days, what is the PERT estimate?
   A. 2.00 days
   B. 4.00 days
   C. 4.67 days
   D. 5.00 days

165. Which of the following represents the WORST response to an identified risk?
   A. Avoid the risk
   B. Mitigate the risk
   C. Accept the risk
   D. Reject the risk

166. Of the following, which BEST describes a backward pass?
   A. A backward pass is an American football sports term that has nothing to do with project management.
   B. A backward pass is performed by moving right-to-left (end-to-start) through the network diagram to determine Late Start (LS) and Late Finish (LF) times for each activity.
   C. Backward pass is a familiar (unofficial) project management term that generally means revisiting a previously applied process to make refinements.
   D. Backward pass is a familiar (unofficial) project management term that means project schedule performance is trending further and further behind.

167. To help determine and justify a cost contingency for your project, you decide to further evaluate four identified risks using EMV analysis. Risk 1 has a 10% probability of occurring, and if it occurs, will result in $10,000 added cost to the project. Risk 2 has a 70% probability of occurring, and if it occurs, will result in $8,000 added cost to the project. Risk 3 has a 60% probability of occurring, and if it occurs, will result in $10,000 less cost to the project. Risk 4 has a 20% probability of occurring, and if it occurs, will result in $800 added cost to the project. What is the combined EMV of these four risks?
   A. −$12,760
   B. $760
   C. −$760
   D. Not enough information

168. Which of the following best describes the Develop Project Management Plan process?
   A. The Develop Project Management Plan process may use a PMIS to help assemble the integrated project plan.
   B. The Develop Project Management Plan process represents the last step in project planning.
   C. The Develop Project Management Plan process is applied to gather the outputs from all other planning processes, along with all subsidiary plans, and assemble them into a single, cohesive document; the Project Management Plan.
   D. The Develop Project Management Plan process is ongoing throughout the project planning phase.

169. Which of the following best describes the Acquire Project Team process?
   A. The Acquire Project Team process is applied to obtain needed human resources (people) from functional managers.
   B. The Acquire Project Team process is applied to assign needed human resources (people) to the project directory.
   C. The Acquire Project Team process is applied to assign project team roles and responsibilities.
   D. The Acquire Project Team process is applied to obtain and assign needed human resources (people) to the project.

170. Which of the following statements is most true?
   A. Collocation can include moving team members into a more central area when team members already work at the same physical location, but should not include relocating team members from other geographic locations.
   B. Team Development is generally easier in functional organizations.
   C. In some organizations, team development can be extra challenging when team members report to both the project manager and to their functional manager.
   D. Team development procedures should be developed during Develop Project Charter.

171. The Manage Project Team process is applied to:
   A. Enhance the performance of project team members, to enhance the overall project performance
   B. Coordinate training for project team members and to create the project's reward and recognition system
   C. Address performance, behavior, issues, and conflicts associated specifically with project team members
   D. Develop options and determine actions to create opportunities for project team member advancement

172. The responsibility for project quality management lies with:
   A. The project manager
   B. The project core team member assigned to manage project quality
   C. The highest ranking QA/QC manager in the performing organization

D. The organization QA/QC manager assigned to oversee quality activities for this particular project

173. You and your project team have just commenced the execution/controlling phases of the project. Today, at the end of week one, your first weekly project performance report was prepared, reviewed/approved by the project core team, and sent to the appropriate distribution list via electronic mail. Based on this information, select the best statement.
    A. Your communication obligation is satisfied. Your weekly performance report, as agreed to in the communication management plan, has been prepared and distributed, on time, to the appropriate stakeholders. Stakeholders must accept ownership of their obligation to acknowledge receipt, then read and understand the information.
    B. Your communication obligation is not yet satisfied. Although your weekly performance report, as agreed to in the communication management plan, has been prepared and distributed, on time, to the appropriate stakeholders, you must verify that the reports were received for communication to be complete. It may be a good idea to use electronic receipt verification to automate this process.
    C. Your communication obligation may not yet be satisfied. Although your weekly performance report, as agreed to in the communication management plan, has been prepared and distributed, on time, to the appropriate stakeholders, you should verify that the reports were received and that the recipients understood the information, as it was intended. It may be a good idea to interview a few recipients to ensure the reports satisfy their intended purpose, especially after distribution of the very first report.
    D. Your communication obligation is satisfied. Your weekly performance report, as agreed to in the communication management plan, has been prepared and distributed, on time, to the appropriate stakeholders. You may confidently move to the next activity.

174. During project execution, a key stakeholder becomes very upset. She claims that she was not aware of a project management plan element that impacts her division. Your best response would be:
    A. As soon as possible, arrange a face-to-face meeting with your sponsor to plan a resolution
    B. As soon as possible, arrange a face-to-face meeting with the stakeholder
    C. As soon as possible, with your project management team, create a work-around plan
    D. As soon as possible, document the stakeholder's concern and communicate it to your sponsor/customer

175. The Conduct Procurements process is performed to _____ _____.
    A. develop and document the project's procurement management plan
    B. obtain responses, select a seller, and award a contract
    C. determine the qualified sellers list
    D. advertise to prospective sellers to add to the company's vendor list

176. Legitimate scope changes may be necessitated/justified by many conditions. Of the following, which does not typify a condition that would justify a scope change?
    A. A sponsor's decision to re-estimate activity costs
    B. A client's decision to add a feature to the product of the project
    C. A newly available technology that was not an option when project scope was initially documented
    D. A newly enacted government regulation

177. Which of the following best describes the intended application of the Control Schedule process?
    A. Control Schedule is the process of effectively monitoring the project progress and managing project schedule baseline changes, then integrating those changes across the entire project.
    B. Control Schedule is the process applied to prevent changes to the schedule baseline.
    C. Control Schedule is the process applied to guide the project manager when making approval/denial decisions with respect to schedule baseline change requests.
    D. Control Schedule is the process applied to determine the potential benefit value of schedule change requests.

178. At the end of month three into a four-month project, you find yourself 50% complete and have spent $600,000. You originally planned to spend $212,500 each month, with your work activities evenly scheduled at 25% each month. The total project budget is $850,000. What is the VAC?
    A. –$425,000
    B. $350,000
    C. $1,200,000
    D. –$350,000

179. Perform Quality Control (QC) is the process of:
    A. Applying statistical testing to detect and analyze quality trends
    B. Monitoring the product of the project to ensure it satisfies product performance specifications
    C. Developing performance tolerance criteria, then documenting actual performance using a control chart
    D. Monitoring specific project results to ensure they comply with the project's quality standards

180. Which of the following statements best depicts the difference between Verify Scope and Perform Quality Control?
    A. Scope Verification is primarily focused on the acceptance of project deliverables; Quality Control is primarily focused on the correctness of deliverables.
    B. Quality Control is primarily focused on the acceptance of project deliverables; Scope Verification is primarily focused on the correctness of deliverables.
    C. Quality Control is always performed before Scope Verification.

D. Scope Verification is primarily focused on whether or not deliverables meet the requirements; Quality Control is primarily focused on the correctness of deliverables.

181. During project execution, an odd risk event occurs, a risk that no one imagined in advance. But now that it has occurred, the project team must act. An appropriate response would be to:
    A. Request guidance from the project sponsor
    B. Create new risk response plan
    C. Create a work-around
    D. Transfer the risk as soon as possible

182. Administer Procurements is:
    A. The procurement process of interfacing with the organization's central contract group
    B. The procurement process of approving and paying sellers' invoices in a timely fashion
    C. The procurement process of ensuring that the seller's performance satisfies contractual obligations
    D. The procurement process of minimizing the number of contractors' change requests

183. The Monitor and Control Project Work process is applied to _____.
    A. monitor all executing processes and take/make corrective/preventive actions, as needed
    B. monitor all other processes through initiation, planning, executing and closing, and implement risk response actions, if/when risk events occur
    C. monitor all other processes through initiation, planning, executing and closing, and take/make corrective/preventive actions, as needed
    D. provide guidance for all other monitoring and controlling processes and take/make corrective/preventive actions, as needed

184. Perform Integrated Change Control is _____ ____.
    A. the process applied to guide the project change control board (CCB) in their decisions to approve or deny project change requests
    B. the process of effectively managing changes and integrating them appropriately across the entire project
    C. the process applied to encourage the project manager to use effective influencing skills to discourage unnecessary changes
    D. the process applied to guide the use of configuration management procedures across the project life cycle

185. Which of the following is a Close Procurements tool/technique?
    A. Procurement audits
    B. Closed procurements
    C. Organizational process assets updates
    D. Procurement documentation

186. _____ best describes the Close Project or Phase process.
A. Preparing and distributing the final project performance report
B. Archiving the performance evaluations of project core team members
C. Bringing an orderly end to the seller's contractual obligations
D. Formally ending either the project or project phase

187. You and the team are preparing detailed information for the engineering review board regarding a major change request. Of all the information you can provide to help the board make an informed approval/rejection decision, what is the MOST important?
A. The impact the change will have on project objectives.
B. The date, time, and source of the change request.
C. Your opinion.
D. The expected monetary value of the change should it be approved.

188. Before releasing your project management core team members at project end, it is most appropriate for you to _____.
A. provide formal input to their respective performance appraisals
B. host an offsite celebration, if budget money is available
C. offer a personal thank-you to each member, individually
D. publicly award incentives, if goals were achieved

189. Of the following activities, which best depicts Verify Scope?
A. Approving a project budget change request
B. Authorizing the project to proceed to its next phase
C. Accepting a newly created operating manual
D. Agreeing to scope definition, as illustrated by the work breakdown structure

190. During project planning, the team identifies a large number of potential negative risks. Most of them have low probability of occurrence and low impact, should they occur. You and the team call these non-critical risks. What is the most appropriate way to manage these non-critical risks?
A. Document them and review them occasionally throughout the project.
B. Ignore them.
C. Establish a collective non-critical risk cost reserve to compensate.
D. Establish a contingency action plan for each.

191. You have been made aware that one of the key stakeholders involved with your new project has a history of requesting numerous changes. Assuming the reputation is true, what is the BEST way to manage this situation?
A. Have a no-nonsense talk with the stakeholder soon.
B. Get the stakeholder actively involved early in planning.
C. Ask your project sponsor to shield the project from this stakeholder.
D. Add resources to the plan to accommodate the higher-than-normal number of anticipated change requests.

192. Upon taking over as project manager for an ongoing project, you discover that your predecessor has been reporting misleading information. Senior management believes the project is on schedule and within budget. However,

your assessment reveals the project is significantly behind schedule and over budget. What is the most appropriate FIRST action on your part?

A. Refuse the assignment.

B. Report your assessment to senior management.

C. Meet with your predecessor to agree on a unified report to senior management.

D. With the team, explore fast-tracking and crashing options to get the project back on track.

193. When quality problems are observed, but the causes are not certain, some project teams apply a diagramming tool that ranks problems by frequency of occurrence. The resulting histogram usually indicates a small percentage of all possible causes contributing to the majority of problems. This allows the team to concentrate their corrective actions on the few root causes creating most of the problems. What is this diagramming tool?

A. Pareto diagram

B. Delphi technique

C. Ishikawa diagram (also termed "fishbone diagram" or "cause-and-effect diagram")

D. Responsibility Assignment Matrix (RAM)

194. For the past twenty-two years, you have worked in the outage planning group at a nuclear power reactor facility. The facility has enjoyed a near-flawless safety record. As part of the plant's expected life cycle, permanent shutdown was scheduled five years from now, with decommissioning activities to begin immediately after shutdown. However, the parent company's executive board decided recently to shut down the facility now, five years ahead of plan. You were asked to stay on to oversee decommissioning as project manager, and agreed. Twelve others have agreed to stay on to help manage the project. You learn that decommissioning will likely be a five-year process and could cost as much as $550 million. You and your twelve peers know very little about managing large projects. Based on this situation, what is your best FIRST action?

A. With your twelve peers, form a committee to find a projectized engineering firm that specializes in decommissioning and contract them to do the work.

B. Form a project management core team with your twelve peers and begin project planning.

C. Respectfully request the parent company to create and issue a formal project charter, and offer to assist them in drafting the document.

D. Make appropriate arrangements for you and your twelve peers to get trained in modern project management concepts, tools, and methodologies.

195. Of the following, your MOST important function as project manager is to _____.

A. prevent and discourage unnecessary changes

B. document all changes

C. communicate all changes

D. evaluate all changes

196. Who performs and documents lessons learned?
   - **A.** You, the project manager
   - **B.** Key project stakeholders
   - **C.** The project sponsor
   - **D.** You and the project team

197. Coaching and mentoring other project personnel in your organization can have beneficial effects. A KEY benefit is _____.
   - **A.** building the capabilities of colleagues to improve overall project management quality
   - **B.** increasing the awareness of project limitations in a functional organization
   - **C.** grooming others, so you can move up
   - **D.** earning personal respect

198. During a review of your project's spending history, you find several suspicious payment authorizations. Upon further investigation, you find strong evidence these payments are kickbacks to one of the project's suppliers. What should you do FIRST?
   - **A.** Post it as an issue to be discussed by the team as soon as possible.
   - **B.** Document it as a newly identified risk.
   - **C.** Seek counsel from your organization's legal group.
   - **D.** With the team, explore alternatives.

199. During project closing, you perform an appraisal for each of your core team members, providing one-on-one discussions, backed up with written appraisal forms. You also perform one for yourself. In your own appraisal, you found several areas across the project where you feel your management style was ineffective, perhaps indicating the need for targeted management training. This exemplifies what?
   - **A.** Self assessment
   - **B.** Self promotion
   - **C.** Career path planning
   - **D.** Learning curve

200. With three months remaining to bring your project to close, the client requests you finish early, in just two months. What is your most appropriate FIRST action?
   - **A.** Respectfully deny the request.
   - **B.** Go to your sponsor for advice.
   - **C.** Prepare a formal, written dispute report and forward it to senior management.
   - **D.** With the project team, explore crashing and fast-tracking options.

End of Lesson 54

Appendix A

Lesson Quiz Solutions

LESSON 3   PM FUNDAMENTALS

1. <u>B</u>   Option B is the correct answer since an ongoing operation is something that has an indefinite time period and also has a flexible definition (in many cases). Options A, C, and D effectively make up the definition of a project: temporary, creating a unique Output and being progressively elaborated. *PMBOK® Guide*, chapter 1.2.

2. <u>C</u>   Option C comes right from the *PMBOK® Guide Fourth Edition*. The other answer options are less correct. Option A is incorrect since the answer is not complete. Answer B is incorrect because it indicates that the project manager would rely on intuition and feelings. (While intuition and feelings may be a useful aid for a project manager, they are not a primary definition or tool). Answer D is also incorrect due to the insertion of art and science into the choice. *PMBOK® Guide*, chapter 1.3.

3. <u>C</u> The main role of the project manager is to integrate all of the activities to achieve the project goals and objectives. Other answers are less correct. While it is true that the project manager is a manager, that does not define the overall role. It is true that the project manager is the project leader and it is true that the project manager is a communicator. The best answer is integrator. *PMBOK® Guide*, chapter 1.6.

4. <u>B</u>   The "triple constraint" has generally been recognized as scope, time, and budget. These are represented by answers A, C, and D for this question. In addition to the traditional triple constraint, many projects and project managers often consider a wider view of project constraints to include quality, resources, and risk. A previous version of the *PMBOK Guide* cited "customer satisfaction" as part of the constraints. *PMBOK® Guide*, chapter 1.3.

5. <u>D</u>   Communicating continues to be the most challenging part of project management. Effective communication will enable almost every other interpersonal skill. It is impossible to lead, motivate, influence, or politic within the organization without the ability to communicate. *PMBOK® Guide*, appendix G.4.

6. <u>B</u>   The main role of the stakeholder on the project is to communicate. The *PMBOK Guide* describes the multiple ways that the project stakeholder is expected to participate and communicate. Answers A, C, and D each have some validity but also define "communicating" as their intent. *PMBOK® Guide*, chapter 2.3.

LESSON 4 MASTERING THE *PMBOK*

1. <u>B</u> In the fourth edition of the *PMBOK® Guide*, there are forty-two processes. Answer A is invalid. Answer C corresponds to the number of processes in the third edition. Answer D corresponds to the number of processes in the second edition. It should be noted at this point that the student should take care to learn, understand, and memorize process relationships to the Knowledge Areas and Process Groups in the *PMBOK Guide*. The table on page 43 is an excellent place to study. *PMBOK® Guide*, table 3.1, page 43.

2. <u>A</u> Process groups are intended to facilitate interaction and activity between other process groups and the processes contained within. In most multiphase projects, each process group is performed in each phase of the project. Answer B is also correct, but not the best answer choice. Answer C is incorrect since Initiating processes are used to ensure that the project is still correctly chartered. Answer D is incorrect since closing processes can be used at the end of each phase to ensure that a checkpoint occurs prior to moving to the next phase. *PMBOK® Guide*, chapter 3.2.

3. <u>A</u> It is generally recognized that the most critical portion of the project is the Initiation and Planning areas. If the project manager and team are not properly informed about project intentions during the Initiating processes (Develop Project Charter and Identify Stakeholders), then planning outcomes will most likely contain errors. *PMBOK® Guide*, chapter 3.3.

4. <u>C</u> Process groups have a high level of interaction throughout the project. This is apparent from the depiction of how project management process groups overlap when being performed. Answer A is incorrect since at least three process groups are performed at the same time during a project (Planning, Executing, and Monitoring and Controlling process groups). Answer B is incorrect due to overlaps. Answer D is incorrect since all process groups are intended to be performed during a typical project life cycle. *PMBOK® Guide*, chapter 3, Figure 3.2.

LESSON 6 DEVELOP PROJECT CHARTER

1. <u>B</u> This is a common sense derivation from the general definition given for product description.

2. <u>D</u> Review your Develop Project Charter process illustration. You will see that expert judgment is a Tool/Technique not an Input.

3. <u>C</u> This is the only answer option that was discussed (and emphasized) in Lesson 6. You can derive the best answer here by eliminating the three options that received no mention in Lesson 6.

4. <u>A</u>   As emphasized in Lesson 6, the Project Charter is typically the responsibility of senior management. It may be prepared by the project manager but is approved and authorized by senior management.

5. <u>B</u>   Hopefully, you found this one to be easy. The Project Charter is the primary Output (deliverable) from the Develop Project Charter process, which is one of the two processes that comprise the Initiating Process Group.

6. <u>B</u>   The lesson here is to understand that the greatest influence anyone has on any project aspect (cost, or any other aspect) is early in the project life cycle. The earlier in the life cycle, the greater the potential influence. In this quiz question "concept" can logically be identified as the earliest phase, and therefore the best answer.

7. <u>C</u>   The lesson here is to understand and respect the high value of "organizational process assets." A project manager can gain valuable insight and readily useful lessons by researching past information on similar projects, which are part and parcel of an organization's process assets. Historical information, part of an organization's process assets, can provide valuable help, more so than any other single resource.

8. <u>A</u>   Review your project charter template illustration in Lesson 6, along with your Must Know items. You will see that answer option A is the only exception, and therefore the best answer.

LESSON 7   IDENTIFY STAKEHOLDERS

1. <u>A</u>   Option A is the best response and is the common sense answer in this group of answers. Option B cites the function of Plan Communications. Option C is closest to a description of Distribute Information. Option D is a combination of several processes. *PMBOK® Guide*, chapter 10.1.

2. <u>B</u>   In this question we must choose the best group of actions that describe the technique. Options A and C partially describe communications requirement analysis, which occurs later in planning. Option D describes a practical approach. Option B is the most accurate and complete answer. *PMBOK® Guide*, 10.1.2.1.

3. <u>B</u>   This question requires you to know your Outputs from the process. Options A, C, and D are not Outputs from the Identify Stakeholders process. *PMBOK® Guide*, chapter 10.1.

LESSON 8 PLANNING

Process Matching Exercise

The following processes are correctly depicted as residing in the Planning Process Group. Reference *PMBOK® Guide*, chapter 3, table 3.1.

Project Integration Management	Develop Project Management Plan
Project Scope Management	Collect Requirements Define Scope Create WBS
Project Time Management	Define Activities Sequence Activities Estimate Activity Resources Estimate Activity Durations Develop Schedule
Project Cost Management	Estimate Costs Determine Budget
Project Quality Management	Plan Quality
Project Human Resource Management	Develop Human Resource Plan
Project Communications Management	Plan Communications
Project Risk Management	Plan Risk Management Identify Risks Perform Qualitative Risk Analysis Perform Quantitative Risk Analysis Plan Risk Responses
Project Procurement Management	Plan Procurements

LESSON 9 PLAN COMMUNICATIONS

1. <u>C</u>   This quiz question is designed to ensure that you understand the intended application of the Plan Communications process. *The Plan Communications process is applied to determine the communications needs of project stakeholders, including what information is needed, when it is needed, and how it will be delivered.* Therefore, Option C is the precise correct answer. Options A, B, and D are only partially true, describing only portions of the process.

2. <u>C</u>   Answer Options A and D are blatantly false statements. Option B may appear reasonable to some, but is not true. All forms of communication (formal, informal, verbal, written, non-verbal) are acceptable and encouraged when applied appropriately. Formal written communication is normally encouraged for performance reports, legal matters, contractual matters, and other issues of similar importance. Option C is a true statement and therefore the correct (most correct) answer. Non-verbal communication is actually much more expressive than any type of verbal or written communication.

3. <u>B</u>   This is a straightforward test of your ability to understand and apply the communication channels equation $N(N-1)/2$. Note the importance of reading the question correctly here. You are asked to determine the <u>number of additional channels</u> resulting from an increase in stakeholders. To derive the correct answer, you must perform three mathematical steps. (1) You must determine the number of communication channels with 6 stakeholders. (2) You must determine the number of communication channels with 2 more stakeholders, 8. (3) You must then determine the resulting increased number of channels. With 6 stakeholders, the number of communication channels is 15. With 8 stakeholders, the number of communication channels is 28. The increase is 13. Therefore, the correct answer is Option B. Note that answer Options C and D could represent reasonable answers if an error is made in understanding precisely what the question is asking. Option A could seem reasonable to someone who doesn't know the equation. Make a special note that the overall importance of this exercise is to reinforce the concept of communication channels growing exponentially in size and complexity with every added person in the project communications loop.

4. <u>D</u>   This quiz question is intended to test your ability to simply recognize and identify practical examples of communication types. It is presented as a long situational type question, but is simple in nature. Presentations fall under the formal verbal category of communication types. Therefore, answer Option D is the only possible correct answer.

LESSON 10   COLLECT REQUIREMENTS

1. <u>A</u>   This quiz question is designed to help ensure that you understand the intended application of the Collect Requirements process. During the Collect Requirements process, stakeholder needs are defined and documented. This documentation provides the basis for defining and managing customer expectations throughout the project. Therefore, Option A is the preferred answer. Option B is a true statement, but not fully complete. Option C describes product requirements and Option D describes project requirements.

2. <u>C</u>   This quiz question is intended to ensure that you understand the difference between group decision techniques and negotiating techniques. Group decision making techniques are utilized to process alternatives and generate future actions and include unanimity, majority, plurality, and dictatorship. Option C (forcing) is a negotiating technique and therefore is the correct (exception) answer.

3. <u>C</u>   This is a straightforward test of your ability to recognize the processes contained within the Project Scope Management knowledge area. There are five processes included in the Project Scope Management knowledge area: (1) Collect Requirements, (2) Define Scope, (3) Create WBS, (4) Verify Scope, and (5) Control Scope. Option C contains three of these five processes and therefore is the preferred answer.

4. <u>A</u>   This quiz question provides a real-world scenario that is very commonly encountered by project managers; their boss or sponsor wants immediate results. Refusing to take immediate action is usually a career-altering experience. The choices in B, C, and D offer an alternative to refusing to take immediate action and somewhat protect the project and allow definitions to take place.

LESSON 11   DEFINE SCOPE

1. <u>C</u>   Review your Define Scope process illustration. You will see that the project scope statement is the intended Output of the process, not an Input. Therefore Option C represents the best answer.

2. <u>D</u>   Each of the answer Options A, B, and C are equally true. Once developed, the project scope statement serves many important functions across the entire project life cycle. Therefore Option D, all of the above, represents the best answer.

3. <u>C</u>   This quiz question is designed to ensure that you understand the development and intended application of the Define Scope process. *The Define Scope process is intended to create the project scope statement.* Options A, B, and D describe activities intended by processes other than Define Scope. Therefore Option C represents the best answer.

4. <u>A</u> Options B, C, and D are false statements. Option A represents the only true statement and is therefore the best, most correct, answer. It is important to know the difference between a Project Scope Statement and a Scope Management Plan. Refer to your template illustrations (Lessons 5 and 6).

5. <u>B</u> This is a logical or common sense question. You should understand intuitively that stability (of any project parameter, including scope) will decrease as a project becomes more complex. Another way to view this is, "the level of uncertainty increases as the size and complexity of a project increases." Based on this, Option B represents the best answer.

6. <u>C</u> Options A, B, and D are true statements. Option C is false. As a PMP, you should understand that a Project Scope Statement and Scope Management Plan are two different documents with different intended purposes. Therefore Option C, the exception, represents the best answer.

7. <u>A</u> This is a straightforward question requiring you to identify the Tools & Techniques associated with the Define Scope process. Refer to your Define Scope process illustration.

LESSON 12   CREATE WBS
. . . .

1. <u>C</u> This quiz question is intended to ensure that you can differentiate the WBS from other types of breakdown structures. You can refer to *PMBOK Guide* section 5.3.3.2 for a more detailed discussion.

2. <u>C</u> This is a straightforward definition type question. Only Option C represents a reasonable choice, and is therefore the best answer.

3. <u>D</u> Review your Create WBS process illustration. Options A and D are named Inputs. Option C, WBS templates, is contained within the OPA input. Option B is an Output, and is the correct (exception) answer.

4. <u>D</u> You will have to think a bit deeper to derive the correct answer here. Option A is blatantly wrong. Options B and C could seem reasonable. Some WBS software tools will identify critical path components but only after the project's schedule has been developed. The WBS can be used as an effective reference to help identify potential project risks, but the WBS does not automatically identify risks or single-out key risks. Option D is the best answer. The WBS can serve as an excellent communication tool, especially to create common understanding of scope among stakeholders (including project team members). Thus, it is reasonable to conclude that the WBS can enhance team buy-in, by creating better understanding.

5. <u>A</u> Options B, C, and D are false, leaving Option A as the only true statement. Option B is false because the WBS has no timeframe, thus no schedule information. Option C is false because the WBS defines work, not the need or justification. Option D is false because the WBS does not assign work; it identifies subdivided work elements.

6. **D** This is a straightforward definition question. Refer to *PMBOK Guide* section 5.3.2 for a more detailed discussion.

7. **C** This is another straightforward definition question. You can refer to your *PMBOK Guide* section 5.3.3.2 for a more detailed discussion.

8. **D** While the formal process of subdividing major deliverables into smaller, more manageable pieces is termed Create WBS, the defined methodology (*Tool/Technique*) used to facilitate the process is *decomposition*. You can refer to *PMBOK Guide* section 5.3.2.1 for a more detailed treatment of the subject.

9. **A** Options B, C, and D represent selections that have no direct association to the context of the question. Options C and D are somewhat fabricated. The lesson here is to understand the primary application of the Create WBS process. That is, to subdivide the project scope into manageable pieces which can be confidently estimated, managed, and measured.

10. **A** Review your Create WBS process illustration for the answer source. Note that only five or six questions typically appear on the PMP Exam that test your detailed mastery of specific *Inputs, Tools & Techniques* and *Outputs*. There is no need to memorize them. After completing the course, you will have sufficient familiarity to logically derive the correct answers, without having to rely on rote memory.

LESSON 13 DEFINE ACTIVITIES

1. **C** This quiz question is intended to ensure that you can differentiate *activities* from *deliverables*. The WBS is deliverables-oriented. The Define Activities process essentially converts the WBS deliverables into action-oriented activities.

2. **A** Option B is false. It is the intent of the activity list to identify project activities. WBS Work Packages are still deliverables-oriented. Option C is false. Again, Work Packages should be deliverables-oriented. The Define Activities process is applied to further subdivide Work Packages into manageable sized activities. Option A is the only true statement, and therefore represents, as the exception, the best answer.

3. **D** Review your Define Activities process illustration. You will see that "milestone list" is an intended Output of the process, not an Input. Option D, as the exception, is therefore the best answer.

4. **D** Options A, B, and C are true statements. This question is intended to help reinforce *decomposition* as a key methodology in applying both the Create WBS process (creating the WBS) and Define Activities process (creating the activity list).

LESSON 14 SEQUENCE ACTIVITIES
· ·

1. <u>D</u> *Critical path* is one of the most important terms used by project managers. It is important to know and understand its definition: *the longest path through a network diagram.* It is also important to know that the critical path defines the *shortest period of time in which a project may be completed.*

2. <u>A</u> Although, this was not directly discussed in Lesson 11, it is possible for a project to have more than one critical path through its network. When more than one critical path exists, it typically increases project risk. It is usually advisable for the project team to brainstorm some solution to avoid multiple critical paths. Option B is not true, by default. Option C is not true (good judgment should dictate that it is not conventional to attempt the creation of hybrid network diagramming methods). Option D is not true: the WBS identifies all of the deliverables-oriented work within project scope; the network diagram illustrates all activities and their logical interdependencies, from project start to project finish.

3. <u>C</u> Review your Sequence Activities process illustration. Project schedule network diagrams represents an *Output,* not an *Input.*

4. <u>C</u> There are five possible paths: (1) Start-A-B-D-E-Finish, (2) Start-A-C-E-Finish, (3) Start-A-B-C-E-Finish, (4) Start-A-B-C-D-E-Finish, and (5) Start-A-C-D-E-Finish.

5. <u>C</u> The critical path is the longest path through a network diagram. Option A cannot be correct because Start-A-C-D-Finish is not a complete path through the network. Option B does represent one of the five possible complete paths through the network and, when durations are added, requires 26 days, start to finish. Option C represents a complete path and, when added, requires 32 days. Option D is a complete path and requires 30 days. When all five paths are analyzed for total time duration, the longest path through the network is Start-A-B-C-D-E-Finish (32 days). Therefore, C is the correct answer. Hint: Remember, critical path is typically identified with a heavier arrowed line. In some cases, the illustration will already identify the critical path for you. Don't be surprised to find such clues in real-world environments.

6. <u>D</u> *The critical path defines the shortest period of time in which a project may be completed.* All four options represent actual path times through this network diagram. The longest path is Start-A-B-C-D-E-Finish and therefore defines both the critical path and the shortest time to complete the project. If you identified the wrong path as being the critical path, then one of the other answer options may have appeared correct. In many exam question situations, you will encounter wrong answer options that appear correct if a calculation error is made.

7. <u>C</u> To answer this question, you must first construct a network diagram from the given information. Be prepared to do the same in real-world project environments. The proper network diagram appears below. There are three possible paths through this network from start to finish: (1) Start-A-C-E-F-G-Finish, (2) Start-B-D-E-F-G-Finish, and (3) Start-B-C-E-F-G-Finish.

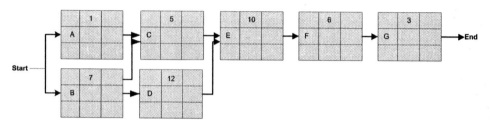

8. <u>B</u> To answer this question, you must (a) construct a network diagram from the given information, (b) identify each path from start to finish, and (c) determine which path is the longest. Remember, the longest path is the critical path. We find three possible paths: (1) Start-A-C-E-F-G-Finish (25 weeks), (2) Start-B-D-E-F-G-Finish (38 weeks), and (3) Start-B-C-EF-G-Finish (31 weeks). Path 2 is the longest and therefore the correct answer.

9. <u>C</u> Once again, to answer this question, you must first construct a network diagram from the given information. Then you must identify all possible paths through the network and determine which path is longest. The longest path is the critical path, which defines the shortest period of time in which the project may be completed. In this example, Start-B-D-E-F-G-Finish represents the critical path, and the shortest time to complete (38 weeks).

10. <u>B</u> Slack (also referred to as "float," "total float," "path float," or "reserve") is determined by subtracting Early Start (ES) from Late Start (LS). The result will be in work units (in this example, days), either positive or negative. While negative slack is unusual, it is possible in some cases. Option A is partially true, in that activities on the critical path typically have zero slack. However, nowhere in this question does it say this activity is on the critical path. Option C could appear correct if the factors are reversed doing the calculation. Option D is wrong, in that it is expressed in percentage, not work units.

11. <u>A</u> The correct answer is taken directly from your Lesson 14 Must Know Review Sheet. Option B defines a *backward pass*. Options C and D are simply incorrect definitions.

12. <u>A</u> Precedence Diagramming is also known as "Activity on Node" diagramming; therefore nodes represent activities and arrows show interrelationships. Answer B describes Arrow Diagramming (which was cited in previous *PMBOK* editions but not in the current version). Answers C and D contain descriptive errors.

13.   <u>C</u>   This quiz question is intended to ensure that you understand the application of the Sequence Activities process. Answers A, B, and D refer to outputs from other processes.

LESSON 15   ESTIMATE ACTIVITY RESOURCES

1.   <u>B</u>   *Resource* is one of the most important key terms in a project manager's vocabulary. This quiz question is intended to ensure that you are familiar with the simple, yet critical, accepted definition of resource(s).

2.   <u>A</u>   Each answer Option here is true. However, B, C, and D are incomplete. Option A represents the most complete description of the Estimate Activity Resources process and is therefore the best answer.

3.   <u>A</u>   Review your Estimate Activity Resources process illustration. Only Option A correctly identifies defined Tools & Techniques associated with Estimate Activity Resources. Options B, C, and D include items other than proper Tools & Techniques.

4.   <u>A</u>   Only answer Option A is a true statement. Option B refers to role and responsibility assignments.

LESSON 16   ESTIMATE ACTIVITY DURATIONS

1.   <u>C</u>   Analogous estimating (top-down) is fast, efficient, and less costly, but also less confident. It bases its estimate on the actual performance of a past similar activity. Option A, *bottom-up*, is actually a formal estimating technique that we will discuss soon, but it is the opposite of analogous. Options B and D are legitimate types of estimates, but neither satisfies the given definition.

2.   <u>D</u>   This question is intended to test your understanding of the term *work unit* (also termed *work period*). Most modern project management software tools need to define activity durations in terms of work units to create the project schedule. Work units are simply the defined time periods used to report duration estimates. In most projects, they are hours, shifts, days, or weeks. The project team usually decides what specific work units make the most sense for their project. Answer Options A and B are boldly incorrect statements. Both A and B confuse *work units* with *duration estimates*. Option C could appear reasonable, but the project manager should always encourage the *team* to make these types of decisions, making C not universally true. Statement D is always correct, and therefore the *most* true.

3. __A__ This is a straightforward test of your ability to recognize the defined Inputs, the Tools & Techniques, and the Outputs associated with the Estimate Acitivity Durations process. Know that there is no need to memorize all the Inputs, Tools and Techniques, and Outputs. In this question, Option B includes *three-point estimating*, which is a Tool/Technique, not an Output. Option C includes *reserve analysis*, which is also a Tool/Technique. Option D includes *resource calendar*, which is an Input.

4. __D__ Modern project management encourages many themes. One of the most important themes dictates that estimates should be prepared by the person or people most knowledgeable about the activity, ideally by the person or people that will actually perform the work. This question is intended to reinforce that theme. Answer Options A, B, and C each may appear reasonable to some extent. However, only Option D hits the mark 100%. This is a question where all of the answer options appear reasonable. But generally, one option will stand out as the *best* or *most correct*.

LESSON 17   DEVELOP SCHEDULE

1. __D__ This quiz question is designed to ensure that you understand the intended application of the Develop Schedule process. *The Develop Schedule process is applied to determine the start/finish dates for project activities and to create the Schedule Management Plan.* Therefore, Option D is the precise correct answer. Options A, B, and C are all somewhat true, but incomplete.

2. __A__ This question is intended to test your understanding of schedule compression techniques. The two most often applied techniques are *crashing* (adding resources) and *fast-tracking* (performing normally sequential activities in parallel). Answer Option B identifies *resource leveling*. Resource leveling is applied to eliminate peaks and valleys in human resource needs across a project schedule. Resource leveling actually extends the schedule in most cases. Answer Option C has nothing to do with schedule compression, but could appear reasonable to someone who's mistaken priority is to avoid schedule changes at all costs. Option D could be viewed as an application of fast-tracking and therefore could be somewhat correct. However, only Option A presents a complete correct statement and is therefore the best answer. Note that it is the responsibility of the project manager and team to explore the feasibility of crashing and fast-tracking, then choose the lowest cost and least risk alternatives. Note that crashing and fast-tracking are not always feasible.

3. __D__ This is a straightforward test of your ability to recognize the defined Inputs, the Tools & Techniques and the Outputs associated with the Develop Schedule process. Option D, *activity duration estimates* represents an Input to Develop Schedule, not an Output. Therefore, Option D is the correct (exception) answer.

4. <u>C</u>   This quiz question is intended to test your ability to identify and reinforce correct schedule development concepts. Option A is a true statement, *Completed project schedules are typically illustrated using bar charts (also called Gantt charts), milestone charts or dated network diagrams.* Option B is also a true statement: *There are two primary methods used to shorten schedules: crashing and fast-tracking.* Option C is not true: *Resource leveling heuristics <u>are not</u> necessarily used to reduce the number of estimated resources, and <u>do not</u> necessarily result in lower project costs.* Option D is a true statement: *Lead time and lag time allow project teams to add realism and flexibility to their schedule. Lead time may be viewed as an overlap between tasks. Lag time is waiting time.* Therefore, Option C is the correct (least true) answer.

5. <u>A</u>   This quiz question is intended to test your ability to identify the four most often used techniques to develop the project schedule. They are (1) Critical Path Method (CPM), (2) Resource Leveling, (3) Critical Chain Method, and (4) What-if Scenario Analysis. Therefore, answer Option A is correct. Option B includes GERT, PERT, and crashing. GERT and PERT are outmoded techniques and crashing is not a schedule development technique. Crashing is refinement technique, applied to compress (shorten) the schedule. Option C also includes GERT and PERT. Simulation (typically Monte Carlo based) is used to support What-if Scenario Analysis. Option D includes PERT and flowcharting, which is not a schedule development technique. A dated network diagram is sometimes used to illustrate the project schedule, and a network diagram may be considered a flowchart. However, flowcharting is not viewed as an accepted schedule development technique on its own.

6. <u>A</u>   This quiz question is intended to test your practical understanding of aspects of the Critical Path Method (CPM). Option B describes PERT, not CPM. PERT uses the weighted average of three estimates (three-point estimates) to determine durations. Option C describes simulation. Simulation involves running numerous computer simulations, using variable data, to determine durations. Option D is a blatantly false statement. CPM, PERT, GERT, and simulation are not the same. Option A accurately describes CPM as using one, single-point estimate to determine durations. Therefore, Option A is the correct (most correct) answer.

7. <u>C</u>   This quiz question is intended to test your ability to properly apply the PERT equation. The PERT equation is: (P + 4M + O) / 6, where P = the pessimistic estimate, M = the most probable estimate, and O = the optimistic estimate. In this question, the given variables yield the equation [14 + 4(9) + 6] / 6. When calculated, this gives us the correct PERT estimate of 9.33 (days). Therefore, Option C is the precise correct answer. Option A should be recognized as an unreasonable answer under any circumstances. This value is even lower than the optimistic estimate. Option B would appear correct if you ignored the PERT equation and simply accepted the most probable estimate. Option D would appear correct if you simply averaged the three estimates.

LESSON 18 DEVELOP HUMAN RESOURCE PLAN

1. <u>B</u>   This quiz question is designed to ensure that you understand the intended application of the Develop Human Resource Plan process. The Develop Human Resource Plan process is applied to develop, document, and assign project roles, responsibilities, and reporting relationships. Therefore, Option B is the correct answer. Options A and C represent activities you may perform during organizational planning, but they do not represent the primary purpose of applying the process. Option D more closely represents the description of quality planning, not organizational planning.

2. <u>D</u>   Option A is a true statement: In Matrix Organizations, project managers typically share responsibility and authority with functional managers. Option B is also a true statement: In strong Matrix Organizations, project managers may have more authority than functional managers. Option C is another true statement: Project managers in Functional Organizations may have very little authority and are often termed project coordinators or project expeditors. Option D is a false statement. To make it true, it would have to be revised to read: "In projectized organizations, the project manager typically assumes full profit/loss responsibility/authority and staffs the project with human resources dedicated to the project". The question asks us to identify the least true statement. Option D is the only false statement and is therefore the correct answer.

3. <u>B</u>   This is a question to test your knowledge of process Tools and Techniques. Answer B is the only completely correct answer. *PMBOK® Guide*, chapter 9.1.

LESSON 19 ESTIMATE COSTS

1. <u>B</u>   This quiz question is intended to help ensure that you have a general understanding of the *life cycle costing* concept. Answer Option B correctly defines it. Option A can be true for any term in the group of accounting terms, but it is not true for *life cycle costing*. Option C defines project *costs* in general. Option D generally defines *bottom-up* estimating.

2. <u>C</u>   This quiz question is intended to measure your knowledge of estimate allowances. The ROM range is ≠50%. *PMBOK® Guide*, chapter 7.1.

3. <u>C</u>   This is a straightforward test of your ability to recognize the defined Inputs, the Tools & Techniques, and the Outputs associated with the Estimate Costs process. Know that it is not necessary to memorize all Inputs, Tools & Techniques, and Outputs. In this question, Options A, B, and D include items that are not defined Estimate Costs Inputs, Tools/Techniques, or Outputs.

4.   <u>A</u>   This question asks you identify the *least* true statement. Options B, C, and D all represent clearly correct statements. Option A is false and therefore the correct answer. The cost baseline (or *budget*) is developed during the Determine Budget process, not during Estimate Costs.

5.   <u>C</u>   This question is a simple test to help ensure that you know *price* and *cost* are two different things. The question asks you to identify the *most* correct statement. Option A is clearly false, by definition. Option B is a misleading incorrect answer, but could appear reasonable to anyone who is not familiar with the differences. Option D is another incorrect misleading mismatch of terms.

6.   <u>A</u>   All PMP Exam questions require you to select the *best* answer. In some cases, all four options will appear reasonable, but one generally stands out as being the *best*. The same is true for this quiz question. Answer Options B, C, and D could be true under specific circumstances, but not always. Option A is true and correct in *all* circumstances, and therefore the best answer.

7.   <u>B</u>   A chart of accounts is often used to document, report, and track project costs, by category. The chart of accounts is a coding structure designed to capture cost information in an organized and generally accepted fashion. Option B fits the given definition and is therefore the correct answer. Option A *analogous estimating* does not fit the given definition, even remotely. Options C and D could be somewhat true, but one would have to stretch far to justify either as a possible correct answer.

8.   <u>D</u>   This is another question intended to reinforce a modern project management theme: *estimates should be developed by the person, or people, who are best qualified to prepare the estimates ... namely, the person, or people, who will be doing the actual work.* Only answer Option D can be correct.

9.   <u>C</u>   You are very likely to encounter the terms *analogous*, *top-down*, and *bottom-up* on your PMP Exam. This quiz question is intended to reinforce your familiarity with *bottom-up estimating*. Bottom-up estimating generally produces the most reliable estimates, but is more costly and time consuming than analogous estimating. Typically, bottom-up estimating is performed by developing detailed estimates for each activity at the Work Package level of the WBS. They are then rolled-up to derive a project total. Answer Option C satisfies the given definition and is therefore the correct answer. Options A, B, and D simply do not satisfy the given definition and are incorrect.

LESSON 20 DETERMINE BUDGET

1. <u>B</u> This quiz question is designed to ensure that you understand the intended application of the Determine Budget process. *The Determine Budget process is applied to formally organize all activity cost estimates into a cohesive project budget.* Therefore, Option B is the precise correct answer. Options A, C, and D all describe legitimate activities more closely associated with the Cost Estimating process, not Determine Budget. Note: You may have noticed a seeming inconsistency in the way we present process nomenclature. Sometimes you see a process with capital letters: Determine Budget. Other times, you may see it with small letters: determine budget. This is by design. One version refers to a process, the other an action. You should become familiar recognizing processes presented both ways, with capital letters and with small letters.

2. <u>C</u> This question is intended to test your understanding of *cost baseline. The cost baseline is a time-phased budget, used to monitor and measure project cost performance.* Therefore, Option C is precisely the best answer. Option A is a statement that is loosely associated with the cost control process, not the cost baseline. Option B describes the intended purpose of the cost management plan, not the cost baseline. Option D is simply a reasonable-sounding statement that actually makes little logical sense. Note the importance of all project baselines (scope baseline, schedule baseline, cost baseline) in establishing the planned objectives by which monitoring and performance will be measured throughout project execution and controlling phases. Note also that planned baselines should remain intact, regardless of changes made across the project life cycle. Only in extreme cases should a fundamental baseline change be considered.

3. <u>A</u> This is a straightforward test of your ability to recognize the defined Inputs, the Tools & Techniques, and the Outputs associated with the Determine Budget process. Options B, C, and D each correctly identifies one of the Determine Budget process Inputs. Option A, *cost performance baseline,* is an *Output* and is therefore the correct (exception) answer.

4. <u>A</u> This quiz question is intended to further test your understanding of *cost baseline.* Option A is exactly correct: *Cost baselines are typically illustrated using graphs. Plotted cost baselines usually form an S-curve appearance.* Option B is blatantly incorrect. Cost baselines, like all planned baselines, should not be subject to frequent changes. Option C more accurately describes the cost management plan, not the cost baseline. Option D more accurately describes the project schedule, not the cost baseline. Therefore, Option A is the best (most true) answer.

LESSON 21 PLAN QUALITY

1. **D** This quiz question is designed to ensure that you understand the intended application of the Plan Quality process. *The Plan Quality process is applied to identify which quality standards are applicable to the project, then determine how to satisfy them.* Therefore, Option D is the correct answer. Option A is simply incorrect. Option B could appear somewhat correct if the question was referring to the Quality Assurance process, but not for Plan Quality. *Quality improvement* is a defined Output of the Quality Assurance process. Therefore B is incorrect. Option C offers a distracting incorrect answer. While cause-and-effect diagrams are useful quality tools, there is not necessarily any such thing as a "project cause-and-effect diagram."

2. **B** This quiz question is intended to reinforce the modern project management theme: *Quality must be planned into a project, not inspected in.* Answer Option A is an outright false statement. *ISO 9000 is an international quality standard used by organizations to ensure adherence to their own quality policies. It is a brief document.* Options C and D are incorrect statements also. *Just in Time (JIT) is the manufacturing management concept/ practice of maintaining minimal inventory (ideally zero). Total Quality Management (TQM) is a concept/practice intended to help organizations achieve quality improvement objectives.* The question asks to identify the *most correct* statement. Option B is the only true statement, and therefore the correct answer.

3. **A** This is a straightforward test of your ability to recognize the defined Inputs, the Tools & Techniques, and the Outputs associated with the Plan Quality process. In this question, only Option A properly lists Plan Quality Tools/Techniques, and is therefore the best answer. Option B includes *quality baseline*, which is not a Tool/Technique. Option C includes *quality checklists*, which is an intended Output, not a Tool/Technique. Option D includes *quality metrics*, which is also an Output, not a Tool/Technique.

4. **D** This quiz question is intended to reinforce key quality terms and concepts. Option A is a correct statement. *Flowcharts (also termed "process maps" or "systems flowcharts") are graphical illustrations that show how elements of a system relate.* Option B is also correct. *Cause-and-effect diagrams (also termed "fishbone diagrams" or "Ishikawa diagrams") are often used to illustrate how different factors are linked to problems and are especially helpful in generating ideas and thinking when analyzing quality problems.* Option C is another correct statement. Cost of quality includes all costs expended to achieve product/service quality objectives. Option D is incorrect. *Grade is <u>not</u> another term for quality in some application areas. The two terms may <u>not</u> be used interchangeably.* This question asks you to identify the *least* true statement. Option D is the only false statement, and therefore the correct answer.

5. <u>C</u> This quiz question is intended to test your applied understanding of the term *benchmark* (or *benchmarking*). *Benchmarks are established standards and/or practices that may be used for comparison when the project team establishes its standards for measuring project performance.* Options A, B, and D can each appear to be reasonably correct, and arguments can be made to justify either of them as being correct. However, the given scenario describes the use of *benchmarking* much closer than *historical data*, *templates*, or *lessons learned*. Therefore, C is the best choice and the correct answer. This quiz question requires you to select the *best* answer. Many PMP Exam questions will feature correct statements for all four options. In these questions, your job is to select the *best* of the four.

6. <u>A</u> This quiz question is intended to test your applied understanding of quality in project management: *In project management, quality means delivering precisely what is promised. When a project team delivers on time, within budget, and has satisfied all scope requirements, then quality has been achieved.* Option A is the correct response. Options B, C, and D represent possible responses in some cases, but Option A is the best.

LESSON 22   PLAN RISK MANAGEMENT
· ·

1. <u>C</u> Project risk is formally defined as *any uncertain event or condition that, if it occurs, has a negative or positive effect on a project objective. Uncertain* is key in this definition. If an event or condition is certain, then it is not a risk. Only Option C fully satisfies the definition. Options A, B, and D represent partial, misleading, and incorrect answers.

2. <u>D</u> This question is intended to reinforce the important concept that project risks can be positive as well as negative. Positive risks are called *opportunities* and should be pursued. Negative risks are called *threats* and should be avoided. The question asks you to identify the most incorrect statement. Option A is a correct statement. Recall reading it in your *PMBOK Guide.* Option B is correct, reinforcing the point. Option C is also true, reinforcing the point. Option D is false (while we would certainly like to eliminate negative risks, it is not possible) and therefore the most incorrect statement.

3. <u>B</u> This is a straightforward test of your ability to recognize the defined Inputs, the Tools & Techniques, and the Outputs associated with the Plan Risk Management process. In this question, you are asked to identify the exception. Option A, *organizational process assets,* is indeed an Input. Option C, *the project scope statement,* is also an Input. Option D, the *communications management plan,* is another proper Input. Only Option B is incorrect, and therefore, the exception. The *risk management plan* is an Output, not an Input.

4. __A__ The six risk management processes are, in logical application order, (1) Plan Risk Management, (2) Identify Risks, (3) Perform Qualitative Risk Analysis, (4) Perform Quantitative Risk Analysis, (5) Plan Risk Responses, and (6) Monitor and Control Risks.

LESSON 23 IDENTIFY RISKS

1. __B__ This quiz question is designed to ensure that you understand the intended application of the Identify Risks process. The Identify Risks process is applied to (1) determine which risks may affect the project and (2) to document their characteristics. Therefore, Option B is the correct answer. Options A, C, and D are all legitimate objectives in project risk management, but not objectives of the Identify Risk process.

2. __A__ There are four recognized categories of project risk: technical risks (technical, quality, performance), project management risks, organizational risks, and external risks. Therefore, Option A is the correct answer. Options B, C, and D represent proper risk management terms, but they do not represent *risk categories*.

3. __D__ This is a straightforward test of your ability to recognize the defined Inputs, the Tools & Techniques, and the Outputs associated with the Identify Risks Process. Know that your PMP Exam will likely include only five or six questions that ask you to identify specific sets of Inputs, Tools & Techniques, and Outputs. In this question, Options A, B, and C all identify accepted Tools and Techniques. Therefore, Option D *all of the above* is the best answer.

4. __C__ This quiz question is intended to reinforce the modern project management theme: *Identifying risks is a process that should be encouraged frequently throughout the project life cycle. In many projects, new risks can surface daily.* Therefore, Option C is the best answer. Option A is directly contrary to the theme and incorrect. Option B is incorrect. Identify Risk should encourage participation by as many knowledgeable people as possible, inside and outside of the immediate project team. Option D is incorrect for the same reason Option B is incorrect.

5. __D__ This quiz question is intended to test your ability to identify diagramming techniques typically used to help identify risks. These techniques include: cause and effect diagrams (also termed "fishbone diagrams" or "Ishikawa diagrams"), systems flowcharts also termed "process maps") and influence diagrams. Options A, B and C all identify proper diagramming techniques. Therefore, D *all of the above* is the correct answer.

6. __B__ This quiz question is intended to test your ability to identify proper risk management terms. Indications that a risk has occurred, or is about to occur, are termed "triggers" (or *risk symptoms* or *warning signs*). Therefore, Option B is the correct answer. Options A, C, and D are proper risk management terms, but not in the context of the question.

7. <u>D</u> This quiz question is intended to reinforce the key definition of project risk. *Project risk is an uncertain event or condition that, if it occurs, has a positive or negative effect on a project objective. A risk has a <u>cause</u>, and if it occurs, a <u>consequence</u>.* Therefore, Option D is the correct answer. Options A, B, and C are simply incorrect.

LESSON 24   PERFORM QUALITATIVE RISK ANALYSIS

1. <u>D</u> This quiz question is designed to ensure that you understand the intended application of the Perform Qualitative Risk Analysis process. *The Perform Qualitative Risk Analysis process is applied to assess the impact and likelihood of identified risks. It is intended to help prioritize identified risks and identify those risks serious enough to warrant further analysis.* Option D defines the process perfectly and is therefore the correct answer. Option A is an incorrect hodgepodge of risk management terms. Option B defines the application of the Identify Risk process, not Qualitative Risk Analysis. Option C defines a portion of Quantitative Risk Analysis, not Qualitative Risk Analysis.

2. <u>D</u> This quiz question is intended to test your applied understanding of a probability/impact (P-I) risk rating matrix. *A probability/impact (P-I) risk rating matrix is a tool that combines both risk probability and risk impact into a single score. It is used to help determine qualitative risk rankings.* Option A is correct. It is a defined Tool/Technique. Option B is incorrect. It is not a defined process Output. Option C is also true. This is a proper definition for the P-I matrix. Therefore, Option D (*A and C*) is the best answer.

3. <u>B</u> This is a straightforward test of your ability to recognize the defined Inputs, the Tools & Techniques, and the Outputs associated with the Perform Qualitative Risk Analysis process. In this question, Options A, C, and D all identify defined Tools/Techniques. You may reference them directly on your Qualitative Risk Analysis process illustration. Option B *risk register* is an Input, not a Tool/Technique. This is the exception you were asked to identify in the quiz question, and therefore, the best answer.

4. <u>A</u> This is another quiz question intended to test your applied understanding of a probability/impact (P-I) risk rating matrix. Risks that are assessed with scores in the lower left portion of a typical P-I matrix indicate low-probability with low-impact. Risks that are assessed with scores in the upper right portion of a typical P-I matrix indicate high-probability with high-impact. Middle areas indicate high-low or low-high scores. Therefore, Option A is the only correct statement, and therefore the best answer.

5. <u>B</u> This is a quiz question designed to test your practical ability to use a simple probability/impact (P-I) risk rating matrix. To derive the correct answer, a simple multiplication calculation is necessary: $(0.3)(7) = 2.10$. Therefore, Option B is the best answer. Options A or C could appear to be correct answers if a math error is made.

6. <u>A</u>   This is another quiz question designed to test your practical ability to use a simple probability/impact (P-I) risk rating matrix. To derive the correct answer, two simple multiplication calculations are necessary: First, multiply the two highest chart values $(0.9)(10) = 9.0$. Second, multiply the two lowest chart values $(0.1)(1) = 0.1$. Answer Option A identifies the two correct values: $9, 0.1$. Options B, C, or D could appear to be correct answers if a math error is made.

7. <u>C</u>   This is yet another quiz question designed to test your practical ability to use a simple probability/impact (P-I) risk rating matrix. To derive the correct answer, you must back-fit the 0.1 score to find it is the result of a risk assessed with a probability of 0.1 and an impact of 1. With this example matrix, it is the only possible combination to derive a score of 0.1. Plotted, it appears in the lowest-left corner, signifying low-probability and low-impact. Therefore, Option C is the best answer.

LESSON 25   PERFORM QUANTITATIVE RISK ANALYSIS
. . . .

1. <u>D</u>   This quiz question is designed to ensure that you understand the intended application of the Perform Quantitative Risk Analysis process. *The Perform Quantitative Risk Analysis process is applied to* guide *the additional analysis of individual risks, to determine the numerical value of its probability of occurrence and the numerical value of its consequence on project objectives, should it occur.* Option D defines the process perfectly and is therefore the correct answer. Option A describes the application of Risk Management Planning. Option B describes the application of Identify Risk. Option C describes the application of Qualitative Risk Analysis.

2. <u>D</u>   This quiz question is intended to test your applied understanding of sensitivity analysis. *Sensitivity analysis is a simple risk analysis technique used to help make project decisions based on the general risk sensitivity of an organization, person, or group of people.* Based on the given scenario in this question, it appears that the primary rationale behind the sponsor's decision was the lower level of risk (by comparison), which satisfied her apparent risk-averse policies. This certainly fits the definition of sensitivity analysis. Option A is not a recognized risk management term. Option B could be correct in some situations, but it is not directly consistent with this particular scenario. Option C could also be correct in some situations, but is not consistent with this scenario. Option D *sensitivity analysis* is a proper risk management technique, it is consistent with the scenario, and therefore the best (correct) answer.

3. <u>C</u> This is a straightforward test of your ability to recognize the defined Inputs, the Tools & Techniques, and the Outputs associated with the Perform Quantitative Risk Analysis process. In this question, only Option C properly identifies Tools/Techniques, as asked. You may reference them directly on your Perform Quantitative Risk Analysis process illustration.

4. <u>D</u> This is a quiz question intended to test your understanding of (Monte Carlo) simulation. *Simulation is a quantitative analysis tool that can produce probability-based predictions for many project parameters. Monte Carlo algorithms provide the underlying engines in many of today's simulation software programs. Monte Carlo simulation works by running numerous simulations with project-specific information.* Options A, B, and C are all correct statements regarding Monte Carlo and simulation. Option D may appear to be somewhat true, if justification is stretched, but it is an awkward statement at best. This question asks to identify the *least* true statement. Option D qualifies as the best choice and is therefore the best answer.

5. <u>C</u> This quiz question is intended to test your practical understanding of EMV. *Expected Monetary Value Analysis (EMV) is a quantitative risk analysis tool. EMV is calculated by multiplying the value of each possible outcome by its probability of occurrence, then adding them all together. EMV = V (value $) × P (probability).* To select the correct answer to this quiz question, you must perform a series of simple calculations. Risk 1 = –$10,000 × 0.10 = –$1,000. Risk 2 = –$8,000 × 0.70 = –$5,600. Risk 3 = +$10,000 × 0.60 = +$6,000. Risk 4 = –$800 × 0.20 = –$160. Added together, the total equals -$760. (remember to recognize the plus and minus values associated with positive and negative risks).

LESSON 26 PLAN RISK RESPONSES

1. <u>B</u>   This quiz question is designed to ensure that you understand the intended application of the Plan Risk Responses process. *The Plan Risk Responses process is applied to develop options and determine actions to enhance opportunities (positive risks) and develop options and determine actions to reduce threats (negative risks).* Therefore, Option B is the correct answer. Options A, C, and D all represent incorrect variations of the proper definition. Notice how each of these incorrect answer options use legitimate terms, but in the wrong context, to act as distracters. Options A, C, or D could appear reasonable to someone who has only a cursory knowledge of the subject material.

2. <u>D</u>   This quiz question is intended to test your applied understanding of the risk response planning Tools/Techniques: avoidance, transference, mitigation, and acceptance. In this scenario, the team has opted to act on the risk by handing over direct responsibility to a party outside of the organization. The team has apparently negotiated a guarantee and a fixed price from the supplier. This indicates the supplier is willing to assume the consequence, if the risk occurs. This is all indicative of risk *transference.* Therefore, Option D is the best answer. Options A and B, *active/passive acceptance,* are not correct because the team is acting now on the risk. Acceptance typically involves advance contingency planning, but no immediate action. Option C *mitigation* is not correct, because contracting does not always reduce the impact or probability of a risk — it simply assigns the consequence elsewhere. Remember, transference does not eliminate the risk — it transfers the consequence, should it occur.

3. <u>A</u>   This is a straightforward test of your ability to recognize the defined Inputs, the Tools & Techniques, and the Outputs associated with the Plan Risk Responses process. Know that it is not necessary to memorize all Inputs, Tools & Techniques, and Outputs. In this question, only Option A correctly identifies process Outputs, as asked. Refer to your Plan Risk Responses process illustration.

4. <u>C</u>   This quiz question is intended to reinforce risk response planning key term definitions: Option A is a correct definition: *Contingency allowance (or contingency reserve) is a cost buffer or time buffer included in the project plan to compensate for risk and to help reduce the probability of overruns.* Option B is also a correct definition: *Residual risks are those risks that remain after response actions have been implemented.* Residual risks also include those risks that have been accepted. Option D is another correct definition: *Secondary risks are those risks that arise from the implementation of risk response actions.* Option C is an incorrect definition (the correct definition of *contingency allowance* was given in Option A). Therefore, Option C is the *least true* statement, and best answer.

LESSON 27   PLAN PROCUREMENTS

1. <u>C</u>   This quiz question is intended to test your applied understanding of SOWs. *The Contract Statement of Work (SOW) describes, in detail, the complete scope of work expected from the supplier, along with other applicable terms.* The scenario presented in this question describes the intended application of a statement of work (SOW). Therefore, Option C is the correct answer. Option A *work package* could seem reasonable to someone who does not understand SOW, but is incorrect. Option B *contractor's project charter* may also appear reasonable to some, but is incorrect in this question's context (note that an SOW can, in fact, serve as a contractor's project charter in some cases). Option D *risk transference* is the intent of the team's *buy decision*, but does not properly describe the "document," as asked.

2. <u>A</u>   This quiz question is designed to help ensure that you understand the intended application of the Plan Procurements process. Option A is the only true statement and therefore the best answer. Option B is incorrect in that the make-or-buy decision analysis includes all costs (direct and indirect). Option C is incorrect in that the amount of risk that is shared between buyer and seller is determined by the type of contract implemented between the parties. Option D provides an incorrect definition of the procurement management plan — the selection of a seller for a particular item is accomplished in the Conduct Procurements process.

3. <u>D</u>   This quiz question is intended to reinforce *contract types*. Options A, B, and C are all correct descriptions of their respective contract types. Option D is incorrect. The last portion of this statement indicates that fixed price contracts can *increase* cost risk to the buyer. The exact opposite is true. Fixed price contracts can *reduce* overall project cost risk for the buyer. Therefore, Option D is the *least true* statement, and the correct answer.

4. <u>A</u>   This is a straightforward test of your ability to recognize the defined Inputs, the Tools & Techniques, and the Outputs associated with the Plan Procurements process. The Outputs associated with the Plan Procurement process include procurement management plan, procurement statements of work, make-or-buy decisions, procurement documents, source selection criteria, and change requests. Option A best represents the Outputs and therefore is the preferred answer.

5. <u>C</u>   This quiz question is intended to test your applied understanding of *source selection criteria*. Consistent evaluation criteria give the project team a fair and consistent basis from which to compare prospective suppliers. Some project teams establish numerical rating systems to evaluate bids. Many times, price is not the only consideration in selecting a vendor. Financial stability, technical depth, management depth, and understanding of scope may all be important considerations to factor. A low price bidder will not serve the project very well if they have poor financial stability and go out of business during project execution. Option C is the best choice, and the best answer.

LESSON 28 DEVELOP PROJECT MANAGEMENT PLAN

. . . .

1. <u>C</u>   This quiz question is designed to ensure that you understand the intended application of the Develop Project Management Plan process. *The Develop Project Management Plan process is applied to gather the Outputs from all other planning processes and assemble them into a single, cohesive document, the project plan.* Therefore, Option C is the precise correct answer. Options A, B, and D are all partially true, but describe only portions of the process. Option C is the only complete choice.

2. <u>D</u>   The project management plan is used to document project planning decisions, strategies, alternatives, and assumptions. It serves as the baseline for monitoring and measuring project performance during the project's execution, monitoring and controlling, and closing phases. The project management plan also serves to guide all aspects of the project through execution, monitoring and controlling, and closing. Therefore, Options A, B, and C are all equally true statements, making Option D *all of the above* the best answer.

3. <u>C</u>   This quiz question is a straightforward choice between Inputs and Tools. Choices A, B, and D are Inputs (B is part of Organizational Process Assets, D is part of Enterprise Environmental Factors).

4. <u>A</u>   This quiz question is intended to reinforce the modern project management concept: *Plans should be sized in sensible proportion to the size and complexity of the project.* Option A correctly communicates this concept and is therefore the best answer. Options B and C both contradict the proper concept. Based on the incorrectness of Options B and C, answer Option D *all of the above* cannot be correct.

5. <u>C</u>   This quiz question is designed to ensure that your understanding of the component plans of the project management plan. Option C, Scope Verification Plan, is not a valid plan created during the Planning process.

LESSON 29 EXECUTING

The following processes are correctly depicted as residing in the Executing Process Group. Reference *PMBOK® Guide*, chapter 3, table 3.1.

Project Integration Management	Direct and Manage Project Execution
Project Scope Management	None
Project Time Management	None
Project Cost Management	None
Project Quality Management	Perform Quality Assurance
Project Human Resource Management	Acquire Project Team
	Develop Project Team
	Manage Project Team
Project Communications Management	Distribute Information
	Manage Stakeholder Expectations
Project Risk Management	None
Project Procurement Management	Conduct Procurements

LESSON 30 DIRECT AND MANAGE PROJECT EXECUTION

1. <u>C</u>   This quiz question is designed to ensure that you understand change requests. Options A, B, and D are all characteristics of a change request. Option C, while it may be true for a particular change request, is not indicative of all change requests and therefore is the (exception) answer to this question.

2. <u>A</u>   This quiz question is designed to ensure that you understand conflict resolution techniques and their impacts. Bargaining (Compromising) is the technique where each side in the conflict resolution must compromise or give up something in order to come to resolution.

3. <u>D</u>   Options A, B, and C all represent perfectly true statements. Option D is not true. Work authorization systems are used primarily to manage and control scope, not to account for spending. Therefore, Option D is the preferred (least true) answer.

4. <u>B</u>   This is a straightforward test of your ability to recognize the defined Inputs, Tools & Techniques, and the Outputs associated with the Direct and Manage Project Execution process. Option B is the only answer which correctly identifies two Outputs and is therefore the preferred answer.

5. <u>A</u>   This quiz question is intended to test your ability to recognize characteristics associated with different sources of leadership power. Expert

power is a type of power earned when the leader is respected as a successful expert in his/her specialty. The scenario described in this question perfectly satisfies the definition of expert power. Therefore, Option A is the correct answer. Options B, C, and D are correct types of leadership power, but do not represent the type of earned power described in the scenario.

6. <u>D</u> This quiz question is designed to reinforce the fact that resources in a project are not just people. Resources include people, physical space (meeting rooms), and equipment (PCs, assembly machines); therefore Option D is the correct answer.

LESSON 31 ACQUIRE PROJECT TEAM

1. <u>D</u> This quiz question is designed to ensure that you understand the intended application of the Acquire Project Team process. *The Acquire Project Team process is applied to obtain and assign needed human resources (people) to the project.* Options A and B are somewhat true, but not complete. Option C better describes the Plan Human Resources process, not Acquire Project Team. Option D is the preferred answer.

2. <u>C</u> Option A is a true statement: *In matrix organizations, project managers may have to negotiate with functional managers to obtain needed people.* Option B is true: *In strong matrix organizations, project managers may have more authority than functional managers.* Option D is also true: *A Responsibility Assignment Matrix (RAM) illustrates assignments and levels of authority/responsibility, as a function of WBS elements. There is no time associated with a RAM.* Option C is false and therefore the preferred answer (least true): *In functional organizations, it is <u>not necessarily</u> the project sponsor's responsibility to assign project staff.*

3. <u>B</u> This is a straightforward case of choosing the correct tools for this process. Option B cites two of the four tools used by this process. All other answers have at least one correct tool along with distracting information.

4. <u>B</u> This quiz question is intended to reinforce acceptable reasons why staff may be assigned early. Option B is a legitimate reason: specific staff members may be proposed in competitive bids before a contract is ever awarded, thereby identifying project staff, if the bid is won. Note: Options A, C, and D represent unacceptable reasons, but more importantly they represent *unvalidated assumptions.*

LESSON 32   DEVELOP PROJECT TEAM

1.   C   In this question you are asked to choose the option that is not an Input to the process. Team Building activities are a Tool to be used in the process, not an Input.

2.   B   This quiz question is designed to ensure that you understand the intended application of the Develop Project Team process. *Develop Project Team is the process of enhancing the ability of individual team members to enhance overall project performance.* Therefore, Option B is the preferred answer. Options A, C, and D could be correct statements in some, but not all, situations.

3.   C   This question calls on your general management knowledge to choose the correct selection. The highest level of need under Maslow's Hierarchy of Need is self-actualization. All other answers are distracters.

4.   C   This quiz question is intended to test your understanding of some of the potential challenges faced by project managers in different types of organizations. Options A, B, and D represent incorrect statements. In Option A, colocation *can* involve moving team members (sometimes even team members' families) to/from different parts of the world. In Option B, team development is nearly always more challenging in functional organizations, where resources are typically borrowed on a temporary basis. In Option D, team development procedures typically represent far too much detail for inclusion in the project charter. Option C is exactly true and is therefore the preferred (most true) answer.

LESSON 33   MANAGE PROJECT TEAM

1.   B   This is a straightforward test of your ability to recognize the defined Inputs, the Tools & Techniques, and the Outputs associated with the Manage Project Team process. The Inputs associated with the Manage Project Team process include project staff assignments, project management plan, team performance assessments, performance reports, and organizational process assets. Option B best represents the Inputs and therefore is the preferred answer.

2.   B   This quiz question is intended to test your knowledge of the intended application of the Manage Project Team process. Options A, C, and D are all false statements. Answer Option B which defines an Issue Log is true and therefore the best answer.

3.   C   This quiz question is designed to help ensure that you understand the intended application of the Manage Project Team process. *The Manage Project Team process is applied to address performance, behavior, issues, and conflicts associated specifically with project team members.* Therefore,

Option C is the preferred answer. Options A, B, and D are more closely associated with the Develop Project Team process. Only Option C provides a complete, accurate description of the Manage Project Team process.

LESSON 34   PERFORM QUALITY ASSURANCE

1. <u>A</u>   This quiz question is designed to ensure that you understand the intended application of the Perform Quality Assurance process. *The Perform Quality Assurance process is applied to provide confidence that the project will satisfy relevant quality standards.* Therefore, Option A is the preferred answer. Options B and C are not correct because the Perform Quality Assurance process is not intended to *measure* any parameters. Measurement is associated more closely with the controlling process Perform Quality Control. Option D is not correct because Perform Quality Assurance in the project management context is primarily concerned with project management processes, not the product/service of the project.

2. <u>A</u>   This question is intended to test your ability to recognize with whom the responsibility for project quality lies. While various team members and/or organizational groups may support project quality objectives, overall project quality is the responsibility of the project manager. Therefore, Option A is the preferred answer.

3. <u>B</u>   This is a straightforward test of your ability to recognize the defined Inputs, the Tools & Techniques, and the Outputs associated with the Perform Quality Assurance process. Only Option B correctly identifies one of the four defined Perform Quality Assurance Outputs, and therefore represents the preferred answer.

4. <u>D</u>   This quiz question is intended to reinforce critical project quality concepts. Option A is a true statement: *Quality Assurance (QA) is the collective total of all activities intended to ensure the project satisfies recognized quality requirements.* Option B is another true statement: *Quality activities should be applied across the entire project life cycle.* Option C is also a true statement: *Process improvement is sometimes termed Kaizen, representing the quality philosophy of achieving improvement via small incremental steps.* Option D is not true: *Process improvement is focused on improving project performance (to increase stakeholder value), <u>not</u> improving functionality of the product of the project.* Option D is therefore the preferred (least true) answer.

LESSON 35   DISTRIBUTE INFORMATION

1. <u>B</u>   This quiz question is designed to help ensure that you understand the intended application of the Distribute Information process. *Distribute Information is the communications process of making project information available to project stakeholders, as determined and documented in the communications management plan.* Therefore, Option B is the preferred answer. Option A is not complete, because it is limited to project performance reports. Option C is not complete, because it is limited to earned value reports. Option D is not complete, because it is limited to presentations.

2. <u>C</u>   This is a long situational type question that is intended to test your understanding of a simple communication concept: *Communication is a two-way process. Communication is not complete until the sender verifies that the receiver has received the communication, and understood it as intended by the sender.* Based on this, Option C represents the best, most complete, answer. Options A and D, while partially true, both contradict the proper concept. Option B is much closer to the best answer, but omits the need to verify the communication being understood as intended. Verifying physical receipt is just one part of the two-part equation.

3. <u>D</u>   This is a simple question that asks you to choose which of the choices is incorrect. Communications Methods would be a Tool for this process.

LESSON 36   MANAGE STAKEHOLDER EXPECTATIONS

1. <u>C</u>   This quiz question is designed to help ensure that you understand the intended application of the Manage Stakeholder Expectations process. *The Manage Stakeholder Expectations process is applied to satisfy the needs of project stakeholders and to resolve issues with project stakeholders.* Therefore, Option C represents the preferred answer. Options A, B, and D represent remotely true statements. Only Option C provides a complete, accurate description of the Manage Stakeholder Expectations process.

2. <u>B</u>   This question tests your ability to recognize that an immediate face-to-face meeting directly with the other party is always the preferred method in issue/conflict resolution situations … opposed to e-mails, phone calls, or other less direct approaches. Therefore, Option B represents the preferred answer.

3. <u>C</u>   This is a straightforward test of your ability to recognize the defined Inputs, the Tools & Techniques, and the Outputs associated with the Manage Stakeholder Expectations process. Manage Stakeholder Expectations Tools & Techniques include (1) communications methods and (2) interpersonal skills.

Only Option B correctly identifies these defined process Tools/Techniques and is therefore the preferred answer.

LESSON 37   CONDUCT PROCUREMENTS

1. <u>A</u>   This is a straightforward test of your ability to recognize the defined Inputs, the Tools & Techniques, and the Outputs associated with the Conduct Procurements process. The Tools & Techniques associated with the Conduct Procurements process include bidder conferences, proposal evaluation techniques, independent estimates, expert judgment, advertising, and Internet search and procurement negotiations. Option A, *bidder conferences*, is the only correct Tool/Technique of the Conduct Procurements process and is therefore the preferred answer.

2. <u>C</u>   This quiz question is intended to reinforce the intended application of the Conduct Procurements process. The Conduct Procurements process is the process of obtaining seller responses, selecting seller(s), and awarding contracts. A key Tool/Technique in this process is bidder conference, which ensures that all prospective sellers are provided with the same information so procurements are made in a fair and impartial manner.

3. <u>B</u>   This quiz question is intended to reinforce the intended application of the Conduct Procurements process. The Conduct Procurements process is the process of obtaining seller responses, selecting seller(s), and awarding contracts. Option A describes the Plan Procurements process. Options C and D are somewhat correct; however Option A provides the most detailed description of the Conduct Procurements process and is therefore the preferred answer.

LESSON 38   MONITORING AND CONTROLLING

The following processes are correctly depicted as residing in the Monitoring and Controlling Process Group. Reference *PMBOK® Guide*, chapter 3, table 3.1.

Project Integration Management	Monitor and Control Project Work
	Perform Integrated Change Control
Project Scope Management	Verify Scope
	Control Scope
Project Time Management	Control Schedule
Project Cost Management	Control Costs
Project Quality Management	Perform Quality Control
Project Human Resource Management	None
Project Communications Management	Report Performance
Project Risk Management	Monitor and Control Risks
Project Procurement Management	Administer Procurements

LESSON 39   CONTROL SCOPE

1.   <u>A</u>   This question is intended to test your practical judgment in recognizing legitimate reasons for scope change. Options B, C, and D each present a valid reason for considering/justifying scope change. Option A represents a situation that has nothing to do with project scope. Therefore, Option A is the preferred (exception) answer.

2.   <u>C</u>   This is a straightforward test of your ability to recognize the defined Inputs, the Tools & Techniques, and the Outputs associated with the Control Scope process. Option C, change requests, is actually an Output of the Control Scope process.

3.   <u>D</u>   Options A, B, and C are all true statements. Option D is a false statement and provides the best answer for this question.

4.   <u>D</u>   This quiz question is designed to ensure that you understand the intended application of the Control Scope process. *Control Scope is the process of effectively managing changes in project scope, then integrating those changes with other control processes across the entire project.* Therefore, Option D is the preferred answer. Option A is simply a false statement. Option B describes the Develop Project Management Plan process, not the scope change control process. Option C is another blatantly false statement.

5.   <u>B</u>   This is an order-of-priority type question. In these type questions, all options may represent correct actions, but only one is the best first action. In this question, Options A, B, and C all represent reasonable actions with respect to change control. Option D is the only false statement (the sponsor review requirement, as well as your authority to approve changes, are unvalidated assumptions). Upon closer examination of Options A, B, and C, B should logically surface as the best first priority. It stands to reason that the first priority in change control is to discourage unnecessary change requests in the first place. Placing this priority first (directly at the source) will help reduce the overall number of change requests, and the need for subsequent actions. Therefore Option B represents the preferred answer.

LESSON 40   CONTROL SCHEDULE

1.   <u>A</u>   This quiz question is designed to help ensure that you understand the intended application of the Control Schedule process. *Control Schedule is the process of effectively managing changes to the project schedule baseline, then integrating those changes with other control processes across the entire project.* Therefore, Option A is the preferred answer. Options B, C, and D represent remotely true statements. Only Option A provides a complete, accurate description of schedule control.

2.   <u>A</u>   This question tests your understanding of a schedule change control system. *A schedule change control system is intended to provide the procedural guidance by which the schedule may be changed.* Option A is therefore the best and preferred answer.

3.   <u>C</u>   This is a straightforward test of your ability to recognize the defined Inputs, the Tools & Techniques, and the Outputs associated with the Control Schedule process. Options A, B, and D each correctly identifies one of the eight defined Control Schedule Tools/Techniques. Option C, *project schedule*, is a process Input, not a Tool/Technique. Therefore, Option C is the preferred (exception) answer.

LESSON 41   CONTROL COSTS

1.   <u>A</u>   This quiz question is designed to help ensure that you understand the intended application of the Control Costs process. *Control Costs is the process of effectively managing changes to the cost baseline, then integrating those changes with other control processes across the entire project.* Therefore Option A is the correct answer. Options B, C, and D are all somewhat true, but not as complete and accurate as Option A.

2.   <u>D</u>   This is a judgment question. With respect to proper cost control, Option D represents the most reasonable statement, and is therefore the

correct answer. Options A, B, and C would all require validating the stated assumptions to be considered true. Remember, answer options that include unvalidated assumptions should be rejected.

3. <u>A</u> This question tests your understanding of a cost change control system. *A cost change control system is intended to provide the procedural guidance by which cost change requests will be managed.* Option A is therefore the best and preferred answer.

4. <u>D</u> This is a straightforward test of your ability to recognize the defined Inputs, the Tools & Techniques, and the Outputs associated with the Control Costs process. Options A, B, and C each identify one of the six defined Control Costs Tools/Techniques. Option D, Cost Change Control System is not a toll/technique. Therefore, Option D is the preferred (exception) answer.

5. <u>D</u> Variance at Completion (VAC) is determined by applying the equation, VAC = BAC – EAC. In this question, BAC (total planned budget) is given as $850,000. EAC is determined by applying the equation EAC = BAC / CPI. CPI is determined by applying the equation, CPI = EV / AC. In this question, EV is $425,000 (50% of the work is complete and 50% of the total planned budget is $425,000). AC is given as $600,000 (the actual cost of work completed). Now we have all the variables necessary to complete the VAC calculation. CPI = $425,000 / $600,000 = 0.708. EAC = $850,000 / 0.708 = $1,200,560. VAC = $850,000 – $1,200,560 = –$350,560 . Note that calculated values on the PMP Exam typically use 'rounding' for large numerical values. Option D (–$350,000) is therefore the correct answer. This answer generally indicates the project will be over budget by roughly $350,000 at completion.

6. <u>C</u> This is another deceptively easy question. Earned value (EV or BCWP) is given directly in the question as $6,000. No calculations are necessary to identify the correct answer, Option C.

7. <u>D</u> Schedule Performance Index (SPI) is determined by applying the equation, SPI = EV / PV. Therefore, Option D is the correct answer. Remember EV and BCWP are interchangeable terms. PV and BCWS are also interchangeable.

8. <u>D</u> Schedule Variance (SV) is determined by applying the equation, SV = EV – PV. Cost Variance (CV) is determined by applying the equation, CV = EV – AC. In this question, EV (BCWP) is given as $650,000. PV (BCWS) is given as $750,000. AC (ACWP) is given as $800,000. Therefore, SV = $650,000 – $750,000 = –$100,000. CV = $650,000 – $800,000 = –$150,000. Option D is the correct answer. This answer generally indicates the project is behind schedule, and over budget by $150,000.

9. <u>B</u> Estimate to Complete (ETC) is determined by applying the equation, ETC = EAC – AC. AC (ACWP) is given as $600,000. EAC was calculated earlier, in quiz question 5, as $1,200,560. Therefore, ETC = $1,200,560 – $600,000 = $600,560. Rounded, Option B presents the best correct answer.

This answer generally indicates that roughly $600,000 is needed to complete the project from this point forward.

LESSON 42   REPORT PERFORMANCE

1. <u>D</u>   The Report Performance process relies heavily on preparing and disseminating project performance status reports and forecasts, most using earned value analysis (EVA). Your PMP Exam will likely feature five or six questions to test your understanding of earned value analysis, especially with respect to associated equations, calculations, and analysis. In this question, EAC is determined by applying the equation, $EAC = BAC / CPI$. Therefore, Option D is the preferred answer.

2. <u>D</u>   Schedule Variance (SV) is determined by applying the equation, $SV = EV - PV$ (or $BCWP - BCWS$). In this question, EV (BCWP) = 3,000. PV (BCWS) = 4,000. Therefore, SV = –1,000, making Option D the correct answer. Note that ACWS, although given, is not needed to perform the calculation. Note all of the extraneous information in this quiz question.

3. <u>A</u>   Budgeted Cost of Work Performed (BCWP) is an alternate term for Earned Value (EV). In this question, Earned Value is given as $8,000. Therefore, Option A is the correct answer. No calculation is necessary. This is not a trick question. It is designed to challenge your confidence.

4. <u>D</u>   Cost Performance Index (CPI) is a measure of project cost efficiency. A CPI value greater than 1 indicates under-budget performance. Less than 1 indicates over-budget performance. The actual value may be used to determine the degree of over/under performance. In this question, the given CPI of 1.13 indicates under-budget performance, yielding a positive cost efficiency that may be interpreted as getting $1.13 for each dollar planned/invested. Therefore, Option D is the preferred answer.

LESSON 43   PERFORM QUALITY CONTROL

1. <u>D</u>   This quiz question is designed to help ensure that you understand the intended application of the Perform Quality Control process. *The Perform Quality Control process is applied to monitor specific project results to ensure they comply with the project's quality standards.* Option D describes the process precisely this way and is therefore the preferred answer. Options A and C are somewhat true, but not as complete or accurate as D. Option B is not true.

2. <u>D</u> The PMP Exam will require you to understand a few statistical QC fundamentals. This question tests your understanding of certain characteristics of typical QC control charts, specifically Upper Control Limit (UCL) and Lower Control Limit (LCL). Option D correctly describes UCL and LCL and is therefore the preferred answer. Specification Limits, as alluded to in Options A, B, and C, are not the same as UCL and LCL. Specification Limits are generally further away from the mean (average) than LCLs and UCLs.

3. <u>D</u> This is a straightforward test of your ability to recognize the defined Inputs, the Tools & Techniques, and the Outputs associated with the Perform Quality Control process. Options A, B, and C each correctly identifies a defined process Tool/Technique. Option D, *quality metrics*, is a process Input, not a Tool/Technique. Therefore, Option D is the preferred (exception) answer.

4. <u>B</u> This quiz question is intended to test your general understanding of standard deviation (sigma) with respect to project quality control. *Standard deviation in project quality control is a measure of how far you are from a determined mean (average)*. Therefore, Option B is the preferred answer. Options A, C, and D represent statements that may seem somewhat reasonable at first glance. But upon closer examination, each should be recognized as inaccurate.

5. <u>C</u> This is another question intended to test your understanding of certain quality control chart characteristics, specifically *out-of-control*. Generally, an out-of-control condition exists when a data point falls outside an established Upper or Lower Control Limit or when seven or more consecutive data points fall on one side of the mean (above or below) (*rule of seven*). In this question, Option C best describes an out-of-control condition and is therefore the preferred answer. Options A and B are simply not true. Option D could appear reasonable at first, but upon closer examination it describes only one data point. The rule of seven involves seven consecutive data points.

6. <u>A</u> This quiz question tests your ability to identify the correct values associated with 1 sigma, 2 sigma, 3 sigma, and 6 sigma. In this question, only Option A is correct. For project Quality Control purposes, 1 sigma = ±68.26%, 2 sigma = ±95.46%, 3 sigma = ±99.73%, and 6 sigma = ±99.99%.

7. <u>D</u> This quiz question is intended to help reinforce critical project quality control concepts. Option A is true: *Prevention over inspection is a preferred project quality concept*. Option B is also true: *Pareto diagrams typically identify the 20% of all possible root causes that are responsible for 80% of the problems*. Option C is another true statement: *Project QC monitors both product-related deliverables (work packages) and project management deliverables (cost/schedule/scope performance)*. Option D (*Statistical sampling is a QC technique that requires inspection of only 50%, instead of 100% of the population, thus reducing testing time by half.*) is not true. While statistical

sampling is a valid technique that can save time and money, the actual percentage of items sampled is determined using statistical analysis, not fixed to the 50% suggested in this answer option. Therefore, Option D is the preferred (least true) answer.

LESSON 44   VERIFY SCOPE

1. <u>A</u>   This quiz question is designed to reinforce the difference between Verify Scope and Perform Quality Control. It is important to know the difference between the two. Scope verification focuses on the formal acceptance of the project deliverable while quality control focuses on the how the deliverables meet quality requirements.

2. <u>D</u>   This is a straightforward test of your ability to recognize the defined Inputs, the Tools & Techniques, and the Outputs associated with the Verify Scope process. Option D, scope management plan is not one of the Inputs related to the Verify Scope process.

3. <u>C</u>   This quiz question is designed to help ensure that you understand the intended application of the Verify Scope process. *Scope verification is the process of obtaining <u>formal acceptance</u> of project deliverables.* Therefore, Option C is the correct answer. Options B and D erroneously allude to verifying the "correctness" of project deliverables. Verify Scope is applied to obtain *formal acceptance*, not verify correctness. It is possible to correctly complete a deliverable, but fail to obtain formal acceptance … and vice-versa. Option A wrongly alludes to guiding parallel performance.

LESSON 45   MONITOR AND CONTROL RISKS

1. <u>C</u>   This quiz question is designed to ensure that you understand the intended application of the Monitor and Control Risks process. *The risk monitoring and control process is applied to monitor identified risks, identify new risks, ensure proper execution of the Risk Response Plan, and evaluate overall effectiveness of the risk management plan in reducing risk.* Therefore, Option C is the correct answer. Options B and D are more descriptive of the risk response planning process, not risk monitoring and control. Option A is somewhat correct, but only partially. Only Option C describes risk monitoring and control completely and accurately.

2. <u>C</u>   This question tests your understanding of the term *workaround. A workaround is a response to an unanticipated risk event, typically executed after the risk event occurs.* Therefore, Option best C satisfies the proper response to the scenario presented in this question, and is the correct answer. Note that Option A describes going to your sponsor for guidance. You should begin to take note that issues, problems, and challenges should

be handled at the project level. Only very significant issues (that can't be resolved at the project level) should be escalated to the sponsor level.

3.　A　This is a straightforward test of your ability to recognize the defined Inputs, the Tools & Techniques, and the Outputs associated with the Monitor and Control Risks process. Only Option A correctly identifies defined process Tools/Techniques, as asked, and is therefore the preferred answer.

4.　A　This quiz question is intended to help reinforce critical risk monitoring and control concepts. Option B is true: *Project team members and stakeholders should be vigilant in looking for risk symptoms, as well as for new project risks.* Option C is also true: *Risk monitoring is intended to be a daily, ongoing process across the entire project life cycle, from project start to project finish.* Option D is another true statement: *Workarounds (or workaround plans) are responses to unanticipated (surprise) risk events after they occur.* Option A (*Unanticipated risks that occur during project plan execution must be ignored, because no advance plans exist to deal with them. The project must simply accept the consequences.*) is not true. Risks can be accepted, mitigated, avoided, and/or transferred, but they cannot be ignored. Therefore, Option A is the preferred (least true) answer.

LESSON 46　ADMINISTER PROCUREMENTS

1.　C　This quiz question is designed to help ensure that you understand the intended application of the Administer Procurements process. *The Administer Procurements process is applied to ensure that the seller's performance satisfies contractual obligations.* Therefore, Option C is the correct answer. Options A, B, and D are all somewhat true, but not as complete and precise as Option C.

2.　D　This question is intended to test your judgment. There is no clear, right or wrong, reference to cite here. However, proper thinking is intended to have you arrive at the conclusion that, *with a well-defined scope of work,* the need for contractual changes should be minimal. In this question scenario, the well-defined scope of work should significantly mitigate the only identified risk with this particular seller. Therefore, Option D is probably the best response. Options A and B represent unvalidated assumptions and may be rejected (remember … you can confidently reject answer options that present unvalidated assumptions). Option C represents a position of mistrust, a position that should never be knowingly entered.

3.　C　This is a straightforward test of your ability to recognize the defined Inputs, the Tools & Techniques, and the Outputs associated with the Administer Procurements process. Options A, B, and D each correctly identifies one of the six defined Administer Procurements Inputs, as asked.

Option C, *change requests*, represents a process Output, not an Input. Therefore, Option C is the preferred (exception) answer.

4. <u>A</u>   This question is intended to reinforce critical project procurement concepts. Option B is a true statement: If *a contract is well-planned and negotiated, then the need for contract changes should be minimized.* Option C is another true statement: *Contract changes that will lead to improved project performance should be facilitated, but in accordance with the project's change control system.* Option D is also a true statement: *Unnecessary contract changes should be discouraged.* Option A (*Once negotiated and executed, a buyer/ seller contract becomes a legally binding agreement and cannot be changed*) is not true. While contracts *are* legally binding agreements, they may certainly be changed, if both parties agree. Therefore, Option A is the preferred (least true) answer.

LESSON 47   MONITOR AND CONTROL PROJECT WORK

1. <u>C</u>   This quiz question is designed to help ensure that you understand the intended application of the Monitor and Control Project Work process. *The Monitor and Control Project Work process is applied to (1) monitor all other processes through initiation, planning, executing and closing and (2) take/make corrective/preventive actions, as needed.* Therefore, Option C is the preferred answer. Options A, B, and D are all somewhat true, but not as complete and precise as Option C.

2. <u>B</u>   This question is intended to test your understanding of "preventive action." *Preventive actions are actions required to reduce the probability of negative consequences associated with project risks.* Option B best describes the actions presented in the root question, and is therefore the preferred answer.

3. <u>C</u>   This is a straightforward test of your ability to recognize the defined Inputs, the Tools & Techniques, and the Outputs associated with the Monitor and Control Project Work process. Monitor and Control Project Work Outputs include: (1) change requests, (2) project management plan updates, and (3) project document updates. Only Option C correctly identifies process Outputs, as asked, and therefore represents the preferred answer.

LESSON 48   PERFORM INTEGRATED CHANGE CONTROL

1.   <u>C</u>   This question is designed to test your understanding of the Perform Integrated Change Control process' interrelation with the project life cycle. The Perform Integrated Change Control process is conducted from the beginning to the end of a project. Answer Option C, project life cycle, best reflects this timeframe and therefore is the preferred answer.

2.   <u>D</u>   This is a straightforward test of your ability to recognize the defined Inputs, the Tools/Techniques, and the Outputs associated with the Perform Integrated Change Control process. Answer Options A, B, and C each correctly identifies defined process Outputs. Option D, change control meetings, is a Tools/Techniques associated with Perform Integrated Change Control. Therefore, Option D is the exception (correct) answer.

3.   <u>B</u>   This quiz question is designed to help ensure that you understand the intended applications of the Perform Integrated Change Control process. Perform Integrated Change Control is the process of effectively managing changes and integrating them appropriately across the entire project. Option B describes the process precisely this way and is therefore the preferred answer. Options A, C, and D are all somewhat true, but incomplete compared to Option B.

LESSON 50   CLOSE PROCUREMENTS

1.   <u>B</u>   This quiz question is designed to help ensure that you understand the intended application of the Close Procurements process. *Close Procurements is the procurement process of formally accepting and closing contracted work.* Therefore, Option B is the preferred answer. Options A, C, and D could all be somewhat correct statements in some situations, but certainly not universally. Only Option B provides a complete and accurate description of the contract closeout process.

2.   <u>C</u>   This question further tests your understanding of activities typically associated with the Close Procurements process. Option A is true: *Close Procurements is performed by verifying that contracted work was completed correctly and contract terms and conditions were satisfied.* Option B is true: *During Close Procurements, formal acceptance is documented and contract records are archived.* Option D is true: *Close Procurements is applied only if services/supplies are contracted/purchased to support the project.* Option C (*Close Procurements is applied once, at the very end of the final project phase, like all closing processes*) is not true. Close Procurements must be applied to formally end every project contract, regardless of the number of contracts or

the point in time when each ends. Therefore, Option C is the preferred (least true) answer.

3. <u>A</u>   This is a straightforward test of your ability to recognize the defined Inputs, the Tools/Techniques, and the Outputs associated with the Close Procurements process. There are only two defined Close Procurements Tools/Techniques: (1) procurement audits and (2) records management system. Only Option A identifies one of these two defined Tools/Techniques, and therefore represents the preferred answer.

LESSON 51   CLOSE PROJECT OR PHASE

1. <u>D</u>   This quiz question is designed to help ensure that you understand the intended application of the Close Project or Phase process. *The Close Project or Phase process is applied to formally end either the project or project phase.* Therefore, Option D is the preferred answer. Options A and B are true statements, but not complete descriptions. Option C better describes the Close Procurements process, not the Close Project or Phase process.

2. <u>B</u>   This question is intended to reinforce the concept that administrative closure is applied to formally end *each* phase in the project life cycle, not just the end of the entire project. Based on this, Option B best describes the concept, and is therefore the preferred answer. Options A and D are blatantly false. Option C is true, but not complete.

3. <u>C</u>   This is a straightforward test of your ability to recognize the defined Inputs, the Tools & Techniques, and the Outputs associated with the Close Project or Phase process. There is only one tool, expert judgment. Only Option C identifies this defined tools/technique, and therefore represents the preferred answer.

4. <u>D</u>   This quiz question is intended to reinforce the concept that lessons learned should be performed by the project manager and project management team, not by any one individual. Option D best describes this concept, and is therefore the preferred (most true) answer. Options A and C contradict the concept and can be eliminated quickly. Option B is somewhat true, in that you and your team members are key stakeholders. However, Option D is the best, most accurate and complete answer.

LESSON 52 PROFESSIONAL RESPONSIBILITY

1. <u>C</u>   Professional and Social Responsibility questions typically require experience and logical judgment to select the correct answers. In many cases, it could be difficult to cite a specific text source to justify a correct answer. More often, the correct answer is based upon the intended application of a good-practices concept. In this question, four loosely related statements are presented. You are asked to select the most correct. Option A presents an interesting approach, but probably not practical, and without a basis in common literature. Option B is not a universally true statement. Option C presents an interesting and practical approach, with some justification based on current global practices in project management. Option D is not universally true, probably even a rare exception. After examining all four Options, C is probably the most true (at minimum, it is the Option that represents the fewest objections).

2. <u>B</u>   In this Question, Options B, C, and D each represent reasonable sources of potential communication challenges. The cultural communication matrix in Option B is a fabricated term. Therefore, Option B is the preferred (exception) answer.

3. <u>A</u>   This is a question that can be answered correctly by simply selecting the Option that best represents doing the right thing. After examining all four options, you should be able to quickly recognize Options B, C, and D as being less than forthright, sheepish approaches. Only Option A presents an honest, open, and responsive course of action. Option A is the preferred answer. Note that, in many cases, it is the responsibility of the project manager to directly address the public.

Appendix B

Answers and Explanations for

LESSON 54—SIMULATED PMP EXAM

1. $\underline{A}$ *PMBOK® Guide Fourth Edition*, 4.1.1. The business case provides the necessary information from a business standpoint to determine whether or not the project is worth the required investment. Typically the business need and the cost benefit analysis are contained in the business case to justify the project.

2. $\underline{B}$ *PMBOK® Guide Fourth Edition*, 7.3.2. Using the cost variance (CV) formula it will show that you have a positive variance of cost to work performed. CV = (EV) – (AC). So the simple calculation is 105 – 100 = 5, indicating a positive result that the budget is still under, ever so slightly. All other answers are misleading to the question.

3. $\underline{C}$ *PMBOK® Guide Fourth Edition*, 4.1. This came about due to a business need. Staff members were spending unproductive hours producing information for the management report that wasn't consistent or meaningful.

4. $\underline{B}$ An integrated project management plan is a compilation of all planning outputs, including the cost and schedule baselines. Therefore it cannot yet exist without the completed cost and schedule baselines.

5. $\underline{A}$ *PMBOK® Guide Fourth Edition*, 4.1. The project charter authorizes a project or phase to begin. The project management plan contains the project charter. A project statement of work is a description that may be included in the project charter. Feasibility plans are a distracter in this question.

6. $\underline{B}$ *PMBOK® Guide Fourth Edition*, 7.3.2. The To Complete Performance Index (TCPI) is the calculated projection of cost performance that must be achieved on the remaining work, when project performance results show that BAC or EAC are no longer valid. All other answers are misleading to the question.

7. $\underline{D}$ *PMBOK® Guide Fourth Edition*, 12.4.2. A Records Management System contains an archive of contract documentation and correspondence. All other answers are misleading to the question.

8. $\underline{B}$ *PMBOK® Guide Fourth Edition*, 4.6. Close Project or Phase formally will close the design phase. Close Procurements will verify that all contracted work and deliverables are acceptable.

9. **B** *PMBOK® Guide Fourth Edition*, 10.1. Identifying stakeholders is the process of identifying all people or organizations impacted by the project. Answer A is incorrect since it involves determining the needs and expectations of identified stakeholders. Answer C is a tool, and not a process, for identifying stakeholders. Answer D is a fictional answer.

10. **C** *PMBOK® Guide Fourth Edition*, 4.1. The project charter formally authorizes a project and documents the first view of the stakeholders' needs and expectations. Answer A is developed in the next integration process and Answer D is an input to the development of the project charter. Answer B is a distracter.

11. **B** *PMBOK® Guide Fourth Edition*, 10.3.1. Policies and procedures are organizational process assets and are another input to the Distribute Information process and have no connection to the data in the performance reports. Answer D is misleading to the question.

12. **C** *PMBOK® Guide Fourth Edition*, 4.3. Answer C is part of Monitor and Control Project Work process. All other answers are valid activities in the Direct and Manage Project Execution.

13. **B** *PMBOK® Guide Fourth Edition*, 12.2. Determining the source selection criteria to rate seller proposals is an output of the Plan Procurements process. All other answers are valid to the question.

14. **D** *PMBOK® Guide Fourth Edition*, 4.2. The question narrative clearly gives the reader clues that are related to planning and creation of the overall project management plan.

15. **D** Of the options listed, the most likely source of issues will stem from language, cultural, and time-zone differences. The other options represent straightforward project management processes.

16. **A** *PMBOK® Guide Fourth Edition*, 4.1. The project charter documents the business needs, current understanding of the customer's needs, and the new product, service, or result that is intended to satisfy stakeholder expectations. The project charter properly documents the project manager's authority to proceed with the project and apply organization resources to project execution processes.

17. **C** *PMBOK® Guide Fourth Edition*, 7.3.2. The budget at completion is the original estimated costs of the project. All other answers are misleading to the question.

18. **B** *PMBOK® Guide Fourth Edition*, 12.4. Economic factors are the least correct choice from the above choices for a reason of early termination of a contract. A contract is valid unless terms are available to terminate it. Contracts are only invalid and would be terminated if deemed illegal. All other answers present valid reasons.

19. <u>A</u> Close Procurements process can happen first or concurrent to the Close Project or Phase process. All other answers are distracters to the question.

20. <u>A</u> *PMBOK® Guide Fourth Edition*, 10.2. The key to the statement is that a stakeholder strategy has been created, so the next process is Plan Communications. Answer B is another process, and Answers C and D are processes later in the Communication Management knowledge area.

21. <u>B</u> *PMBOK® Guide Fourth Edition*, 4.1. Answer B is correct as the project is authorized by someone external to the project and is at a level that is appropriate to funding the project. Answers A and D are incorrect as someone within the project management team should not author the project charter unless they are delegated by the official sponsor. Answer C is misleading to the question.

22. <u>A</u> *PMBOK® Guide Fourth Edition*, 10.3.3. This process does include an output for feedback from stakeholders and is used to modify or improve future performance of the project. All other answers are valid to the question.

23. <u>C</u> *PMBOK® Guide Fourth Edition*, 4.3. Answer C is correct. All other answers are misleading to the question.

24. <u>D</u> *PMBOK® Guide Fourth Edition*, 12.2.3. A procurement contract award will be given to each selected seller from the Conduct Procurements process. All other answers are misleading to the question.

25. <u>A</u> *PMBOK® Guide Fourth Edition*, 4.3. The project manager, along with the project management team, directs the performance of the planned project activities, and manages the various technical and organizational interfaces that exist within the project. The most difficult aspect of the Direct and Manage Project Execution process is coordinating and integrating all the project elements.

26. <u>D</u> Communications in the project environment cannot be controlled. They can be managed, but not controlled.

27. <u>B</u> Projects are temporary, progressively elaborated, and create a unique output. Operations are open ended and their outputs are repetitive. Clearly an ongoing operation is not part of a project.

28. <u>A</u> *PMBOK® Guide Fourth Edition*, 12.1.1.1. The scope baseline is fully developed at the end of the Create WBS process. Other answers here are incorrect options for this question.

29. <u>D</u> *PMBOK® Guide Fourth Edition*, 7.3.2. Schedule variance is the amount of progress achieved compared to the progress planned on a project. It is equal to the earned value minus the planned value. So, EV is $146,000 – $150,000 for a SV = –$4,000. All other answers are misleading to the question.

30. <u>A</u> *PMBOK® Guide Fourth Edition*, 12.4.2. Closed procurements are not a valid Tool and Technique of the Close Procurements process; instead it is an output of the process. All other answers are valid to the question.

31. <u>C</u> *PMBOK® Guide Fourth Edition*, 4.6. The team is in the Closing phase. The question describes the lessons learned process; Monitoring, Controlling and Executing phases are already completed.

32. <u>C</u> *PMBOK® Guide Fourth Edition*, 10.1.3. Answers A, B, and D are details that can be included in the stakeholder register. Answer C contains details related to a risk register.

33. <u>D</u> *PMBOK® Guide Fourth Edition*, 4.1. Answers A, B, and C are valid statements for how a project manager would manage a project with three sponsors, since this can imply that are three unique areas of the project. Answer D is the least correct since there is no standard that a project should only have a single sponsor.

34. <u>B</u> *PMBOK® Guide Fourth Edition*, 10.3. Creating and publishing an agenda before a meeting is a communication method to have an organized and effective meeting. All other answers are misleading to the question.

35. <u>C</u> *PMBOK® Guide Fourth Edition*, 4.4. Answer C is incorrect and is part of the Monitor and Control Project Work process. All other answers are valid activities of the Direct and Manage Project Execution process.

36. <u>A</u> *PMBOK® Guide Fourth Edition*, 12.2.2. The complexity of the project has no bearing on using an independent estimate prepared by an outside professional estimator. All other answers are valid to the question.

37. <u>B</u> *PMBOK® Guide Fourth Edition*, 4.4. Comparing actual results to plan, making forecasts, and identifying corrective actions are all part of Monitor and Control Project Work. Other answer choices are incorrect for this question.

38. <u>A</u> There is no obligation. With a firm fixed-price contract, there is no requirement for the contractor to share cost and margin information.

39. <u>C</u> Option C comes right from the *PMBOK® Guide Fourth Edition*. The other answer options are less correct. Option A is incorrect since the answer is not complete. Answer B is incorrect because it indicates that the project manager would rely on intuition and feelings. (While intuition and feelings may be a useful aid for a project manager, they are not a primary definition or tool). Answer D is also incorrect due to the insertion of art and science into the choice. *PMBOK® Guide*, 1.3.

40. <u>A</u> *PMBOK® Guide Fourth Edition*, 12.1.1.3. Teaming agreements are temporary agreements used to gain the best work efficiency and outcomes during a project. Teaming agreements usually end with the project. There is no set time when the teaming agreement must be started or concluded. Teaming agreements are generally made with external sources.

41. B   *PMBOK® Guide Fourth Edition*, 7.3.2. Cost variance is a measurement of cost performance on a project. It is equal to the earned value minus the actual costs. So first, you calculate the earned value (($500 * 100%) + ($600 * 95%) + ($400 * 90%) = $500 + $570 + $360 = $1,430). Then sum the actual costs of each task ($550 + $530 + $420 = $1,500). CV = EV – AC = $1,430 – $1,500 = –$70.

42. B   *PMBOK® Guide Fourth Edition*, 12.4.3. Procurement terms and conditions updates are misleading to the question. All other answers are valid to the question.

43. B   *PMBOK® Guide Fourth Edition*, 4.6. "The Close Project or Phase process reviews the accepted deliverables output from the Verify Scope process before considering the project closed" is a true statement. All other answers are misleading to the question.

44. D   *PMBOK® Guide Fourth Edition*, 4.1. Answer D is correct since it is typically the sponsor's role to pay for the project and own it when it completes. All other answers are misleading to the question.

45. C   Lessons learned documentation should take place throughout the project life cycle. All other answers are not the best answer, although each potential answer has some level of correctness; a project manager will probably perform lessons learned at the end of the project, the phase, and when dealing with issues on the project.

46. C   *PMBOK® Guide Fourth Edition*, 4.3.3. When issues are found while a project is being managed and executed, change requests are issued which may modify project policies, scope, cost or budget, schedule, or quality. Thus, these change requests are an Output of the Manage and Direct Project Execution process and are Input to the Perform Integrated Change Control process. Answers A and B are misleading to the question.

47. D   *PMBOK® Guide Fourth Edition*, 12.2. The Conduct Procurements process obtains seller responses, selects a seller and awards a contract. All other answers are misleading to the question.

48. C   *PMBOK® Guide Fourth Edition*, 4.5. Perform Integrated Change Control is the process of reviewing all change requests, approving changes and managing changes to the deliverables, organizational process assets, project documents, and the project management plan.

49. B   Bottom-up estimating involves developing an estimate for each WBS work package, then rolling them all up to derive the project total.

50. B   The "triple constraint" has generally been recognized as scope, time, and budget. These are represented by answers A, C, and D for this question. In addition to the traditional triple constraint, many projects and project managers often consider a wider view of project constraints to include quality, resources, and risk. A previous version of the *PMBOK Guide* cited "customer satisfaction" as part of the constraints (*PMBOK® Guide*, 1.3).

51. <u>A</u> *PMBOK® Guide Fourth Edition*, 7.3.2. The question provides enough information to calculate CPI, but not enough information to calculate SPI. CPI = EV/AC = $1,430 / $1,500 = 0.95. Thus you are trending over budget by 5%.

52. <u>C</u> *PMBOK® Guide Fourth Edition*, 12.4. The correct choice is perform the Close Procurements process; all other answers are misleading to the question.

53. <u>B</u> *PMBOK® Guide Fourth Edition*, 4.6.3. All other answers are valid to the question.

54. <u>C</u> *PMBOK® Guide Fourth Edition*, 4.1.1. Marketplace conditions are an environmental factor to the production of the project charter and are not part of the business case. All other answers are valid to the question.

55. <u>B</u> *PMBOK® Guide Fourth Edition*, 10.3.3. Lessons learned documentation is not done to boast of the team's accomplishments. All other answers are correct to the question.

56. <u>B</u> *PMBOK® Guide Fourth Edition*, 4.3.3. Quality assurance metrics are not included in work performance information of the execution process. It includes deliverable status, schedule progress, and costs incurred as Outputs of the Direct and Manage Project Execution process.

57. <u>A</u> *PMBOK® Guide Fourth Edition*, 12.2.2. Bidder conferences can allow vendors that are considering bidding to learn about the work and ask questions. All other answers are misleading to the question.

58. <u>B</u> *PMBOK® Guide Fourth Edition*, 4.6. The work performance information is reviewed to determine the status of project activities and make certain the project goals and objectives are met. This is an Input to the Close Project process.

59. <u>C</u> This question is intended to test your understanding of "progressive elaboration." Although we attempt to illustrate project management as a process-oriented endeavor, it is not reasonable to initiate, plan, execute/control, and close a project in a strict, straight-line, logical manner. In actuality, each element of a project gradually unfolds with increasing detail as more is learned and experienced. We can "elaborate" with more detail as the project "progresses." This concept of progressive elaboration is especially evident during project planning. Options A and D are difficult to justify as possible answers. Option B could appear reasonable. But, Option C is perfectly correct and therefore the best answer.

60. <u>A</u> *PMBOK® Guide Fourth Edition,* 3.3. It is generally recognized that the most critical portion of the project is the Initiation and Planning areas. If the project manager and team are not properly informed about project intentions during the Initiating processes (Develop Project Charter and Identify Stakeholders), then planning outcomes will most likely contain errors.

61. <u>B</u> *PMBOK® Guide Fourth Edition*, 12.4.3. The buyer does not use the procurement audit results to determine the deliverable acceptance. The procurement audit is a Tool and Technique of the Close Procurements process. All other answers are valid to the question.

62. <u>C</u> *PMBOK® Guide Fourth Edition*, 5.1. Many organizations categorize requirements into project requirements and product requirements. Project requirements can include business requirements, project management requirements, delivery requirements, etc. Product requirements can include information on technical requirements, security requirements, performance requirements, etc.

63. <u>A</u> The primary function of a work authorization system is to help control scope.

64. <u>B</u> This is a common sense derivation from the general definition given for product description.

65. <u>D</u> *PMBOK® Guide Fourth Edition*, 12.4.2. Only as a last option would litigation in the courts become a desirable option. All other answers are valid to the question.

66. <u>A</u> *PMBOK® Guide Fourth Edition*, 5.2. The project scope statement describes, in detail, the project's deliverables and the work required to create those deliverables. The project scope statement provides a common understanding of the project scope among project stakeholders.

67. <u>D</u> Cost of quality (COQ) includes all costs expended to achieve project quality objectives.

68. <u>D</u> Review your Develop Project Charter process illustration. You will see that expert judgment is a Tool/Technique, not an Input.

69. <u>A</u> *PMBOK® Guide Fourth Edition*, 5.3. The WBS details the entire scope of the project and includes all deliverables. It is an Output of the Create WBS process, and the technique of elaborating some deliverables at a later date is called rolling wave planning.

70. <u>B</u> Of the options listed, seeking permission from the first client represents the most responsible action.

71. <u>A</u> *PMBOK® Guide Fourth Edition*, 10.1. Answer A is the best response and is the common sense answer in this group of answers. Answer B cites the function of Plan Communications. Answer C is closest to a description of Distribute Information. Answer D is a combination of several processes.

72. <u>C</u> *PMBOK® Guide Fourth Edition*, 5.4. Verify Scope process should document the level and degree of completion of the project. If you come back at a later date and restart this project, Scope Verification will describe how far the project progressed and give you an idea of where to start.

73. C *PMBOK® Guide Fourth Edition*, 5.5. Project performance measurements are used to assess the magnitude if a variation from the original scope baseline. Important aspects of project scope control include determining the cause and degree of variance relative to the scope baseline and deciding whether corrective or preventative action is required.

74. A *PMBOK® Guide Fourth Edition*, 6.1. Developing a project schedule uses outputs from the Define Activities, Sequence Activities, Estimate Activity Resources, and Estimate Activity Durations in combination with the scheduling tool to produce the project schedule. The first task is to define schedule activities by decomposing the project scope baseline (WBS) into smaller components called activities.

75. A Expected monetary value (EMV) is determined by applying the equation, EMV = Probability (in percentage) × Impact (in value). In this case, EMV = 0.30 × –$10,000 = –$3,000. If the risk is negative, then the EMV is negative. If the risk is positive, then the EMV is positive.

76. B *PMBOK® Guide Fourth Edition,* 10.1. In this questions we must choose the best group of actions. Options A and C partially describe communications requirements analysis. Option D describes a practical approach. Option B is the most accurate answer in this process.

77. B This question requires you to know your outputs from the process. Answers A, C, and D are not Outputs from the Identify Stakeholders process. *PMBOK® Guide*, 10.1.

78. B *PMBOK® Guide Fourth Edition*, 6.2. The initiation of the successor activity depends on the completion of the predecessor activity.

79. B *PMBOK® Guide Fourth Edition*, 6.3. Estimate Activity Resources is the process of estimating the type and quantities of material, people, equipment, or supplies required to perform each activity.

80. D *PMBOK® Guide Fourth Edition*, 6.4. Three-point estimates are based on determining the three types of estimates: most likely, optimistic (best-case), and pessimistic (worst-case).

81. B Lag time (wait time) is a mandatory constraint between two sequential activities. The need to wait for poured concrete to set is a good example.

82. A Forcing is generally the least preferred method of conflict resolution. However, it is sometimes the best choice when other approaches fail or when time does not allow other approaches. Forcing can produce a definitive, lasting resolution.

83. C Answer Options A and D are blatantly false statements. Option B may appear reasonable to some, but is not true. All forms of communication (formal, informal, verbal, written, non-verbal) are acceptable and encouraged when applied appropriately. Formal written communication is

normally encouraged for performance reports, legal matters, contractual matters, and other issues of similar importance. Option C is a true statement and therefore the correct (most correct) answer. Non-verbal communication is actually much more expressive than any type of verbal or written communication.

84.   <u>B</u>   This is a straightforward test of your ability to understand and apply the communication channels equation $N(N-1)/2$. Note the importance of reading the question correctly here. You are asked to determine the <u>number of additional channels</u> resulting from an increase in stakeholders. To derive the correct answer, you must perform three mathematical steps. (1) You must determine the number of communication channels with six stakeholders. (2) You must determine the number of communication channels with two more stakeholders, 8. (3) You must then determine the resulting increased number of channels. With six stakeholders, the number of communication channels is 15. With eight stakeholders, the number of communication channels is 28. The increase is 13. Therefore, the correct answer is Option B. Note that answer Options C and D could represent reasonable answers if an error were made in understanding precisely what the question is asking. Option A could seem reasonable to someone who doesn't know the equation. Make a special note that the overall importance of this exercise is to reinforce the concept of communication channels growing exponentially in size and complexity with every person added to the project communications loop.

85.   <u>C</u>   *PMBOK® Guide Fourth Edition*, 6.5. The Critical Path Method calculates a single early and late start date and a single early and late finish date for each activity. Once these dates are known, float time is calculated for each activity to determine the critical path. The other answers contain elements of PERT calculations.

86.   <u>D</u>   *PMBOK® Guide Fourth Edition*, 6.6. Variance analysis is performed during the Control Schedule process and is a key function of schedule control. Comparing target (planned) schedule dates with the actual completion dates provides useful information and can be used to forecast start and finish dates of future schedule activities.

87.   <u>B</u>   *PMBOK® Guide Fourth Edition*, 7.2. Analogous cost estimating uses the values of parameters, such as scope, cost, budget, and duration or measures of scale such as size, weight, and complexity, from a previous, similar project as the basis for estimating the same parameter or measure for a current project.

88.   <u>C</u>   *PMBOK® Guide Fourth Edition*, 7.2. The cost performance baseline is an authorized time-phased budget at completion used to measure, monitor, and control cost performance on the project. In the earned value technique the cost performance baseline is referred to as the performance measurement baseline (PMB).

89. <u>D</u> *PMBOK® Guide Fourth Edition*, 7.3.

CPI = EV / AC

CPI = 168,750 ÷ 300,000

CPI = 0.5625

90. <u>A</u> *PMBOK® Guide Fourth Edition*, 8.1. Benchmarking involves comparing actual or planned project practices to those of comparable projects to identify best practices, generate ideas for improvement, and provide a basis for measuring performance. These other projects can be within the performing organization or outside of it and can be within the same or general application area.

91. <u>C</u> *PMBOK® Guide Fourth Edition*, 8.2. Process analysis follows the steps outlined in the process improvement plan to identify any needed improvements. This analysis also examines problems experienced, constraints experienced, and non-value-added activities identified during the process operation. Process analysis includes root cause analysis—a specific technique to identify a problem, discover the underlying causes that lead to it, and develop preventative actions.

92. <u>C</u> This question is intended to test your understanding of the Conduct Procurements process and practical judgment. Answer Options A, B, and D are simply not true. Options B and D actually represent generally poor practices. Option C is the only true statement and therefore the preferred (most true) answer.

93. <u>A</u> Quality and grade should not be confused. Grade has to do with the features of a product or service. Quality is conformance to specifications and requirements. Low quality is a problem; low grade is not.

94. <u>A</u> This quiz question is designed to help ensure that you understand the intended application of the Collect Requirements process. During the Collect Requirements process, stakeholder needs are defined and documented. This documentation provides the basis for defining and managing customer expectations throughout the project. Therefore, Option A is the preferred answer. Answer B is a true statement, but not fully complete. Answer C describes product requirements and Answer D describes project requirements.

95. <u>D</u> Each of the answer Options A, B, and C are equally true. Once developed, the project scope statement serves many important functions across the entire project life cycle. Therefore Option D, all of the above, represents the best answer.

96. <u>B</u> *PMBOK® Guide Fourth Edition*, 8.3. A Pareto chart, also referred to as a Pareto diagram, is a specific type of histogram, ordered by frequency of occurrence. It shows how many defects were generated by type or category of identified causes.

97. D	*PMBOK® Guide Fourth Edition*, 9.1. The human resource plan documents the project roles and responsibilities, project organization, and the staffing management plan. Important consideration should be given to the availability of, or competition for, scarce or limited human resources within or outside of the organization performing the project and their impact on project resource availability. Project roles can be designated for persons or groups.

98. D	*PMBOK® Guide Fourth Edition*, 9.2. The enterprise environmental factors that influence the Acquire Project Team process include, but are not limited to: existing information for human resources including who is available, their competency levels, their experience, their interest in working on the project, and their cost rate.

99. C	*PMBOK® Guide Fourth Edition*, 9.3. Proper development of the team is critical to a successful project. Since teams are made up of individuals, individual development becomes a critical factor to project success. Individual team members need the proper development and training to perform the activities of the project or to enhance their existing knowledge and skills. The development needed will depend on the project.

100. A	There is a wide body of knowledge about interpersonal skills that is appropriate to project work and nonproject work. See the Appendix of the *PMBOK® Guide Fourth Edition* for a treatment of relevant interpersonal skills.

101. A	Earned value analysis is a method that integrates cost, scope, and schedule to derive measurement values that accurately assess project progress to date, as well as forecasted future performance.

102. A	Option B is false. It is the intent of the activity list to identify project activities. WBS work packages are still deliverables-oriented. Option C is false. Again, work packages should be deliverables-oriented. Define Activities is applied to further subdivide work packages into manageable sized activities. Option A is the only true statement, and therefore represents, as the exception, the best answer.

103. C	Since the risks and cost were not taken into account at the beginning of the project, the project should not go forward as planned. Project initiation should be revisited to examine the project plan and determine how changes can be made to accommodate the added network security requirements. Conflicts between stakeholders should always be resolved in favor of the customer. This question emphasizes the importance of identifying your stakeholders and their needs as early as possible in the project.

104. C	*PMBOK® Guide Fourth Edition*, 10.2. Plan communications is the process of determining the project stakeholder information need and defining a communication approach. The communication plan is the primary output of the Plan Communications process.

105. <u>D</u> *PMBOK® Guide Fourth Edition*, 10.3. Virtual teams are teams that do not necessarily work in the same location or have the same hours but all share the goals of the project and have a role on the project. The web conferencing and e-mail references describe the information distribution tools.

106. <u>B</u> *PMBOK® Guide Fourth Edition*, 10.4 and 10.5. This question describes the Report Performance process (concerned with collecting and reporting information regarding project progress and project accomplishments to the stakeholders) and the Manage Stakeholders process. Both processes are part of the Project Communications Management Knowledge area.

107. <u>C</u> *PMBOK® Guide Fourth Edition*, 10.5. Report Performance is the process of collecting and distributing performance information, including status reports, process improvements, and forecast.

108. <u>B</u> Based on the information given, your project finished on-schedule, within budget, and satisfied contractual requirements. Your contract is complete.

109. <u>A</u> Of the options listed, the scenario best exemplifies contributing to the project management knowledge base to improve quality and build capabilities.

110. <u>D</u> Transference is a risk response strategy. Risk transfer involves shifting the consequence and ownership of a risk to a third party. Transfer does not eliminate the risk.

111. <u>D</u> *Critical path* is one of the most important terms used by project managers. It is important to know and understand its definition: *the longest path through a network diagram*. It is also important to know that the critical path defines the *shortest period of time in which a project may be completed*.

112. <u>A</u> Although this was not directly discussed in Lesson 11, it is possible for a project to have more than one critical path through its network. When more than one critical path exists, it typically increases project risk. It is usually advisable for the project team to brainstorm some solution to avoid multiple critical paths. Option B is not true, by default. Option C is not true (good judgment should dictate that it is not conventional to attempt the creation of hybrid network diagramming methods). Option D is not true; the WBS identifies all of the deliverables-oriented work within project scope; the network diagram illustrates all activities and their logical interdependencies, from project start to project finish.

113. <u>D</u> *PMBOK® Guide Fourth Edition*, 1.1. This question describes risk tolerance levels of the stakeholders. Risk triggers are recorded in the risk register during the Plan Risk Responses process. The risk of using a new vendor for language translations and cultural coexistence testing would pose a threat to the project, not an opportunity. Interviewing could be used but this answer is not as complete as D.

114. <u>D</u> *PMBOK® Guide Fourth Edition*, 11.2. Brainstorming, Delphi technique, interviewing, root cause identification, and root cause analysis are all project identify risk process techniques. In answer A, PERT is an estimating technique. In answer B, benchmarking is used in Quality processes. Answer C erroneously includes sensitivity analysis.

115. <u>D</u> *PMBOK® Guide Fourth Edition*, 11.3. Perform Qualitative Risk Analysis is the process of prioritizing risks for further analysis or action by assessing and combining their probability of occurrence and impact.

116. <u>B</u> *PMBOK® Guide Fourth Edition*, 11.4. Distributions graphically display the probability of risk to the project objectives as well as the time and or cost elements.

117. <u>C</u> *PMBOK® Guide Fourth Edition*, 11.5. Transference is shifting the negative impact risk and responsibility of risk response to a third party. Acceptance is a strategy that the project team has decided not to change the project management plan to deal with the risk. Avoidance involves changing the project plan to eliminate the risk. Mitigation is a technique for reducing the level of risk to an acceptable threshold.

118. <u>D</u> *PMBOK® Guide Fourth Edition*, 11.6. Implementing contingency plans or workarounds sometimes results in a change request. Change requests are prepared and submitted to the Perform Integrated Change Control process (see *PMBOK® Guide Fourth Edition*, Sec. 4.5). Change requests can include recommended corrective and preventative actions as well.

119. <u>D</u> Upgrading scheduling software will not likely change your project's scope of work.

120. <u>A</u> The two project closing processes are contract closure and close project.

121. <u>C</u> To answer this question, you must first construct a network diagram from the given information. Be prepared to do the same in real-world project environments. The proper network diagram appears below. There are three possible paths through this network from start to finish: (1) Start-A-C-E-F-G-Finish, (2) Start-B-D-E-F-G-Finish, and (3) Start-B-C-E-F-G-Finish.

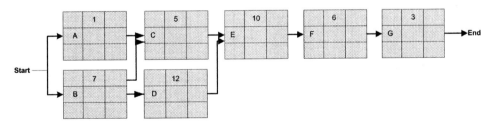

122. <u>B</u> To answer this question, you must (a) construct a network diagram from the given information, (b) identify each path from start to finish, and (c) determine which path is the longest. Remember, the longest path is the critical path. We find three possible paths: (1) Start-A-C-E-F-G-Finish (25 weeks), (2) Start-B-D-E-F-G-Finish (38 weeks), and (3) Start-B-C-E-F-G-Finish (31 weeks). Path 2 is the longest and therefore the correct answer.

123. <u>B</u> *PMBOK® Guide Fourth Edition*, 12.1. The scenario in this question is an example of a make-or-buy analysis, a Tool and Technique of the Plan Procurements process. The monthly cost of the vendor solution is $61,200 (estimate 12,000 users at $5 per month, plus $1,200 per month for the accountant). Subtract your cost of $30,000 from the vendor cost of $61,200, this equals $31,200. Divide that number into the cash outlay of $250,000 for internal code creation and you get 8.01 months. Of the choices presented, 8 months is the best choice.

months. Of the choices presented, 8 months is the best choice.

124. <u>C</u> *PMBOK® Guide Fourth Edition*, 12.2. Bidder conferences are meetings to ensure that all prospective sellers have a clear and common understanding of the procurement. Advertising is a technique of expanding the potential seller list by placing advertisements in newspapers, business journals, etc. The qualified sellers list includes those sellers who are asked to submit a proposal and does not represent a meeting or a bidder conference. Contract negotiation clarifies the structure and requirements of the contract so that mutual agreement can be reached prior to signing the contract. This takes place after a bid is accepted. Bidder conferences are meetings to ensure that all prospective sellers have a clear and common understanding of the procurement.

125. <u>A</u> *PMBOK® Guide Fourth Edition*, 12.3. Administer Procurements is the process of managing procurement relationships, monitoring contract performance, and making changes and corrections as needed. Both the buyer and the seller will administer the procurement contract for similar purposes. Each must ensure that both parties meet their contractual obligations and that their own legal rights are protected.

126. <u>C</u> *PMBOK® Guide Fourth Edition*, 12.4. A procurement audit is a structured review of the procurement process originating from the Plan Procurements process through Administer Procurements and is a Tool and Technique of the Close Procurements process. The objective of a procurement audit is to identify successes and failures that warrant recognition in the preparation or administration of other procurements on the project, or other current and future projects within the performing organization.

127. <u>D</u> The project management plan is not typically used as a general educational reference.

128. <u>A</u> When project deliverables completely satisfy the client's requirements, specifications, and fitness of use, then quality is achieved.

129. <u>C</u> This question is designed to ensure you understand the practical definition of "assumption." Assumptions are factors that are deemed to be certain. They are important to help the project team get past unknowns. For example, if the project involves an outdoor event, the project team may assume the weather will be fine, and plan around that assumption. Of course, all assumptions include some degree of risk and they should be validated and elaborated upon as planning progresses. Initial assumptions should be identified in the high-level project scope statement. Answer Options A, B, and D could each appear somewhat reasonable, but only Option C is correct in all interpretations, and is therefore the best answer.

130. <u>D</u> The idea of 80% of the problems stemming from 20% of all possible causes is associated with Pareto diagrams, not control charts.

131. <u>C</u> If the team applied risk management processes during planning, they would have identified and analyzed most potential risk events and developed response strategies in advance, should any of the risk events occur. Planned responses for unidentified risks would also have been developed.

132. <u>A</u> Statistical sampling involves testing a representative sample of the entire population, as opposed to testing every item. Statistical sampling can be effective and can reduce time and costs.

133. <u>A</u> This scenario represents an extreme situation, justifying the immediate involvement of senior management.

134. <u>C</u> Once again, to answer this question, you must first construct a network diagram from the given information. Then you must identify all possible paths through the network and determine which path is longest. The longest path is the critical path, which defines the shortest period of time in which the project may be completed. In this example, Start-B-D-E-F-G-Finish represents the critical path, and the shortest time to complete: 38 weeks.

135. <u>D</u> The communications management plan describes who will receive what project information and when, how the information will be gathered, and how the information will be distributed.

136. <u>B</u> This is a common sense derivation from the general definition given for product description.

137. <u>C</u> *PMBOK Guide*, 6.1. The Sequence Activities process identifies and documents relationships among the project activities to create the project schedule network diagram.

138. <u>B</u> *Resource* is one of the most important key terms in a project manager's vocabulary. This quiz question is intended to ensure that you are familiar with the simple, yet critical, accepted definition of resource.

139. <u>A</u> The procurement management plan is developed during project planning. It describes how subsequent procurement processes will be applied. Procurement management helps ensure the most efficient use of contractors and suppliers.

140. <u>D</u> This question is intended to reinforce the important concept that project risks can be positive, as well as negative. Positive risks are called opportunities and should be pursued. Negative risks are called threats and should be avoided. The question asks you to identify the most incorrect statement. Answer Option A is a correct statement. Recall reading it in your *PMBOK® Guide*. Option B is correct, reinforcing the point. Option C is also true, reinforcing the point. Option D is false (while we would certainly like to eliminate negative risks, it is not possible) and therefore the most incorrect statement.

141. <u>D</u> Changes must be properly integrated across the entire project, and original performance baselines should be maintained.

142. <u>A</u> Each answer Option here is true. However, B, C, and D are incomplete. Option A represents the most complete description of the Activity Resource Estimating process, and is therefore the best answer.

143. <u>C</u> Analogous estimating (top-down) is fast, efficient, and less costly, but also less reliable. It bases its estimate on the actual performance of a past similar activity. Option A, bottom-up, is actually a formal estimating technique that we will discuss soon, but it is the opposite of analogous. Options B and D are legitimate types of estimates, but neither satisfies the given definition.

144. <u>D</u> This quiz question is designed to ensure that you understand the intended application of the Develop Schedule process. *The Develop Schedule process is applied to determine the start/finish dates for project activities and to create the schedule management plan.* Therefore, Option D is the precise correct answer. Options A, B, and C are all somewhat true, but incomplete.

145. <u>A</u> Review your project charter template illustration in *Ultimate PMP® Exam Prep Workbook*, Lesson 6, along with your Must Know items. You will see that answer Option A is the only exception, and therefore the best answer.

146. <u>B</u> Indications that a risk has occurred, or is about to occur, are termed triggers (or risk symptoms or warning signs).

147. <u>C</u> This quiz question is intended to test your ability to properly apply the PERT equation. The PERT equation is (P + 4M + O) / 6, where P = the pessimistic estimate, M = the most probable estimate, and O = the optimistic estimate. In this question, the given variables yield the equation [14 + 4(9) + 6] / 6. When calculated, this gives us the correct PERT estimate of 9.33 (days). Therefore, Option C is the precise correct answer. Option A should be recognized as an unreasonable answer under any circumstances.

This value is even lower than the optimistic estimate. Option B would appear correct if you ignored the PERT equation and simply accepted the most probable estimate. Option D would appear correct if you simply averaged the three estimates.

148. <u>B</u>   This quiz question is designed to ensure that you understand the intended application of the Organizational Planning process. The Organizational Planning process is applied to develop, document, and assign project roles, responsibilities, and reporting relationships. Therefore, Option B is the correct answer. Options A and C represent activities you may perform during organizational planning, but they do not represent the primary purpose of applying the process. Option D more closely represents the description of quality planning, not organizational planning.

149. <u>D</u>   Presentations of this nature represent formal verbal communication.

150. <u>D</u>   There is a wide range of uses for what constitutes a project office.

151. <u>B</u>   Discussing observed weaknesses then together developing an improvement plan represents the most appropriate way to conduct appraisals in this situation.

152. <u>C</u>   Upon any change request, it is almost always necessary to evaluate the impact of the change before an effective decision can be made or action taken.

153. <u>C</u>   This question is intended to test your understanding of *cost performance baseline. The cost performance baseline is a time-phased budget, used to monitor and measure project cost performance.* Therefore, Option C is precisely the best answer. Options A and B describe the cost management plan. Option D is simply a reasonable-sounding statement that actually makes little logical sense.

154. <u>D</u>   This quiz question is designed to ensure that you understand the intended application of the Plan Quality process. *The Plan Quality process is applied to identify which quality standards are applicable to the project, then determine how to satisfy them.* Therefore, Option D is the correct answer. Option A is simply incorrect. Option B could appear somewhat correct if the question were referring to the Quality Assurance process, but not for Plan Quality. Option C offers a distracting incorrect answer. While cause-and-effect diagrams are useful quality tools, there is not necessarily any such thing as a "project cause-and-effect diagram."

155. <u>C</u>   Project risk is formally defined as, *any uncertain event or condition that, if it occurs, has a negative or positive effect on a project objective. Uncertain* is key in this definition. If an event or condition is certain, then it is not a risk. Only answer Option C fully satisfies the definition. Options A, B, and D represent partial, misleading, and incorrect answers.

156. <u>B</u> This quiz question is designed to ensure that you understand the intended application of the Identify Risk process. The Identify Risk process is applied to (1) determine which risks may affect the project and (2) to document their characteristics. Therefore, Option B is the correct answer. Options A, C, and D are all legitimate objectives in project risk management, but not objectives of the Identify Risk process.

157. <u>B</u> This question is designed to ensure that you understand the intended application of the Develop Project Team process. Develop Project Team is the process of enhancing the ability of individual team members to enhance overall project performance. Therefore, Option B is the preferred answer. Options A, C, and D could be correct statements in some, but not all, situations.

158. <u>A</u> Of the options listed, practicing and promoting formal project reviews and lessons learned represents the best method.

159. <u>C</u> Slack is determined by applying the equation, Slack = LS – ES. In this case, Slack = 15 days – 6 days = 9 days.

160. <u>A</u> There are four recognized categories of project risk: technical risks (technical, quality, performance), project management risks, organizational risks, and external risks. Therefore, Option A is the correct answer. Options B, C, and D represent proper risk management terms, but they do not represent *risk categories*.

161. <u>D</u> This quiz question is designed to ensure that you understand the intended application of the Qualitative Risk Analysis process. *The Qualitative Risk Analysis process is applied to assess the impact and likelihood of identified risks. It is intended to help prioritize identified risks and identify those risks serious enough to warrant further analysis.* Option D defines the process perfectly and is therefore the correct answer. Option A is an incorrect hodgepodge of risk management terms. Option B defines the application of the Identify Risk process, not Qualitative Risk Analysis. Option C defines a portion of Quantitative Risk Analysis, not Qualitative Risk Analysis.

162. <u>C</u> This is yet another quiz question designed to test your practical ability to use a simple probability/impact (P-I) risk rating matrix. To derive the correct answer, you must back-fit the 0.1 score to find it is the result of a risk assessed with a probability of 0.1 and an impact of 1. With an example matrix, it is the only possible combination to derive a score of 0.1. Plotted, it appears in the lowest-left corner, signifying low-probability and low-impact. Therefore, Option C is the best answer.

163. <u>D</u> This quiz question is intended to test your applied understanding of sensitivity analysis. *Sensitivity analysis is a simple risk analysis technique used to help make project decisions based on the general risk sensitivity of an organization, person or group of people.* Based on the given scenario in this question, it appears that the primary rationale behind the sponsor's decision was the lower level of risk (by comparison), which satisfied her apparent risk averse policies. This certainly fits the definition of sensitivity analysis. Option A is not a recognized risk management term. Option B could be correct in some situations, but it is not directly consistent with this particular scenario. Option C could also be correct in some situations, but is not consistent with this scenario. Option D *sensitivity analysis* is a proper risk management technique, it is consistent with the scenario, and therefore the best (correct) answer.

164. <u>C</u> PERT = [P + 4(M) + O] / 6. [2 days + (4)(5 days) + 6 days] / 6 = [2 days + 20 days + 6 days] / 6 = 28 days / 6 = 4.67 days.

165. <u>D</u> Risks may be accepted, mitigated, transferred, and/or avoided, but not rejected.

166. <u>B</u> A backward-pass is performed by moving right-to-left (end-to-start) through the network diagram to determine Late Start (LS) and Late Finish (LF) times for each activity. A forward-pass is performed by moving left-to-right (start-to-end) through the network diagram to determine Early Start (ES) and Early Finish (EF) times for each activity.

167. <u>C</u> This quiz question is intended to test your practical understanding of EMV. *Expected Monetary Value Analysis (EMV) is a quantitative risk analysis tool. EMV is calculated by multiplying the value of each possible outcome by its probability of occurrence, then adding them all together. EMV= V (value $) × P (probability).* To select the correct answer to this quiz question, you must perform a series of simple calculations. Risk 1 = –$10,000 × 0.10 = –$1,000. Risk 2 = –$8,000 × 0.70 = –$5,600. Risk 3 = +$10,000 × 0.60 = +$6,000. Risk 4 = –$800 × 0.20 = –$160. Added together, the total equals –$760 (remember to recognize the plus and minus values associated with positive and negative risks).

168. <u>C</u> This quiz question is designed to ensure that you understand the intended application of the Develop Project Management Plan process. *The Develop Project Management Plan process is applied to gather the outputs from all other planning processes and assemble them into a single, cohesive document, the project plan.* Therefore, Option C is the precise correct answer. Options A, B, and D are all partially true, but describe only portions of the process. Option C is the only complete choice.

169. <u>D</u> This quiz question is designed to ensure that you understand the intended application of the Acquire Project Team process. *The Acquire Project Team process is applied to obtain and assign needed human resources (people) to the project.* Answer Options A and B are somewhat true, but not complete. Option C better describes the Plan Human Resources process, not Acquire Project Team. Option D is the preferred answer.

170. <u>C</u> This quiz question is intended to test your understanding of some of the potential challenges faced by project managers in different types of

organizations. Answer Options A, B, and D represent incorrect statements. In Option A, colocation *can* involve moving team members (sometimes even team members' families) to/from different parts of the world. In Option B, team development is nearly always more challenging in functional organizations, where resources are typically borrowed on a temporary basis. In Option D, team development procedures typically represent far too much detail for inclusion in the project charter. Option C is exactly true and is therefore the preferred (most true) answer.

171. <u>C</u>   This quiz question is designed to help ensure that you understand the intended application of the Manage Project Team process. *The Manage Project Team process is applied to address performance, behavior, issues and conflicts associated specifically with project team members.* Therefore, Option C is the preferred answer. Options A, B, and D are more closely associated with the Develop Project Team process. Only Option C provides a complete, accurate description of the Manage Project Team process.

172. <u>A</u>   This question is intended to test your ability to recognize with whom the responsibility for project quality lies. While various team members and/or organizational groups may support project quality objectives, overall project quality is the responsibility of the project manager. Therefore, Option A is the preferred answer.

173. <u>C</u>   This is a long situational type question that is intended to test your understanding of a simple communication concept: Communication *is a two-way process. Communication is not complete until the sender verifies that the receiver has received the communication, and understood it as intended by the sender.* Based on this, Option C represents the best, most complete, answer. Options A and D, while partially true, both contradict the proper concept. Option B is much closer to the best answer, but omits the need to verify the communication being understood as intended. Verifying physical receipt is just one part of the two-part equation.

174. <u>B</u>   This question tests your ability to recognize that an immediate face-to-face meeting directly with the other party is always the preferred method in issue/conflict resolution situations … as opposed to e-mails, phone calls, or other less direct approaches. Therefore, Option B represents the preferred answer.

175. <u>B</u>   Conduct Procurements is intended to notify the prospective sellers of your need via an RFP or other procurement document, then to receive proposals from vendors, and to ultimately negotiate the contract. All other answer selections are incorrect.

176. <u>A</u>   This question is intended to test your practical judgment in recognizing legitimate reasons for scope change. Options B, C, and D each present valid reasons for considering/justifying scope change. Option A represents a situation that has nothing to do with project scope. Therefore, Option A is the preferred (exception) answer.

177. <u>A</u>   This quiz question is designed to help ensure that you understand the intended application of the Control Schedule process. *Control Schedule is the process of effectively managing changes to the project schedule baseline, then integrating those changes with other control processes across the entire project.* Therefore, Option A is the preferred answer. Options B, C, and D represent remotely true statements. Only Option A provides a complete, accurate description of schedule control.

178. <u>D</u>   Variance at Completion (VAC) is determined by applying the equation, VAC = BAC − EAC. In this question, BAC (total planned budget) is given as $850,000. EAC is determined by applying the equation EAC = BAC / CPI. CPI is determined by applying the equation, CPI = EV / AC. In this question, EV is $425,000 (50% of the work is complete and 50% of the total planned budget is $425,000). AC is given as $600,000 (the actual cost of work completed). Now we have all the variables necessary to complete the VAC calculation. CPI = $425,000 / $600,000 = 0.708. EAC = $850,000 / 0.708 = $1,200,560. VAC = $850,000 − $1,200,560 = −$350,560 . Note that calculated values on the PMP Exam typically use rounding for large numerical values. Option D (−$350,000) is therefore the correct answer. This answer generally indicates the project will be over budget by roughly $350,000 at completion.

179. <u>D</u>   This quiz question is designed to help ensure that you understand the intended application of the Perform Quality Control process. *The Perform Quality Control process is applied to monitor specific project results to ensure they comply with the project's quality standards.* Option D describes the process precisely this way and is therefore the preferred answer. Options A and C are somewhat true, but not as complete or accurate as D. Option B is not true.

180. <u>A</u>   This quiz question is designed to reinforce the difference between scope verification and quality control. It is important to know the difference between the two. Scope verification focuses on the formal acceptance of the project deliverable while quality control focuses on the how the deliverables meet quality requirements.

181. <u>C</u>   This question tests your understanding of the term *workaround. A workaround is a response to an unanticipated risk event, typically executed after the risk event occurs.* Therefore, Option C best satisfies the proper response to the scenario presented in this question, and is the correct answer. Note that Option A describes going to your sponsor for guidance. You should begin to take note that issues, problems, and challenges should be handled at the project level. Only very significant issues (that can't be resolved at the project level) should be escalated to the sponsor level.

182. <u>C</u>   This quiz question is designed to help ensure you understand the intended application of the Contract Administration process. *The Contract Administration process is applied to ensure that the seller's performance satisfies contractual obligations.* Therefore, Option C is the correct answer.

Options A, B, and D are all somewhat true, but not as complete and precise as Option C.

183. <u>C</u> This quiz question is designed to help ensure that you understand the intended application of the Monitor and Control Project Work process. *The Monitor and Control Project Work process is applied to (1) monitor all other processes through initiation, planning, executing, and closing and (2) take/ make corrective/preventive actions, as needed.* Therefore, Option C is the preferred answer. Options A, B, and D are all somewhat true, but not as complete and precise as Option C.

184. <u>B</u> This quiz question is designed to help ensure that you understand the intended applications of the Perform Integrated Change Control process. Perform Integrated Change Control is the process of effectively managing changes and integrating them appropriately across the entire project. Option B describes the process precisely this way and is therefore the preferred answer. Options A, C, and D are all somewhat true, but incomplete compared to Option B.

185. <u>A</u> This is a straightforward test of your ability to recognize the defined Inputs, the Tools and Techniques, and the Outputs associated with the Close Procurements process. There are three defined Contract Closure Tools/ Techniques: (1) procurement audits, (2) records management system, and (3) negotiated settlements. Only Option A identifies one of these two defined Tools/Techniques, and therefore represents the preferred answer.

186. <u>D</u> This quiz question is designed to help ensure that you understand the intended application of the Close Project or Phase process. *The Close Project or Phase process is applied to formally end either the project or project phase.* Therefore, Option D is the preferred answer. Options A and B are true statements, but not complete descriptions. Option C better describes the Contract Closure process, not the Close Project process.

187. <u>A</u> Upon any change request, it is most important to evaluate the impact of the change before an effective decision can be made or action taken.

188. <u>A</u> Of the options listed, the only universally appropriate action is to provide input to your team member's performance appraisals.

189. <u>C</u> This question is intended to reinforce your understanding of Verifiy Scope. Remember, Verifiy Scope is obtaining formal acceptance, regardless of correctness. Only Option C has the distinguishing term, acceptance. Options A, B, and D use the terms authorize, agree, and approve, but not accept. Option C is therefore the preferred answer.

190. <u>A</u> Risks with low probability and low impact may be passively accepted, but should be documented and revisited at appropriate frequencies.

191. <u>B</u> Generally, early involvement of key stakeholders helps to reduce the need for changes later in the project life cycle.

192. <u>B</u> Of the options listed, reporting your assessment to senior management represents the most responsible action.

193. <u>A</u> Pareto diagrams are used to identify the few causes (typically 20%) that create the majority of the problems (typically 80%).

194. <u>D</u> Training is the best first choice. A solid understanding of project management will be essential to begin conceptualizing a project of this size and complexity.

195. <u>A</u> One of the project manager's most important responsibilities across the project life cycle is to proactively prevent and discourage unnecessary changes.

196. <u>D</u> Lessons learned are performed together by the project manager and the project management team.

197. <u>A</u> One way to build the capabilities of colleagues is through coaching and mentoring.

198. <u>C</u> Of the options listed, seeking counsel from your organization's legal group represents the most responsible action. This could represent criminal activity.

199. <u>A</u> Of the options given, this scenario best exemplifies self assessment.

200. <u>D</u> Fast-tracking and crashing are two effective schedule compression techniques that can be explored when the schedule needs to be shortened.

Appendix C

Bonus Practice Questions -Earned Value-

Your PMP Exam will likely include five or six earned-value questions. But due to the random nature of the test structure, some students have reported as many as twenty earned value questions. These questions typically ask you to either interpret given information or perform a simple calculation to derive the preferred answer. Here is a set of bonus practice questions to help you develop an intuitive familiarity with earned value terms, meanings, and equations.

1. EV is $3,000. BAC is $4,000. How much of the total work have you completed?
   A. 25%
   B. 50%
   C. 75%
   D. Unknown

2. CV is –$6,000. EV is $18,000. AC is what?
   A. –$6,000
   B. $12,000
   C. $24,000
   D. $18,000

3. EV = $350, AC = $400 and PV = $325. CV is _____.
   A. –$25
   B. $25
   C. $50
   D. –$50

4. Which of the following statements is *most* true?
   A. EAC is the cost of work completed to date.
   B. EAC is the estimated value of what it will cost to complete the project from this point forward.
   C. EAC is the estimated total cost at project completion.
   D. EAC is the estimated value of work scheduled.

5. Your project has an SPI of 0.87. This means what?
   A. The project is over budget by 33%.
   B. The project is progressing at only 87% of the rate originally planned.
   C. The project is progressing at only 13% of the rate originally planned.
   D. The project is ahead of schedule by 13%.

6. Upon reviewing the most recent progress report, you see that your project currently has a CPI of 0.77. This means _____.
   A. your project is going to cost 77% more than originally planned
   B. your project is progressing at only 77% of the rate originally planned
   C. your project is progressing at only 23% of the rate originally planned
   D. your project is getting only $0.77 for every $1.00 invested

7. Your project has an SPI of 1.13. This means _____.
   A. the project is over budget by 13%
   B. the project is progressing at 113% of the rate originally planned
   C. the project is progressing at only 87% of the rate originally planned
   D. the project is under budget by 33%

8. VAC may be determined by _____.
   A. subtracting estimate at completion (EAC) from budget at completion (BAC)
   B. subtracting actual cost (AC) from estimate at completion (EAC)
   C. dividing budget at completion (BAC) by the cost performance index (CPI)
   D. dividing earned value (EV) by budgeted cost of work scheduled (BCWS)

9. SV may be determined by _____.
   A. subtracting estimate at completion (EAC) from budget at completion (BAC)
   B. subtracting planned value (PV) from earned value (EV)
   C. dividing budget at completion (BAC) by the cost performance index (CPI)
   D. dividing budgeted cost of work performed (BCWP) by budgeted cost of work scheduled (BCWS)

10. CV may be determined by _____.
   A. subtracting estimate at completion (EAC) from budget at completion (BAC)
   B. dividing budget at completion (BAC) by the cost performance index (CPI)
   C. subtracting actual cost of work performed (ACWP) from budgeted cost of work performed (BCWP)
   D. dividing budget cost of work performed (BCWP) by budgeted cost of work scheduled (BCWS)

11. CPI may be determined by _____.
   A. subtracting estimate at completion (EAC) from budget at completion (BAC)
   B. dividing earned value (EV) by the actual cost of work performed (ACWP)
   C. subtracting actual cost (AC) from budgeted cost of work performed (BCWP)
   D. dividing earned value (EV) by planned value (PV)

12. Which formula would you use to calculate the TCPI of your project if you do not intend to exceed the overall original budget for the project?
    A. TCPI = (BAC – EV) / (EAC – AC)
    B. TCPI = (BAC – PV) / (EAC – AC)
    C. TCPI = (BAC – EV) / (BAC – AC)
    D. TCPI = (BAC – PV) / (BAC – EV)

13. ETC may be determined by _____.
    A. subtracting estimate at completion (EAC) from budget at completion (BAC)
    B. dividing earned value (EV) by the actual cost of work performed (ACWP)
    C. subtracting actual cost (AC) from estimate at completion (EAC)
    D. dividing budget cost of work performed (BCWP) by planned value (PV)

14. Your project has a CV of –$5,250. This means what?
    A. Your project is over budget by $5,250.
    B. Your project is behind schedule.
    C. Your project is ahead of schedule.
    D. Your project is under budget by $5,250.

15. Your project has an SV of 400. This means _____.
    A. your project is ahead of schedule
    B. your project is behind schedule
    C. your project is behind schedule by 400%
    D. your project is ahead of schedule by 400%

16. It is currently the end of month nine of a planned twelve month project. You find yourself 50% complete and have spent $700,000. You originally planned to spend $83,333 each month, with your work activities evenly scheduled at 8.33% each month. The total project budget is $1 million. Your earned value (EV) is _____.
    A. $1,000,000
    B. $500,000
    C. $700,000
    D. $750,000

17. It is currently the end of month nine of a planned twelve month project. You find yourself 50% complete and have spent $700,000. You originally planned to spend $83,333 each month, with your work activities evenly scheduled at 8.33% each month. The total project budget is $1 million. Your PV is

    _____.
    A. $1,000,000
    B. $500,000
    C. $700,000
    D. $750,000

18. Which formula would you use to calculate the TCPI of your project if you will use the new EAC as the overall budget for the project?
    A. TCPI = (BAC − EV) / (EAC − AC)
    B. TCPI = (BAC − PV) / (EAC − AC)
    C. TCPI = (BAC − EV) / (BAC − AC)
    D. TCPI = (BAC − PV) / (BAC − EV)

19. It is currently the end of month nine of a planned twelve month project. You find yourself 50% complete and have spent $700,000. You originally planned to spend $83,333 each month, with your work activities evenly scheduled at 8.33% each month. The total project budget is $1 million. Your BCWP is

    _____.
    A. $1,000,000
    B. $500,000
    C. $700,000
    D. $750,000

20. It is currently the end of month nine of a planned twelve month project. You find yourself 50% complete and have spent $700,000. You originally planned to spend $83,333 each month, with your work activities evenly scheduled at 8.33% each month. The total project budget is $1 million. Your AC is

    _____.
    A. $1,000,000
    B. $500,000
    C. $700,000
    D. $ 750,000

21. It is currently the end of month nine of a planned twelve month project. You find yourself 50% complete and have spent $700,000. You originally planned to spend $83,333 each month, with your work activities evenly scheduled at 8.33% each month. The total project budget is $1 million. Your BAC is

    _____.
    A. $1,000,000
    B. $500,000
    C. $700,000
    D. $750,000

22. It is currently the end of month nine of a planned twelve month project. You find yourself 50% complete and have spent $700,000. You originally planned to spend $83,333 each month, with your work activities evenly scheduled at 8.33% each month. The total project budget is $1 million. Your TCPI to complete the project under the original budget is _____.
    A. 1.40
    B. 0.50
    C. 0.67
    D. 1.66

23. It is currently the end of month nine of a planned twelve month project. You find yourself 50% complete and have spent $700,000. You originally planned to spend $83,333 each month, with your work activities evenly scheduled at 8.33% each month. The total project budget is $1 million. Your CV is

    _____.

    A. –$200,000
    B. +$200,000
    C. +$300,000
    D. –$300,000

24. It is currently the end of month nine of a planned twelve month project. You find yourself 50% complete and have spent $700,000. You originally planned to spend $83,333 each month, with your work activities evenly scheduled at 8.33% each month. The total project budget is $1 million. What is the CPI?

    A. 0.83
    B. 1.50
    C. 0.67
    D. 0.71

25. It is currently the end of month nine of a planned twelve month project. You find yourself 50% complete and have spent $700,000. You originally planned to spend $83,333 each month, with your work activities evenly scheduled at 8.33% each month. The total project budget is $1 million. What is the SV?

    A. +250,000
    B. –500,000
    C. +750,000
    D. –250,000

26. It is currently the end of month nine of a planned twelve month project. You find yourself 50% complete and have spent $700,000. You originally planned to spend $83,333 each month, with your work activities evenly scheduled at 8.33% each month. The total project budget is $1 million. Your SPI is

    _____.

    A. 1.40
    B. 0.50
    C. 0.67
    D. 0.71

27. It is currently the end of month nine of a planned twelve month project. You find yourself 50% complete and have spent $700,000. You originally planned to spend $83,333 each month, with your work activities evenly scheduled at 8.33% each month. The total project budget is $1 million. What is the EAC?

    A. $731,000
    B. $1,000,000
    C. $1,408,451
    D. $1,492,537

28. The calculation factor that can be part of the formula used to forecast project cost at completion is what?
    A. CPI
    B. SPI
    C. BCWP
    D. ACWP

29. Your project was estimated to cost $1.8 million and was scheduled for eight months, start to finish. After four months, a performance report indicates:

    EV = $750,000
    PV = $850,000
    AC = $900,000

    What is the schedule variance?
    A. SV = +100,000
    B. SV = +150,000
    C. SV = –50,000
    D. SV = –100,000

30. Your project was estimated to cost $1.8 million and was scheduled for eight months, start to finish. After four months, a performance report indicates:

    EV = $750,000
    PV = $850,000
    AC = $900,000

    What is the cost variance?
    A. CV = +$150,000
    B. CV = –$100,000
    C. CV = +$150,000
    D. CV = –$150,000

Bonus Answer Key

Question	Answer	Question	Answer	Question	Answer
1	C	11	B	21	A
2	C	12	C	22	D
3	D	13	C	23	A
4	C	14	A	24	D
5	B	15	A	25	D
6	D	16	B	26	C
7	B	17	D	27	C
8	A	18	A	28	A
9	B	19	B	29	D
10	C	20	C	30	D

Appendix D

Rapid Review Sheets

LESSON 4 MASTERING THE *PMBOK® GUIDE*
. . . .
Rapid Review Sheets are a high level review of key elements for each project process. In some cases the information will be abridged.

The *PMBOK Guide (A Guide to the Project Management Body of Knowledge)* published by the Project Management Institute, PMI) is the defacto global standard for managing projects. In September 1999, the *PMBOK Guide* was formally adopted as an ANSI standard. The *PMBOK Guide* has been updated twice since being adopted; the current version is the *PMBOK® Guide Fourth Edition*, ANSI/PMI 99-001-2008.

As a PMP candidate and eventually as a PMP, it is essential that you understand the intent, content, and context of the *PMBOK Guide*. Many exam questions are designed specifically to test your content knowledge of the *PMBOK Guide*. However, the *PMBOK Guide* is a reference standard, not a learning text. Therefore, the *PMBOK Guide* can be difficult to quickly master. In this lesson, we will begin to master the *PMBOK Guide* by developing a high-level understanding of its intent, content, and presentation structure.

Ultimate PMP Exam Prep Guide — Must Know Concepts

1. The *PMBOK Guide* identifies and describes generally recognized best practices that are applicable to most projects most of the time.

2. The level of project management effort should be sensibly proportional to the size and complexity of the project.

3. The *PMBOK Guide* organizes much of its content as an interrelated set of forty-two well defined processes, further grouped into five progress groups.

4. The Process Groups are: Initiating, Planning, Executing, Monitoring and Controlling, and Closing.

5. The *PMBOK Guide* organizes detailed discussions of the forty-two processes in a set of nine Knowledge Areas: Project Integration Management, Project Scope Management, Project Time Management, Project Cost Management, Project Quality Management, Project Human Resource Management, Project Communications Management, Project Risk Management, and Project Procurement Management.

6. Each of the forty-two *PMBOK Guide* processes is presented as a set of well-defined Inputs, Tools & Techniques, and Outputs.

7. The *PMBOK Guide* is the defacto global standard for managing projects. The *PMBOK Guide* is an ANSI standard: ANSI/PMI 99-001-2208.

8. Projects should be organized in terms of phases or stages to form an overall project life cycle.

9. The relationship of project processes to specific project management knowledge areas and process groups is an important element to learn for the PMP Exam.

LESSON 6   DEVELOP PROJECT CHARTER

The Develop Project Charter process is intended to ensure that any project chartered and authorized by management is well thought-through and justified. With a solid beginning, any project has a greater probability of ultimate success.

Applying the Develop Project Charter process encourages management to thoroughly consider all high-level aspects of a proposed project, and then to make an informed selection decision. The process suggests that management employ expert judgment to make good decisions. While not specifically specified as tools in the process of Develop Project Charter, informed selection methods usually include Benefit Measurement tools or some form of mathematical models (or application programs) to determine whether or not a project would be valuable to the organization.

Develop Project Charter (4.1)		
INPUTS	**TOOLS & TECHNIQUES**	**OUTPUTS**
• Project Statement of Work (SOW) • Business Case • Contract • Enterprise Environmental Factors • Organizational Process Assets	• Expert Judgement	• Project Charter

Formally sanctions a new project or authorizes a project into its' next phase
- **Project Statement of Work (SOW)**   Narrative description of the products/services to be delivered by the project
- **Business Case**   Describes the reason the project is worth investing in from the business standpoint
- **Contract**   Used as an input if the project is undertaken for an external customer/client
- **Enterprise Environmental Factors**   Consideration factors such as; culture, systems, procedures, industry standards
- **Organizational Process Assets**   Consideration factors such as; processes, procedures and corporate knowledge base

- **Expert Judgement**   Expert technical and/or managerial judgment (from any qualified source)

- **Project Charter**   High-level document that authorizes this project and assigns/authorizes the project manager

Ultimate PMP Exam Prep Guide — Must Know Concepts

1. The Develop Project Charter process is intended to formally authorize a new project, or authorize an ongoing project to continue into its next phase.

2. Projects must be aligned with the organization's strategic plan (strategic objectives).

3. The primary deliverable (Output) of the Develop Project Charter process is the Project Charter.

4. The Project Charter is a high-level document that communicates preliminary project characteristics, authorizes the project, and identifies and authorizes the project manager.

5. The Project Charter is typically issued by a project initiator or sponsor, external to the immediate project organization, at a funds-providing management level.

6. The project's business need should be clearly defined and documented in the Project Charter.

7. The project's product or service description should be clearly defined during Develop Project Charter and documented in the Project Charter.

8. Chartering a project links the project to the ongoing work of the performing organization.

9. The project manager should be assigned as early as possible, prior to project planning, preferably during Project Charter development.

10. The Project Charter should be relatively brief (broad, not deep), perhaps one to five pages in length.

11. Decisions made early in the project life cycle (in Initiating or Planning) tend to have the greatest overall influence on the project outcome.

LESSON 7 IDENTIFY STAKEHOLDERS

Very early in the life of a project, it is critical to identify all of the organizations and people who may have an impact on the project, and all those who may be impacted by the project.

A "stakeholder" is any person or organization that is actively involved in a project, or whose interests may be affected positively or negatively by execution of a project. Stakeholders can be internal to the organization or external. In many projects, the public at large will become a stakeholder to be considered on the project. The challenge for the project manager when the public is a stakeholder will be to act while considering public needs. Often there is no direct representative of the public to be consulted during project planning and execution.

A project manager must be sure to identify and list all potential stakeholders for a project.

Identify Stakeholders (10.1)		
INPUTS	**TOOLS & TECHNIQUES**	**OUTPUTS**
• Project Charter • Procurement Documents • Enterprise Environmental Factors • Organizational Process Assets	• Stakeholder Analysis • Expert Judgment	• Stakeholder Register • Stakeholder Management Strategy

Identify all persons/organizations impacted by a project and document their interests, involvement, and impact on the project

- **Project Charter** High-level document that authorizes the project and assigns/authorizes the project manager
- **Procurement Documents** Identifies procurement contract stakeholders
- **Enterprise Environmental Factors** Consideration factors such as; culture, systems, procedures, industry standards
- **Organizational Process Assets** Consideration factors such as processes, procedures and corporate knowledge base

- -

- **Stakeholder Analysis** Gathering and assessing information to determine whose interests should be taken into account for a project
- **Expert Judgment** Expert technical and/or managerial judgment (from any qualified source)

- -

- **Stakeholder Register** A document identifying all project stakeholder information
- **Stakeholder Management Strategy** Defines the approach to increase stakeholder support and reduce negative impacts

Ultimate PMP Exam Prep Guide — Must Know Concepts

1. A "stakeholder" is any person or organization that is actively involved in a project, or whose interests may be affected positively or negatively by execution of a project

2. The Identify Stakeholders process is used to identify all people or organizations that may be impacted or have an impact on a project.

3. A key output of the Identify Stakeholders process is the Stakeholder Register which lists the project's stakeholders and relevant information for each stakeholder or stakeholder group.

4. Stakeholder Analysis is a technique used to determine each stakeholder's interest, influence, participation, and expectations for a project.

LESSON 9 PLAN COMMUNICATIONS

The Plan Communications process is applied to determine the communication needs of project stakeholders. This includes determining: what information is needed, when it is needed, and how it will be delivered.

Communications needs for the project are typically determined by first engaging identified project stakeholders (communication requirements analysis), to determine their detailed information needs, then documenting the details in a Communications Management Plan. The initial identification of stakeholders occurs early in the project during project initiation. During the initial identification of stakeholders, communications requirements are identified at a high level. In the Plan Communications process, the initial requirements are further detailed and recorded. The Plan Communications process will be executed at the beginning of planning processes. The fact that this process is performed so early in the project attests to the overall importance of having an effective communications plan.

Plan Communications (10.2)

INPUTS	TOOLS & TECHNIQUES	OUTPUTS
• Stakeholder Register • Stakeholder Management Strategy • Enterprise Environmental Factors • Organizational Process Assets	• Communications Requirements Analysis • Communications Technology • Communications Models • Communications Methods	• Communications Management Plan • Project Document Updates

Determines who needs what information, when, and how they get it

- **Stakeholder Register**   A document identifying all project stakeholder information
- **Stakeholder Management Strategy**   Defines the approach to increase stakeholder support and reduce negative impacts
- **Enterprise Environmental Factors**   Consideration factors such as; culture, systems, procedures, industry standards
- **Organizational Process Assets**   Consideration factors such as processes, procedures and corporate knowledge base

- **Communications Requirements Analysis**   Determining the total of information needs among project stakeholders
- **Communications Technology**   The methodologies used to transfer information among project stakeholders
- **Communications Models**   A model demonstrating how communications occur between two parties
- **Communication Methods**   Individual/group meetings, video/audio conferences, other communication methods

- **Communications Management Plan**   Details the management of all project communications
- **Project Document Updates**   Updates to other project documentation

---

Ultimate PMP Exam Prep Guide — Must Know Concepts

1. Effective communications in project management is a critical success factor.

2. It is an accepted heuristic that good project managers spend up to 90% of their time communicating.

3. The primary deliverable (Output) of the Plan Communications process is the Communications Management Plan.

4. The Plan Communications process is applied to determine the communications needs of project stakeholders. This includes what information is needed, when it is needed, and how it will be delivered.

5. Communication requirements analysis is a formal activity performed in communications planning to identify project stakeholders, determine their needs and expectations, then decide how best to manage their needs and expectations.

6. Communication is a two-way activity. Communication is not complete until the sender confirms that the receiver has understood the intended message.

7. There are five categories of interpersonal communication: Informal Verbal, Informal Written, Non-Verbal, Formal Verbal, and Formal Written.

8. The number of communication channels within a project increases exponentially as the number of stakeholders increases. The equation used to calculate communications channels is $N(N - 1) / 2$.

LESSON 10 COLLECT REQUIREMENTS

The Collect Requirements process defines and documents the product and project features that are required to meet the expectations and requirements of the project's stakeholders. These "requirements" are the conditions and capabilities that must be achieved through the project's execution. The requirements must be documented in sufficient detail to allow measurement in determining the status of project completion and in determining whether or not the documented requirements have been met.

The identified expectations and requirements will be used in other processes, such as cost, quality, and schedule planning, to ensure that the project is properly planned and will meet stakeholder expectations.

There are many tools and techniques that can be used to help facilitate identifying requirements, such as: focus groups, workshops, brainstorming, mind mapping, surveys, observation, and others.

A key output of this process is the Requirements Documentation. This documentation is normally progressively elaborated as a project progresses. As part of this process, a Requirements Management Plan is created.

A project's success is directly influenced by the accuracy and completeness in identifying all of the requirements and expectations through this process.

Collect Requirements (5.1)

INPUTS	TOOLS & TECHNIQUES	OUTPUTS
• Project Charter • Stakeholder Register	• Interviews • Focus Groups • Facilitated Workshops • Group Creativity Techniques • Group Decision Making Techniques • Questionnaires and Surveys • Observations • Prototypes	• Requirements Documentation • Requirements Management Plan • Requirements Traceability Plan

Defines and documents the project and product features and functions needed to fill stakeholder's needs and expectations

- **Project Charter** High-level document that authorizes the project and assigns/authorizes the project manager
- **Stakeholder Register** A document identifying all project stakeholder information

- **Interviews** Formal and informal approach to determine stakeholder information requirements and expectations
- **Focus Groups** Brings together prequalified stakeholders and subject matter experts to determine expectations about a proposed product, service, or result
- **Facilitated Workshops** Focused sessions with key cross-functional stakeholders to define requirements
- **Groups Creativity Techniques** Group activities organized to identify project and product requirements
- **Group Decision Making Techniques** Groups assessment process of multiple alternatives with an expected outcome in the form of future actions resolution
- **Questionnaires and Surveys** Written sets of questions to quickly accumulate information from a wide number of respondents
- **Observations** Directly viewing individuals or groups in their environment to determine how they perform their jobs or tasks and carry out processes
- **Prototypes** Obtaining early feedback by providing a model of a product before actually building it

- **Requirements Documentation** Documentation describing how individual requirements meet the business needs of the project
- **Requirements Management Plan** Documents how requirements will be analyzed, documented, and managed throughout the project
- **Requirements Traceability Plan** A table that links requirements to their origins and traces them throughout the project life cycle

---

Ultimate PMP Exam Prep Guide — Must Know Concepts

1. The Collect Requirements process defines and documents the product and project features that are required to meet the expectations and requirements of the project's stakeholders.

2. "Requirements" are the conditions and capabilities that must be achieved through the project's execution.

3. A key output of the Collect Requirements process is the Requirements Documentation.

4. The Requirements Documentation describes how the identified requirements meet the business needs of the project.

5. A Requirement Traceability Matrix links requirements to business objectives to ensure that each requirement is adding value to the project and organization

6. A project's success is directly influenced by the accuracy and completeness in identifying all of the requirements and expectations through this process.

7. The Collect Requirements process defines the Requirements Management Plan which is a component of the overall Project Management Plan.

LESSON 11   DEFINE SCOPE

The Define Scope process is applied to create the Project Scope Statement. The Project Scope Statement defines the project's deliverables and the work required to create those deliverables.

During scope definition, you and your team build upon the major deliverables, assumptions, and constraints that were defined during project initiation. Stakeholders' needs and desires, as defined in the Requirements Document, are analyzed and developed into firm work requirements. Assumptions and constraints can be further analyzed and the opinions of domain experts can be solicited.

It is important to understand that your Project Scope Statement will provide a common understanding of the project scope among stakeholders. The process of Define Scope creates a detailed Project Scope Statement. The Project Scope Statement is required to complete detailed project planning. The Work Breakdown Structure, Activity List, and Project Schedule will derive from key information that is documented in this process.

During project execution, the original Project Scope Statement will be used to guide decisions. When changes to the project scope are approved, the Project Scope Statement will be updated.

A detailed and thorough Project Scope Statement is critical to the success of a project. The Project Scope Statement is one of three required documents that must be defined for the project. The other two required documents are the Project Charter and Project Management Plan.

Define Scope (5.2)

INPUTS	TOOLS & TECHNIQUES	OUTPUTS
• Project Charter • Requirements Documentation • Organizational Process Assets	• Expert Judgment • Product Analysis • Alternatives Identification • Facilitated Workshops	• Project Scope Statement • Project Document Updates

Defines and documents the project and product features and functions needed to fill stakeholder's needs and expectations

- **Project Charter**   High-level document that authorizes the project and assigns/authorizes the project manager
- **Requirements Documentation**   Documentation describing how individual requirements meet the business needs of the project
- **Organizational Process Assets**   Consideration factors such as processes, procedures and corporate knowledge base

- **Expert Judgment**   Expert technical and/or managerial judgment (from any qualified source)
- **Product Analysis**   Generally accepted methods for translating high-level product descriptions into tangible deliverables
- **Alternatives Identification**   Technique used to generate different approaches to accomplish the work of the project
- **Facilitated Workshops**   Focused sessions with key cross-functional stakeholders to define requirements

- **Project Scope Statement**   Detailed description of a project deliverables and work required to create them
- **Project Document Updates**   Updates to other project documentation

---

Ultimate PMP Exam Prep Guide — Must Know Concepts

1.   The Define Scope process is intended to create the Project Scope Statement.

2.   The Project Scope Statement defines the project's deliverables and the work required to create those deliverables.

3.   The Project Scope Statement provides a documented basis for common understanding of project scope among stakeholders.

4.   The Project Scope Statement provides a documented basis for making many project decisions.

5.   Alternatives identification that is used during Define Scope can serve as a useful technique for generating different approaches for defining and performing project work.

LESSON 12   CREATE WBS

Experienced project managers understand it is simply not possible to visualize and manage an entire project without some sort of tool. Instead of trying to manage the whole project at once, all the time, the project must be broken down into manageable pieces, and then the pieces can be easily managed. The Create Work Breakdown Structure process facilitates this goal by decomposing (subdividing) major project deliverables into smaller, more manageable components.

This process is typically the first process applied after the Project Scope Statement has been developed.

The primary deliverable from the Create Work Breakdown Structure process is the Work Breakdown Structure (WBS). The WBS may be the most important tool for management of a project. When properly developed, the WBS illustrates all of the work elements that define the project and serves as the basis for most planning activities from this point forward.

The WBS documents all the work required to successfully complete the project. The WBS must identify all of the work required, and only the work required, to successfully complete the project. "Scope creep" or continual changes in a project's work requirements can be eliminated by carefully defining scope and managing it using the WBS.

Effective application of the Create Work Breakdown Structure process is critical to project success. Work Packages are critical to developing the budget, the schedule, and in tracking the project during monitoring and controlling. The completed Project Scope Statement, WBS, and WBS Dictionary form the Scope Baseline for the project.

Create WBS (5.3)		
INPUTS	**TOOLS & TECHNIQUES**	**OUTPUTS**
• Project Scope Statement • Requirements Documentation • Organizational Process Assets	• Decomposition	• Work Breakdown Structure (WBS) • WBS Dictionary • Scope Baseline • Project Document Updates
Subdivides major deliverables into manageable components		
• **Project Scope Statement** Detailed description of a projects deliverables and work required to create them • **Requirements Documentation** Documentation describing how individual requirements meet the business needs of the project • **Organizational Process Assets** Consideration factors such as processes, procedures and corporate knowledge base		
• **Decomposition** The process of subdividing WBS work packages into manageable-sized schedule activities		
• **Work Breakdown Structure (WBS)** The deliverables-oriented organization/illustration of all project work (scope) • **WBS Dictionary** Companion document to the WBS that details the content of each WBS element • **Scope Baseline** Scope Baseline = the approved project scope statement + the WBS + the WBS dictionary • **Project Document Updates** Updates to other project documentation		

Ultimate PMP Exam Prep Guide — Must Know Concepts

1. The Create Work Breakdown Structure process is intended to decompose (subdivide) major project deliverables into manageable components.

2. The primary deliverable from the Create Work Breakdown Structure process is the Work Breakdown Structure (WBS).

3. The WBS may be the single most important project management tool.

4. The WBS serves as the basis for most subsequent planning activities.

5. WBS deliverables should be decomposed to a level where adequate cost and duration estimates are possible.

6. The WBS should be subdivided to a level where acceptance criteria can be easily defined and the work can be effectively assigned, managed, and measured.

7. There is no predefined limit to the number of sublevels in a WBS.

8. The WBS has no time frame.

9. The WBS defines work only.

10. The lowest-level elements of the WBS are termed "Work Packages."

11. Work packages should require no more than eighty hours to complete.

12. Detailed work package descriptions are documented and collected to form a WBS Dictionary.

13. The detailed Project Scope Statement, the WBS and the WBS Dictionary combine to form the Project Scope Baseline.

LESSON 13 DEFINE ACTIVITIES

The process of Define Activities logically follows the Create WBS process. The WBS identifies the total of all project work in terms of deliverables. The WBS is deliverables-oriented. To adhere to this definition, our WBS should identify work using descriptive nouns, as opposed to action-oriented verbs. We apply the Define Activities process to convert our WBS work packages (lowest-level elements) into action-oriented activities.

The Define Activities process identifies the specific activities necessary to complete the project deliverables.

The primary deliverable from the Define Activities process is the project's Activity List; the Activity List becomes an extension of the WBS.

The primary Tool & Technique used to create the Activity List is "decomposition." This is basically the same decomposition method used to create the WBS. The difference is that, in Define Activities, decomposition is used to further subdivide work packages into manageable activities, and the final output is described in terms of activities rather than deliverables. These tasks represent what is needed to complete a work package.

Ideally, Define Activities is applied immediately following Create WBS. In real-world practice, however, the two processes are many times applied in parallel. In many projects, Rolling Wave Planning can be an effective tool to support activity definition. In Rolling Wave Planning, only near-term work is planned in detail, leaving future work summarized with less detail. As future work draws nearer, detailed planning is performed.

Define Activities (6.1)		
INPUTS	**TOOLS & TECHNIQUES**	**OUTPUTS**
• Scope Baseline • Enterprise Environmental Factors • Organizational Process Assets	• Decomposition • Rolling Wave Planning • Templates • Expert Judgment	• Activity List • Activity Attributes • Milestone List

The process of specifically identifying all schedule activities

• **Scope baseline**   Scope baseline = the approved project scope statement + the WBS + the WBS dictionary
• **Enterprise Environmental Factors**   Consideration factors such as; culture, systems, procedures, industry standards
• **Organizational Process Assets**   Consideration factors such as processes, procedures and corporate knowledge base

• **Decomposition**   The process of subdividing WBS work packages into manageable-sized schedule activities
• **Rolling Wave Planning**   A form of progressive elaboration planning where only near term work is planned in detail
• **Templates**   Any existing form (i.e. an activity list from a similar project) that may be used as a template for this process
• **Expert Judgment**   Expert technical and/or managerial judgment (from any qualified source)

• **Activity List**   The comprehensive list and description of all schedule activities
• **Activity Attributes**   An extension of the activity attributes identified in the activity list, intended to provide more detail
• **Milestone List**   The documented list of both mandatory and optional schedule milestones

Ultimate PMP Exam Prep Guide — Must Know Concepts

1. The Define Activities process is identifying the specific activities necessary to complete the project deliverables.

2. The Define Activities process is intended to decompose or subdivide WBS work packages into manageable activities.

3. The primary deliverable (Output) from the Define Activities process is the Activity List.

4. The Activity List may be viewed as an extension of the WBS.

5. Decomposition is the primary methodology (Tool/Technique) used to create the Activity List.

6. In some projects, Rolling Wave Planning can be an effective tool to support activity definition. In Rolling Wave Planning, only near-term work is planned in detail, leaving future work summarized with less detail. As future work draws nearer, detailed planning is performed.

7. Decomposition in Define Activities differs from decomposition in Create WBS, in that it is used to further subdivide WBS work packages into manageable activities, and the final output is described in terms of activities rather than deliverables.

LESSON 14 SEQUENCE ACTIVITIES

Sequence Activities is the process of identifying the interrelationships between individual project activities, then documenting them using what is generically termed a "Network Logic Diagram." This is an essential step for schedule planning.

There are four possible interactivity relationships.

Finish-to-Start: One activity must finish before the next activity may start. F-S is the most common interdependency

Finish-to-Finish: One activity must finish before the next activity may finish

Start-to-Start: One activity must start before the next activity may start

Start-to-Finish: One activity must start before the next activity may finish. S-F is the least common interdependency.

These relationships must be identified and documented in some form of Network Logic Diagram.

Sequence Activities (6.2)		
INPUTS	**TOOLS & TECHNIQUES**	**OUTPUTS**
• Activity List • Activity Attributes • Milestone List • Project Scope Statement • Organizational Process Assets	• Precedence Diagramming Method (PDM) • Dependency Determination • Applying Leads and Lags • Schedule Network Templates	• Project Schedule Network Diagrams • Project Document Updates

Identifies and documents dependencies among schedule activities

- **Activity List**   The comprehensive list and description of all schedule activities
- **Activity Attributes**   An extension of the activity list, intended to provide more attribute details
- **Milestone List**   The documented list of both mandatory and optional schedule milestones
- **Project Scope Statement**   Detailed description of a projects deliverables and work required to create them
- **Organizational Process Assets**   Consideration factors such as processes, procedures and corporate knowledge base

- **Precedence Diagramming Method (PDM)**   Activity-on-Node (AON) project network diagramming technique
- **Dependency Determination**   Mandatory dependencies, discretionary dependencies, external dependencies
- **Applying Leads and Lags**   Further defined 'overlaps (leads)' and 'delays (lags)' in activity dependencies
- **Schedule Network Templates**   Standardized networks used to expedite the creation of the schedule network diagram

- **Project Schedule Network Diagrams**   Schematic displays of the project's activities and their logical relationships
- **Project Document Updates**   Updates to other project documentation

Ultimate PMP Exam Prep Guide — Must Know Concepts

1. The Sequence Activities process is intended to identify and document interactivity logical relationships.

2. The primary deliverable (Output) of the Sequence Activities process is the project schedule network diagram.

3. The project schedule network diagram becomes the primary input to develop the project schedule.

4. The project schedule network diagram illustrates all project activities and their predecessor/successor relationships/interdependencies. It also identifies the project's Critical Path and all of the activities on the Critical Path.

5. The Critical Path is the longest path through a network diagram. It defines the shortest project complete time.

6. Network Diagrams are often (inaccurately) referred to as PERT charts.

7. Network Diagrams are typically created and documented using the Precedence Diagramming Method (PDM).

8. PDM is also referred to as Activity-on-Node (AON). In AON diagrams, activities are represented by nodes which are connected by arrowed lines to illustrate their interdependencies.

9. AON diagrams can show four types of interdependencies (F-S), (S-F), (F-F), and (S-S).

10. A Forward Pass (left-to-right through the network) may be performed to determine Earliest Starting times (ES) and Earliest Finish times (EF) for each project activity.

11. A Backward Pass (right-to-left through the network) may be performed to determine Latest Starting times (LS) and Latest Finish times (LF) for each project activity.

12. Slack (also referred to as "float," "reserve," "path float," or "total float") for any given activity may be determined by subtracting ES from LS. Activities on the Critical Path typically have zero slack.

13. Subnet (or fragnet or subnetwork) is a subdivision of a network diagram.

14. Hammock is a group of related activities illustrated as a single summary activity.

15. Lead time and lag time allows project teams to add realism and flexibility to their schedules. Lead time may be viewed as an overlap between tasks. Lag time is waiting time.

LESSON 15 ESTIMATE ACTIVITY RESOURCES

Estimate Activity Resources is the simple, yet important, process of determining the type and quantities of material, people, equipment, or supplies (physical resources) needed. . Ideally, resource needs are determined at the lowest level of the WBS (work package elements), then rolled-up to higher levels (major deliverables).

The primary deliverable of the Estimate Activity Resources process is a documented description of Activity Resource Requirements. Typically, the resource needs identified here will be obtained by later applying the Acquire Project Team process and the Procurement processes.

The Activity Attributes provide the primary data input for Estimate Activity Resources. The Estimate Activity Resource process is closely coordinated with several processes, including Estimate Costs, Acquire Project Team, Activity Duration Estimating, and Plan Procurements process.

Estimate Activity Resources (6.3)

INPUTS	TOOLS & TECHNIQUES	OUTPUTS
• Activity List • Activity Attributes • Resource Calendars • Enterprise Environmental Factors • Organizational Process Assets	• Expert Judgment • Alternatives Analysis • Published Estimating Data • Bottom-up Estimating • Project Management Software	• Activity Resource Requirements • Resource Breakdown Structure (RBS) • Project Document Updates

Determines the types and quantities of resources needed

- **Activity List** The comprehensive list and description of all schedule activities
- **Activity Attributes** An extension of the activity list, intended to provide more attribute details
- **Resource Calendars** Information on the availability of resources over the planned activity duration
- **Enterprise Environmental Factors** Consideration factors such as; culture, systems, procedures, industry standards
- **Organizational Process Assets** Consideration factors such as processes, procedures and corporate knowledge base

- **Expert Judgment** Expert technical and/or managerial judgment (from any qualified source)
- **Alternatives Analysis** Used to identify alternatives to account for various resource capabilities, skills, and availability
- **Published Estimating Data** Available published information on production rates and costs for an array of trades, materials, and equipment, and other resources
- **Bottom-Up Estimating** Deriving project totals by estimating individual activities, then rolling-up the summary
- **Project Management Software** Any software that may help plan, organize, manage resource estimates and pools

- **Activity Resource Requirements** Types and quantities of resources needed for each schedule activity
- **Resource Breakdown Structure (RBS)** Hierarchal structure of identified resources (by category and type)
- **Project Document Updates** Updates to other project documentation

---

Ultimate PMP Exam Prep Guide — **Must Know Concepts**

1. The Estimate Activity Resources process is intended to estimate the type and quantities of material, people, equipment, or supplies required to perform each activity.

2. Physical resources include people, equipment, supplies, and materials.

3. The primary deliverable (Output) from the Estimate Activity Resources process is the documented description of Activity Resource Requirements.

4. Bottom-up estimating generally produces the most reliable estimates, but is more costly and time-consuming than it's opposite, analogous estimating. Typically, bottom-up estimating is performed by developing detailed estimates for each activity at the work package level of the WBS. They are then rolled-up to derive a project total.

5. Identified resource requirements will typically be obtained later by applying the Acquire Project Team process and the Procurement processes.

6. The Estimate Activity Resource process is closely coordinated with the Estimate Cost Process.

LESSON 16 ESTIMATE ACTIVITY DURATIONS

Estimate Activity Durations is the process of estimating time durations for each defined activity resource, which will serve as an essential input for the Develop schedule process.

In simpler projects, estimates are typically documented as deterministic, single-point values (one number). For example, a single-point estimate may be documented as: 7 days (with no plus/minus flexibility). Single point estimates use expert judgment or an analogous estimate (also known as a "top-down estimate").

In more complex projects, it is common to use sophisticated mathematics to determine probabilistic distributions for each activity, resulting in a time-range estimate instead of a single-time estimate. For example, a probabilistic estimate may be documented as a graphical curve indicating the probability of an activity finishing at any given time on the curve. Probabilistic estimates generally provide for more reliable expectations. Probabilistic estimates usually use a method like three-point estimating to predict a range of outcomes. Duration estimates do not include any lags.

Estimate Activity Durations (6.4)

INPUTS	TOOLS & TECHNIQUES	OUTPUTS
• Activity List • Activity Attributes • Activity Resource Requirements • Resource Calendars • Project Scope Statement • Enterprise Environmental Factors • Organizational Process Assets	• Expert Judgment • Analogous Estimating • Parametric Analysis • Three-Point Estimates • Reserve Analysis	• Activity Duration Estimates • Project Document Updates

Estimates the number of work periods for each schedule activity

- **Activity List**   The comprehensive list and description of all schedule activities
- **Activity Attributes**   An extension of the activity list, intended to provide more attribute details
- **Activity Resource Requirements**   Types and quantities of resources needed for each schedule activity
- **Resource Calendars**   Information on the availability of resources over the planned activity duration
- **Project Scope Statement**   Detailed description of a projects deliverables and work required to create them
- **Enterprise Environmental Factors**   Consideration factors such as; culture, systems, procedures, industry standards
- **Organizational Process Assets**   Consideration factors such as processes, procedures and corporate knowledge base

- **Expert Judgment**   Expert technical and/or managerial judgment (from any qualified source)
- **Analogous Estimating**   Using actual results from a previous similar project to base current estimates
- **Parametric Analysis**   Use of project parameters to calculate predicted durations i.e. Total labor hours = 6,000
- **Three-Point Estimates**   Factoring most likely, optimistic, and pessimistic estimates to derive a forecasted estimate
- **Reserve Analysis**   Determining the appropriate amount of contingency reserve to compensate for project risk

- **Activity Duration Estimates**   Quantitative assessments of the time likely needed to complete each schedule activity
- **Project Document Updates**   Updates to other project documentation

---

Ultimate PMP Exam Prep Guide — Must Know Concepts

1. The Estimate Activity Durations process is estimating time durations for each defined activity resource. These estimates will ultimately be used to create the project schedule.

2. Care must be taken to differentiate the actual effort time (performance time) required to perform the activity work and the calendar time (elapsed time) required to complete the activity. Some activities have waiting time involved.

3. Deterministic (single-point) estimates are typically documented with only one value. Probabilistic (range) estimates typically report estimates in terms of probabilities, instead of hard numbers.

4. Estimating should originate from the person, or group of people, who are most knowledgeable about the activity, ideally by the person or people who will be doing the work.

5. Analogous estimating (also termed "top-down estimating") typically involves basing an estimate on a known previous activity performed in the past. Analogous estimates are relatively quick to perform and inexpensive, because no detailed estimating protocols are necessary. Analogous estimates are also the least reliable.

6. Three-Point Estimates uses the three estimates (Pessimistic, Most Probable, and Optimistic) and may be used as a tool to help determine an approximate range for an activity's duration. PERT analysis calculates an Expected activity duration using a weighted average of these estimates $t_E = t_O + 4t_M + t_{P/6}$.

7. Estimators may choose to include reserve time to proportionately compensate for the level of associated risk.

8. Duration estimates are typically documented in terms of work periods. Work periods are determined by the project team and are typically defined as shifts, hours, days, or weeks.

9. Ideally, estimates should be reported with ranges of possible results such as: 8 days ±2 (indicating 6–10 days).

LESSON 17 DEVELOP SCHEDULE
. . . .

Develop Schedule is the process to create the project schedule based on activity sequences, durations, resource requirements, and schedule constraints The project schedule is developed as the result of many detailed iterations and progressive elaboration across the entire planning phase.

Scheduling software has become an essential tool to help create the schedule. Most scheduling software today will allow project teams to input raw data, then automate the process of maneuvering it to create the schedule baseline. Once baselined, software can automate changes and tracking throughout the project's remaining phases.

Developing and maintaining a project schedule file can be quite time consuming and require expert support. In large projects, it is not unusual to assign one full-time scheduler for every thousand lines in the schedule.

The Develop Schedule process is applied to determine the start/finish dates for project activities.

Develop Schedule (6.5)		
INPUTS	**TOOLS & TECHNIQUES**	**OUTPUTS**
• Activity List • Activity Attributes • Project Schedule Network Diagrams • Activity Resource Requirements • Resource Calendars • Activity Duration Estimates • Project Scope Statement • Enterprise Environmental Factors • Organizational Process Assets	• Schedule Network Analysis • Critical Path Method • Critical Chain Method • Resource Leveling • What-If Scenarios Analysis • Applying Leads and Lags • Schedule Compression • Scheduling Tool	• Project Schedule • Schedule Baseline • Schedule Data • Project Document Updates

Analyzes activities and constraints to create the project schedule

- **Activity List**   The comprehensive list and description of all schedule activities
- **Activity Attributes**   An extension of the activity list, intended to provide more attribute details
- **Project Schedule Network Diagrams**   Schematic displays of the project's activities and their logical relationships
- **Activity Resource Requirements**   Types and quantities of resources needed for each schedule activity
- **Resource Calendars**   Information on the availability of resources over the planned activity duration
- **Activity Duration Estimates**   Quantitative assessments of the time likely needed to complete each schedule activity
- **Project Scope Statement**   Detailed description of a projects deliverables and work required to create them
- **Enterprise Environmental Factors**   Consideration factors such as; culture, systems, procedures, industry standards
- **Organizational Process Assets**   Consideration factors such as processes, procedures and corporate knowledge base
- -
- **Schedule Network Analysis**   Technique that generates the project schedule, employs various schedule models
- **Critical Path Method**   Calculates schedule dates without regard to resource limitations
- **Critical Chain Method**   Uses activity duration buffers to account for limited resources
- **Resource Leveling**   Technique applied to create efficient resource-limited schedules
- **What-If Scenario Analysis**   Explores various scenarios using simulations tools (Monte Carlo)
- **Applying Leads and Lags**   Further defined 'overlaps (leads)' and 'delays (lags)' in activity dependencies
- **Schedule Compression**   Shortens the project schedule without changing scope (fast-tracking, crashing)
- **Scheduling Tool**   Tool used to facilitate creation of the project schedule documentation
- -
- **Project Schedule**   Graphic presentation illustrating planned start and planned finish dates for each project activity
- **Schedule Baseline**   Specific version of the project schedule, accepted by the team as the project's schedule baseline
- **Schedule Data**   The schedule milestones, activities, activity attributes, and all documented assumptions and constraints
- **Project Document Updates**   Updates to other project documentation

Ultimate PMP Exam Prep Guide — **Must Know Concepts**

1.   The Develop Schedule process is applied to create the project schedule based on activity sequences, durations, resource requirements and schedule constraints.

2.   There are four primary methods used to calculate theoretical early/late start/finish dates for project activities: Critical Path Method (CPM), Critical Chain Method, What-if Scenario Analysis, and Resource Leveling.

3.   The primary deliverables (Outputs) of the Develop Schedule process include the Project Schedule and the Schedule Baseline.

4.   There are two primary methods used to shorten schedules: Crashing and Fast-Tracking.

5.   Completed project schedules are typically illustrated using bar charts (also called Gantt charts), milestone charts, or Project Schedule Network Diagrams.

6.   Resource leveling is a resource management tool sometimes used to "level" resources across the project schedule, to minimize exaggerated peaks and valleys.

7.   Heuristic is an academic term that means "thumb rule." Some modern project management conventions are generally described as heuristics, such as resource-leveling heuristics.

LESSON 18   DEVELOP HUMAN RESOURCE PLAN

The Develop Human Resource Plan process is applied to develop, document, and assign project roles, responsibilities, and reporting relationships. This typically involves creating a project organization chart, the Human Resource Plan, and defining team policies/procedures.

Logically, human resource planning is one of the earliest processes applied in project planning. Because the organizational structure will greatly influence the project's communications requirements, human resource planning is closely linked with communications planning.

Projects can be staffed by people external to the organization, internal to the organization, or by a mix of both. As you may imagine, a project team comprised of staff members who are temporarily borrowed from various groups within an organization will be quite different from a project team comprised of members who are all hired from the outside. To better understand the dynamics of different project organizations, it is helpful to understand the way different organizations tend to staff their projects.

Develop Human Resource Plan (9.1)		
INPUTS	**TOOLS & TECHNIQUES**	**OUTPUTS**
• Activity Resource Requirements • Enterprise Environmental Factors • Organizational Process Assets	• Organizational Charts and Position Descriptions • Networking • Organizational Theory	• Human Resource Plan
Documents project roles, responsibilities and reporting relationships		
• **Activity Resource Requirements** Types and quantities of resources needed for each schedule activity • **Enterprise Environmental Factors** Consideration factors such as; culture, systems, procedures, industry standards • **Organizational Process Assets** Consideration factors such as processes, procedures and corporate knowledge base		
• **Organization Charts and Position Descriptions** Displays illustrating project reporting relationships and positions • **Networking** Informal interaction to better understand political and interpersonal factors in an organization or industry • **Organizational Theory** The body of knowledge that describes how people, teams, and organizations behave		
• **Human Resource Plan** Describes how and when human resources will be applied to the project team		

Ultimate PMP Exam Prep Guide — **Must Know Concepts**

1.   The Develop Human Resource Plan process is applied to develop, document, and assign project roles, responsibilities, and reporting relationships.

2.   The primary output of the Develop Human Resource Plan process is the project's Human Resource Plan.

3.   The Human Resource Plan describes how/when human resources will be brought into the project and how/when human resources will leave the project. A Resource Histogram is often used to illustrate some of this information.

4.   A Resource Histogram illustrates human resource needs as a function of time.

5.   Roles (who does what) and responsibilities (who decides what) are often illustrated using a Responsibility Assignment Matrix (RAM).

6.   A Responsibility Assignment Matrix (RAM) illustrates assignments and levels of authority/responsibility, as a function of WBS elements. There is no time associated with a RAM.

7.   A RACI chart (Responsible, Accountable, Consult, Inform) is a type of RAM.

8.   Functional organizations typically do not perform much work as cross-functional projects. When they do, projects are usually the full responsibility of a functional manager. Project managers in functional organizations typically have very little authority and are often termed "project coordinators" or "project expediters."

9.   In matrix organizations, projects are performed using human resources borrowed from functional areas within the organization. In matrix organizations, project managers typically share responsibility and authority with functional managers.

10.   In projectized organizations, most work is performed as projects. In projectized organizations, the project manager typically assumes full profit/loss responsibility and authority and staffs the project with dedicated (not borrowed) human resources.

LESSON 19 ESTIMATE COSTS

Estimate Costs is the process of determining the estimated costs of resources that will be applied to complete all project schedule activities. This includes direct resources such as labor, materials, and equipment plus other indirect costs such as contingency cost reserves, inflation allowances, and overhead. Cost estimates may be in detail or in summary form.

It is important to distinguish between cost and price. For example, in a competitive bid scenario, a construction company may estimate its total cost to build an office complex then submit a bid with its price to the client. Typically the price will be higher than the cost. Generally, price is negotiable, whereas cost is not.

The Estimate Costs process is applied not only to produce cost estimates, but to create the Cost Management Plan as well. The Cost Management Plan serves as a subsidiary plan to the overall project management plan.

Estimate Costs (7.1)

INPUTS	TOOLS & TECHNIQUES	OUTPUTS
• Scope Baseline • Project Schedule • Human Resource Plan • Risk Register • Enterprise Environmental Factors • Organizational Process Assets	• Expert Judgment • Analogous Estimating • Parametric Estimating • Bottom-up Estimating • Three-Point Estimates • Reserve Analysis • Cost of Quality • Project Management Estimating Software • Vendor Bid Analysis	• Activity Cost Estimate • Basis of Estimates • Project Document Updates

Approximating the costs of resources needed to complete project activities

- **Scope Baseline** Scope Baseline = the approved project scope statement + the WBS + the WBS Dictionary
- **Project Schedule** Graphic presentation illustrating planned start and planned finish dates for each project activity
- **Human Resource Plan** Describes how and when human resources will be applied to the project team
- **Risk Register** List of identified risks
- **Enterprise Environmental Factors** Consideration factors such as culture, systems, procedures and industry standards
- **Organizational Process Assets** Consideration factors such as processes, procedures and corporate knowledge base

- **Analogous Estimating** Using actual results from a previous project to base current estimates
- **Parametric Estimating** Use of project parameters to calculate predicted costs
- **Bottom-Up Estimating** Deriving a project total by estimating individual activities, then rolling-up the summary
- **Reserve Analysis** Determining appropriate amount of contingency reserve to compensate for cost risk
- **Cost of Quality** Total costs incurred to achieve project quality (conformance to requirements)
- **Project Management Estimating Software** Cost estimating software applications, spreadsheets, simulations, and statistical tools
- **Vendor Bid Analysis** Analyzing vendor bids (in competitive bid situations) to determine project costs
- **Expert Judgment** Expert technical and/or managerial judgment (from any qualified source)
- **Three-Point Estimates** Factoring most likely, optimistic, and pessimistic estimates to derive a forecasted estimate

- **Activity Cost Estimates** A quantitative assessment of the probable costs required to complete an activity
- **Basis of Estimates** Documentation that supports the cost estimates by defining how the estimates were derived
- **Project Document Updates** Updates to other project documentation

Ultimate PMP Exam Prep Guide — Must Know Concepts

1. The Estimate Costs process is applied to develop cost estimates for each identified project activity. Costs include direct costs plus indirect costs.

2. Estimating should be performed by the person, or group of people, who are most knowledgeable about the activity.

3. Cost estimates should be prepared and documented with ranges of possible outcomes, instead of inflexible single-point values. For example, $9,300 –10% +25%.

4. An Order of Magnitude (or Rough Order of Magnitude [ROM]) estimate defines the estimate to be ±50%.

5. A Budget(ary) estimate defines the confidence level of an estimate to be ±25%.

6. A Definitive estimate defines the confidence level of an estimate to be ±10%.

7. Analogous estimating (also termed "top-down estimating") typically involves basing an estimate on a known previous activity performed in the past.

8. Bottom-up estimating generally produces the most reliable estimates, but is more costly and time consuming than analogous estimating.

9. Life Cycle Costing is an important concept to factor into project planning. It suggests that post-project operating costs should be considered when planning project strategies. Avoid strategies that will lower immediate costs but will increase post-project operating costs.

10. In addition to the cost estimates themselves, the cost management plan is defined as a key output of the estimating cost process. The cost management plan is intended to describe how cost will be managed across the project.

LESSON 20 DETERMINE BUDGET

The Determine Budget process is applied to formally aggregate all activity (and/or work package) cost estimates into a cohesive project budget and approved cost baseline

The project budget is sometimes termed the "Project Cost Performance Baseline" or "Performance Measurement Baseline" (PMB). Formally, the cost performance baseline is the time-phased budget. It is used to monitor and measure project cost performance across remaining project phases. When measuring the project using Earned Value Techniques, the Performance Measurement Baseline is represented by the Budget at Complete (BAC) value. Cost performance baselines are typically illustrated using graphs. Plotted cost baselines usually form an S-curve.

Management and contingency reserves are established in the Determine Budget Process. However, reserves are excluded in the baseline.

Determine Budget (7.2)

INPUTS	TOOLS & TECHNIQUES	OUTPUTS
• Activity Cost Estimates • Basis of Estimates • Scope Baseline • Project Schedule • Resource Calendars • Contracts • Organizational Process Assets	• Cost Aggregation • Reserve Analysis • Expert Judgment • Historical Relationships • Funding Limit Reconciliation	• Cost Performance Baseline • Project Funding Requirements • Project Document Updates

Aggregates individual activity costs to establish the project's Cost Performance Baseline

- **Activity Cost Estimates**   A quantitative assessment of the probable costs required to complete an activity
- **Basis of Estimates**   Documentation that supports the cost estimates by defining how the estimates were derived
- **Scope Baseline**   Scope Baseline = the approved project scope statement + the WBS + the WBS Dictionary
- **Project Schedule**   Graphic presentation illustrating planned start and planned finish dates for each project activity
- **Resource Calendars**   Information on the availability of resources over the planned activity duration
- **Contracts**   Applicable contract information for products and services to be purchased from external sources
- **Organizational Process Assets**   Consideration factors such as processes, procedures and corporate knowledge base

- **Cost Aggregation**   The process of aggregating schedule activity cost estimates by work packages
- **Reserve Analysis**   Determining the appropriate amount of contingency reserve to compensate for project risk
- **Expert Judgment**   Expert technical and/or managerial judgment (from any qualified source)
- **Historical Relationships**   Analogous and Parametric Models used for cost estimation
- **Funding Limit Reconciliation**   The scheduling of work to avoid large variations in periodic expenditures

- **Cost Performance Baseline**   The time-phased budget used to measure, monitor, and control project cost performance
- **Project Funding Requirements**   Simply the funding needed and when it will be needed
- **Project Document Updates**   Updates to other project documentation

---

Ultimate PMP Exam Prep Guide — Must Know Concepts

1.   The Determine Budget process is applied to formally aggregate all activity cost estimates into a cohesive project budget, also known as the Cost Performance Baseline.

2.   The primary deliverable (Output) of the Determine Budget process is the cost performance baseline (performance measurement baseline [PMB]).

3.   The Cost Performance Baseline is the project's time-phased budget.

4.   The Cost Performance Baseline is used to monitor and measure project cost performance across project phases.

5.   Cost Performance baselines are typically illustrated using graphs. Plotted cost performance baselines usually form an S-curve.

6.   Reserves are excluded in the Cost Performance Baseline.

LESSON 21 PLAN QUALITY

The Plan Quality process is applied to identify which quality standards are applicable to the project and then determine how to satisfy them. Quality planning is often applied in parallel with other processes during project planning.

The term quality means different things to different people, depending on their specific orientation and application environment. For our purposes in project management, quality means delivering precisely what is promised. When a project team delivers on time, within budget, and has satisfied all scope requirements, then high quality has been achieved.

It is important to understand that quality must be "planned in" to the project, not "inspected in."

It is also helpful to understand that the terms "quality" and "grade" are not identical. Quality is the totality of characteristics to satisfy requirements. Grade is a measurement of technical characteristics.

Plan Quality (8.1)

INPUTS	TOOLS & TECHNIQUES	OUTPUTS
• Scope Baseline • Stakeholder Register • Cost Performance Baseline • Schedule Baseline • Risk Register • Enterprise Environmental Factors • Organizational Process Assets	• Cost-Benefit Analysis • Cost of Quality • Control Charts • Benchmarking • Design of Experiments • Statistical Sampling • Flowcharting • Proprietary Quality Management Methodologies • Additional Quality Planning Tools	• Quality Management Plan • Quality Metrics • Quality Checklists • Process Improvement Plan • Project Document Updates

Identifies project quality standards and defines how they will be satisfied

- **Scope Baseline**   Scope Baseline = the approved project scope statement + the WBS + the WBS dictionary
- **Stakeholder Register**   A document identifying all project stakeholder information
- **Cost Performance Baseline**   The time-phased budget used to measure, monitor, and control project cost performance
- **Schedule Baseline**   Specific version of the project schedule, accepted by the team as the project's schedule baseline
- **Risk Register**   List of identified risks
- **Enterprise Environmental Factors**   Consideration factors such as; culture, systems, procedures, industry standards
- **Organizational Process Assets**   Consideration factors such as processes, procedures and corporate knowledge base

- **Cost-Benefit Analysis**   The use of financial measures to assess the desirability of identified alternatives
- **Cost of Quality**   Total costs incurred to achieve project quality (conformance to requirements)
- **Control Charts**   Charts used to determine if processes are stable and performing in a predictable manner
- **Benchmarking**   Comparing performance to a selected 'standard', primarily to generate ideas for improvement
- **Design of Experiments**   A statistical method to help identify optimal solutions, factoring-in specific variables
- **Statistical Sampling**   Statistical analysis using a small group from an entire population
- **Flowcharting**   Diagramming methods that can help analyze how problems in a system occur
- **Proprietary Quality Management Methodologies**   Other quality management methodologies (Ex: Lean 6 Sigma)
- **Additional Quality Planning Tools**   Affinity diagrams, force field analysis, matrix diagrams, and others

- **Quality Management Plan**   Describes how the team will implement the organization's quality policy
- **Quality Metrics**   Operational definitions. Project elements, and how they are to be measured by quality control
- **Quality Checklists**   Structured forms used to verify that a set of required steps has been performed
- **Process Improvement Plan**   Describes the steps for analyzing processes to eliminate wasteful activities
- **Project Document Updates**   Updates to other project documentation

---

Ultimate PMP Exam Prep Guide — **Must Know Concepts**

1. The Plan Quality process identifies which quality standards are applicable to the project and how to satisfy them.

2. The primary outputs of Plan Quality are the Quality Management Plan and Process Improvement Plan.

3. In project management, quality means delivering precisely what is promised. When a project team delivers on time, within budget, and has satisfied all scope requirements, then high quality has been achieved.

4. Quality must be planned in to a project, not inspected in.

5. Quality and grade are not the same. Low quality is a problem; low grade is not.

6. A quality policy is an organization's quality commitment.

7. Cost of quality includes all costs expended to achieve product/service quality objectives.

8. Quality metrics are the specific parameters a project team selects for measuring quality performance.

9. Process improvement is any action taken to improve efficiency and effectiveness in project performance, providing increased benefits to project stakeholders.

10. Total Quality Management (TQM) is a concept/practice intended to help organizations achieve quality improvement objectives.

LESSON 22   PLAN RISK MANAGEMENT

Project risk management is a knowledge area that has been largely overlooked in the past, but is now recognized as one of the most important areas in all of modern project management.

Risk infiltrates each and every aspect of a project. Even though risk is found everywhere in the project environment, it can be identified, analyzed, and managed to minimize potential negative impacts and maximize potential positive impacts.

There are six closely associated processes in project risk management. The first is Plan Risk Management. In Plan Risk Management, we decide how to approach and plan our risk management activities for a particular project. The Plan Risk management process is applied to develop the project's Risk Management Plan.

Plan Risk Management (11.1)

INPUTS	TOOLS & TECHNIQUES	OUTPUTS
• Project Scope Statement • Cost Management Plan • Schedule Management Plan • Communications Management Plan • Enterprise Environmental Factors • Organizational Process Assets	• Planning Meetings and Analysis	• Risk Management Plan

Defines how risk management will be accomplished for a project

- **Project Scope Statement**   Detailed description of a projects deliverables and work required to create them
- **Cost Management Plan**   Defines how risk budgets, contingencies, and management reserves will be managed
- **Communications Management Plan**   Details the management of all project communications
- **Schedule Management Plan**   Defines how changes to the project schedule will be managed
- **Enterprise Environmental Factors**   Consideration factors such as; culture, systems, procedures, industry standards
- **Organizational Process Assets**   Consideration factors such as processes, procedures and corporate knowledge base

- **Planning Meetings and Analysis**   Project team meetings held to develop the risk management plan

- **Risk Management Plan**   Describes how project risk management will be structured and performed across the project

---

Ultimate PMP Exam Prep Guide — Must Know Concepts

1. Project risk is any uncertain event or condition that, if it occurs, has a positive or negative effect on a project objective.

2. Project risks can be positive or negative.

3. Negative risks are threats and should be avoided.

4. Positive risks are opportunities and should be pursued.

5. Project risk management is comprised of six closely associated processes.

6. Plan Risk Management is the first of the five risk management processes used in planning and is applied to decide and document how project risk will be approached and planned.

7. The primary deliverable (Output) of the Plan Risk Management process is the Risk Management Plan.

LESSON 23   IDENTIFY RISKS

Identify Risks is the second of the five risk processes that occur in the Planning process group. The Identify Risks process is applied to determine which risks may affect the project and to document their characteristics.

The primary objective of this process is to create a list of identified risks, along with the indications that the risk has occurred or is about to occur. These indications are termed "triggers," "risk symptoms," or "warning signs." Each identified risk will be analyzed during the application of subsequent risk management processes. To help identify as many risks as possible, many knowledgeable people should participate in the process. Several iterations are likely before the list of risks is done.

While most risk identification is done during planning, identifying risks is a process that should be done frequently.

Identify Risks (11.2)

INPUTS	TOOLS & TECHNIQUES	OUTPUTS
• Risk Management Plan • Activity Cost Estimates • Activity Duration Estimates • Scope Baseline • Stakeholder Register • Cost Management Plan • Schedule Management Plan • Quality Management Plan • Project Documents • Enterprise Environmental Factors • Organizational Process Assets	• Documentation Reviews • Information Gathering Techniques • Checklist Analysis • Assumptions Analysis • Diagramming Techniques • SWOT • Expert Judgment	• Risk Register

Determines potential project risks and documents their characteristics

- **Risk Management Plan**   Describes how project risk management will be structured and performed across the project
- **Activity Cost Estimates**   A quantitative assessment of the probable costs required to complete an activity
- **Activity Duration Estimates**   Quantitative assessments of the time likely needed to complete each schedule activity
- **Scope Baseline**   Scope Baseline = the approved project scope statement + the WBS + the WBS dictionary
- **Stakeholder Register**   A document identifying all project stakeholder information
- **Cost Management Plan**   Defines how risk budgets, contingencies, and management reserves will be managed
- **Schedule Management Plan**   Defines how changes to the project schedule will be managed
- **Quality Management Plan**   Describes how the team will implement the organization's quality policy
- **Project Documents**   Additional project documentation that aids in identification of risks
- **Enterprise Environmental Factors**   Consideration factors such as; culture, systems procedures, industry standards
- **Organizational Process Assets**   Consideration factors such as; processes, procedures and corporate knowledge base

- **Documentation Reviews**   A structured review of all project documentation
- **Information Gathering Techniques**   Various techniques used to help in identification of risks
- **Checklist Analysis**   Checklists based on historical risks identified for previous similar projects
- **Assumptions Analysis**   Analysis of project assumptions to identify possible risks associated with those assumptions
- **Diagramming Techniques**   Risk diagramming techniques (Ex: Cause and Effect diagrams)
- **SWOT**   Strengths, Weaknesses, Opportunities, and Threats (SWOT) Analysis
- **Expert Judgment**   Expert technical and/or managerial judgment (from any qualified source)

- **Risk Register**   List of identified risks

Ultimate PMP Exam Prep Guide — Must Know Concepts

1. Project risk is an uncertain event or condition that, if it occurs, has a positive or negative effect on a project objective. A risk has a cause, and if it occurs, a consequence.

2. The Identify Risks process determines which risks may affect the project and their characteristics.

3. Identifying risks is a process that should be encouraged frequently throughout the project life cycle.

4. There are four generally accepted categories of risk in project environments: technical risks (technical, quality, and performance), project management risks, organizational risks, and external risks.

5. Information gathering techniques used to help identify project risks include: brainstorming, Delphi technique, interviewing, and root cause identification.

6. Diagramming techniques can be applied to help identify project risks including: cause and effect diagrams, systems flowcharts and influence diagrams.

7. SWOT analysis is another technique that analyzes the organization's Strengths, Weaknesses, Opportunities, and Threats can bring risks to the surface.

8. Indications that a risk has occurred, or is about to occur, are termed "triggers" (or "risk symptoms" or "warning signs").

9. The primary output of the Identify Risks process is the Risk Register. The Risk Register is created during risk identification and then used to capture the outputs of all subsequent risk processes. The Risk Register becomes a subsidiary plan to the overall project management plan.

LESSON 24   PERFORM QUALITATIVE RISK ANALYSIS

Perform Qualitative Risk Analysis is the process of assessing the impact and likelihood of identified risks. It is the third of five risk planning processes, and is logically applied as the next step after the Identify Risks process.

Perform Qualitative Risk Analysis is intended to help prioritize identified risks and identify those risks serious enough to warrant further analysis. As you may imagine, some identified risks have very little probability of occurring and, if they occur, would have only a slight impact. As a result of the Perform Qualitative Risk Analysis process, these risks would be appropriately listed low in priority. Other identified risks may have high probabilities of occurring and/or significant impact if they occur. These risks may be listed high in priority.

A probability/impact (P-I) risk rating matrix is used as the primary tool in Qualitative Risk Analysis to determine the impact and likelihood of identified risks.

A probability/impact (P-I) matrix is a tool that combines both risk probability and risk impact into a single score. It is used to help determine qualitative risk rankings.

Perform Qualitative Risk Analysis (11.3)		
INPUTS	**TOOLS & TECHNIQUES**	**OUTPUTS**
• Risk Register • Risk Management Plan • Project Scope Statement • Organizational Process Assets	• Risk Probability and Impact Assessment • Probability and Impact Matrix • Risk Data Quality Assessment • Risk Categorization • Risk Urgency Assessment • Expert Judgment	• Risk Register Updates

Prioritizes risks by analyzing their combined probability and impact

- **Risk Register**   List of identified risks
- **Risk Management Plan**   Describes how project risk management will be structured and performed across the project
- **Project Scope Statement**   Detailed description of a projects deliverables and work required to create them
- **Organizational Process Assets**   Consideration factors such as processes, procedures and corporate knowledge base

- **Risk Probability and Impact Assessment**   Qualitative assessment of individual risk probability/impact
- **Probability and Impact Matrix**   A matrix that rates/prioritizes risks by combining probabilities and impacts
- **Risk Data Quality Assessment**   Technique to determine the level (confidence) to which a risk is useful
- **Risk Categorization**   Technical risks, external risks, project management risks, organizational risks
- **Risk Urgency Assessment**   Identification of risks which may require near-term responses
- **Expert Judgment**   Expert technical and/or managerial judgment (from any qualified source)

- **Risk Register Updates**   Updates to the list of identified risks

Ultimate PMP Exam Prep Guide — Must Know Concepts

1. The Perform Qualitative Risk Analysis process is applied to assess the impact and likelihood of identified risks. It is intended to help prioritize identified risks and identify those risks serious enough to warrant further analysis.

2. A probability/impact (P-I) risk rating matrix is a tool that combines both risk probability and risk impact into a single score. It is used to help determine qualitative risk rankings.

3. The primary output of the Perform Qualitative Risk Analysis process is new input to the Risk Register, including a list of risks for additional analysis, a list of prioritized risks, a list of risks requiring near-term response, risks grouped by category, and more.

LESSON 25   PERFORM QUANTITATIVE RISK ANALYSIS

The Perform Quantitative Risk Analysis process is applied to guide the additional analysis of individual risks, to determine the numerical value of its probability of occurrence and the numerical value of its consequence on project objectives should it occur. This process is also applied to determine a numerical value for overall project risk. Perform Quantitative Risk Analysis is the fourth of five risk planning processes and is normally applied as the logical next step following perform qualitative risk analysis.

Today's powerful desktop computers and application software allows project teams to perform sophisticated quantitative risk analyses, which contributes to higher confidence in schedule estimates, cost estimates, and overall quality. Monte Carlo simulation and expected monetary value analysis are commonly used tools to apply perform quantitative risk analysis.

Perform Quantitative Risk Analysis (11.4)		
INPUTS	**TOOLS & TECHNIQUES**	**OUTPUTS**
• Risk Register • Risk Management Plan • Cost Management Plan • Schedule Management Plan • Organizational Process Assets	• Data Gathering and Representation Techniques • Quantitative Risk Analysis and Modeling Techniques • Expert Judgment	• Risk Register Updates
Numerically analyzes the effect of risks on overall project objectives		
• **Risk Register** List of identified risks • **Risk Management Plan** Describes how project risk management will be structured and performed across the project • **Cost Management Plan** Defines how risk budgets, contingencies, and management reserves will be managed • **Schedule Management Plan** Defines how changes to the project schedule will be managed • **Organizational Process Assets** Consideration factors such as processes, procedures and corporate knowledge base		
• **Data Gathering and Representation Techniques** Interviewing, probability distributions, expert judgement • **Quantitative Risk Analysis and Modeling Techniques** Sensitivity analysis, EMV, decision tree, simulation • **Expert Judgment** Expert technical and/or managerial judgment (from any qualified source)		
• **Risk Register Updates** Updates to the list of identified risks		

Ultimate PMP Exam Prep Guide — **Must Know Concepts**

1. The Perform Quantitative Risk Analysis process is applied to guide the additional analysis of individual risks, to determine the numerical value of its probability of occurrence and the numerical value of its consequence on project objectives should it occur. This process is also applied to determine a numerical value for overall project risk.

2. Sensitivity analysis is a simple risk analysis technique used to help make project decisions based on the general risk sensitivity of an organization, person, or group of people.

3. Simulation is a quantitative risk analysis tool that can produce probability-based predictions for many project parameters. Monte Carlo algorithms provide the underlying engines in many of today's simulation software programs. Monte Carlo simulation works by running numerous simulations with project-specific information.

4. Expected Monetary Value Analysis (EMV) is a quantitative risk analysis tool. EMV is calculated by multiplying the value of each possible outcome by its probability of occurrence, then adding them all together. $EMV = V \times P$, where V is value in dollars and P is probability. Decision tree analysis illustrates the decision being considered, along with all the implications of choosing various alternatives. Solving a decision tree yields the path with the greatest expected value.

5. The primary output of the Perform Quantitative Risk Analysis process is new input information to the Risk Register including probabilistic analysis of the project, probability of achieving cost and time objectives, a prioritized list of quantified risks, and more.

616   Ultimate PMP® Exam Prep Study Guide

LESSON 26   PLAN RISK RESPONSES

The Plan Risk Responses process is applied to develop options and determine actions to enhance opportunities (positive risks), and to develop options and determine actions to reduce threats (negative risks).

A primary objective of the Plan Risk Responses process is to create the project's Risk Response Plan as part of the Risk Register.

Once a risk has been identified and analyzed (qualitatively and quantitatively), a decision must be made on what to do about the risk. It is the intent of Plan Risk Responses to guide that decision, by planning an appropriate response to the risk.

Plan Risk Responses (11.5)		
INPUTS	**TOOLS & TECHNIQUES**	**OUTPUTS**
• Risk Register • Risk Management Plan	• Strategies for Negative Risks or threats • Strategies for Positive Risks or Opportunities • Contingent Response Strategies • Expert Judgment	• Risk Register Updates • Risk-Related Contract Decisions • Project Management Plan Updates • Project Document Updates
Develops options & actions to reduce threats and enhance opportunities		
• **Risk Register** List of identified risks • **Risk Management Plan** Describes how project risk management will be structured and performed across the project		
• **Strategies for Negative Risks or Threats** Avoid, transfer, mitigate • **Strategies for Positive Risks or Opportunities** Exploit, share, enhance • **Contingent Response Strategy** Responses planned for implementation if/when certain conditions occur • **Expert Judgment** Expert technical and/or managerial judgment (from any qualified source)		
• **Risk Register Updates** Updates to the list of identified risks • **Risk-Related Contract Decisions** Insurance, services and/or other items contracted to address specific risks • **Project Management Plan Updates** Updates to the Project Management Plan as a result of this process • **Project Document Updates** Updates to other project documentation		

Ultimate PMP Exam Prep Guide — Must Know Concepts

1.   The Plan Risk Responses process is applied to develop options and determine actions to enhance opportunities (positive risks), and to develop options and determine actions to reduce threats (negative risks).

2.   The primary output of the Plan Risk Responses process is the project's completed Risk Register.

3.   Avoidance is one of the strategies for negative risks or threats. Avoidance involves changing the project plan, or condition within the plan, to eliminate the risk.

4.   Transference is one of the strategies for negative risks or threats. Risk transfer involves shifting the consequence and ownership of a risk to a third party. Transfer does not eliminate the risk.

5.   Mitigation is one of the strategies for negative risks or threats. Mitigation involves reducing the probability and/or impact of a negative risk to an acceptable threshold.

6.   Acceptance is a strategy for both threats and opportunities. With active acceptance, a contingency plan is developed in advance to respond to the risk, should it occur. With passive acceptance, a response action is developed only if and when the risk event occurs.

7.   Exploit, Share, and Enhance are strategies for positive risks or opportunities.

8.   Secondary risks are those risks that arise from the implementation of risk response actions.

9.   Residual risks are those risks that remain after response actions have been implemented. Residual risks also include those risks that have been accepted.

10.   Contingency action is any planned response action to a risk, should it occur.

11.   Contingency allowance (or contingency reserve) is a cost buffer or time buffer included in the project plan to compensate for risk and to help reduce the probability of overruns.

LESSON 27   PLAN PROCUREMENTS

The Plan Procurements process is the planning process used to document decisions regarding the purchasing and acquisition of required project resources. In addition, this process identifies potential sellers for required resources.

It is important to understand that the required resources include more than just physical materials or components, but can include services and labor from outside the immediate project organization.

There are three primary activities during Plan Procurements: make or buy decision making, contract selection and creation of the Procurement Management Plan.

The Plan Procurements process is closely related to the Develop Schedule and Estimate Activity Resources processes. It also must factor in consideration for project risks involved in purchasing decisions.

Plan Procurements (12.1)		
INPUTS	**TOOLS & TECHNIQUES**	**OUTPUTS**
• Scope Baseline • Requirements Documentation • Teaming Agreements • Risk Register • Risk-Related Contract Decisions • Activity Resource Requirements • Project Schedule • Activity Cost Estimates • Cost Performance Baseline • Enterprise Environmental Factors • Organizational Process Assets	• Make or Buy Analysis • Expert Judgment • Contract Types	• Procurement Management Plan • Procurement Statements of Work • Make-or-Buy Decisions • Procurement Documents • Source Selection Criteria • Change Requests

Document purchasing decisions, the procurement approach, and identify potential sellers

- **Scope Baseline**   Scope baseline = the approved project scope statement + the WBS + the WBS dictionary
- **Requirements Documentation**   Documentation describing how individual requirements meet the business needs of the project
- **Teaming Agreements**   Legal contractual agreements between parties to form partnerships or joint ventures
- **Risk Register**   List of identified risks
- **Risk-Related Contract Decisions**   Insurance, services, and/or other items contracted to address specific risks
- **Activity Cost Estimates**   A quantitative assessment of the probable costs required to complete an activity
- **Cost Performance Baseline**   The time-phased budget used to measure, monitor, and control project cost performance
- **Enterprise Environmental Factors**   Consideration factors such as; culture, systems, procedures, industry standards
- **Organizational Process Assets**   Consideration factors such as processes, procedures, and corporate knowledge base

- **Make-or-Buy Analysis**   General management technique used to determine which resources must be purchased outside of the organization
- **Expert Judgment**   Expert technical and/or managerial judgment (from any qualified source)
- **Contract Types**   Consideration and selection of an appropriate contract types for the intended purchases

- **Procurement Management Plan**   Describes how the procurement process will be managed from documentation through contract closure
- **Procurement Statements of Work**   Detailed description of the 'procurement item,' for prospective suppliers (sellers)
- **Make-or-Buy Decisions**   The documented decisions of what will be developed in-house and what will be purchased
- **Procurement Documents**   Documents used to solicit proposals from prospective sellers
- **Source Selection Criteria**   Criteria used to help score or rate proposals submitted by prospective project suppliers (sellers)
- **Change Requests**   Request for changes to scope, schedule, costs, or processes or other project documentation

Ultimate PMP Exam Prep Guide — Must Know Concepts

1.   The Plan Procurements process is the planning process used to document decisions regarding the purchasing and acquisition of required project resources.

2.   A primary output of the Plan Procurements process is the Procurement Management Plan.

3.   If it is determined during Plan Procurements that there are no products or services that need to be acquired externally, then the remaining Procurement Management processes do not need to be performed.

4.   There are three primary activities during the Plan Procurements process: Make-or-buy decision making, Selecting the type of contract(s) to be negotiated with suppliers, and Creating the Procurement Management Plan.

5.   There are the three broad categories of contract types: Fixed Price, Cost Reimbursable, and Time and Materials (T&M).

6.   The Plan Procurements process is also applied to develop documents to be used to support the Conduct Procurements process.

7.   Statements of work are prepared in sufficient detail to allow prospective sellers to bid on the work.

8.   Procurement documents are prepared to inform sellers of the project need. Common procurement document forms include RFP (Request for Proposal), RFQ (Request for Quote), and IFB (Invitation for Bid).

9.   Evaluation criteria should be developed during this process to ensure that procurement is handled in a fair and equitable manner.

LESSON 28   DEVELOP PROJECT MANAGEMENT PLAN

The Develop Project Management Plan process represents the final step in project planning. It simply defines, integrates, and coordinates all subsidiary plans and the outputs from other planning processes into a single, cohesive document: the Project Management Plan.

Once approved and authorized, the Project Management Plan is used to:

serve as the baseline for monitoring and measuring project performance during execution and control

- facilitate stakeholder communications during execution and control
- guide all aspects of the project through execution, monitoring and control, and closing
- document project planning decisions, strategies, alternatives, and assumptions

The Project Management Plan is progressively elaborated through updates throughout a project's life cycle.

The Project Management Plan and a Project Schedule are not one and the same. In common application, many persons, including project managers, tend to use "project plan" to mean a Microsoft Project Schedule; however these documents are two distinct things.

Develop Project Management Plan (4.2)		
INPUTS	**TOOLS & TECHNIQUES**	**OUTPUTS**
• Project Charter • Outputs from Planning Processes • Enterprise Environmental Factors • Organizational Process Assets	• Expert Judgment	• Project Management Plan

Documenting all actions required to define, prepare, integrate, and coordinate all subsidiary plans

- **Project Charter**   High-level document that authorizes the project and assigns/authorizes the project manager
- **Outputs from Planning Processes**   Planning documents from the other project planning processes
- **Enterprise Environmental Factors**   Consideration factors such as; culture, systems, procedures, and industry standards
- **Organizational Process Assets**   Consideration factors such as processes, procedures and corporate knowledge base

- **Expert Judgment**   Expert technical and/or managerial judgment (from any qualified source)

- **Project Management Plan**   The consolidated package of the subsidiary management plans and baselines

Ultimate PMP Exam Prep Guide — Must Know Concepts

1.   The Develop Project Management Plan process represents the final step in project planning.

2.   The Develop Project Management Plan process is applied to gather the outputs from all other planning processes, all subsidiary plans, then assemble them into a single, cohesive document: the Project Management Plan.

3.   The primary deliverable (Output) of the Develop Project Management Plan process is the Project Management Plan.

4.   The Project Management Plan documents project planning decisions, strategies, alternatives, and assumptions.

5.   The Project Management Plan serves as the baseline for monitoring and measuring project performance during execution, monitoring and control, and closing.

6.   The Project Management Plan facilitates stakeholder communications during execution, monitoring and control, and closing.

7.   The Project Management Plan guides all aspects of the project through execution, monitoring and control, and closing.

LESSON 30   DIRECT AND MANAGE PROJECT EXECUTION

Direct and Manage Project Execution is the process of coordinating and directing all the resources that exist across the project, in carrying out the Project Management Plan. To successfully execute the Project Management Plan, the project manager and team must constantly monitor and measure performance against baselines, so that timely corrective action can be taken, as appropriate. Also, final cost and schedule forecasts must be updated periodically, as appropriate.

Typically, most project costs are expended during project execution.

The understanding and appropriate use of general management skills are most important during project execution.

Direct and Manage Project Execution (4.3)

INPUTS	TOOLS & TECHNIQUES	OUTPUTS
• Project Management Plan • Approved Change Requests • Enterprise Environmental Factors • Organizational Process Assets	• Expert Judgment • Project Management Information System	• Deliverables • Work Performance Data • Change Requests • Project Management Plan Updates • Project Document Updates

Executes the work defined in the project management plan

- **Project Management Plan**   The consolidated package of the subsidiary management plans and baselines
- **Approved Change Requests**   Documented, authorized changes that expand or reduce scope
- **Enterprise Environmental Factors**   Consideration factors such as; culture, systems, procedures, industry standards
- **Organizational Process Assets**   Consideration factors such as processes, procedures and corporate knowledge base

- **Expert Judgment**   Expert technical and/or managerial judgment (from any qualified source)
- **Project Management Information System (PMIS)**   Automated system to help the team execute planned activities

- **Deliverables**   Results, products, and/or capabilities (unique, verifiable outcomes) of activities performed
- **Work Performance Data**   Raw data related to deliverable status, schedule progress, and costs incurred
- **Change Requests**   Requests for changes to scope, cost, budget, schedule, or policies and procedures
- **Project Management Plan Updates**   Updates to the Project Management Plan as a result of this process
- **Project Document Updates**   Updates to other project documentation

---

Ultimate PMP Exam Prep Guide — Must Know Concepts

1. The Direct and Manage Project Execution process is applied by the project manager and project team to coordinate and direct all the resources that exist across the project, in carrying out the Project Management Plan.

2. To successfully execute the Project Management Plan, the project manager and team must constantly monitor and measure performance against baselines, so that timely corrective action can be taken.

3. The primary deliverable (Outputs) of the Direct and Manage Project Execution process are work results (deliverables).

4. The effective use of people skills is essential to achieve success during project execution.

5. In most projects, most of the project budget is spent during the project execution phase.

6. Formal work authorization systems are helpful to control project work, especially with respect to minimizing unnecessary scope expansion (so-called "Scope creep").

7. Sources of conflict in projects often include (in rank order): schedules, budgets, priorities, human resources, technical trade-offs, personalities. and administrative procedures.

8. The six commonly applied techniques for conflict resolution include: withdrawing, forcing, smoothing, confronting, collaborating, and compromising.

9. Items typically requiring negotiation in projects include: human resources, budgets, schedules, changes, performance criteria, issues, scope, and supplies.

10. Negotiation in projects typically involve people such as: functional managers, executive managers, contractors, other project managers, and clients.

11. Sources/Types of leadership power in projects include: reward power, punishment power, referent power, expert power, title power, information power, charismatic power, and contacts power.

LESSON 31 ACQUIRE PROJECT TEAM

The Acquire Project Team process is applied to get needed human resources assigned and working on the project.

When considering people to support the project, the project team should factor in things such as experience, availability, competencies, personal characteristics, and whether or not the potential resource has an interest in working on the project. Many times, especially in matrix organizations, you as project manager may need to use your best negotiating skills to get the people you want from their functional manager(s).

The Acquire Project Team process is defined as an executing process in the *PMBOK® Guide Fourth Edition*. This does not mean that the project manager has to wait until late in the project to acquire the project team. Best practice guidelines would suggest that a core project team will be acquired early in the project — immediately after the project charter is issued. Other human resources will be brought on throughout the project as needed. It will be important that the project manager plan carefully and not acquire resources without first considering the Develop Human Resource Plan process and its outcomes: the Staffing Management Plan and Roles and Responsibilities for the project.

An important consideration for the project manager will be to negotiate for and acquire resources which have the needed levels of competency that are required to execute the project. If the available resources do not have the required competencies and experience, if there are not sufficient resources available to perform project activities, or if resources cannot be acquired in a timely manner, the project manager will return to the planning processes and replan portions of the project that are affected by differences in planned human resources.

The Acquire Project Team process is complete when the project is reliably staffed with appropriate people. Many project teams publish a formal team directory when staffing is complete.

Acquire Project Team (9.2)

INPUTS	TOOLS & TECHNIQUES	OUTPUTS
• Project Management Plan • Enterprise Environmental Factors • Organizational Process Assets	• Pre-Assignment • Negotiation • Acquisition • Virtual Teams	• Project Staff Assignments • Resource Calendars • Project Management Plan Updates

Obtains needed project human resources

- **Project Management Plan** The consolidated package of the subsidiary management plans and baselines
- **Enterprise Environmental Factors** Consideration factors such as; culture, systems, procedures, industry standards
- **Organizational Process Assets** Consideration factors such as processes, procedures and corporate knowledge base

- -

- **Pre-Assignment** Predefined project staff assignments. Example: Staff was identified in the project charter
- **Negotiation** Influential discussions (typically with Functional Managers) to fill project staff assignments
- **Acquisition** Obtaining project staff from outside sources (if necessary), using project procurement management
- **Virtual Teams** Teams with shared goals working with little or no face-to-face communications

- -

- **Project Management Plan Updates** Updates to the Project Management Plan as a result of this process
- **Project Staff Assignments** The appropriate people, reliably assigned to staff the project
- **Resource Calendars** Documents the time periods each team member can work on the project

---

Ultimate PMP Exam Prep Guide — Must Know Concepts

1. The Acquire Project Team process is applied to obtain and assign needed human resources (people) to the project.

2. The project manager will negotiate with functional managers and other sources of possible project team members as necessary to obtain the people a project manager desires.

3. The project manager will use procurement processes to acquire staff if external staff are used for the project

4. The primary deliverable (Output) of the Acquire Project Team process is project staff assignments.

LESSON 32   DEVELOP PROJECT TEAM

Develop Project Team is the process of enhancing the ability of individual team members (skills and team cohesiveness) to enhance overall project performance. In practice, team development is a continuous process applied from the time the project team comes together until the team disbands. In concept, stronger individuals will naturally create a stronger team.

Generally, Develop Project Team tools include:

- training
- team-building activities
- reward and recognition systems
- colocation

Some project managers like to establish a project war room where core team members can be colocated to work in close proximity during the project.

In some matrix organizations, team development can be extra challenging when team members report to both the project manager and to their functional manager. In most organizations, the resources will be more closely aligned with their functional managers and will minimize input from the project manager on any organizational issues other than those directly relating to the project.

Develop Project Team (9.3)

INPUTS	TOOLS & TECHNIQUES	OUTPUTS
• Project Staff Assignments • Project Management Plan • Resource Calendars	• Interpersonal Skills • Training • Team-Building Activities • Ground Rules • Co-Location • Recognition and Rewards	• Team Performance Assessment • Enterprise Environmental Factors Updates

Improves people competencies to enhance project performance

- **Project Staff Assignments**   The appropriate people, reliably assigned to staff the project
- **Project Management Plan**   The consolidated package of the subsidiary management plans and baselines
- **Resource Calendars**   Documents the time periods each team member can work on the project

---

- **Interpersonal Skills**   The broad set of 'soft skills' important to team development
- **Training**   Activities designed to enhance the competencies of project team members
- **Team-Building Activities**   Actions designed to enhance interpersonal relationships among team members
- **Ground Rules**   Documented team rules to establish clear expectations with respect to acceptable behavior
- **Co-Location**   The placing of team members in the same physical location, to enhance team performance
- **Recognition and Rewards**   Formal management actions that recognize and reward desirable behavior

---

- **Team Performance Assessments**   Formal and/or informal assessments of the team's effectiveness
- **Enterprise Environmental Factors Updates**   Updates to employee training records and skill assessments

---

Ultimate PMP Exam Prep Guide — Must Know Concepts

1. Develop Project Team is the process of enhancing the ability of individual team members (skills and team cohesiveness) to enhance overall project performance.

2. In some matrix organizations, team development can be extra challenging when team members report to both the project manager and to their functional manager.

3. The primary deliverables (Output) of the Develop Project Team process are team performance assessments.

4. It may be helpful to colocate team members to a single work location during the project.

5. A war room is sometimes established to serve as a temporary office to function as a single working headquarters for the project team.

6. Rewards and recognition are management actions intended to encourage desired behavior.

7. Important content theories of motivation include Maslow's Hierarchy of Needs and Herzberg's Motivator/Hygiene Theory.

8. Important process theories of motivation include McGregor's Theory X/Theory Y.

LESSON 33 MANAGE PROJECT TEAM

We apply the Manage Project Team process to address performance, behavior, issues, and conflicts associated specifically with project team members.

The process involves tracking and appraising team member performance, resolving issues, observing team behavior, managing conflicts, and providing feedback. In matrix organizations, dual reporting roles of team members typically create complications that must be managed properly by the project manager. Effectively managing these dual reporting situations is often a critical success factor in project environments.

The intended outcome of the Manage Project Team process is enhanced overall project performance.

Manage Project Team (9.4)

INPUTS	TOOLS & TECHNIQUES	OUTPUTS
• Project Staff Assignments • Project Management Plan • Team Performance Assessment • Performance Reports • Organization Process Assets	• Observation and Conversation • Project Performance Appraisals • Conflict Management • Issue Log • Interpersonal Skills	• Enterprise Environmental Factors • Organization Process Assets • Change Requests • Project Management Plan Updates

Tracks team members performance to enhance overall project performance

- **Project Staff Assignments**   The appropriate people, reliably assigned to staff the project
- **Project Management Plan**   The consolidated package of the subsidiary management plans and baselines
- **Team Performance Assessments**   Formal and/or informal assessments of the team's effectiveness
- **Performance Reports**   S-curves, bar charts, tables, histograms, etc. that summarize team member performance
- **Organizations Process Assets**   Consideration factors such as processes, procedures, and corporate knowledge base

- -

- **Observation and Conversation**   Used to stay in touch with project work and team member attitudes
- **Project Performance Appraisals**   Formal and/or informal appraisals to provide feedback to team members
- **Conflict Management**   Used to enhance productivity and create positive working relationships
- **Issue Log**   Written log identifying specific issues, issue owners and resolution target dates
- **Interpersonal Skills**   The broad set of 'soft skills' important to team development

- -

- **Enterprise Environmental Factors**   Updates to employee training records and skill assessments
- **Organizational Process Asset**   Updates to corporate docs, guidelines, procedures, historical information, etc.
- **Change Requests**   Request for changes to scope, schedule, costs, or processes or other project documentation
- **Project Management Plan Updates**   Updates to the Project Management Plan as a result of this process

---

Ultimate PMP Exam Prep Guide — Must Know Concepts

1. The Manage Project Team process is applied to address performance, behavior, issues, and conflicts associated specifically with project team members.

2. Observation and conversation are key methods to stay in touch with the work and attitudes of project team members.

3. Successful conflict management results in greater productivity and positive working relationships.

LESSON 34 PERFORM QUALITY ASSURANCE

Quality assurance (QA) is the application of all quality activities intended to ensure that the project will employ all processes necessary to satisfy recognized requirements. Quality activities should be applied across the entire project life cycle.

An intended outcome of applying the Perform Quality Assurance process is continuous process improvement. Continuous process improvement includes all actions to reduce waste and non-value-added activities, to increase project efficiency and effectiveness. An example of process improvement could be reducing the overall project cost by 2% through more efficient use of resource leveling. Continuous process improvement is sometimes termed "Kaizen," representing the quality philosophy of achieving improvement via small incremental steps. Note that process improvement is focused on improved project performance, not improved functionality of the product of the project.

While many organizations support quality assurance with dedicated departments, it is important to understand that project quality management is the responsibility of the project manager.

Perform Quality Assurance (8.2)

INPUTS	TOOLS & TECHNIQUES	OUTPUTS
• Quality Metrics • Project Management Plan • Work Performance Information • Quality Control Measurements	• Plan Quality and Perform Quality Control Tools and Techniques • Quality Audits • Process Analysis	• Organizational Process Assets Updates • Change Requests • Project Management Plan Updates • Project Document Updates

Ensures the project employs all processes needed to meet requirements

- **Quality Metrics**   Operational definitions, Project elements, and how they are to be measured by quality control
- **Project Management Plan**   The consolidated package of the subsidiary management plans and baselines
- **Work Performance Information**   Raw data related to deliverables status, schedule progress, and costs incurred
- **Quality Control Measurements**   Results of all quality control activities

- **Plan Quality and Perform Quality Control Tools and Techniques**   The same T&Ts used to for the Plan Quality process
- **Quality Audits**   Structured reviews to identify ineffective/inefficient processes/procedures
- **Process Analysis**   Implements the process improvement plan, to identify needed improvements

- **Organizational Process Assets Updates**   Updates to corporate docs, guidelines, procedures, historical information, etc
- **Change Requests**   Requests for changes to scope, cost, budget, schedule, or politics and procedures
- **Project Management Plan Updates**   Updates to the Project Management Plan as a result of this process
- **Project Document Updates**   Updates to other project documentation

---

Ultimate PMP Exam Prep Guide — **Must Know Concepts**

1. Quality assurance is the application of all quality activities intended to ensure that the project will employ all processes necessary to satisfy recognized requirements.

2. Quality activities should be applied across the entire project life cycle.

3. An intended outcome of applying the Perform Quality Assurance process is continuous process improvement.

4. Continuous process improvement (quality improvement) is sometimes termed "Kaizen," representing the quality philosophy of achieving improvement via small incremental steps.

5. Continuous process improvement is focused on improved project performance, not improved functionality of the product of the project.

6. Project quality management is the responsibility of the project manager.

LESSON 35   DISTRIBUTE INFORMATION

Distribute Information is the communications process of making project information available to project stakeholders, as determined and documented in the Communications Management Plan.

It should be noted that information distribution may be facilitated by keeping orderly records. Orderly record keeping can assist in information distribution only when there are effective distribution methods chosen. Information distribution methods should be appropriate to the project, the timeliness required, and the culture of the organization that you are working in.

Distribution of information can be done effectively if there are effective retrieval systems available and put into use. And finally, in order to effectively distribute information, the project manager must possess good general communications skills. Information is often distributed to stakeholders that is clouded with technical terms or acronyms which are not readily understandable by managers or customers.

Effective distribute information techniques include:

- Sender-receiver models — understanding feedback and barriers to communication
- Choice of media — written, verbal, or electronic: based on needs of project
- Writing styles — using active vs. passive
- Meeting management — agendas and effective means for addressing conflict
- Presentation — body language and presentation aids
- Facilitation — obtaining consensus and overcoming obstacles

It is important to be mindful that communication is not complete until the sender is confident that the receiver understands the information, as intended. In a later process, Manage Stakeholders Expectations, the project manager will address any issues that arise from the distribution of information. Project success is most likely when all stakeholders have a common understanding of the current condition of the project.

Distribute Information (10.3)		
INPUTS	**TOOLS & TECHNIQUES**	**OUTPUTS**
• Project Management Plan • Performance Reports • Organizational Process Assets	• Communication Methods • Information Distribution Tools	• Organizational Process Assets Updates
Provides needed information to stakeholders in a timely fashion		
• **Project Management Plan** The consolidated package of the subsidiary management plans and baselines • **Performance Reports** S-curves, bar charts, tables, histograms, etc., that summarize team member performance • **Organizational Process Assets** Consideration factors such as processes, procedures and corporate knowledge base		
• **Communication Methods** Individual/group meetings, video/audio conferences, other communication methods • **Information Distribution Tools** Hard copy documents, electronic distribution, web-based distribution, etc.		
• **Organizational Process Assets Updates** Updates to corporate docs, guidelines, procedures, and historical information		

Ultimate PMP Exam Prep Guide — Must Know Concepts

1. Distribute Information is the communications process of making project information available to project stakeholders, as determined and documented in the communications management plan.

2. Communication is not complete until the sender is confident that the receiver understands the information, as intended.

3. Orderly record keeping, effective distribution methods (meetings, project intranet, presentations, or e-mail), effective retrieval systems, and good general communication skills facilitate information distribution.

LESSON 36 MANAGE STAKEHOLDER EXPECTATIONS

The Manage Stakeholder Expectations Process is used to ensure that communications with project stakeholders is productive and meets the needs and desires of those stakeholders. This process also deals with resolving problems that arise from communications issues.

There is often a great deal of communication between the project management team and the project stakeholders. For the project to be managed effectively and efficiently, the project manager should ensure that the stakeholder communications needs and desires are being met and that stakeholders are not being flooded with excessive and unnecessary communications.

In addition, successfully managing stakeholder expectations helps foster project acceptance and support and helps to reduce overall project risk. This will also limit disruptions during the project.

Manage Stakeholder Expectations (10.4)

INPUTS	TOOLS & TECHNIQUES	OUTPUTS
• Stakeholder Register • Stakeholder Management Strategy • Project Management Plan • Issue Log • Change Log • Organizational Process Assets	• Communication Methods • Interpersonal Skills • Management Skills	• Organizational Process Assets Updates • Change Requests • Project Management Plan Updates • Project Document Updates

Manages communications to satisfy stakeholder requirement

- **Stakeholder Register**   A document identifying all project stakeholder information
- **Stakeholder Management Strategy**   Defines the approach to increase stakeholder support and reduce negative impacts
- **Project Management Plan**   The consolidated package of the subsidiary management plans and baselines
- **Issue Log**   Written log identifying specific issues, issue owners and resolution target dates
- **Change Log**   A log used to track changes that occur during a project
- **Organizational Process Assets**   Consideration factors such as processes, procedures and corporate knowledge base

- **Communication Methods**   Individual/group meetings, video/audio conferences, other communication methods
- **Interpersonal Skills**   The broad set of 'soft skills' important to team development
- **Management Skills**   Presentation, writing, and public speaking skills as well as other general management skills

- **Organizational Process Assets Updates**   Updates to corporate docs, guidelines, procedures and historical information
- **Change Requests**   Request for changes to scope, schedule, costs, or processes or other project documentation
- **Project Management Plan Updates**   Updates to the Project Management Plan as a result of this process
- **Project Document Updates**   Updates to other project documentation

---

Ultimate PMP Exam Prep Guide — Must Know Concepts

1. The Manage Stakeholder Expectations process is applied to ensure that communications with project stakeholders is productive and meets the needs and desires of those stakeholders

2. Actively managing project stakeholders increases the likelihood that the project will not be negatively impacted by unresolved stakeholder issues.

3. An issue log (or action-item log) is used to document and monitor the resolution of issues.

LESSON 37   CONDUCT PROCUREMENTS

The Conduct Procurements process is used to solicit and obtain the project's external resources. This process includes obtaining seller responses and bids, selection of a seller or sellers, and awarding contracts. During the process of Conduct Procurements, the project manager (or purchasing department) will notify sellers of the potential need by providing appropriate procurement documents to the sellers. In response, the project manager (or purchasing department) will receive proposals from the seller on how the need can be satisfied by the vendor. Statements of work and evaluation criteria developed during Plan Procurements may be used in conjunction with notifying the vendor and evaluating their response or proposal.

This process is often repeated many times within the life cycle of the project. In its simplest form, this may include searching for parts via the Internet (for example) and placing an order from the cheapest source, or it can be a more complicated process of submitting procurement packages, reviewing seller bids, seller evaluations, negotiations, and contract award.

Successful procurement is often very critical to project success and can greatly impact the project's expenses.

Conduct Procurements (12.2)

INPUTS	TOOLS & TECHNIQUES	OUTPUTS
• Project Management Plan • Procurement Documents • Source Selection Criteria • Qualified Seller List • Seller Proposals • Project Documents • Make-or-Buy Decisions • Teaming Agreements • Organizational Process Assets	• Bidder Conferences • Proposal Evaluation Techniques • Independent Estimates • Procurement Negotiations • Expert Judgment • Advertising • Internet Search	• Selected Sellers • Procurement Contract Award • Resource Calendars • Change Requests • Project Management Plan Updates • Project Document Updates

Obtaining seller responses, selecting sellers, and awarding contract

- **Project Management Plan**   The consolidated package of the subsidiary management plans and baselines
- **Procurement Documents**   Documents used to solicit proposals from prospective sellers
- **Source Selection Criteria**   Criteria used to help score or rate proposals submitted by prospective project suppliers (sellers)
- **Qualified Seller List**   Final list of prospective suppliers (sellers)
- **Seller Proposals**   Supplier (seller) responses that describe ability and willingness to provide requested services
- **Project Documents**   Risk Register and Risk Related Contract Decisions
- **Make-or-Buy Decisions**   The documented decisions of what will be developed in-house and what will be purchased
- **Teaming Agreements**   Legal contractual agreements between parties to form partnerships or joint ventures
- **Organizational Process Assets**   Consideration factors such as processes, procedures, and corporate knowledge base

- **Bidder Conferences**   Q&A-type meetings with prospective project suppliers (sellers) prior to proposal preparation
- **Proposal Evaluation Techniques**   Formal evaluation process defined by procurement policies
- **Independent Estimates**   Prepared estimates used for benchmark on proposed seller responses
- **Procurement Negotiations**   Used to clarify structure and requirements for purchases between seller and purchaser
- **Expert Judgment**   Expert technical and/or managerial judgment (from any qualified source)
- **Advertising**   Public advertisements used to solicit potential sellers for contracted project goods and/or services
- **Internet Search**   Use of the Internet to research and procure required resources or materials

- **Selected Sellers**   List of sellers selected using the process tools & techniques
- **Procurement Contract Award**   The contract package for selected sellers
- **Resource Calendars**   Information on the availability of resources over the planned activity duration
- **Change Requests**   Request for changes to scope, schedule, costs, or processes or other project documentation
- **Project Management Plan Updates**   Updates to the Project Management Plan as a result of this process
- **Project Document Updates**   Updates to other project documentation

---

Ultimate PMP Exam Prep Guide — Must Know Concepts

1. Conduct Procurements is the process of obtaining bids and proposals from sellers and selecting a seller to provide resources for the project.

2. The primary deliverable from this process is selected sellers.

3. Objective bid evaluations should be performed to determine the successful bidders

4. When performing a large procurement, it may be helpful to narrow the field to a short list then enter into more detailed negotiations with the remaining bidders.

5. The project manager should play an integral role throughout the contracting process.

6. Contracts are legally binding agreements between buyer and seller. The project team should be aware of the project's contractual legal obligations.

7. Contracts may be simple or complex, proportional to the size and complexity of the procurement.

LESSON 39 CONTROL SCOPE

Control Scope is the process of effectively managing changes in project scope, then integrating those changes across the entire project through the Perform Integrated Change Control process. In Scope Control, scope changes are identified by utilizing the variance analysis tool. After a scope change has been identified it becomes an output from this process (as a change request), which becomes an input to Integrated Change Control.

It is important to understand that it is the project manager's responsibility to discourage unnecessary scope changes. It is also important to understand that when changes are warranted, they must be made in strict accordance with the project's scope change control process, and the established scope baseline must remain intact. Rebaselining scope is appropriate only in extreme situations.

Some organizations utilize a change control board (CCB) to evaluate and approve/disapprove scope change requests.

Control Scope (5.5)		
INPUTS	**TOOLS & TECHNIQUES**	**OUTPUTS**
• Project Management Plan • Work Performance Information • Requirements Documentation • Requirements Traceability Matrix • Organizational Process Assets	• Variance Analysis	• Work Performance Measurements • Change Requests • Organizational Process Assets Updates • Project Management Plan Updates • Project Documentation Updates

Controls changes to project scope

- **Project Management Plan** The consolidated package of the subsidiary management plans and baselines
- **Work Performance Information** Raw data related to deliverable status, schedule progress, and costs incurred
- **Requirements Documentation** Documentation describing how individual requirements meet the business needs of the project
- **Requirement Traceability Matrix** A table that links requirements to their origins and traces them throughout the project life cycle
- **Organizational Process Assets** Consideration factors such as processes, procedures, and corporate knowledge base

- -

- **Variance Analysis** Comparing scope performance objectives to actuals, to assess the magnitude of variation

- -

- **Work Performance Measurements** Collection of project status information; technical performance measures, etc.
- **Change Requests** Request for changes to scope, schedule, costs, or processes or other project documentation
- **Organizational Process Assets Updates** Updates to corporate docs, guidelines, procedures, historical information, etc.
- **Project Management Plan Updates** Updates to the Project Management Plan as a result of this process
- **Project Document Updates** Updates to other project documentation

Ultimate PMP Exam Prep Guide — **Must Know Concepts**

1. Control Scope is the process of effectively managing changes in project scope, then integrating those changes across the entire project through the Perform Integrated Change Control process.

2. The primary deliverables (Outputs) of the Control Scope process include updates to all associated project plans and documents.

3. It is the project manager's responsibility to discourage unnecessary scope changes.

4. When legitimate scope changes are warranted, they should be made in accordance with the project's scope change control system.

5. For monitoring and performance measurement purposes, the established project scope baseline should remain unchanged.

6. Rebaselining project scope is appropriate only in extreme situations.

7. Some organizations utilize a change control board (CCB) to evaluate and approve/disapprove project scope change requests.

LESSON 40   CONTROL SCHEDULE

Control Schedule is the process of monitoring the status of the project to update project progress and manage changes to the schedule baseline, then integrating those changes across the entire project through the Perform Integrated Change Control process. In Control Schedule, schedule changes are identified using various tools, including variance analysis. After a schedule change has been identified it becomes an output from this process in the form of a change request, which then becomes an input to Perform Integrated Change Control.

It is important to understand that it is the project manager's responsibility to discourage unnecessary schedule changes. It is also important to understand that when changes are warranted, they must be made in strict accordance with the project's schedule change control process that is defined in the Schedule Management Plan, and the established schedule baseline must remain intact. Rebaselining the schedule is appropriate only in extreme situations.

Some organizations utilize a change control board (CCB) to evaluate and approve/disapprove schedule change requests.

Control Schedule (6.6)

INPUTS	TOOLS & TECHNIQUES	OUTPUTS
• Project Management Plan • Project Schedule • Work Performance Information • Organizational Process Assets	• Performance Reviews • Variance Analysis • Project Management Software • Resource Leveling • What-If Scenario Analysis • Adjusting Leads and Lags • Schedule Compression • Schedule Tool	• Work Performance Measurements • Change Requests • Organizational Process Assets Updates • Project Management Plan Updates • Project Documentation Updates

Controls changes to project scope

- **Project Management Plan**   The consolidated package of the subsidiary management plans and baselines
- **Project Schedule**   Graphic presentation illustrating planned start and planned finish dates for each project activity
- **Work Performance Information**   Raw data related to deliverables status, schedule progress, and costs incurred
- **Organizational Process Assets**   Consideration factors such as processes, procedures and corporate knowledge base

- **Performance Reviews**
- **Variance Analysis**   Comparing scope performance objectives to actuals, to assess the magnitude of variation
- **Project Management Software**   Any software that may help plan, organize, manage resource estimates and pools
- **Resource Leveling**   Technique applied to create efficient resource-limited schedules
- **What-If Scenario Analysis**   Explores various scenarios using simulation tools (Monte Carlo)
- **Applying Leads and Lags**   Further defined 'overlaps (leads)' and 'delays (lags)' in activity dependencies
- **Schedule Compression**   Shortens the project schedule without changing scope (fast-tracking and crashing)
- **Scheduling Tool**   Tool used to facilitate creation of the project schedule documentation

- **Work Performance Measurements**   Collection of project status information; technical performance measures, etc.
- **Change Requests**   Request for changes to scope, schedule, costs, or processes or other project documentation
- **Organizational Process Assets Updates**   Updates to corporate docs, guidelines, procedures, historical information, etc.
- **Project Management Plan Updates**   Updates to the Project Management Plan as a result of this process
- **Project Document Updates**   Updates to other project documentation

---

Ultimate PMP Exam Prep Guide — Must Know Concepts

1. Control Schedule is the process of effectively monitoring the project progress and managing project schedule baseline changes, then integrating those changes across the entire project through the Perform Integrated Change Control process.

2. The primary deliverables (Outputs) of the Control Schedule process include updates to all associated project plans and documents.

3. Control Schedule uses earned value to calculate Schedule Variance (SV) and Schedule Performance Index (SPI) values for the project schedule.

4. It is the project manager's responsibility to discourage unnecessary schedule changes.

5. When legitimate schedule changes are warranted, they should be made in accordance with the project's schedule change control system.

6. For monitoring and performance measurement purposes, established project schedule baselines should remain unchanged, regardless of project changes.

7. Schedule rebaselining is appropriate only in extreme situations.

8. Some organizations utilize a change control board (CCB) to evaluate and approve/disapprove project schedule change requests.

LESSON 41 CONTROL COSTS

Control Costs is the process of effectively managing changes to the project budget, then integrating those changes across the entire project through the Integrated Change Control process. Using the project's cost change control process, and that established cost baseline must remain intact. Rebaselining the budget is appropriate only in extreme situations.

In Control Costs, the application of earned value measurement (EVM) is a key tool used to measure project performance. Earned value analysis integrates cost, scope, and schedule to derive measurement values that accurately assess project progress to date, as well as to forecast future performance.

As well as managing change to the cost parameter for the project, a key element to the process of Control Costs is the use of Earned Value Measurement to measure project performance.

Control Costs (7.3)

INPUTS	TOOLS & TECHNIQUES	OUTPUTS
• Project Management Plan • Project Funding Requirements • Work Performance Information • Organizational Process Assets	• Earned Value Measurement • Forecasting Methods • To-Complete Performance Index • Performance Reviews • Variance Analysis • Project Management Software	• Work Performance Measurements • Budget Forecasts • Change Requests • Organizational Process Assets Updates • Project Management Plan Updates • Project Document Updates

Controls changes to project scope

- **Project Management Plan**   The consolidated package of the subsidiary management plans and baselines
- **Project Funding Requirements**   Simply the funding needed and when it will be needed
- **Work Performance Information**   Raw data related to deliverables status, schedule progress, and costs incurred
- **Organizational Process Assets**   Consideration factors such as processes, procedures and corporate knowledge base

- -

- **Earned Value Measurement**   The earned value technique commonly used to measure cost performance
- **Forecasting Methods**   Predicting future project performance trends based on actual performance to date
- **To-Complete Performance Index**   Calculated projection of cost performance to meet management goals
- **Performance Reviews**   Comparison of cost performance over time, schedule under-runs/over-runs, and future expenditure forecasts
- **Variance Analysis**   Comparing scope performance objectives to actuals, to assess the magnitude of variation
- **Project Management Software**   Any software that may help plan, organize, manage resource estimates and pools

- -

- **Work Performance Measurements**   Collection of project status information; technical performance measures, etc.
- **Budget Forecast**   The calculated Estimate at Completion (EAC) and/or Estimate to Completion (ETC)
- **Change Requests**   Request for changes to scope, schedule, costs, or processes or other project documentation
- **Organizational Process Assets Updates**   Updates to corporate docs, guidelines, procedures, historical information, etc.
- **Project Management Plan Updates**   Updates to the Project Management Plan as a result of this process
- **Project Document Updates**   Updates to other project documentation

Ultimate PMP Exam Prep Guide — Must Know Concepts

1. Control Cost is the process of effectively managing changes to the project budget.

2. It is the project manager's responsibility to discourage unnecessary cost changes.

3. When legitimate budget changes are warranted, they should be made in accordance with the project's cost change control system.

4. Earned value measurement (EVM) is a key tool used to measure project performance. Earned value analysis integrates cost, scope, and schedule to derive measurement values that assess project progress.

5. Planned Value (PV) (also termed "Budgeted Cost of Work Scheduled" [BCWS]) is the established baseline that indicates the amount of money planned for spending to date, at any particular point in time.

6. Earned Value (EV) (also termed "Budgeted Cost of Work Performed" [BCWP]) is the established baseline that indicates the amount of money planned for spending on the actual work performed to date, at any particular point in time (regardless of other planned objectives).

7. Actual Cost (AC) (also termed "Actual Cost of Work Performed" [ACWP]) is the amount of money spent on the actual work performed to date, at any particular point in time (regardless of other planned objectives).

8. Budget at Completion (BAC) is simply the amount of money planned for spending on the entire project.

9. Schedule Variance (SV): SV = EV – PV (SV > 0 = ahead of schedule. SV < 0 = behind schedule.).

10. Cost Variance (CV): CV = EV – AC (CV > 0 = under budget. CV < 0 = over budget.).

11. Variance at Completion (VAC): VAC = BAC – EAC (VAC > 0 = under budget. VAC < 0 = over budget.).

12. Schedule Performance Index (SPI): SPI = EV / PV (SPI > 1 = ahead of schedule. SPI < 1 = behind schedule.).

13. Cost Performance Index (CPI): CPI = EV / AC (CPI > 1 = under budget. CPI < 1 = over budget.).

14. Estimate to Complete (ETC): ETC = EAC – AC (ETC forecasts remaining project costs.).

15. Cost Estimate at Completion (EAC): EAC = BAC / CPI (EAC forecasts final project cost total.).

16. TCPI (based on BAC) – TCPI = (BAC – EV) / (BAC – AC) this is the forecast of how efficient future project performance must be in order to conform to the planned BAC for the project.

17. TCPI (based on EAC) – TCPI = (BAC – EV) / (EAC – AC) this is the forecast of how efficient future project performance must be in order to conform to the planned EAC (based on new outcome predictions) for the project.

LESSON 42   REPORT PERFORMANCE

Report Performance is the communications process of providing project stakeholders with performance information, through the use of status reporting, progress reporting, and forecasting. Information included in forecasts and reports typically includes scope, cost, schedule, quality, risk, and procurement. The most common form of performance reporting is the periodic project status report.

In project management, the application of earned value analysis (EVA) is a key tool used to measure project performance. Earned value analysis integrates cost, scope, and schedule to derive measurement values that accurately assess project progress to date, as well as forecasted future performance.

The level and detail of reporting should be appropriate to the intended audience. Providing an excessive amount of performance data where it is unneeded or unwanted should be avoided.

In many industries, performance reports rely heavily on earned value analysis, presented in the form of bar charts, S-curves, histograms, and/or spreadsheets.

Report Performance (10.5)

INPUTS	TOOLS & TECHNIQUES	OUTPUTS
• Project Management Plan • Work Performance Information • Work Performance Measurements • Organizational Process Assets • Budget Forecasts	• Variance Analysis • Forecasting Methods • Communication Methods • Reporting Systems	• Performance Reports • Organizational Process Assets Updates • Change Requests

Collects and distributes status reports and forecasts

- **Project Management Plan**   The consolidated package of the subsidiary management plans and baselines
- **Work Performance Information**   Raw data related to deliverables status, schedule progress, and costs incurred
- **Work Performance Measurements**   Collection of project status information; technical performance measures, etc.
- **Organizational Process Assets**   Consideration factors such as processes, procedures and corporate knowledge base
- **Budget Forecasts**

- **Variance Analysis**   Comparing scope performance objectives to actuals, to assess the magnitude of variation
- **Forecasting Methods**   Predicting future project performance trends based on actual performance to date
- **Communication Methods**   Individual/group meetings, video/audio conferences, other communication methods
- **Reporting Systems**   Typically software related; spreadsheet, graphics, presentation, table reporting

- **Performance Reports**   S-curves, bar charts, tables, histograms, etc. that summarize project performance
- **Organizational Process Assets Updates**   Updates to corporate docs, guidelines, procedures, historical information, etc.
- **Change Requests**   Request for changes to scope, schedule, costs, or processes or other project documentation

---

Ultimate PMP Exam Prep Guide — Must Know Concepts

1. Report Performance is the communications process of providing project stakeholders with performance information, through the use of status reporting, progress reporting, and forecasting.

2. Information included in performance reports typically includes scope, cost, schedule, quality, risk, and procurement.

3. Normally, performance reports reflect current project status and forecasted future performance.

4. In many industries, performance reports rely heavily on earned value analysis, presented in the form of bar charts, S-curves, histograms, and/or tables.

LESSON 43   PERFORM QUALITY CONTROL

Perform Quality Control is the process of monitoring specific project results to ensure they comply with the project's quality standards. Like quality assurance (QA), quality control (QC) should be applied across the entire project life cycle. The quality control process is also intended to identify ways to eliminate quality problems such as causes of weak processes or poor product quality. Process improvement is a natural adjunct of the Perform Quality Control process.

Quality control monitors both product-related deliverables (work packages) and project management deliverables (cost/schedule/scope performance). This process focuses on outputs and uses tools that measure these outputs.

Perform Quality Control (8.3)

INPUTS	TOOLS & TECHNIQUES	OUTPUTS
• Project Management Plan • Quality Metrics • Quality Checklists • Work Performance Measurements • Approved Change Requests • Deliverables • Organizational Process Assets	• Cause and Effect Diagrams • Control Charts • Flowcharting • Histogram • Pareto Chart • Run Chart • Scatter Diagram • Statistical Sampling • Inspection • Approved Change Request Review	• Quality Control Measurements • Validated Changes • Validated Deliverables • Change Requests • Organizational Process Assets Updates • Project Management Plan Updates • Project Document Updates

Monitors project results against relevant quality standards

- **Project Management Plan**   The consolidated package of the subsidiary management plans and baselines
- **Quality Metrics**   Operational definitions. Project elements, and how they are to be measured by quality control
- **Quality Checklists**   Structured forms used to verify that a set of required steps has been performed
- **Work Performance Measurements**   Collection of project status information; technical performance measures, etc
- **Approved Change Requests**   Documented, authorized changes that expand or reduce scope
- **Deliverables**   Results, products, and/or capabilities (unique, verifiable outcomes) of activities performed
- **Organizational Process Assets**   Consideration factors such as processes, procedures and corporate knowledge base

- -

- **Cause and Effect Diagrams**   (fishbone, Ishikawa). Illustrate how various factors may be linked to a problem or effect
- **Control Charts**   Charts used to determine if processes are stable and performing in a predictable manner
- **Flowcharting**   Diagramming methods that can help analyze how problems in a system occur
- **Histogram**   Bar chart showing distribution of variables. Can help identify cause of problems
- **Pareto Chart**   A specific type of histogram that can help identify nonconformities. Pareto's law = 80/20 principle
- **Run Chart**   A line graph that illustrates the history and pattern of variation in a process, to determine trends
- **Scatter Diagram**   Illustrates the pattern of relationship between two variables, to study changes in the two variables
- **Statistical Sampling**   Statistical analysis using a small group from an entire population
- **Inspection**   Measuring, examining, testing (reviews, audits, walkthroughs) to ensure results conform to requirements
- **Approved Change Request Review**   A review of all approved change requests to verify implementation

- -

- **Quality Control Measurements**   Results of all quality control activities
- **Validated Changes**   Notification of acceptance or rejection of changed or repaired items
- **Validated Deliverables**   Completed deliverables checked using the Perform Quality Control process
- **Change Requests**   Request for changes to scope, schedule, costs, or processes or other project documentation
- **Organizational Process Assets Updates**   Updates to corporate docs, guidelines, procedures, historical information, etc.
- **Project Management Plan Updates**   Updates to the Project Management Plan as a result of this process
- **Project Document Updates**   Updates to other project documentation

---

Ultimate PMP Exam Prep Guide — Must Know Concepts

1. Perform Quality Control is monitoring specific project results to ensure compliance with the quality standards.

2. The primary deliverable (Output) of the Perform Quality Control process is validated deliverables.

3. Perform Quality Control monitors both product-related deliverables (work packages) and project management deliverables (cost/schedule/scope performance).

4. "Prevention" is defined as keeping errors out of the process. "Inspection" is keeping errors away from customers.

5. "Attribute Sampling" determines if results are compliant or not compliant: go/no-go.

6. "Variables Sampling" is when results are measured on a continuous scale indicating degree of conformity.

7. "Special Causes" are unusual events.

8. "Random Causes" means normal process variation.

9. "Tolerances" are ranges of acceptable results.

10. "Control Limits" define where a result is in-control if it is within specified control limits.

LESSON 44   VERIFY SCOPE

Verify Scope is the process of obtaining formal acceptance of project deliverables. It must be understood that a project deliverable is not complete until it has been formally accepted, by the individual or group authorized to accept it.

Scope verification differs from quality control. Quality control focuses on the correctness of work. Scope verification focuses on formal acceptance of the work. In practice, both are normally performed in parallel.

Formal acceptance must be documented. Scope verification can occur at any level of the project; it can be done for work, for a specific deliverable, for a milestone, for a phase, or for the project overall. Verify Scope is often a predecessor to the closure of a project phase or when closing the overall project.

Verify Scope (5.4)

INPUTS	TOOLS & TECHNIQUES	OUTPUTS
• Project Management Plan • Requirements Documentation • Requirements Traceability Matrix • Validated Deliverables	• Inspection	• Accepted Deliverables • Change Requests • Project Document Updates

Formalizes acceptance of completed project deliverables

- **Project Management Plan**   The consolidated package of the subsidiary management plans and baselines
- **Requirements Documentation**   Documentation describing how individual requirements meet the business needs of the project
- **Requirements Traceability Matrix**   A table that links requirements to their origins and traces them throughout the project life cycle
- **Validated Deliverables**   Completed deliverables checked using the Perform Quality Control process

---

- **Inspection**   Measuring, examining, and testing (reviews, audits, walkthroughs) to ensure results conform to requirements

---

- **Accepted Deliverables**   Documentation of accepted deliverables from the Verify Scope process
- **Change Requests**   Request for changes to scope, schedule, costs, or processes or other project documentation
- **Project Document Updates**   Updates to other project documentation

---

Ultimate PMP Exam Prep Guide — **Must Know Concepts**

1. Verify Scope is the process of obtaining formal acceptance of project deliverables.

2. The primary deliverable (Output) of the Verify Scope process is formally accepted deliverables.

3. A project deliverable is not complete until it has been formally accepted, in writing by the individual or group authorized to accept it.

4. Scope verification differs from quality control which focuses on the correctness of work while scope verification focuses on formal acceptance of the work.

LESSON 45   MONITOR AND CONTROL RISKS

The Monitor and Control Risks process is applied to perform several functions for the project:
- monitor identified risks
- identify new risks
- ensure the proper execution of planned risk responses
- evaluate the overall effectiveness of the risk management plan in reducing risk

If a risk event occurs during project execution, there is a likelihood it was identified sometime earlier, it was then analyzed, and an appropriate response action was planned to deal with it (captured in the Risk Register). For the most part, Monitor and Control Risks is the process of putting into action all of the risk planning done earlier in the project life cycle.

It is important to understand that risk monitoring is intended to be a daily, ongoing process across the entire project life cycle. Project team members and stakeholders should be encouraged to be vigilant in looking for risk symptoms, as well as for new project risks. It is suggested that project risk always be an agenda item for all team meetings. Newly identified risks and symptoms of previously identified risks should be communicated immediately for evaluation and/or action.

Monitor and Control Risks (11.6)

INPUTS	TOOLS & TECHNIQUES	OUTPUTS
• Risk Register • Project Management Plan • Work Performance Information • Performance Reports	• Risk Assessment • Risk Audits • Variance and Trend Analysis • Technical Performance Measurement • Reserve Analysis • Status Meetings	• Risk Register Updates • Organizational Process Assets Updates • Change Requests • Project Management Plan Updates • Project Document Updates

Executes risk response plans and evaluates their effectiveness

- **Risk Register**   List of identified risks
- **Project Management Plan**   The consolidated package of the subsidiary management plans and baselines
- **Work Performance Information**   Raw data related to deliverables status, schedule progress, and costs incurred
- **Performance Reports**   S-curves, bar charts, tables, histograms, etc. that summarize project performance

- **Risk Assessment**   New risk identification and frequent reassessment of existing risks
- **Risk Audits**   Examination and documentation of the effectiveness of risk responses and risk management processes
- **Variance and Trend Analysis**   Examination of project trends to help determine the impact of threats/opportunities
- **Technical Performance Measurement**   Comparison of planned technical accomplishments to actual achievements
- **Reserve Analysis**   Determining appropriate amount of contingency reserve to compensate for project risk
- **Status Meetings**   Typically, risk management is an agenda item at each project status meeting

- **Risk Register Updates**   Updates to the list of identified risks
- **Organizational Process Assets Updates**   Updates to corporate docs, guidelines, procedures, historical information, etc.
- **Change Requests**   Request for changes to scope, schedule, costs, or processes or other project documentation
- **Project Management Plan Updates**   Updates to the Project Management Plan as a result of this process
- **Project Document Updates**   Updates to other project documentation

---

Ultimate PMP Exam Prep Guide — Must Know Concepts

1.   The Monitor and Control Risks process is applied to monitor identified risks, identify new risks, ensure proper execution of planned risk responses, and evaluate overall effectiveness of the Risk Management Plan in reducing risk.

2.   Workarounds (or workaround plans) are responses to unanticipated (surprise) risk events after they occur. Workarounds are for risk events that were not previously identified, and have no planned response action. Workaround plans should be documented and incorporated into the Risk Register as soon as they are developed.

3.   Risk monitoring is intended to be a daily, ongoing process across the entire project life cycle, from project start to project finish.

4.   Project team members and stakeholders should be vigilant in looking for risk symptoms, as well as for new project risks.

LESSON 46   ADMINISTER PROCUREMENTS

Monitoring the relationships created by a project's procurement needs, monitoring contract performance, and making procurement changes and corrections are accomplished through the Administer Procurements process. Part of this process includes validating that the seller's performance is meeting requirements and contract obligations.

In many organizations, the role of contract monitoring and control is performed by a specialized contracts department. This is often done because of the legalities associated with contracts.

During the application of this process, each seller's performance should be recorded and documented. A performance review of sellers can lead to identification of issues to be resolved, and provides additional data for similar future projects in regards to contracts with and purchases from the sellers.

When applying this process the project manager will have a high degree of interaction with several other processes. Some processes that may be closely coordinated with Administer Procurements are:

- Direct and Manage Project Execution
- Monitor and Control Project Work
- Verify Scope
- Perform Quality Control
- Develop Project Team
- Manage Project Team
- Control Scope
- Control Schedule
- Control Cost
- Perform Integrated Change Control
- Close Procurements
- Close Project

Administer Procurements (12.3)

INPUTS	TOOLS & TECHNIQUES	OUTPUTS
• Procurement Documents • Project Management Plan • Performance Reports • Approved Change Requests • Work Performance Information • Contract	• Contract Change Control • Procurement Performance Reviews • Inspections and Audits • Performance Reporting • Payment Systems • Claims Administration • Records Management System	• Procurement Documentation • Organizational Process Assets Updates • Change Requests • Project Management Plan Updates

Managing procurement relationships and contract performance

- **Procurement Documents**   Documents used to solicit proposals from prospective sellers
- **Project Management Plan**   The consolidated package of the subsidiary management plans and baselines
- **Performance Reports**   S-curves, bar charts, tables, histograms, etc., that summarize project performance
- **Approved Change Requests**   Documented, authorized changes that expand or reduce scope
- **Work Performance Information**   Raw data related to deliverables status, schedule progress, and costs incurred
- **Contract**   Procurement contract and information

- -

- **Contract Change Control System**   A system that defines the process by which a contract may be modified
- **Procurement Performance Reviews**   A procurement performance review of seller's conformance to contract terms
- **Inspections and Audits**   Required by the buyer, supported by the seller, conducted to identify seller weaknesses
- **Performance Reporting**   Management information to assess the contractual performance of project suppliers
- **Payment Systems**   Reviews, approvals, payments made in accordance with contract terms
- **Claims Administration**   Procedures for resolving disputed/contested changes between buyer and seller
- **Records Management System**   Used by the project manager to manage contract documentation and records

- -

- **Procurement Documentation**   Contract, supporting schedules, requested contract changes, and approved change requests
- **Organizational Process Assets Updates**   Updates to corporate docs, guidelines, procedures, historical information, etc.
- **Change Requests**   Request for changes to scope, schedule, costs, or processes or other project documentation
- **Project Management Plan Updates**   Updates to the Project Management Plan as a result of this process

Ultimate PMP Exam Prep Guide — Must Know Concepts

1. The Administer Procurements process is used to manage procurement relationships, monitor contract performance, and make changes and corrections to procurements.

2. Many organizations utilize a contract administration department or office to administer procurement contracting due to the legalities involved in formal contracting.

3. Seller performance should be formally documented for use in future decisions and in evaluation of sellers.

4. Contract changes can be kept to a minimum by proper and thorough procurement planning but can be used to reduce risk, or when such amendments are beneficial for the buyer, the seller, or both.

LESSON 47 MONITOR AND CONTROL PROJECT WORK

The U.S. Apollo space missions to the moon during the 1960s and 1970s were proud successes shared by the entire world. What few people realize is that at any given moment during a space capsule's flight to the moon, the trajectory is considerably off course. Allowed to continue on its path at any given time, the capsule would miss its target by a significant margin. Technology at that time was not capable of automating the capsule's flight path.

To compensate, ground controllers would continuously monitor the flight path and, using tiny on-board jets, make frequent corrective adjustments to bring the capsule back on course. Ultimately, the capsule reached its objective.

This is a good example of Monitoring and Controlling Project Work.

As project managers, it is our responsibility to continuously monitor project work, and when we detect some aspect is heading off course, we make controlling adjustments, as necessary, to bring the project back in alignment, to ultimately achieve our defined objectives.

We apply the Monitor and Control Project Work process to:
- monitor all other processes through initiation, planning, executing, and closing
- take/make corrective/preventive actions, as needed

Monitor and Control Project Work (4.4)		
INPUTS	**TOOLS & TECHNIQUES**	**OUTPUTS**
• Project Management Plan • Performance Reports • Enterprise Environmental Factors • Organizational Process Assets	• Expert Judgment	• Change Requests • Project Management Plan Updates • Project Document Updates
Monitors and controls the processes used by the team		
• **Project Management Plan** The consolidated package of the subsidiary management plans and baselines • **Performance Reports** S-curves, bar charts, tables, histograms, etc. that summarize team member performance • **Enterprise Environmental Factors** Consideration factors such as; culture, systems, procedures, industry standards • **Organizational Process Assets** Consideration factors such as processes, procedures, and corporate knowledge base		
• **Expert Judgment** Expert technical and/or managerial judgment (from any qualified source)		
• **Change Requests** Request for changes to scope, schedule, costs, or processes or other project documentation • **Project Management Plan Updates** Updates to the Project Management Plan as a result of this process • **Project Document Updates** Updates to other project documentation		

Ultimate PMP Exam Prep Guide — Must Know Concepts

1. The Monitor and Control Project Work process is applied to monitor all other processes through initiation, planning, executing, and closing, to take/make corrective/preventive actions, as needed.

2. Corrective actions are actions required to bring expected future project performance into conformance with the project management plan.

3. Preventive actions are actions required to reduce the probability of negative consequences associated with project risks.

4. Defect repairs identify a flaw or defect in a project component and recommend to either repair or replace the component.

LESSON 48   PERFORM INTEGRATED CHANGE CONTROL

Perform Integrated Change Control is the process of effectively managing changes and integrating them appropriately across the entire project. It is important to understand that it is the project manager's responsibility to discourage unnecessary changes. It is also important to understand that when changes are warranted, they must be made in strict accordance with the project's change control system, and established project baselines must remain intact. Rebaselining is appropriate only in extreme situations.

In most application areas, configuration management is applied to control changes to the product of the project.

Project changes, although often initiated verbally, should always be documented to allow tracking and control. Additionally, all project changes should be formally approved or rejected.

Change Requests that are used as inputs to the Perform Integrated Change Control process come from many sources. This process works closely with Control Scope and Control Schedule to manage change requests for formal approval or rejection. Other processes like Direct and Manage Project Execution, Monitor and Control Project Work, Perform Quality Assurance, Perform Quality Control, and others also provide change requests to this process.

Some organizations utilize a change control board (CCB) to evaluate and approve/disapprove project change requests.

Perform Integrated Change Control (4.5)		
INPUTS	**TOOLS & TECHNIQUES**	**OUTPUTS**
• Change Requests • Organizational Process Assets • Project Management Plan • Work Performance Information • Enterprise Environmental Factors	• Expert Judgment • Change Control Meetings	• Change Request Status Update • Project Management Plan Updates • Project Document Updates

Reviews, approves and controls changes to project deliverables

- **Change Requests**   Request for changes to scope, schedule, costs, or processes or other project documentation
- **Organizational Process Assets**   Consideration factors such as processes, procedures, and corporate knowledge base
- **Project Management Plan**   The consolidated package of the subsidiary management plans and baselines
- **Work Performance Information**   Raw data related to deliverable status, schedule progress, and costs incurred
- **Enterprise Environmental Factors**   Consideration factors such as; culture, systems, procedures, industry standards

- -

- **Expert Judgment**   Expert technical and/or managerial judgment (from any qualified source)
- **Change Control Meetings**   Change Control Board meetings to review change requests and approve/reject changes

- -

- **Change Request Status Updates**   Processed change requests
- **Project Management Plan Updates**   Updates to the Project Management Plan as a result of this process
- **Project Document Updates**   Updates to other project documentation

Ultimate PMP Exam Prep Guide — Must Know Concepts

1.   Perform Integrated Change Control is the process of effectively managing changes and integrating them appropriately across the entire project.

2.   The primary deliverables (Outputs) of the Perform Integrated Change Control process include Project Management Plan Updates and Project Document Updates.

3.   Configuration management applies mostly to the framework or specifications for the product and project processes. Configuration management is an especially useful tool when the product of the project is very complex.

4.   It is the project manager's responsibility to discourage unnecessary changes.

5.   When legitimate changes are warranted, they should be made in accordance with the project's change control system.

6.   For monitoring and performance measurement purposes, established project baselines should remain unchanged, regardless of project changes. Re-baselining is appropriate only in extreme situations.

7.   Some organizations utilize a change control board (CCB) to evaluate and approve/disapprove project change requests.

LESSON 50 CLOSE PROCUREMENTS

The Close Procurements process is used to formally validate that all of the requirements for each of the project's procurement activities have been met and are acceptable for both seller and buyer.

This process, in conjunction with the Close Project or Phase process, is used to complete a project. This process is also used throughout the project's life cycle to bring a formal termination to a procurement or procurement contract.

This process is usually preceded by the Verify Scope process and Perform Quality Control process in order to verify that work was completed and that the work or deliverables created are acceptable for project use.

The process of Close Procurements is similar to, but slightly different from the process of Close Project or Phase. First of all, Close Procurements is closing only a portion of the overall project, whereas Close Project or Phase is used to close the overall project or phase. In addition to that difference, there is a difference in activity flow in the process.

Close Procurements (12.4)		
INPUTS	**TOOLS & TECHNIQUES**	**OUTPUTS**
• Project Management Plan • Procurement Documentation	• Procurement Audits • Negotiated Settlements • Records Management System	• Closed Procurements • Organizational Process Assets Updates
Formally closes the project procurements		
• **Project Management Plan** The consolidated package of the subsidiary management plans and baselines • **Procurement Documentation** Contract, supporting schedules, requested contract changes, and approved change requests		
• **Procurement Audits** Structured lessons learned-type reviews of the project's procurement process • **Negotiated Settlements** Final settlement of all outstanding issues, claims, and disputes • **Records Management System** Used by the project manager to manage contract documentation and records		
• **Closed Procurements** Formal written notice of the closure of the procurement • **Organizational Process Assets Updates** Updates to corporate docs, guidelines, procedures, historical information, etc.		

Ultimate PMP Exam Prep Guide — Must Know Concepts

1. The Close Procurements process is used to formally validate that all of the requirements for each of the project's procurement activities have been met and are acceptable for both seller and buyer.

2. The deliverables (Outputs) of the Close Procurements process are the closed procurements and updates to the organizational process assets.

LESSON 51   CLOSE PROJECT OR PHASE

Close Project or Phase is the process of formally ending either the project or project phase. This process documents project results to formalize the acceptance of the product of the project or project phase. Close Project or Phase is also utilized for projects that are terminated prior to their completion.

Close Project or Phase is performed by collecting project records, analyzing project performance, analyzing lessons learned, and archiving all project information for future review and use.

This process is intended to deliver two primary outputs:
- The final product/service/result of the project (formally accepted)
- Organizational process updates

Close Project or Phase (4.6)		
INPUTS	**TOOLS & TECHNIQUES**	**OUTPUTS**
• Project Management Plan • Accept Deliverables • Organizational Process Assets	• Expert Judgment	• Final Product, Service or Result Transition • Organizational Process Assets Updates
Formally closes the project or project phase		

- **Project Management Plan**   The consolidated package of the subsidiary management plans and baselines
- **Accepted Deliverables**   Documentation of accepted deliverables from the Verify Scope process
- **Organizational Process Assets**   Consideration factors such as processes, procedures, and corporate knowledge base

- **Expert Judgment**   Expert technical and/or managerial judgment (from any qualified source)

- **Final Product, Service, or Result Transition**   The final product, service, or result of the project or project phase
- **Organizational Process Assets Updates**   Updates to corporate docs, guidelines, procedures, historical information, etc.

Ultimate PMP Exam Prep Guide — Must Know Concepts

1.   Close Project or Phase is the process of formally ending either the project or project phase.

2.   Close Project or Phase documents project results to formalize the acceptance of the product/service/result of the project (or project phase).

3.   The primary deliverables (Outputs) of the Close Project or Phase process include the formally accepted product/service/result/transition and organizational process assets updates.

4.   Close Project or Phase is performed by collecting project records, analyzing project performance, analyzing lessons learned, and archiving all project information for future review and use.

LESSON 52 PROFESSIONAL RESPONSIBILITY

Your PMP Exam will include approximately eighteen questions designed to test your knowledge, competency, and judgment in the area of professional and social responsibility. This represents a significant overall percentage of exam questions and may actually provide a benefit to the exam taker. For many PMP candidates, professional and social responsibility questions are considered easy to answer.

Many professional responsibility questions can be answered simply by using common sense.

Part of your essential reading assignment is to read the "Project Management Institute Code of Ethics and Professional Conduct." This standard governing the conduct of project managers and PMPs has been developed since the 1980s. This "Code of Ethics and Professional Conduct" responds to changes in the world or project management that have occurred during that time. The new code applies to all members of PMI and certification holders. This code addresses Mandatory Standards which have to be met and Aspirational Standards which are desirable.

In general, this code is intended to instill confidence in the profession of project management by providing a common frame of behavior for project managers. In general, compliance with this code should facilitate each practitioner becoming more proficient as they comply with the code.

Ultimate PMP Exam Prep Guide — Must Know Concepts

1. Perceptions and behaviors are different between cultures.

2. It is important to maintain a professional sensitivity to cultural differences.

3. It is important to respect cultural differences.

4. As a PMP or a member of PMI you agree to adhere to and support the "PMI Code of Ethics and Professional Conduct."

5. As a PMP or PMI member you agree to maintain high integrity in all professional activities and commitments.

6. As a PMP or PMI member you agree to respond to ethical challenges by choosing to do the right thing.

CD Content

In many technical or exam preparation books, you might find a CD with an interactive test simulator or other additional information inserted here.

TSI has chosen not to provide a CD with this book. We think CDs are so "yesterday," so 1990s. Instead, we want to provide you with some materials that are easier to use and easy to access. We think this is a more economical and environmentally friendly approach to learning and disseminating information.

On the inside of this book, we provide the book buyer with instructions on how to access our PMP Exam Sample Questions online. We also provide information for the book buyer on how to access our audio files so they can download them to their MP3 player for review.

For more information, go to: www.truesolutions.com.